Hoo Nam Seelmann

Korean Temple Cooking

with photographs by Véronique Hoegger

Hardie Grant
NORTH AMERICA

CONTENTS

VEN. JEONGKWAN SNIM

Bitter Oranges and Time — 9
In the Temple — 23
Interview — 55

TEMPLE FOOD

History — 71
Rice — 83
Noodles — 91
Tofu — 99
Namul — 105
Kimchi — 113
Meju and Ganjang — 137
Jangajji — 161
Cheong — 167
Rice Syrup — 190
Flavorings — 197
About the Recipes — 198

SEASONAL RECIPES

Winter — 201
Spring — 231
Summer — 269
Autumn — 299

Tea and Buddhism — 331

BUDDHISM IN KOREA

History — 341
The Buddha — 349
The Worldview — 350
The Teachings — 351
The Path — 353
Seon Buddhism — 354
Architecture of the Temple Complex — 365
Robes — 370
Sounds and Rituals — 376
Death in Buddhism — 382

APPENDIX

Glossary of Ingredients — 399
Index — 441
Acknowledgments — 447

BITTER ORANGES AND TIME

It was about bitter oranges and time—a simple, beautiful story that Jeongkwan Snim told me. We were sitting in the kitchen of her temple and drinking tea she had prepared. It was a sunny day in late autumn, and the tea was fragrant and warm. At that time of year, the sunlight has a different luster and warmth—it's softer and mellower—and stories told then often possess a magical power, resonating in the hearer's ears long after they're told, as if they want to unfurl their hidden significance only with the passage of time.

It was just such a story that she told me. We spoke of cooking and her life at the temple. She never says much at one time, and when she does speak, she does so slowly and deliberately, gently raising her tone when she is curious, excited, or laughing. How different she can be when she's at work in the kitchen would become apparent to me later. As I listened to her, I sensed that this story would serve as a signpost that would guide me nearer to Jeongkwan Snim, her cooking, and her life with Buddhism.

I had set off from Seoul early that morning to visit her. It was 2018. Her temple is located deep in the South of Korea, and I had first visited her in spring the year before. Between then and now, we had also met in Seoul and in Switzerland.

Since childhood, visiting a temple has always been a special experience for me because it removes the day's mundanity. Just thinking about visiting a temple has always inspired a vague contentment and inexplicable tranquility in me even though the journey there is usually long and tiring. But autumn is a beautiful season for traveling in Korea, because the humid heat of the summer monsoon retreats and the air becomes dry, fresh, and clear. Freed from the weight of the rain-soaked air, the bright blue sky seems higher and broader, and the view into the distance is clear and almost transparent. But the beauty of autumn is most noticeable in the mountains, where most of Korea's temples are located, including Cheonjinam, where Snim lives.

I disembarked from the bus at the last stop and started walking along the path to the temple. It was not just a single building, but rather a large complex with various gates, buildings, courtyards, and pagodas. Whenever I visit a temple, it always feels special to leave the noise of the world behind and hike deeper into the mountains. Although at that point, you can't see anything of the temple yet—it's still hidden by the landscape—there's a sense of anticipation. I love the way the paths lead you into the world of Buddhism without you even sensing the transition! The woods surrounding temples are extensive and are specially protected areas; the paths leading to temples are old and well-trodden. They are the paths of people searching for comfort, warmth, beauty, and spirituality; their footsteps have carved the paths into the landscape.

The age of a path is revealed by the ancient trees—mostly pine, but also yew—that stand by its borders like witnesses of time, lending it a unique splendor. Often, a small mountain stream meanders along next to the path, which in turn follows the water's route. As you walk along, hopefully you progress into a state of contemplation, introspection, and attunement as you approach the world of the Buddha. This way of thinking is characteristic of Buddhism: all things are becoming, and one should achieve consciousness through one's own path.

After walking through the landscape for a while and passing under a number of red gates, you'll suddenly find yourself in the middle of the temple grounds. The transition is imperceptible, similar to the inner transformation that's also underway. I realize that spirituality needs its own space in order to be present and unfold.

For the moment, Baekyangsa Temple was my destination. The path leading there slopes gently upwards for a long stretch. Cheonjinam, Jeongkwan Snim's small temple, lies farther beyond it. At the pond pavilion, I turned right and hiked for a while longer into the narrow side valley.

Suddenly, the path became steep and led up a small mountain. I was nearly out of breath. Up on the slope is her small temple complex, consisting of a stone pagoda, two halls, and two residences. Once you arrive at the top, if you look back, you see nothing but the mountains, the valley, and the trees. There's a soft rush of water. The human world has been transported far away and has become invisible.

Baekyangsa is a temple for men; Snim lives at Cheonjinam. She is the only snim there, but she is perpetually surrounded by mostly younger people who want to learn from her. During big events, the atmosphere becomes hectic and she commands everyone like a general, speaking the slightly rural dialect of her home province. Below her residence, which sits on a steep mountain slope, she has a simple kitchen, and next to that, she has set up a neat, modest room for dining and drinking tea. A somewhat larger building was later added to that.

She also often cooks outside on the spacious terrace, where there are three large cast-iron pots, and on wide wooden tables, she dries all kinds of vegetables, nuts, and fruits. This is her realm, and this

is where she entertains guests who come from far and wide and whose numbers increase each year.

Now I was sitting opposite of her, tea between us. I had watched how she prepared it; her serene, practiced movements have always been somewhat calming.

The autumn sun with its particular luster shone through the glass door, and the air of the room carried aromas from the dishes that had been served there a short time before. At lunchtime, 23 guests from Sweden had visited, each one marveling at the various vegan dishes with great curiosity and eating them with quiet gratitude. (They were particularly captivated by a braised mushroom dish.) As the guests arrived, Snim removed her chef's apron and put on her light gray robe to greet them. She briefly explained what she had prepared and the overall context of temple food.

After the meal, the guests had questions, and everyone relaxed and had a brief conversation. As is so often the case on such occasions, time was short, and the language barrier made open conversation difficult. Everything had to be interpreted into English, and much was lost in the process. The Buddhist view of humans and nature arises from a wholly different tradition of thought than the Christian-influenced European view does, and it can be impossible to find the right words to reproduce Snim's meaning because each language has evolved alongside its traditions.

It was apparent that the visitors had arrived with many questions: unresolved life questions and doubts in need of answers, painful experiences that demanded clarity. But of course, a brief encounter like the one the Swedes had with Snim is not enough—farewells are always tinged with regret, and many go home without answers. Still, they are one rare experience richer.

Despite the language barrier, however, Snim always tries to engage her visitors in conversation. She says that food nourishes the body and the spirit; it's the connecting force that brings people together. Even without words, there's a sense of closeness when we sit and eat together. The food, the atmosphere, and the personal way in which Snim interacts with people must replace direct communication. At the end of the visit, she hugs each guest, they take photos, and she watches from the terrace for a while as they descend the steep mountain and return to the tumultuous world.

As I sat with her, suddenly the noisy room was still, and we looked at each other and laughed. Her bare face has a healthy genuineness and a distinct beauty. To be sure, the areas around her eyes show some wrinkles, and I saw a certain softness in her features that caught my eye almost immediately. It belongs not just to her, but to many other snims, both men and women. It must be the result of years in the temple, their lives, their meditation. I've often asked myself if what's inside them manifests itself externally in this way.

Her shorn head reflected the light as she moved to and fro, the reflection making her round face appear even rounder. Both men and women shave off their hair when they join a Buddhist order, as removing one's hair signifies forsaking vanity and embracing humility. Once in a while, Snim rubs her hand over her head, which she must carefully protect. To keep her head safe from the cold in the winter, she first puts on a thin cotton cap, then a wool cap over that. In the summer, she often wears a wide-brimmed straw hat.

I observed her small-yet-powerful, unadorned hands—they seemed to work magic as soon as they touched anything. She conjures the most wonderful dishes from nature.

In the autumn, from a distance, you can smell if there's a ginkgo tree in the area. At the Cheonjinam Temple, two old ginkgo trees stand near the small mountain stream that flows past the temple and into the valley. Where there are ginkgo trees, water is never far off! The lovely leaves are a luminous yellow; with every gust of wind, they flutter down to adorn the ground with gold. Their ripe yellow fruits emit an intense aroma of putrefaction. The soft fruits that have already fallen and burst open—with their delicious nuts inside—cannot be touched with bare hands because they can cause an allergic reaction, so people put on gloves to gather and rinse the fruits so that their nuts can be harvested.

Every temple complex has at least one ginkgo tree. Ginkgoes are among the oldest trees on Earth and also among the most beautiful. But that isn't their only appeal—when roasted, the ginkgo nuts have a delicious fragrance and flavor. They also contain protein, so they're an important source of nutrition in temple cooking.

Most Buddhist temples in Korea are situated deep in the mountains. Such a location is best suited for meditation and has protected temples from destruction in times of war. But the sites where temples are erected don't just stand out because of their beautiful landscapes—according to traditional geomancy, they're also places of power. And besides, their beauty and their seclusion make it easier to find and walk the Buddhist path. At night, when all is still and dark, there's a sense of being removed from the world.

Taking a walk with Snim is a special experience—she moves through the world differently. Nature is familiar to her in a special way.

She bends down again and again and touches the plants; sometimes she plucks a leaf and chews on it. She knows all of the plants by name, and she knows their scent and when they will grow, bloom, bear fruit, and wither. She can also tell you how all these things will taste depending on the season and their stage of growth. Cabbages that have been outside through the winter and survived the cold have a different fiber content, texture, and flavor, she says. She also knows how different ingredients affect our bodies and become part of us. We are what we eat, and our health depends on how we nourish ourselves and live. By cooking and eating, we are continually creating our relationship with the world and connecting ourselves to it.

Every year, Snim picks the bitter oranges that are called *taengja*. There's a taengja tree in her temple garden whose knobby form reveals its great age. The lives of trees conceal many mysteries about which we know very little, she told me, but in the spring of every year, the branches of this 500-year-old tree bore white blooms as if by a miracle.

Taengja fruits are green at first, but by autumn, they take on a beautiful orange color. This knobby tree isn't large because it can't grow tall due to the icy winds and heavy snowfalls of winter. Moss has settled onto its branches. The tree exhibits the power of nature and the mystery of life; it carries the weight of the Earth and condenses the traces of time.

Snim gathers these fruits, slices and sugars them, and puts them in earthen jars to make *cheong*, which is a type of fermented syrup. The fruits sit in the jars until she sifts them out after a year. Over time, sugar—which hinders the process—breaks down, and fermentation can begin. After three years, the liquid transforms into cheong.

Snim says, "Time does the work, and I don't have to do much besides wait. Time is the real master." Flavors and aromas form and mature with this process. The work of time and nature is so sublime that her own work is small and humble in comparison. Sun, fog, rain, wind, dew, and even moonlight work together to make the fruit, but it's primarily made by the power of the Earth, which is the source of all life. She only adds a bit of energy to the whole process.

To listen to Snim is to sense the magnitude of nature all around us and to see humans encapsulated within it. We can only live in symbiosis with nature. The breath alone shows us our direct connection with nature and with the world outside. It's no coincidence that correct breathing is central to meditation! When we breathe, we should visualize humanity's oneness with nature. *Our* oneness with nature.

In a similar way, Snim says that when she cooks, she thinks of the people who will eat the food she's preparing. You can sense her dedication when you watch her cook: she's attentive in everything she does, so she calls her actions meditation, and her energy flows into the ingredients. She leaves the preserved bitter oranges to ferment and ripen for many years in order to develop their tart, sweet-and-sour flavor, and then she adds both the fruit and the cheong to dishes to enhance their flavor.

Snim uses the word "mature" often when she talks about cooking. Maturing is the combined work of time and nature, a process that releases a variety of flavors and creates new nutrients. Food that's mature and fermented is easier to digest, more wholesome, and more aromatic. Snim shows me the chamber where she keeps her treasures. Inside are flavorings she has prepared herself; she cannot cook without them. The numerous onggis and bottles contain all of the things that time has created. Many more containers stand outside on the terrace.

Snim says that we must let nature take its course—when we do, we're rewarded with wonderful flavors. As I listened to her and ate the dishes she had prepared, everything seemed so simple and natural that I asked myself, "How could it ever be otherwise?"

IN THE TEMPLE

Jeongkwan Snim has a small garden where she plants different kinds of vegetables. Whenever she stops in the garden or elsewhere in the temple complex, she asks, "How are you?" as if she were speaking to good friends, and she squats down next to them. Snim likes this stance; it's common to see her crouching next to the three huge, steaming cast-iron pots outside in the courtyard.

She uses the pots when she needs to cook a larger quantity of food—she'll stand with a long cooking spoon in her hand, stirring and seasoning. From time to time, she'll add a stick of wood to the fire in order to achieve the right amount of heat.

The vegetable garden is next to a small mountain stream below her temple, where the mountain loses some of its steepness and frees up a level piece of land. Cabbage, carrot, lettuce, squash, and zucchini grow there, depending on the season. Bordering the vegetable patch, all kinds of wild plants and flowers grow wildly in vibrant colors. There's quite a bit of life on this little chunk of land! "A lot of animals come by," she says, laughing.

Tea plants can be found in the rugged mountains surrounding the temple, and Snim collects their leaves in spring to make tea out of them. She harvests mushrooms that grow on tree trunks and dries them in the sun so she can cook with them later. A persimmon tree shares its fruits with her, and in autumn, Snim picks the taengja (the bitter oranges) to preserve them. However, what she harvests for the many foods she prepares is never enough. To supplement her own gathering efforts, she often drives her car to the market in the nearby small town to buy vegetables, fruit, rice, oil, or flour.

Everyone there knows her; she walks around and happily buys what the farmers from the area offer from their own harvests, inquiring about their health. Once in a while, she'll buy knives from the blacksmith. She says her own somewhat unwieldy knives are better than the expensive ones she has been gifted. And of course, cooking requires good organization and logistics; Snim requires a great deal of that as well.

She was sent to Cheonjinam—where she has now lived and worked for 10 years—by her order to bring more life to Baekyangsa Temple. She was already famous in Korea long before Netflix discovered her and brought her culinary skills to the world, and the temple has been there for far, far longer.

Founded in 632, Baekyangsa Temple is snuggled into a beautiful landscape—behind it, rugged, craggy Baekamsan Mountain juts up into the sky, its peak offering a gorgeous panoramic view of the majestic mountain range that gradually disappears into the distance. Far below, you can see the entire temple complex nestled between the hills, and alongside the temple, a broad mountain stream meanders through the long valley filled with old trees.

Yew trees are particularly prolific here—the oldest among them are a good 400 years old. The yew trees give her seasonings a particular aroma and flavor. Snim says that her soy sauce, for example, smells of yew. Yew berries have been used as a remedy here in traditional medicines since time immemorial.

Baekyangsa Temple is mid-sized, with around 30 large and small buildings: gates, halls, a residential wing, a kitchen, a tea house, and pavilions. There are also several courtyards, a pond, and a small lake.

Built deep in the mountains and far away from the city, Baekyangsa is a typical Korean temple.

Since the temple was founded amidst this mountain solitude, countless snims have come, stayed awhile, and then departed again. Their steps have carved the paths; the halls nestled into the quiet valley still ring with the sounds of their rhythmic voices chanting the sutras and the sounds of the *moktak*. The drums and bells have proclaimed the Buddha's message for as long as anyone can remember.

In earlier times, the path must have been long and arduous— even today, it's not easy to reach the temple. Still, temple enthusiasts are happy to come to this valley, as are hikers, especially in autumn when the maple leaves turn red. Jeongkwan Snim's order believed that her culinary skills could draw more attention and visitors, so she moved to the nearby small Cheonjinam Temple. Nowadays, Baekyangsa even offers a temple stay program. The members of Snim's order were right: diverse groups of guests come from all over the world to see her and have the opportunity to taste the food she prepares.

She is the only snim in Cheonjinam, and she is responsible for everything that goes on at the temple. In her temple courtyard, there are a number of *onggis*—large, reddish-brown earthenware containers used for fermentation. They're believed to be particularly well-suited to the task because they breathe. The containers, which are kiln-fired at 1,200°C, are light and very sturdy, and it's said that foods stored in them stay fresh longer.

Active breathing has a beneficial effect on the fermentation process, and the longer the process takes, the better the result

will be. Fermentation is a natural process that's activated when microorganisms break down organic materials, transforming them and creating something new. The resulting marvelously aromatic flavorings, beverages, and dishes are one of nature's great wonders.

In Korea, certain trees and flowers are planted around onggis in order to influence the development of flavors. Pine trees are popular and so are plantain lilies, because not only do they have antibacterial properties, their strong fragrance improves flavor.

Snim stores her treasures—flavorings she has made herself—in onggis. The most important ones are the various kinds of what are called *jang* in Korean. These are *ganjang* (soy sauce), *doenjang* (soybean paste), and *gochujang* (spicy chili paste). Producing them is complicated and requires much time, patience, and skill. Covered with a lid, onggis are exposed to the forces of nature the whole time; the heat of day and the nighttime chill both play a part.

Ganjang and doenjang are started with protein-rich soybeans, salt, and water as their primary materials. As a product of the fermentation process, they form an essential flavoring component in temple cooking. Onggis are also needed for kimchi, which has a huge number of variations and has become known worldwide as a classic fermented Korean dish. However, the temple's kimchi is a bit different from what's consumed in most households because it contains neither garlic nor animal enzymes—this kimchi is lighter and has a milder flavor. (Today, most Koreans have a special kimchi refrigerator in their homes rather than an onggi.)

Each year in November, Snim organizes *kimjang*, an event where she works together with others for several days to make various kinds of kimchi for the winter. More than 70 people will come to help, some of whom travel here from other countries. About 300 heads of napa cabbage, 100 radishes, and many other vegetables are used. Each participant takes something home, but the rest is placed in onggis for storage. Then the fermentation begins. Kimchi must last through the coming winter until next spring.

Snim preserves a number of other things as well: she makes vinegar (or cheong) from fruit, berries, and rice; vegetables, mushrooms, and fruits are dried in the sun and then stored or pickled. She has to prepare all of these things each year to ensure that there's always enough food in storage.

The most important thing to take into account for jang is durability, because the older it gets, the better it gets. A 28-year-old soy sauce has its own unique creaminess and a singular, sweetish flavor.

Not surprisingly, Snim doesn't have much of that particular sauce, so she's treating it preciously. At one point while I was there, she opened the onggi where the vintage soy sauce was being stored, peered into it lovingly, took out a spoonful, and said, "Smell that!" Using just salt, soybeans, and water, time creates this wonderful sauce. At the same time, it's also Snim's achievement.

The world comes together in her temple kitchen. There's always something to do, and people come from all over not only to eat but also to learn and help. When a big event is coming up, things become hectic and stressful. She rushes about the kitchen, issuing commands and giving loud instructions. It's not easy to be Snim on days like that! Those days are when the sharp edges of her southern dialect become especially conspicuous.

For example, on the Buddha's birthday—April 8 according to the lunar calendar—about 300 visitors will arrive who will enjoy food for free. Many of them will bring donations such as rice or fruit, or they'll place money in the wooden donation boxes. Snim has no regular staff of employees, so she must manage everything with the help of students and volunteers.

Fortunately, there are always young people around who want to learn how to cook. The length of their stay varies—it can be three months, six months, or even a year. While they're at the temple, they must start completely from scratch and they must work hard. Most of them come from Korea, but some eager students come from the USA, Europe, and the rest of Asia. The dinner table is always fully occupied, because helpers from the cities also always turn up on weekends. Even professional chefs from Seoul will come by for specific occasions, and former students who have gone on to work abroad often visit Snim when they're home on vacation. On top of that, there's always a team of filmmakers from Korea or abroad or several journalists who want to interview her.

Snim talks about young people from Europe arriving who are looking for direction in life—they simply stand outside the door and wait. Snim takes them in whenever possible. I once met a tall Dutchman who had flown to Korea at age 17 and had come to Snim unannounced. Back at home in the Netherlands, he had been unhappy and hadn't known what to do with his life, so he sought her out. He stayed there for three months. She took him with her everywhere, his head shorn bald like hers, and they often cooked together. Since Snim doesn't speak English, they couldn't communicate verbally, but cooking brought them closer and they got on well together. He returned to the

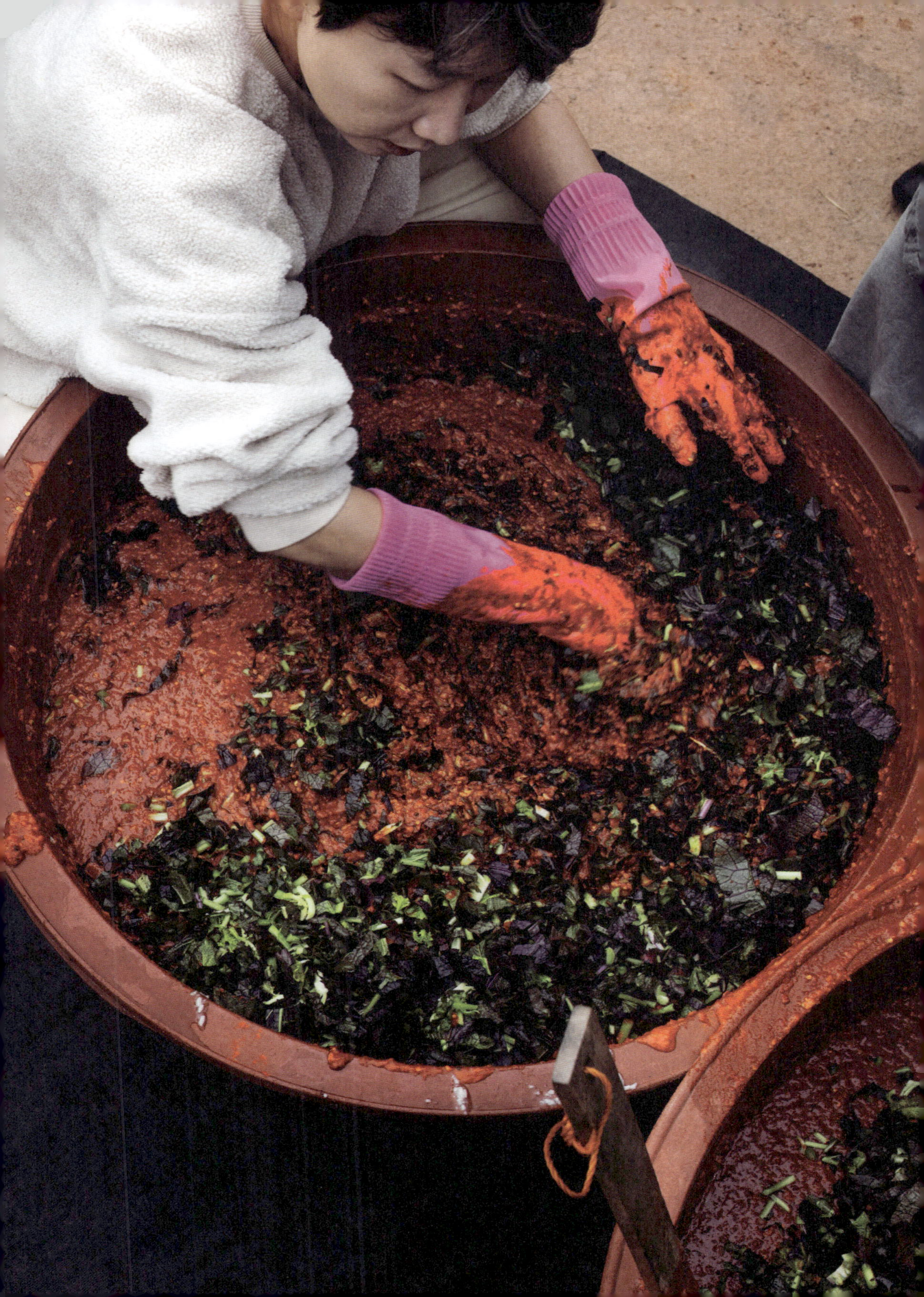

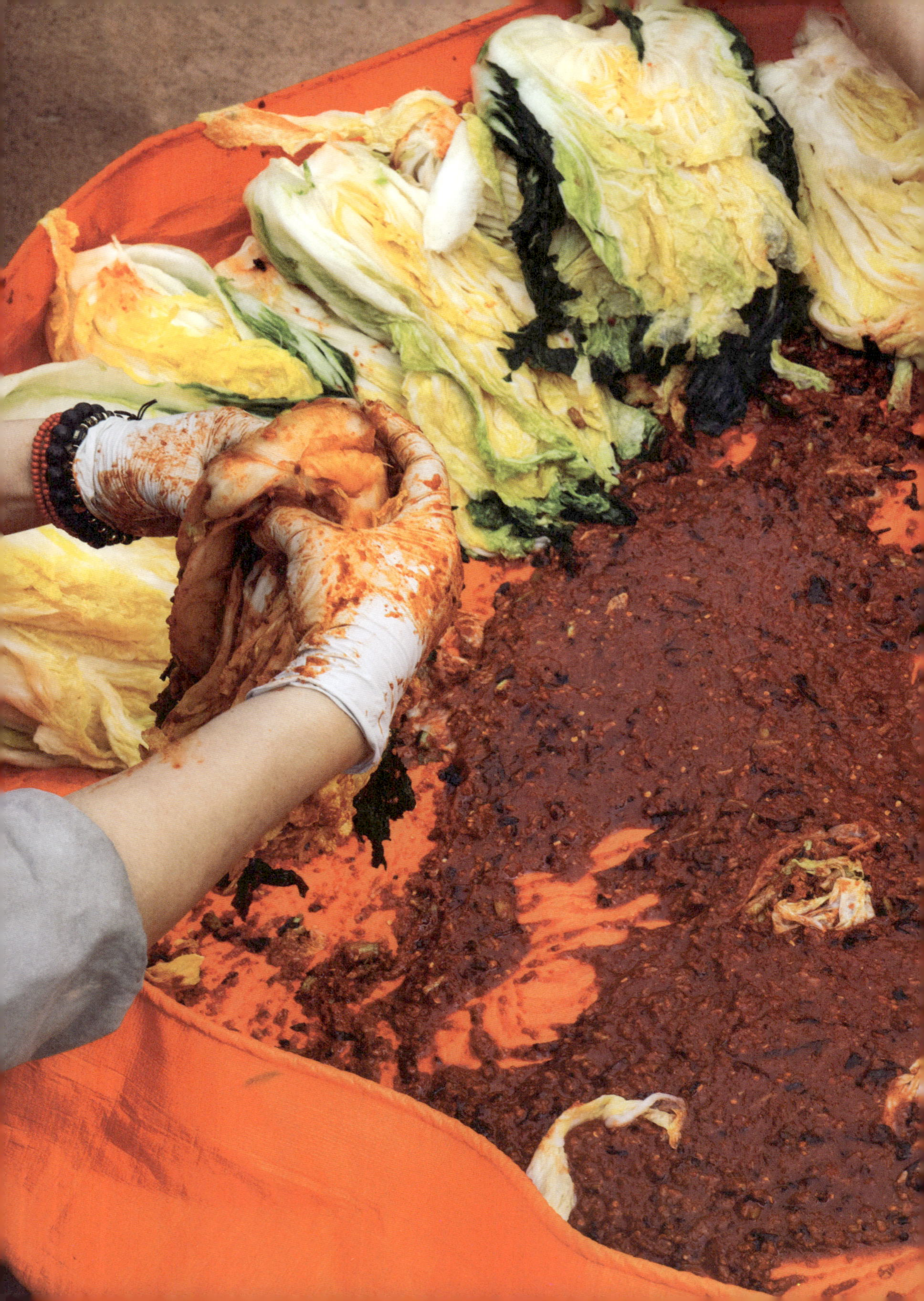

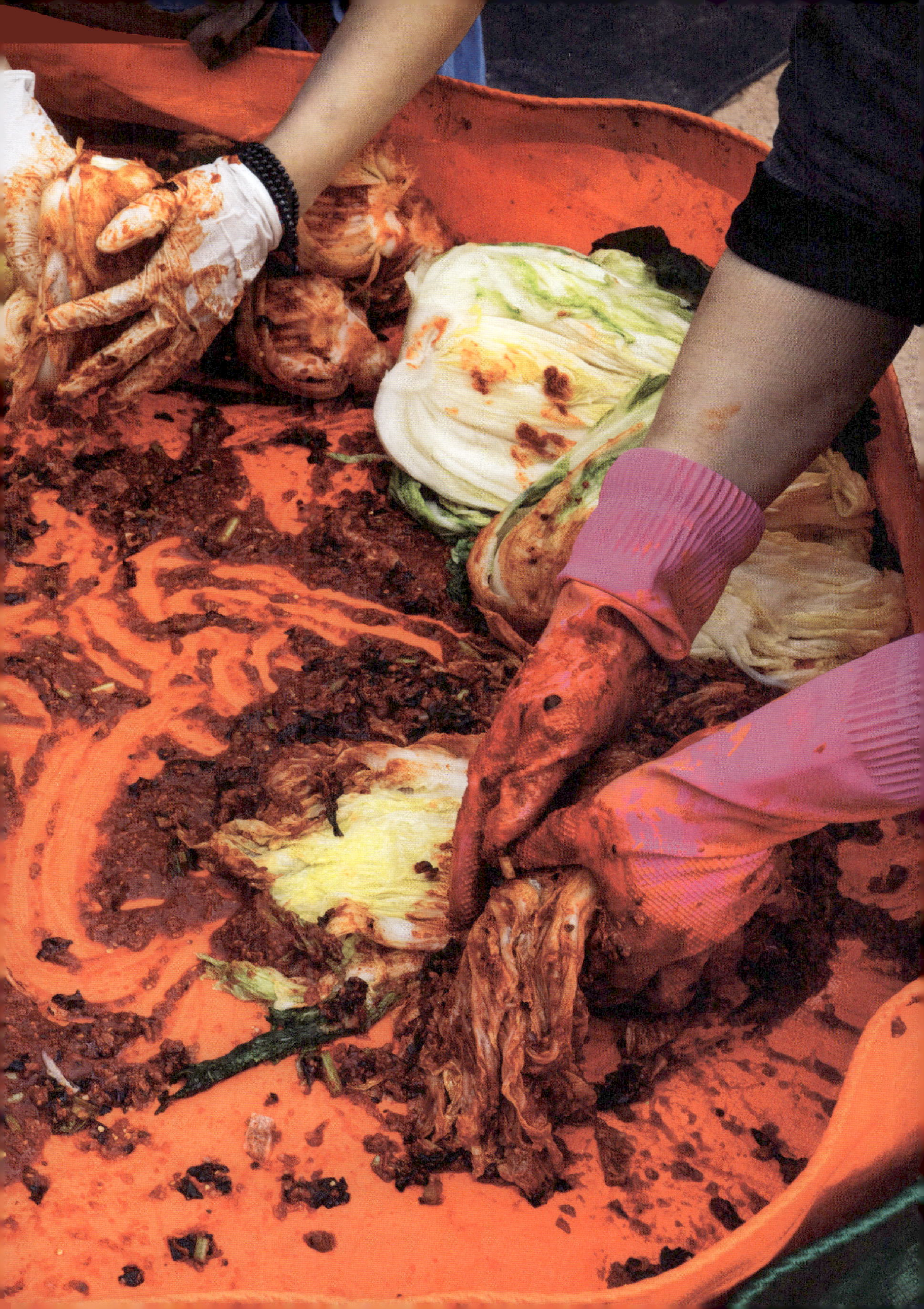

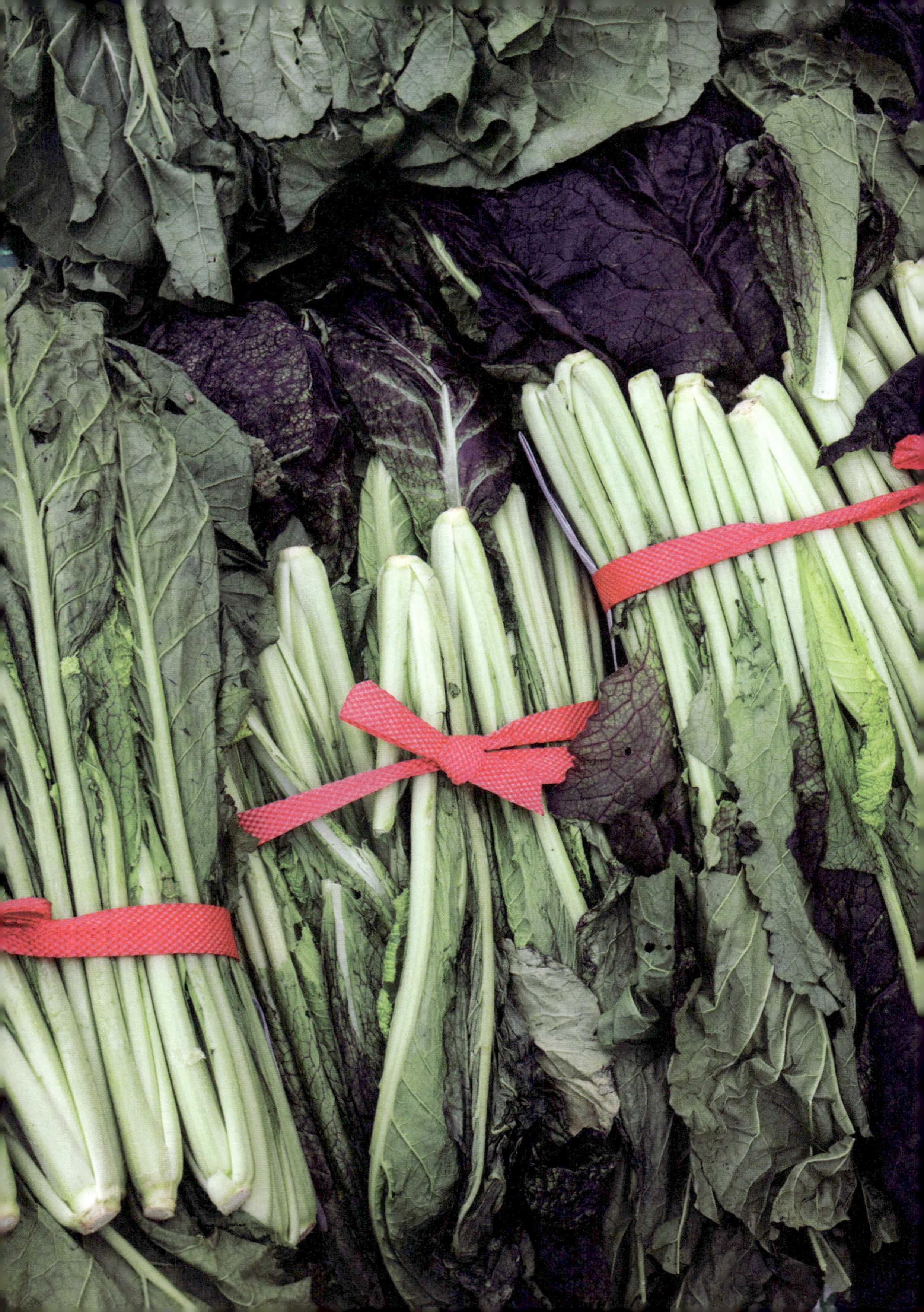

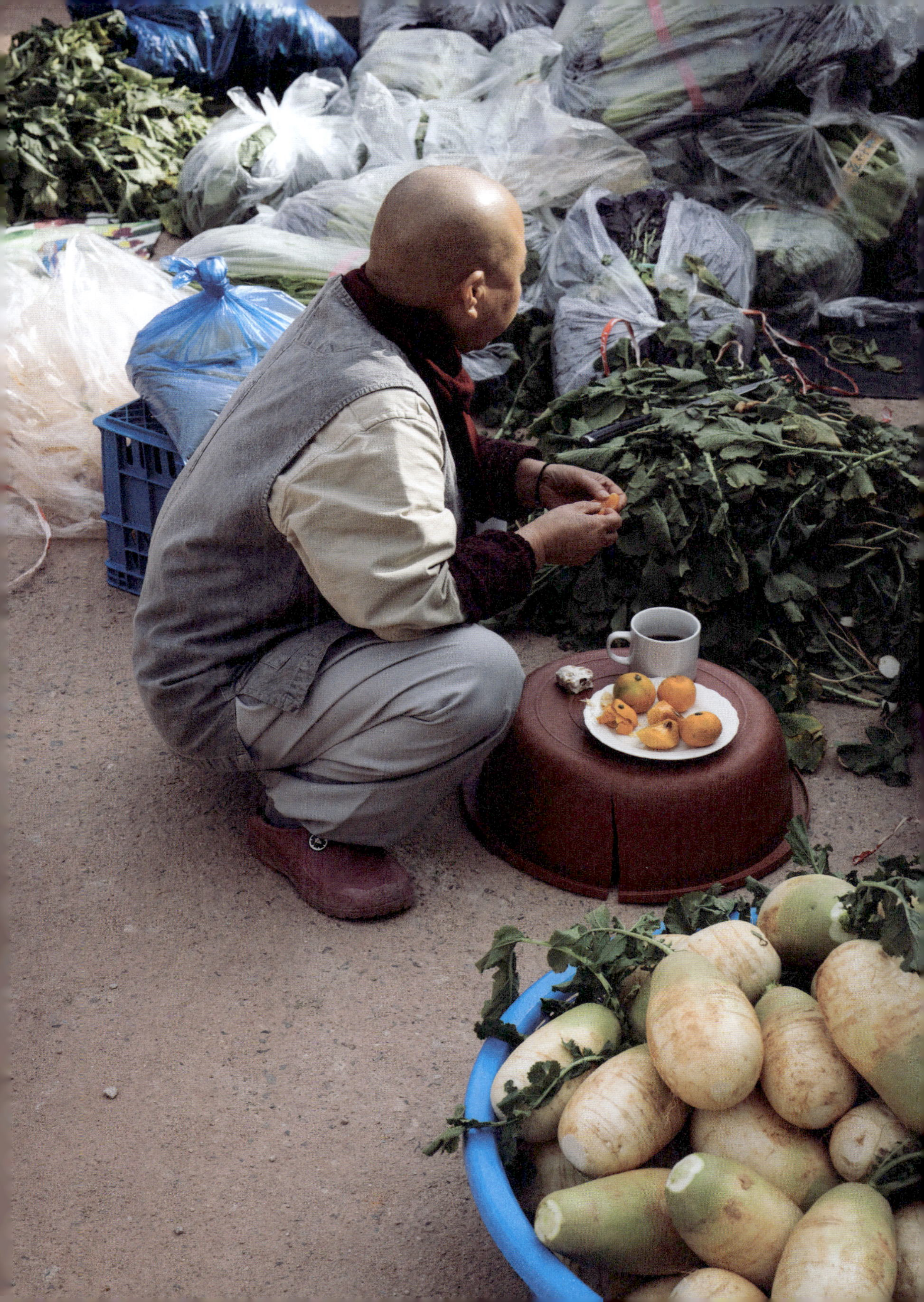

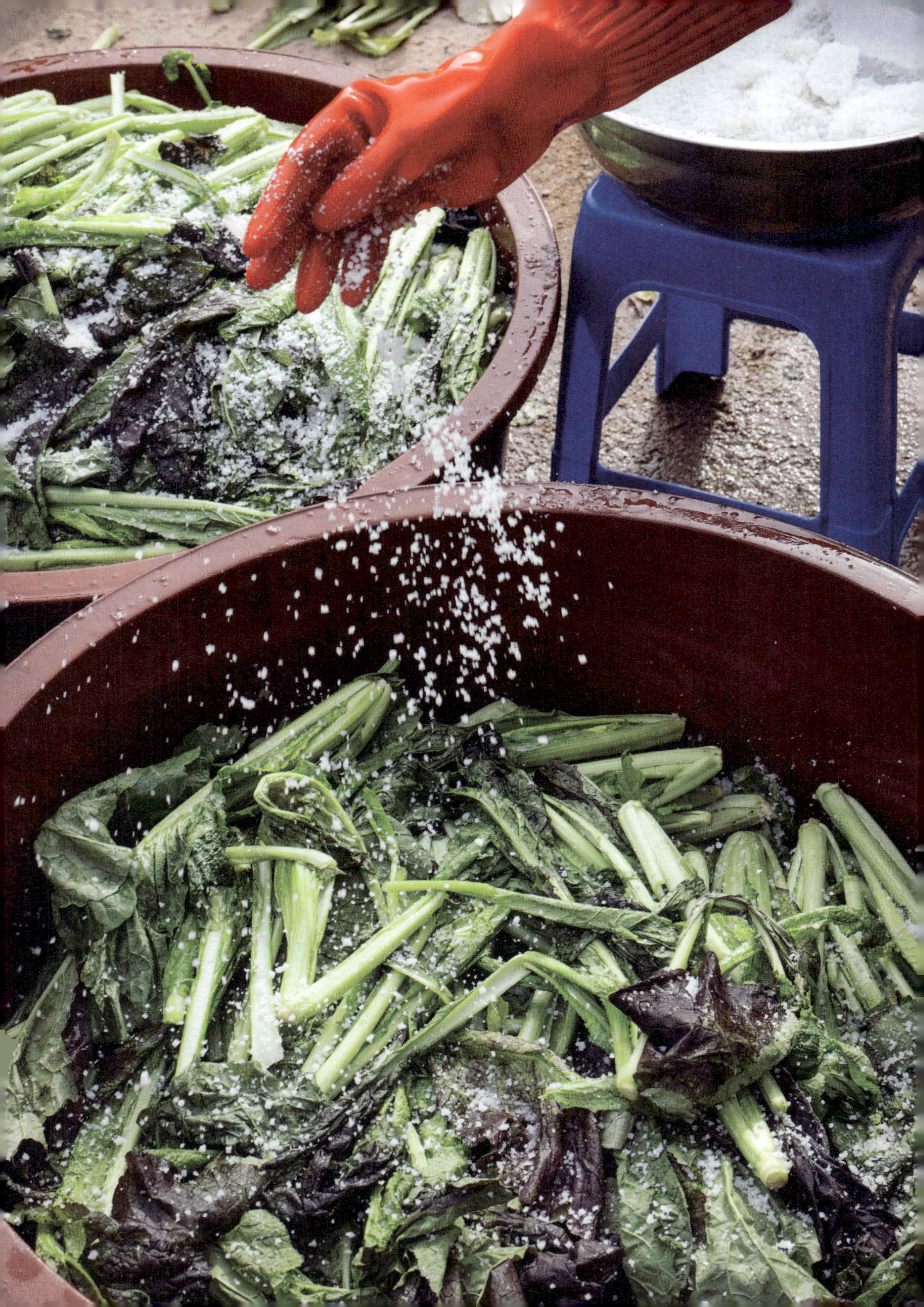

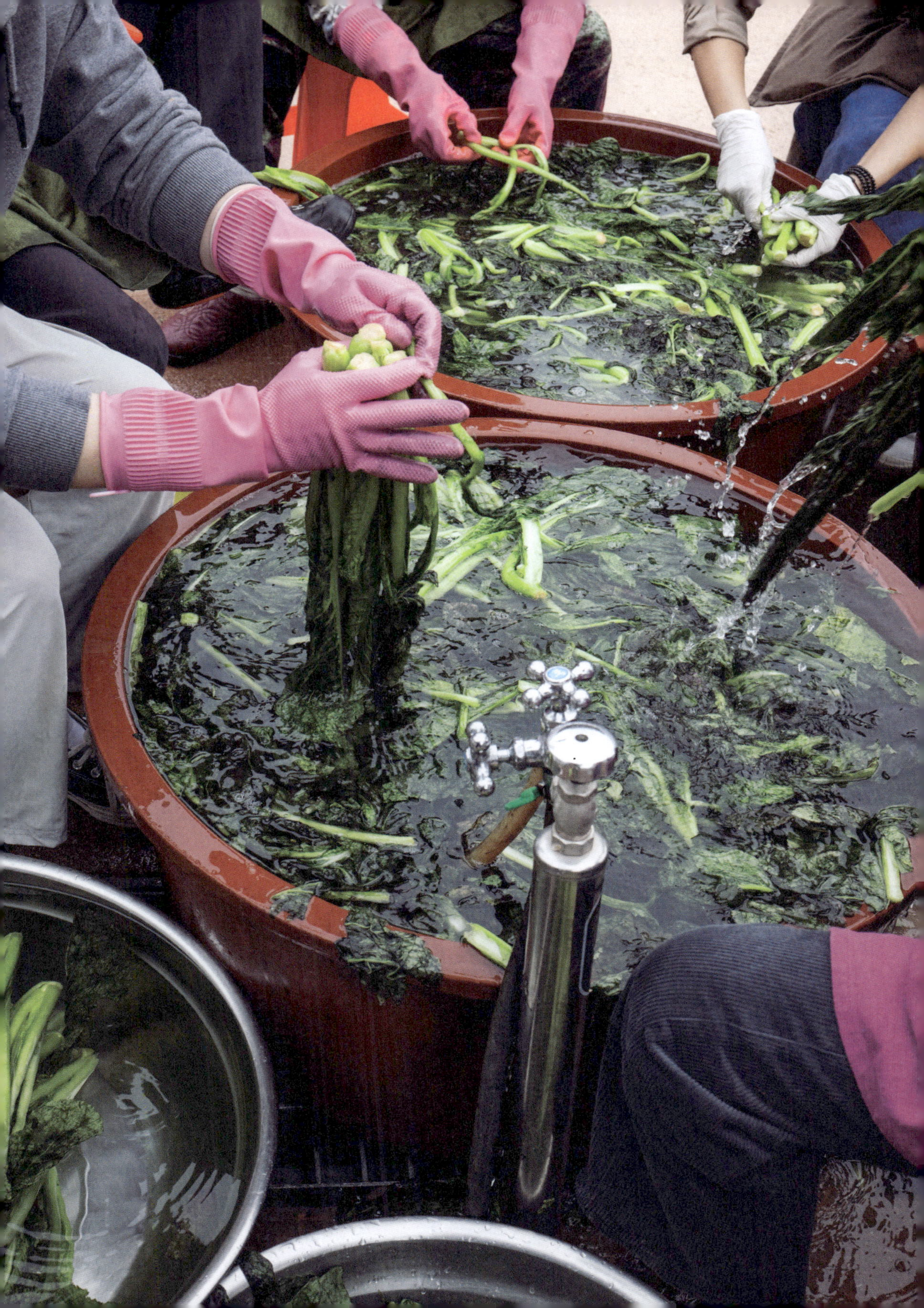

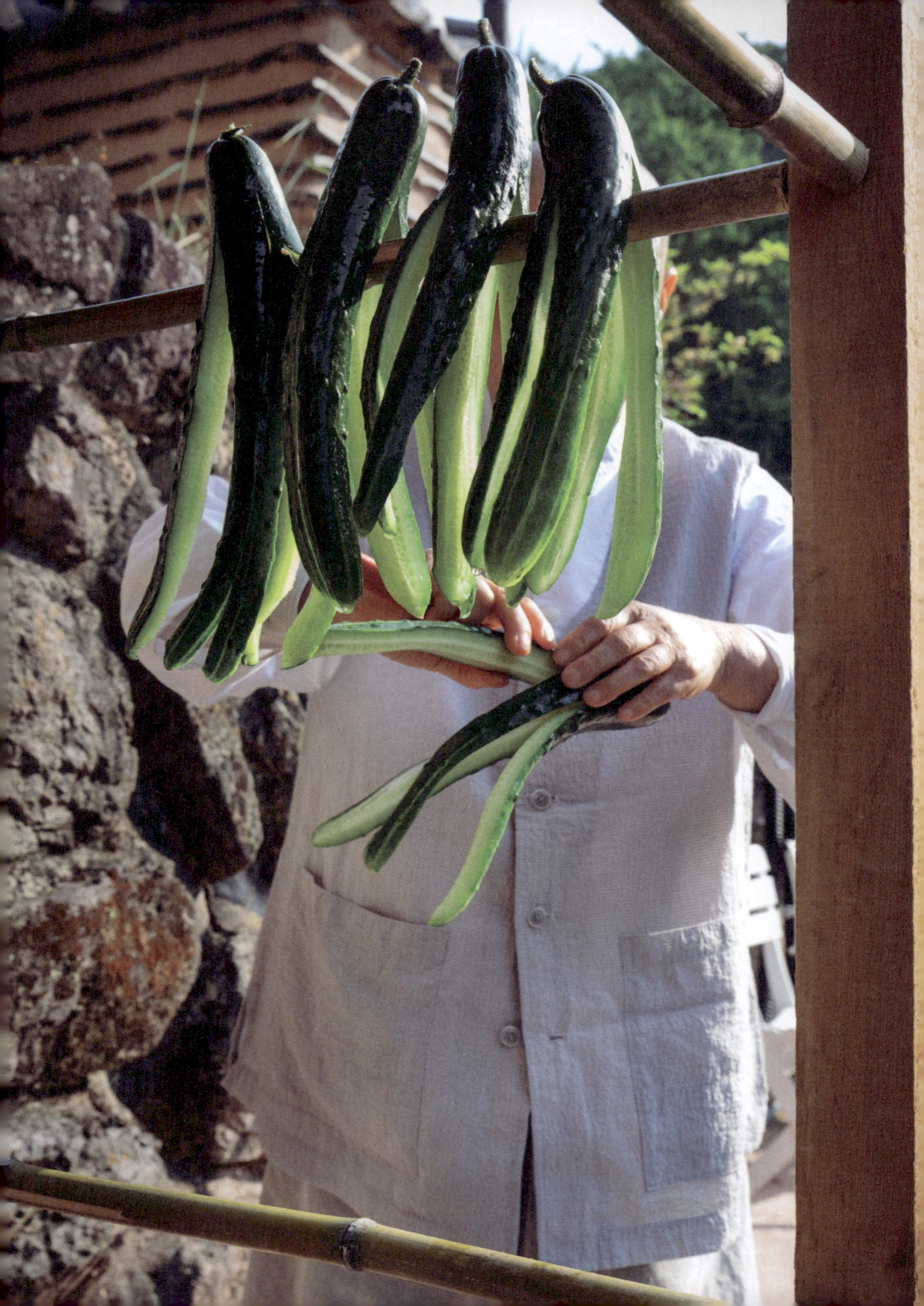

Netherlands and completed an apprenticeship as a chef, and today he works in a restaurant in Amsterdam.

Jeongkwan Snim's everyday life looks somewhat different from life in other temples. That's because the Netflix documentary about her brought her to worldwide fame overnight. And it had some consequences. In Korean temples, all snims lead strictly regulated lives apart from when they're ill. Their days are divided up and times are scheduled in accordance with a daily rhythm: get up, participate in *yebul* or rituals, eat, study, work, meditate, receive visitors, and go to bed.

Jeongkwan Snim, however, must organize her day quite differently if she wants to complete all of the tasks she wishes to complete *and* those that are expected of her. She accepts many additional tasks and meets with people who seek spiritual or life advice from her, and she also meditates with others. If all of that weren't enough, she has become an ambassador for temple food, a role that often takes her on the road. She receives numerous invitations from other countries, and the government sends her abroad; she gives cooking classes and holds lectures in many different places. But her primary duty is being responsible for her temple and for the guests who come to visit her. There's a lot to do, even on days when there are no visitors! Her hands are seldom idle.

Snim speaks often of the significance of hands. They possess power, skill, and beauty, and they enable us to live life by creating a connection to the world. Hands can deliver hard blows and even kill, but they also carry a lot of warmth and are ready to reach out at any time to help others or offer someone support. A touch of the hand appeals to the humanity in us, and in fact babies cannot develop into emotional beings if they are deprived of touch.

The most important thing that hands do, however, is provide us with food. Snim says that they transfer our life energy into the ingredients. We are one with nature because our energy penetrates natural ingredients and forms them into dishes. In an interview with the *New York Times*, she said that "I become the cucumber, and the cucumber becomes me" when she prepares and eats something from the cucumbers she has grown in the garden.

When it comes to food, our own energy meets with the energy of nature, and together they form a single unit. Therein lies the magic that hands work: we incorporate nature into ourselves, and nature then becomes part of us. Our view of things is also important, as Snim says: "When you think of napa cabbage, don't just see it as a vegetable, but consider as well that it will become a part of your body and your self. So, the cabbage becomes the self. This means that it should be handled with the same care and delicacy as if it were your own body. If you make kimchi with this mindset, it will be good."

Snim's hands are slightly plump and not especially large, but her hands are nonetheless powerful. Her palms have lost some of their suppleness because objects, water, heat, and steam have taken the softness from her hands and somewhat faded the enigmatic lines that adorn all hands. Snim has prepared countless dishes for many people all over the world; it's as if you can see the traces of every one of those dishes in her hands.

Snim tells how she handles vegetables when she's in the garden or the kitchen. "You have to be familiar with the individual plants in order to be able to prepare them well," she says. "When they grow, when they bloom, how they taste at what stage, when is the best moment to harvest them. That depends on whether something is tender, tough, or bitter, on whether it tastes sweet or sour."

When she cuts ingredients like squash, bamboo shoot, or lotus root, she shows the cross section and remarks on how diverse and incomparably beautiful it is. If she has a basket full of various kinds of greens, she'll pick up this or that and take a bite to test its flavor. One wonders just how much knowledge she has to share!

"Many plants contain substances that are toxic for us humans and other animals," she explains. "This is because all living things want to stay alive and protect themselves from others. This is completely natural and is a basic principle of life. It is not only animals that defend themselves—so do plants. They produce substances or chemicals that can be toxic. You also have to know that these substances can vary in strength through each stage of growth. When a plant is blossoming and when fruits form and ripen, the effect is the strongest, which means that the toxicity for others is the greatest.

"The goal of plant life is to leave fruits to ensure the plant's own survival. When you want to prepare vegetables, it's important to be aware of these circumstances so that you can neutralize the harmful effects and prepare healthy food from the ingredients. Much has to be controlled in the method of food preparation. You can cook, blanch, or steam the vegetables, but you can also season them with certain fermented flavorings."

In Snim's view, not only do soy sauce and soybean paste make vegetables tastier, they help neutralize unwholesome elements and aid digestion. They also stimulate gut flora. Listening to her, you realize how complex the process of living and surviving in nature is.

Snim loves vegetables and knows all about them. Korean temple cooking plays to her strengths, because temple food in Korean is called *chaesik*, which basically means "plant-based food." The Western word "vegan" is close in meaning. Because temples are located in the mountains, inhabitants there have collected wild vegetables, mushrooms, roots, nuts, and fruits on the mountain slopes since ancient times. There's such a great variety! And the flavors are incomparable.

Snim likes to talk about vegetables when she has free time. She says that every type of vegetable has its own special characteristics. The varieties differ from one another not only in form and color, but also in their fibrousness. That means it's not always a good idea to cut everything with a knife—for some kinds of vegetables, whether you start with it raw or after it's been blanched or steamed, it's better to rip or pull it apart with your fingers. Only vegetables that you can't handle with your fingers should be cut with a knife.

Fingers are essential to cooking because of their agility, sensitivity, tactile sense, and subtle ability to feel. Fingers do the work and conjure up good food, she says. Although because the palms usually contain too much warmth, it's advisable not to handle ingredients for too long.

The Korean view of food as medicine is best preserved in temple cooking. Because they're secluded in the mountains, snims must acquire a lot of medical knowledge to maintain their health and to heal themselves when they become ill. For this reason, most snims have historically had a good understanding of the curative effects of everything people eat. Since the foods differ in their ingredients, each of them has a different effect on us. It's a wonder that we can obtain such diverse nutrients and elements from the soil! And that we can integrate them into our own growth and transform them into other substances and nourish ourselves with them.

Snim also knows what each ingredient is good for. She says that if you know the various ingredients well, you can substitute missing ingredients with something else during food preparation. Some foods are neutral, some warm up the body from the inside, and still others have a cooling effect. For example, rice—which ripens in the heat of summer—contains a lot of warmth. That differs from, say, barley, which as a winter crop cools the body. (In the summer heat, Koreans drink a lot of tea made from roasted barley to draw the heat from the body.) Warming ingredients also include garlic, ginger, gochu, and potatoes.

Vegetables and lettuce, however, are cold by nature. Snim says that if you eat too much uncooked produce, the cold will collect in your body and prevent your organs from functioning properly. Cold and warmth must be balanced to keep the body healthy. This means it's better to eat vegetables cooked (and even to season them with soy sauce) or to supplement them with protein (like tofu) and carbohydrates in order to get enough calories, to make the food tasty, and to balance out the cold.

According to Snim, when cooking, it's important to maintain the vividness of the natural flavors and aromas of the ingredients and develop them fully. The ingredients should also be as visible as possible, because each one has its own individuality and beauty. The simpler the preparation, the better! Snim uses only ingredients whose origin she's familiar with, and she uses mostly natural, homemade seasonings to improve her control over the flavor nuances. She's proud of her 20-plus-year-old soy sauce, her 8-year-old soybean paste, her 10-year-old persimmon vinegar, and her cheong made from rice, plums, and berries. Time has done the work of creating these flavors—their uniqueness depends on it.

The food that Snim prepares is based on the long-standing traditions of Korean temple cooking, which have from the beginning been guided by Buddhism. If you see Snim cooking and talking, you can sense the presence of this inherited spirit of Buddhism. When she announces a meal, she says *gongyanghaseyo*. In other, larger temples where many snims live, the moktak calls everyone to eat. You also hear the word *gongyang* three times a day when you live in a temple—it's an old Buddhist word that's uncommon outside of temple grounds. Gongyang represents respectfully offering the meal that has been prepared with care and devotion. It also resonates with a certain celebratory spirit and with an appreciation for the food that gives us life.

It's no coincidence that according to Buddhism, the entire universe is contained within a single grain of rice. This concept is more than just symbolic: the grain of rice contains the power of the soil, the sunlight, the rain, the wind, the moonlight, the fog, and the dew. The final step is the energy that humans infuse the grain with through their work. We must sense the mysterious power concealed therein, and we must view the grain as being something valuable, and we must handle it with respect. This attitude applies not only to the rice but to *all* of the ingredients we use to prepare food.

The temple regulates who is responsible for the food. It's usually the *haengjas*, or those who are completing a probationary period and the novices who begin their temple lives in this way. Each one must perform work in the temple kitchen for a specified period of time.

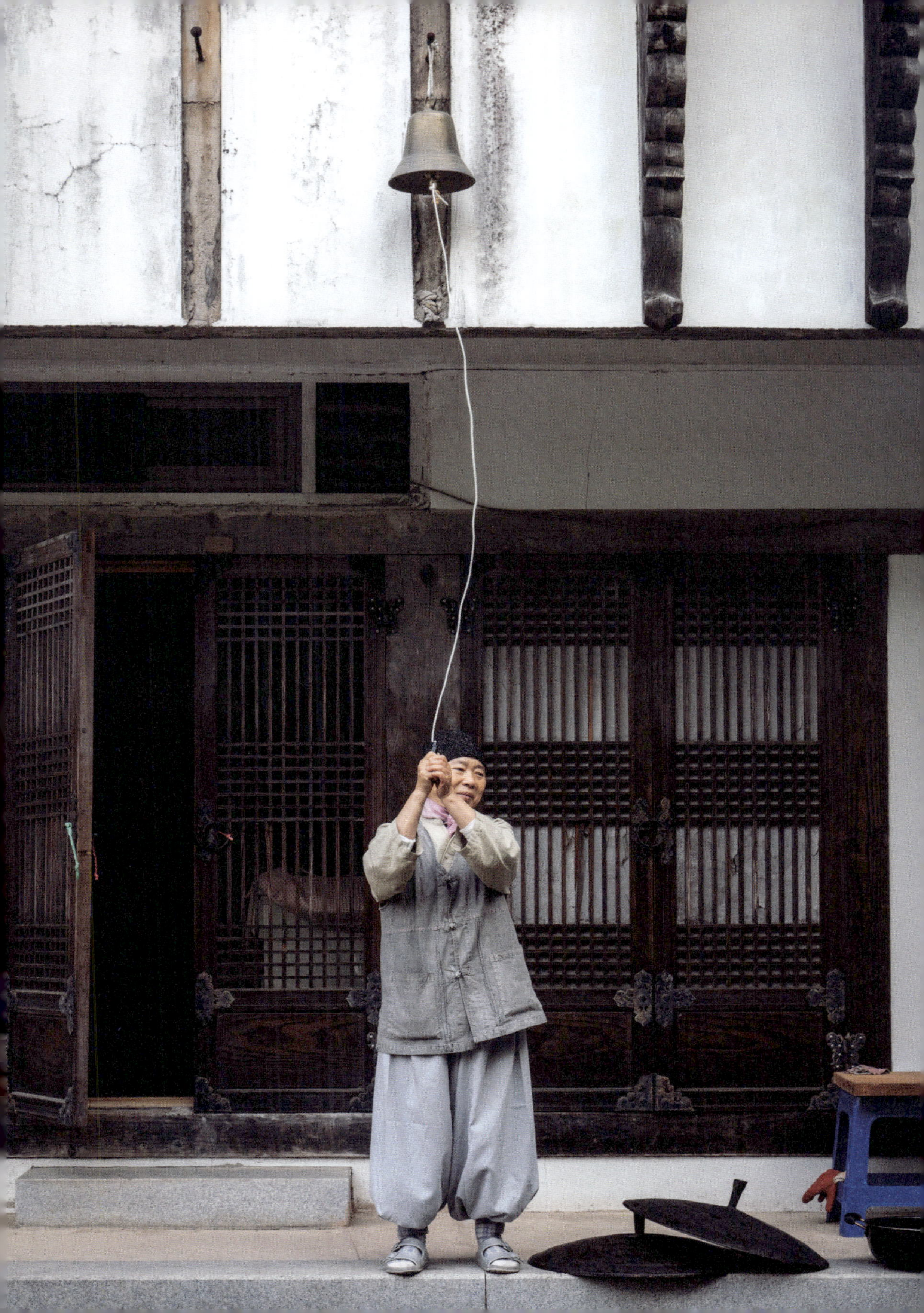

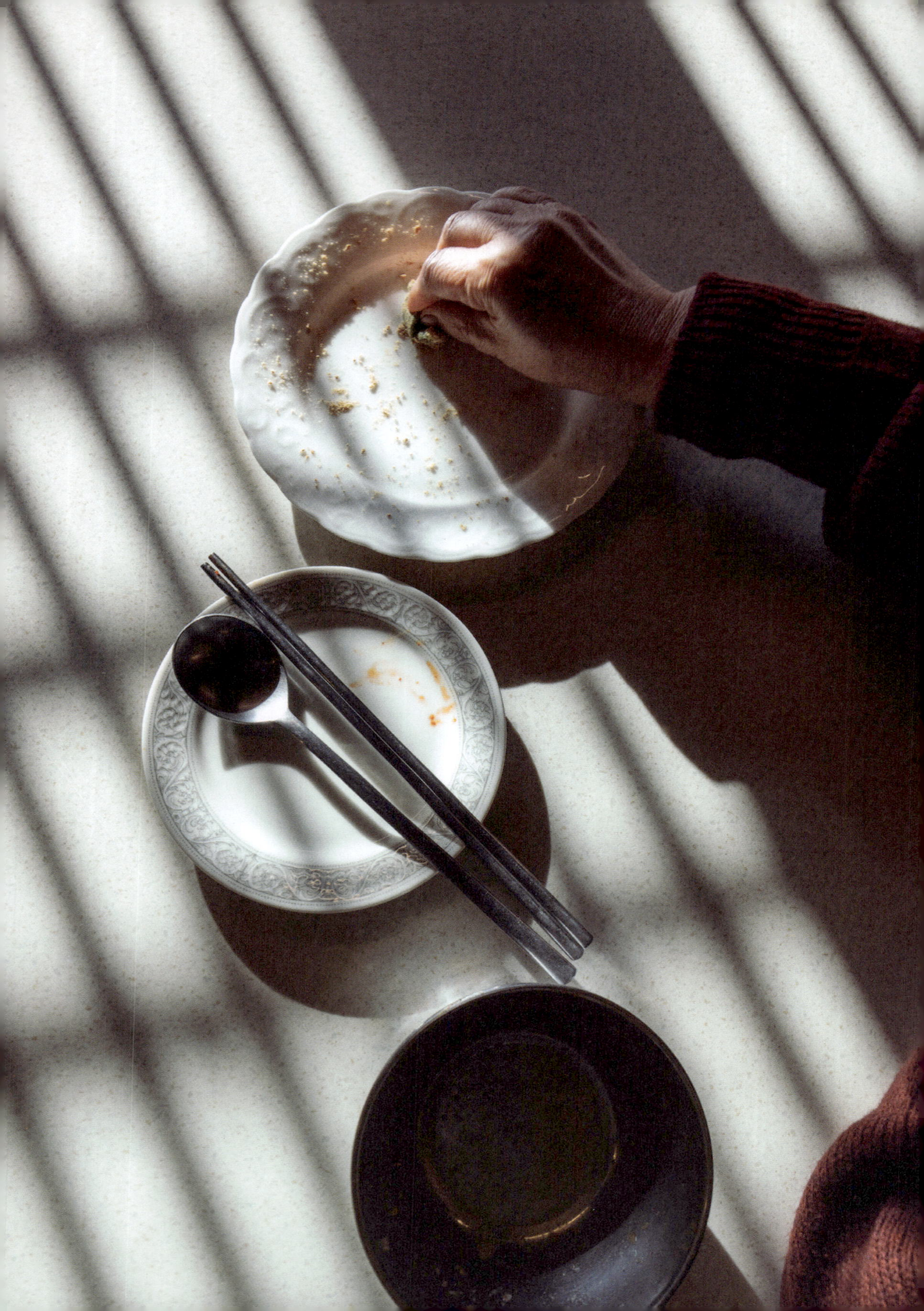

On one hand, kitchen work is a lesson in service and humility, and on the other hand, it teaches that all work is of equal value. Cooking for others sharpens an awareness of what it means to be there for others and for the community.

During the four years of the novitiate, a novice learns to cook something new each year. This teaches them how to cook from the ground up. Cleaning is the simplest task and is how they begin, then comes the preparation of vegetables. Then they learn how to cook soup and finally rice, because cooking rice perfectly is its own art. Nowadays, an electric rice cooker does the work, but before its arrival, you had to use a heavy cast-iron pot, and that required good intuition to wield successfully.

Breakfast in the temple is served at 6 a.m. and usually consists of a simple rice porridge and some vegetables. For lunch, along with the rice, a certain number of varied side dishes are served. These may contain vegetables, tofu, beans, bean sprouts, seaweed, mushrooms, kimchi, vegetable pancakes, corn, potatoes, sweet potatoes, buckwheat dishes, acorn jelly, and fruit. Tea or coffee is served afterwards. Various noodle dishes with an extra-delicate broth, pastries, and rice cakes are also popular. What is cooked depends on the season and the weather.

Dinner is eaten at 6 p.m., and it's usually as simple and light as possible to avoid burdening the body during the night. On Buddhist holidays, a wider variety of dishes is offered; these take the work of many snims and their helpers several days to make.

The temple kitchen has traditionally been seen as a place full of vital energy: this is where energy is created, preserved, and distributed. Another lovely label for the temple kitchen is the "place of fragrances," because all of the smells and aromas nature is able to produce find their way into the kitchen, and from there, once they are transformed into food, they find their way into our bodies.

Giving the kitchen these kinds of names illustrates the significance that food has within Buddhism. While the supply of sustenance is foundational for the survival of all living things, life should be protected as much as possible, which is the basis for the vegan food tradition of Buddhism. In Buddhism, food is seen not only as something material but as something that directly builds the connection between body and spirit. The path to spirituality also goes through the right food.

Temple food is food for suhaengjas: it should provide vital energy, but it should also nourish the soul. Jeongkwan Snim says that even if you use the same ingredients, food tastes differently depending on the inner attitude and devotion of the person who prepares it. When she's working in the kitchen, she thinks of those who come to her to eat. She wants to make other people happy with her food—that's why she told me about noodle dishes.

When she was still young, Snim spent some years in Donghwasa Temple in the South of Korea. One Sunday, she cooked a large batch of a noodle dish purely for the joy of cooking, and then she invited the mountain climbers who happened to come by. They were happy to accept the food, and they continued on afterwards with warmth in their bodies and a lingering flavor in their mouths. She did this for several Sundays in a row. At first, people were surprised, but they accepted the food with gratitude. Later, many came to visit her, and some even became Buddhists. Food moves people; it changes them. If one nourishes oneself properly, this purifies the spirit, and thinking becomes more clear. Even the color of a person's face and their appearance change.

"I'm not a professional chef, but rather a suhaengja," Jeongkwan Snim has often said in interviews. She means that she is a snim and so her cooking has a different significance than a chef's cooking has in a restaurant. Her actions have no commercial purpose, of course, and she also has a different attitude toward cooking and food. The term *suhaengja* cannot be translated into English, but it's a central concept in Korean Buddhism. *Suhaeng* means "changing one's conduct and everyday habits," and *ja* means "someone who does that thing." So, a suhaengja is someone who has made the decision to follow a Buddhist way of life.

A new beginning means giving up previous habits and acquiring new ones. Our lives are controlled by our habits, and we must first become aware of them in order to be able to change them. When we have the right insights, habits, behaviors, way of working, and way of interacting with others, it's simpler to follow the Buddha's teachings, but even then, it's not easy. It's a lifelong process! Study is important—and meditation just as much so—but right action is key. All snims are suhaengja; all try to change themselves so that their own lives follow the Buddha's teachings.

Korean temple food represents an old cooking tradition that is suited to the life of a snim: it supports the body's health, makes meditation easier, and promotes the spiritual life. Temple food also reminds us of nature, which nourishes us. According to the Buddha, health is the most important thing for those who seek enlightenment.

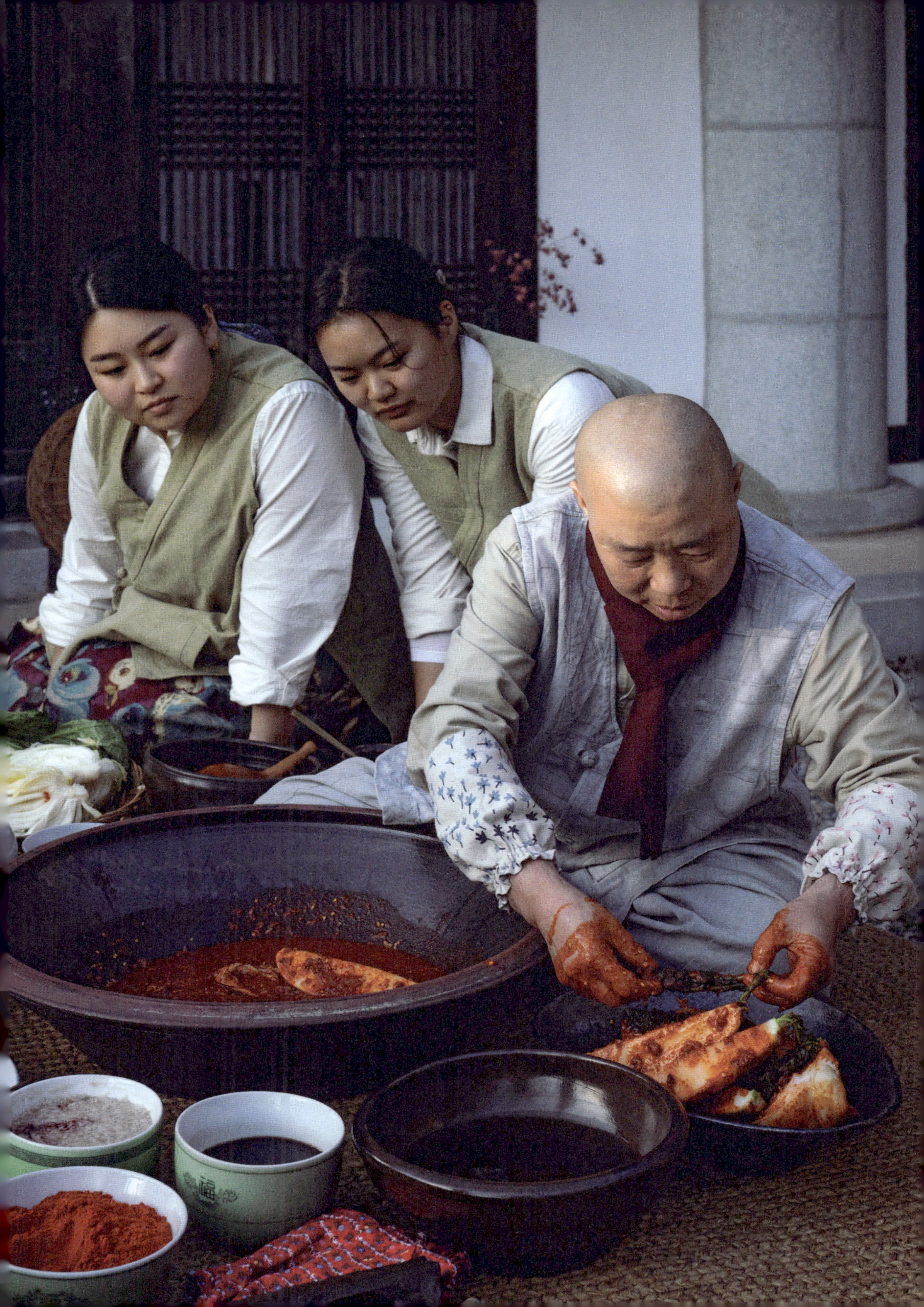

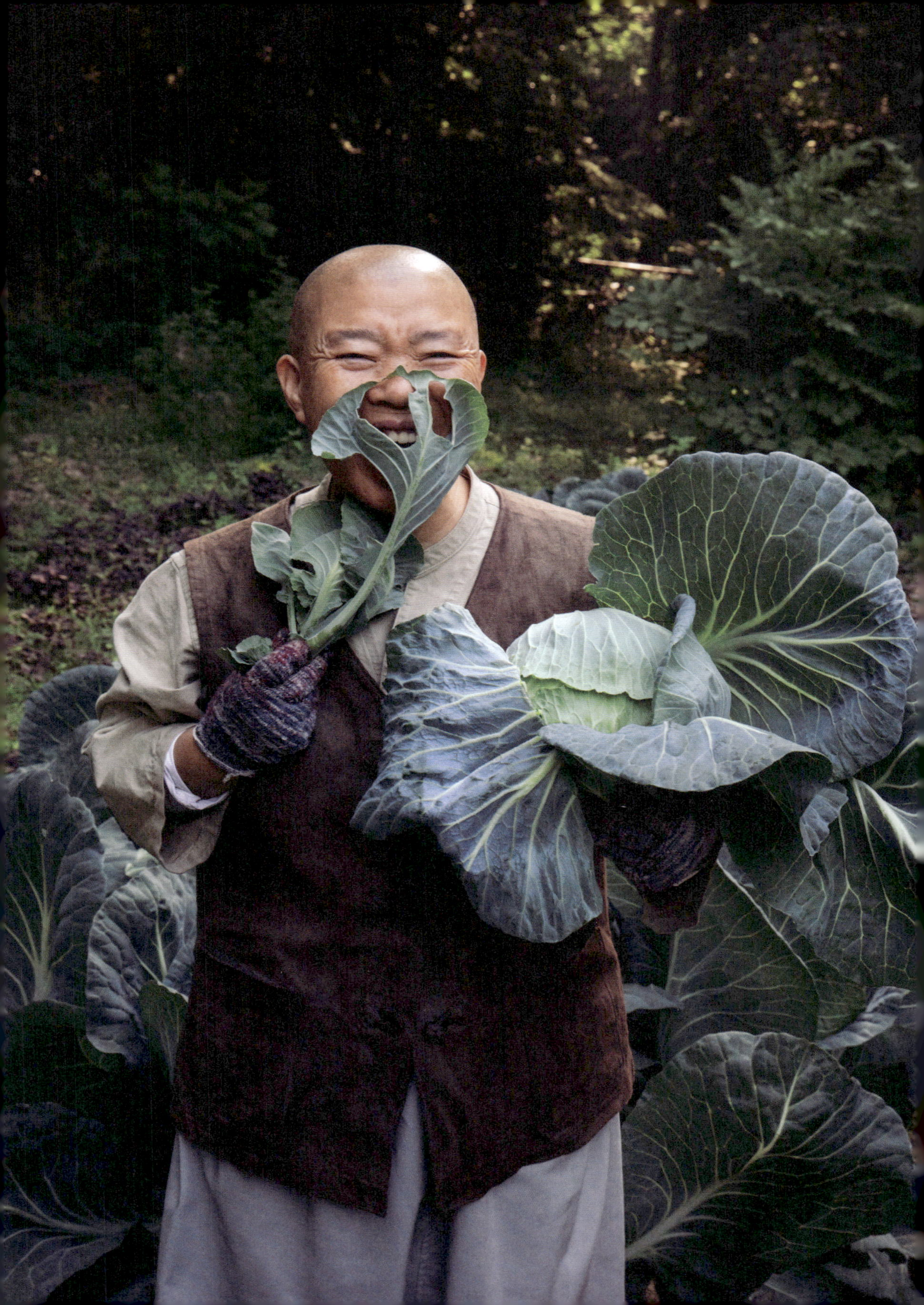

INTERVIEW

May I ask how you came to choose the way of Buddhism and join the order to become a snim? — My family was not Buddhist—they were influenced by Confucianism. However, once a year my mother went to the temple, and as a child I always went with her. When I was up in those mountains, I felt at ease. I kept these visits during my childhood as good memories. There was a Buddhist school in the neighborhood where you could learn a lot about Buddhism. I liked the snims there and went often. I must have been eight or nine years old when I memorized the whole heart sutra. In some ways I was a bit unusual because I already contemplated life and death as a child.

My mother's sudden death was a defining moment. I was in my second year of high school at that point, and I was living away from my parents with my older brother in Daegu. The strange thing was that the night before, I saw her death coming somehow in a dream. The shock was so great that I became ill and dreamed of my mother every night. I lost weight and suffered from insomnia.

One day, I took the bus by myself to Donghwasa, an old traditional temple near Daegu. In the large hall, I bowed down before the Buddha so many times that I lost count. I stayed there for five days and then I went home, but I wanted to return. That must have been early in February 1975.

I traveled to Donghwasa again. I met an older snim there who encouraged me to stay after she had heard my story. She was worried about what my family would say, but still, I stayed there for a week to give it a try and to find out for myself how serious my intentions were. I had a wonderful time! I roamed through the woods, cooked, cleaned, and completed the tasks they gave me. After that, they told me I could officially begin my probationary period as a haengja. I asked to postpone for a week and returned home.

I did not tell anyone what I was planning, but in my way, I did say goodbye to my immediate family, relatives, and friends, I set things in order, and I returned to the temple. I took three things with me: my portable record player, my stamp collection, and three gold rings I had received as a gift when I graduated school. That is how I started on the path of Buddhism.

My mother's death made me think a lot of things over. It hurt so profoundly that she had died and left me behind in the world alone! The pain of saying goodbye and being abandoned was powerful. I did not want to cause the same pain to anyone else, so I never wanted to get married or have children. The path to joining the order seemed like the right one to take. All of the quarrels and conflicts have been resolved in the meantime.

Life as a haengja caused me no difficulty—everything was easy for me. I thought that my mother had led me to Buddhism. On the 49th day after my mother's death, we celebrated the Buddhist death ritual in the temple. That night, my mother appeared dressed all in white in a dream, and she said goodbye to me contentedly.

When I woke up, I felt light and full of energy. From then on, I believed that this was my destiny. I still feel that way to this day. I am no longer anxious, I feel no regret, and each day is like new for me.

Your family didn't know you were in the temple? — Three years later, I visited my family for the first time since leaving and told them where I had been. It was the third anniversary of my mother's death. The snims said I should spend this day with my family. One snim accompanied me back home with special dishes for the death ritual. My family tried to get me to stay—they told me that they needed me at home—but I returned to the temple. One week later, my older brother came to convince me to come home, but I stuck by my decision. I told him that I was happy and content.

How many siblings do you have? — There were seven of us kids: four sons and three daughters, and I'm the fifth child.

There's a story about the braised mushroom dish that is connected with your father. What kind of story is it? — My father first came to see me in the temple seven years after I had left home. I was not there at that time; I was staying at the Buddhist academy in Suwon. I got a letter from the temple saying that my father had come. He had already spent several days waiting for me, and he made his annoyance known to the snims and others in the temple, complaining about this and that. However, he told me that the older snims were very friendly, and what they said appealed to him. What dissatisfied him, though, was the food. He said it was not possible to live only on plants with no fish or meat. "Don't you want to eat meat?" he asked me. He wanted to take me back home.

So, I packed up some dried pyogo mushrooms I had soaked before, along with a pot, some seasonings, and rice syrup, and I climbed

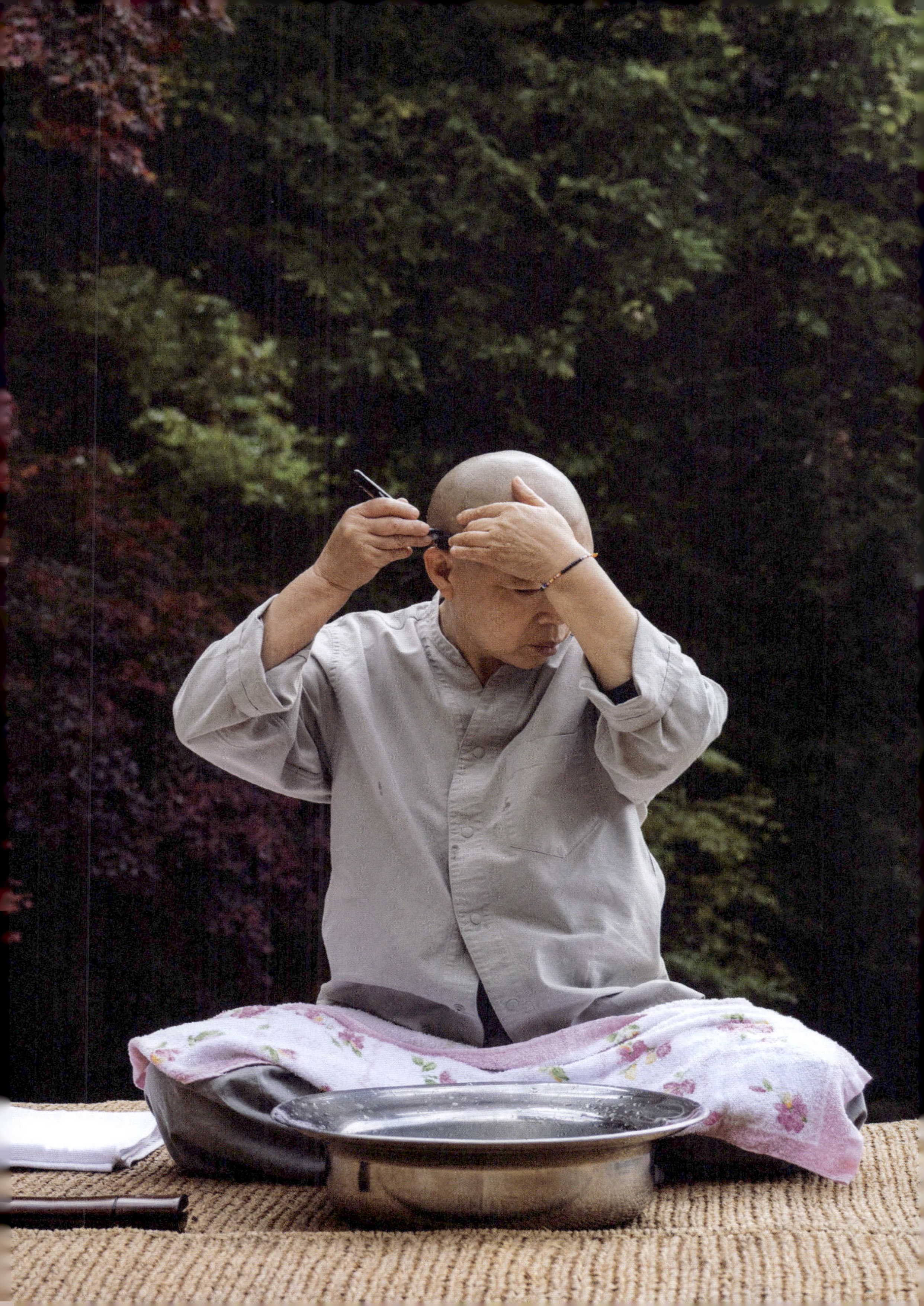

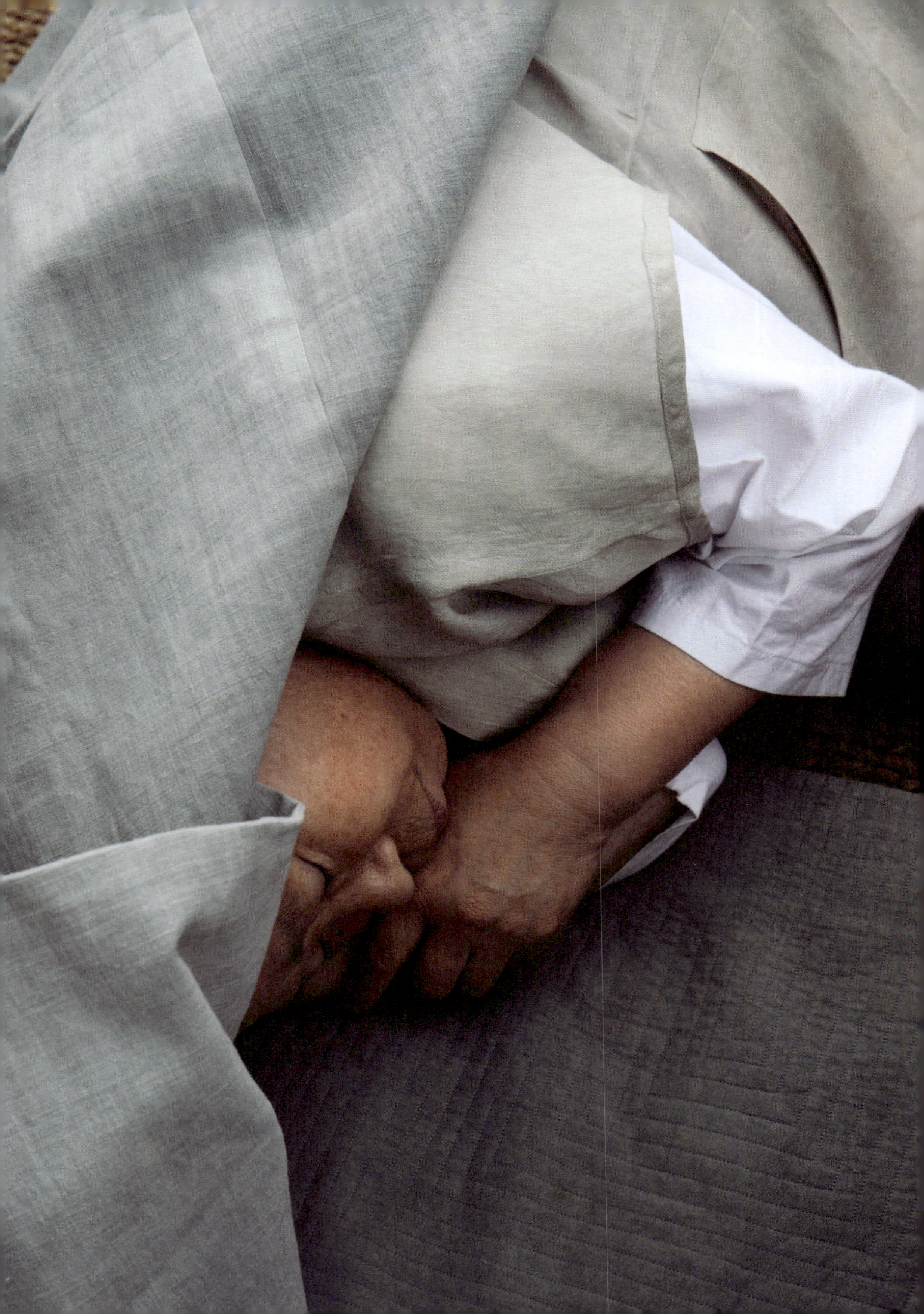

a mountain with my father. I prepared the braised dish for him there, which required time and patience. He ate a large portion of it and said he had never eaten anything so tasty before. He said it tasted better than meat. He left the temple the next day, but before he did, he asked the snims to gather. He had heard that when someone becomes a snim, this brings good luck to three generations of their family. He had also heard that even a king must bow to a snim three times to pay their respects.

He said, "Now I understand what my daughter is doing and how good it is that she is doing it. I was unkind, and I disturbed you while you were working. I would like to apologize for that. Even parents should bow three times to a snim. Now I want to call my daughter by her name for the last time." He did so, and he added that he would be leaving without worry and with joy. Then he bowed to me three times and said goodbye to the other snims, and he left with a light heart. He was whistling because he was happy. When he got home, he told the other members of my family that they should no longer call me by my name, but instead Jeongkwan Snim. One week later, he died peacefully.

You mentioned something before about life as a haengja; can you speak a bit more about that? — It is a probationary period that gives you time to get acquainted with temple life and test out whether that is what you really want. I did not serve as a haengja for long—I already knew a lot and could do some things. It was 1975, and my hair was shaved off on April 15 by the lunar calendar; the ceremony in which I was accepted as a novice took place in July. The period for a haengja is typically six months, but it can be longer or shorter than that depending on a person's skills and the circumstances. The important thing is for the decision to be firm. The men are called *sami* and the women are called *samini*, a term that means "one who makes an effort." Because the ceremony takes place twice a year, sometimes you have to wait even longer.

Everything suited me very well. Three years after I began my novitiate, I visited the Buddhist academy called Kangwon, as well as Seonwon, the meditation center. In 1982, I began studying at the Buddhist university, Joongang Sangha University.

You said before that you suffered from too little sleep. — That's correct. I had to get up at three in the morning each day. I was young and needed a lot of sleep. They wake you up, though. I actually love the wonderful night sky full of stars. In the mountains, you can see the stars at 9 p.m. I often went outside my room to see them, and then my weariness went away. I still do that to this day. But at that time, when I was still young, it was pretty difficult when you hadn't had your morning sleep. During the day, I was very tired and tried to find a place where I could nap, so I slept against a tree or in a quiet back room. Sometimes I would fall asleep in the corner of the bathroom.

There is always a lot of work in the temple that has to do with food: preserving food, cooking rice, making soy sauce and kimchi, and drying vegetables. I was needed, and I was always happy to do it. Because I liked to do all of it, I was assigned a lot of tasks. I learned a lot that way, and I became a part of the community. The best way to learn something is to do it yourself—for example, starting with the details of how to handle heat. When I worked in the kitchen, I discovered and taught myself a lot.

When were you ordained, meaning, when did you become a *biguni* and a proper snim? And which temple were you in? — The ceremony celebrating my becoming a full member of the Korean *jogae* order was in 1980. After that, I went to different temples. In 1991, I took on my first leadership position at Mangwolsa temple in Yongnam, South Korea. The person responsible for a temple is called the *juji*, so I was a juji. I was still young then. In the beginning, there were only a few supporters who came regularly—maybe between 70 and 80. However, their number grew, and later it was around 400 to 500.

I stayed there for 20 years. It was during that time that I really began to take an interest in temple food, and that laid the foundation for what I do today. My idea was that the snims and the temple's supporters should get closer and do something together. I have also organized lessons and events for children. With the supporters, I began to make soy sauce and doenjang regularly. When the sauce and doenjang were fermented and mature, I shared them with the others. Once there was enough money to buy soybeans, I started over again. The first reports about this showed up in the media, and then even more people came. I have also made kimchi together with them. I shared half of it with the others and used the other half in the temple. This gave rise to a new tradition that I continue today in Cheonjinam. My Kimchi Day is well known.

Most Korean Buddhist temples are deep in the mountains, and the snims live in seclusion. So, temple food—which has a tradition going back more than 1,500 years—remains quite hidden from the view of the public and above all the world. Is there something that has caused this to change? — When the Summer Olympic Games were coming to South Korea in 1988, there was a conversation about what parts of our culture and traditions we wanted to show visitors. Since Buddhism has a long history, constitutes a living tradition, and has a rich cultural heritage, the government asked the Buddhist orders to open the temples to the public. A program called Temple Stay was planned and gradually implemented. However, this required renovations and new construction, because up to that point, the temples were not prepared to receive guests. Opening them was meant to give a glimpse into the lives of the snims. Meditation courses were also offered.

In the beginning, only some of the larger temples were selected for this initiative, but more were gradually added. The closed world of Buddhism opened up wide. And if guests were coming, of course there had to be food. We organized a big temple food festival, and many people took part and saw what sorts of old traditions there were.

Another important year was 2007. The government at that time wanted to promote traditional Korean food and bring it to the rest of the world. I went to prepare temple food in other countries, and I was met with great enthusiasm. I brought a tea master along with me and held tea ceremonies.

In this way, temple food gradually became better known to the public. In 2012, I went with some snims to New York for the first time and made temple food. Three hundred people came to see us. Then I went to France and other countries. I wasn't alone, though—others were there. Jeok Mun Snim, a man, Seonje Snim, Dae-Ahn Snim, and Wookwan Snim all cooperated with me to compile, organize, and publicize the traditions of temple food. There were lectures on temple food and cooking courses. Everyone worked together to further develop and therefore preserve the old traditions.

Who determines what temple food should be? What is it based on? — During his lifetime, the Buddha already stipulated quite a bit regarding what a member of a monastic order should eat and what they should be mindful of. So, for example, he said that we should eat only once each day, and the meal should be calm and silent.

The *okwangae* formula was already known. It says that we should thank all living beings and people before we begin to eat. We should think about where the food comes from and how nature makes it possible for us.

The Buddha may have stipulated that we should eat only once per day, but he allowed for exceptions when someone is sick or weak. He left behind a lot of rules regarding details.

Temple food today is viewed differently than it was in the past. However, the basic idea that we should think about where the ingredients come from and who we have to thank for the food—not only should we thank all of the farmers who work in the fields but also all of the living creatures, including insects, who are harmed or killed in the process. It is important to protect life as much as possible and to try to coexist. All of this was already there in the Buddha's time. This is actually where the beauty of temple food comes from.

What do you think about temple food aligning with vegan principles? This term is new, but it has founded a new food tradition. — Temple food was not vegan in the beginning, and you have to ask whether you can automatically equate it with modern veganism. The Buddha himself wasn't vegan since he lived on donated food. In many Buddhist countries, consumption of meat *is* permitted. The temple food tradition that developed in Mahayana Buddhism became increasingly vegetarian and then vegan due to the prohibition of killing. There can be different opinions on whether or not we should eat meat. However, what is really important is contemplating why you want to renounce meat. Is life something that should be respected and not destroyed? It is worth thinking about why the temple food tradition became vegan and why this form is necessary.

Before I came to the temple, of course I ate everything. My mother was a good cook, of both meat and fish, and I emulated her. I still remember the taste of it.

You have a Buddhist name. How do you get this name? — As a haengja, you have no name. This is meant to call awareness to the fact that you have left your previous life behind. You must shed your entire identity. You don't have a new name because you are not yet a member of the order—it is just a probationary period. You are called *haengja-ja*, a vocative form. When you are admitted to your novitiate, you are given a Buddhist name. You typically get it from an older, respected snim whom you have sought out as a teacher and mentor. For women, this is always a woman. Everything has to come together right to create proper relationships, though, because personal connections, trust, and sympathy play an important role.

You chose the name Jeongkwan. Does it have a meaning? — *Jeong* means "honest, righteous," and *Kwan* means "generous and compassionate." However, there is an additional nuance to the meaning of my name: the observation of plants. As the name-bearer, I should observe plants attentively, and I am happy to do it.

The discourse around suhaengjas was often a central category in Korean Seon Buddhism. All snims are suhaengjas, but what exactly does it mean to be suhaengja? — Actually, everyone should be a suhaengja, because everyone wants to live a happy and fulfilling life. You must meditate and work on yourself to achieve this. Because I belong to a Buddhist order, I have greater freedom to do this. The goal of *suhaeng* is that one's inner being should not be in disharmony with the external being—they should be one. Then, one can face everything that comes from the outside freely and calmly.

Inside ourselves we carry a lot of yearnings and desires that can be strong and powerful. It isn't easy to resist them, and this creates internal conflict. You have to be aware of it, have a look at it, and resolve it. Meditation helps to guide you in this practice so that you can free yourself from this inner conflict and become one with yourself. Anyone can learn. However, we snims in the temple have more time to do this. We are ultimately professional suhaengja, even if our profession is not typical because we are not paid. We practice letting go and silently creating an inner world within ourselves.

Through the unusual life that snims lead, they become more aware of conflict than other people. Such conflicts cause a lot of suffering.

All humans have conflicts with themselves and others. This is because every human desires, strives for fame and recognition, and wants possessions. A suhaengja, however, is not dominated by these impulses, but is free from them. If we do not work on ourselves, we remain dependent on them and full of inner discord and dissatisfaction.

Our desires can shackle and dominate us. We lose our freedom. A suhaengja shakes all of this off through daily meditation. Otherwise, the conflicts and unmet desires collect inside of us. We must release them in order to be free. As much as possible, this must be done in a way that will prevent them from flaring up again. Only then can we devote our whole attention to new experiences and the present. We do more of that in the temple because we have more time. The goal is freedom that surpasses even life and death.

How do you deal with conflicts personally? — That really depends on the person, because everyone is different. There are also different suhaeng methods. The famous *Tripitaka Koreana*, which was made in the thirteenth century and is also called *The Eighty Thousand Tripitaka*, lists more than 80,000 ways that a person can be awakened and brought to knowledge. I myself am still only a student.

We think we know all about someone when we have lived together for three days. If coexisting does not work, even though you have both tried your best, it is difficult when you have a lot to do. Sometimes it just doesn't come together. There can be many reasons for this. I also express annoyance when my expectations are not met. Then I have to let it go and take a step back. Discontent lies in the air. I withdraw my attention and my emotions.

It can happen that there will be some cause that will allow you to start over at some point or another. It is important for human relationships that we talk with one another. The Buddha says that we should follow one hundred people and learn from them how to communicate with one. This shows his special generosity.

We all know that interpersonal relationships are complicated and difficult. However, the Buddha already knew a lot about the human psyche more than 2,500 years ago, long before Freud. There are people we can understand without having to communicate verbally with one another—it is a kind of meeting of heart with heart.

When I concentrate on something, I go quiet. If someone speaks, it breaks my concentration and hinders the process of becoming. Then I will go to a quiet place where there is no one. I used to think that I should be among people a lot, that I should talk with them and experience conflicts in order to gain insight and knowledge.

There are two ways to achieve enlightenment: a sudden awakening, which is called *dono*, or the end of a long process of learning and meditation, which is called *jeomsu*. I wanted to combine both ways. Now, in my old age, I think that you can do suhaeng better alone, in a quiet place and surrounded by nature. It may not speak to us directly, but it will still teach us a lot. You can even communicate with it.

If you interact with people, it is easier than you think to cause a lot of pain and suffering without intending to. I only learned this later in life. One example: someone wants to say something to me and, in a hurry, I say, "Not now—later." Of course, I can simply catch up later, but for the entire day, my thoughts will remain on that as an uneasiness in the back of my mind, and it will make it hard to pay attention. That is how it is in the temple, with the many people who are constantly visiting; the quietness is often disturbed. I also have to find my way.

Have you always enjoyed cooking? — Yes, I have. In Buddhism, we say that today's life is determined by yesterday. However, what also seems important to me is the social environment and family situation that you lived in. I grew up in the country; the meadows and fields were my playground. I picked a cucumber when I felt like it and ate it, and I did the same with a lot of other things. I rode cows. I observed closely how the plants and vegetables grew and the fruit ripened. I learned quite young what you can eat and what you cannot, and how something tastes in which stage of growth. I still remember very clearly how things tasted when I was a child. Especially the cucumbers: what kind of noise they made when you bit into them and chewed, how fresh they tasted, and what the consistency was like when you chewed them. When I think about this as I prepare food, I am always very successful. Maybe it also had to do with my early life. The Buddha is supposed to have lived all possible lives.

Temple food has become famous and excites interest all over the world. How do people in other parts of the world react to it? — It is important that I feel fulfilled within in order to be able to give. My mission also requires inner preparedness, because only then can I truly face my mission. Food gives me the energy I need to do this.

Food and the self—the two are inseparably linked together. However, people see them as being separate: eating here and the self there, the body here and the spirit there. They do not reflect enough on what we need to live and to act. Interest in food and nutrition is not great, and many do not know how to cook—rather, many people focus on enjoyment and cultivating their palates. But isn't something missing when we approach food that way? If people prepared food together in a community, they would think more about it.

You can contemplate where the food comes from, what happens to it in our bodies, and how it becomes one with the body in the digestive organs. You can also contemplate how the food transforms inside the body, how it becomes part of the body, and how it enables life. Finally, food helps with the formation of identity. This is because it becomes part of the immune system, the spirit, and the body. This enables me to do everything that I want to—through food, the world outside merges with the world inside of me into one. It is like a work of art that, created from various ingredients, brings the body and soul together, creates balance, and provides us with energy. What we eat is important, because food is life, and it forms the personality.

You have to pay attention to harmony, because not every food is good for us. Even if I have a strong digestive system, food can make me sick if I do not pay attention to the details. I must pay attention to what is good for me in spring, summer, autumn, and winter, and which flavorings are good for me. One should also pay attention to the beauty of things. All of these aspects are important for me, and I would be happy to share my knowledge and experience with many people. When we look at our food, we should feel joy. This makes it easier for it to transform into vital force. When I prepare the temple food, I like to do this together with others and share. Because I give my best each time, I am content and can start anew the next time. If more people sat joyfully around their food, it would be good for the world.

The Netflix documentary that came out in 2017 made you and temple food famous worldwide. You were even invited to the Berlin International Film Festival. Has that sudden interest changed you as a person? — I am asked this question often. What has changed is that I get a lot more invitations than I used to and so I am on the road more. Of course, more visitors come from other countries to my temple, Cheonjinam, to taste my temple food. But apart from that, nothing has changed. I live my life every day as a snim and do the work that I have been doing for years. I prepare all of the flavorings and ingredients that I need for my cooking, and I follow the rhythm of the seasons. Nature sets the beat.

I often say that nature is the great master, not me. Nature grows everything, matures it, and starts fermentation. We are humble next to the greatness of nature. Speaking of recipes sounds too simple when you think of the enormous process through which seeds grow, ripen, and finally end up in my mouth thanks to sunlight, wind, and rain. The energy of the person doing the cooking and their experience can create new food each day.

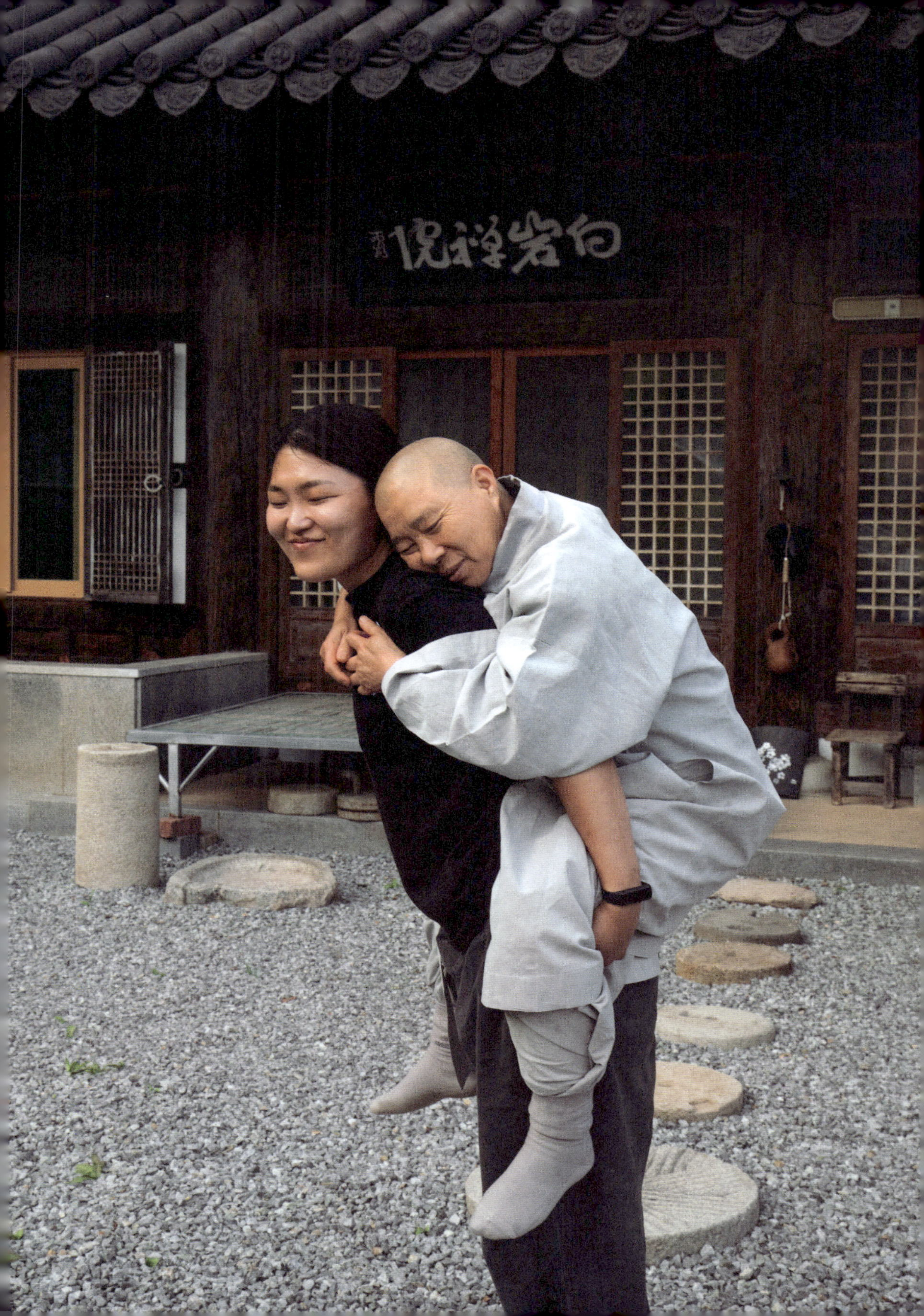
白岩禪院

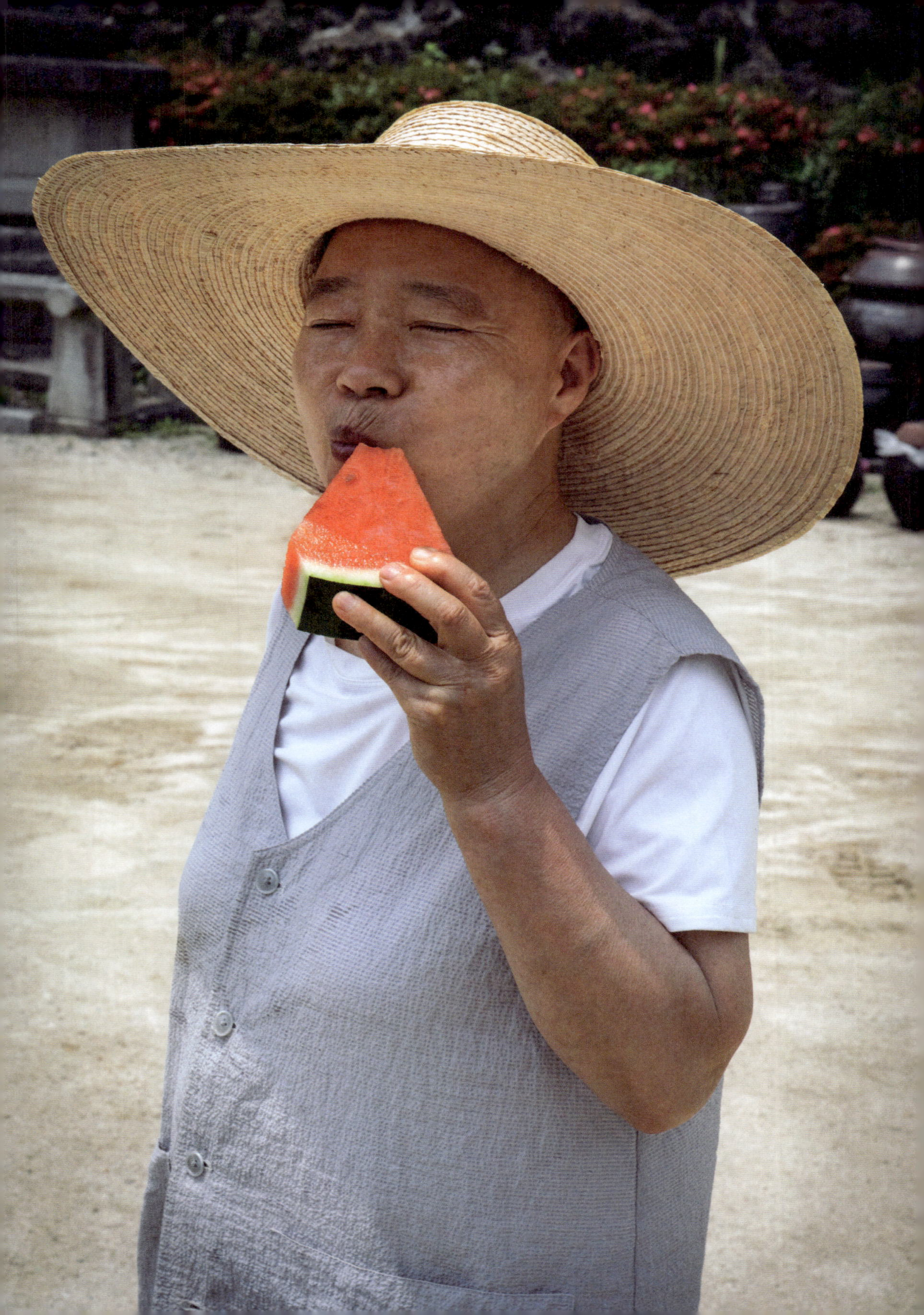

I am often asked for recipes, but I think cooking in itself is not difficult. The reason my food is wholesome and healthy does not have so much to do with my particular cooking skills; it is the flavorings that I prepare myself each year. I have different vintages of soy sauce, doenjang, gochujang, vinegar, oil, and cheong made from fruits and grains, and I have an array of preserved and dried vegetables and fruits. Without this foundation—which takes a lot of time, patience, and love to make—there would be no temple food as I cook it. The secret of my cooking is in the many onggi pots. Recipes are actually ephemeral.

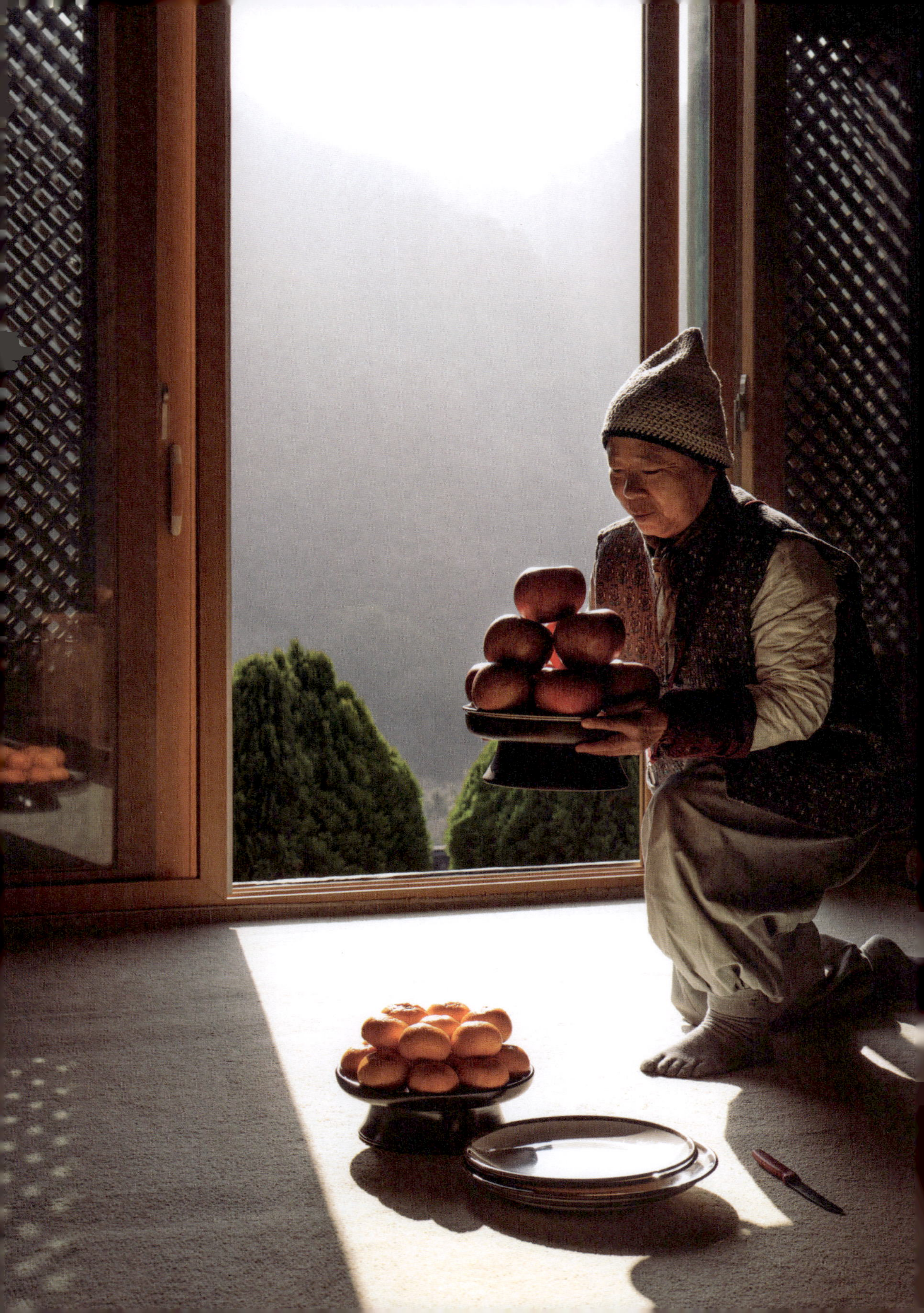

TEMPLE FOOD

Living requires an exchange with nature because all living things depend on one another. Our hands and the work they do transforms nature's gifts into food and provides for us. Eating satisfies a fundamental need—our physical bodies always amount to no more than what we eat. That's because everything we ingest transforms within us, becomes a part of our body, gives it a certain form, awakens the spirit, and keeps it awake.

At the center of every culture lies its culinary tradition. Because food is life, the desire for food is a powerful force that operates within us. We can tame it only with difficulty. Greed arises from this! Because food is central to life, our attitude toward it reveals how we think about ourselves and nature.

HISTORY

Every religion has attached a certain (often symbolic) meaning to food. We've linked food to ideas of purity and impurity, and we've assigned commandments, prohibitions, and taboos to various foods. These helped establish legitimacy and often served as a means of distinguishing one religion from another. Control over food signifies the great power that an institution can exercise over individuals.

The discussion about food in Buddhism began very early on and took an interesting and quite unique course. That said, however, doctrine and practice have changed over the long course of history. Various schools of Buddhism have emerged, and with the spread of Buddhism has come necessary adaptations to local conditions—factors like climate and natural living conditions contribute to the formation of essential food traditions.

The preoccupation with food within a religious context has always had an ethical and spiritual dimension. For Buddhism, the fact that it's a religion of meditation plays a central role. That's why the first thing the Buddha prohibited was the consumption of alcohol: it obscures and eclipses the soul, impedes concentration, and frees us from our inhibitions against violence. As it says in the teaching texts, alcohol destroys the germ of wisdom. Meditation and alcohol are mutually exclusive.

Today, a wide variety of food traditions exist in different Buddhist countries, although they're characterized by the concept that eating food from animal sources became central to the debate very early on.

This debate ultimately resulted in the development of vegan temple cooking within Mahayana Buddhism.

For himself, the Buddha actually had no dietary restrictions, at least not at the beginning of his life, when he was living a life of luxury as a young man. But then he left the palace, gave himself up to austerity, and consumed only very little. After he achieved enlightenment, he lived on donated food.

This need for donated foods is why the temple was not built very far away from the city—every morning, the Buddha went into the city and knocked on different doors to ask for food. He gratefully accepted what was offered and returned to the temple when he had collected a certain quantity. All of the food was heated, distributed, and eaten. If there was too much, the leftovers were buried because it was forbidden to keep food for the next day.

According to the Buddha, no one was allowed to ask for anything specific or to refuse anything. The Buddha ate what residents had laid in his bowl, and he only ate once a day and before noon. After that, only fluids were allowed.

The Buddha was always aware that the desire for food is easily awakened, as is greed, and he was also aware of how powerful this desire can be. If you constantly give in to it, it acts as shackles and controls you. He wanted to live free from that desire, free from the lust for things.

During the Buddha's lifetime, it seems, there were no clear rules regarding what we should eat and what we should not eat. Although his first commandment was the prohibition of killing, the Buddha did not actively undertake to avoid the consumption of meat. He only wanted no animal to be slaughtered for his sake. Despite this, according to tradition, his last meal was a dish with pork that may not have been very fresh. It was said that his death (at 80 years old) was connected with that meal, because he got sick afterwards.

Because his movement was new, the Buddha carefully considered how his teachings were worded and what kinds of rules he stipulated for life in the monastic community. His primary focus was on explaining matters such as what we should do and how we should live. Food regulations are certainly part of that, particularly when they arise from the prohibition of murder. However, the Buddha considered offenses such as killing, committing violence, stealing, lying, betraying others, committing adultery, etc. to be worse than eating meat.

Criticism of meat consumption emerged even during the time of the Buddha, and so in time, it was decided that there was a category of "pure meat" that Buddhists should be permitted to eat. Meat was considered "pure" if it was meat from an animal that a person had not killed themselves or that had not been killed for a member of the order in general. The order member needed to be very certain of this, and they could not have seen or heard how the animal was slaughtered. If there was any uncertainty about the source of the meat, the person should ask exactly for whom the animal had been slaughtered. Meat was also considered "pure" if the animal had been killed as a sacrifice and something was left over.

But despite there being a clearly established category of "pure" meat, consuming meat remained controversial. In order to understand why, it's necessary to understand the contemporary context of Buddhism in India. Buddhism emerged as a countermovement to Hinduism, which dominated India at the time. Hinduism mistrusted Buddhism and saw it as competition. The Hindu priest caste, the Brahmans—who formed the elite class of society—were increasingly eating a vegetarian diet, and they criticized the Buddha's consumption of meat as being inconsistent. This discussion also arose among Buddhists again and again. In response, the Buddha further limited the category of animals whose meat could be eaten—the meat of horses, elephants, snakes, dogs, and leopards was forbidden for various reasons, for example. However, the prohibition on eating meat did not take root in India due to the lifestyle of the Buddhists there: as long as they lived off of donations, they ate anything that residents laid in their bowls.

This changed as Mahayana Buddhism developed in a new direction. Founded in India, it saw rapid expansion in East Asia and began to take on a firmer shape. The discussion about whether a member of a monastic order could eat meat or not was more a matter of principle in these regions. Two main reasons were established that ultimately led to the formation of a vegan food tradition in East Asian temples, one that has remained unique for about 1,500 years. The first reason stated was the commandment not to kill, injure, or inflict suffering: if one takes the prohibition of killing seriously, one must avoid eating meat because it requires the killing of living creatures. This commandment is not absolute, but even eating the meat of an animal that has died of natural causes is discouraged because consuming it could lead to the desire to eat more meat.

As a Buddhist, one must strive to reduce suffering, protect life, and not cause any fresh suffering. If a person consumes meat, it was said that they would lose their core sympathy and empathy for other living creatures. But that concept shouldn't lead to becoming obsessed with avoiding meat—the renunciation is only true when it comes from a place of sympathy for living creatures.

The second reason for prohibiting meat consumption was that meat was perceived as having a strong smell and being hard to digest. It would make the body sluggish, and that makes concentration difficult. Light, plant-based foods not only support meditation and keep the spirit active, but they also promote good health. Striving for spirituality is not compatible with the consumption of meat, says Mahayana Buddhism. For the same reason, it's forbidden to use the five vegetables of garlic, onion, wild chives, garlic chives, and asafetida as ingredients—they have a strong smell, tantalize the senses, develop heat in the body that rises up and pushes outward, and impede the achievement of inner peace and concentration.

When it arrived in China in the first century, Mahayana Buddhism incorporated many local ideas and traditions, resulting in a deep internal transformation. Accompanied by much discussion, vegan temple food soon developed and increasingly established itself in the fifth century. This tradition spread across all of East Asia; even some emperors in China and kings in Korea adhered to it. Such a way of life was possible because the order members in East Asia didn't live off of food donations but rather their own work. The climate in East Asia is different from that in India, too, and agricultural practices were more developed.

The culture, lifestyle, and living conditions in East Asia were also very different from those in India. In East Asia, a temple community was well organized and designed to provide for itself. This development was necessary because the temples often lay deep in the mountains, and while they were happy to take community donations, all of the order members worked, including in the fields. They grew tea, rice, and vegetables, and temple housekeeping also included providing a wide variety of resources for winters that were sometimes long and cold. This meant that fermentation methods played a central role—they were used in a variety of ways and were constantly being refined. That's how a unique tradition of vegan cooking emerged that supported meditation and kept temple residents healthy.

Endeavoring for self-reliance and having a pronounced work ethic are particularly present in Seon Buddhism. That said, the commandment not to eat anything derived from animals cannot be seen as absolute—there are many exceptional situations, like war or illness, in which the rule against eating meat must be flouted so that order members can survive. Buddhism has always recognized this.

The Buddha and his disciples in India didn't work—instead, they dedicated themselves to study and meditation. However, they also gave people advice and counseled them in spiritual matters. Because they didn't physically work, they could get by on one meal per day. Even today, a dish called *maji* is prepared with great care and is laid on the altar at 10 a.m. in Korean temples to commemorate the one daily meal that the Buddha ate.

In Korea, it's customary to eat three meals per day at set times, with breakfast and dinner being light and simple preparations. Temple life in East Asia maintains its own character through its long vegan tradition and special rituals. The category of gratitude is central: when we have food in front of us, we should foster a deep feeling of gratitude toward nature, the farmers, and the people who prepare the food. This certain inner attitude is to be nurtured as well as celebrated; the spiritual atmosphere peculiar to East Asian temples may have its source in this.

While Mahayana Buddhism and its vegan food tradition developed and became the standard in East Asia, both Theravada Buddhism and Tantric Buddhism in Tibet went another way. Consumption of meat and fish is allowed in Theravada Buddhism because the Buddha also ate meat and fish and did not expressly forbid them. No special tradition of temple food developed in Southeast Asia, but in Tibet or Nepal, the living conditions high up in the mountains determine what the people there eat more than anything else—practicing agriculture is much more difficult there, and order members must rely on farming livestock. In the high mountains of Tibet, Buddhists cannot help but consume meat and milk in order to survive.

The special funeral rite of leaving the dead to the vultures is also connected to the peculiarities of this region. The idea of the circle of life is one thing, but the frost and the lack of soil where the dead can be buried are something else. When the monks in Tibet slaughter an animal to eat it, they celebrate a special ritual to thank the animal and ask its forgiveness. Extinguishing another life in order to survive is often unavoidable, and awareness of this situation enables gratitude for the nourishment the animal provides. Life is always a precious thing, and that should not be forgotten; waste should always be avoided. Life should be protected wherever possible.

The history of Korean temple food begins with the arrival of Buddhism at the end of the fourth century. It seems that the unusual idea of vegan food spread gradually. Eventually, though, court annals reported that kings became Buddhists, ate no meat, and prohibited the slaughter of animals.

Buddhism left many traces in Korea's food traditions. The technique of fermentation—and with it the entire jang culture, which is constantly being refined—expanded from the temple outwards to the community and became part of the general food culture in Korea. However, a vegetarian or even vegan food tradition didn't establish itself outside the temple, though in general less meat was consumed. People are considering this old tradition more today, though, because it helps us eat more mindfully, protect nature, and maintain a natural balance.

In summary, you could say that contemplating food and how we interact with it has a long and multifaceted tradition in Buddhism, and different traditions have emerged as a result. Alongside the various interpretations of the Buddha's teachings, different cultures and different natural living conditions of countries play a decisive role in how Buddhists feed themselves. Jeongkwan Snim continues the old tradition of temple food as it has formed in Korea, in the spirit of the Buddha.

MAJI

The Buddha wore a single piece of clothing and went every day with a bowl into the city to request food for the one meal a day he ate. He wasn't begging, because people weren't giving the Buddha some of their leftovers out of sympathy—rather, they gifted him some of the food they had prepared before they ate it themselves. In exchange for this, the Buddha spoke with them, and when he was asked, he gave spiritual advice or guidance.

As a reminder of the Buddha's single daily meal, between 10 and 11 a.m. each day in Korea, cooked rice is offered on the altar in a special brass dish. This is called *maji*, which means "rice prepared with great care and special devotion." It's a simple ceremonial act observed as a celebration.

Jeongkwan Snim fills a bowl with cooked rice and smooths the surface flat with a wet spoon. The bowl is covered and wrapped in a fine red cloth. Clad in her ceremonial robe, she goes to the main hall, holding the maji bowl high in her right hand. She removes the cloth, sets the bowl on the altar before the Buddha, and opens the cover. Then Snim steps back, takes the moktak in her hand, taps in rhythm, and kneels three times. Afterwards, she sits a while in a meditative pose and continues to tap the moktak as if she wants to give the Buddha time to inhale the aroma of the rice and eat some.

Once the ceremony is over, she takes the bowl from the altar. Before closing the cover, she spoons

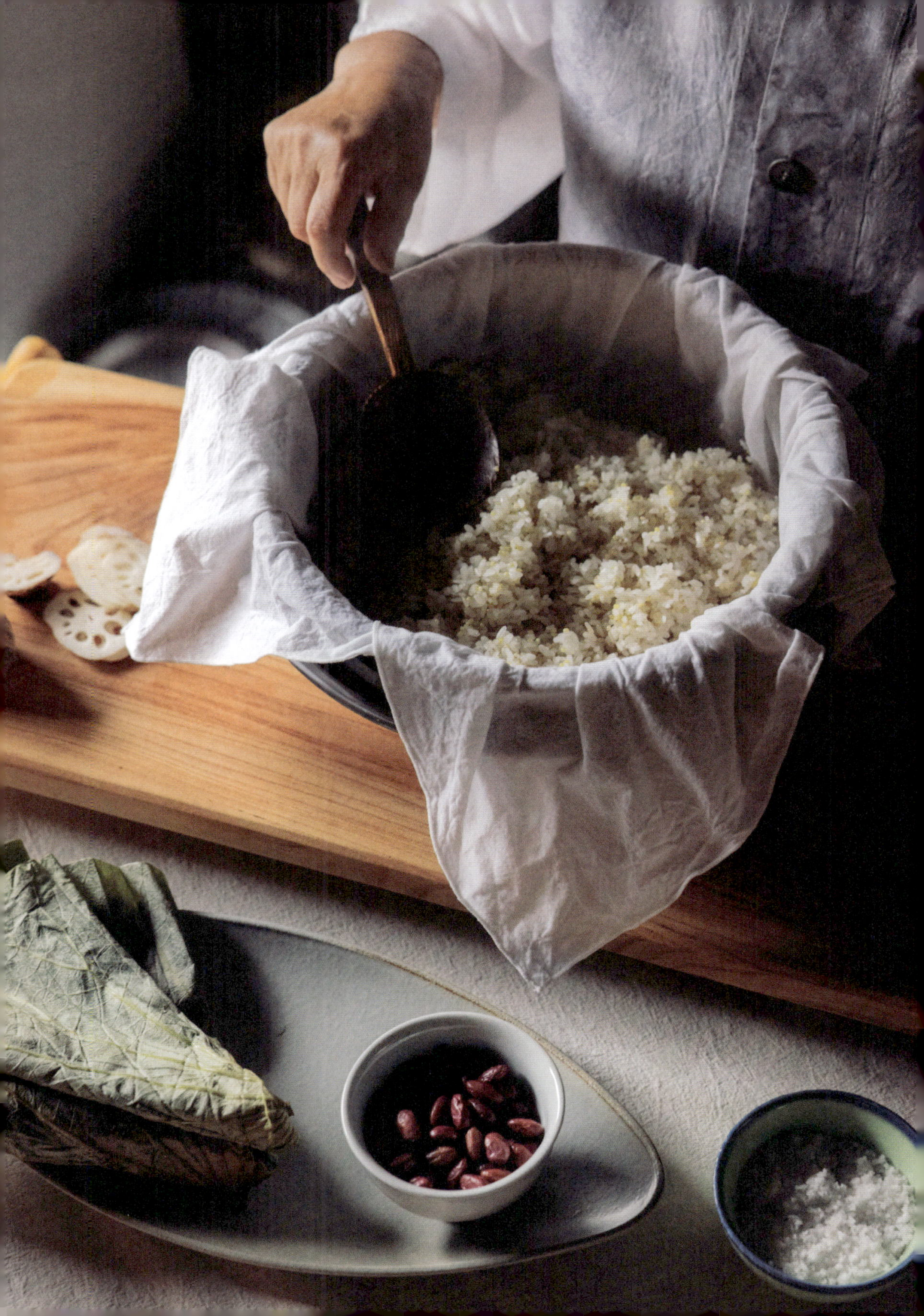

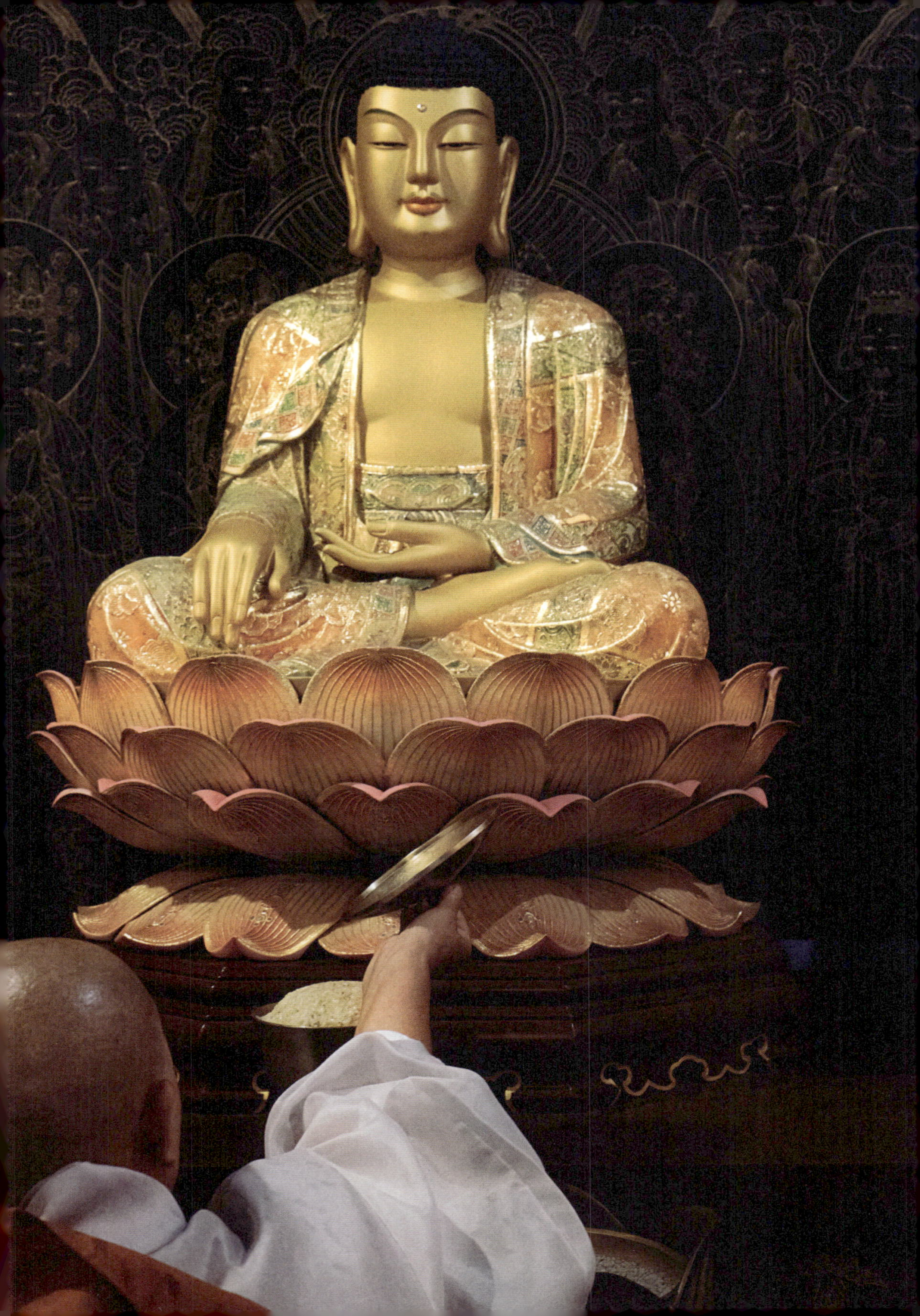

some of the rice into a small dish and puts it outside in the garden for the animals. The monks then eat the rice together. This ceremony is a reminder not only of the Buddha, but also of his teachings about how to treat food.

BARUGONGYANG

The snims eat a meal together (if not every day, then at regular intervals) called *barugongyang*. This is a ritual act in which simplicity, humility, and moderation are practiced. The snims all dress in their official robes and gather in the hall, where they sit next to each other on the floor in a long row.

The sequence of the meal is precisely determined. First, each snim takes their own set of *barus* from the cases along the wall where the sets are kept and lays it in front of themselves. The baru set consists of four wooden bowls of varying sizes, a cover, a wooden spoon, and chopsticks. These bowls are meant to remind them of the one bowl the Buddha took with him each day when he asked for food. In Seon Buddhism, the baru has deviated from the original bowl because Korean food culture is different from Indian. In Korea, the set also includes a long cord, a napkin, and a square cloth.

Barus are lovely yet plain bowls made from the old wood of a ginkgo tree by the hand of a master. Their beauty can be attributed not only to the unique grain and workmanship of the wood but also to the seven layers of lacquer that give the bowls a warm, dark, reddish-brown sheen. Each bowl has a specific purpose: one is for rice, the second is for soup, the third is for vegetables, and the fourth is for water.

The four nested bowls are "unfolded," as the action is called, onto the spread-out square cloth in a particular order. Novices stand ready to serve water and food. The ritual begins with a blow to the *jukbi*, which sends its muted tone into the silence of the room. In a set order, each snim takes only as much food as they would like to eat. The number of side dishes is limited to five.

When everyone has food in their bowl, they recite the following lines together: "Where do these dishes come from? / I have not done enough good to deserve them. / I want to be released from greed. / And to view this food as medicine that nourishes my body. / Because I strive for wisdom and enlightenment, I consume these dishes."

Now the meal begins. Speaking is not allowed; everything must happen in calm and silence. During the meal, a small bowl is passed around, and each person takes a bit of rice out of their own bowl and puts it into the communal bowl. When the meal ends, the little bowl is placed on a stone in the garden for the animals to eat. Birds are aware of this, and they stop by; so do squirrels. It's a simple gesture with deep symbolic meaning: it's a reminder that every living thing needs nourishment, that they all depend on one another, and that we must share what we have.

During the barugongyang, it's important that nothing remains in the bowls. Once a snim has finished eating, they pour water from one bowl into the next, one after the other, and swish it around until everything is clean. After that, they drink the water. Once all of the bowls are empty, they dry them with the cloth. The barus are once again nested within each other, the cover is put on, and the cord is tied. The cloth is also folded up and put away in the cabinet with the barus.

This ritual meal practices eating with gratitude, eating little, eating mindfully, and eating together with company. We should contemplate the preciousness of the food. When we cherish the food, we honor the Earth, which provides us with nourishment.

The significance of food in Korean Buddhism also manifests in how a snim acquires their baru set. When a person is accepted as a novice, they are received into the novitiate through a celebratory ceremony. During the ceremony, a novice will receive, for example, a baru set and novice robes as a gift from an older snim whom they previously sought out as a teacher and mentor. The baru set and the robes symbolize the Buddha and his life. The relationship between the mentor and the student is close—it's a connection that usually lasts a lifetime. The baru set is therefore considered something important and precious; it will be there throughout life's journey until death.

The baru set, like the robes, is among the few personal things that snims may call their own. The baru must be treated with great care and mindfulness and must not be damaged or lost. The snim always takes their baru with them when they change temples, withdraw for long meditation periods, or go to assemblies. If it's lost, it cannot simply be replaced, because there are highly complex rules explaining how one can obtain a new set of barus. Losing a baru is considered to be a great transgression that can only be atoned for with great difficulty. This is an expression of appreciation for both the teacher and the food.

Eating together at a group barugongyang in the temple might look as follows: the largest bowl is always for rice, which is mixed with beans. Next to that is the soup bowl; it may contain a soup of zucchini leaves and soybean powder. The bowl containing water stands behind the rice bowl. The fourth bowl is filled with four kinds of vegetables, such as perhaps *hobak* (squash) and *yangha* (myoga ginger). Everyone takes as much as they want to eat from the communal bowls, and they are required to eat everything they take in order to honor nature and the people who have prepared the food.

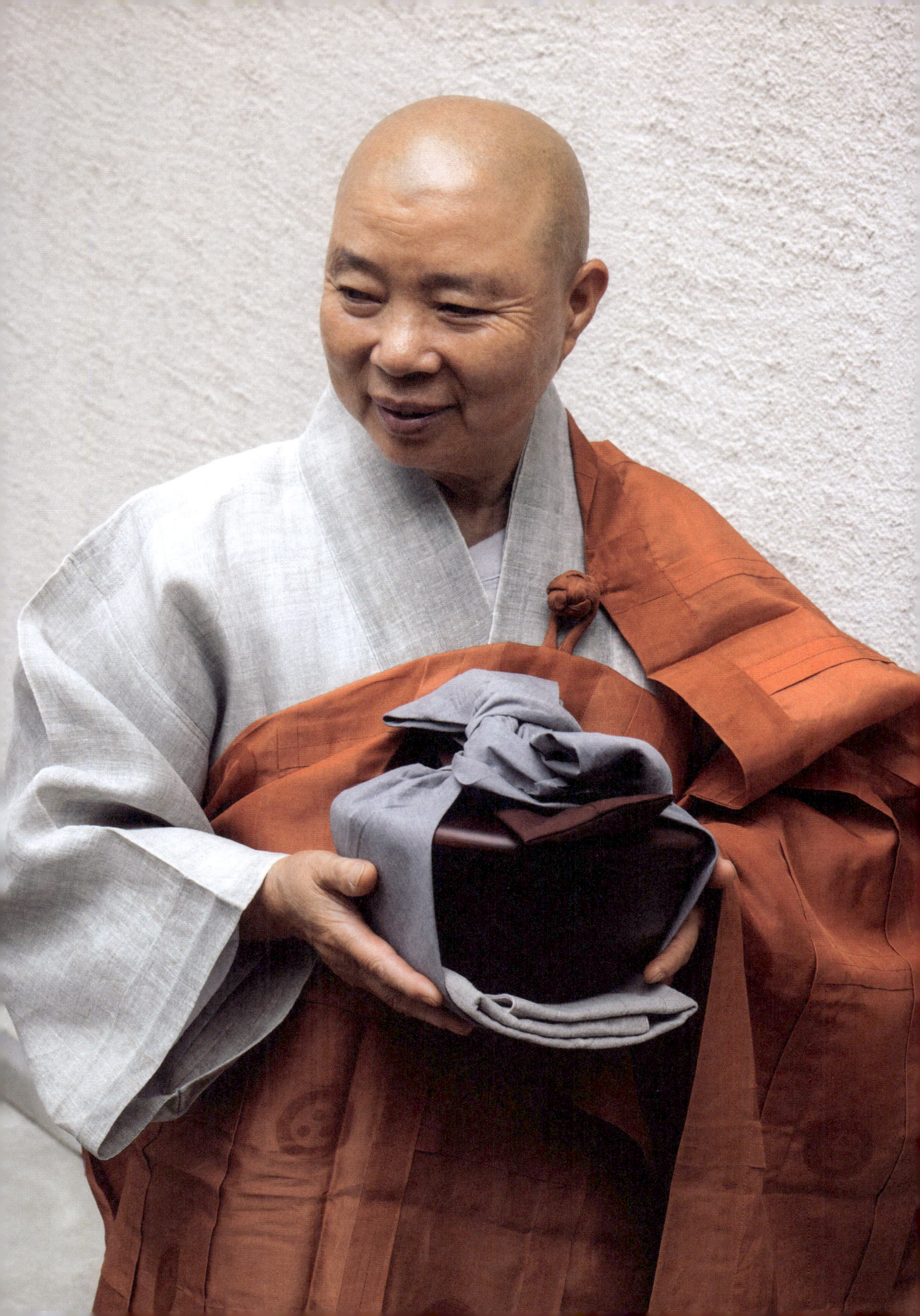

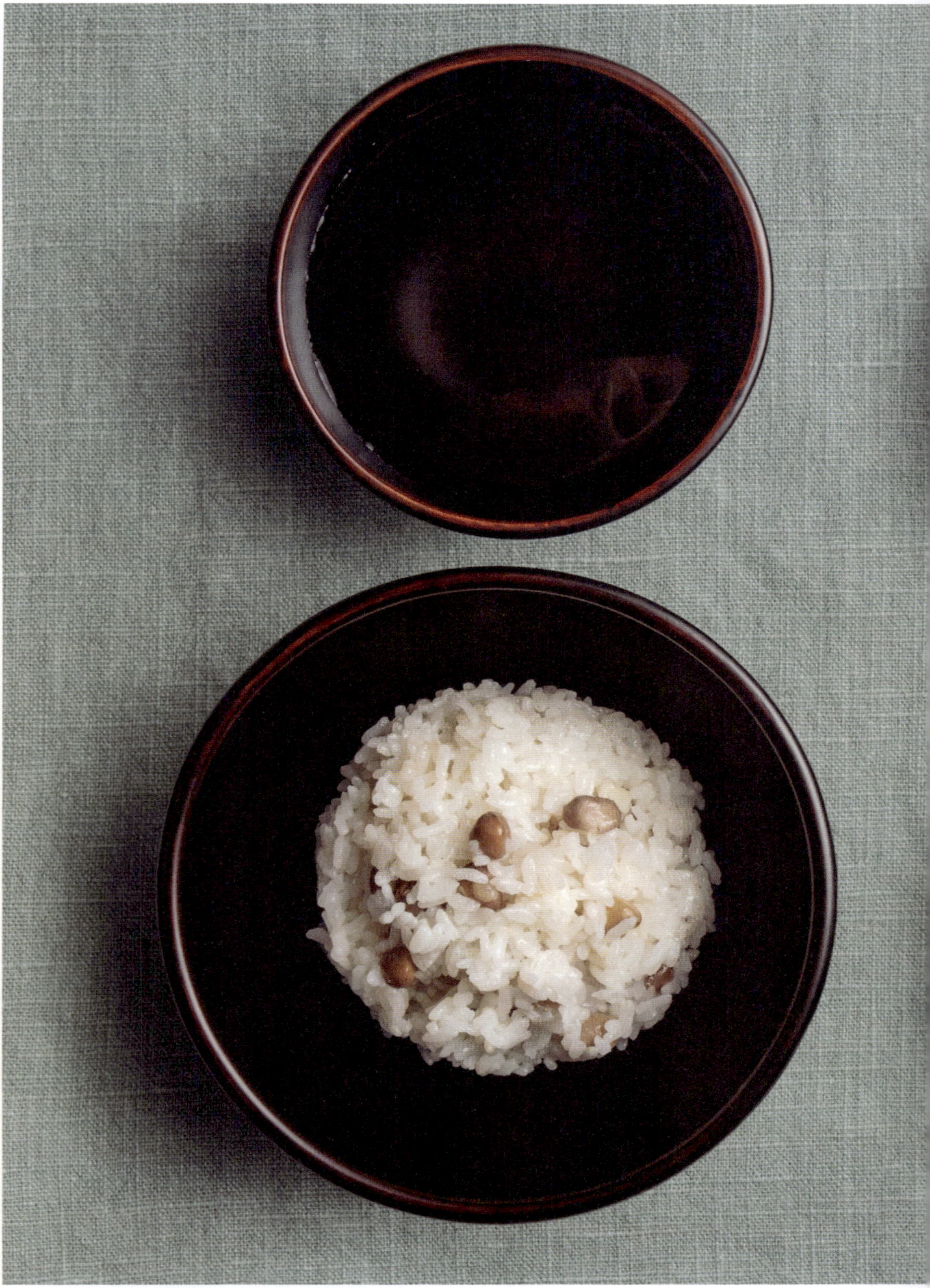

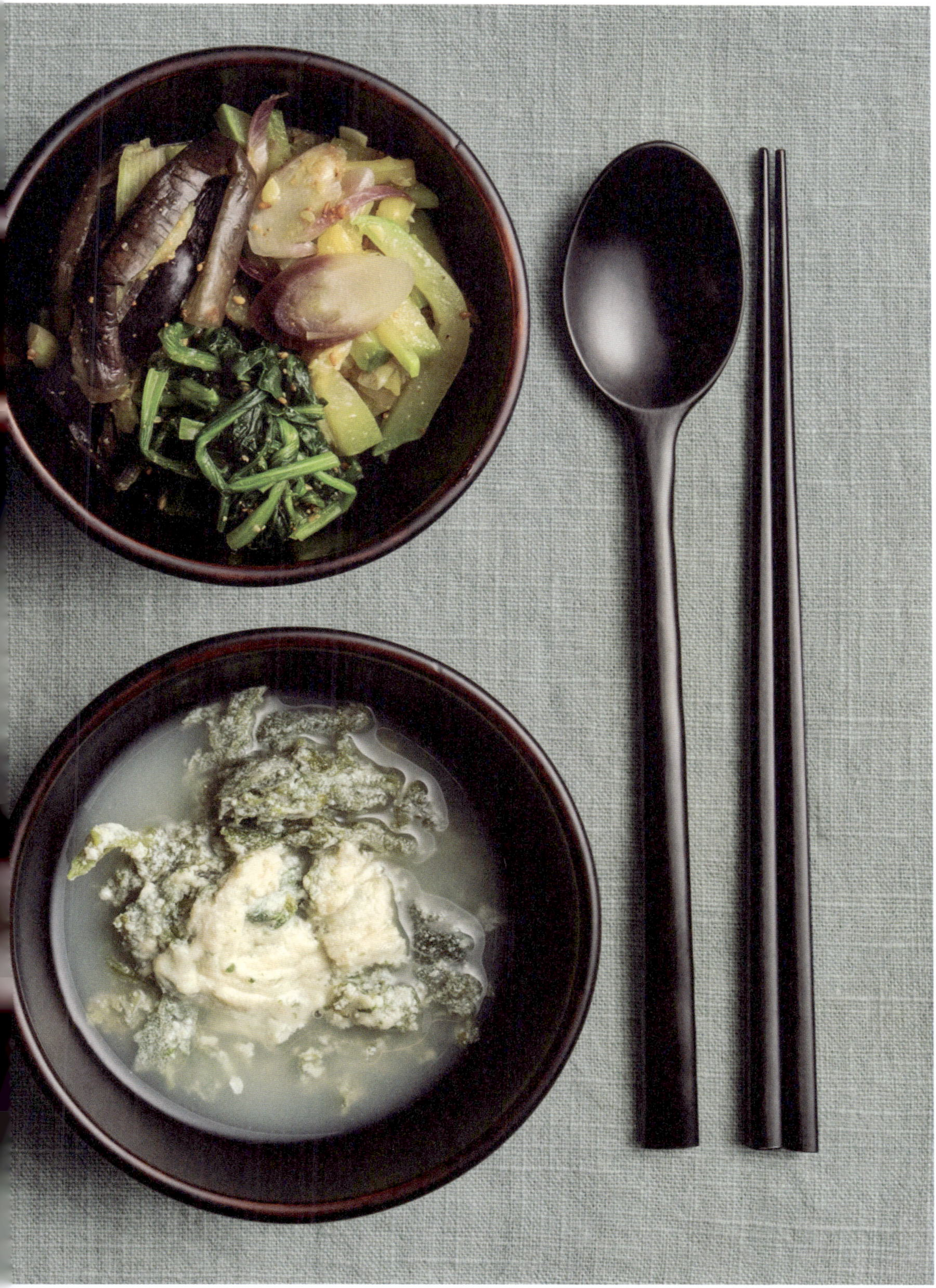

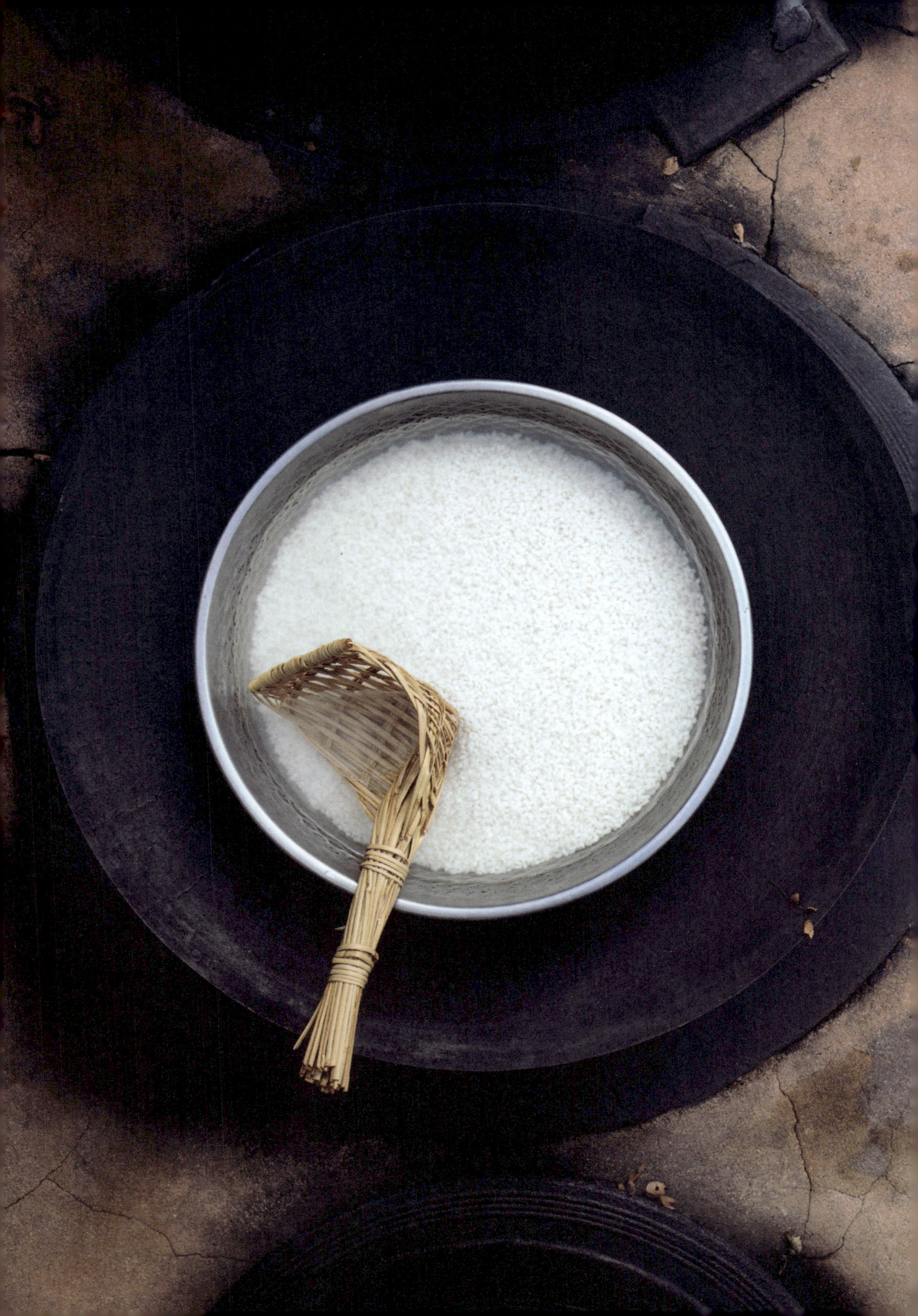

RICE

The fact that rice is the king of foods in Korea makes itself apparent in a number of ways. In autumn, the ripe stalks of rice gleam golden in the valleys, exhibiting how rice has shaped the cultural landscape of the country. Rice was so precious that it was once used to pay taxes. The rice plant is among the oldest crops in East Asia, and in Korea, rice is a staple food. It also symbolizes life because it bestows vital force, and it has a central place in temple food. The preferred type is short-grain rice, which typically must be washed several times and is cooked with only water. There is also glutinous rice, which contains more starch and is therefore better suited to making rice cakes and pastries. Other varieties of rice are also cultivated today, such as red rice.

Rice has great potential and can be used in a variety of ways. The special status of rice can be discerned from the language. When Koreans eat out, they always go for bap, even if they're eating noodles or hamburgers. *Bap*, or "cooked rice," simply means food in general. Because rice is considered a staple food, everything else is arranged around it and is called *banchan*. Banchan is an umbrella term for anything that's eaten as a side to rice. The harmonious synergy between rice and banchan is possible because the rice is unseasoned and cooked only with water. It does have its own flavor and aroma, yes, but overall, the rice is neutral enough that the individual character of each banchan can be experienced to its full effect.

Because it's considered healthy and for the sake of variety, it's also common to steam or boil rice together with other grains or various kinds of beans, as well as chestnuts, pine nuts, ginkgo nuts, and *daechus* on certain occasions. A wide variety of *tteok* (rice cakes) can also be made with rice. They're often filled with beans or nuts and are usually steamed. Rice can also be used to make alcohol.

The smell of freshly cooked rice signifies home and food being ready. Offering someone a bowl of warm rice represents humanity. However, if someone is "treated like cold rice," this means that they were not welcomed.

Jeongkwan Snim prepares rice in different ways. She says that back when there were no electric rice cookers available, cooking rice in a cast-iron pot required great skill. Her signature dish of preparing rice by wrapping it in lotus leaves and steaming it is well known. Snim also often prepares rice as *juk*, a kind of porridge—rice is simmered in plenty of water for a long time and seasoned with salt. Many variations of juk can be made with other ingredients; it's typically eaten for breakfast or during illness. Her cheong made from rice called *jocheong* is famous: it condenses the sweetness of the rice, and she uses it often as a flavoring.

COOKING RICE

In Korea, cooking rice well has always been considered a difficult business that requires experience and skill. This is because rice must be treated differently depending on its variety and freshness. It requires four things: good-quality rice, soft water, an appropriate pot, and well-controlled heat. Every Korean kitchen used to have a cast-iron pot for this purpose. The electric rice cooker used to cook rice in modern Korean households replaced the millennia-old manual preparation method and can cook many varieties of rice automatically.

"Good" rice in Korea means husked short-grain rice accompanied by the quality seal of a region. Freshly harvested rice needs less water and a shorter cooking time; it's more aromatic and has a visible sheen. In other parts of the world, the closest thing to Korean rice is the Italian rice varieties used to make risotto.

Rice can actually be cooked in any kind of pot, but the result is better when rice is cooked in pots that possess certain characteristics. The pot should have the thickest bottom possible in order to distribute the heat better—that way, the rice will rest better in the residual heat at the end of its cooking. Letting the rice rest is important, because that's when all of the remaining water will be absorbed into the grains without the risk of scorching them. The pot should also be a certain height and the lid should have a certain weight. It's easy for rice to boil over, but the pot should remain covered and the lid shouldn't be opened too often, or else the aroma will be lost. Avoid using a light, flat lid.

The first step to cooking rice is rinsing it. Place it in a bowl and add plenty of cold water. Stir the rice steadily with your hand and then drain the water. Repeat this process four or five times. The water will be milky and opaque in the beginning, but it will get clearer as you go. Then add the rice to the pot and spread it evenly along the bottom. Using the right quantity of water is crucial for success, but this amount can differ depending on preference. (In Korea, it's said that marriages have broken up due to differing preferences regarding how much water should be used.) The question is: should the rice be more al dente or a bit more tender? In general, a ratio of one part rice to two parts water works, though a rule of thumb is to add enough water that if you lay your hand on the rice, the water will just cover your hand. With time, you'll discover for yourself how you prefer your rice.

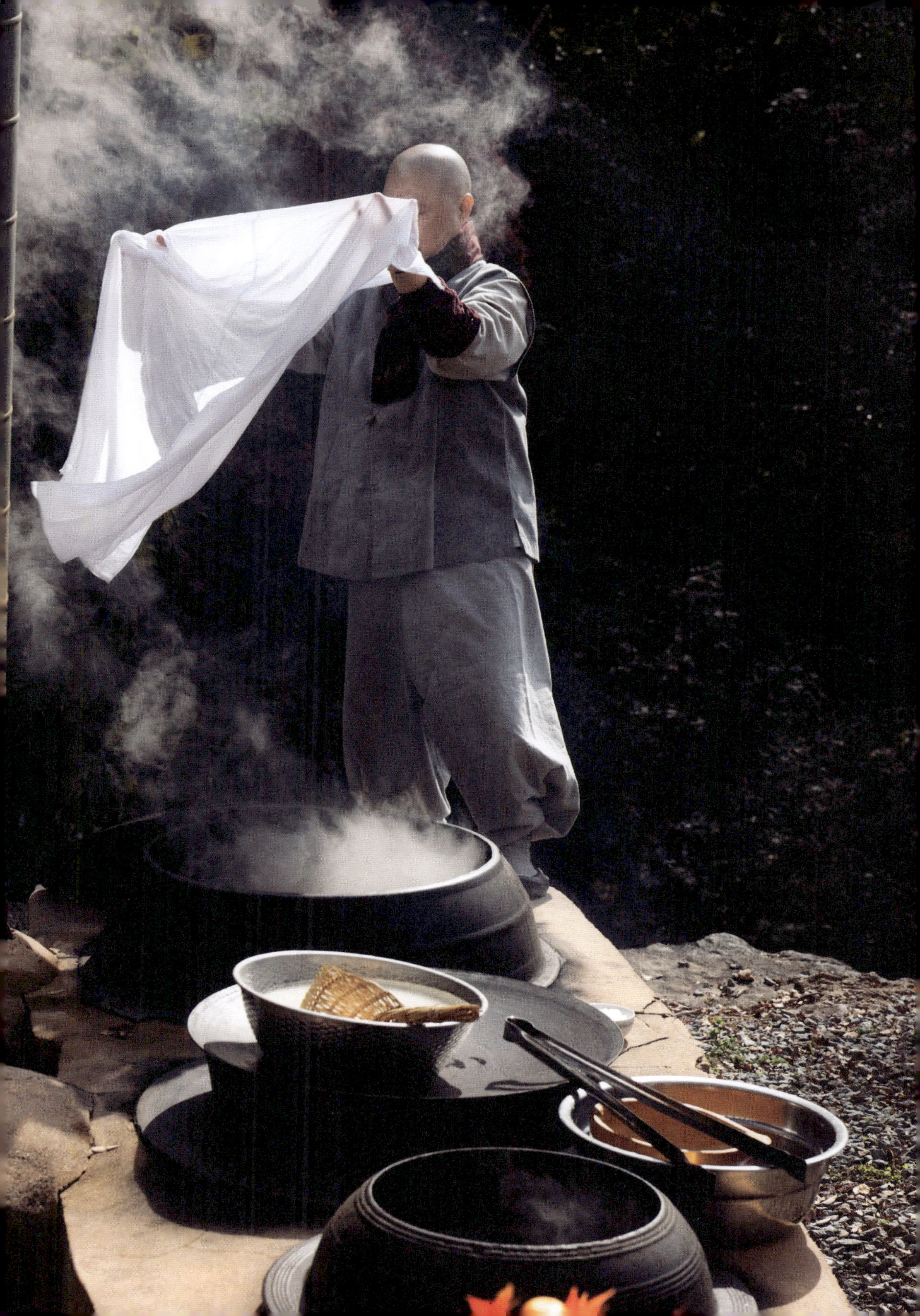

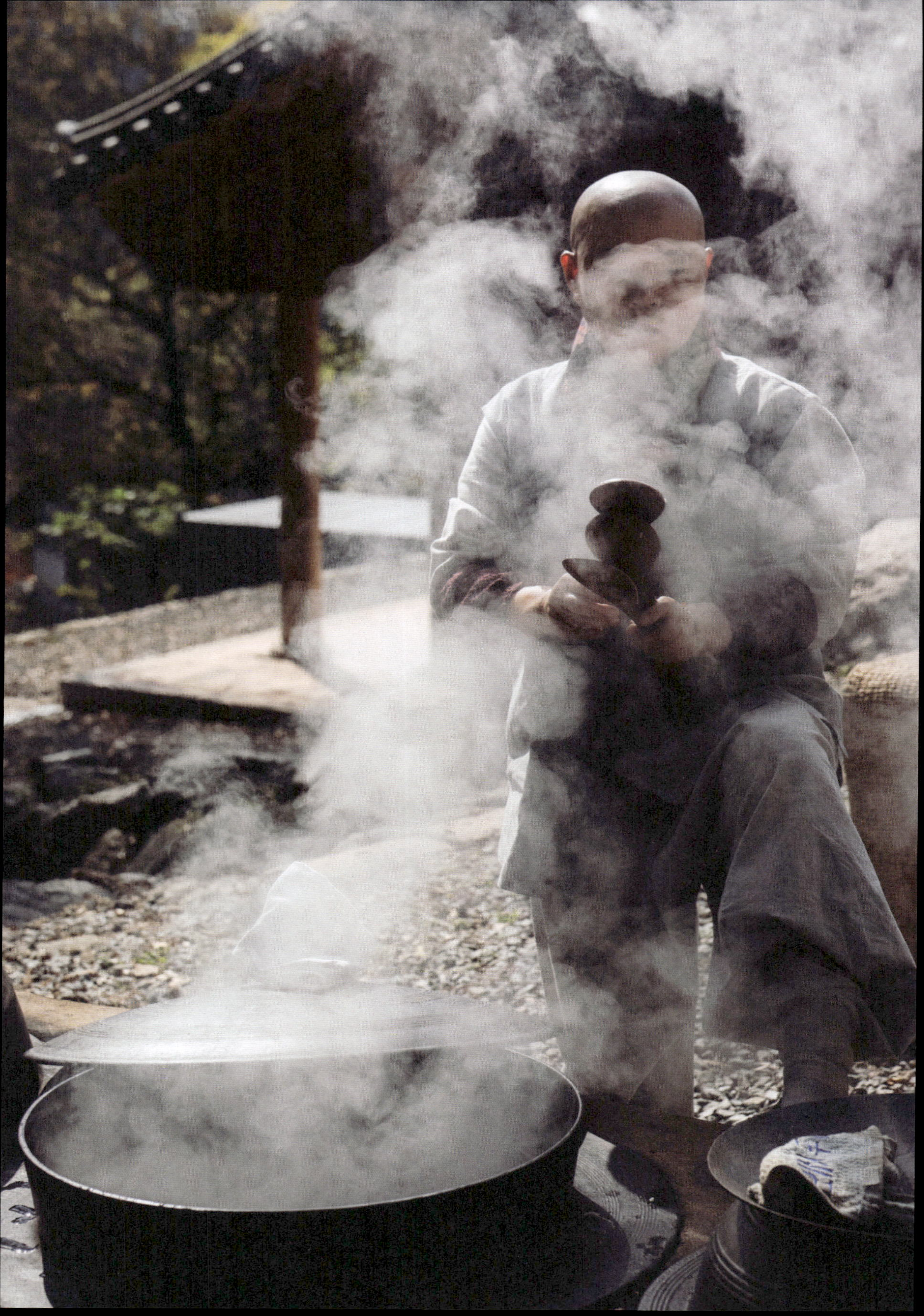

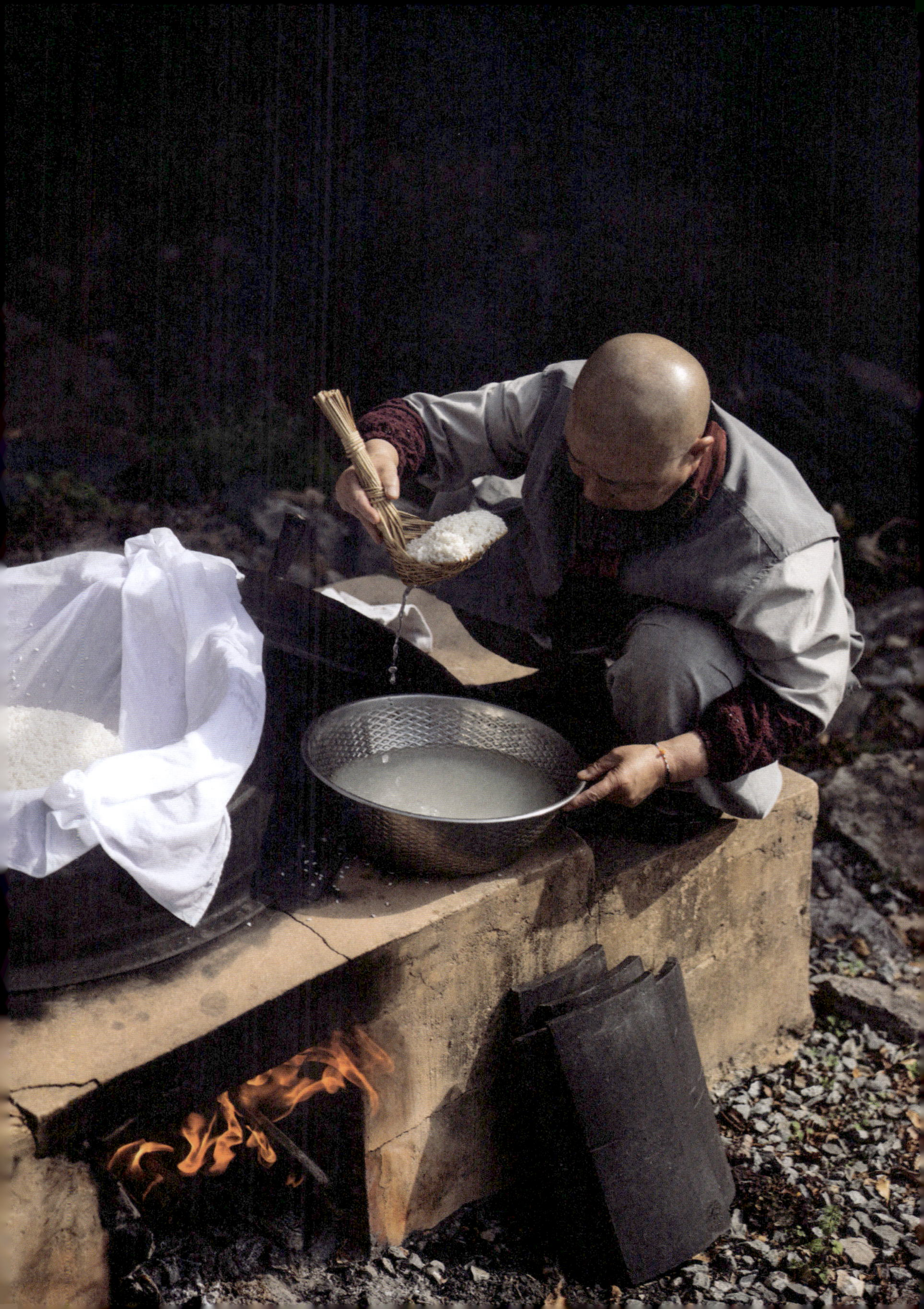

Using the correct heat also plays a significant role in the proper preparation of rice. The heat should be high at first because it takes some time for the cold water and rice to begin to boil. When it does boil, reduce the heat to medium, cover the pot, and let the rice cook for 15 minutes. To avoid the rice boiling over and having to clean the pot and the stove, you can either lift the lid every so often and release the steam or you can cool the lid with a damp cloth. Then reduce the heat to low, and after a few minutes, turn off the stove but leave the pot on the burner. Don't leave the kitchen while you're cooking rice! And give it a good stir with a wide spoon before serving it.

In Korea, many different things are mixed into the rice: other grains like barley or millet, vegetables like diced potatoes or sweet potatoes, chestnuts, daechus, pine nuts, or various kinds of beans. When mixing in other ingredients, pay attention to how much water is in the pot. Especially with beans, there are some things to consider: if they're fresh, they can simply be added and cooked with a little extra water, but if they're dried, they must be soaked for a long time or they won't get soft. The best way to include beans is to rinse them and put them in a bowl with a ratio of one part beans to two parts water. Put them in the fridge and let them sit overnight.

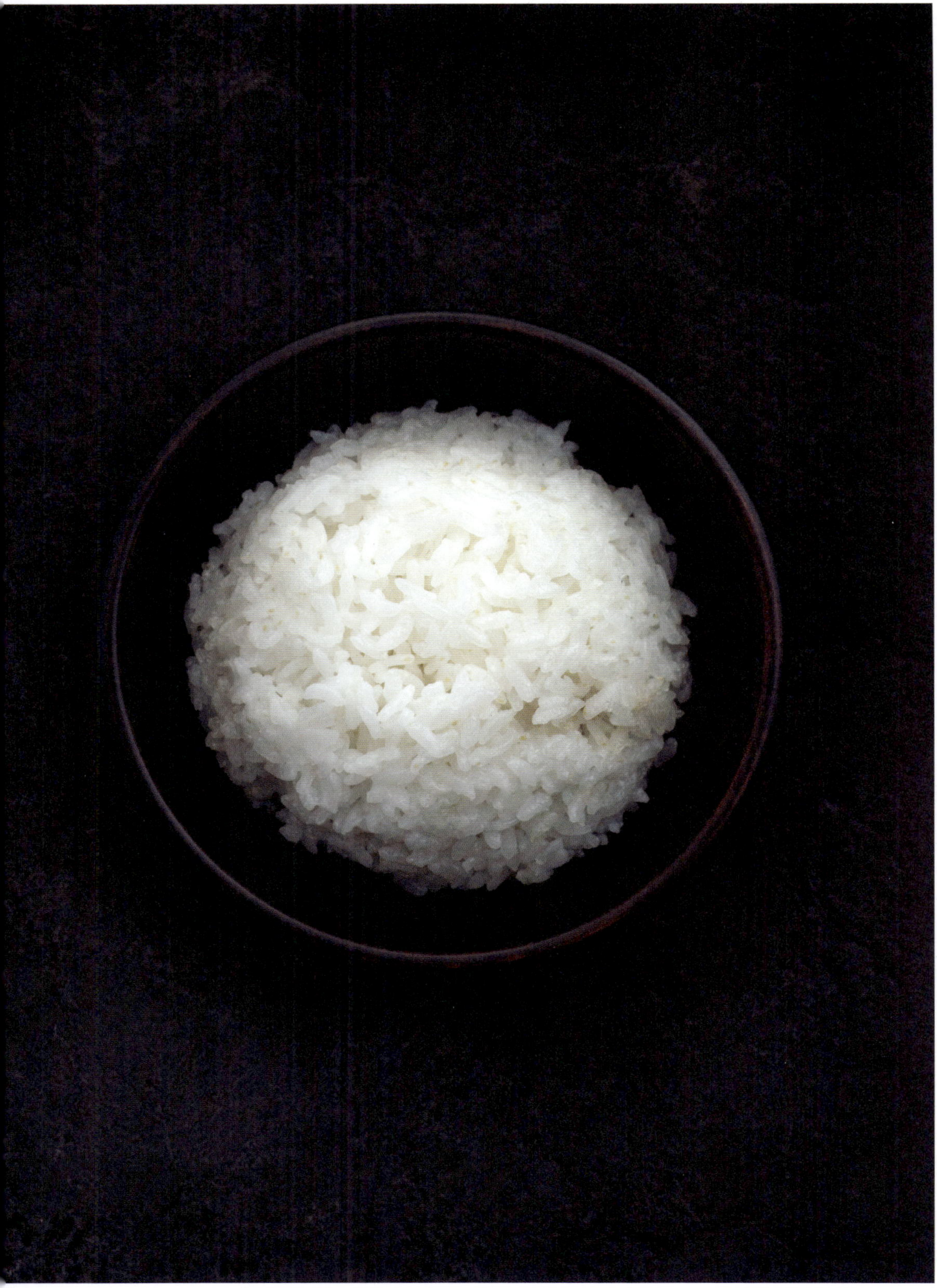

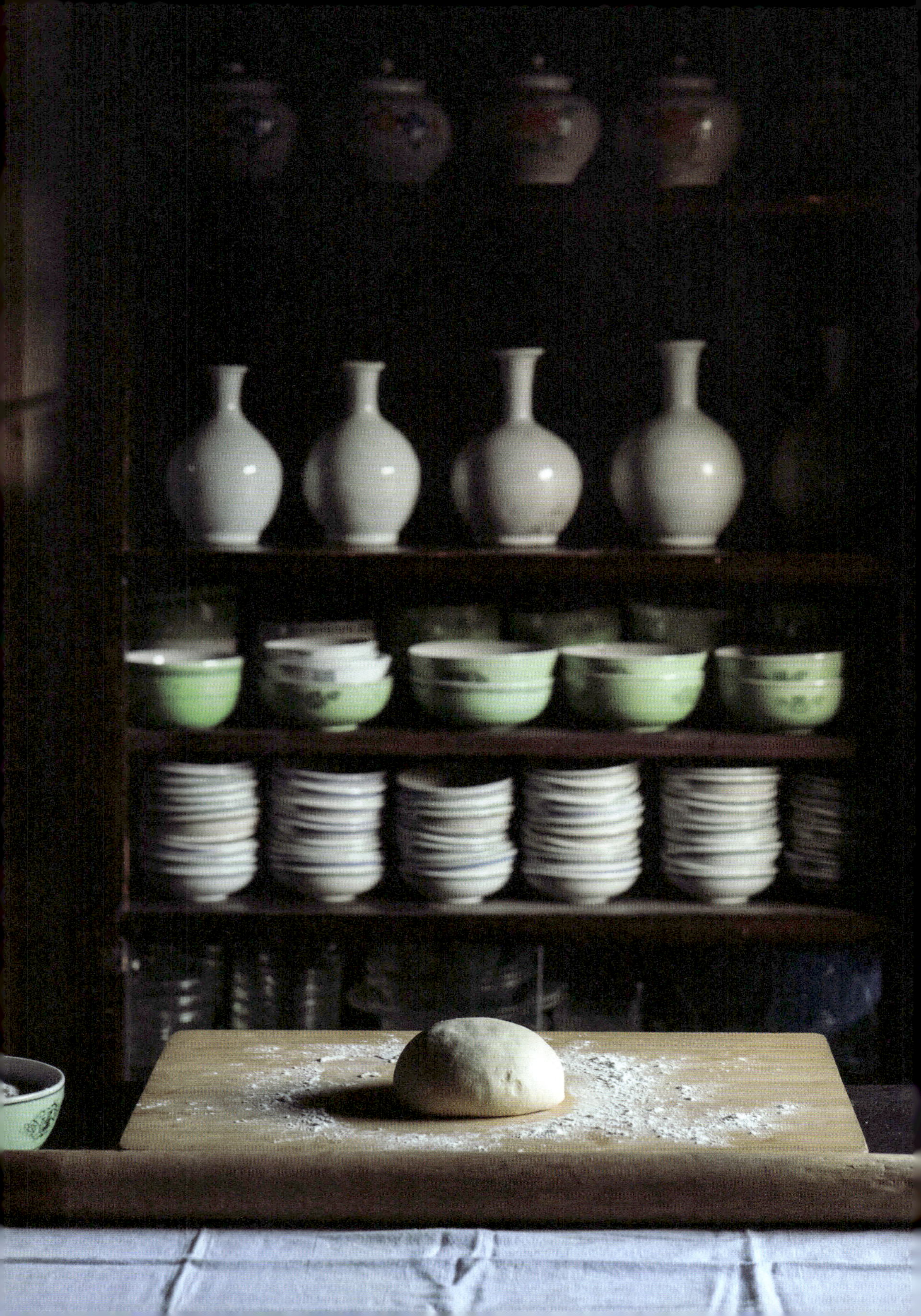

NOODLES

Seungso, or "Snim's smile," is what noodle dishes have been called in temples for as long as anyone can remember. This expresses how popular these dishes are and what a joy they are for the temple residents to prepare. Noodle dishes represent a welcome change, because in the everyday life of the temple, usually rice is what's eaten along with other plant-based dishes. Even today, noodle dishes are treated as a delicacy that all snims look forward to.

Flour used to be a rather scarce commodity because very little wheat was grown in Korea. Demand for it was low because Koreans traditionally didn't eat bread—it only came to the country at the end of the nineteenth century along with a major influx of peoples and cultures coming from other places. Neither cattle nor dairy farming existed in Korea, either.

In contrast to today, in the past, dishes made from flour were rare and prized. On the other hand, there's a long tradition of noodle dishes made from buckwheat flour, and these still enjoy great popularity today, particularly as summer meals.

There are other reasons why noodles bring smiles to the faces of snims. One of them is that temple residents must take care to ensure they're getting enough protein and carbohydrates. (Snims supposedly often experience a physical craving for dishes that contain gluten.) *Jeon*, or vegetable pancakes, are often cooked to supplement what's missing.

Different noodle dishes are eaten in the temple according to the season, with varying ingredients and preparation methods. Along with noodles, this also includes filled, steamed dumplings called *mandu*. On special holidays or on days when they shear their hair, snims prepare mandus, a noodle dish, and a dish with glass noodles made from sweet potato. In other words, they indulge in a deviation from the culinary norm.

Jeongkwan Snim knows a wide variety of noodle dishes; she prepares them depending on the occasion and season. She often makes the noodles herself, patiently rolling out the dough on a large wooden board with a long rolling pin until it has reached its desired thickness. She often mixes various vegetables or *namul* into the dough, too—then it takes on a different color, a unique aroma, and a new flavor.

Snim also cooks namul, vegetables, roots, or mushrooms to produce a special broth. (Koreans especially like to eat noodles in warm broth with vegetables and mushrooms.) Her noodle dishes are seasoned with salt, soy sauce, or doenjang, and she also likes to cook buckwheat noodle dishes that are eaten in the summer months because they have a cooling effect on the body. The broth for these dishes can be cold.

One dish that's considered to be unpretentious is called *sujebi*. It involves preparing a dough that must be left to rest. Once it has, then a piece of the dough is pinched off and pressed flat with the fingers, torn into small pieces, and added to a boiling vegetable broth. If the piece of dough floats to the surface, the sujebi is ready. It's a good dish for rainy days!

Kalguksu

NOODLES WITH VEGETABLES IN BROTH

For the dough
4 cups (500 g) all-purpose flour
1 ¼ cups (150 g) roasted soybean powder (konggaru)
2 tablespoons perilla oil (deulgireum)
2 tablespoons soy sauce (ganjang)
2 teaspoons salt
2 cups (450 ml) water

⅔ pound (300 g) zucchini (aehobak)
Some napa cabbage leaves (baechu), sliced into strips
2 sun-dried red chile peppers (hoenari-gochu)
Light soy sauce (guk-ganjang) for seasoning
Salt for seasoning

Add the flour, soybean powder, perilla oil, and soy sauce to a bowl. Dissolve the salt in the water, then pour the salted water slowly into the bowl with the flour. Knead everything into a smooth dough. Wrap the finished dough in a cloth and let it rest in the refrigerator for 3 hours.

Sprinkle some flour onto a large board or onto a table and use a rolling pin to roll out the dough to a thickness of ⅛ inch (3 mm). Fold the dough together and slice it into noodles ¼ inch (5 mm) wide.

Slice the zucchini into strips ¼ inch (5 mm) wide. In a pot, bring some water to a boil and add the noodles to it. When the water and noodles come back to a boil, add the zucchini strips, napa cabbage strips, and chile peppers. Season to taste with soy sauce and salt. When the vegetables are tender, serve the noodles with the broth in a large bowl.

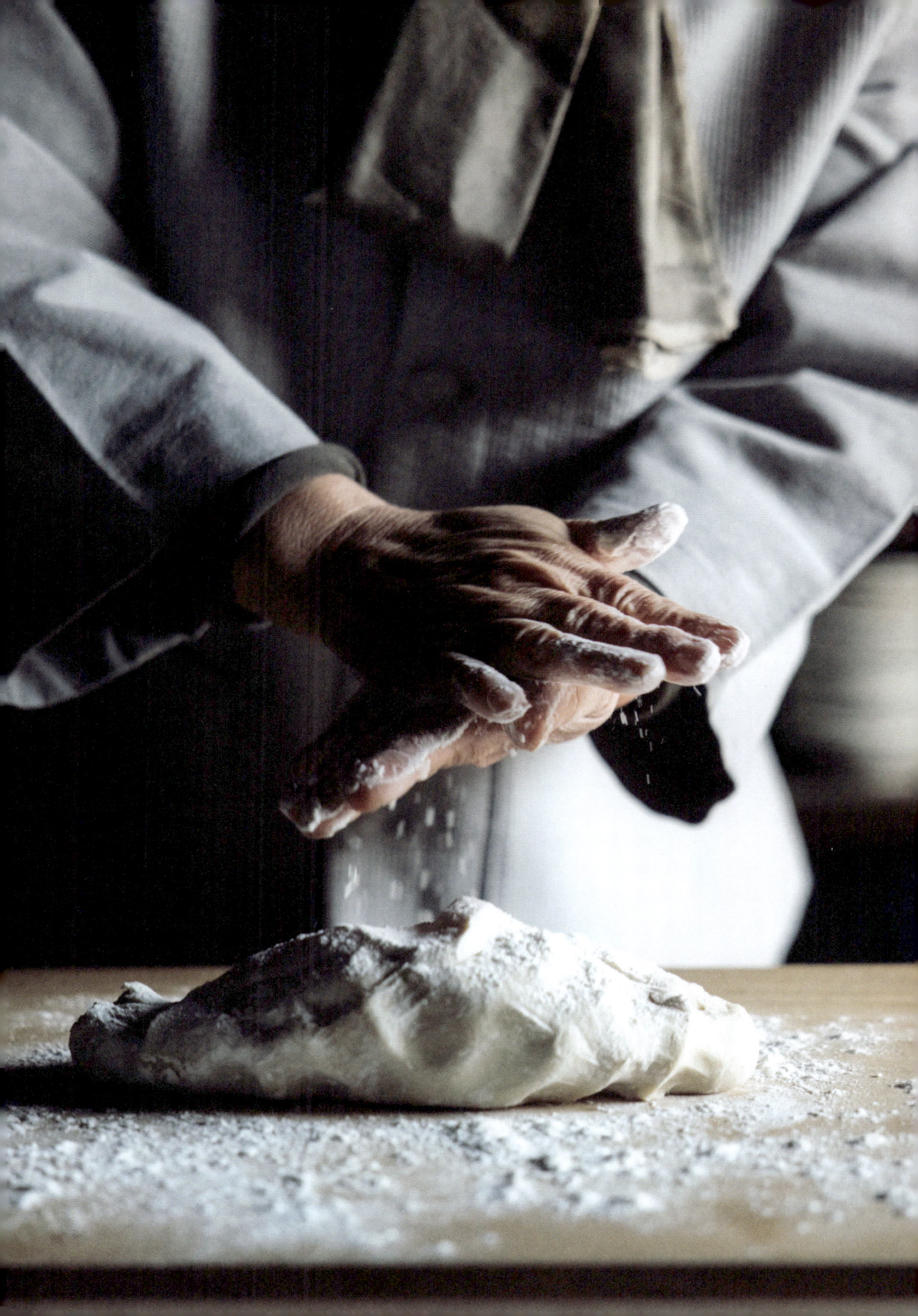

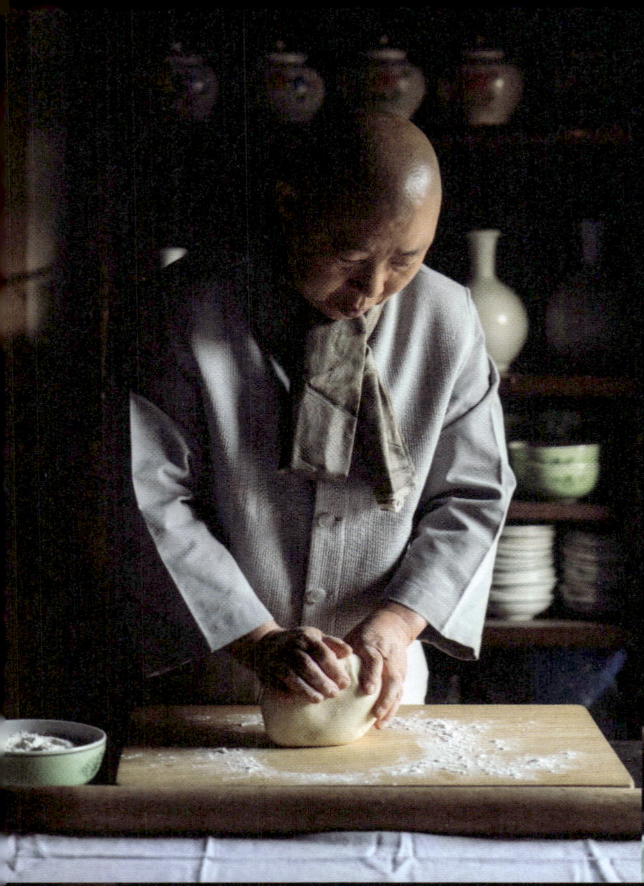
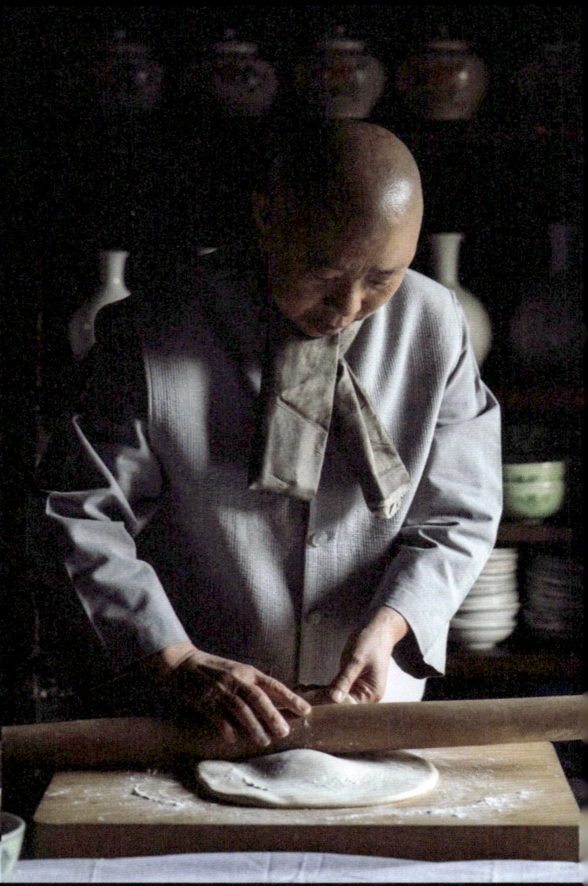
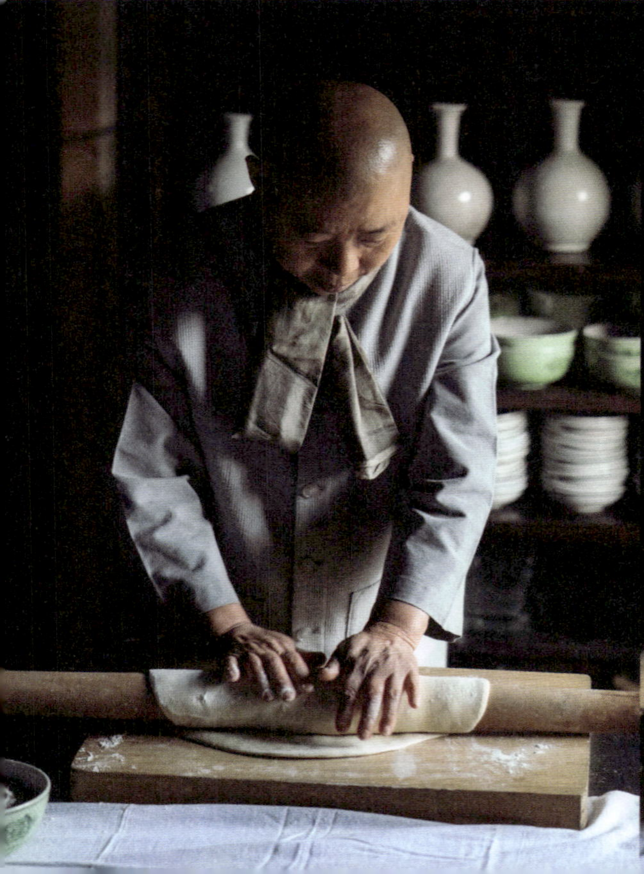
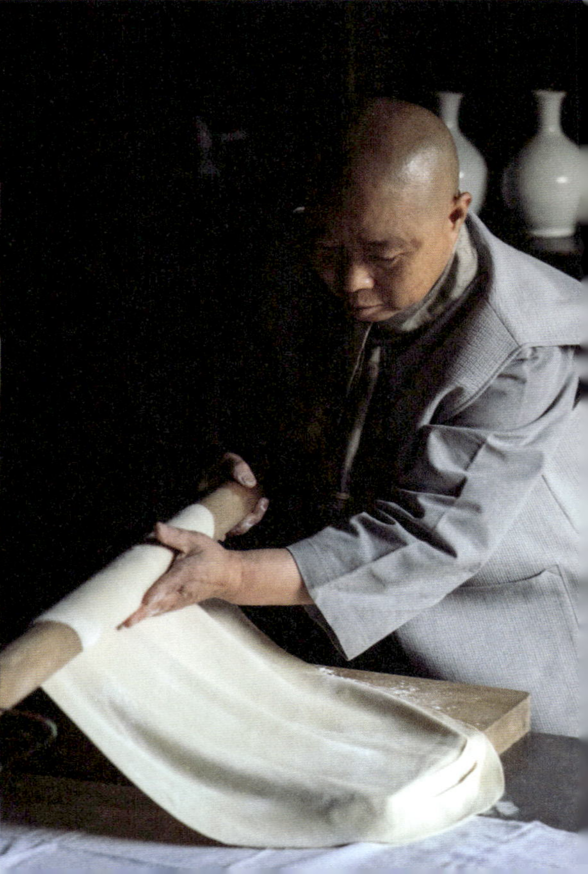

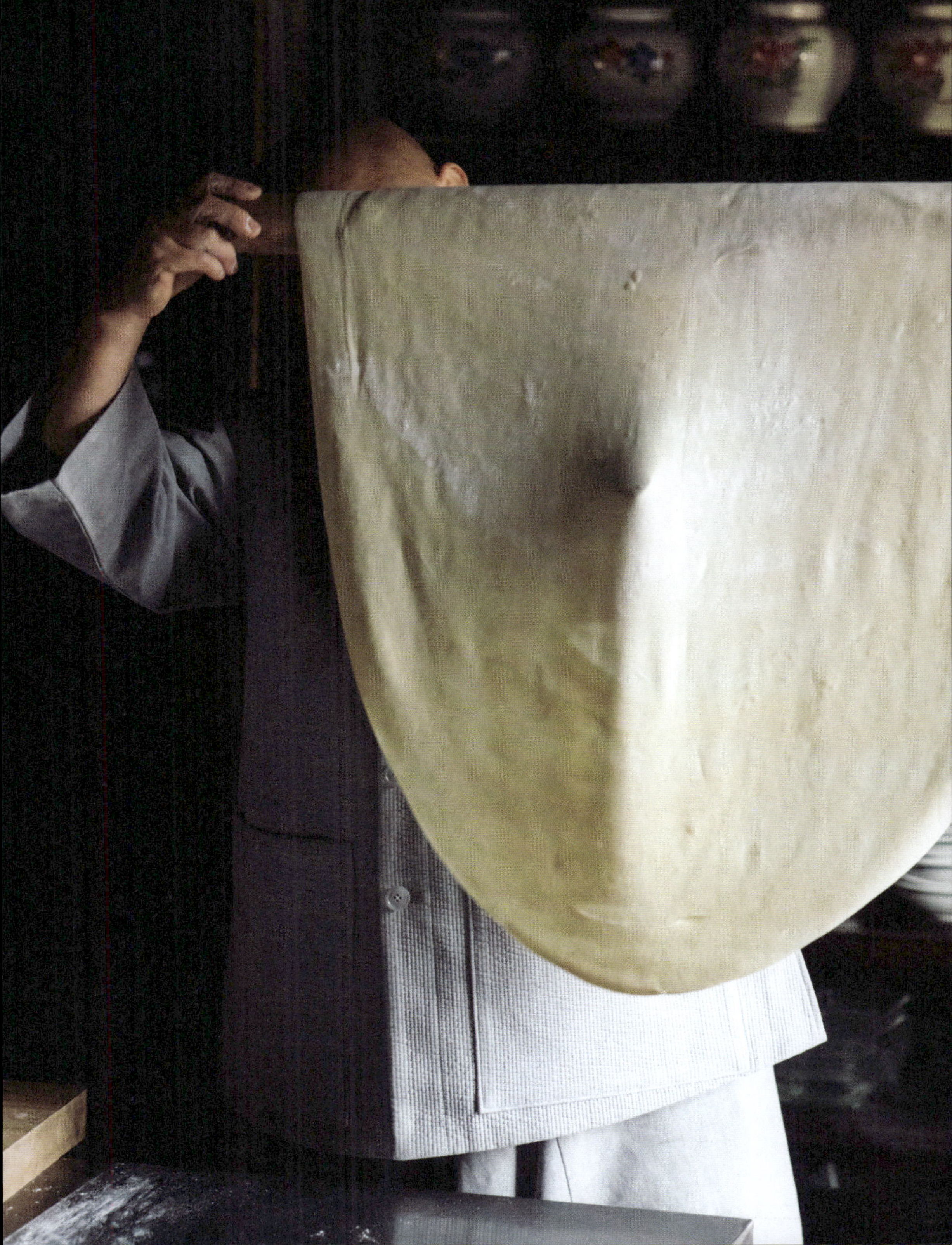

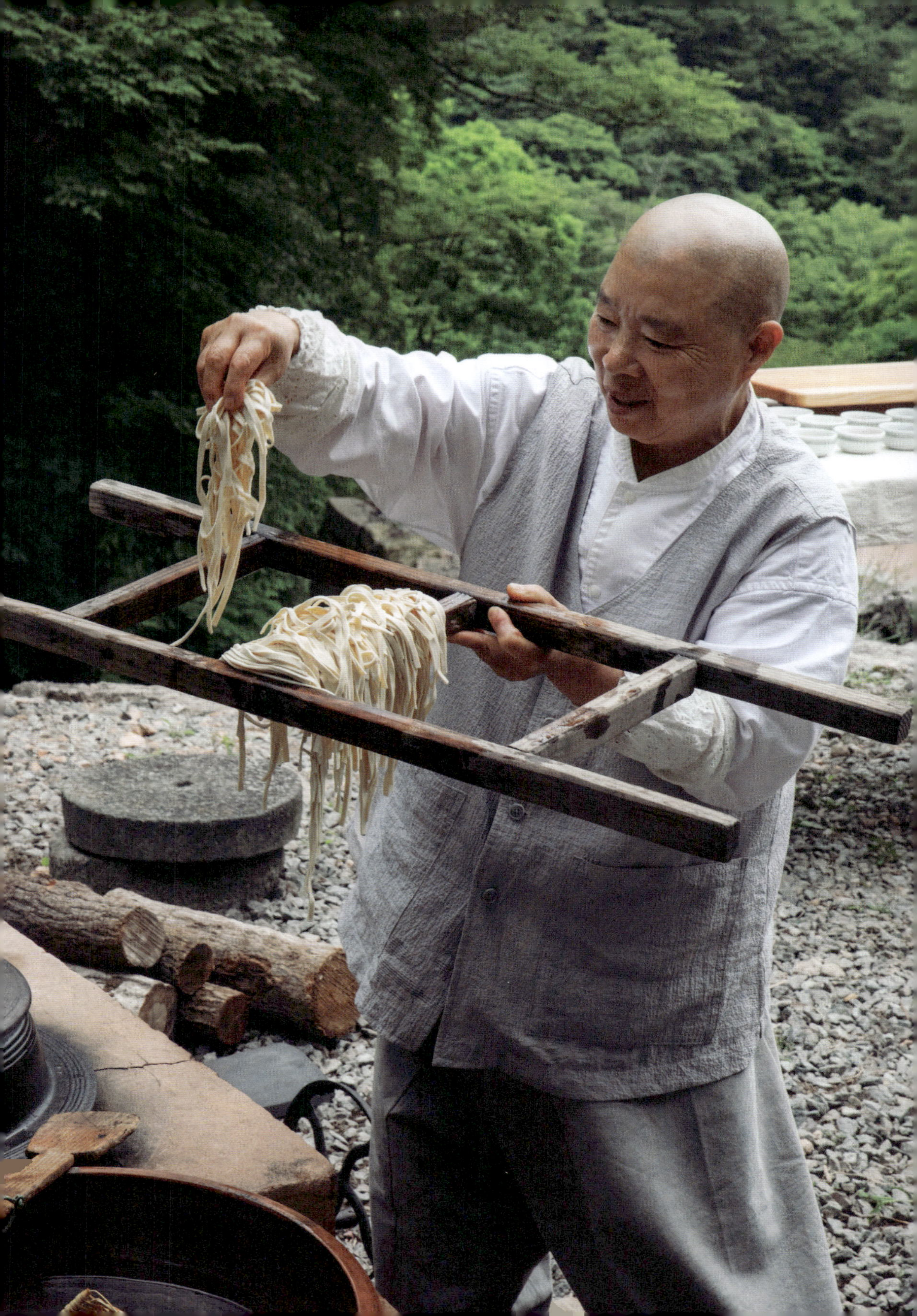

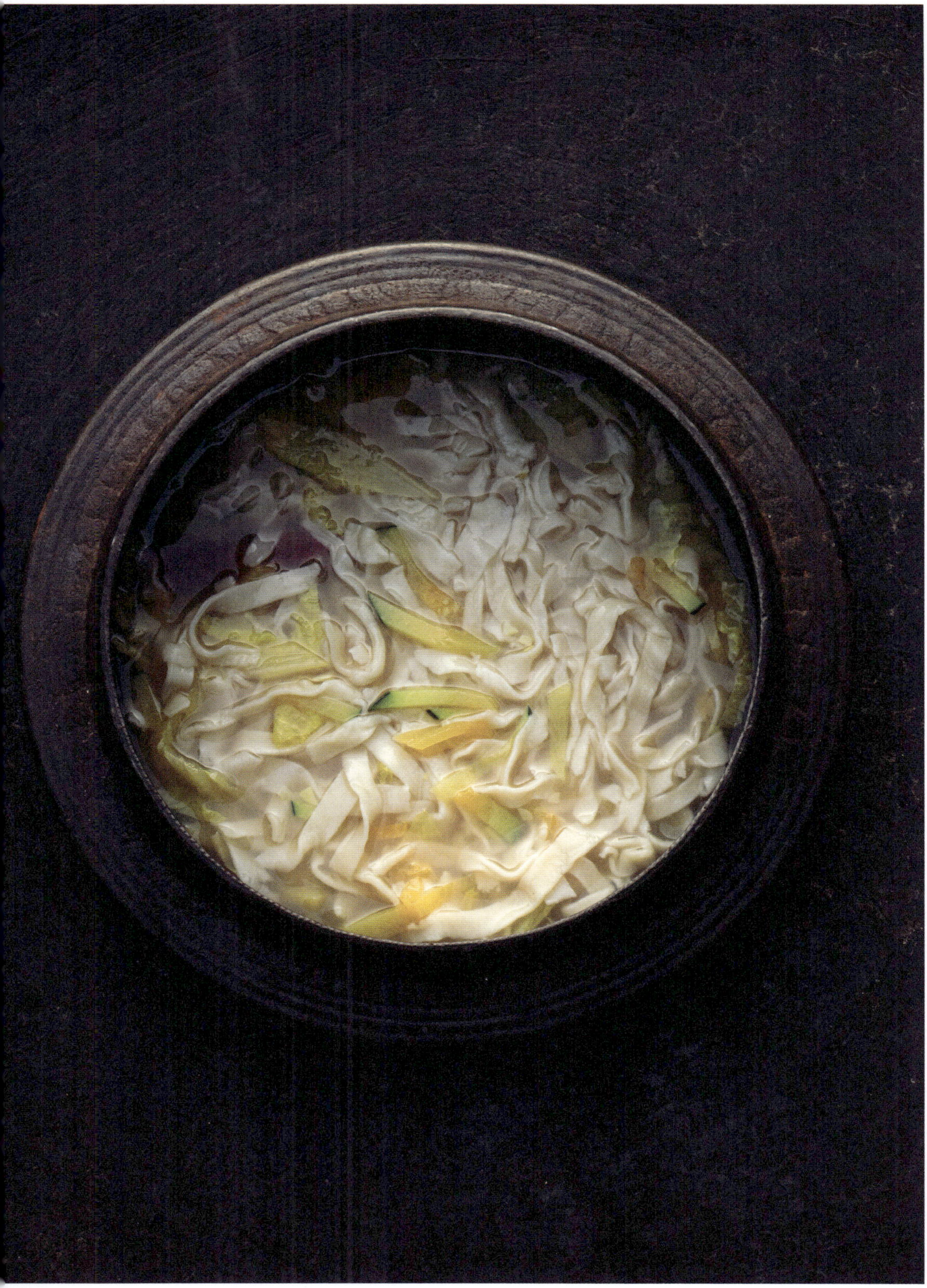

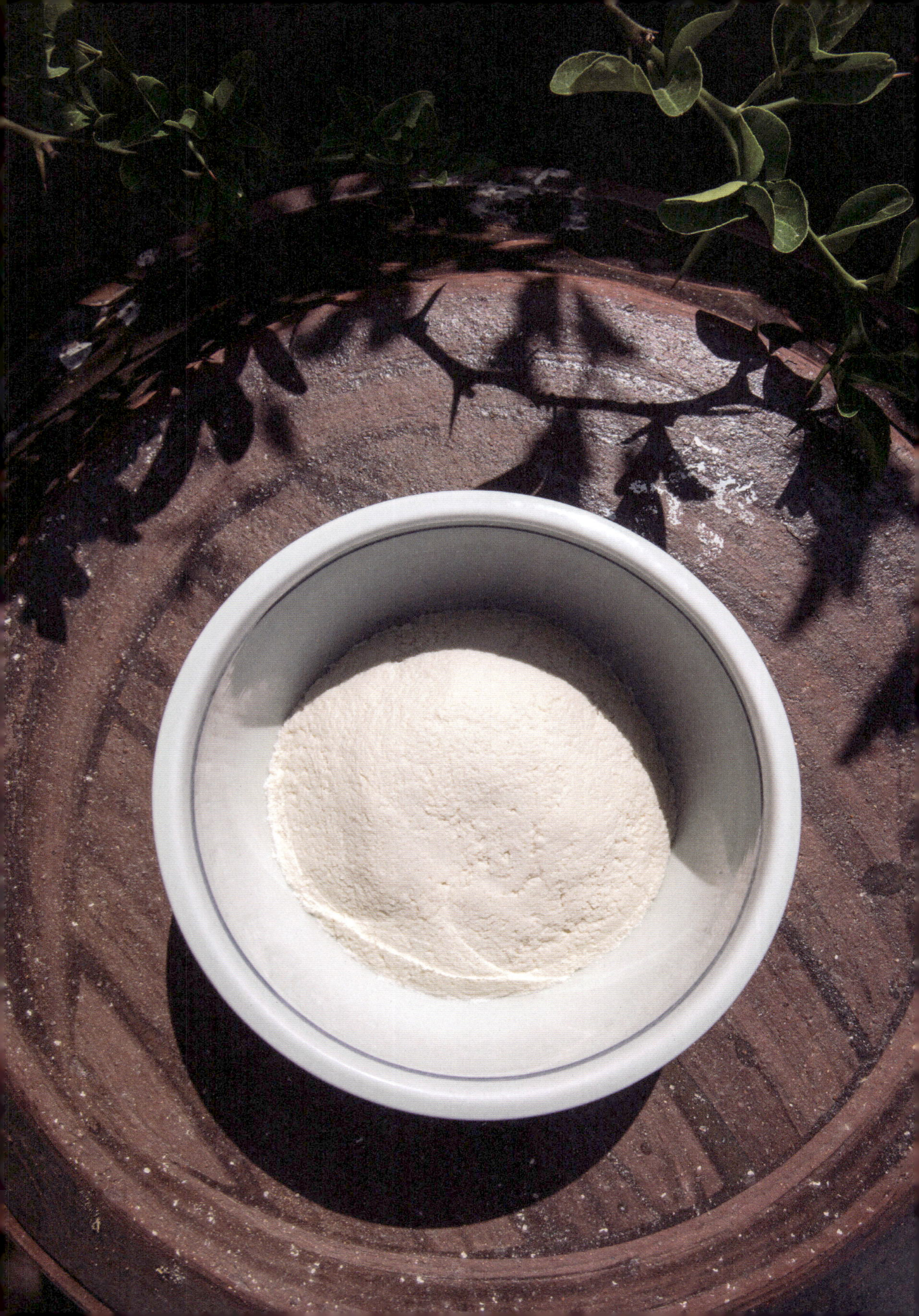

TOFU

The soybean occupies a special position among beans in Korea because it's a fascinating plant and because along with rice and sesame, soybeans are one of the oldest crops in East Asia. Due to the soybean's versatility, it plays an indisputably central role in traditional foods. The soybean is a valuable plant-based source of protein—40 percent of the bean is protein—and has been necessary for survival many times throughout history. It has been consumed primarily in the form of tofu, a soybean product that is popular not only in Korea but throughout East Asia. The beans are soaked, ground, and squeezed in a cloth. The soybean water that's squeezed out is boiled, and the protein solidifies into curds with the help of *gansu*. The water is then squeezed out of the curds, leaving the firm, protein-rich tofu behind.

Tofu can be prepared in a variety of ways—it's impossible to imagine Korean cooking without it! Tofu harmonizes well with flavorings like soy sauce and doenjang, which are themselves made from soybeans.

Homemade Tofu — 100
Tofu with Naengi Braised in Soy Sauce — 222
Tofu Steamed in Zucchini with Fresh Green Tea Leaves — 252
Soup with Tofu and Napa Cabbage — 274
Fried Tofu with Pickled Sansho — 280
Steamed Sweet Squash with Tofu — 300
Tofu-Jang — 306

Dubu mandeulgi

HOMEMADE TOFU

1 cup (300 g) dried soybeans (kong)
8 ½ cups (2 L) water
1 cup (250 ml) gansu (1 tablespoon salt and 2 tablespoons vinegar mixed with ¾ cup (200 ml) water)

Rinse the soybeans well and soak them in the water for 8 hours.

In a blender or food processor, grind the beans finely along with their soaking water.

With a linen cloth, squeeze out the bean mixture to separate the hulls from the bean water. This liquid is soy milk. Pour it into a pot and cook it over medium heat, stirring constantly—it can easily scorch or boil over! When the soy milk comes to a boil, turn off the stove.

Slowly add the gansu to the bean water. The milk will congeal and protein clumps will form. Gently stir them in one direction with a broad, flat wooden paddle, then cover the pot with a lid and let the mixture rest. The *sundubu*, or fresh tofu, is ready. In Korea, tofu may be eaten in this form.

Line a sieve with a damp cotton cloth and use a soup ladle to carefully scoop the sundubu out of the pot and into the sieve. Fold the cloth together, squeeze the sundubu well (it will drip!), weigh it down with a stone, and let it stand. After 40 to 60 minutes, this will become *modubu*, or firm tofu.

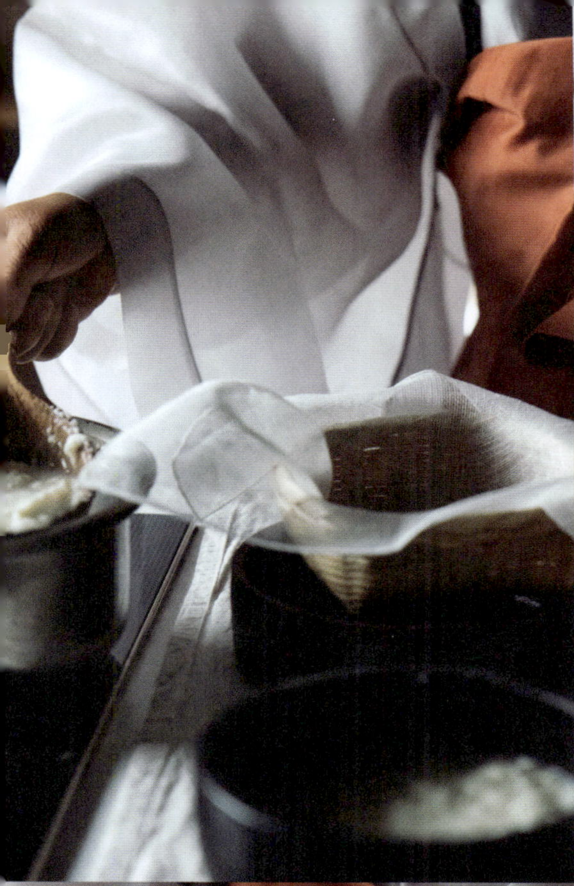
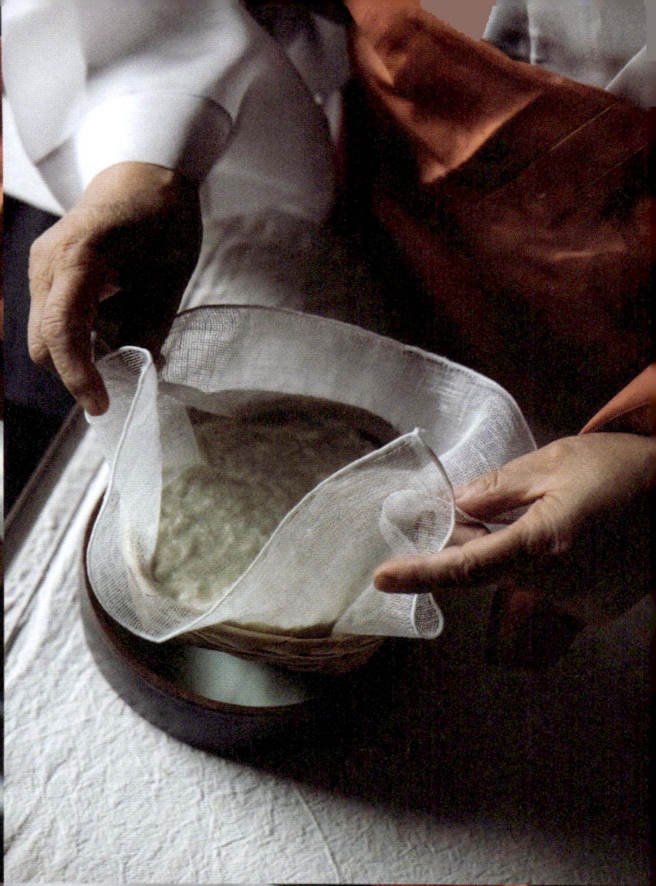
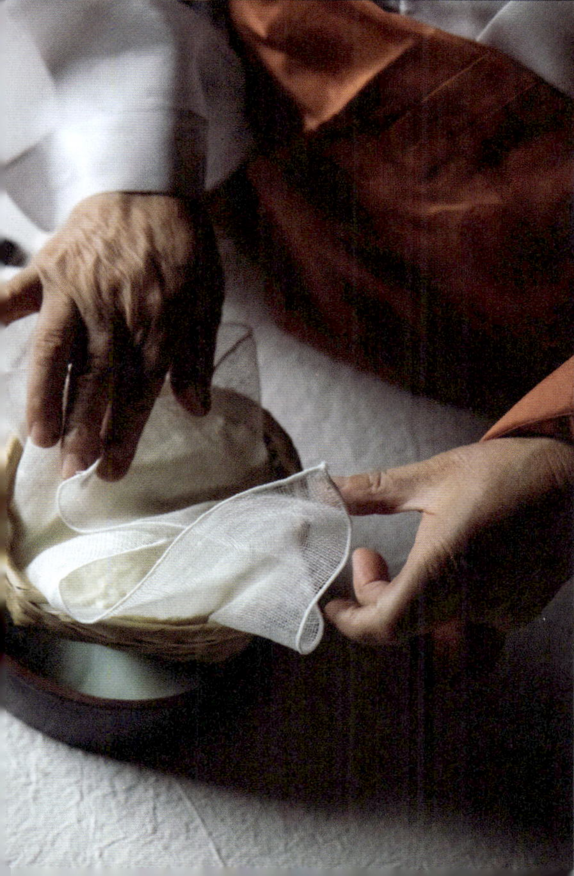
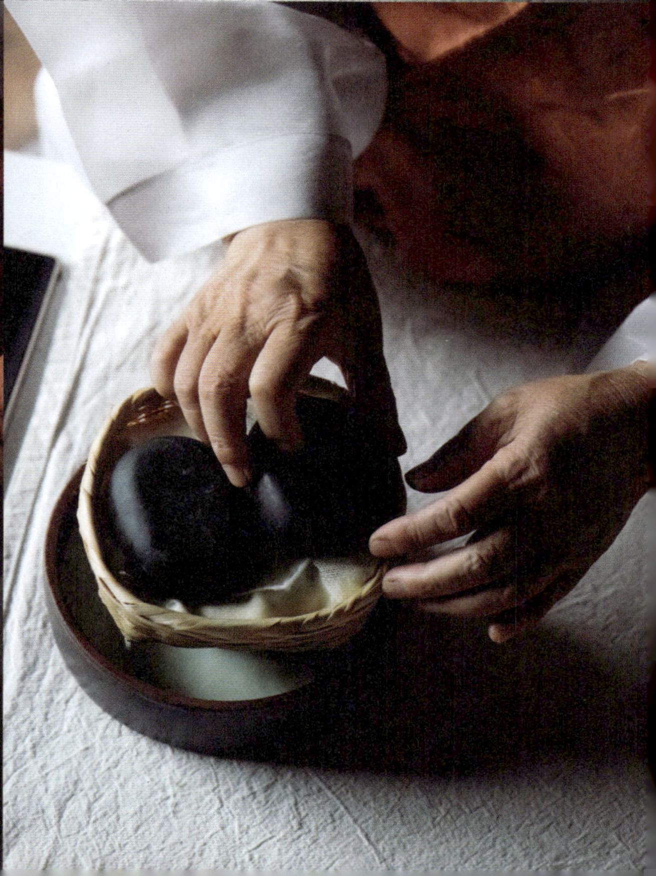

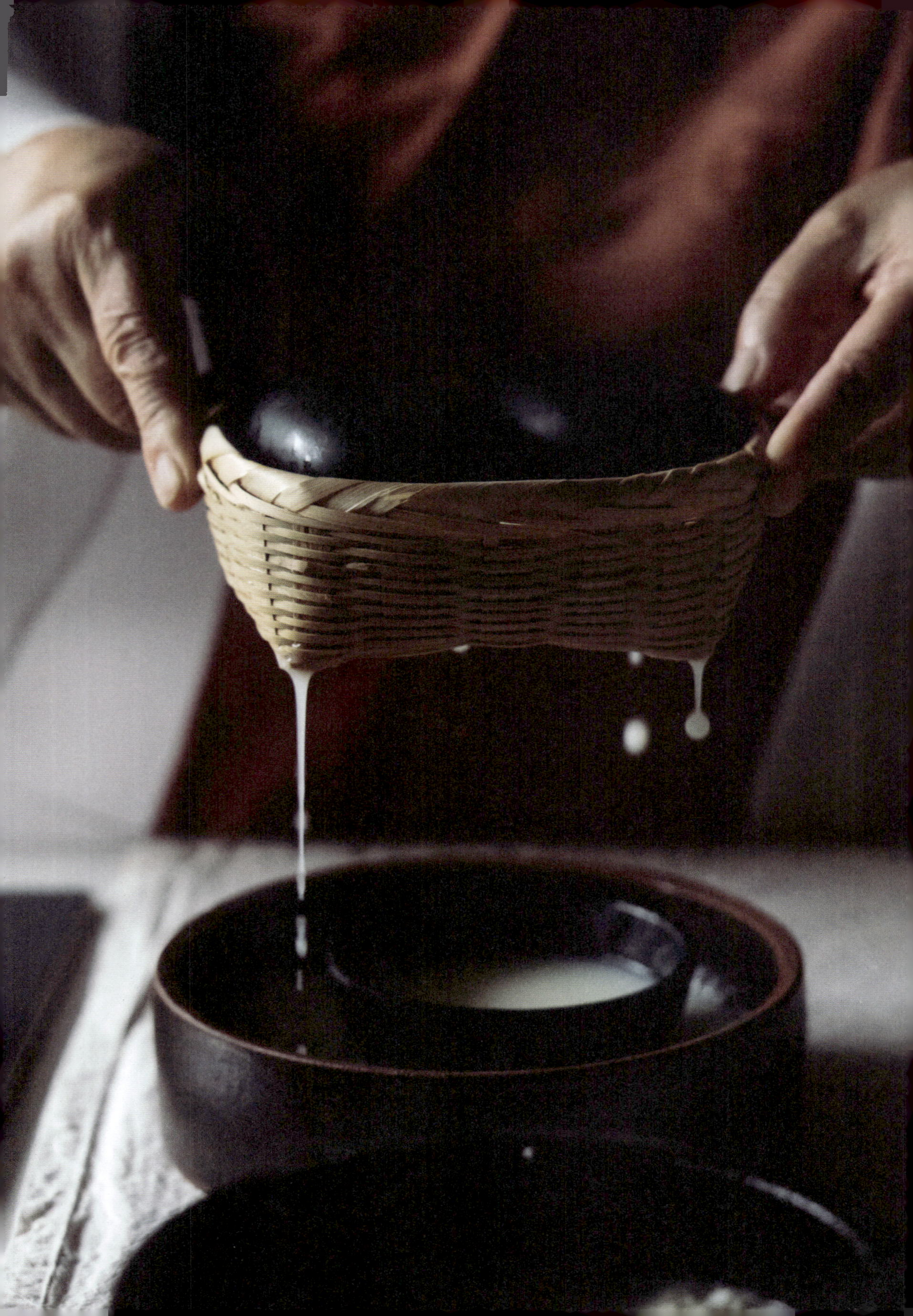

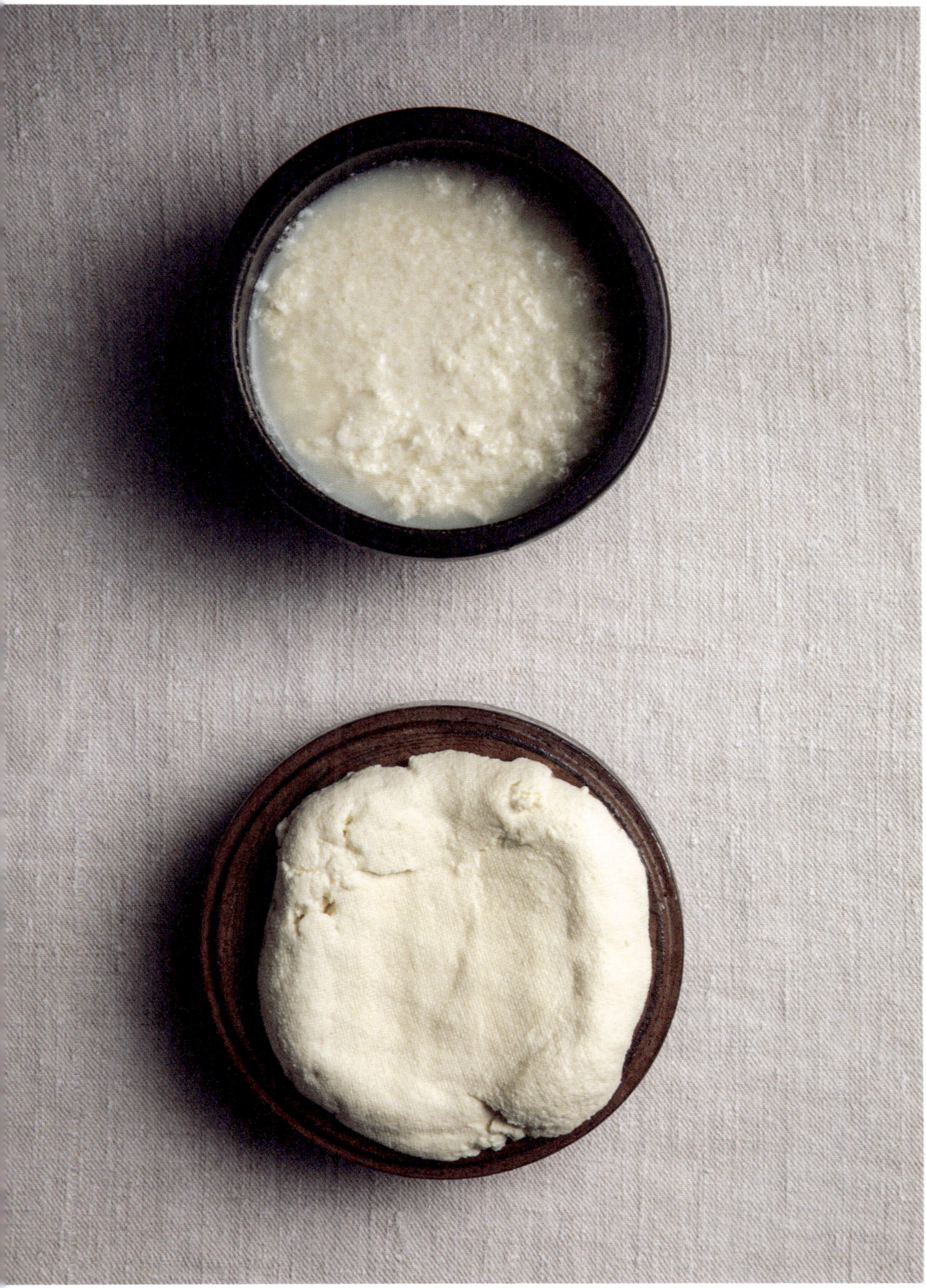

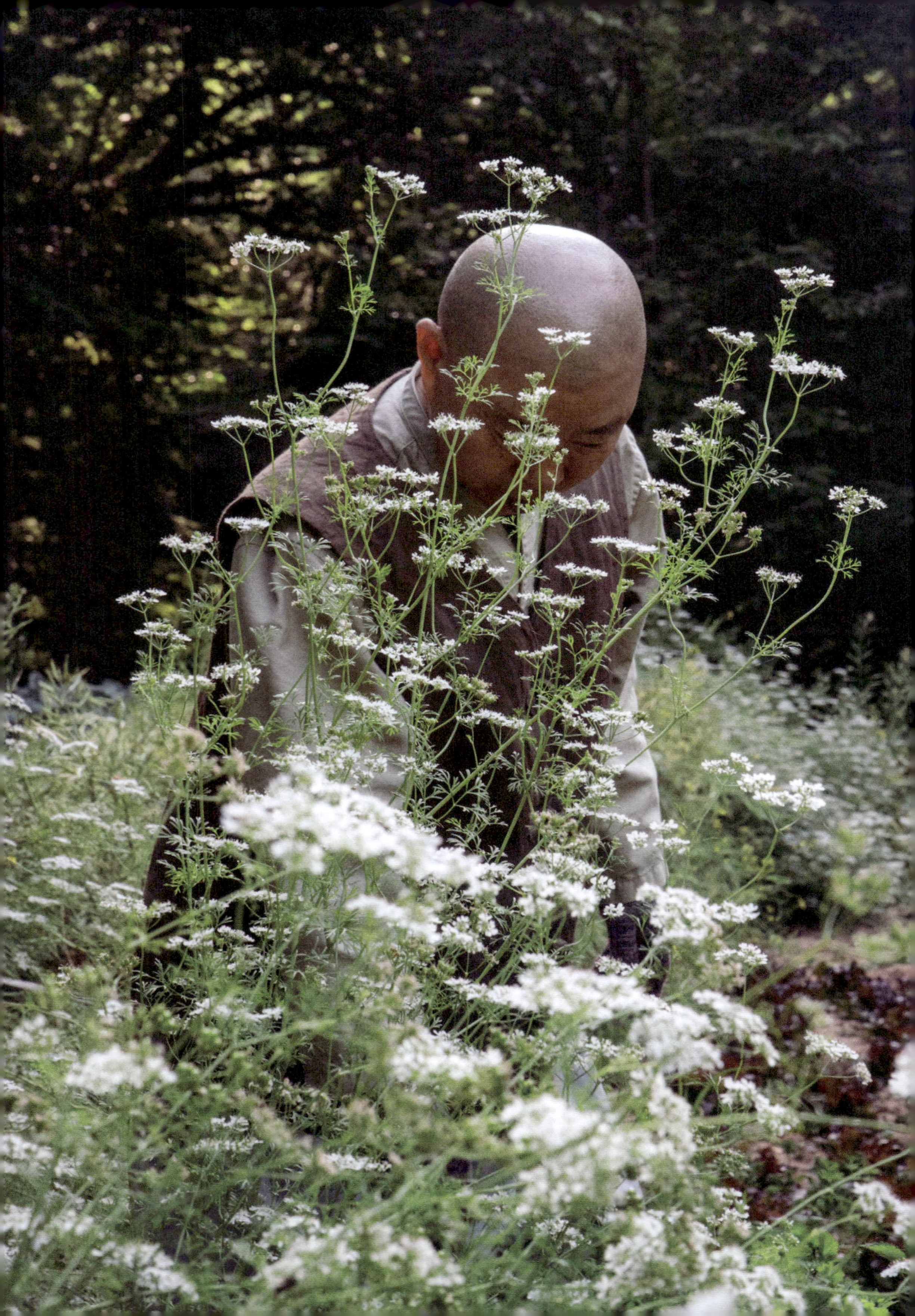

NAMUL

The observation that a food tradition is special can mean different things. For example, it can mean that different ingredients are used in different countries. Korea has its own native flavorings as well as typical foods. *Namul* is one such ingredient that's indispensable to the Korean dinner table—there are supposedly about 300 different types of namul in Korea! This enormous variety is connected to the fact that the therapeutic use of healing plants is an essential component of Korean traditional medicine.

The closest translation of *namul* in English is "vegetable," which generally includes leaves, roots, tubers, seed pods, and stalks. However, namul includes much more than those! There's a wide array of preparation methods for the different types of namul. Because snims don't eat animal-based foods, namul—alongside grains, beans, potatoes, fruits, and nuts—plays a central role in temple cooking. This Buddhist tradition has left lasting traces on traditional Korean food.

Namul can be separated into four categories. The first one is *san-namul*, which means everything that grows wild in the mountains. (*San* means "mountain.") San-namul covers a wide variety of ingredients since roots and mushrooms are included with plants. The distinction between healing plants and vegetables is fluid. Edible shoots of shrubs and trees (like bamboo shoots) also belong in this category.

In spring, when everything begins to grow, professional foragers set out with great cloth sacks to harvest entire plants or to pick their fresh leaves. Since Korea is a very mountainous country with a long tradition of using healing plants to treat illness, professional foragers with a lot of knowledge have always plied their craft in Korea. (Snims used to be among the preeminent experts on healing plants and their effects.) Extensive expertise is required to gather edible items, and to this day, many of those items are still recognized as being medicinal. In fact, there are even special markets for these plants.

San-namul has a strong, highly unique aroma, and each plant has its own flavor and is rich in vitamins. In its natural state, each plant is therefore considered to be healthy. San-namul can be freshly prepared, dried and preserved, or dried and steamed. Edible roots are dug up in late summer or fall because that's when they've taken up enough nutrients to survive the cold of winter and sprout again in the spring. Mushrooms that grow in the mountains are also gathered at the right time, as are nuts and fruits.

Deul-namul means "growing wild in the meadow" because *deul* means "meadow." These plants are also picked in spring, and many flowers are gathered, dried, and made into tea. Different plants grow in the meadow than what grow in the mountains because the soil is different and gets more sunlight.

Edible plants grow in the water or wetlands, too. A typical example is the lotus—not only are the roots edible, but the leaves also have a variety of uses, and tea can be prepared from the lotus flowers. Today, some plants that were once wild are now also cultivated.

Namul from the sea is called *bada-namul*. The sea is inhabited by not only fish, mussels, sea stars, sea cucumbers, and urchins but also by various plants and algae and seaweed. Some of the edible bada-namul are native to sea; others are sometimes cultivated and then harvested. Bada-namul is often used to make soup, but it's also eaten in salads or as a vegetable. It's rich in minerals, usually carries the scent of the ocean, and often tastes lightly salty.

Jaebae-namul means cultivated vegetables that are grown either in the field or in greenhouses. These correspond the most closely to what are called vegetables in Europe. In Korea, this subgroup has now acquired its own name: *chaeso*. (In comparison, the word *namul* clings to the meaning of "wild vegetables" although the distinction has long been fluid.) The variety of chaeso has increased in recent years, with new types like broccoli, bell peppers, green cabbage, and asparagus being added. Even when it comes to these cultivated vegetables, there's a bigger selection in Korea than there is in Europe. That's because there are more types of mushrooms, radishes, and sprouts in comparison.

The four types of namul can be prepared in different ways, from being fried or steamed to being added to soup or stews. The most popular way to prepare them, however, is to blanch the namul in boiling water and then place it in cold water in order to preserve its color and freshness. Then it's squeezed out by hand and a sauce is prepared for it. The sauce can be made from a combination of soy sauce, doenjang, gochujang, sesame oil, salt, garlic, pepper, gochu, perilla oil, or toasted and crushed sesame or perilla seeds. This sauce is then mixed with the namul, so only a little oil is needed. Mushrooms can be braised, added to stews, fried, steamed, or dried.

Namul is also popular as an ingredient in pancakes, or jeon. Scallions, napa cabbage, *minari*, and zucchini are good additions, too.

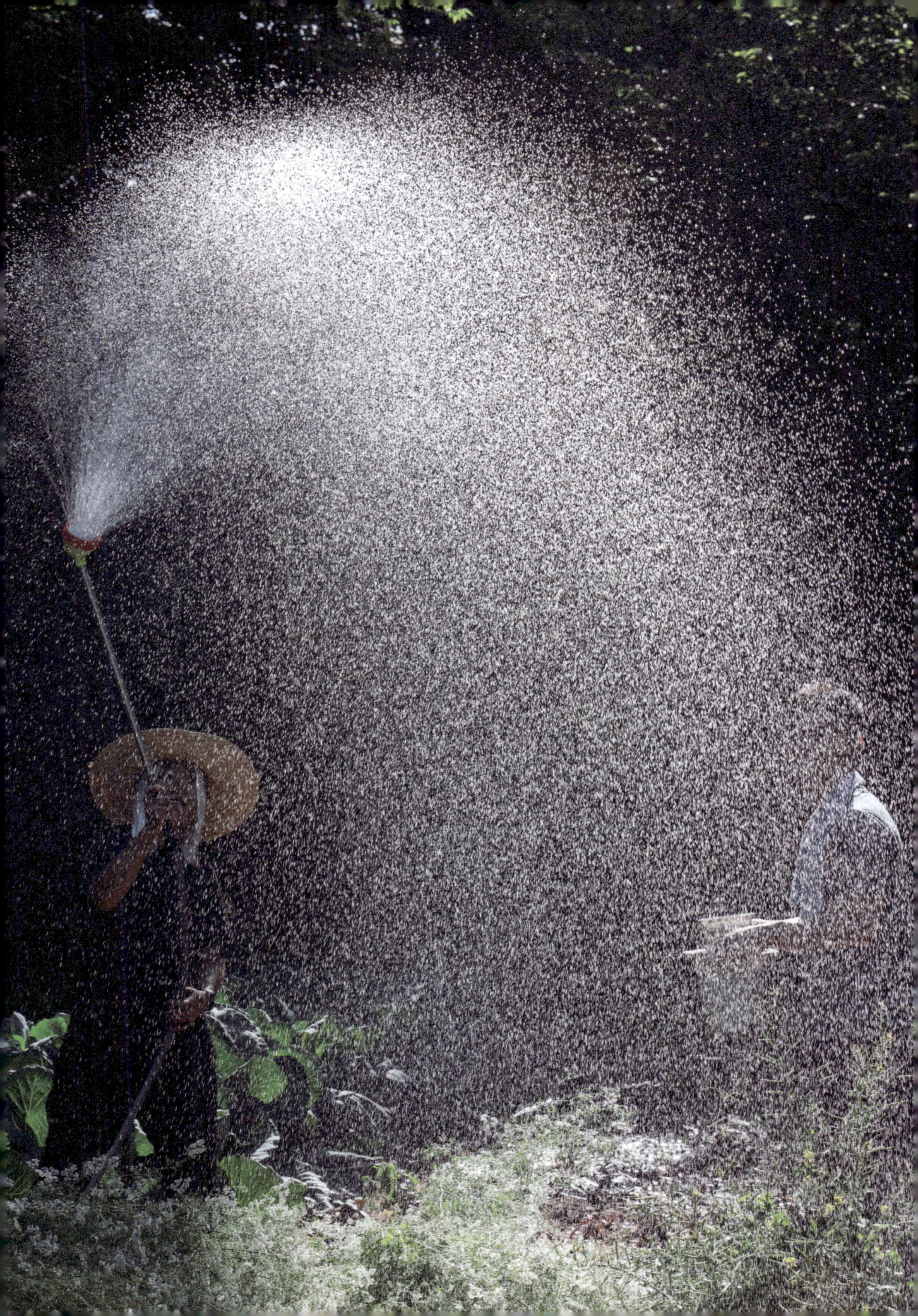

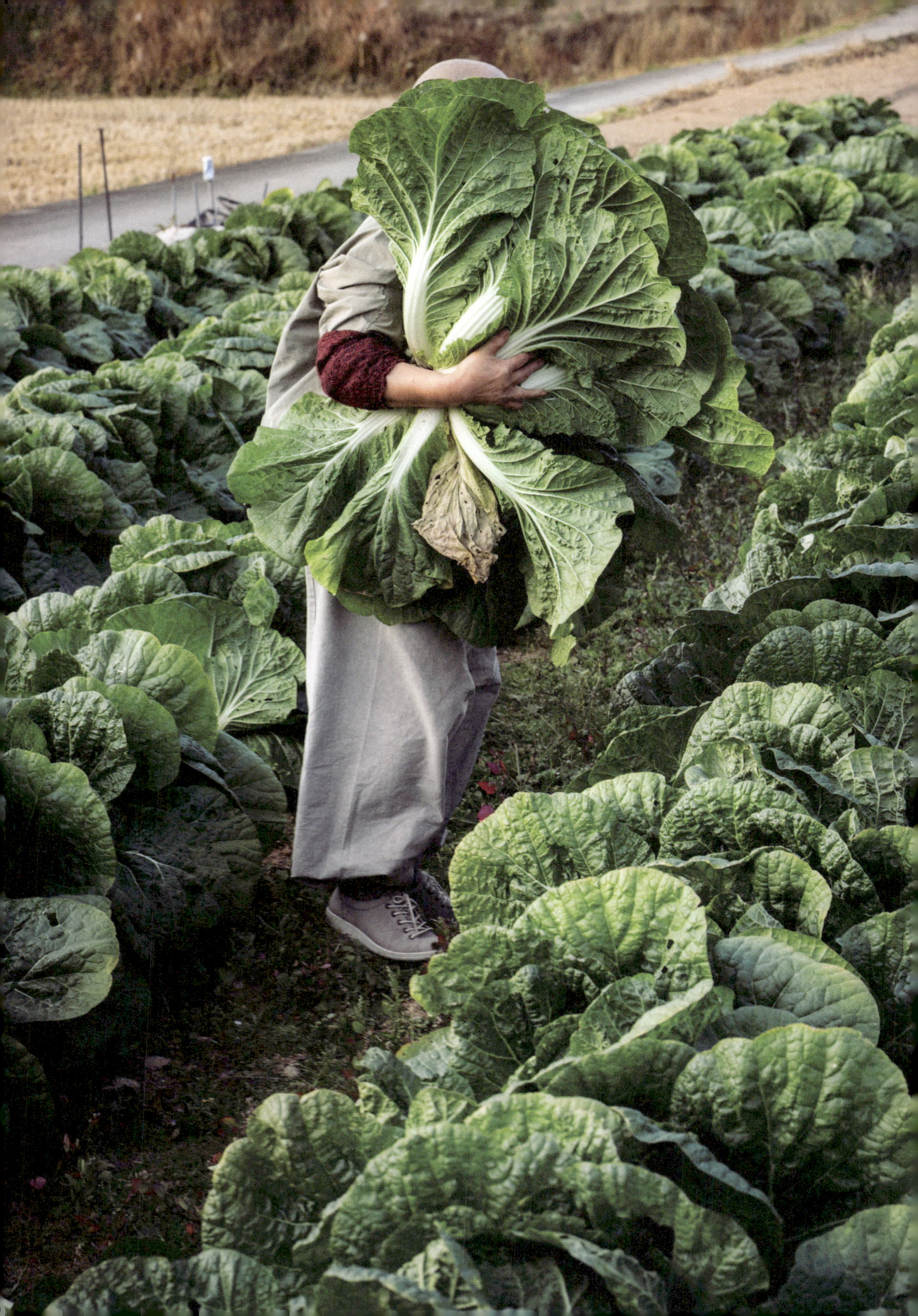

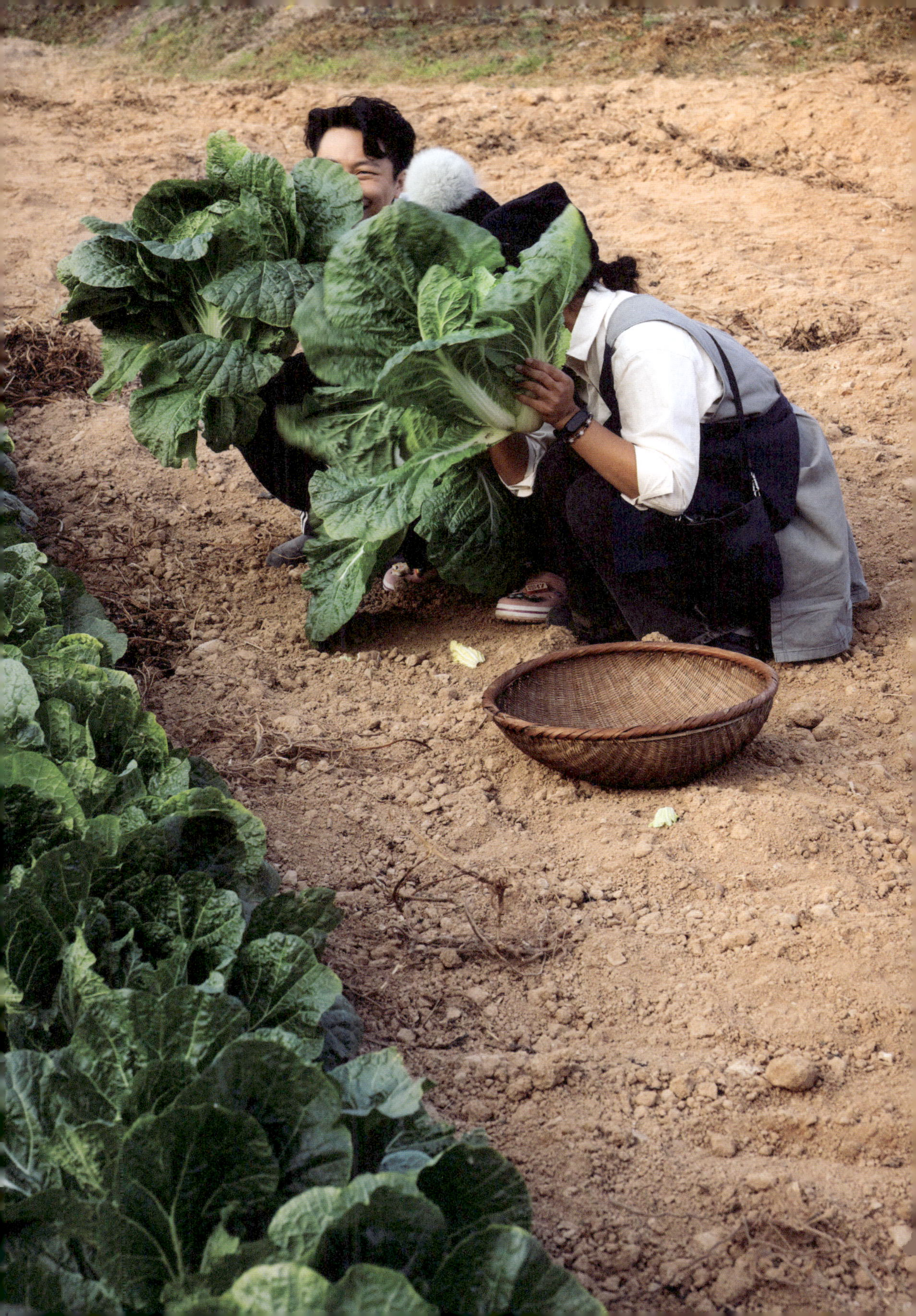

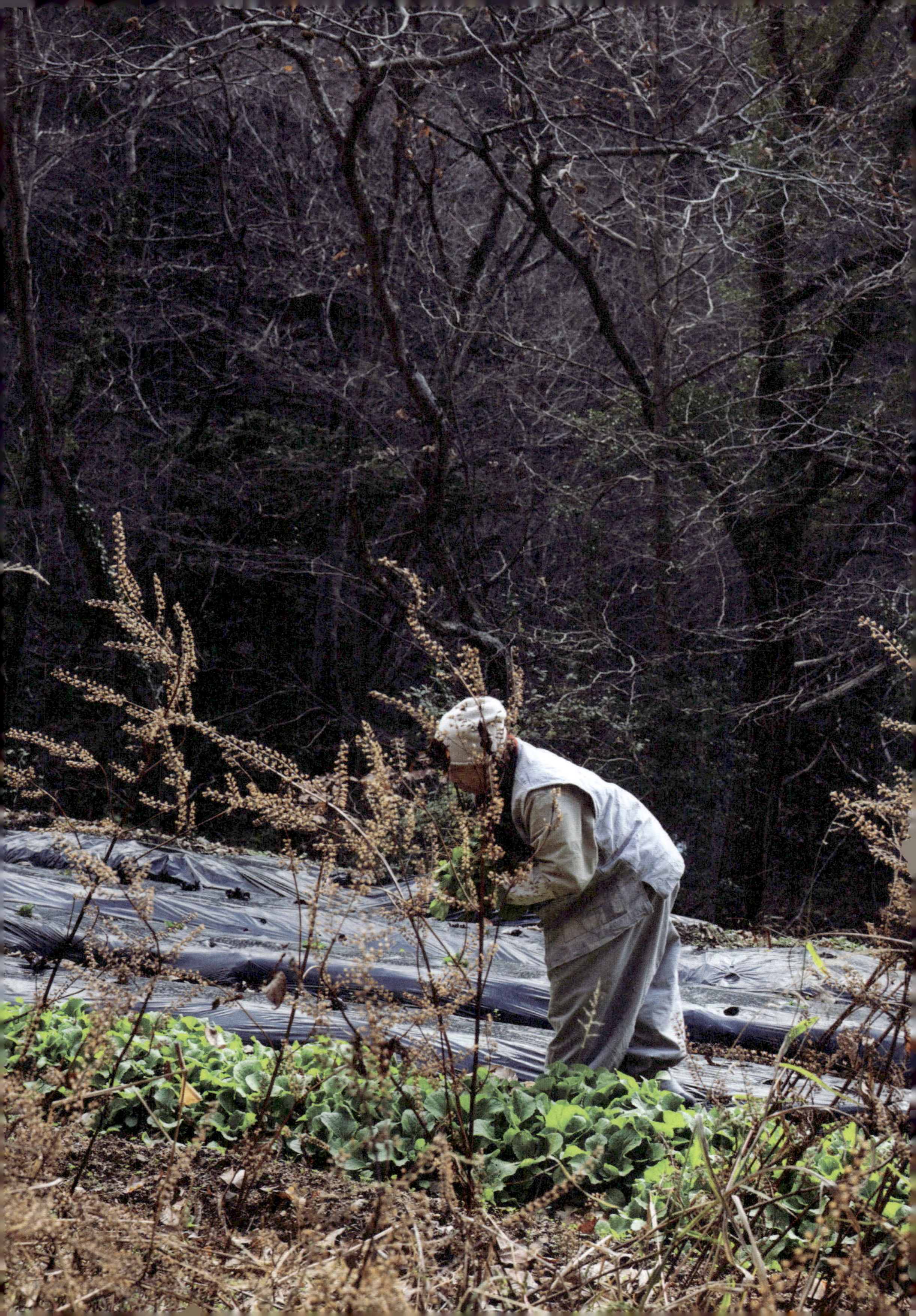

The dough is often made from flour, grated potatoes, buckwheat flour, or mung bean flour. Vegetable pancakes with squid or crab are also popular. According to tradition, the pancakes are always savory—they're never sweet as they typically are in Europe. Small, lightly sweetened pancakes garnished with flowers are made with rice flour and only on certain holidays.

In Korea, namul is also frequently eaten dried, particularly san-namul and bada-namul. If you leave cooked namul to dry in the sun for four or five days, it ferments naturally. Jeongkwan Snim likes to use this method; she dries all kinds of vegetables herself. In the spring and summer, there are more than enough vegetables to ferment them! But in order to prepare dried namul, it must first be soaked in cold water.

Another way to preserve namul is to preserve it as *jangajji* (page 161), with soy sauce and salt. Onions, garlic, cucumbers, radishes, perilla leaves, and even honeydew melons can be processed this way. San-namul and bada-namul are both very well suited for this. The variety of possible preparations is unimaginable! Buddhism awoke the love among Koreans for namul and so created a special tradition.

Spinach with Soy Sauce and Sesame Seeds — 216
Soup with Soybean Sprouts — 238
Bamboo Shoot with Perilla — 242
Chinamul — 246
Mung Bean Sprouts with Minari — 248
Cucumber Namul — 284
Soybean Sprouts with Turmeric — 286

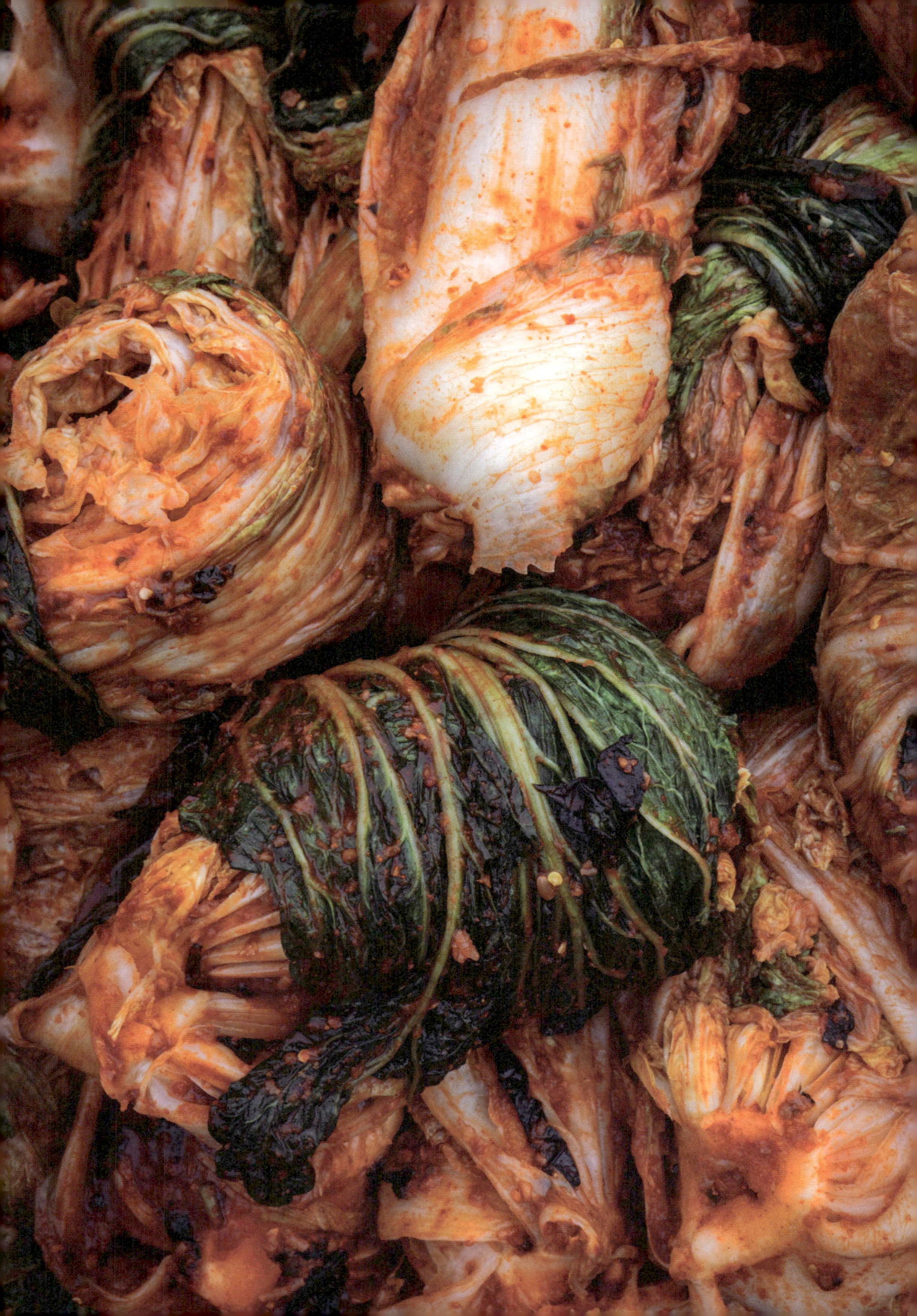

KIMCHI

At the end of November, Jeongkwan Snim organizes Kimjang Days at Cheonjinam. It's an annual autumn tradition that brings together about 70 people from Korea and abroad. Everyone works together as mountains of napa cabbage, radishes, and mustard greens are processed into kimchi and placed in earthenware containers to ferment. Temple kimchi has developed into a unique tradition and differs from other kinds of kimchi—it forms an important component of Korean kimchi culture, which collectively boasts a long history and a great variety.

Kimchi can be recognized by its distinctive appearance, flavor, and aroma—it's a fermented vegetable that has become famous far and wide outside of Korea. Fermentation means that a natural process is underway and a transformation is taking place within. This task involves the work of microorganisms that transform the organic materials into (in the case of kimchi) amino acids and lactic acid, in the process creating new nutrients and releasing new flavors. The ingredients become easier to digest and more beneficial for our health, and they promote healthy gut bacteria. Fermented vegetables like kimchi remain edible for a long time.

Salt—a fundamental material for all life—plays a central role in the making of kimchi. It draws water from the ingredients, preventing the bacteria that are harmful to humans from flourishing. At the same time, salt also enables halophiles, or salt-loving bacteria, to set the fermentation process in motion. This makes kimchi, soy sauce, and doenjang possible. Fermentation is a wonderful natural spectacle that helps us maintain our health in harmony with nature! It's a complex process; many factors come into play. As the Buddha himself taught, life is not possible without mutual support.

Written attestations of kimchi can be traced back to the seventh century, but kimchi may be much older than that—it seems that the principles of fermentation were already known even then. Earlier forms of kimchi may have looked different from the modern version. In Korea, as with the rest of the world, vegetables and fish were preserved in salt to make them last, and tradition suggests that vegetables like radishes, eggplant, leeks, bamboo shoots, and turnips were already being preserved with salt and flavorings. Eventually, new ingredients were added, and people's tastes developed in different directions. Every family set aside several days in late autumn to make kimjang, and various types of kimchi were prepared for the long winter ahead. The filled clay pots were left in a cool storeroom or buried in the ground to keep the temperature of the fermenting vegetables constant. (Refrigeration technology had not yet been invented.) Some very large, very old pots have been discovered in temple complexes, indicating that kimchi was already being made and stored in Buddhist temples.

Obvious changes took place in the seventeenth century that gave kimchi a new appearance. Specifically, *gochu* arrived in Korea from Central and South America. It spread rapidly due to its spicy flavor and soon came to play an important role as a vegetable and as a flavoring. When *baechu* (napa cabbage) came to Korea in the nineteenth century, it became one of the main ingredients in kimchi along with white radishes. This tradition remains today—the many types of baechu kimchi have become synonymous with kimchi.

Although people like to add some radishes to the ingredients in baechu kimchi, radish makes a wonderful kimchi on its own! Various kinds of radishes in Korea are good for this. However, usually kimchi is made from many kinds of vegetables: cucumbers are popular, as are eggplants, minari, scallions, green cabbages, and mustard greens. There's no limit to the number of variations! This has led to the creation of countless regional specialties.

The preparation begins with salt: the vegetables are placed in a brine or sprinkled with salt. This requires good instincts, because everything depends on using the right quantity and type of salt. (Just as important is the length of time that the vegetables should remain in the salt.) Coarse-grained salt is usually used to create the brine. Too much salt will make the vegetables too soft, lengthen the fermentation process, and make the kimchi too salty, but if too little salt is used, the vegetables will remain too firm. The quantity of salt required also depends on the kinds and amounts of vegetables being used. For example, cucumbers need only a little salt and cannot be left to pickle too long, but radishes need more time depending on whether they're cut up or whole.

Baechu is typically halved and salted; it needs a few hours and must be turned several times during the pickling to ensure that the salt gets into all the crevices. Baechu should be neither too firm nor too tender—after it's pickled, it's rinsed thoroughly two or three times in cold water to remove the salt. At this point, the person making it should taste a piece to make sure that it's not too salty. If it *is* too salty, it needs to sit in water for a while. The water will be squeezed out afterwards.

When the baechu or other vegetable is ready, the sauce, or *yangnyeomjang*, is prepared. Everyone has their own preferences as to what to include, but for baechu kimchi, the standard ingredients in the

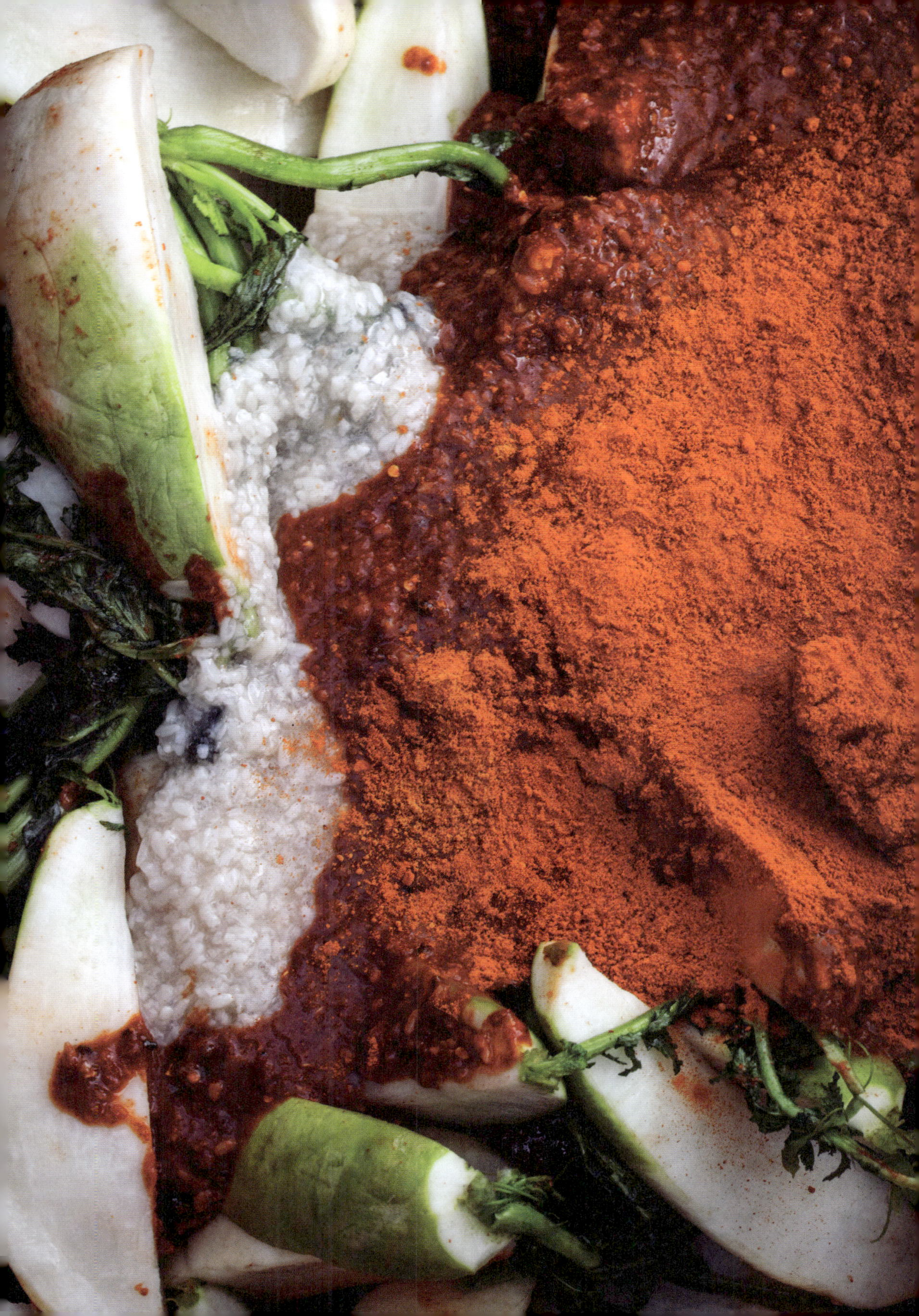

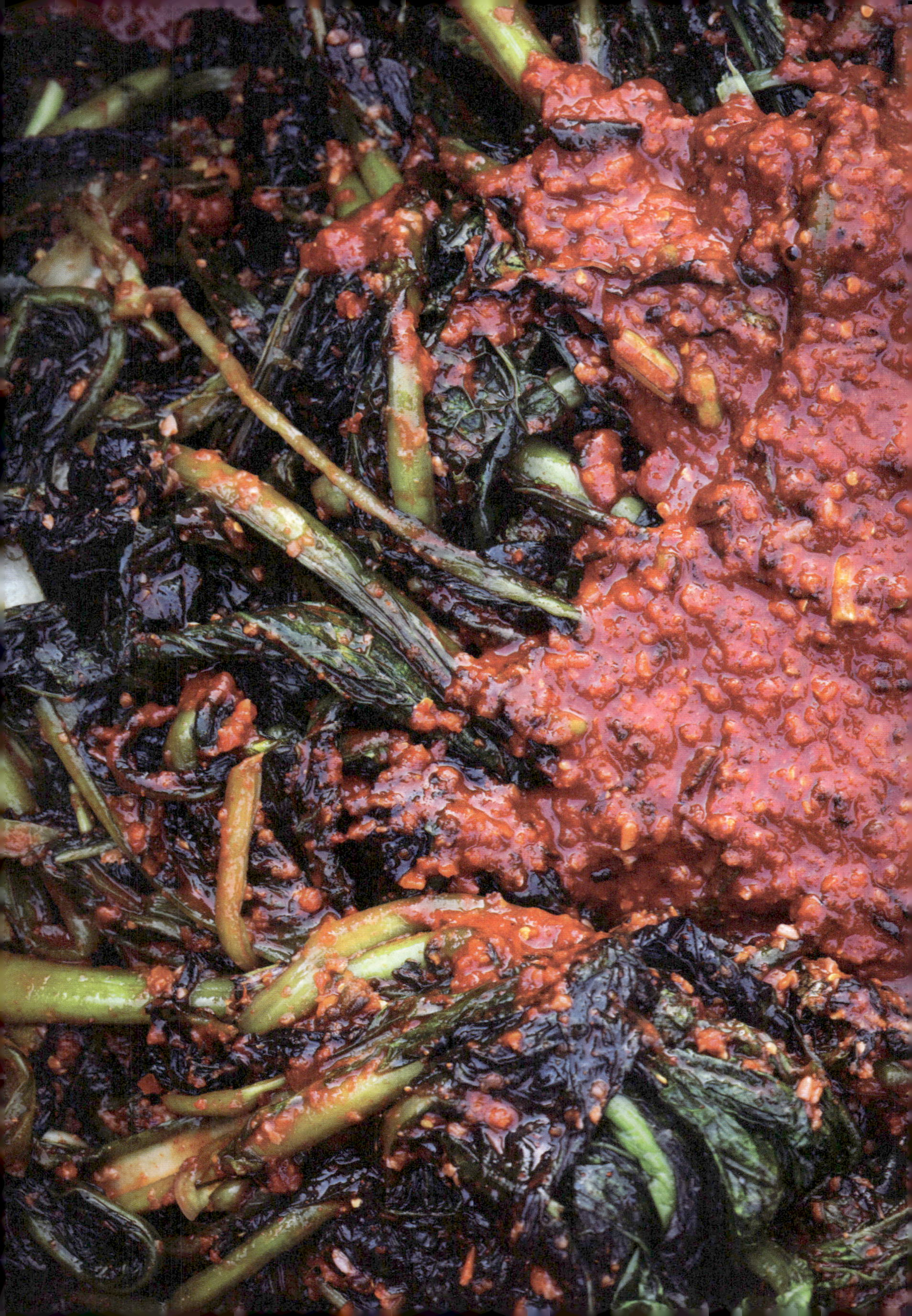

paste are: glutinous rice flour, garlic, ginger, radish, scallion, gochu, gochu powder, pear, and jeotgal. *Jeotgal* is made from little fermented fish or shellfish; they're usually small fish like anchovies, or they're fish eggs or mussels that have been preserved in salt for about a year to ferment them. A certain quantity of jeotgal is added to the kimchi to activate and accelerate its fermentation. Temple kimchi, however, does not use any jeotgal.

It's important that the components for yangnyeomjang are used in the right proportion relative to one another and that they harmonize well. That's especially true for garlic and ginger, because those both have strong flavors. When the sauce is ready, it's spread all over the baechu and between the leaves. The person making the kimchi can decide for themselves how spicy they want it to be. After that, the baechu is wrapped in its outer leaf and placed in an onggi or a container with all of the pieces layered on top of one another. Finally, the remaining sauce is poured over the top and the kimchi is pressed down to ensure that it contains as little air as possible.

The container is closed, left to stand at room temperature for a few days, and then placed in a cool area. The kimchi is ready to eat one week later. However, since the fermentation process will continue, the kimchi can be observed and tasted periodically to see how its flavor develops over time.

Jeongkwan Snim's kimchi distinguishes itself through certain characteristics—although it's temple kimchi, it has its own unique and distinctive character. It's vegan, so there is no jeotgal; it doesn't use garlic; it's less spicy; it tastes fresh and mild. A distinct tradition for making kimchi arose in Buddhist temples over the centuries, and Jeongkwan Snim carries this forward. However, she also tries to create new variations. For the yangnyeomjang, Snim adds grated or pureed tomatoes, red beets, persimmons, pears, or even apples to the glutinous rice paste. To help fermentation along, she adds well-aged soy sauce. But what makes her kimchi unique is that she adds different types of homemade cheong made from fruit, which contain valuable enzymes. This causes her kimchi to develop its own distinctive flavor.

You can taste different levels of maturity as kimchi ages. Each phase has a different flavor, but the longer the kimchi ferments, the more tart it will become. If the temperature remains constant, the kimchi can be kept fresh longer. (That's why a special refrigerator for kimchi was developed in South Korea.) Before the advent of refrigeration, people used to add more salt when they wanted to keep their kimchi longer.

Like those traditional kimchi makers did, Jeongkwan Snim also buries kimchi in onggis and lets it ferment and mature underground. Her kimchi still tastes very good after six months! It's tender and somewhat paler in color, but it has a unique flavor. She also lets kimchi sit for years and then makes stew from it.

The diversity of kimchi is broad. There's watery kimchi made from radishes that's less salty but fresh and effervescent, making it good for hot summer days. Most kimchi contains gochu powder, but there are also varieties without it—for example, *baek-kimchi*, or "white kimchi." Baek-kimchi contains chestnuts, pine nuts, pears, and dates, ingredients that make it taste mild and fruity (although it's expensive to make). You can also make quick kimchi by making yangnyeomjang and then mixing it together with lettuce leaves. In coastal areas, some kimchis are made with various ingredients sourced from fish.

The Korean dinner table is simply not complete without kimchi! Many families still prepare it according to their own traditional recipes, but nowadays, kimchi is also produced in factories and sold in supermarkets. Because kimchi is now consumed worldwide, it won't be long before new, localized variations turn up in other parts of the world. But no matter where kimchi is made or eaten, the smell of it brings a sense of home to Koreans—kimchi is embedded deeply in their body memory.

Summer Water Kimchi — 120
Baechu Kimchi — 126
Quick Kimchi with Oak Leaf Lettuce — 130
Braised Three-Year-Old Kimchi — 132
Watery Mustard Green Kimchi — 250

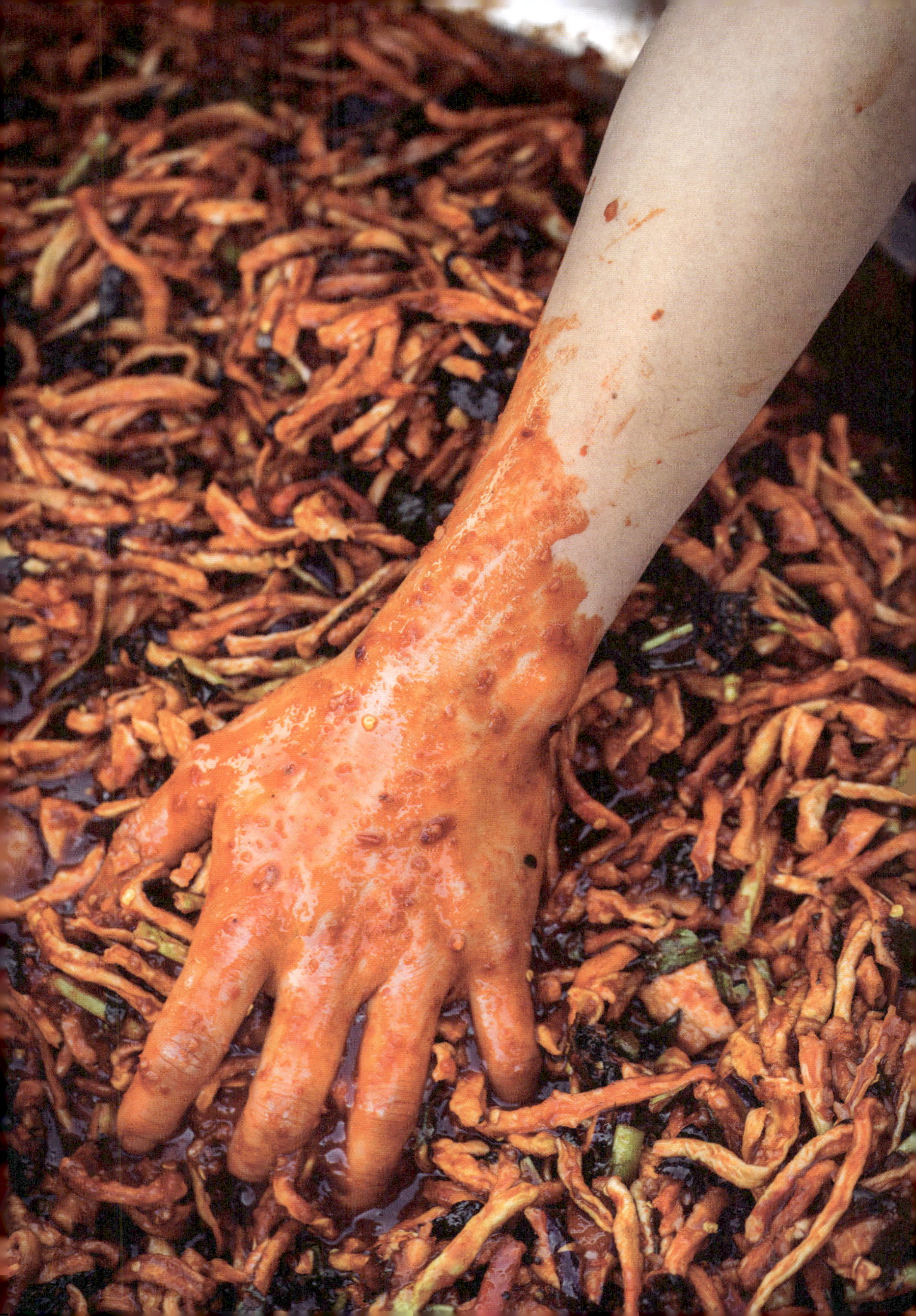

Yeoreum mul-kimchi

SUMMER WATER KIMCHI

2¼ pounds (1 kg) napa cabbage (baechu)
⅔ cup (200 g) coarse salt
2 small white radishes (mu)

Prepare the napa cabbage: cut off some of the core and remove the wilted outer leaves. Use your hands to rip it into two parts, then halve each piece again in the same way.

In a large bowl, mix 8½ cups (2 L) water with 6½ tablespoons (120 g) coarse salt. Press the napa cabbage pieces under the water with your hands and sprinkle the remaining salt over the individual napa cabbage leaves. Place a lid or board over the cabbage and weigh it down. Let it stand for 4 to 5 hours, stirring once or twice.

After that, rinse the cabbage thoroughly three times with cold water to remove the extra salt. Let it drain and then squeeze it out gently.

Prepare the radishes: rinse and halve them (leave the green leaves on them). Place them in a bowl and salt them generously. Let them stand for 2 hours, then rinse and drain them.

For the sauce (yangnyeomjang)
3 tablespoons glutinous rice paste (chapssalpul, page 412)
1 tablespoon salt
2 tablespoons soy sauce (ganjang)
¼ cup (20 g) ginger (saenggang), grated
2 tablespoons Bokbunja-Cheong (page 180)
1 small Asian pear (bae), grated
Red beet (bit), grated

Add the glutinous rice paste to a large bowl along with the salt. Add the soy sauce, ginger, bokbunja-cheong, and pear and mix well. Gradually add water until a thin sauce forms. You should be able to thinly cover the napa cabbage and the radish with it.

Place a piece of napa cabbage in the bowl and use your hands to spread the sauce well between the leaves. Set it aside and do the same with the other pieces. Coat the radish with the sauce as well, then finally wrap it with the radish greens.

Place some radishes in a large container. Wrap the napa cabbage with its outer leaves and coat the outside of it with some grated red beet for a splash of color, then place it in the container. Place more radishes over that and coat them with more of the red beet. Pour the rest of the sauce over everything.

Close the container and leave it to ferment at room temperature for 2 to 3 days, then place it in the refrigerator. The kimchi can be eaten after about a week. To serve it, cut the napa cabbage and radish into small pieces and serve them with the sauce. The kimchi will keep in the refrigerator for up to 6 weeks.

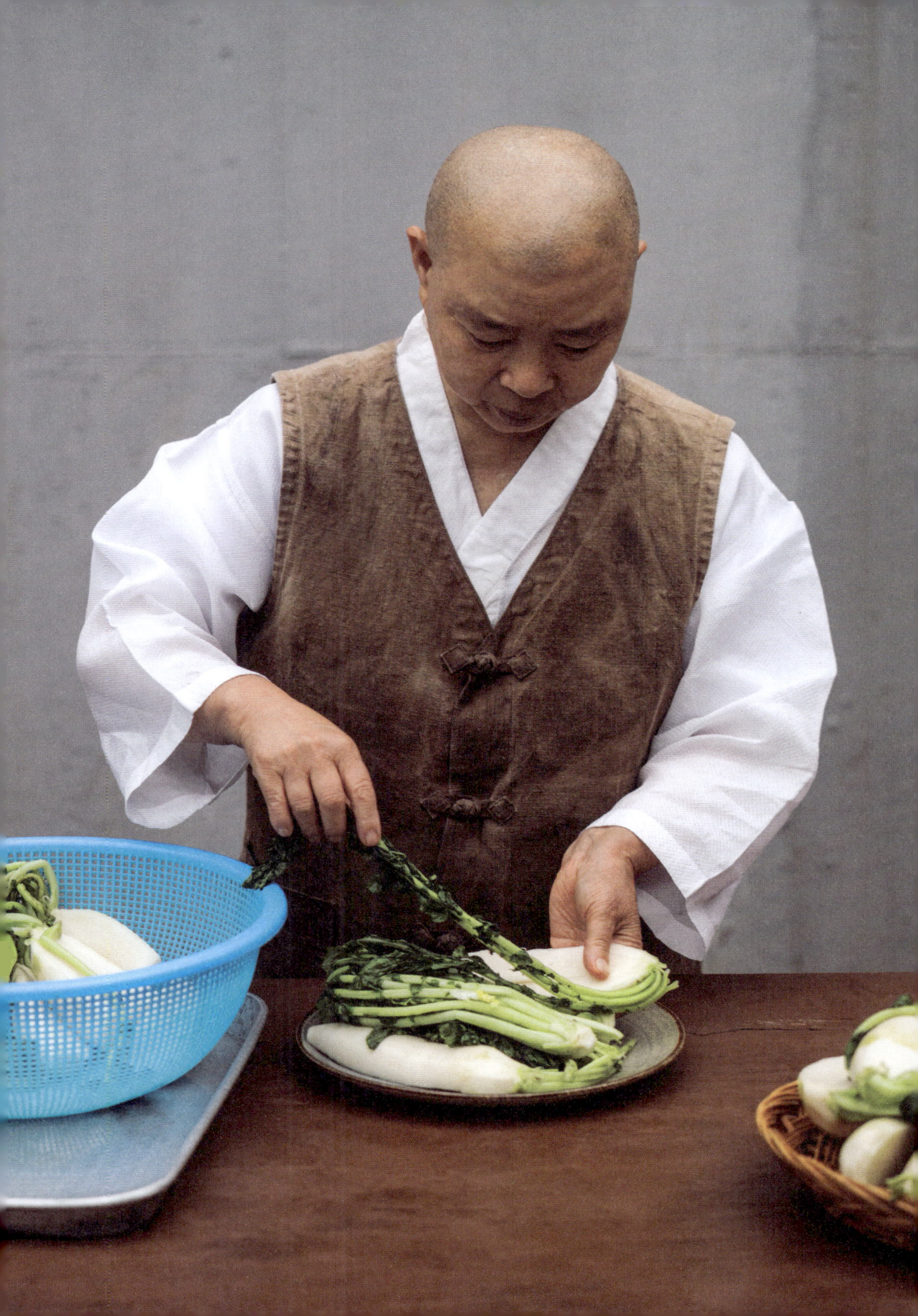

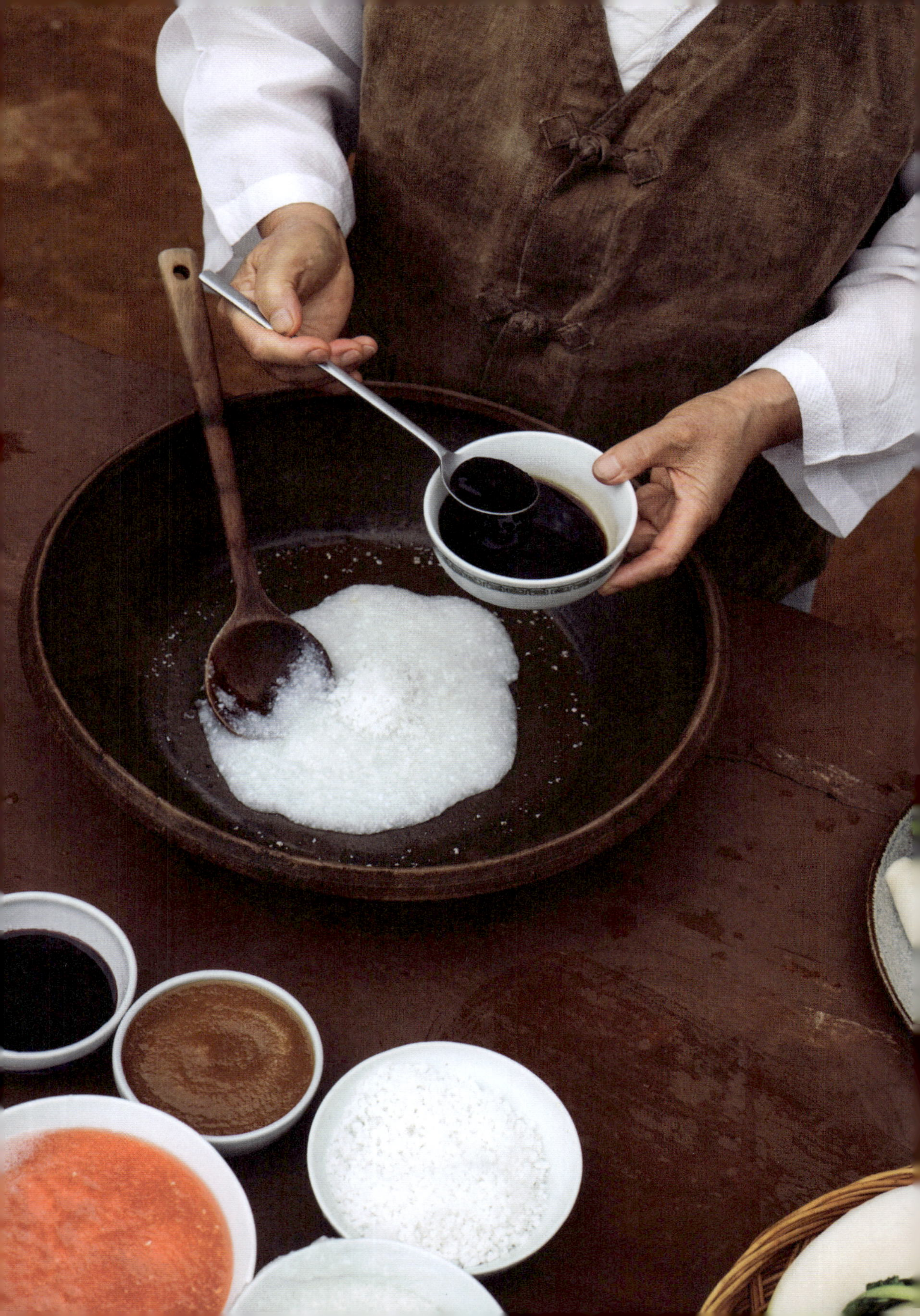

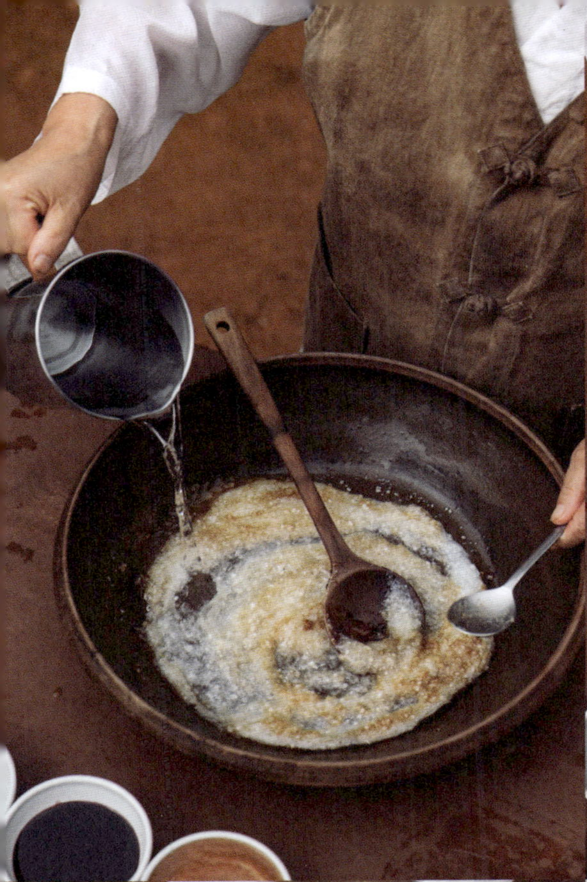
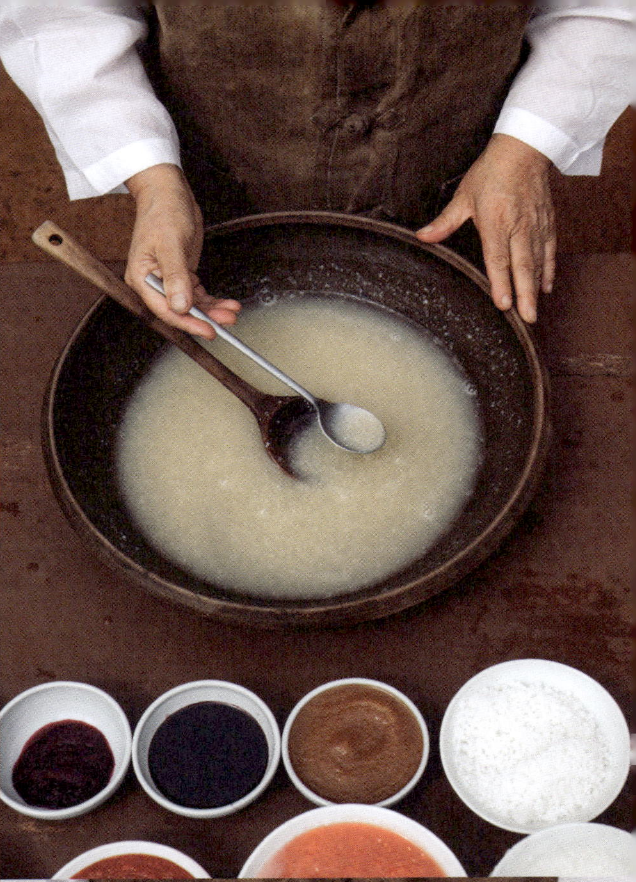
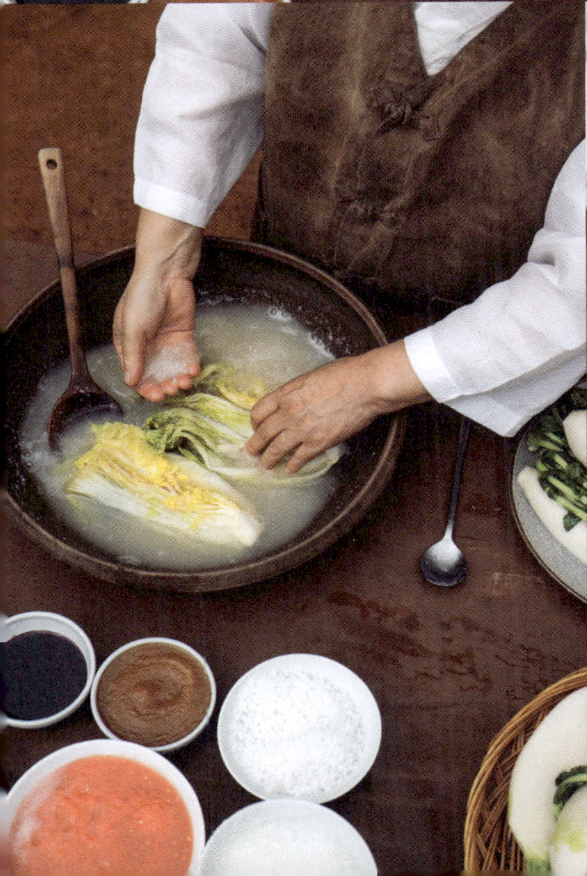
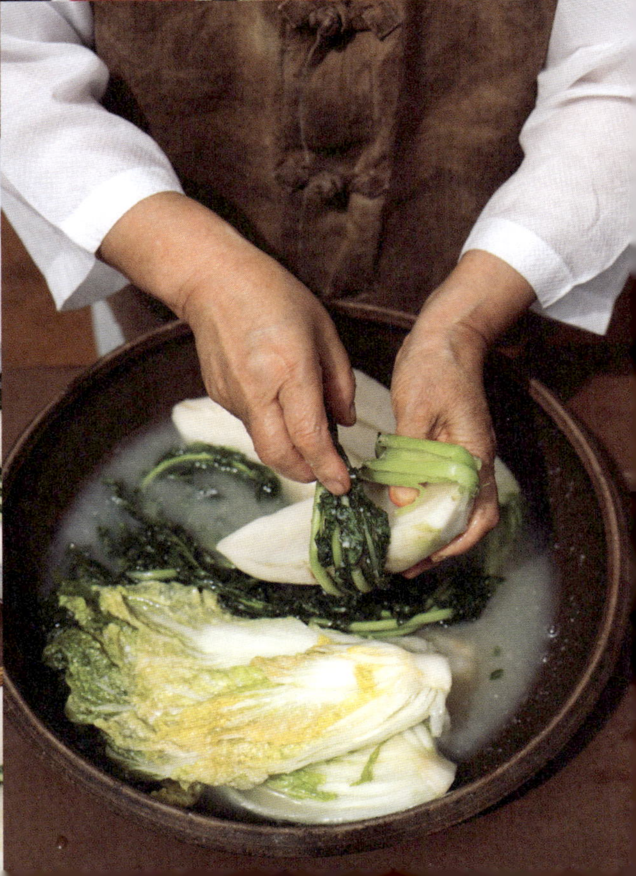

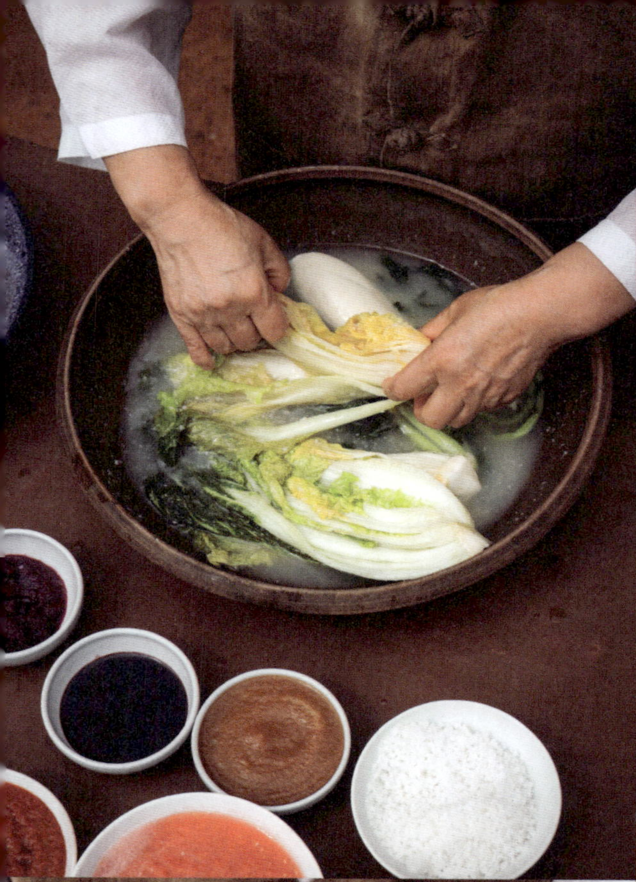
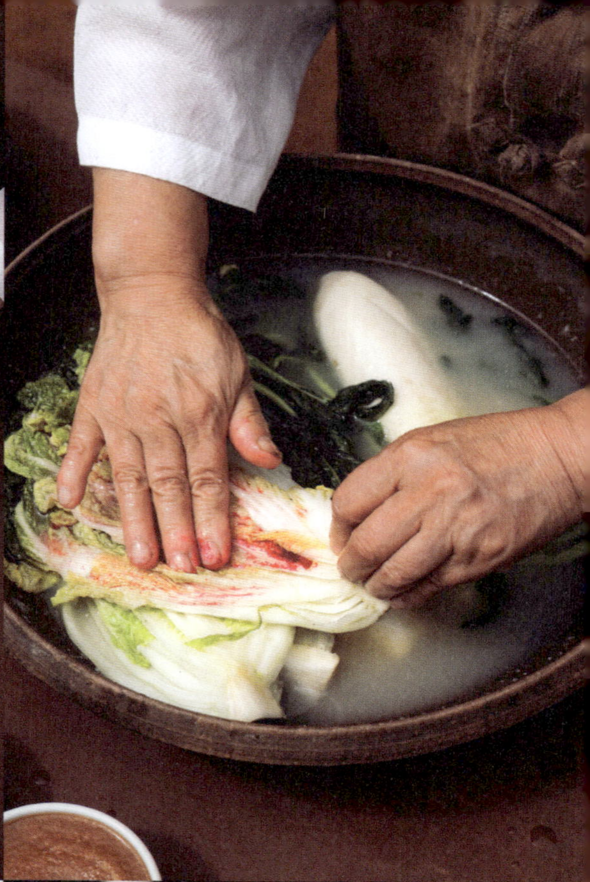
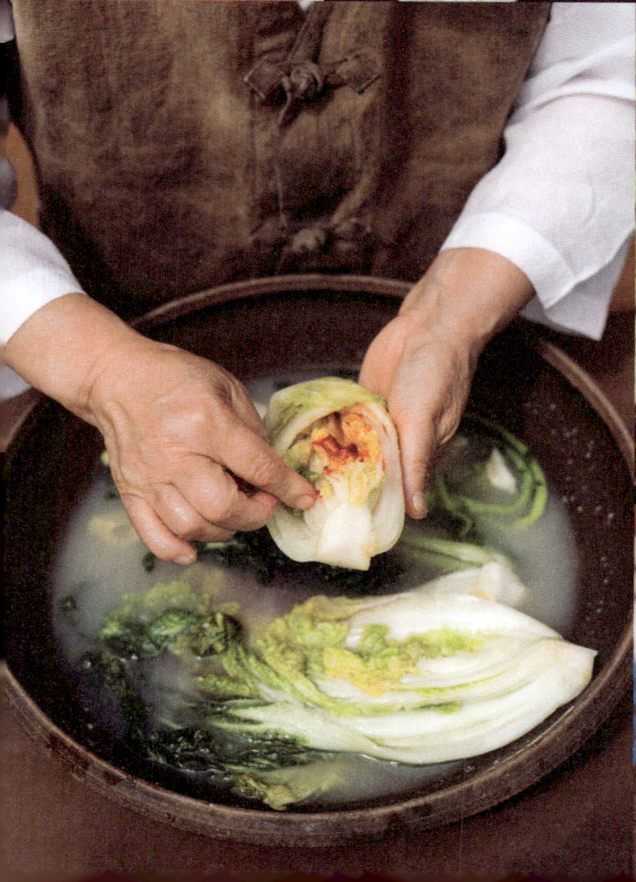
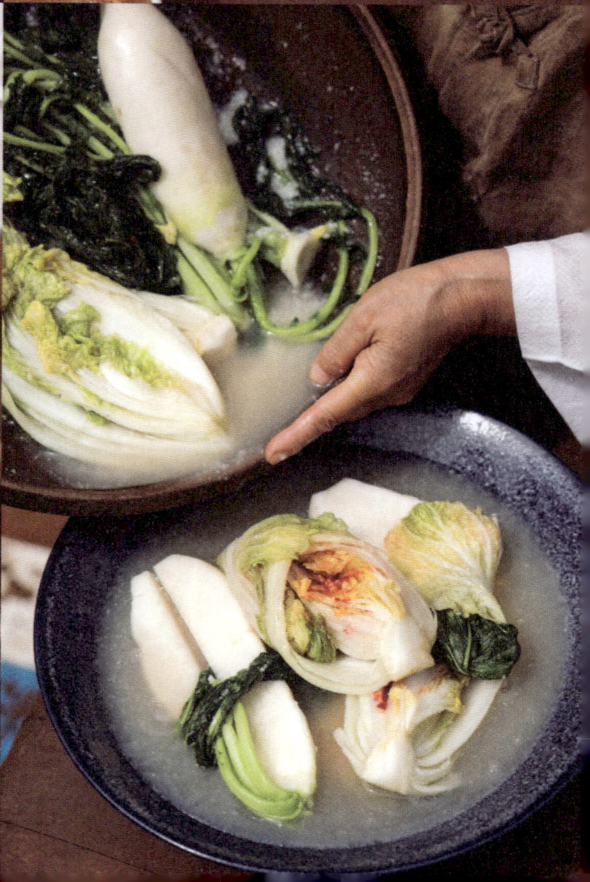

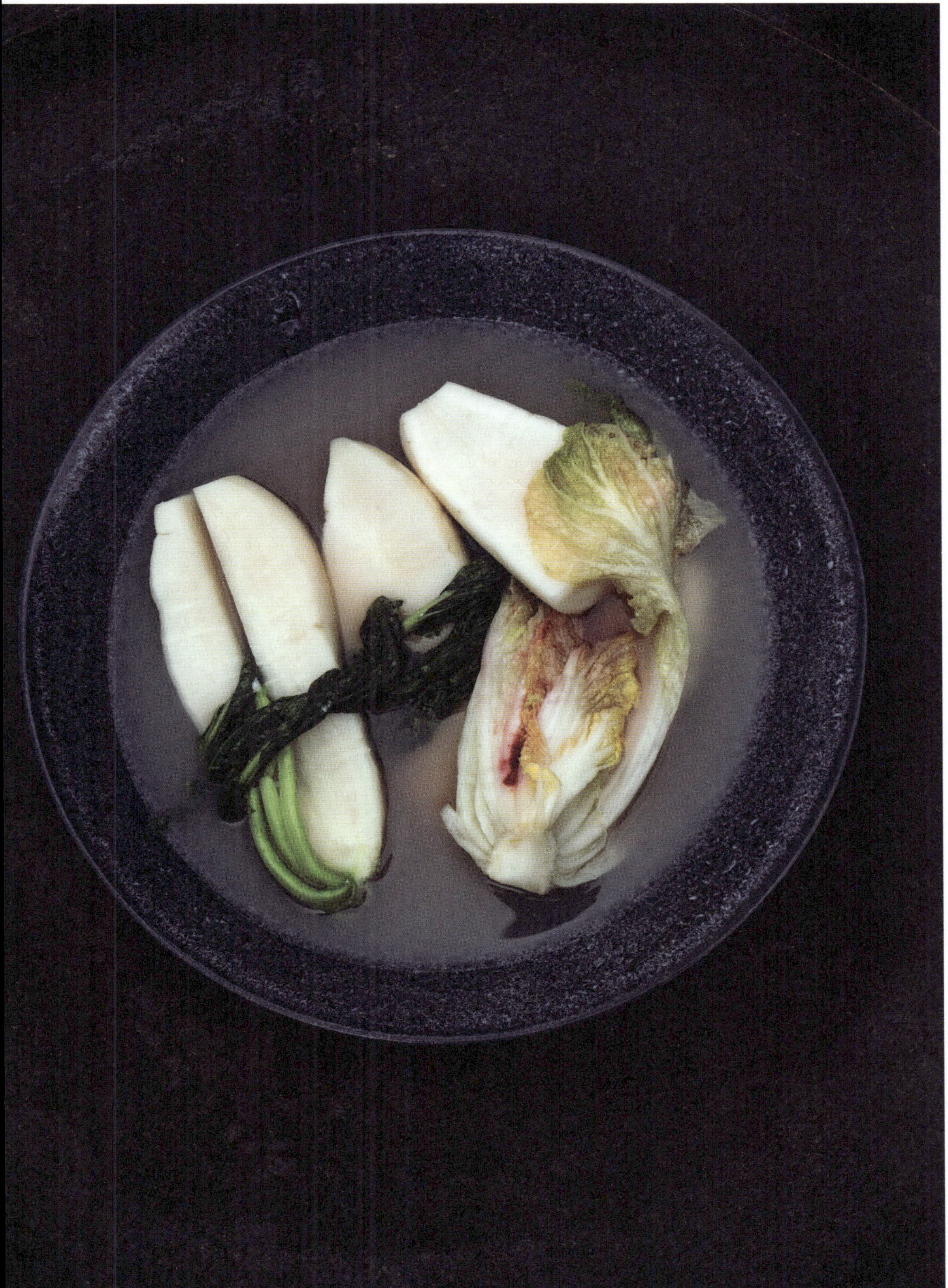

Jeongkwan Snim likes to experiment to create new yangnyeomjang for her temple kimchi, but she also has some proven recipes, some of which are presented here. One of these sauces can be used for different types of kimchi. If there's any left, it can be kept in the refrigerator for another kimchi.

Baechu-kimchi

BAECHU KIMCHI

4 ½ pounds (2 kg) napa cabbage (baechu)
1 cup plus 3 tablespoons (350 g) coarse salt, divided

Prepare the napa cabbage: cut off some of the core and remove the wilted outer leaves. Use your hands to rip it into two parts, then halve each piece again in the same way. In a bowl, mix the baechu with 1 gallon (4 L) water and ⅔ cup plus 3 tablespoons (250 g) of the coarse salt, then sprinkle the individual leaves generously with the rest of the salt.

Place a lid or board over the cabbage and weigh it down. Let it stand for 4 to 5 hours, stirring once or twice. If the baechu is older and the leaves are firmer, it will need more time. Instinct and experience are essential here.

Rinse the baechu in cold water three times. Tear off a piece and taste it to determine whether the salt level is good. Squeeze it out well and drain it in a sieve.

For the sauce (yangnyeomjang)
6 tablespoons glutinous rice paste (chapssalpul, page 412)
1 Asian pear (bae)
2 red apples (sagwa)
2 tomatoes
1 red bell pepper (pimang)
1 piece of ginger (saenggang)
4 tablespoons Bokbunja-Cheong (page 180)
4 tablespoons soy sauce (ganjang)
3 to 4 tablespoons coarse chili powder (gochugaru)
Salt for seasoning

Put the glutinous rice paste in a bowl. Clean the pear, apples, tomatoes, red bell pepper, and piece of ginger and cut them into pieces. Puree them in a blender. Add the puree, the bokbunja-cheong, the soy sauce, and the chili powder to the bowl, mix well, and season to taste with salt.

Coat the baechu well with the yangnyeomjang. There should be enough sauce to cover everything, but not too much. Wrap each of the baechu pieces with one of the outer leaves and place it in a container. When all of the pieces are nestled in next to each other, pour more sauce over them, press them down firmly, and cover them with the lid.

Let the container stand at room temperature for 2 to 3 days, then place it in the refrigerator. The kimchi can be eaten after about a week. It will keep in the refrigerator for up to 6 weeks.

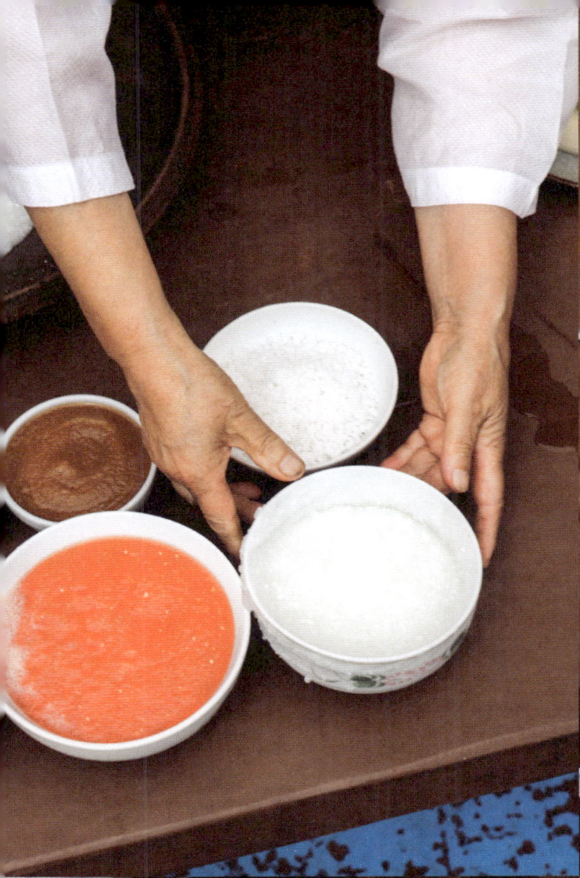
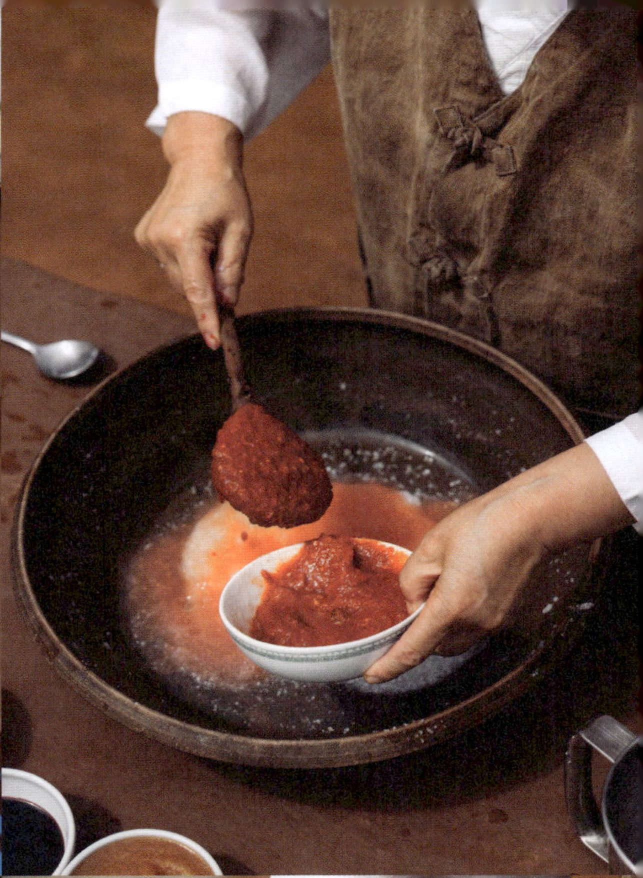
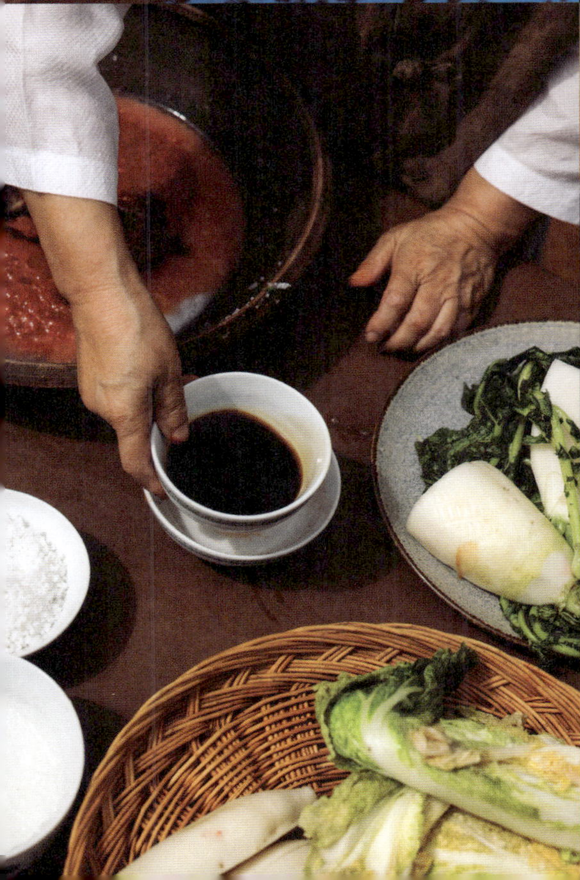
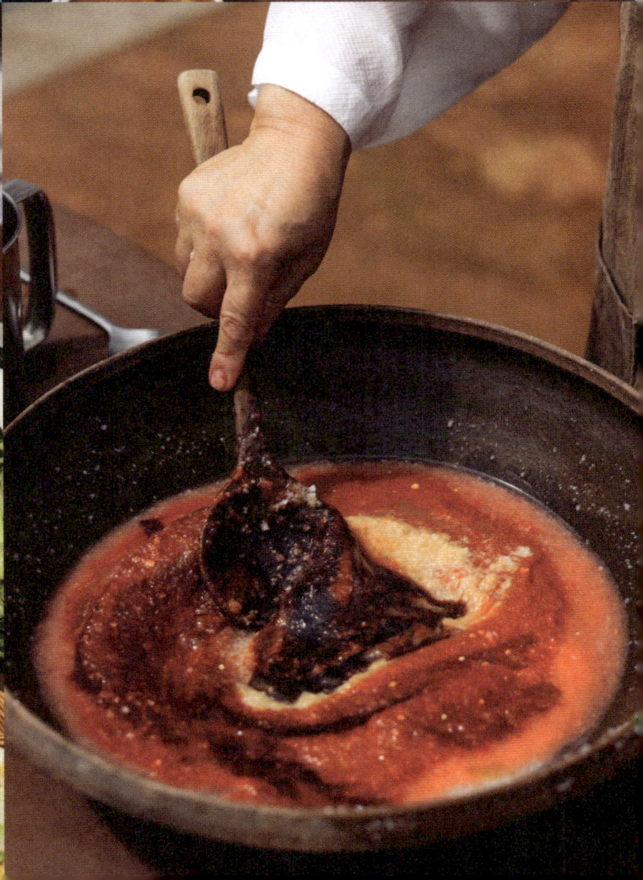

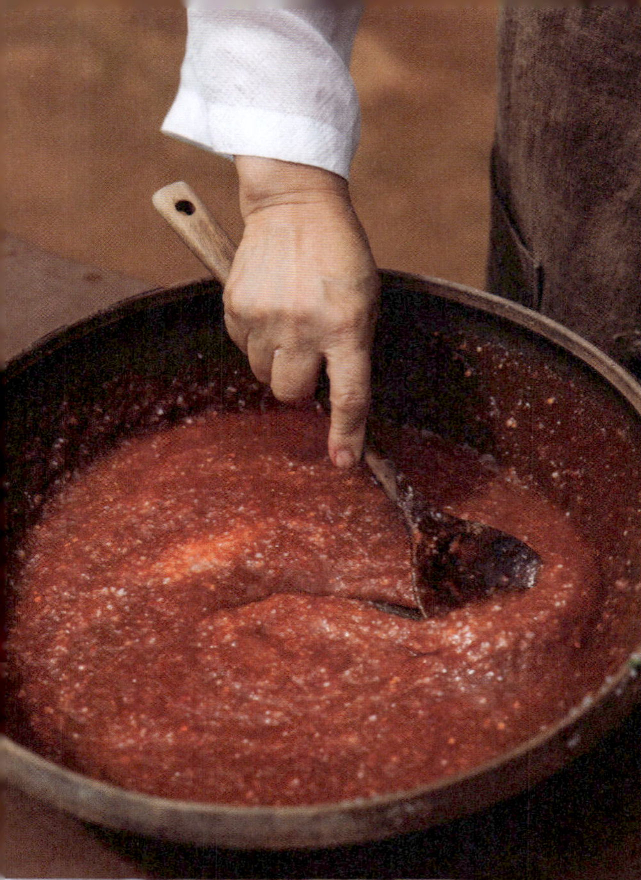
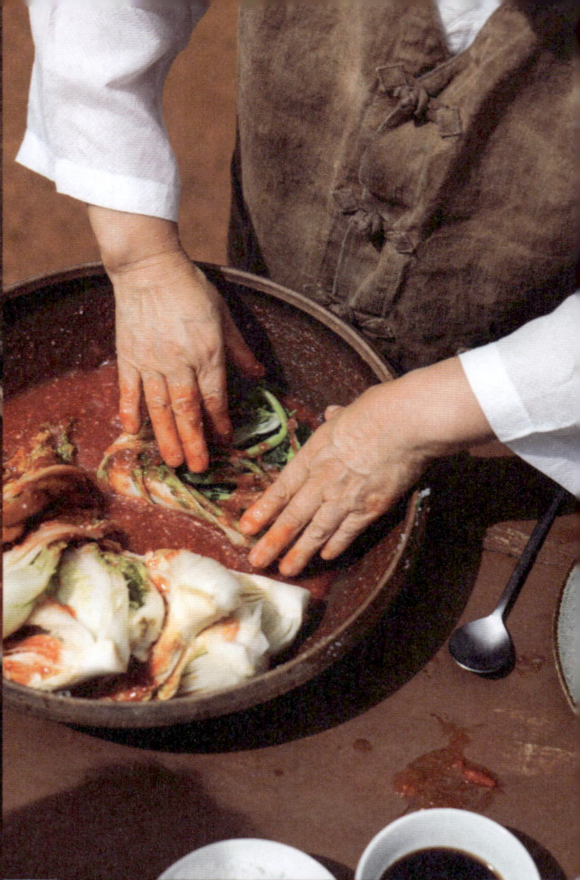
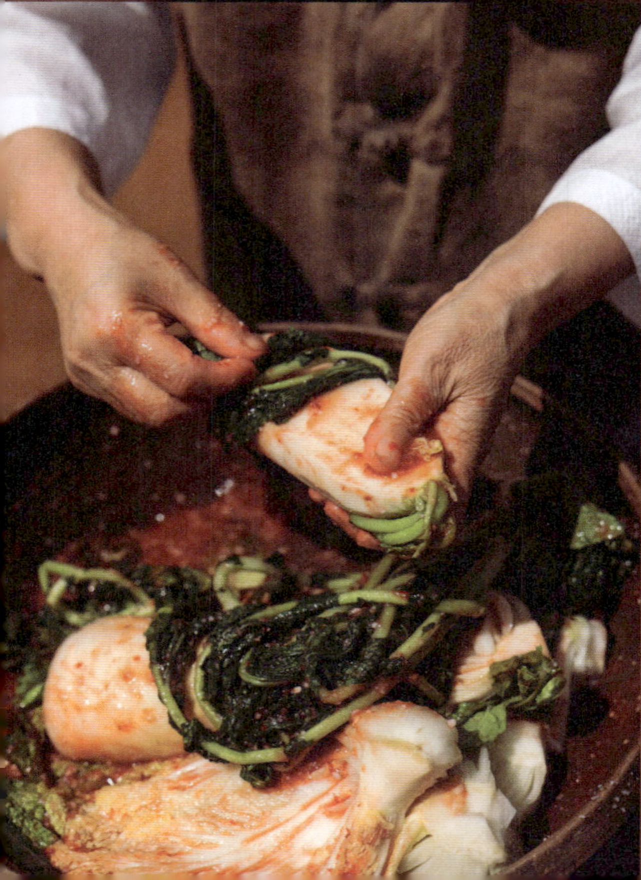
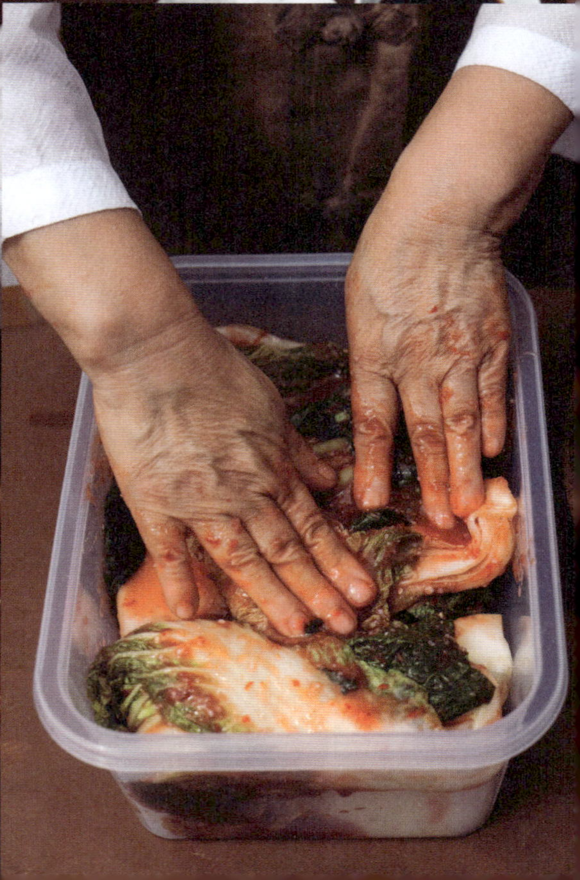

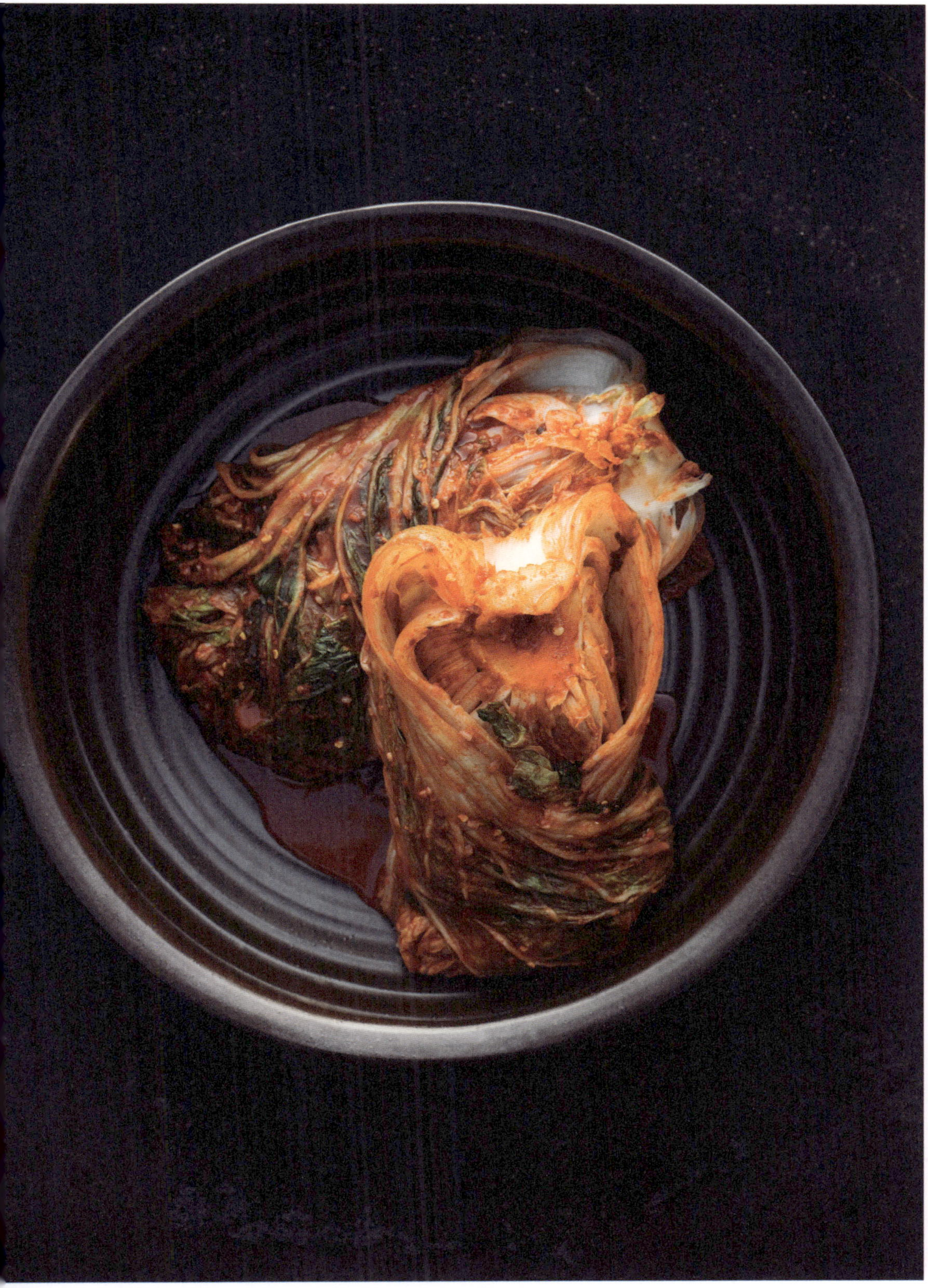

Sangchu-kimchi

QUICK KIMCHI WITH OAK LEAF LETTUCE

1 head of oak leaf lettuce
Salt for seasoning
½ of a small red beet (bit)

Rinse the lettuce leaves or bunch of leaves well and place them in a shallow container of salt water for 10 minutes. It should not be too salty! Then rinse off and drain.

Julienne the red beet.

For the sauce (yangnyeomjang)
2 tomatoes
3 long red chile peppers (cheongyanggochu)
2 tablespoons glutinous rice paste (chapssalpul, page 412)

Cut the tomatoes into thick slices and finely mince the chilies.

In a bowl, mix the glutinous rice paste well with the tomatoes and the chilies.

Mix the lettuce leaves and the red beet well with the yangnyeomjang. This kimchi can be served immediately, but it will also keep in the refrigerator for one or two days.

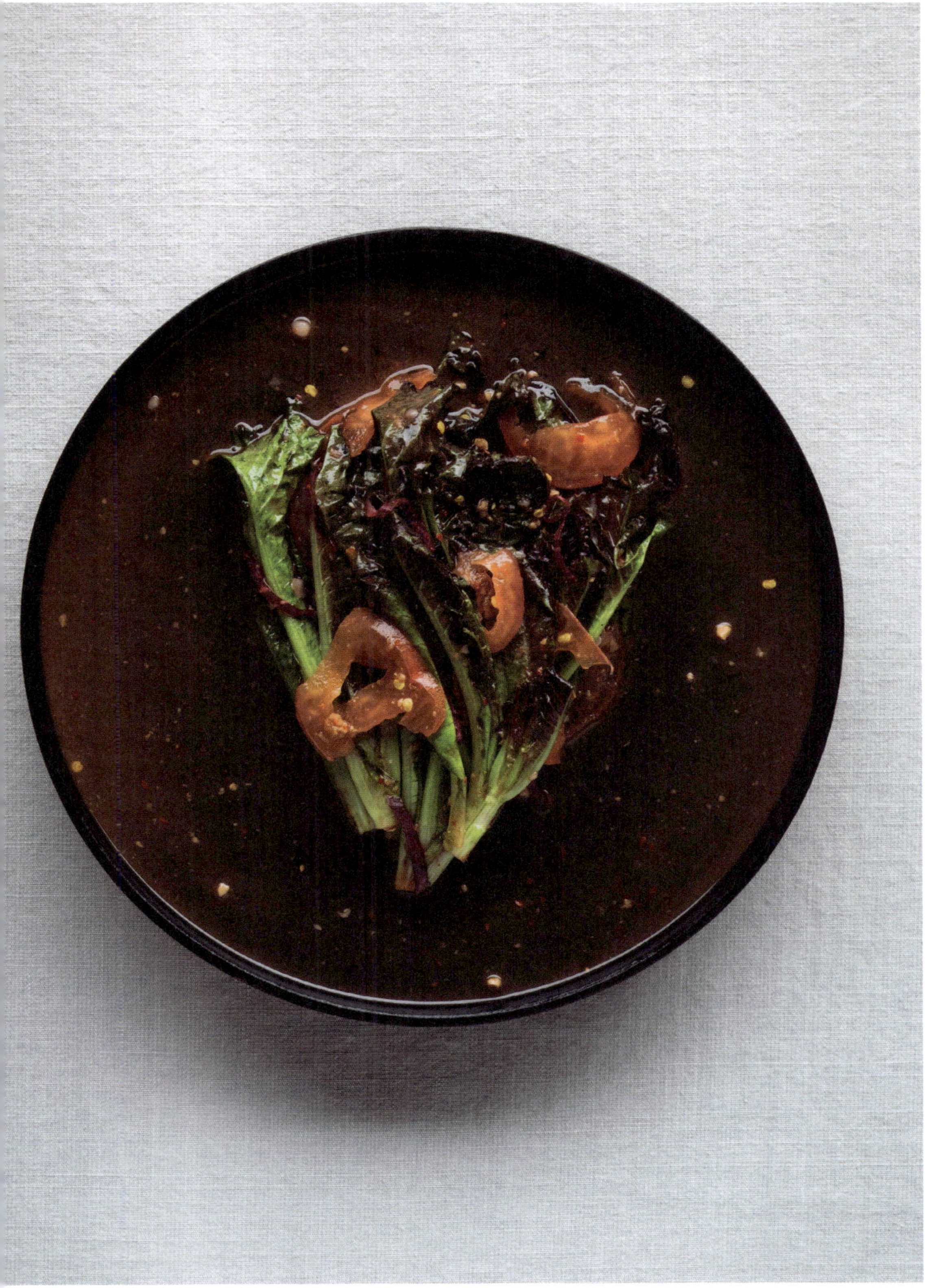

It's not very easy to find three-year-old kimchi, even in Korea. (Jeongkwan Snim has some because she keeps a big inventory of supplies.) Aged kimchi can still be eaten, but it will taste tart. When it's braised, however, it transforms into a rare delicacy.

Samneun-mugeunjijjim

BRAISED THREE-YEAR-OLD KIMCHI

4 pieces of baechu kimchi (note that this braised dish can also be made with a younger kimchi)
2 carrots (danggeun)
½ of a white radish (mu)
4 tablespoons perilla oil (deulgireum)
4 Korean shiitake mushrooms (pyogo beoseot)
¼ cup (20 g) ginger (saenggang), finely sliced
3 long red and 3 long green chile peppers (cheongyanggochu)
1 tablespoon fermented soybean paste (doenjang)
2 tablespoons soy sauce (ganjang)
3 tablespoons Bokbunja-Cheong (page 180)
2 tablespoons rice syrup (jocheong, page 190)
¼ cup (30 g) sesame seeds (kkae), crushed

Rinse the kimchi and let it stand in water for 2 hours to wash off the sauce (yangnyeomjang).

Slice the carrots, then quarter the radish lengthwise and cut it into equally thin slices.

Pour the oil into a deep pot. Place a layer of carrots and radish on the bottom and layer the kimchi on top of that. Then add a layer of shiitake mushrooms, followed by the ginger. Cut the red and green chilies in half and add them to the pot. Pour in enough water to cover the kimchi.

Cook over high heat and boil for a bit, then reduce the heat and braise until half of the water has cooked off.

Now add the doenjang, soy sauce, bokbunja-cheong, jocheong, and sesame seeds and continue to braise over low heat. Periodically baste the sauce over the kimchi.

When all of the ingredients are tender, the dish can be served.

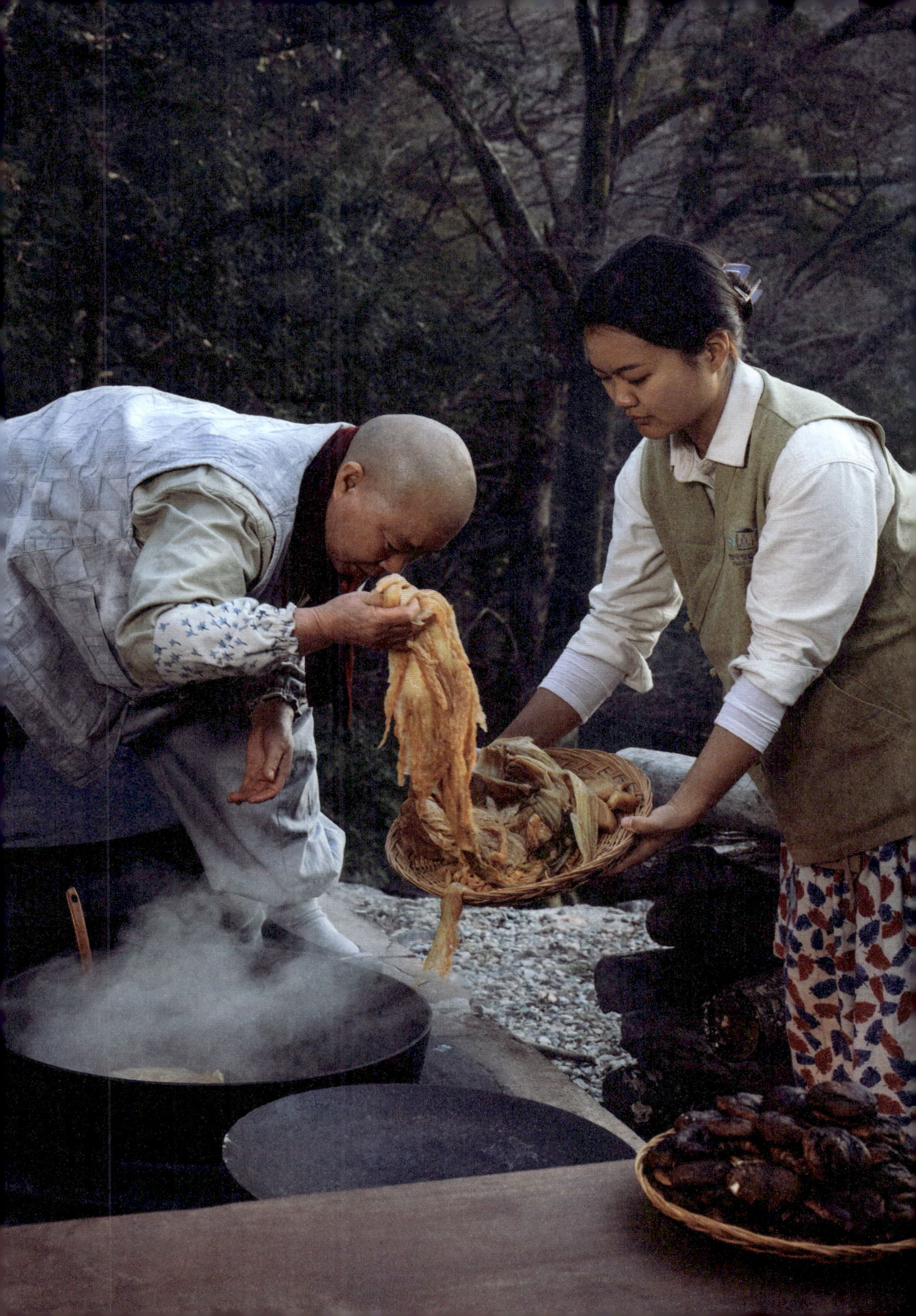

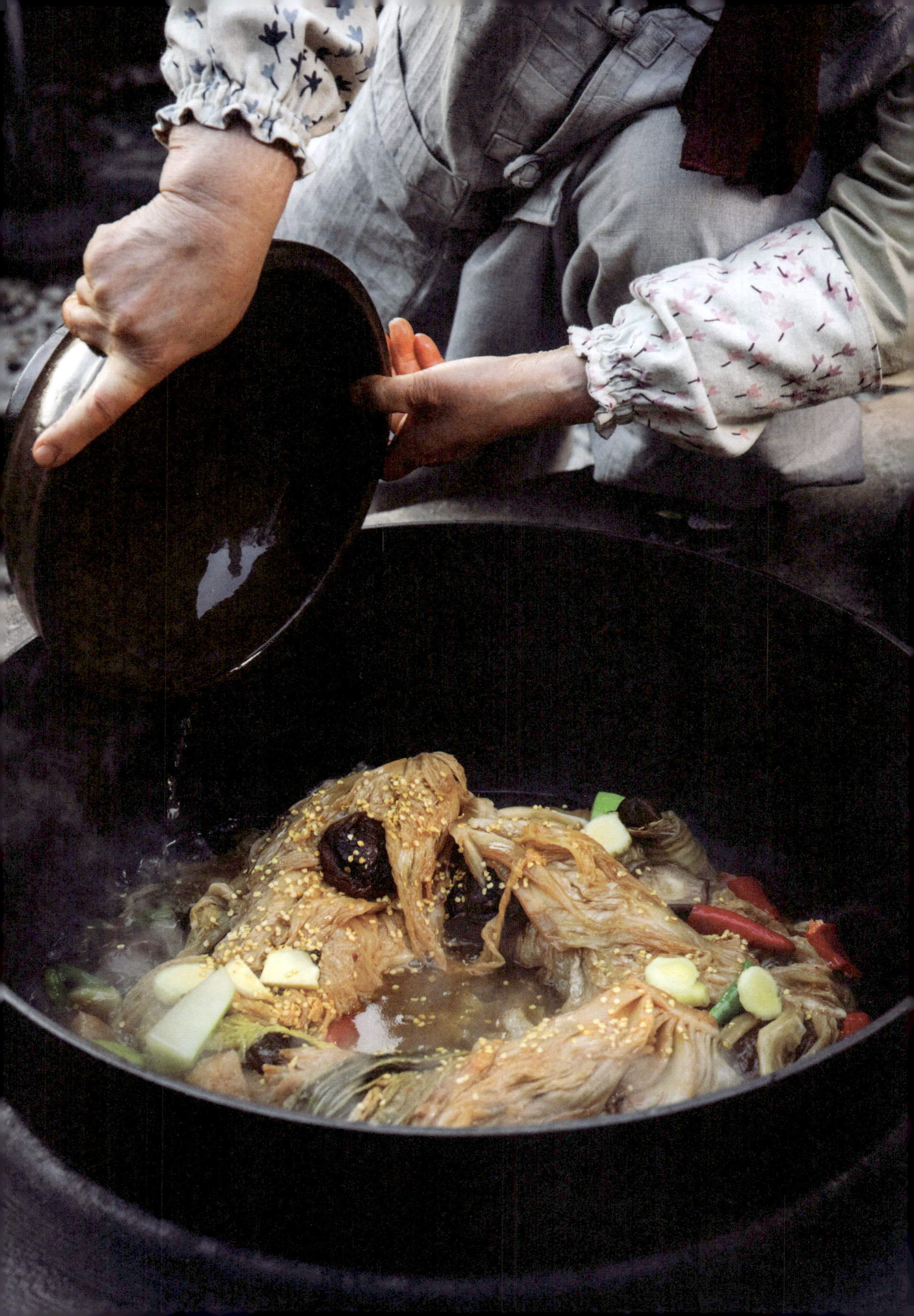

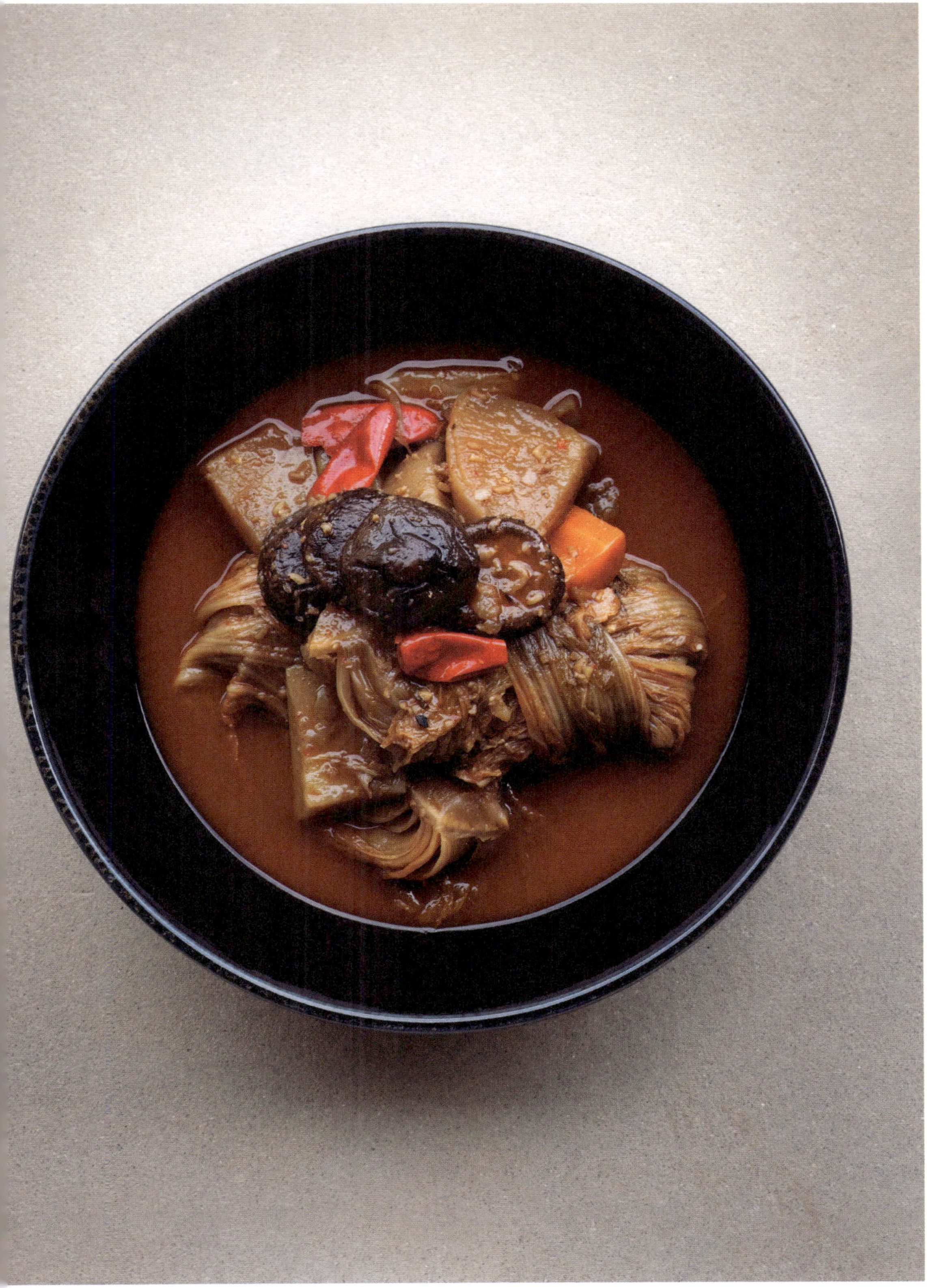

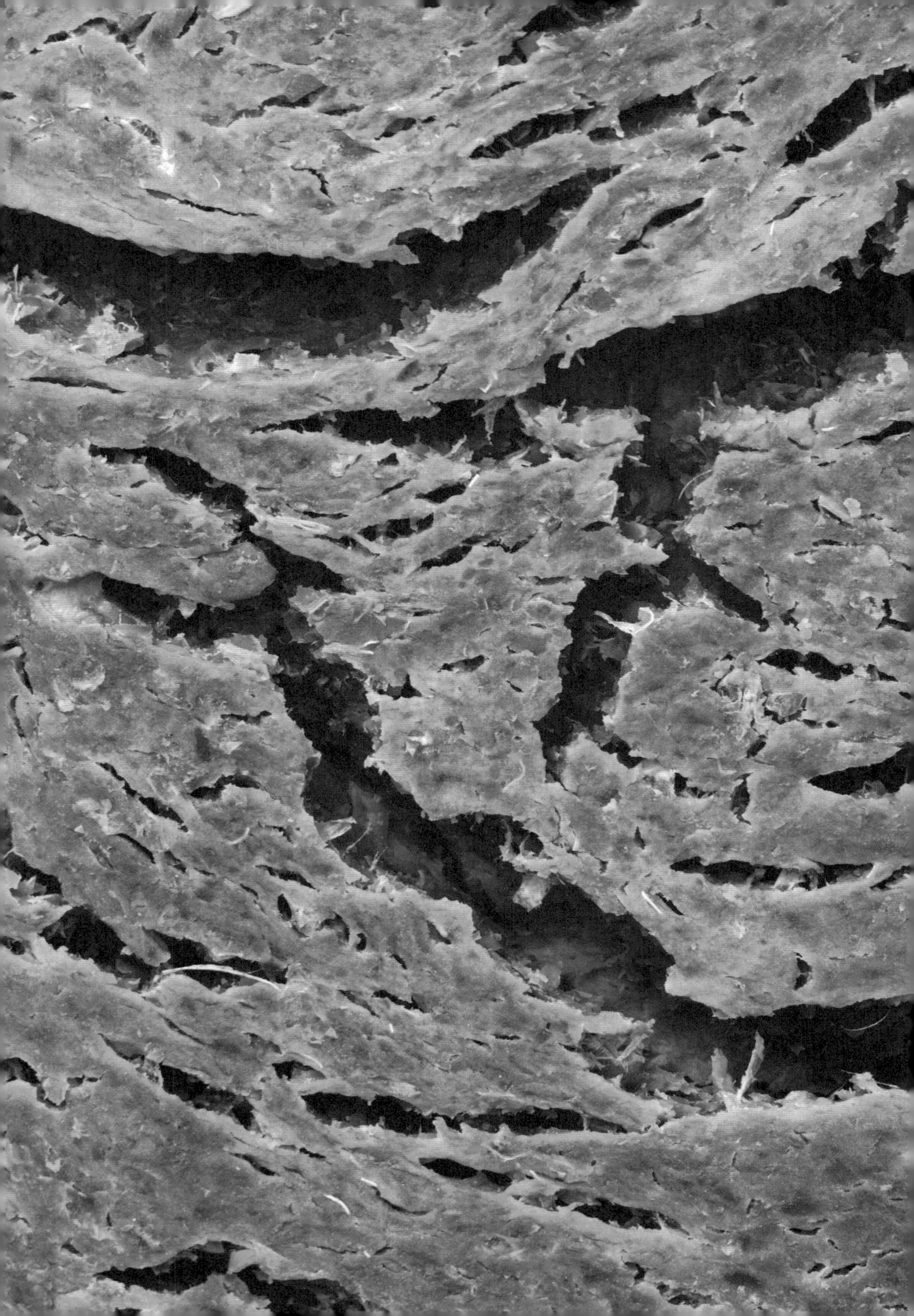

MEJU AND GANJANG

Soy sauce, or ganjang, is among the most important flavorings in Korea and is part of the collective culinary heritage of East Asia. It has a unique flavor and contains within itself the great mystery of fermentation—time causes this flavoring to mature when soybeans are combined with salt and water and nature is allowed to take its course. The quality of ganjang is judged by its color, consistency, smell, flavor, and resonance on the tongue. Age is also an important factor that provides information about the ganjang's level of maturity, and age controls the development of flavor.

Behind this dark, fragrant liquid stand more than 2,000 years of tradition, which also represent the cultural history of food. Conversations about the flavor of soy sauce represent a high art and have given rise to a particular lingo. That's because ganjang does not neatly fit into the standard taste categories of salty, sweet, bitter, and sour—it has a very distinctive flavor that's created when the protein in the soybeans turns into glutamic acid during fermentation. Microorganisms bring this change about with their enzymes; the longer the fermentation process lasts, the more acids emerge and therefore the more intense the flavor of the soy sauce becomes.

Jeongkwan Snim often says that soy sauce must have *gamchilmat*. (*Mat* means "flavor" and *gamchil* means "enveloping" or "surrounding.") Snim tried to explain the meaning of this word to me. The tongue is said to have receptors for glutamic acids. When a food has gamchilmat, she pointed out, it pleasantly envelops the entire tongue—it has "a flavor that caresses the mouth." When one tastes this flavor, it satisfies the mouth. It's a harmonious, unobtrusive taste, but nonetheless it has depth. While gamchilmat is translated into English as "savory taste" or "umami," other languages don't necessarily have a translation for gamchilmat. (There's no German word to express this type of flavor, for example.) Meat also has a lot of gamchilmat because it's also rich in glutamic acids. People say that's why meat is such a popular food.

Snim makes *meju* in late autumn. Meju is later used to make soy sauce. (The kimchi made for the winter season must already be ready by this time.) Although few ingredients are needed to make soy sauce, the process has multiple steps and requires a lot of time, patience, good instincts, and an understanding of how nature works.

Making soy sauce also requires good soybeans. Since they're dried, they must first be soaked in water to make them swell up. Then they're boiled in water in a large pot until they're tender. Next, the beans are ground in a mortar and pestle, crushed, or milled—not too finely, but also not too coarsely.

A firm square called meju is molded from this mass of ground beans. This is wrapped in rope made from rice straw and then either hung up in a room or laid on rice straw on a warm floor and covered with more straw. The straw is very important, says Snim, because it acts as a vehicle for microorganisms and facilitates fermentation. The temperature and humidity must be well regulated so that the right microorganisms will settle in and form healthy mold. Snim lets the meju blocks ferment for several months, until spring comes.

In spring, Snim brings out the meju, rinses them, and dries them in the sun. Then the meju blocks are placed in an onggi and covered with salt water. The correct salt content is important for the flavor! Dried red gochu and Korean dates are also typically added, and sometimes a piece of charcoal is added to act as a purifier. The meju is left to soak and continue fermenting for 30 or 40 days. During this time, the onggi must be placed in a sunny area, because the process requires warmth.

Next, the liquid portion is separated from the solids. Ganjang is made from the liquid; the solid parts are used to make doenjang. Although it's made from the same soybeans and emerges from the same process, doenjang tastes completely different from soy sauce. However, doenjang also plays an important role as a flavoring and can be used in a variety of ways.

While ganjang must be left alone and not moved during storage, doenjang must be stirred and allowed to "breathe" every two or three years. Snim says that her soy sauce and doenjang have particular aromas because the temple is surrounded by ancient yew trees and their flowers and fragrance lend an incomparable character to what she makes.

The soy sauce is made by heating the filtered liquid to 176°F. The heating process slows the fermentation activity but enhances the flavor and intensifies the color. A salt content between 18 and 20 percent is considered ideal. When soy sauce is created in this traditional way, each batch takes on a unique character. That's due to the wide variety of microorganisms that bring forth the different flavor variations. In Korea, people have known since ancient times that a dish cannot be a

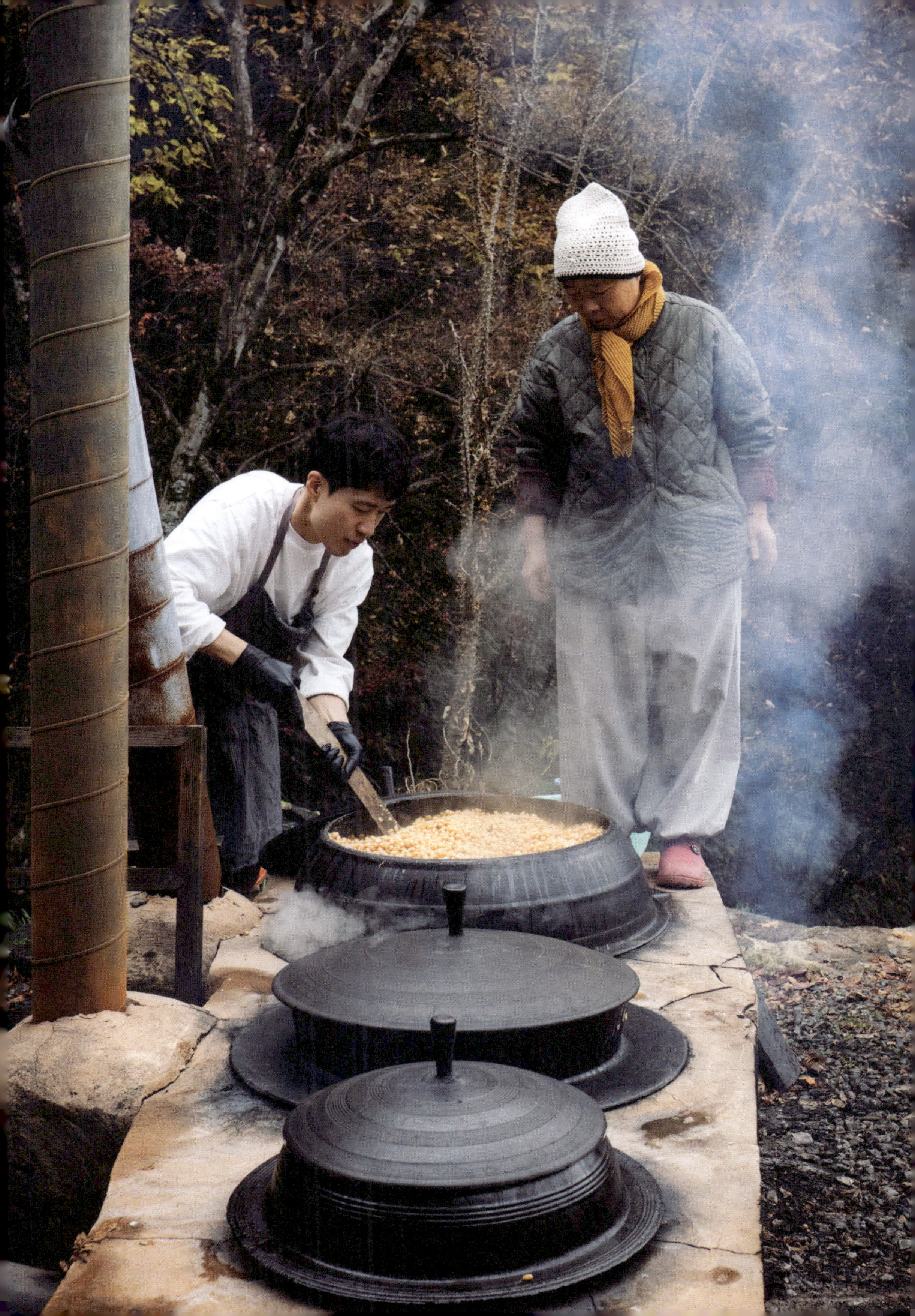

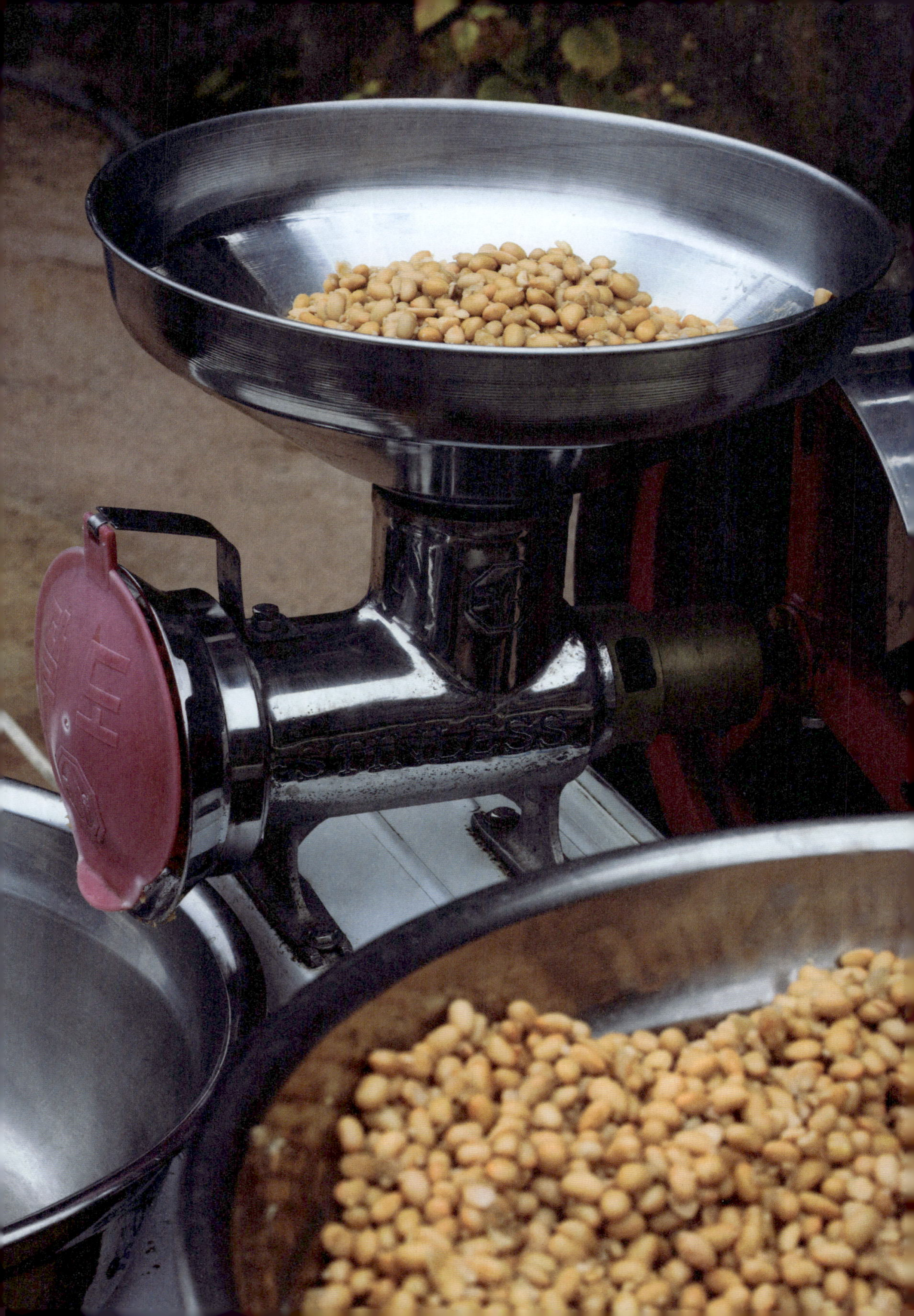

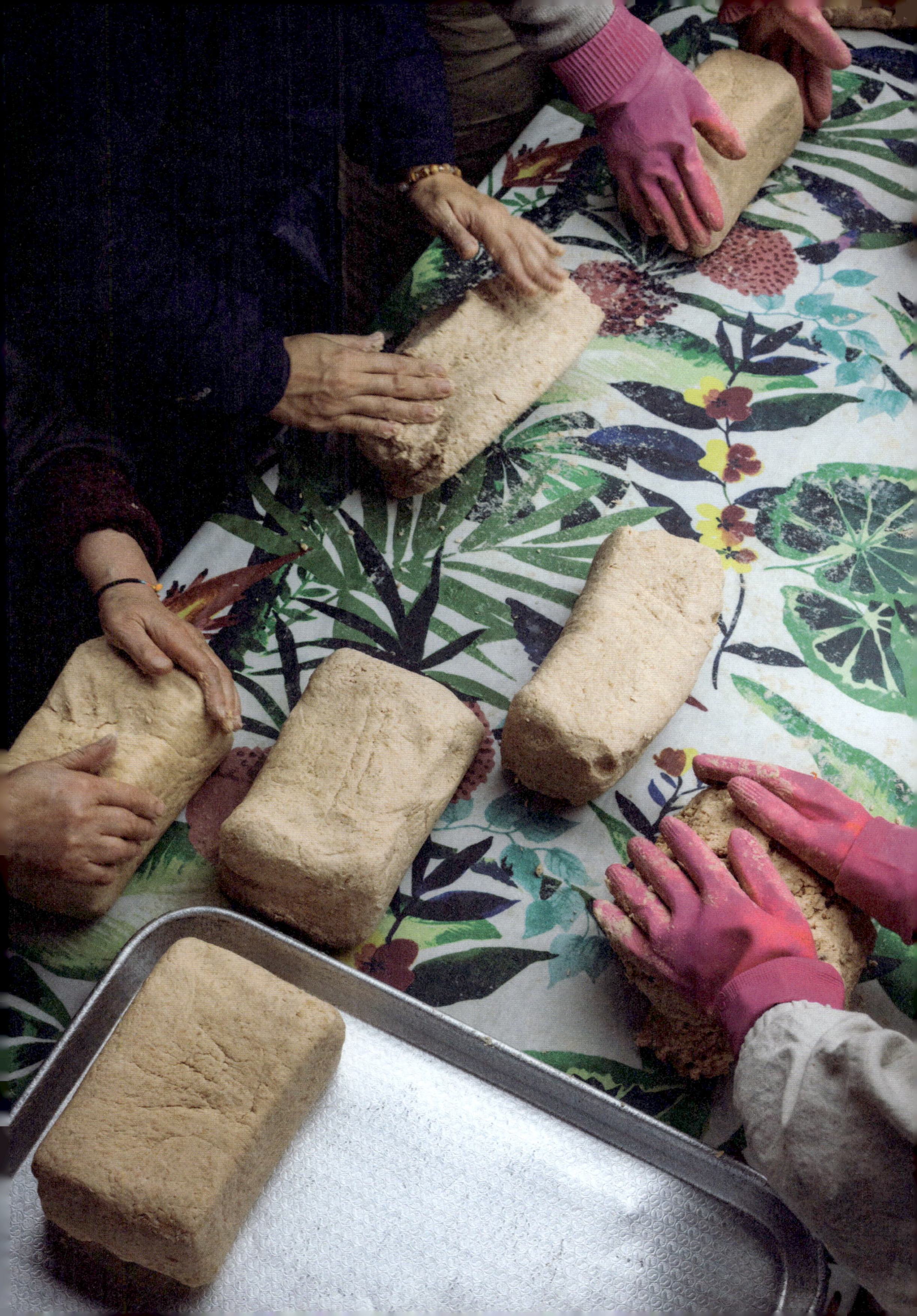

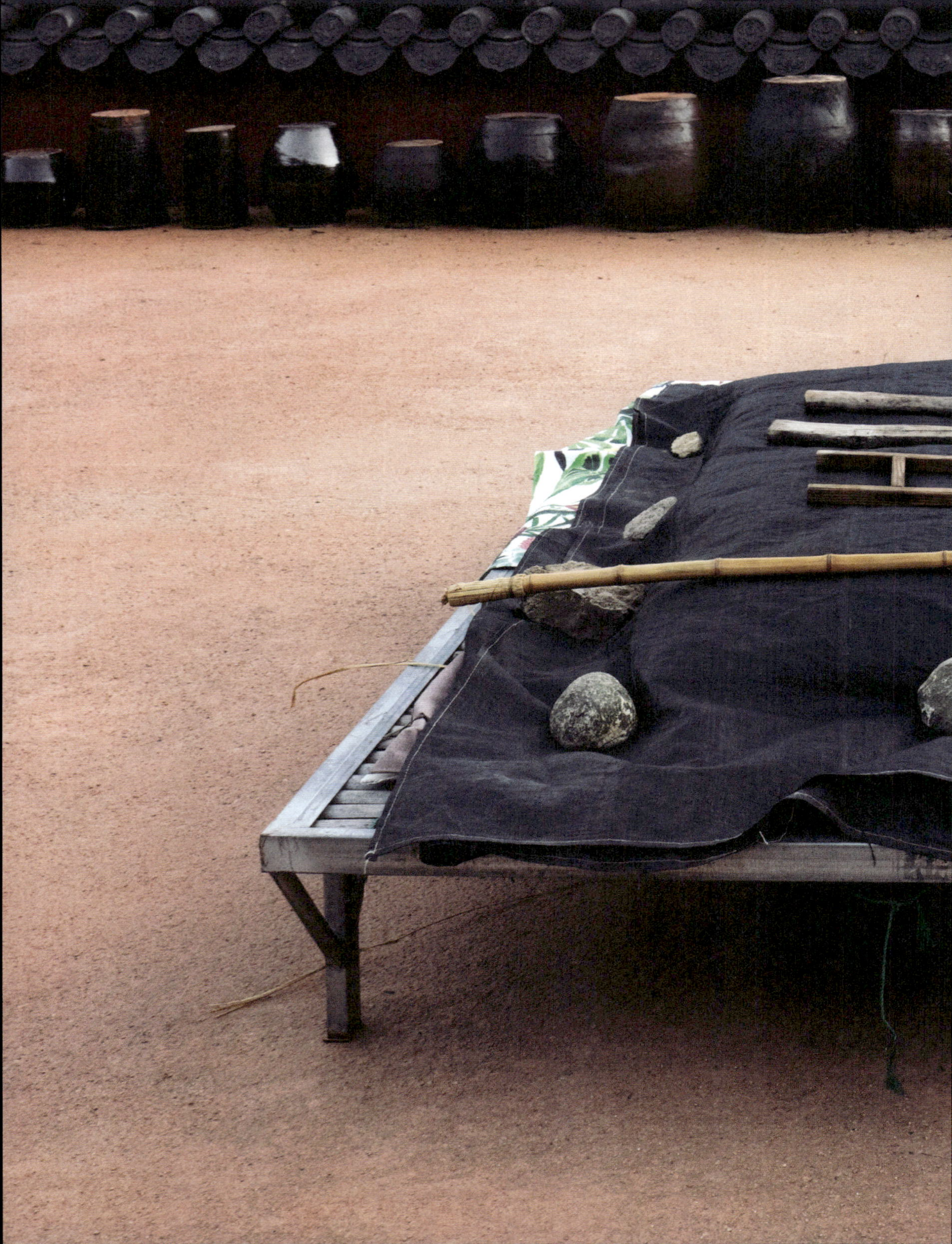

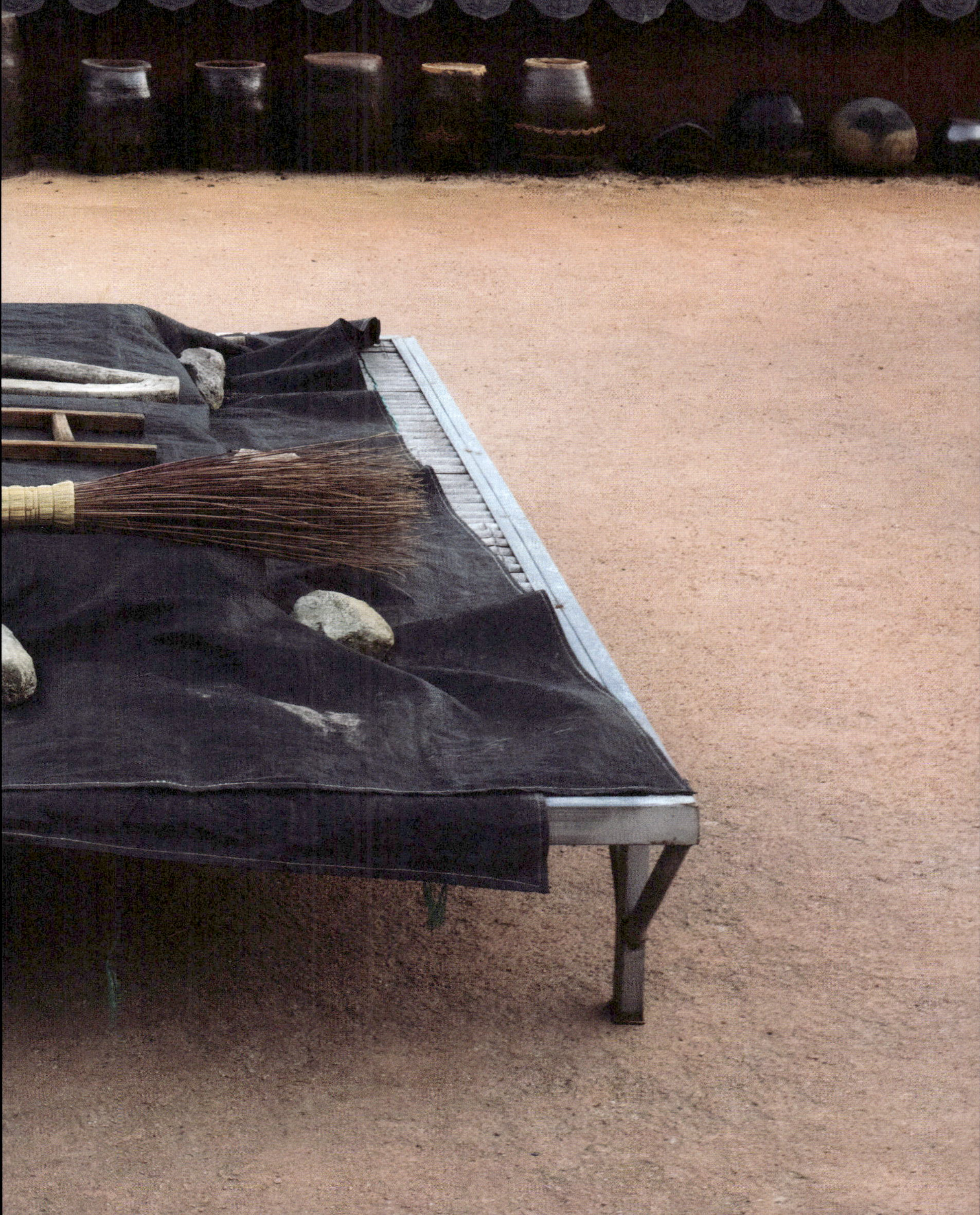

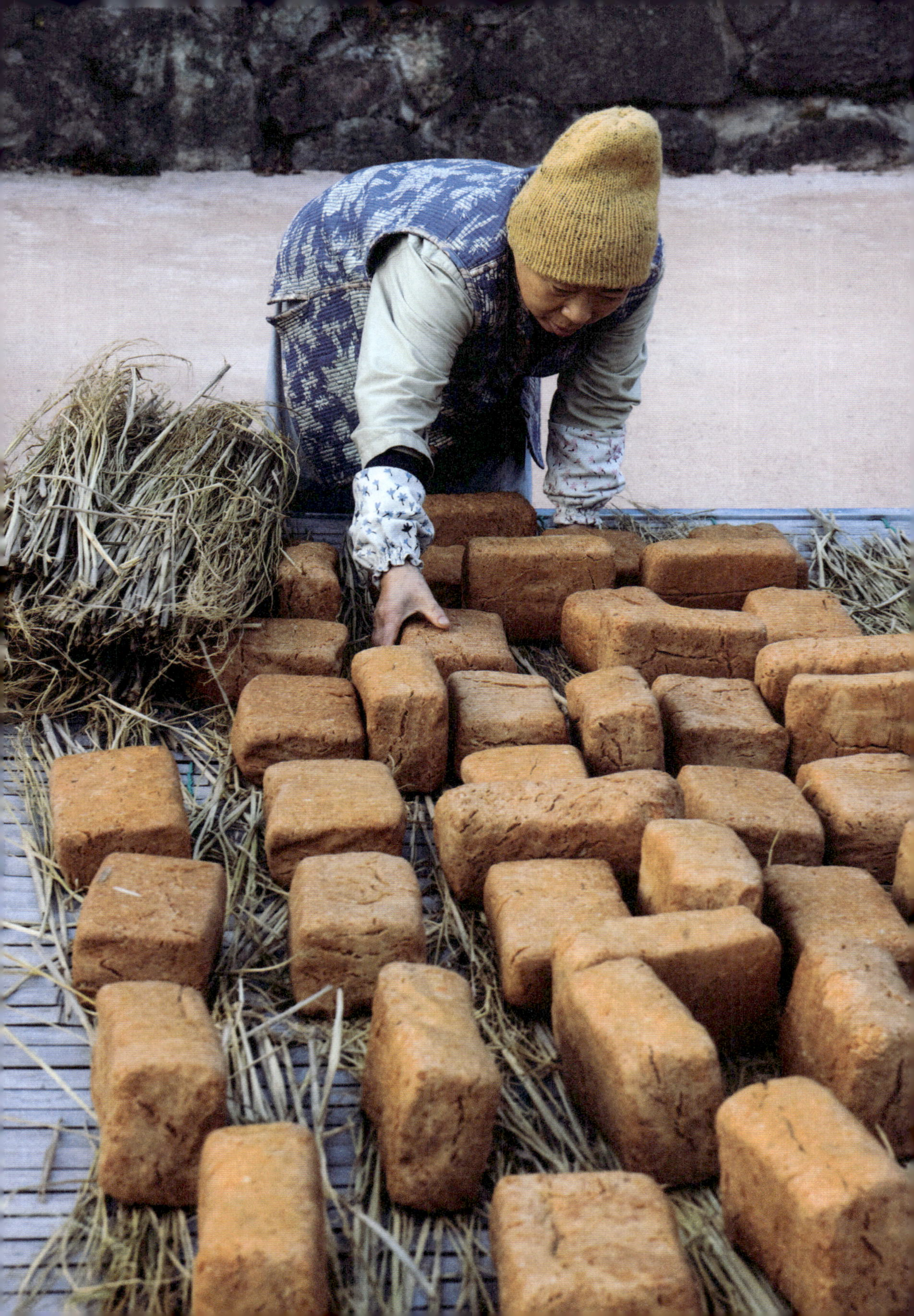

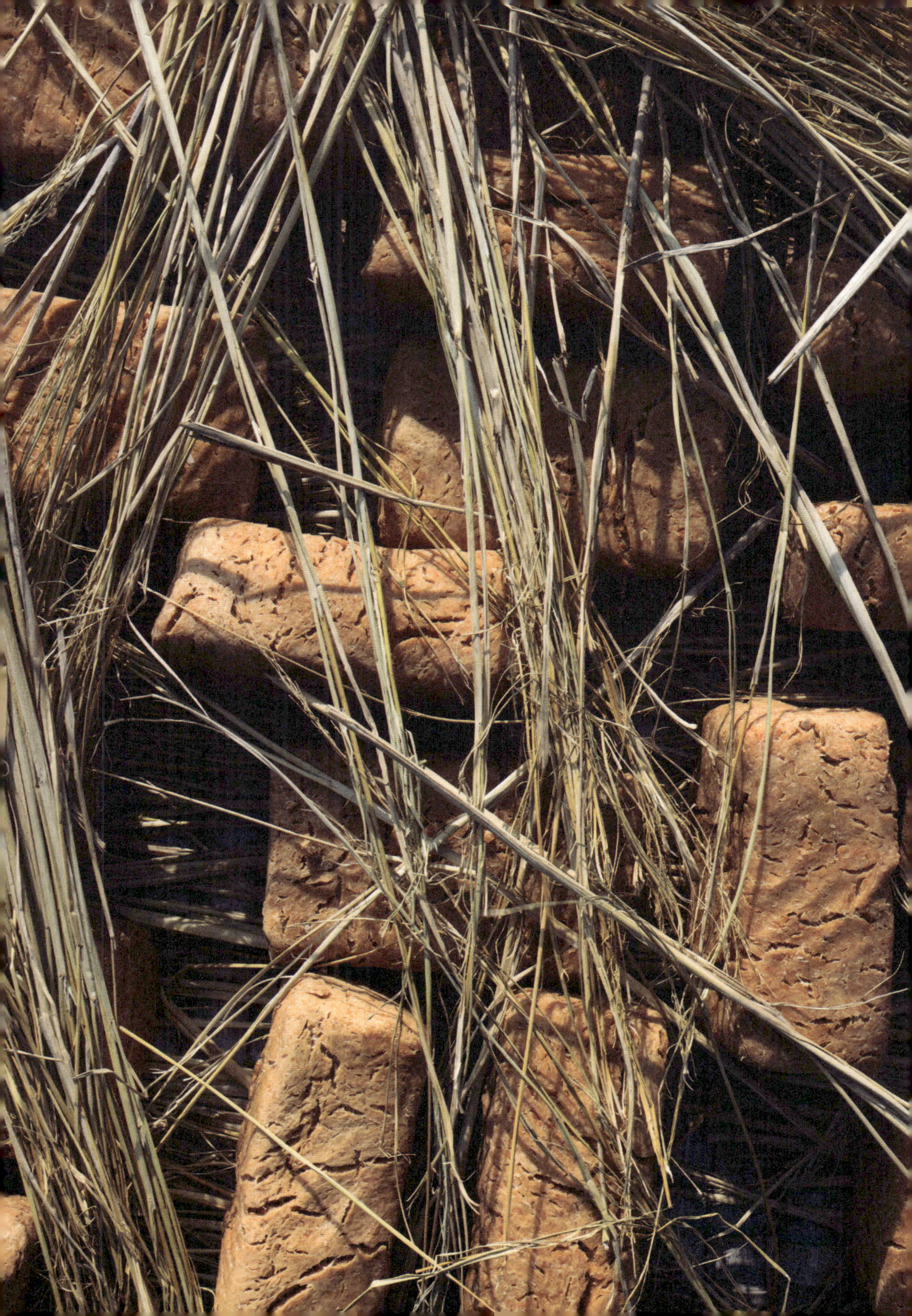

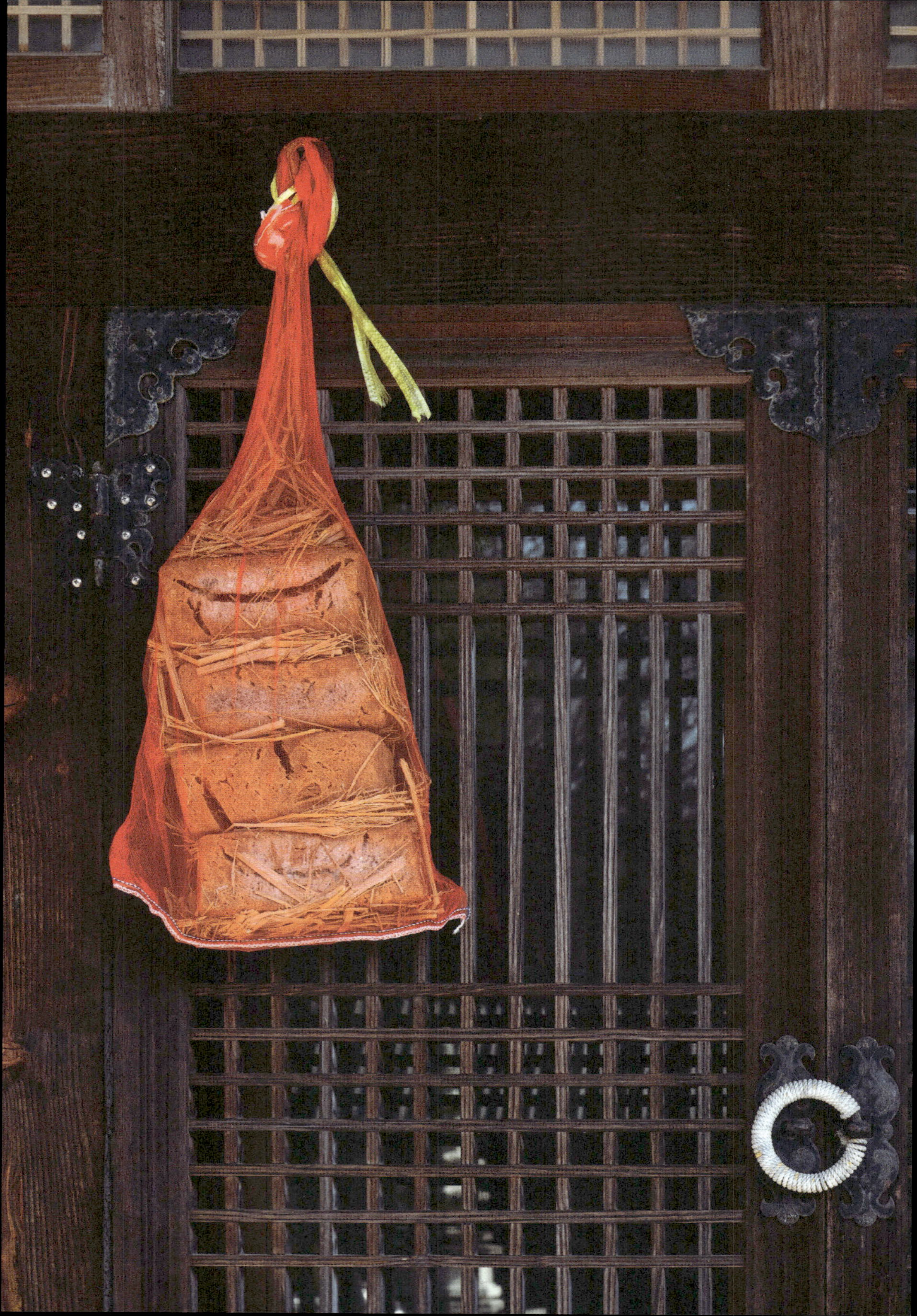

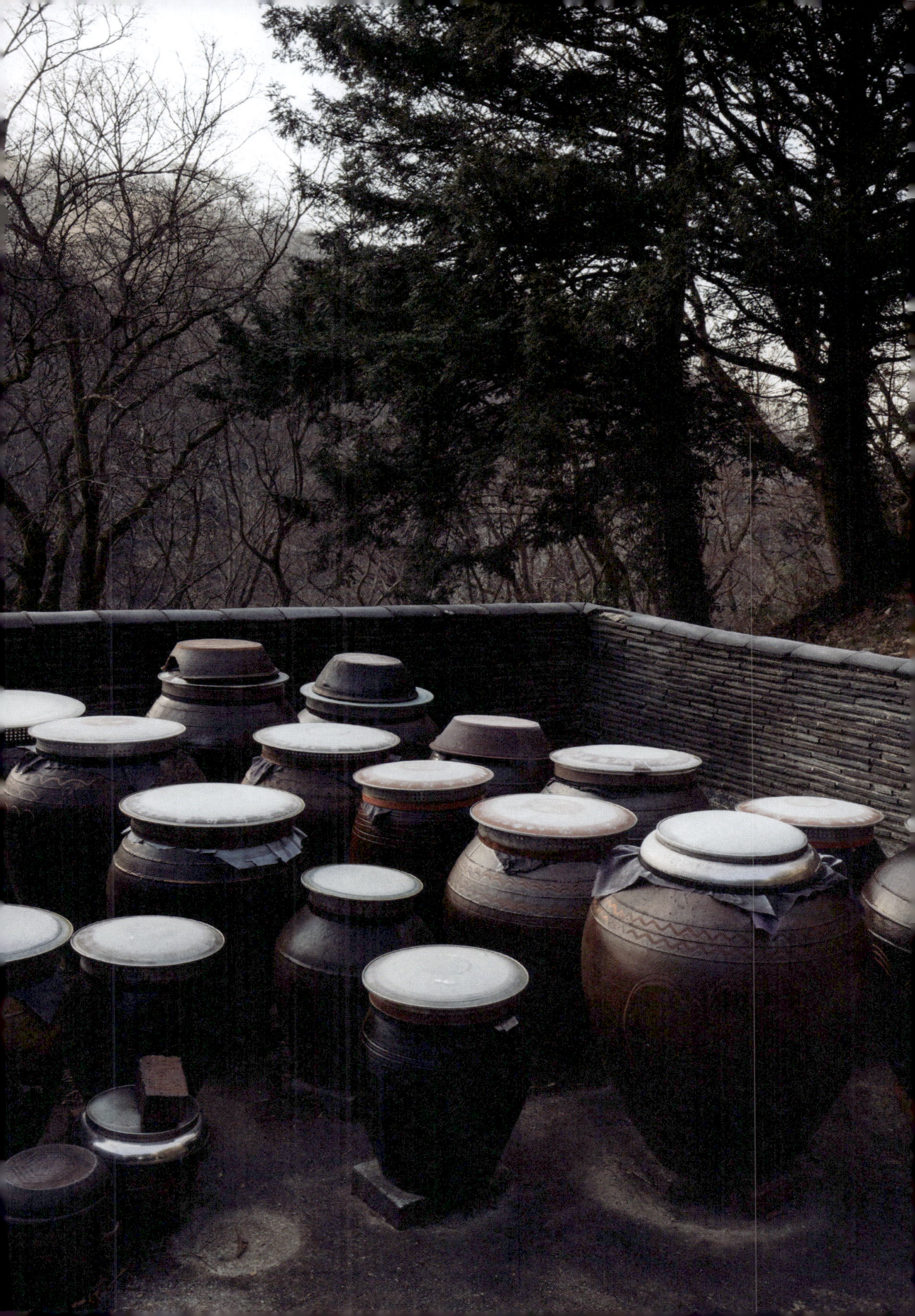

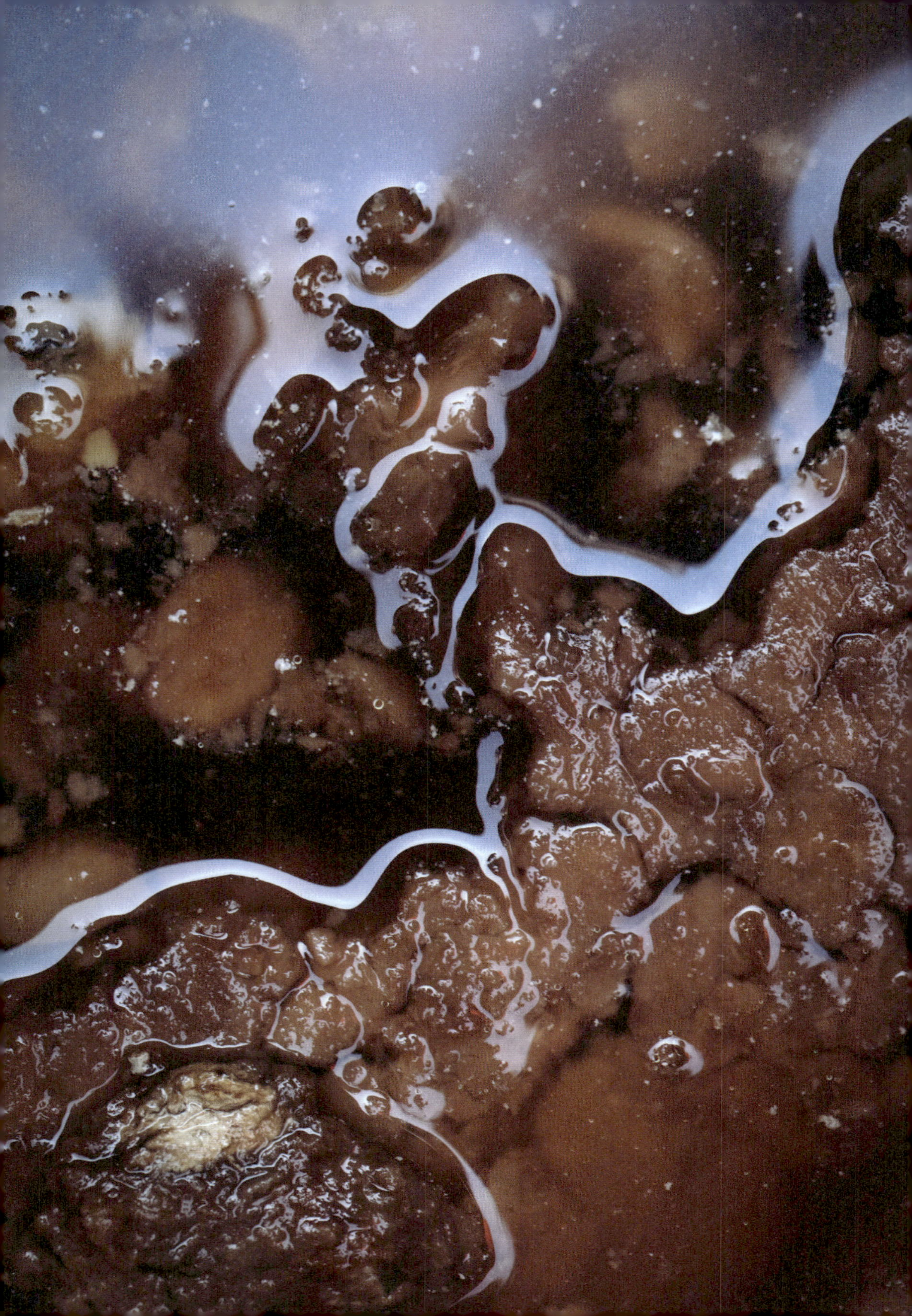

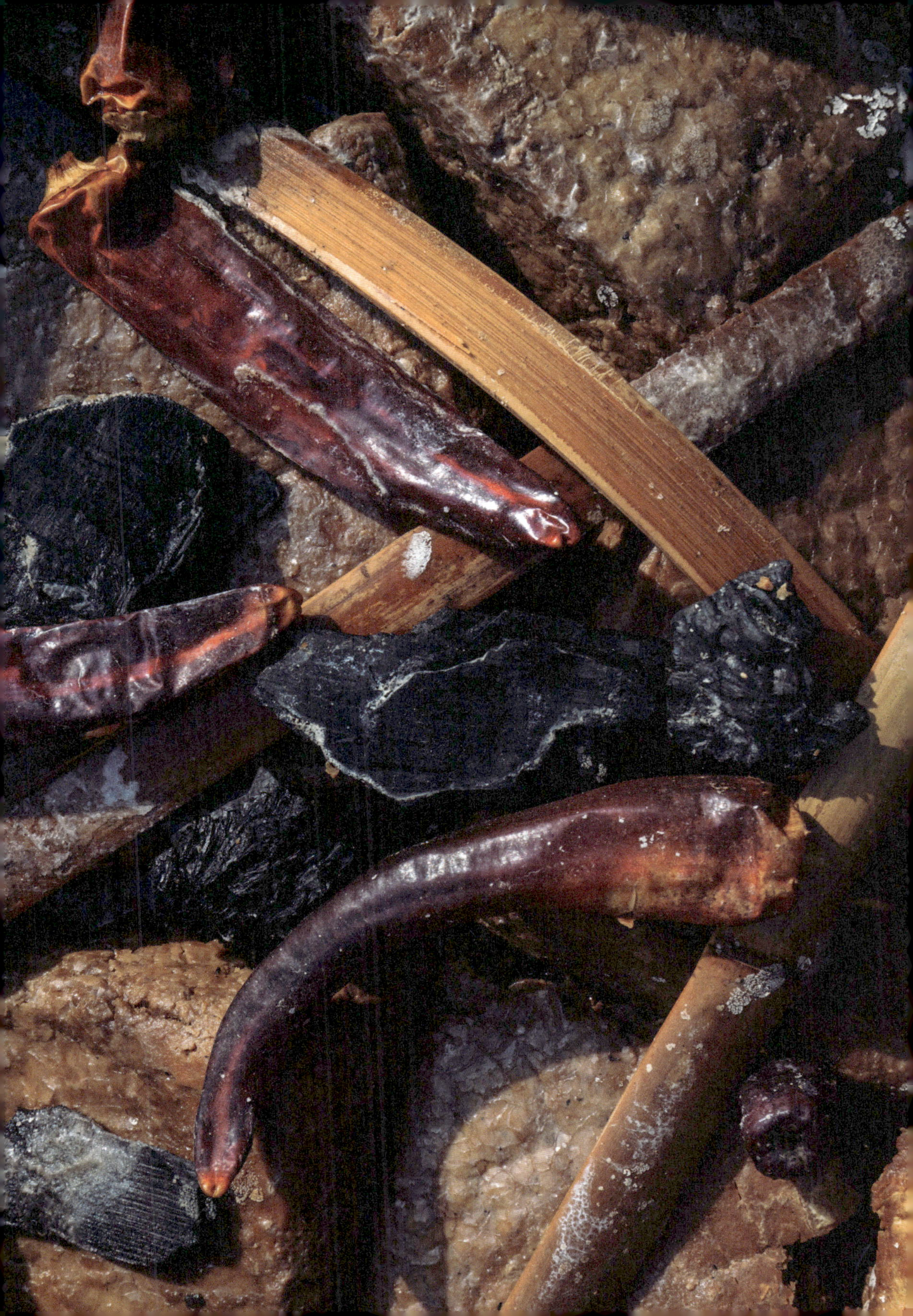

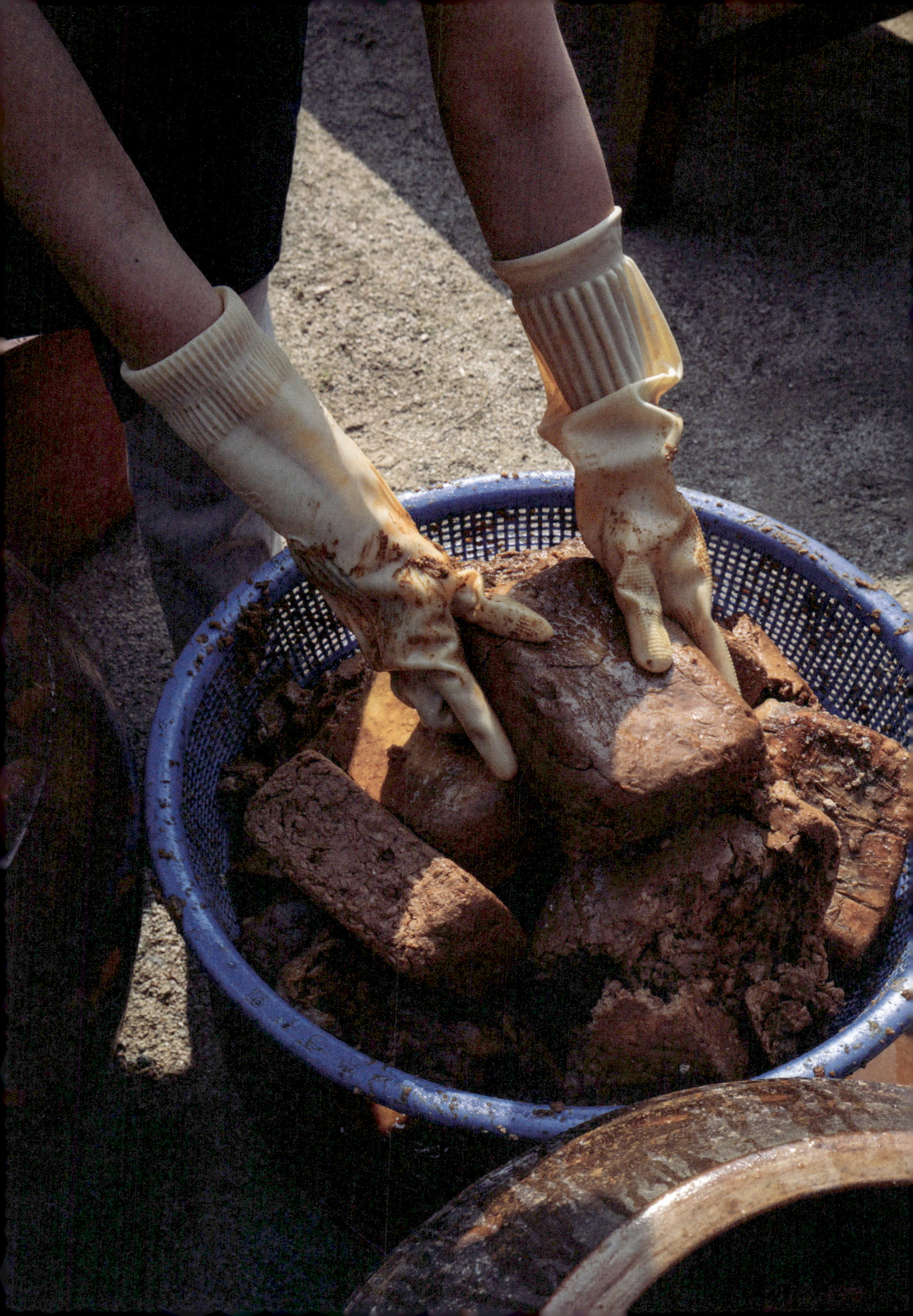

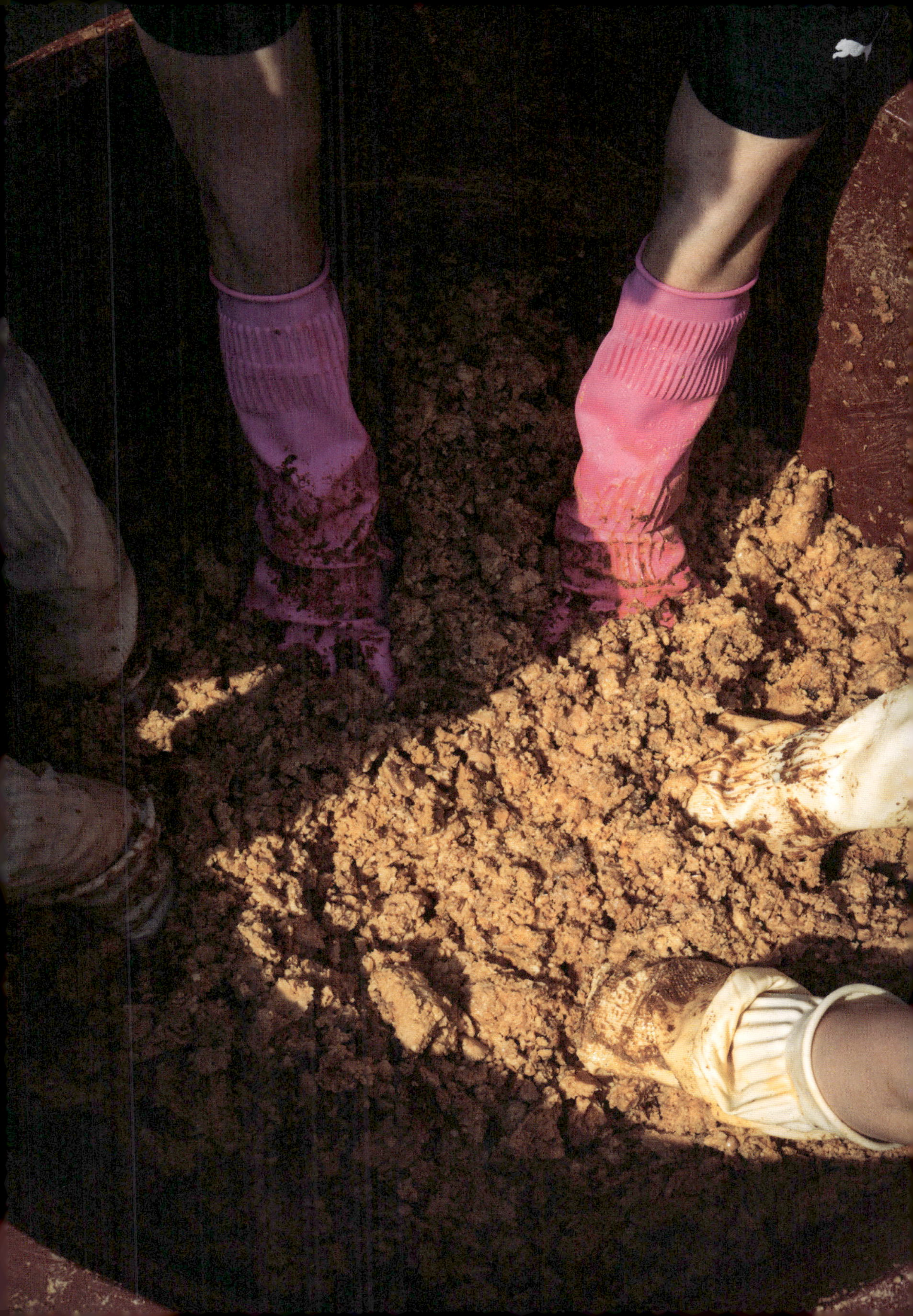

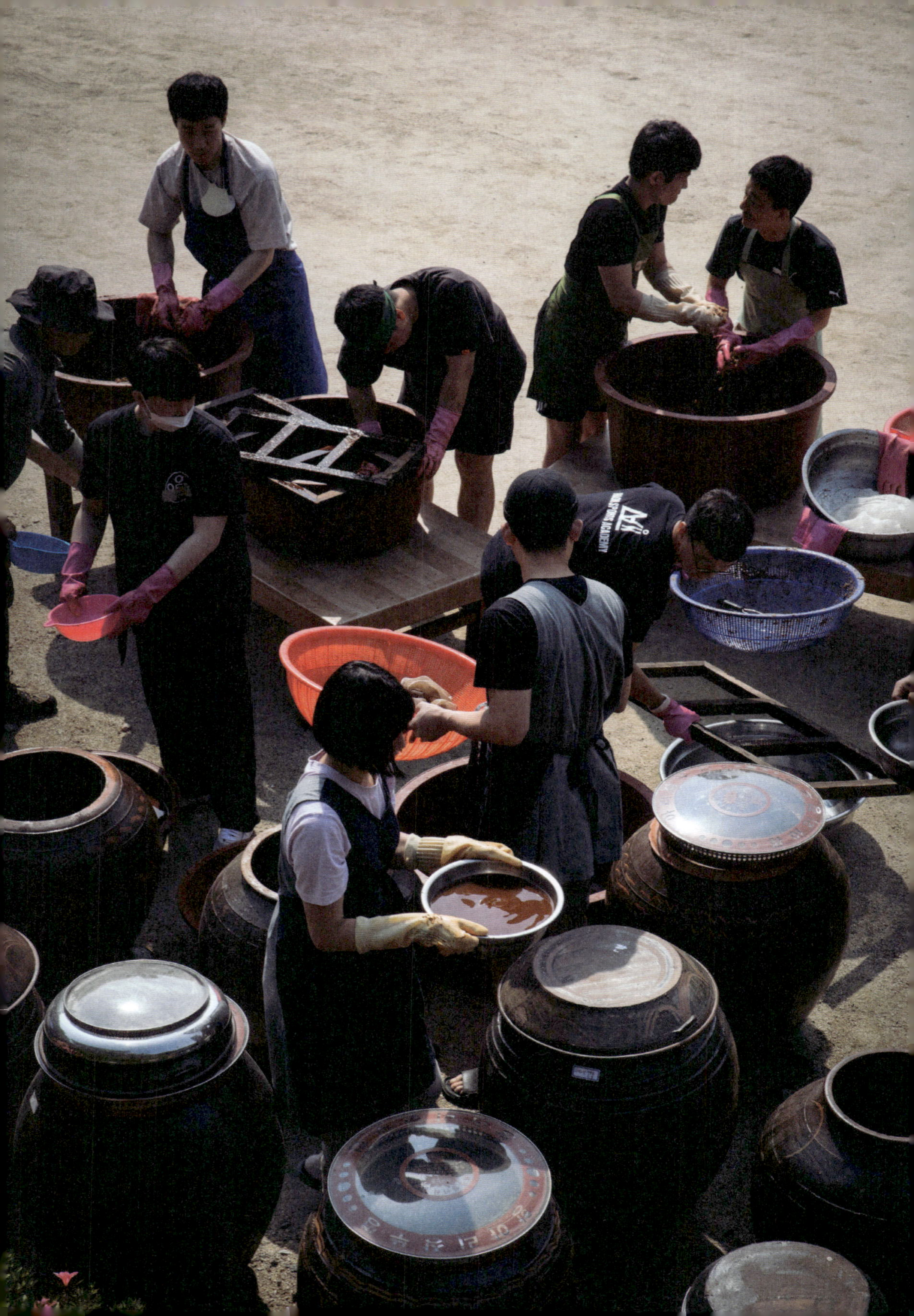

failure if the soy sauce is good! Its quality guarantees a rich flavor for whatever is served.

Preparing soy sauce used to be considered a kind of sacred act and was accompanied by rituals, and different vintages of soy sauce were guarded like precious treasures. In modern Korea, soy sauce is made in two ways, one being the traditional method described above. Jeongkwan Snim follows this tradition. The second way is a modernized version used to produce large quantities: wheat or other grains are mixed into the soybeans, and the meju is produced from that. This accelerates the fermentation process and somewhat reduces the time needed because select strains of microorganisms are added to the meju that are more powerful and better able to break down and convert protein and starches more quickly. Also, in modern production, the production of soy sauce is separate from the production of doenjang. That way, any flavor inconsistencies can be avoided and uniformity and a consistent quality can be achieved. However, the flavor is rather simple—it's flat and it lacks depth.

In the past, every family made their own soy sauce using traditional methods. This was called *jipganjang*, or "house soy sauce." The entire family was proud of their jipganjang; a lot of individual knowledge and experience was passed on to subsequent generations thanks to this tradition. Making jipganjang is less common today, but Snim always uses her own jipganjang.

While various soy sauces are available in Korea, three kinds of soy sauce are differentiated based on certain nuances: their stage of maturity, whether they taste more sweet or more salty, and the intensity of their color. Age is the crucial factor—it's best to use sauces of different ages for different dishes.

One sauce is called *haetganjang*, which basically means "thin soy sauce." This is a young sauce, at most one or two years old; it's lighter in color and has a saltier flavor. This thin sauce is appropriate as a soup ingredient, for example.

The second kind of soy sauce is called *zungganjang*, or "medium soy sauce." It's older than haetganjang, but it's still younger than five years. As its name indicates, it belongs to the medium category of maturity. It's used to flavor namul and to make stew.

The third kind is *jinganjang*, meaning "viscous" or "thick" soy sauce. It's aged for longer than five years, and it develops a creaminess as the salty flavor fades with continued fermentation. Its color is darker and its flavor more intense. It can be eaten with raw fish, but it's good in any application where a smoother yet more intense flavor is needed.

In Korea, soy sauce is more than a flavoring: it tells the story of food and life. Soybeans, salt, and water mix together and transform with time, and in the end, a sauce is created that's dark, flowing, and fragrant. The mystery of nature—which enables life!—seems to live within ganjang.

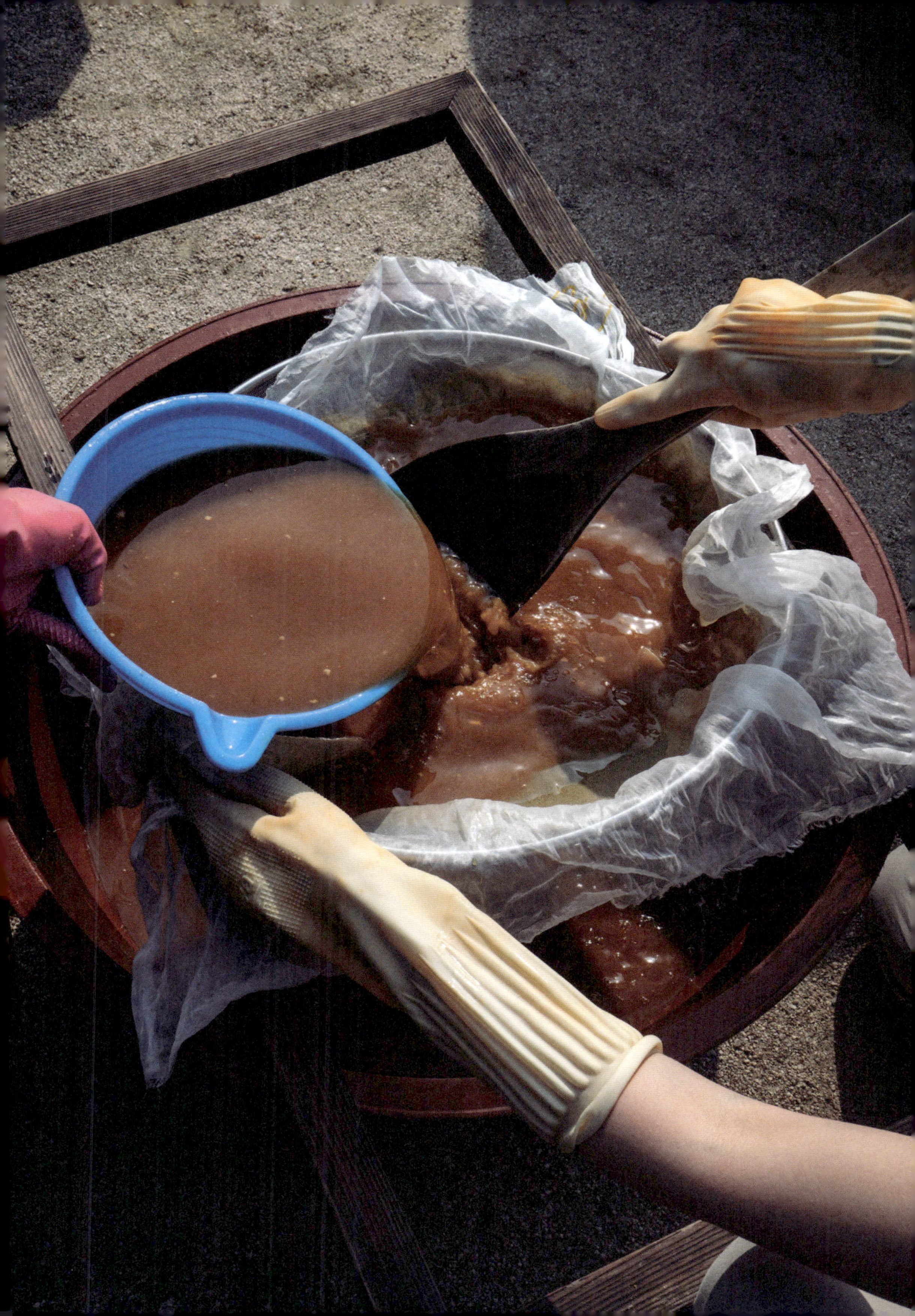

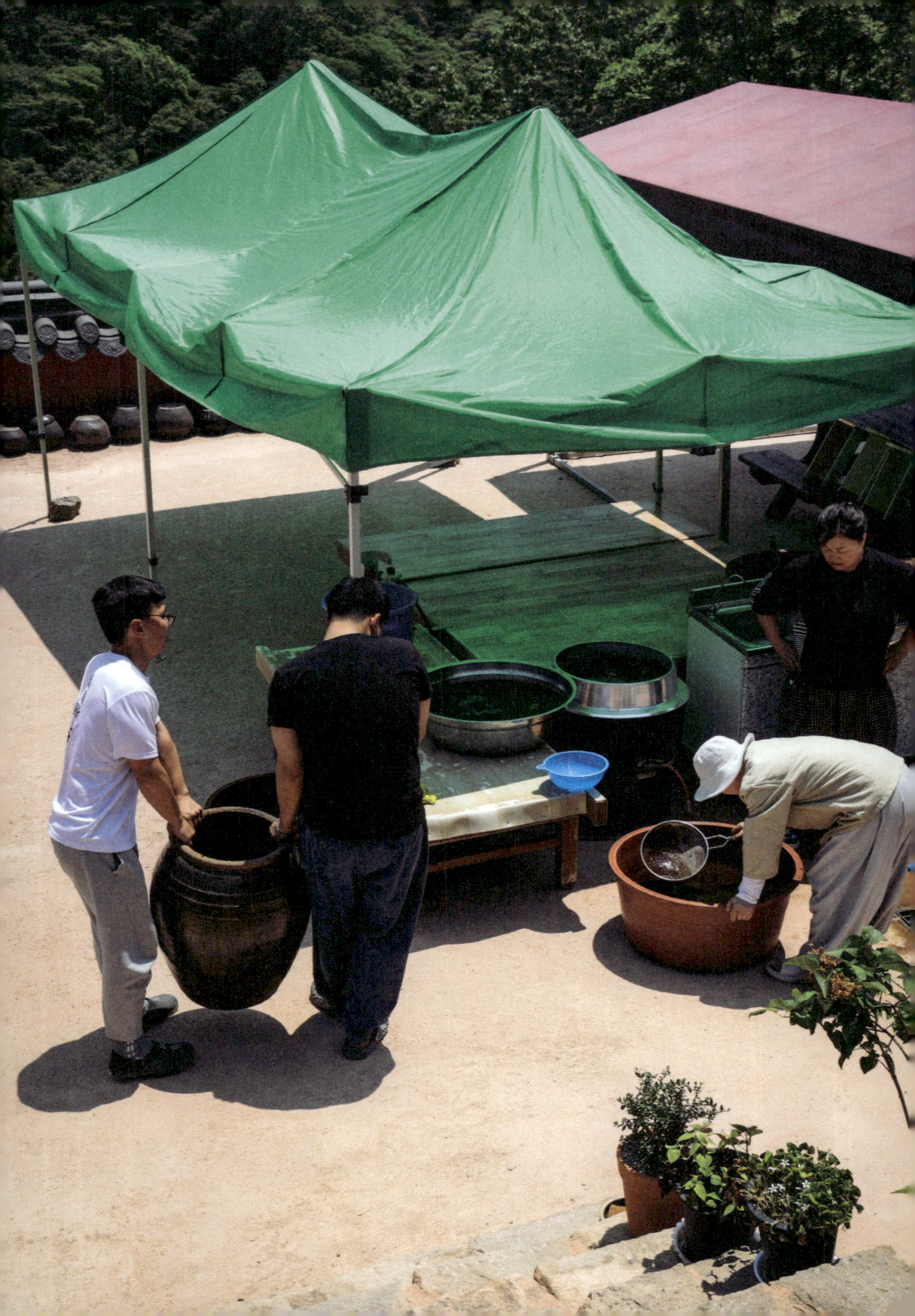

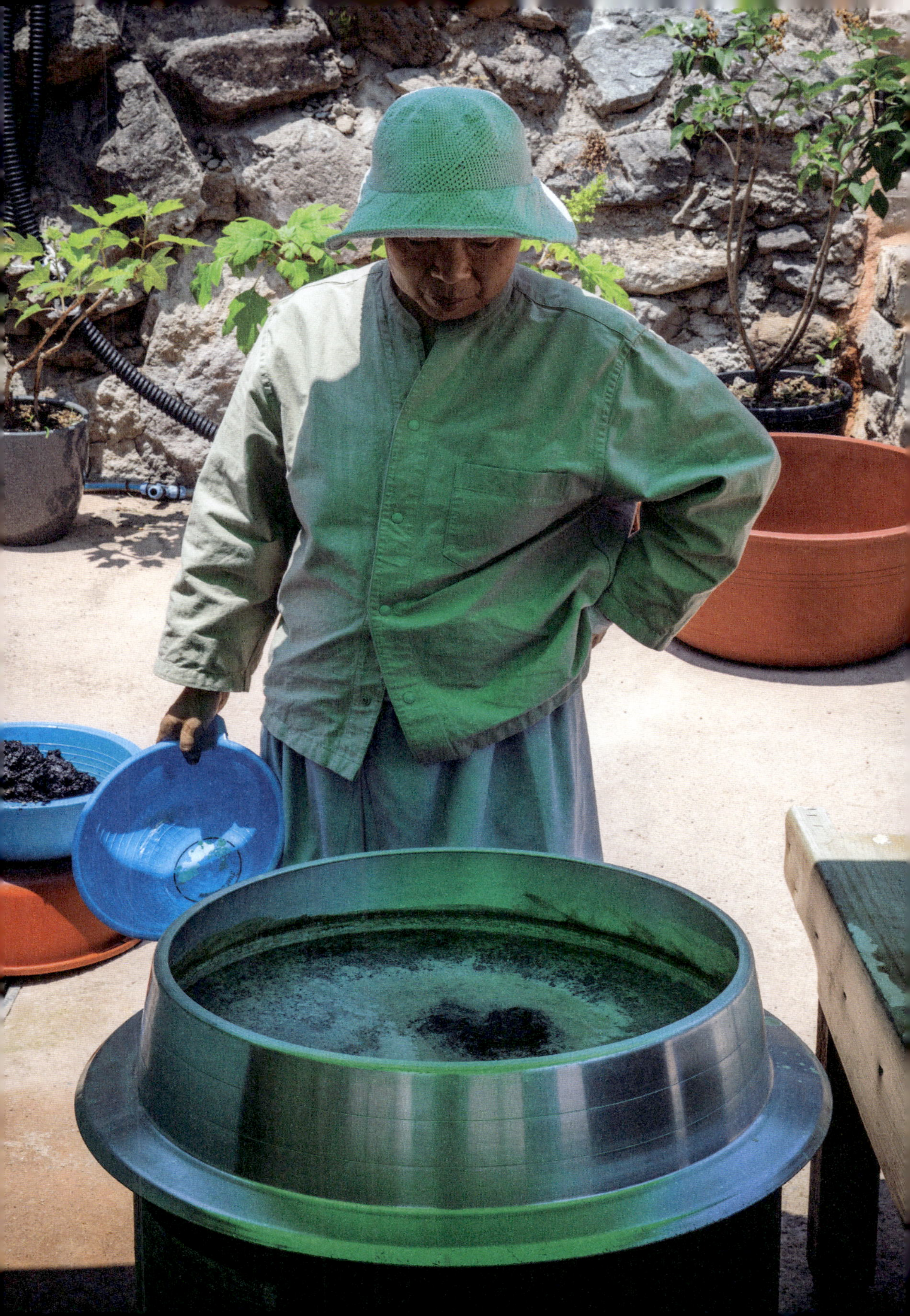

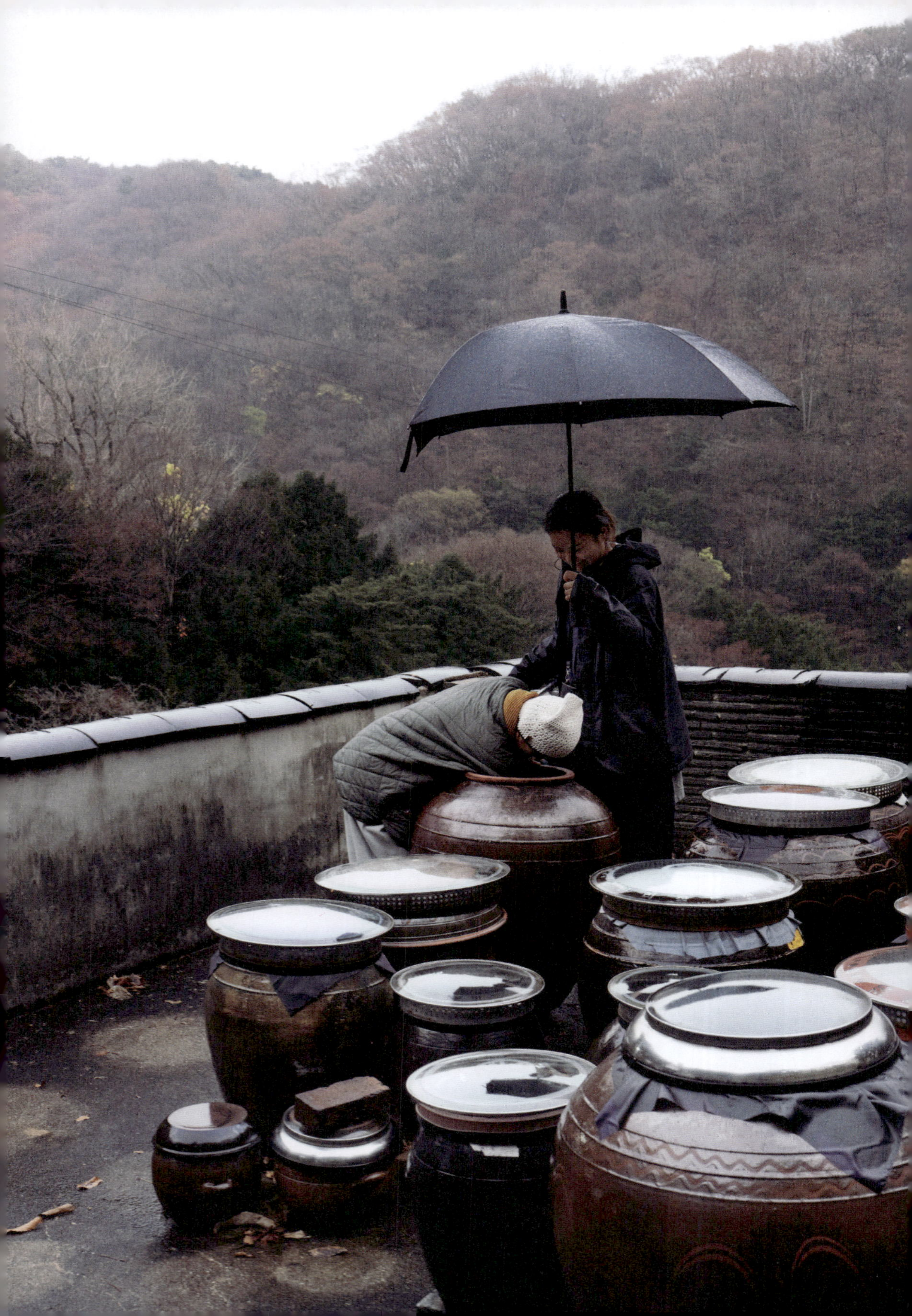

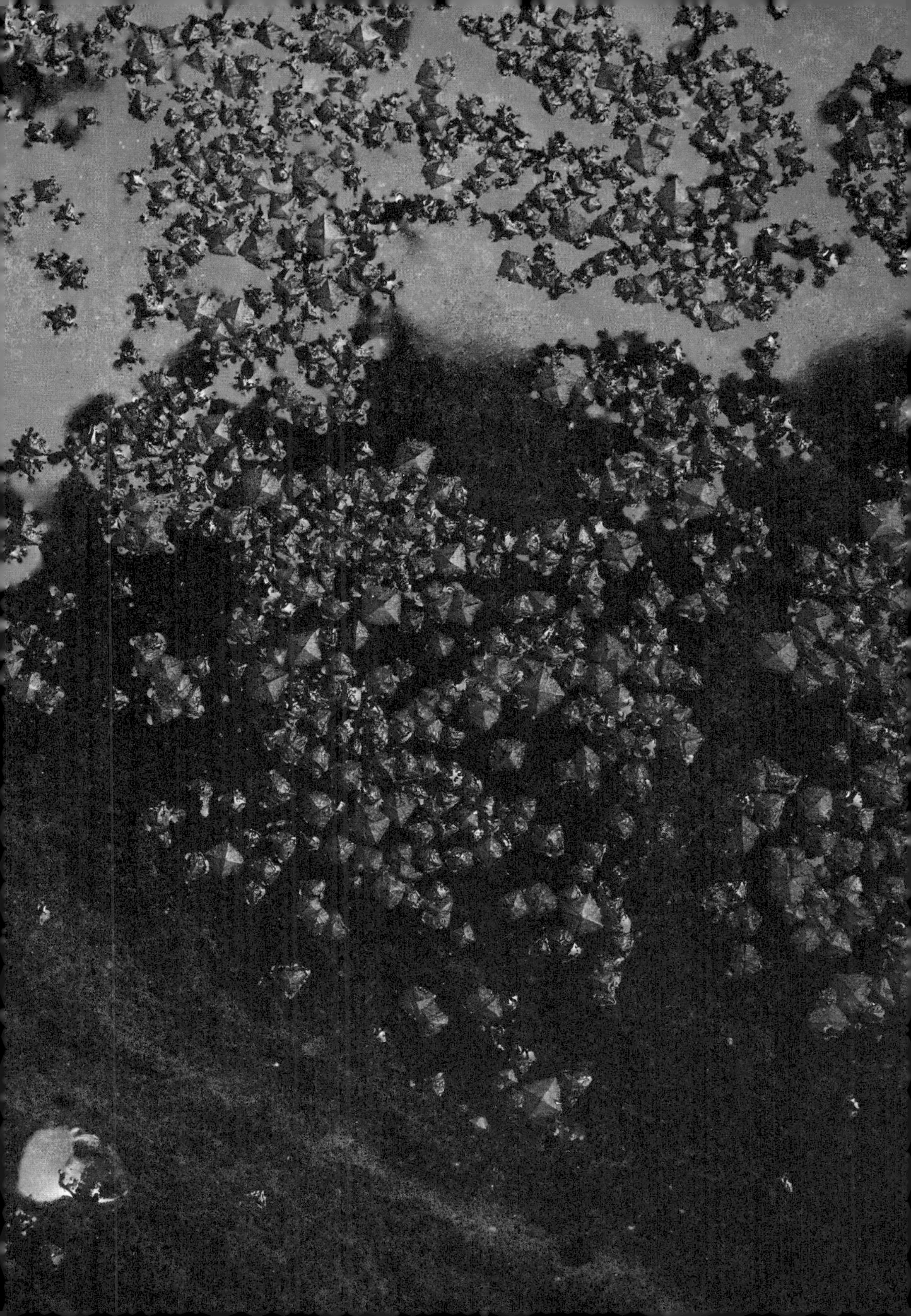

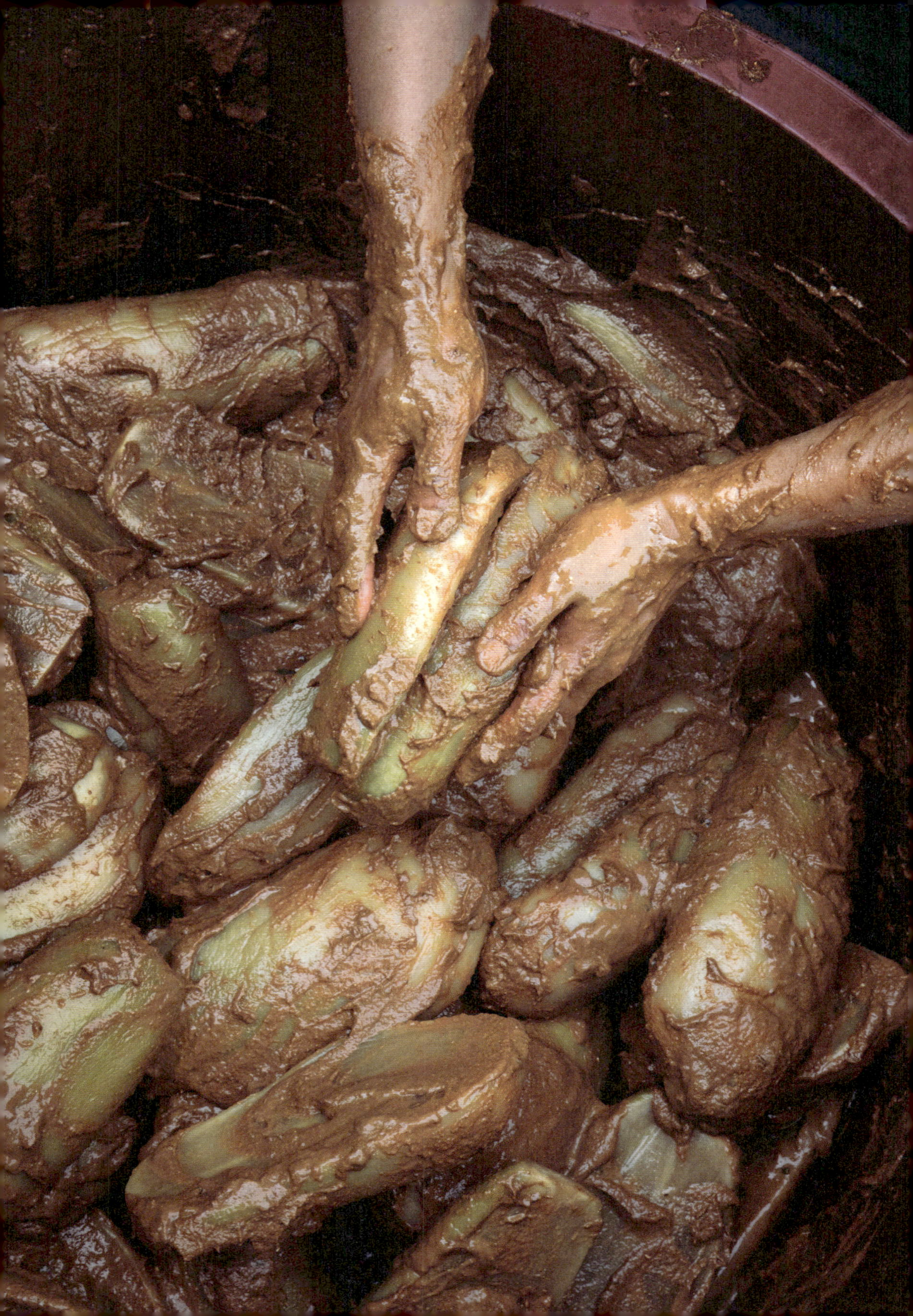

JANGAJJI

Korean cooking has various traditional ways of making food last. One well-established and popular method is called *jangajji*. It's considered a simple way to preserve an ingredient in a sauce—a combination of soy sauce, salt, sugar, doenjang, or gochujang. For some ingredients (like cucumbers), one must pour a boiling mixture of salt and soy sauce over them to prevent them from spoiling. Many vegetables, namul, and fruit are suitable candidates for preserving with jangajji. Cucumber is popular, and so are onions, sansho, maesil, and honeydew melon.

Snim prepares a special kind of jangajji from baechu (napa cabbage) and radish. She rinses the baechu, halves it, and places it in an onggi in layers, adding sufficient salt after each layer. Then she leaves the salt to do its work for one year. After a year, the napa cabbage looks yellow. Next, Snim removes it from the pot and adds it to a sauce that's one half doenjang and one half fermented grain remnants left over from the production of spirits.

Snim has developed her own method for getting the salty flavor out of the baechu: she places sweet omija berries sifted out during the production of cheong over the top of the cabbage and closes the container, then lets it ferment for three years. The *baechu-jangajji*—which is nonperishable yet fresh—can then be eaten. Snim prepares jangajji with radishes in a similar manner, but for that, instead of omija, she uses the remnants of *bokbunja* (blackberries) that are left over from when she makes cheong.

You can observe how the colors of the ingredients change depending on their stage of fermentation. This transition exhibits the work of nature, and nature in turn brings forth new flavors.

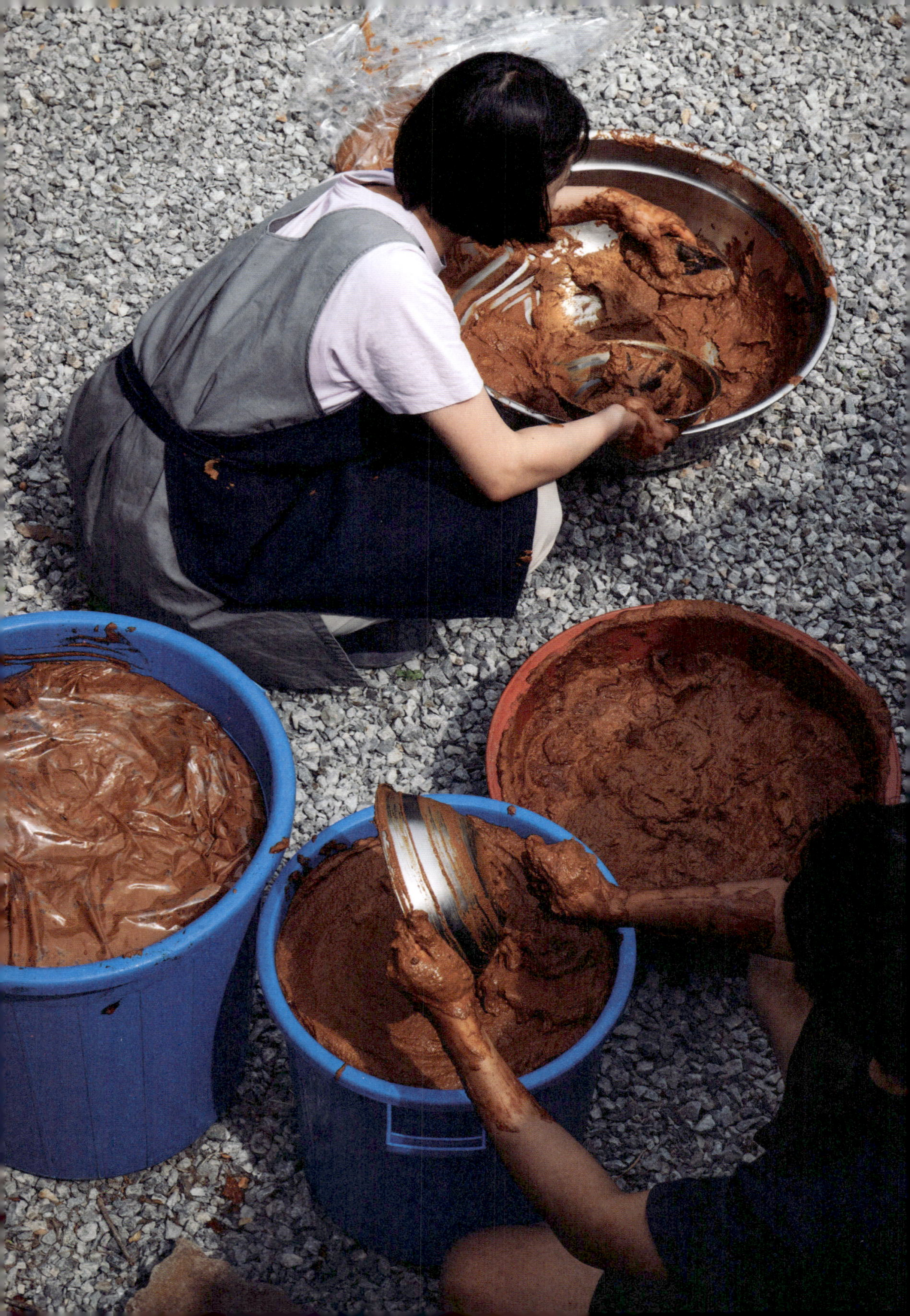

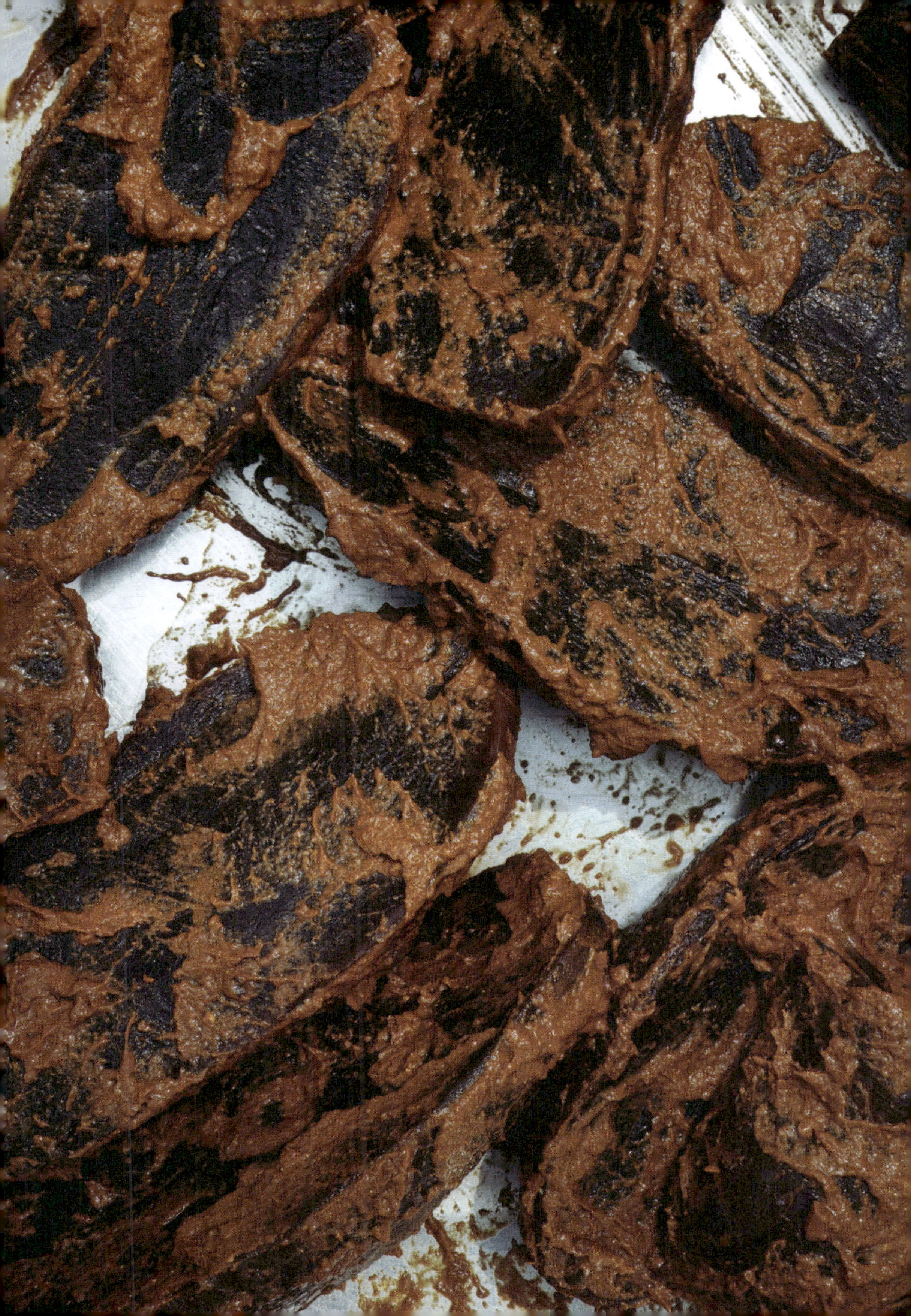

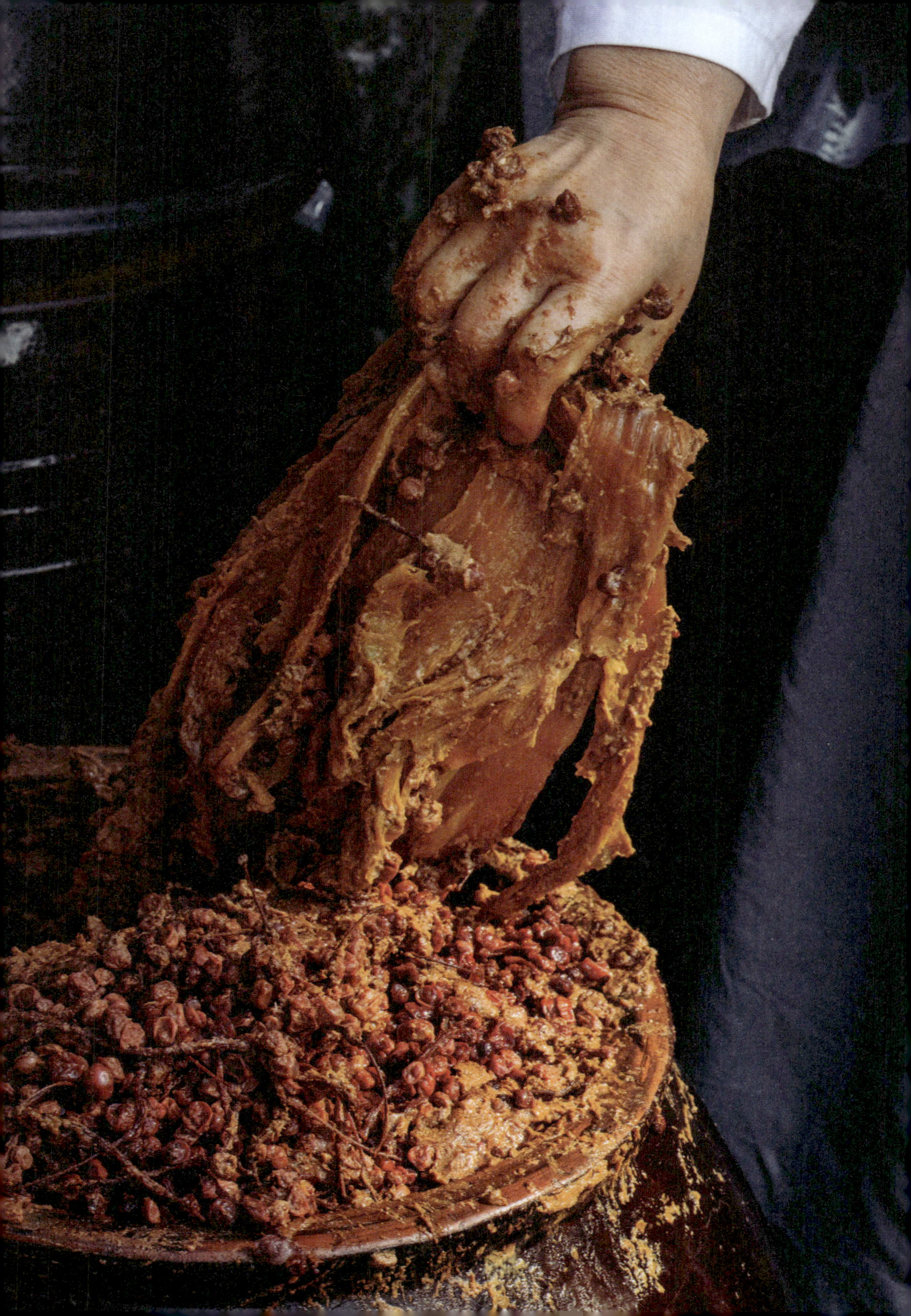

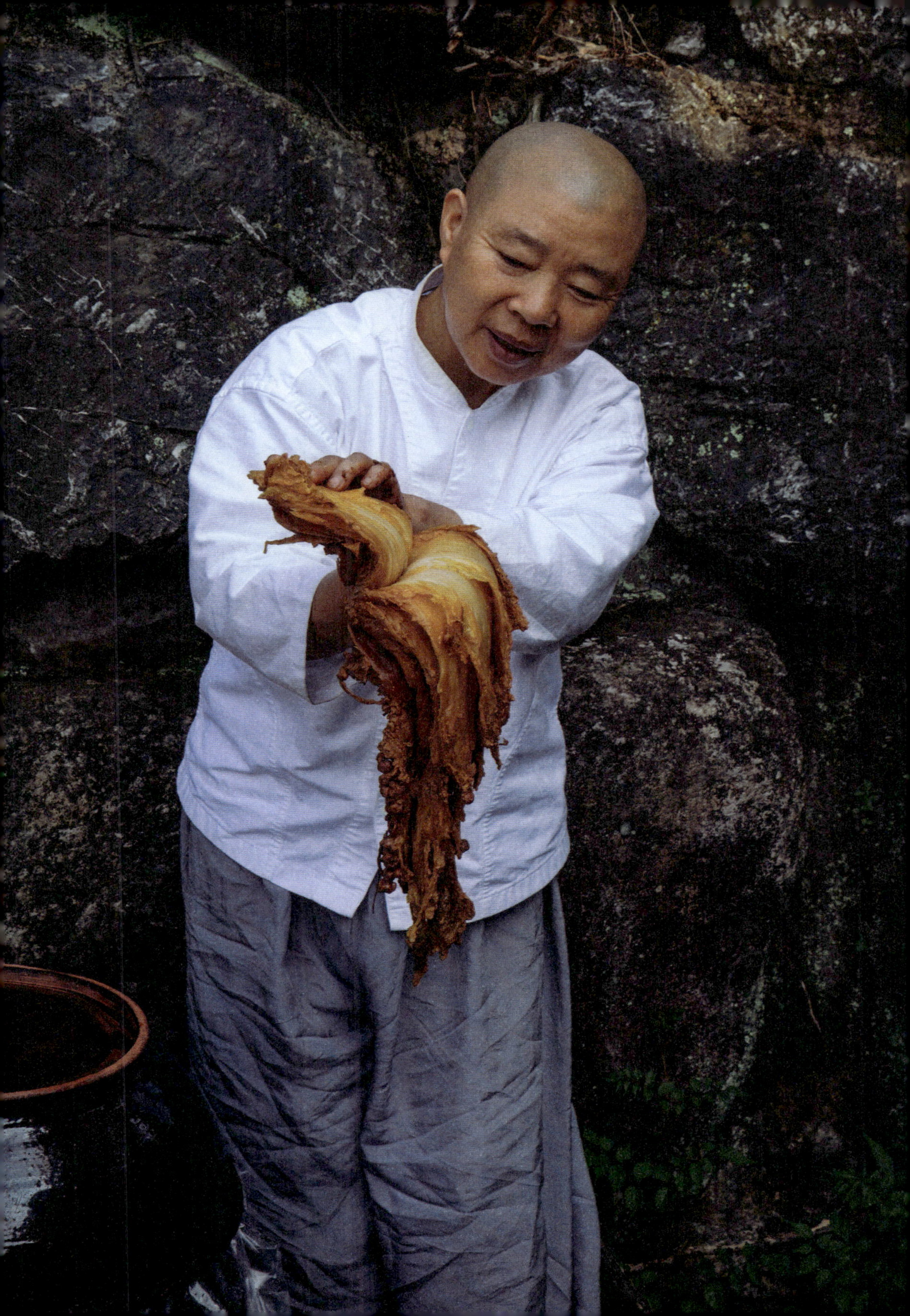

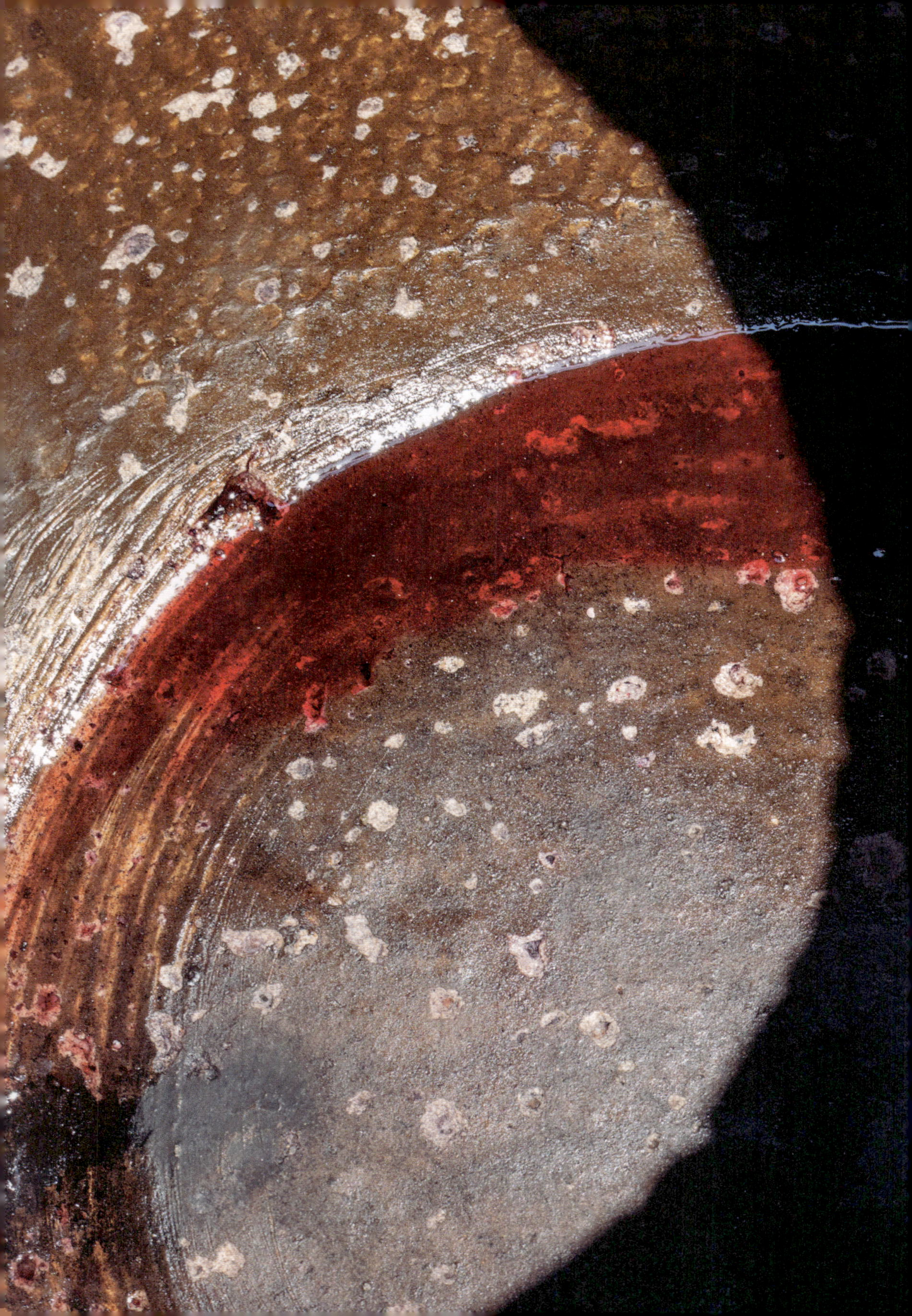

CHEONG

Storing food for long periods of time has been a central concern for as long as cooking has existed. Methods of food storage vary greatly depending on the culture. Jeongkwan Snim maintains a time-honored tradition in temple cooking by making a large number of different kinds of cheong. The kinds she makes from fruits or berries are famous! However, grains, squash, namul, roots, seaweed, and flowers can also be used to make cheong.

Snim makes around 100 different kinds of cheong herself and uses them as flavorings or to elevate dishes. Cheong is one of the categories of foods that utilizes nature's complex transformation process—it's made by preserving fruit, for example, in sugar and leaving it in an onggi for one year in a cool, well-ventilated area. The sugar draws the sweetness and other qualities from the fruit. Next, the fruit is sifted out and the liquid is saved. Fermentation begins once the sugar begins to break down (otherwise, sugar inhibits this process). The fermentation then creates a new flavor and new active agents.

Cheong is the name for a very thick and intensely colorful liquid. It tastes best after three years of fermentation; if it's left to ferment for an additional five or six years, it will turn into vinegar, which has a different aroma and a unique flavor.

Taengja-Cheong — 168
Maesil-Cheong — 174
Bokbunja-Cheong — 180
Omija-Cheong — 186
Rice Syrup (Jocheong) — 190
Yuja-Cheong — 416

Bitter oranges are called *taengja* in Korea. A 500-year-old taengja tree in Snim's temple garden still produces fruit every year! Its white flowers give way to initially green fruits that lighten into orange in the autumn. Harvesting them isn't easy because of the tree's thorns, but they are nonetheless harvested, and then the fruit is rinsed and halved. Snim needs a lot of patience and some helping hands in order to remove all of the seeds, which have a bitter flavor. Harvesting the taengja and processing them to make her famous cheong is one of Snim's annual autumn rituals.

TAENGJA-CHEONG

4½ pounds (2 kg) bitter oranges (taengja)
10 cups (2 kg) sugar

Rinse the taengja thoroughly, drain them, halve them, remove the seeds, and then slice them thinly. Mix them with the sugar and put them into an earthenware container. Cover the top with a layer of sugar to protect the fruit from rotting. Let the container stand in a cool, shady place for one year.

After the year is up, sift out the fruit with a sieve and pour the remaining liquid into an earthenware container. Store it in a cool place. The leftover fruit slices can be stored and reused later as a flavoring or garnish.

Fermentation will begin gradually. The liquid is called taengja-cheong, and its flavor will change each year. It's best after 3 years.

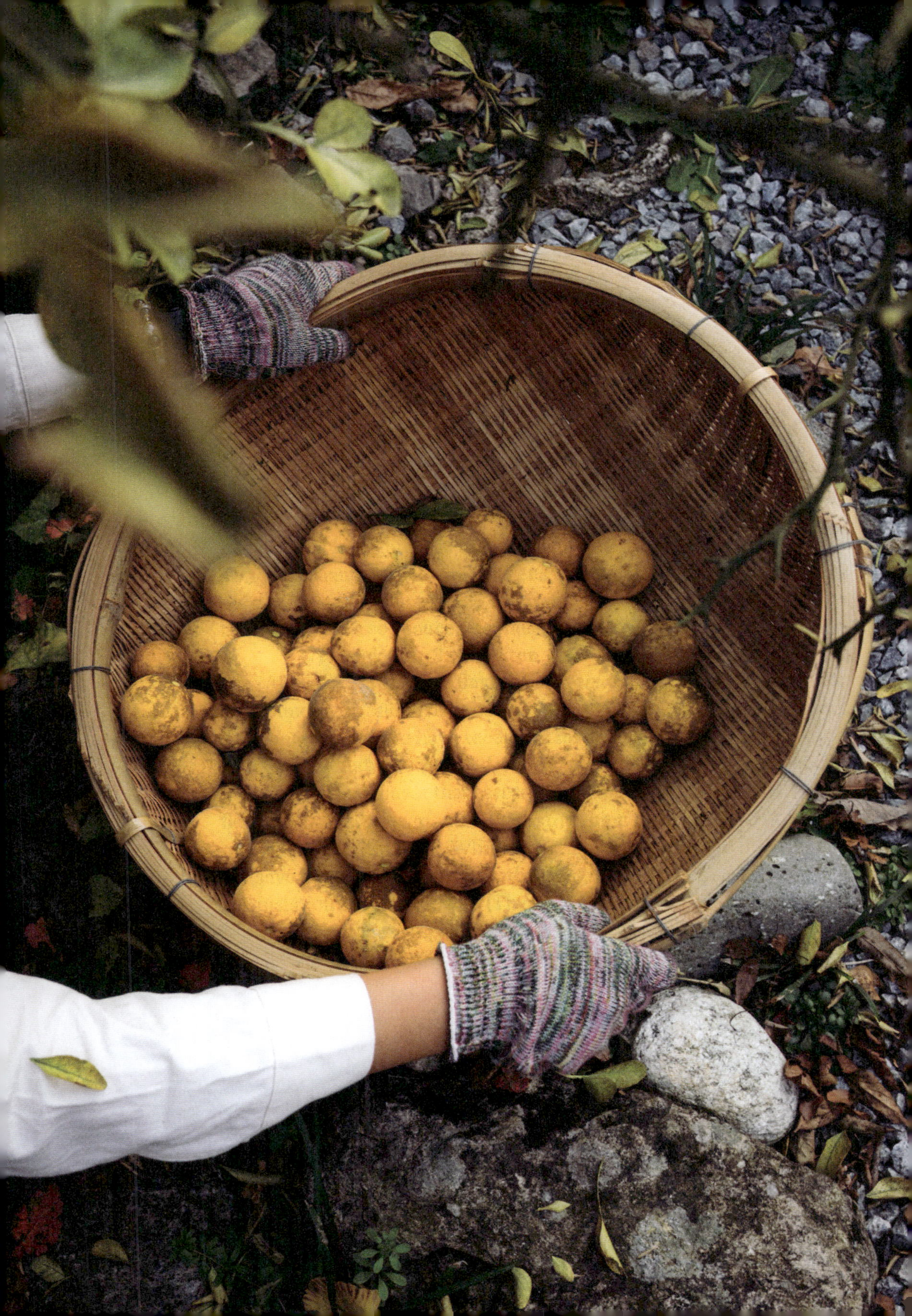

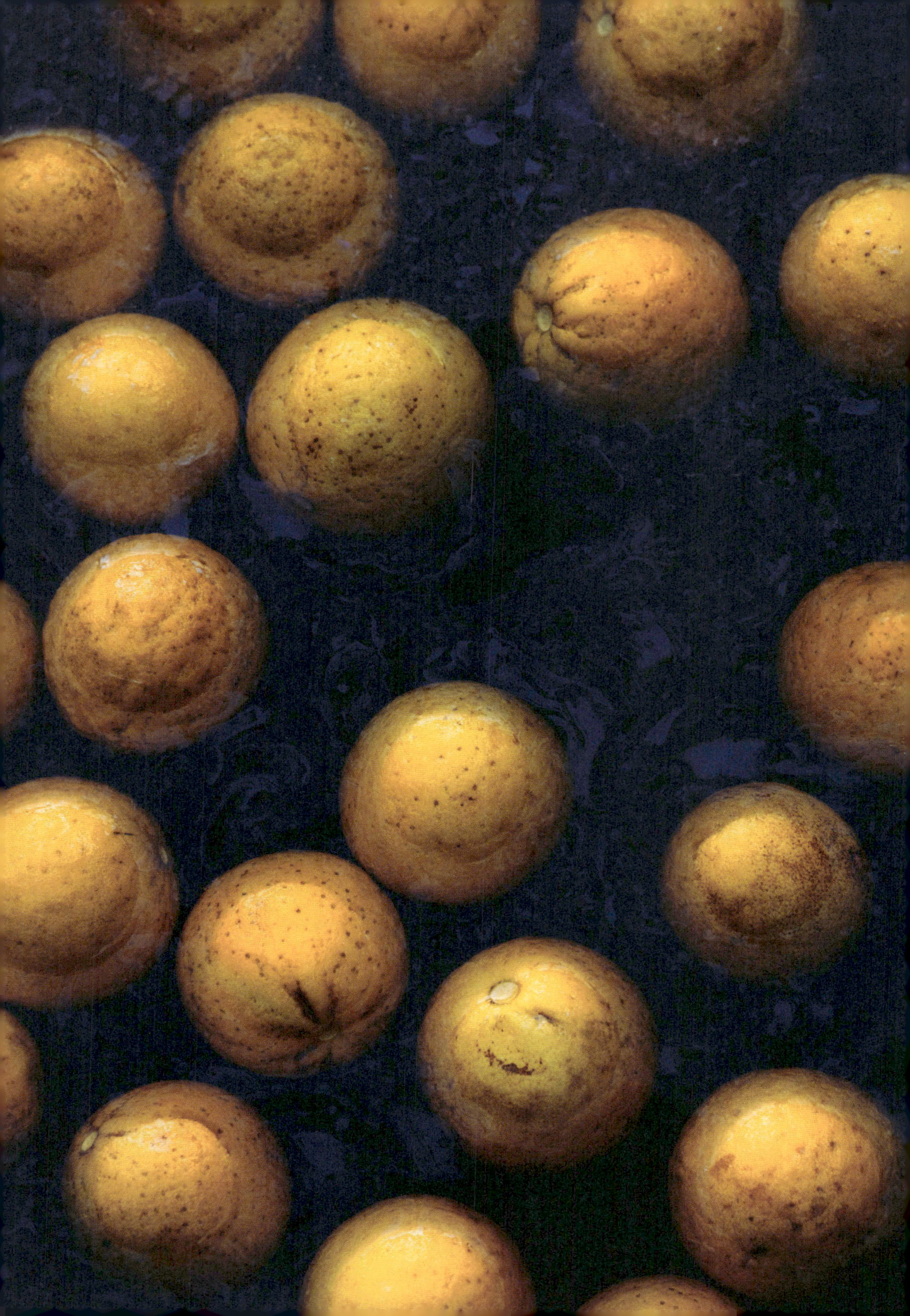

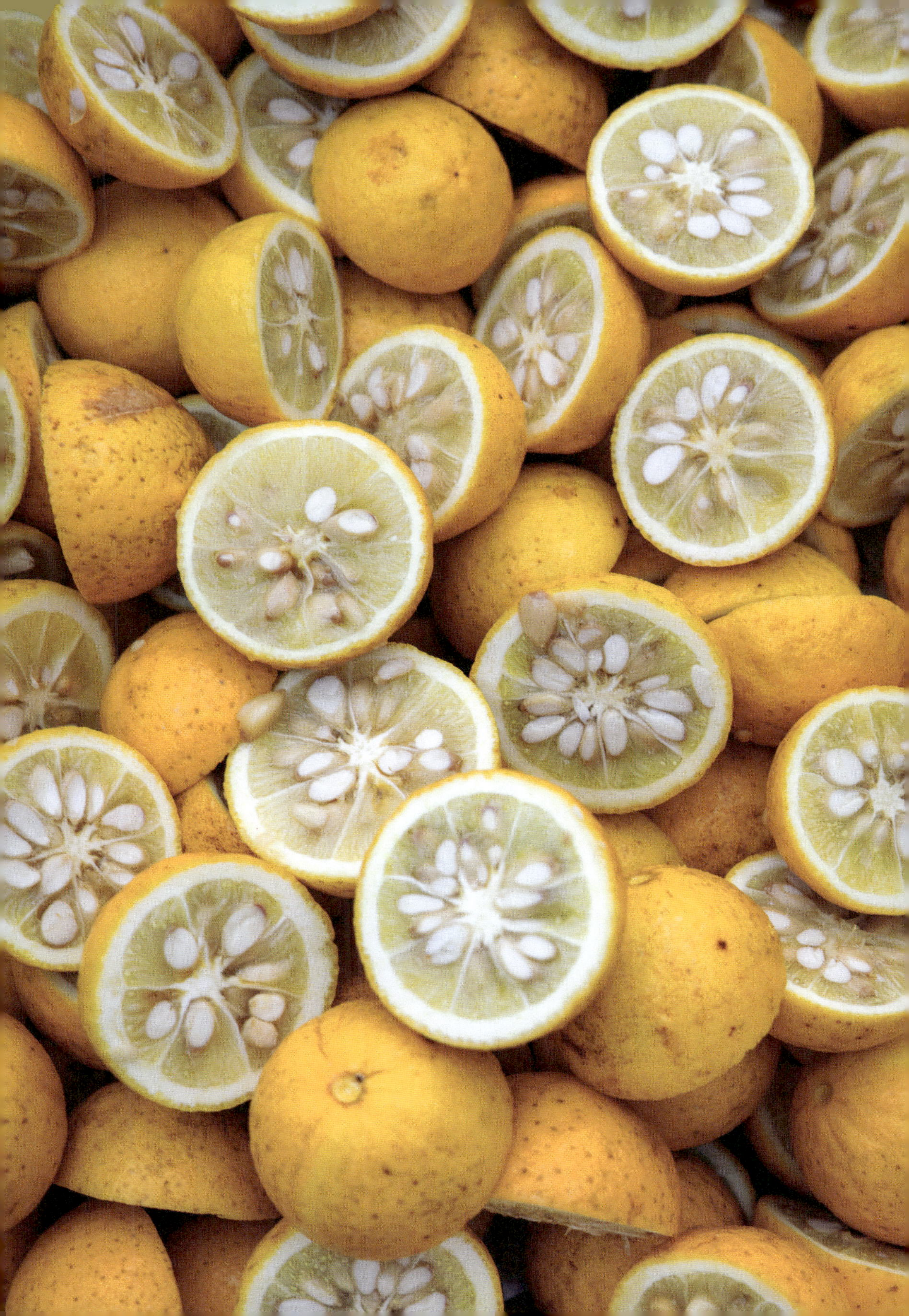

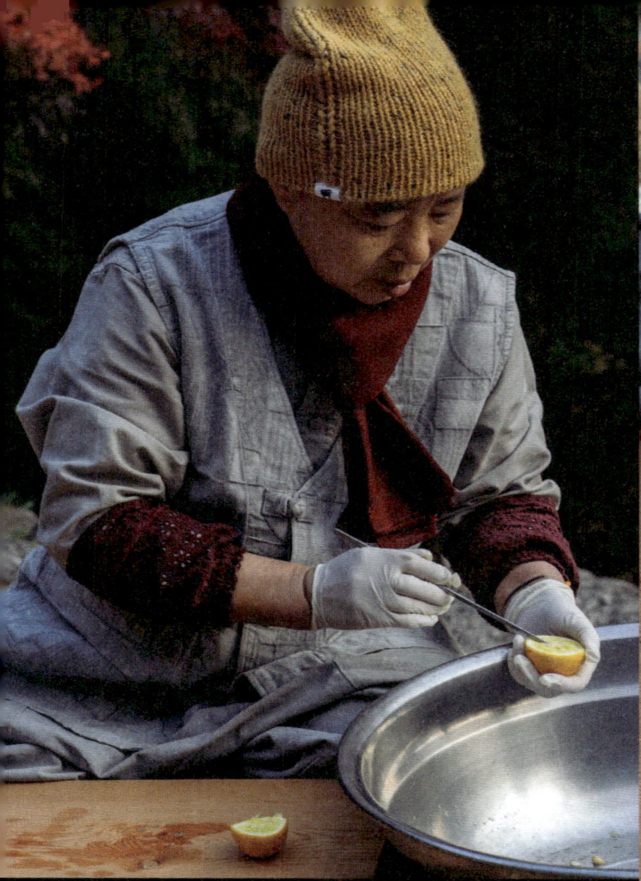

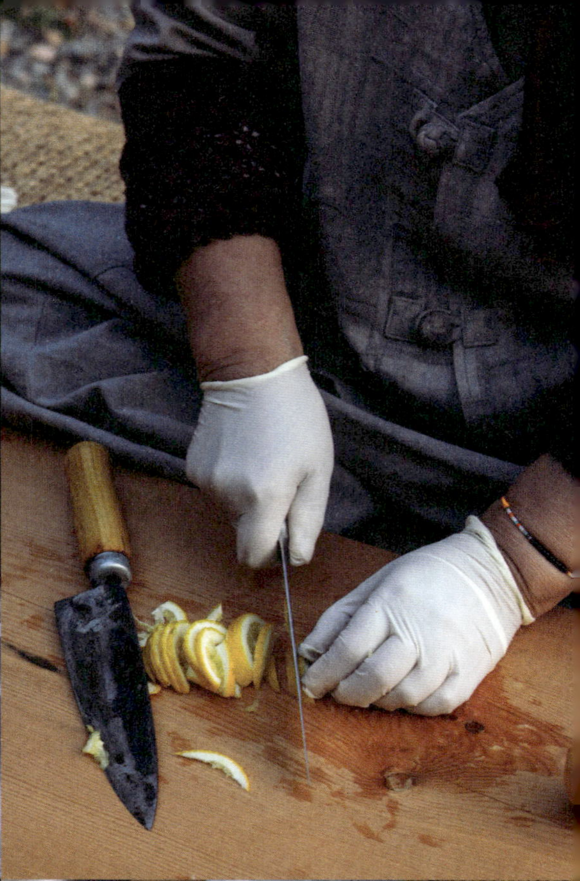

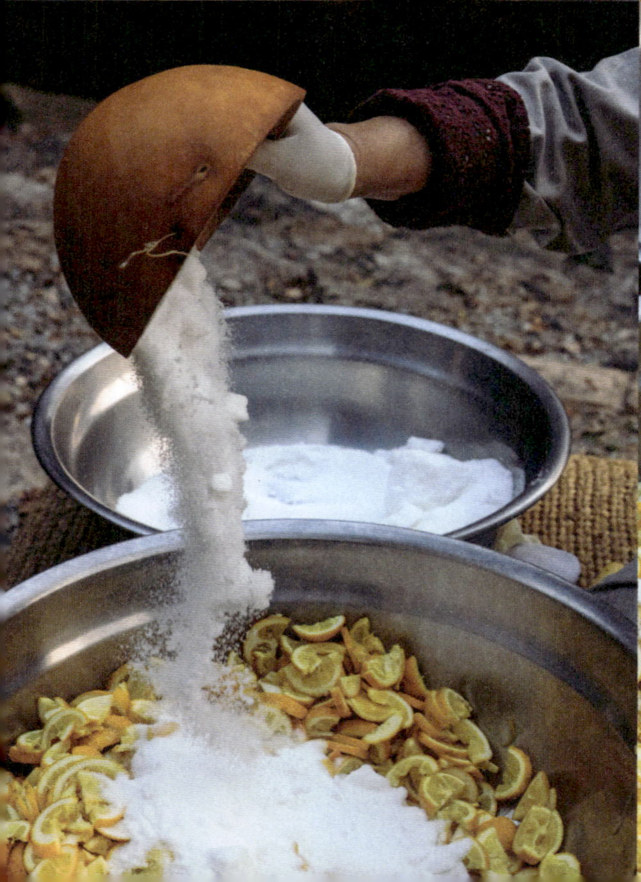

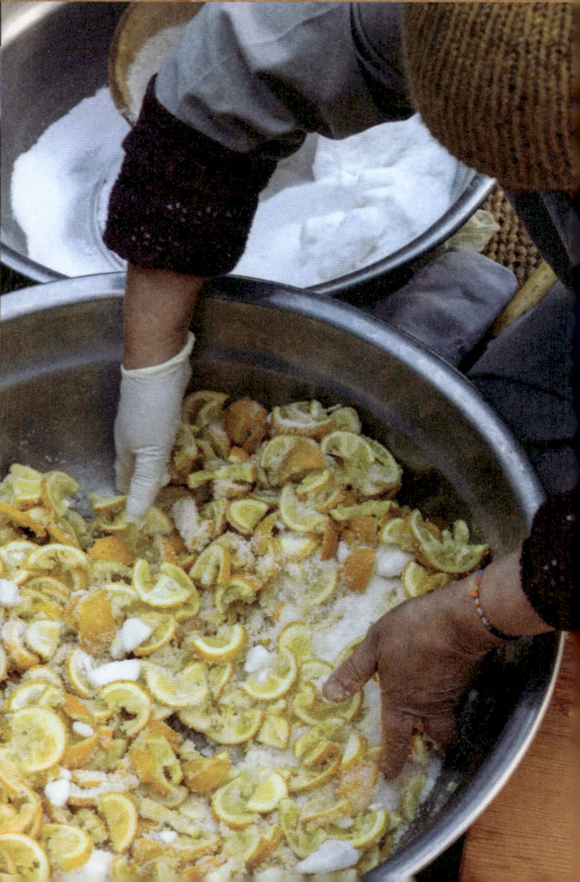

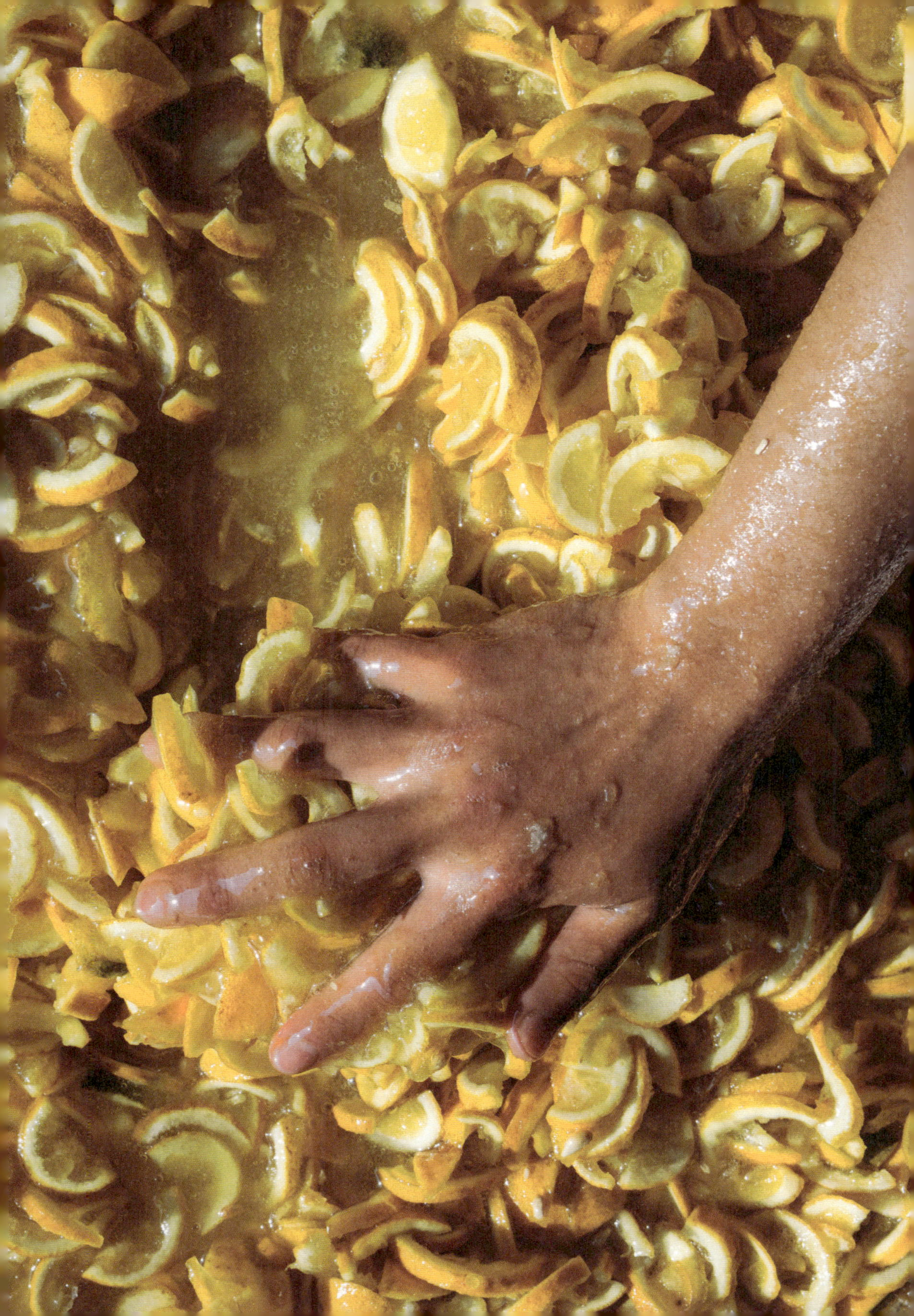

Maesil is a type of plum grown in the southern part of the country and harvested in June. The fruits must be processed quickly! Young maesils are green, but they turn yellow when they're ripe. Ripe plums taste sweeter, while the green ones are quite sour. They're used in a variety of ways: they can be squeezed for juice or processed into jangajji by cutting them into small pieces and preserving them with salt, soy sauce, doenjang, or gochujang. Smoked maesil is used to make *jehotang*, a beverage that quenches thirst and is therefore drunk in the heat of summer. Snim makes maesil-cheong every year in early summer to use as a flavoring ingredient in dishes.

MAESIL-CHEONG

4½ pounds (2 kg) Korean plums (maesil)
10 cups (2 kg) sugar

Rinse the maesils carefully but thoroughly, drain them well, mix them well with the sugar, and place them in an earthenware container. Cover them with a layer of sugar. Let the container stand in a shady spot.

After one year, sift out the fruit with a sieve but keep the remaining liquid in the container. Once the sugar breaks down, fermentation will begin gradually.

New flavor nuances will come forward, and the maesil-cheong will eventually be ready. It tastes best after 3 years.

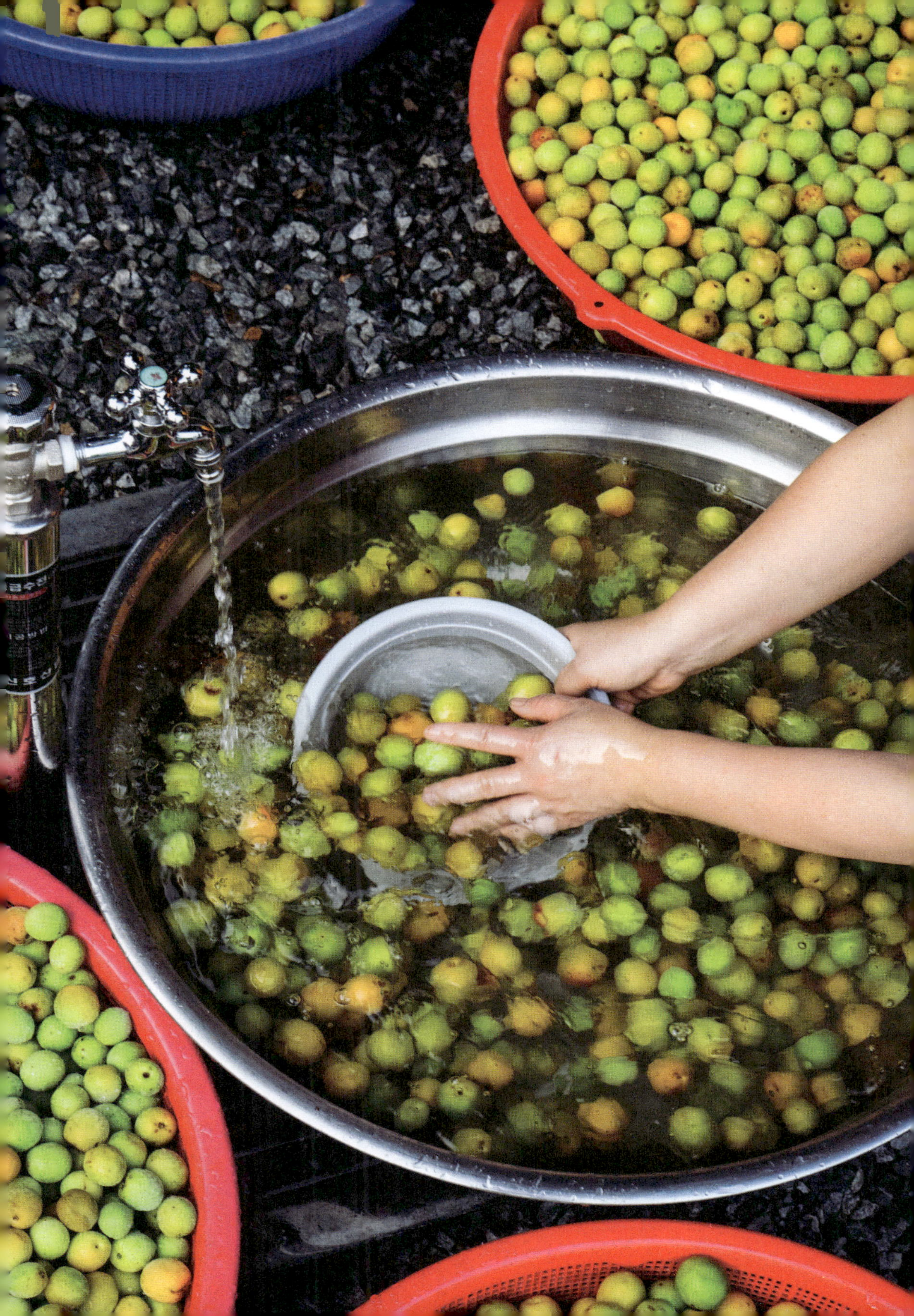

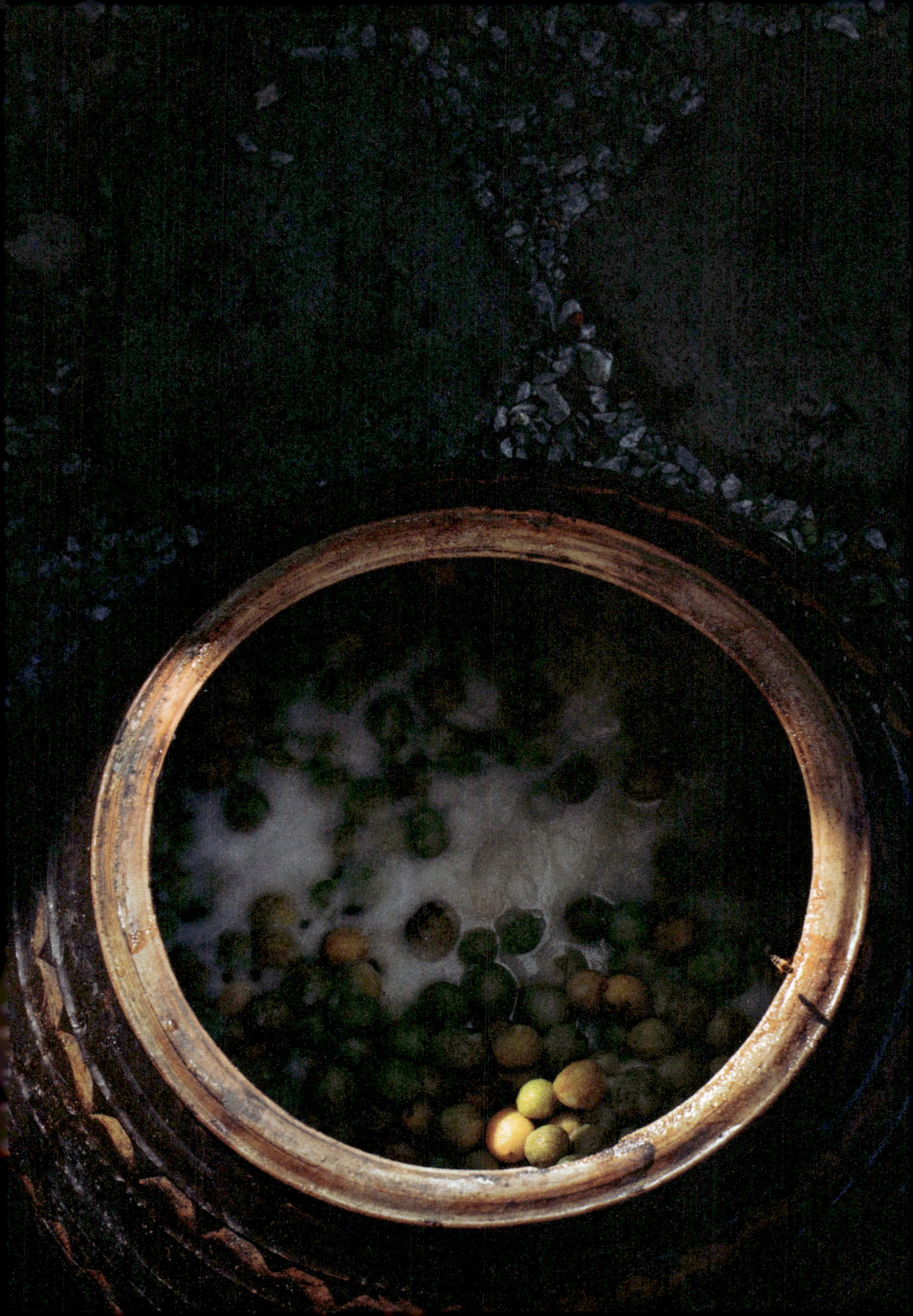

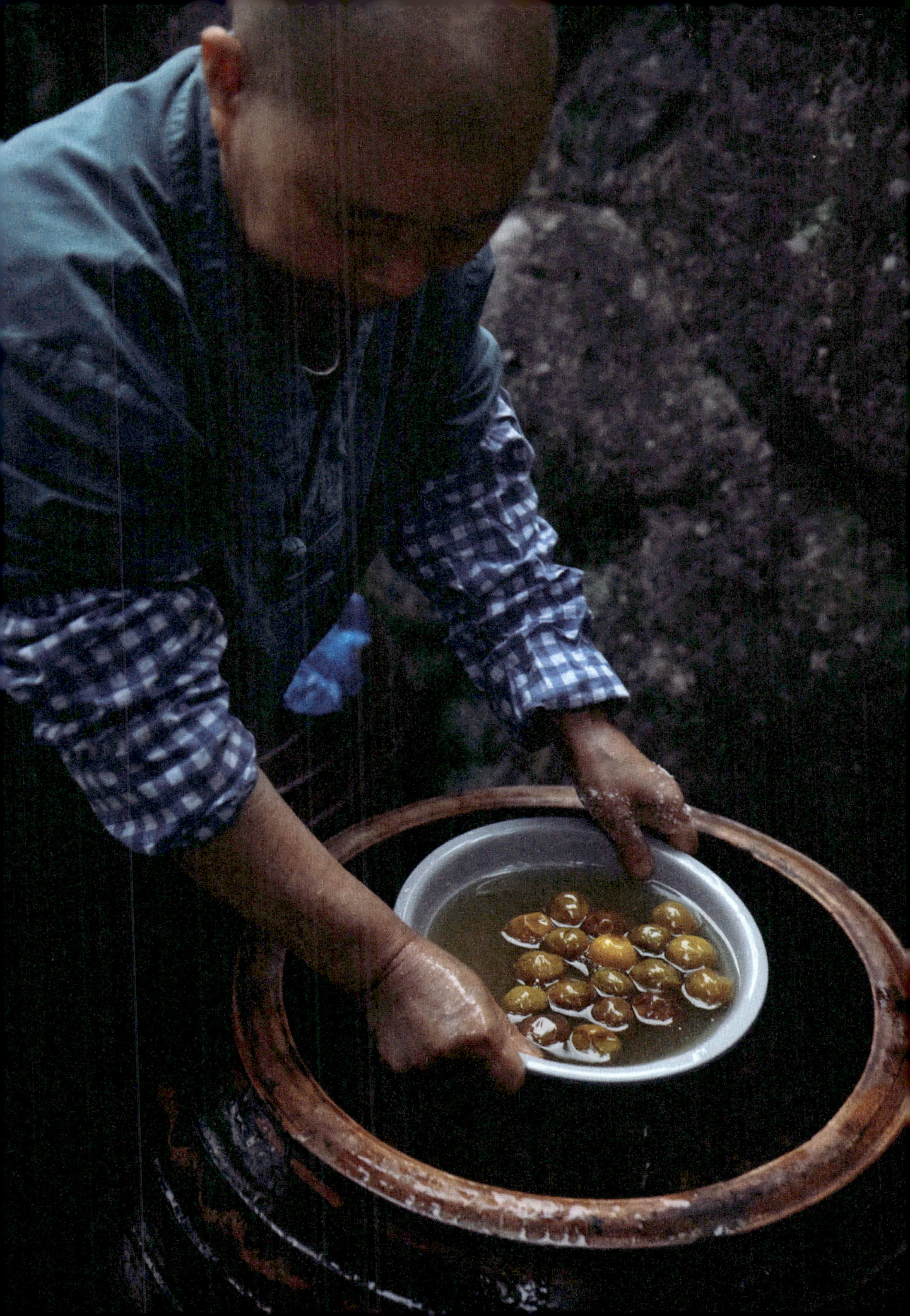

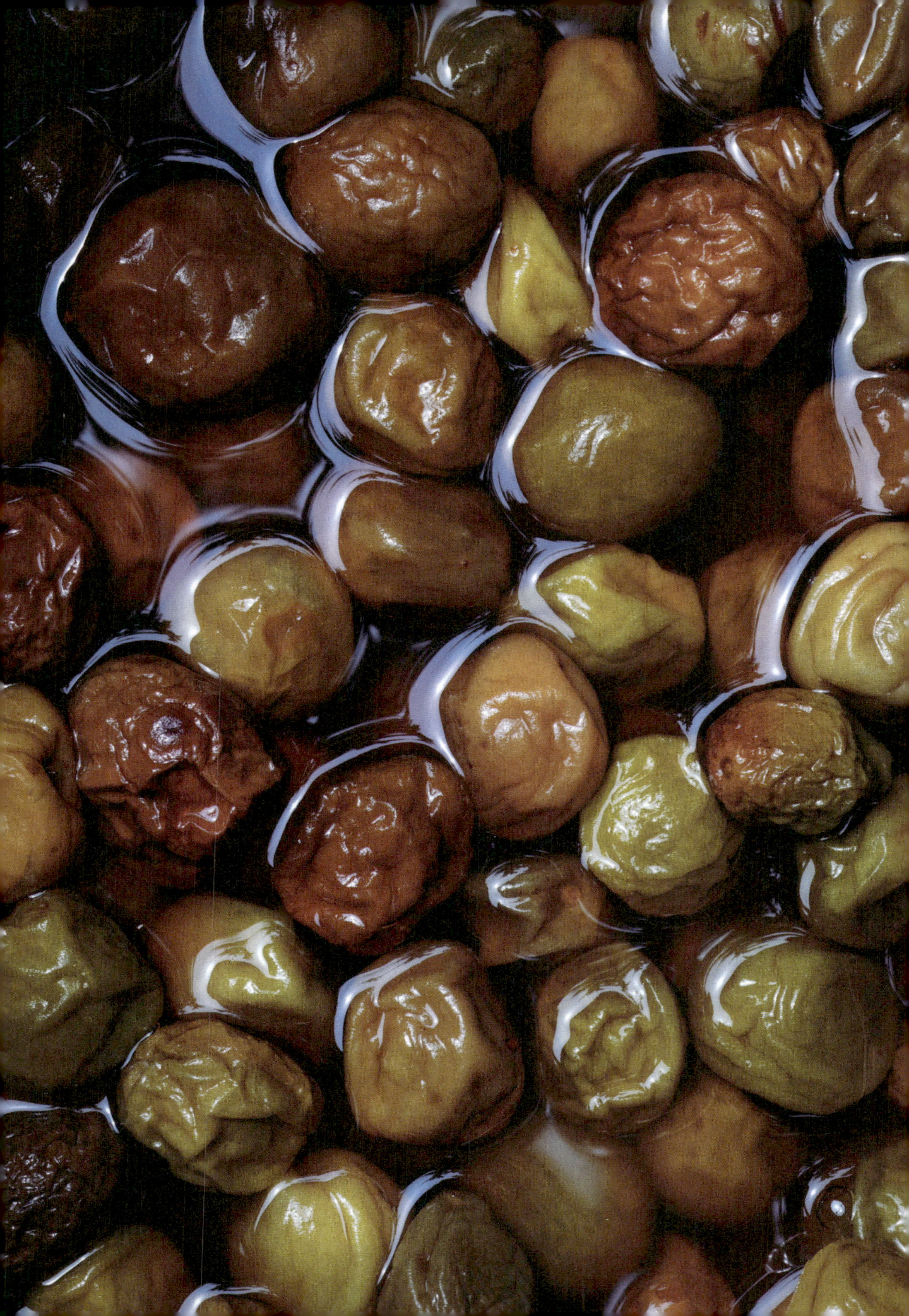

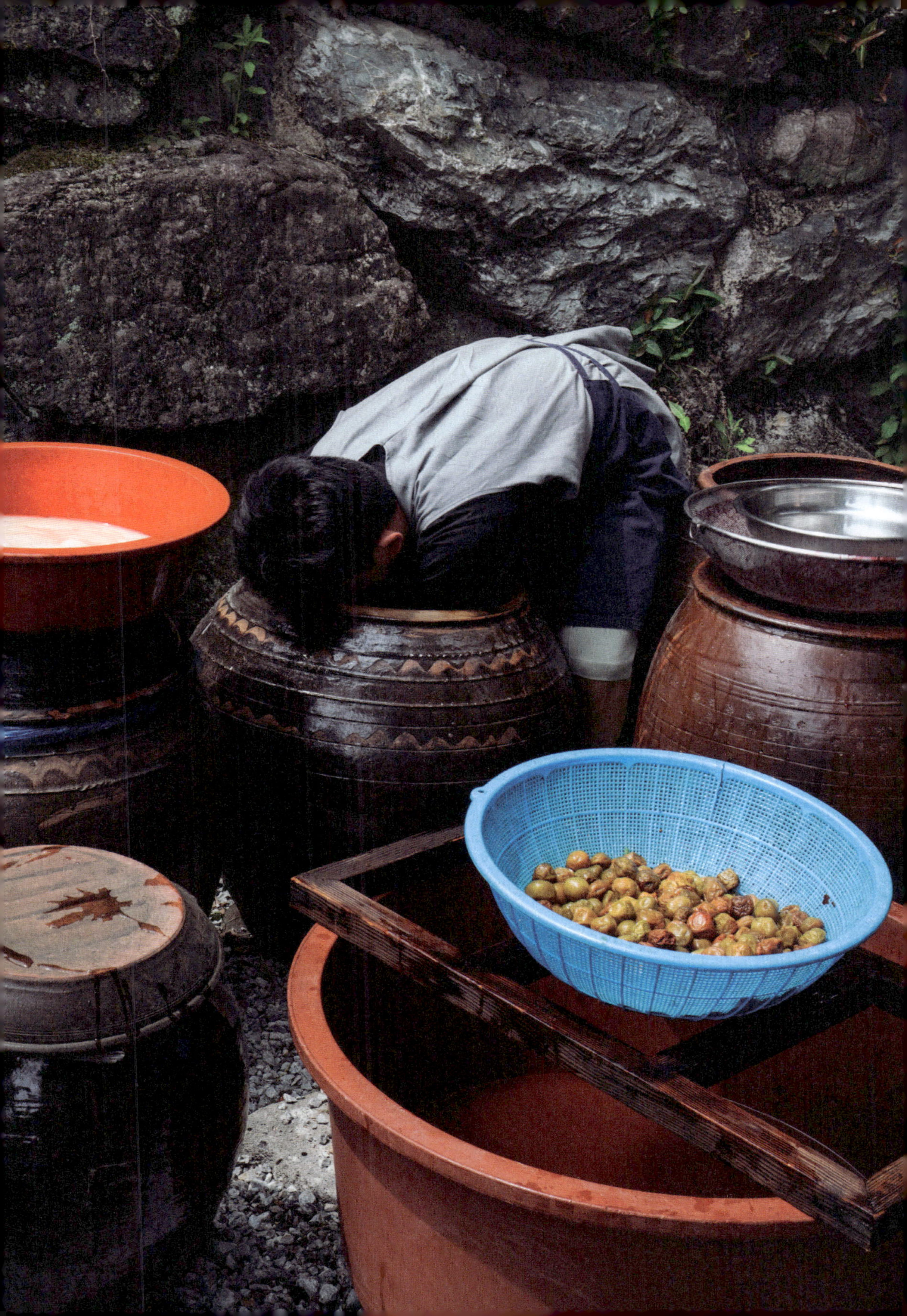

Bokbunja, or Korean blackberries, have a pleasant flavor. They were mentioned as early as the sixteenth century in a book about healing plants. In summer, the fruits first turn red before growing increasingly dark and then turning black. They can be eaten raw or used to make wine or liquor. In their dried form, they've been used as a remedy in traditional medicine. One of Snim's favorite ingredients is the *bokbunja cheong* that she makes fresh each year.

BOKBUNJA-CHEONG

4 ½ pounds (2 kg) Korean blackberries (bokbunja)
10 cups (2 kg) sugar

Rinse the berries carefully, drain them well and mix them with the sugar. Place them in an earthenware container and cover them with a layer of sugar. Let the container stand in a cool place.

After one year, sift the fruit out of the liquid with a sieve. The liquid will begin to gradually ferment.

After 3 years, the bokbunja-cheong will have an intense dark-blue color and a unique aroma. It will have a pleasantly sweet and tart flavor.

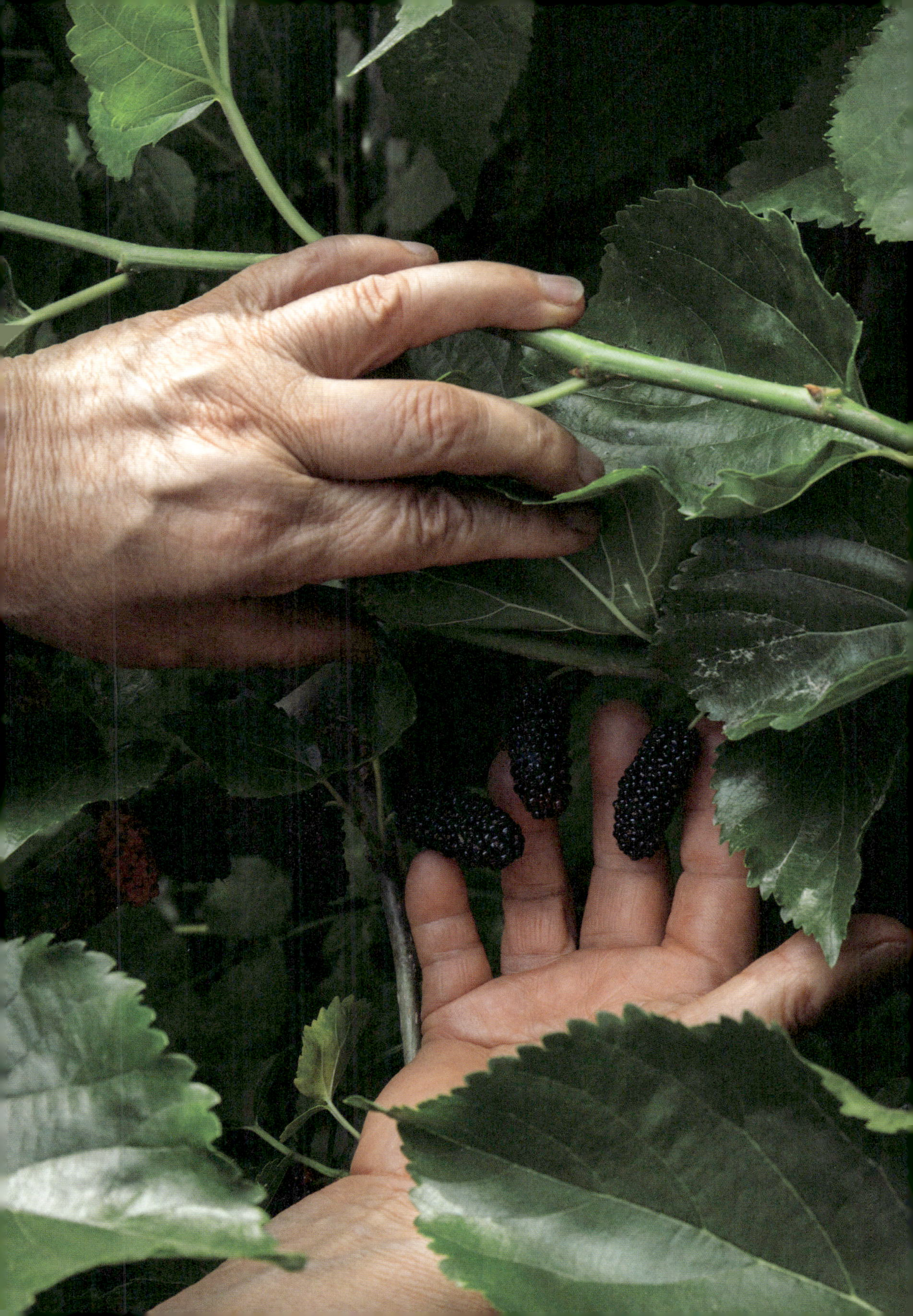

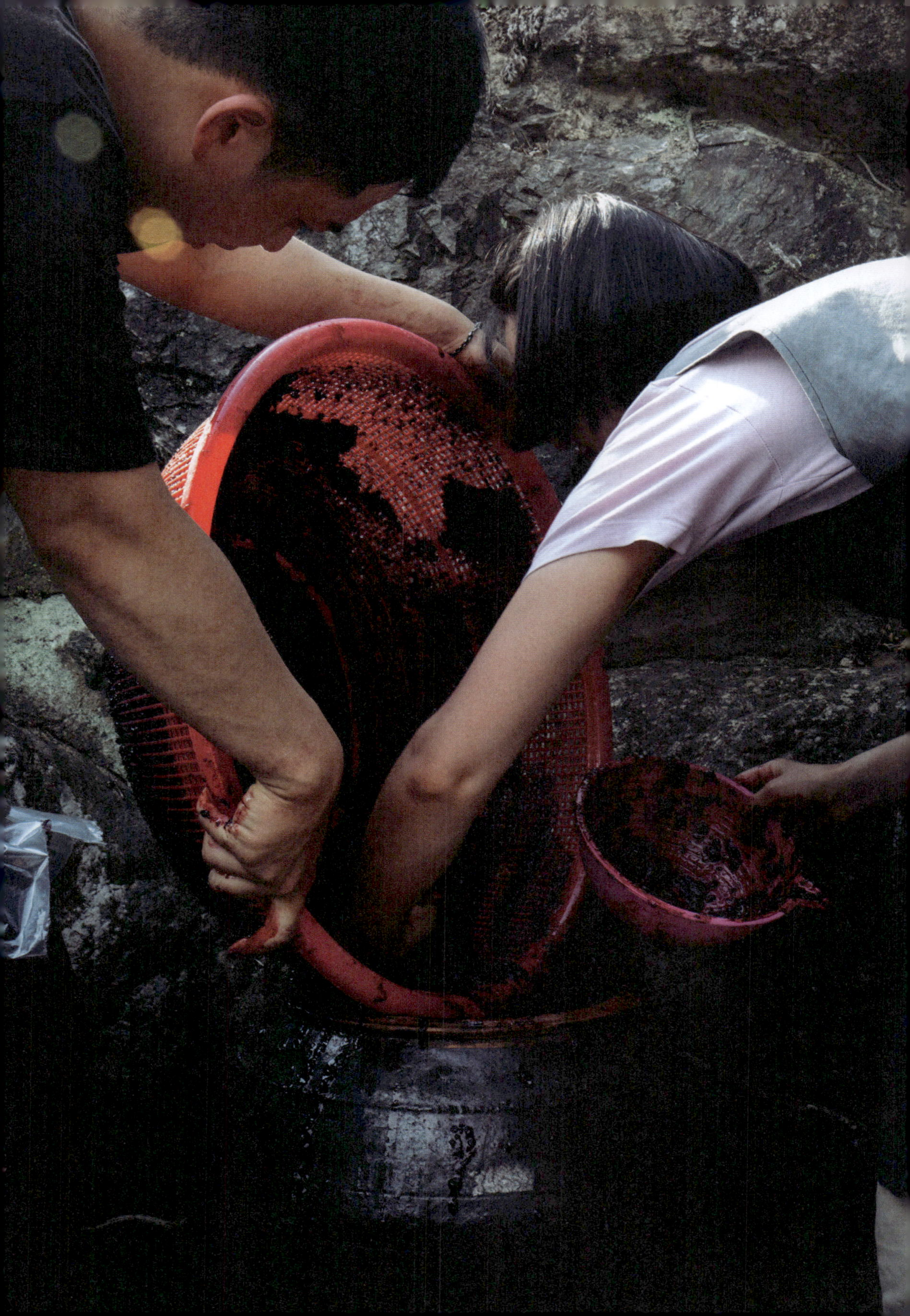

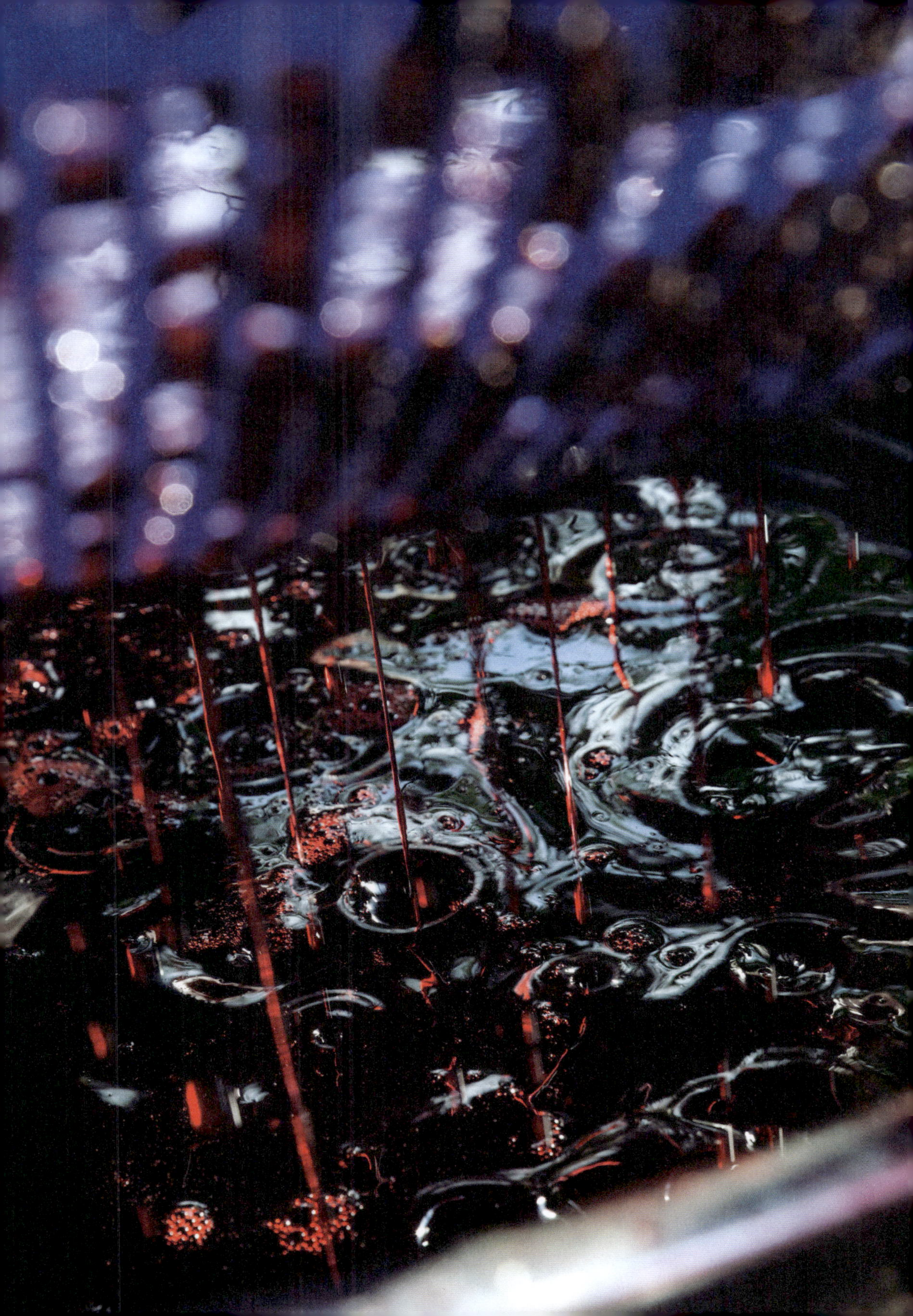

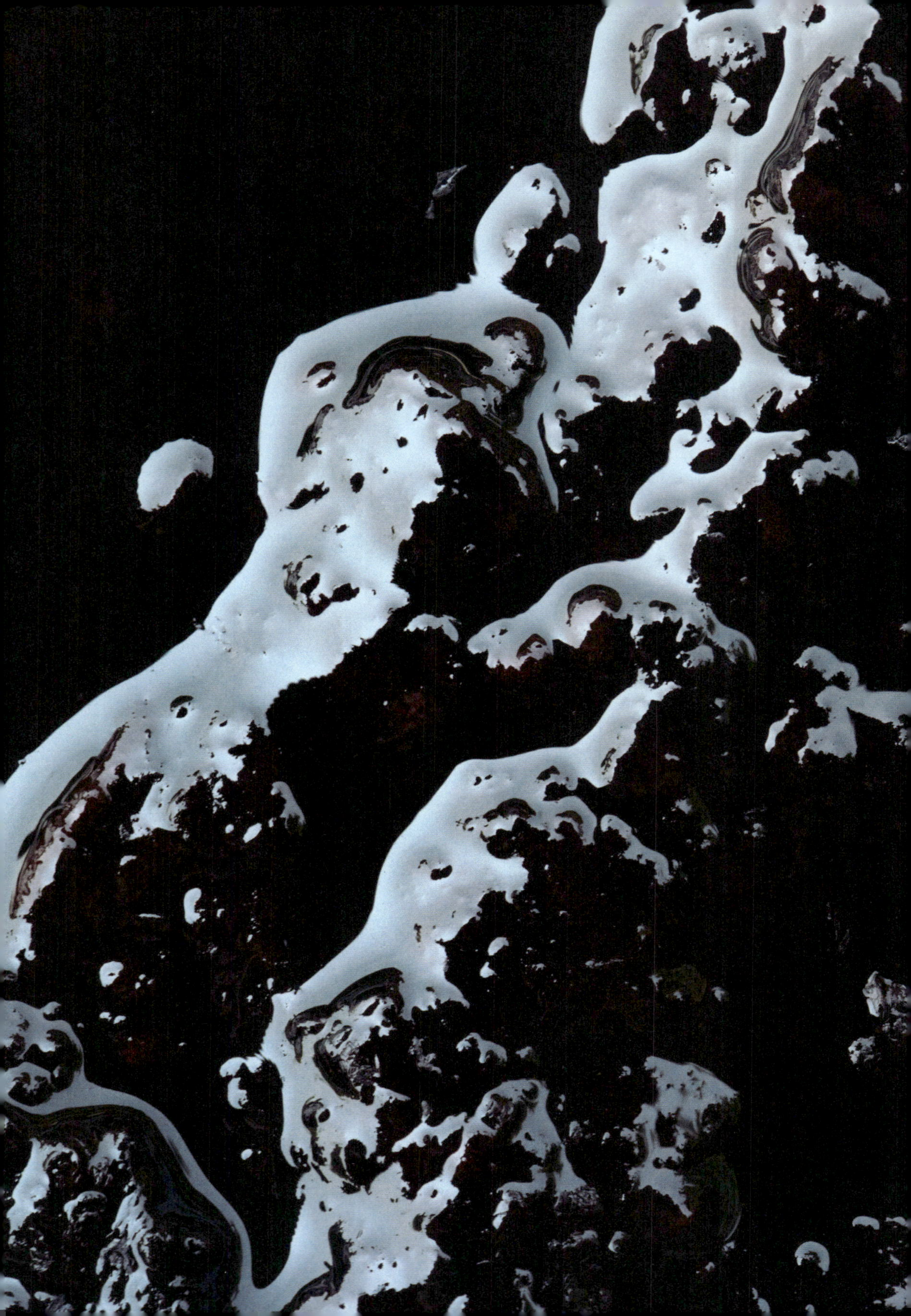

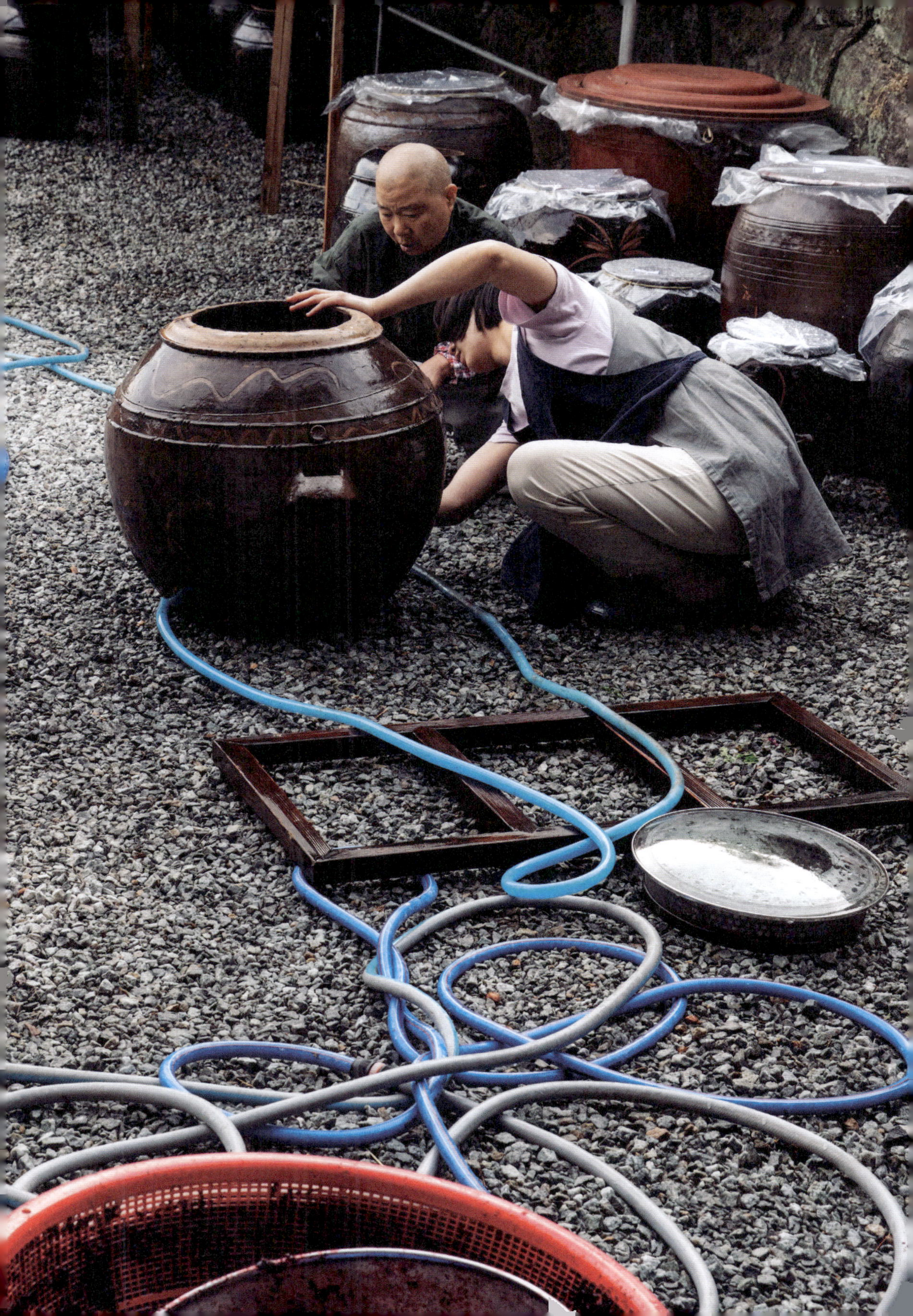

Omija is a red berry that has a long history of use as a remedy in Korea. It grew wild for a long time; today, it's a cultivated crop. There's also a black variety said to protect the lungs and kidneys and be good against coughs and colds. Omija is drunk as a tea and is particularly popular during winter. Its name in Korean means "five-flavor berries" and is derived from the idea that omija are supposed to unite five different flavor nuances: sour, sweet, bitter, salty, and spicy. Omija is also used to make vinegar and cheong.

OMIJA-CHEONG

4½ pounds (2 kg) five-flavor berries (omija)
10 cups (2 kg) sugar

Rinse the omija berries, drain them well, and mix them with the sugar. Let them sit in an earthenware container in a cool place for one year.

Sift out the fruit with a sieve, collecting the berries to use for other fermentation processes.

The liquid will have a red color that grows darker the longer the fermentation continues. The omija-cheong will be ready after 3 years.

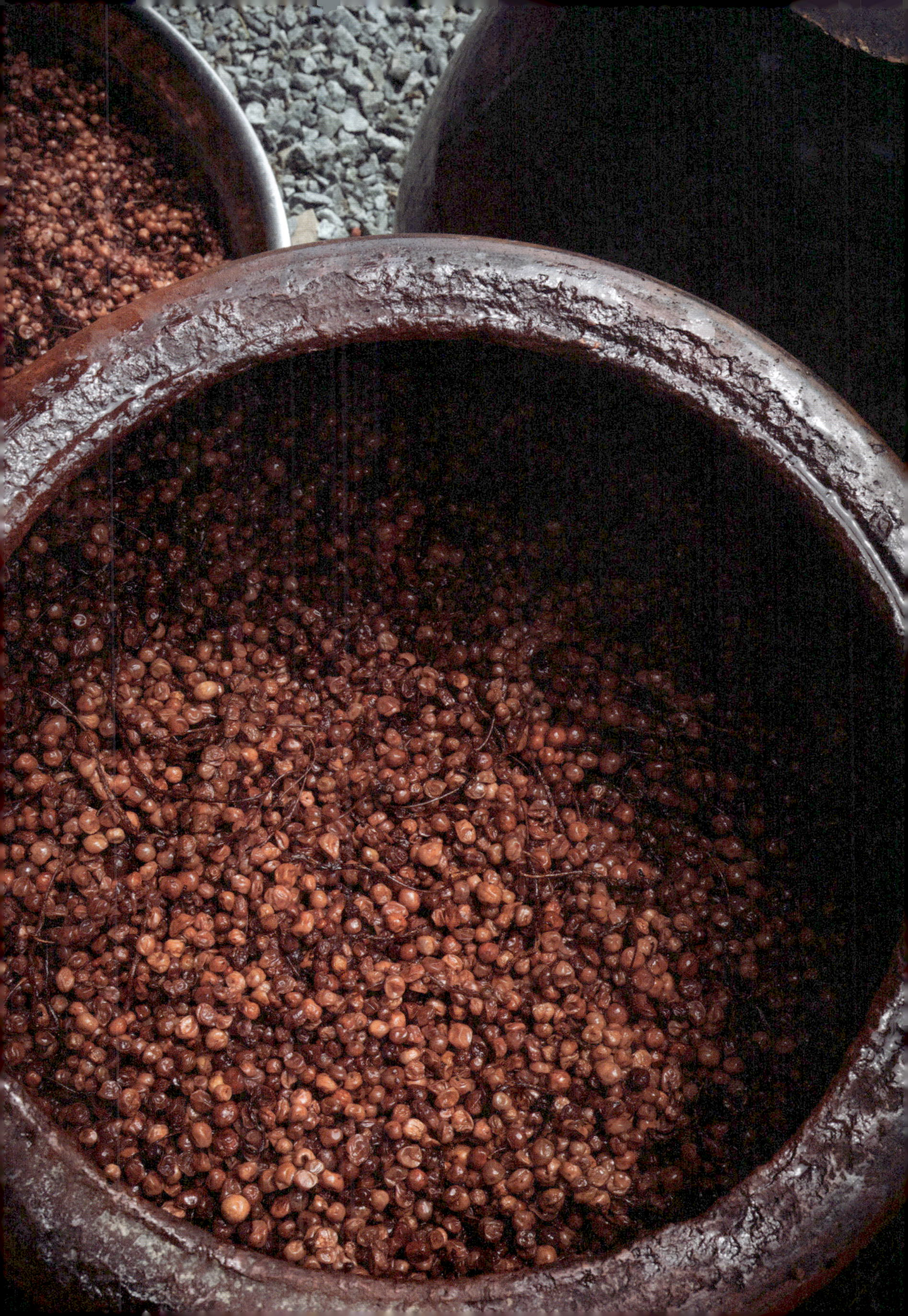

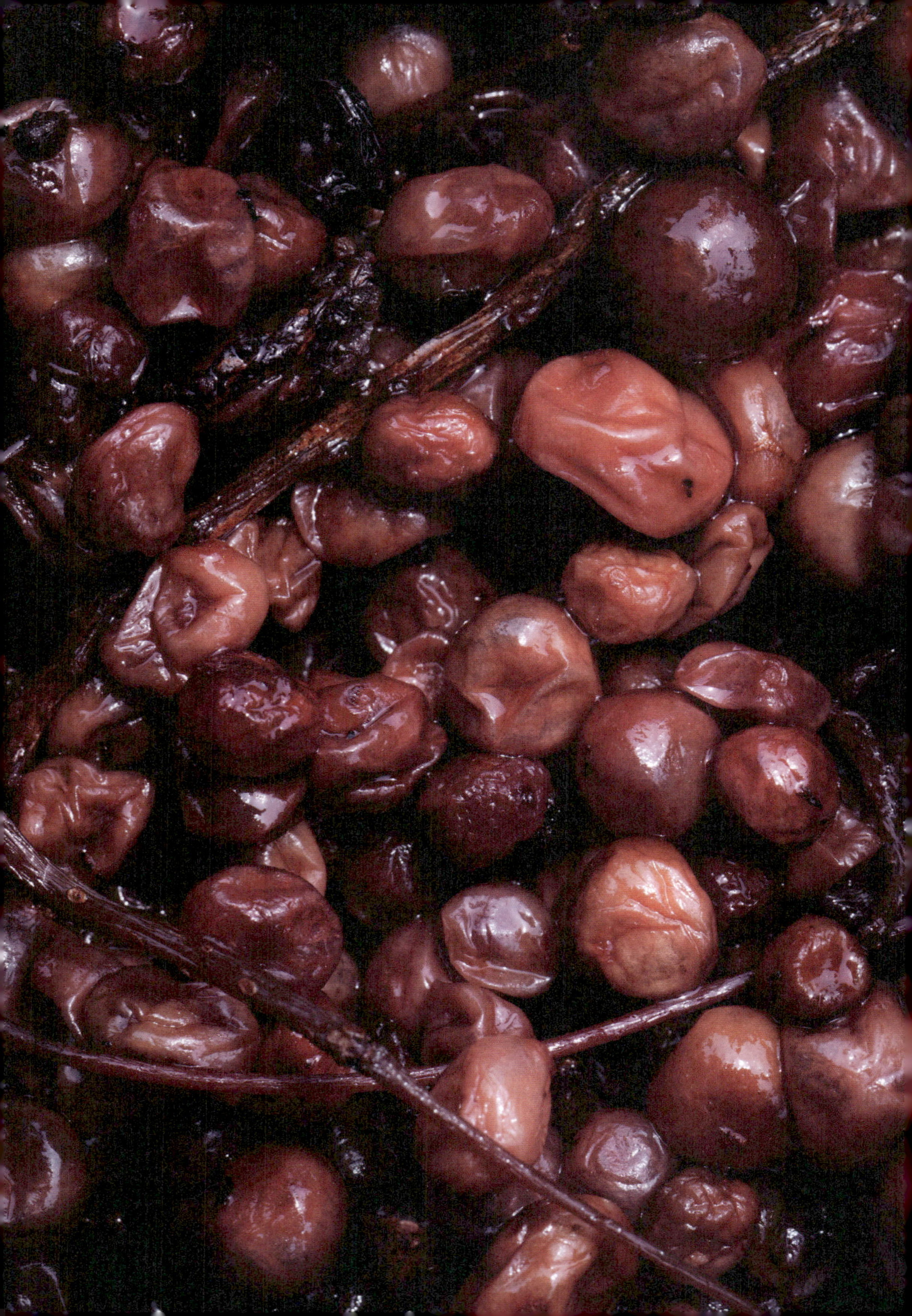

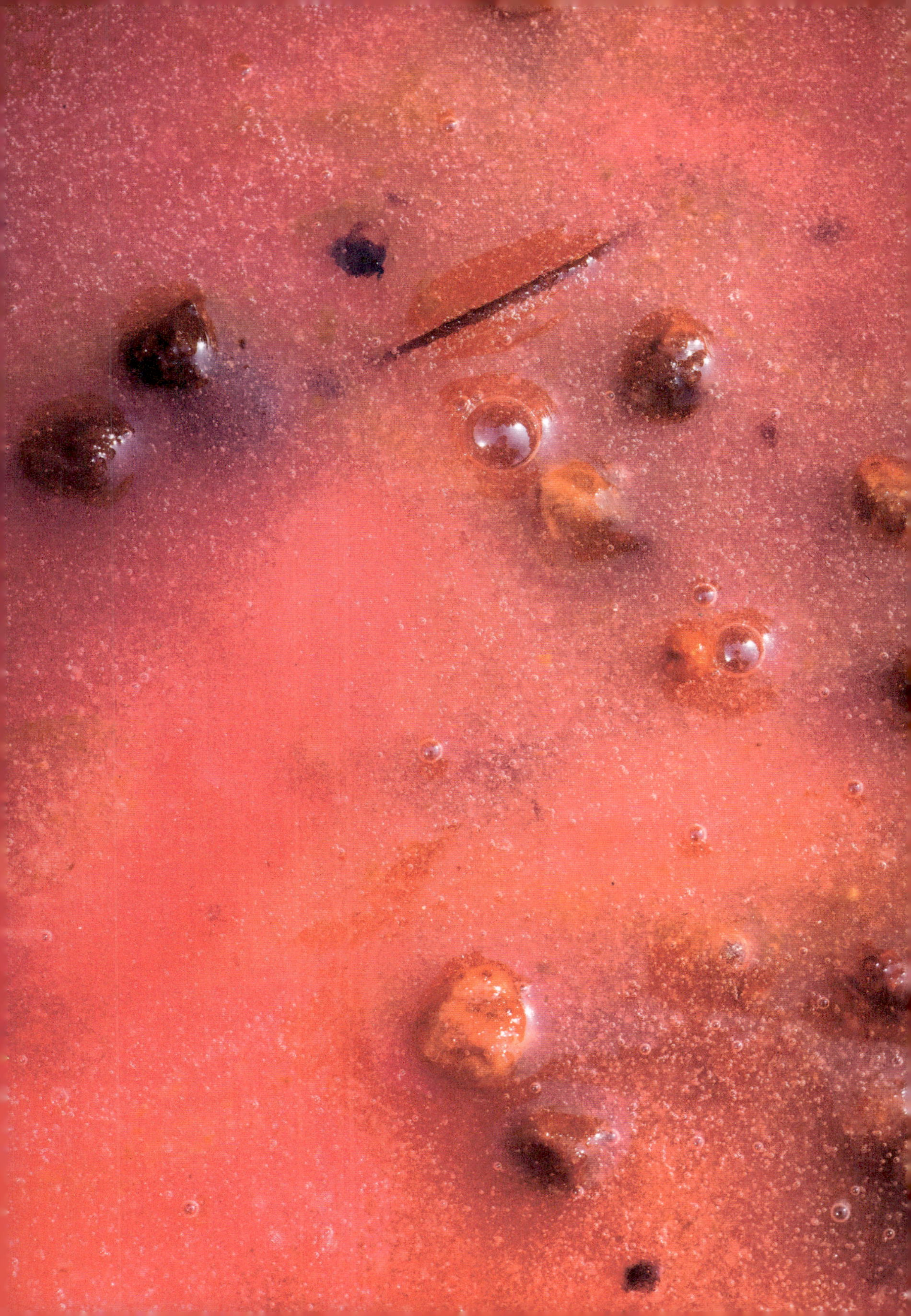

Jocheong is a variety of cheong that uses rice as its base ingredient. It's helped along by dried barley sprouts, also known as malt—they activate the enzymes in the grains and turn the starches into sugar. Jocheong has an intense yet naturally sweet flavor and is very aromatic. Jocheong can also be made from other grains.

Jocheong

RICE SYRUP

5 ½ pounds (2 ½ kg) rice
1 ¾ cups (400 g) dried barley sprouts

Rinse the rice, then steam or boil it (not too tender) and let it cool. Add the dried barley sprouts to it and mix well. Add enough water to cover the mixture completely. Let it sit in a warm place for at least 7 hours, until the rice grains float.

Pour all of the contents into a cloth bag and squeeze out the liquid, squeezing it into a pot. Simmer the liquid slowly until it thickens. This takes a long time! While the pot is bubbling, leave it uncovered—the syrup can boil over easily. Do not allow it to come to a rolling boil. Jocheong must remain thick.

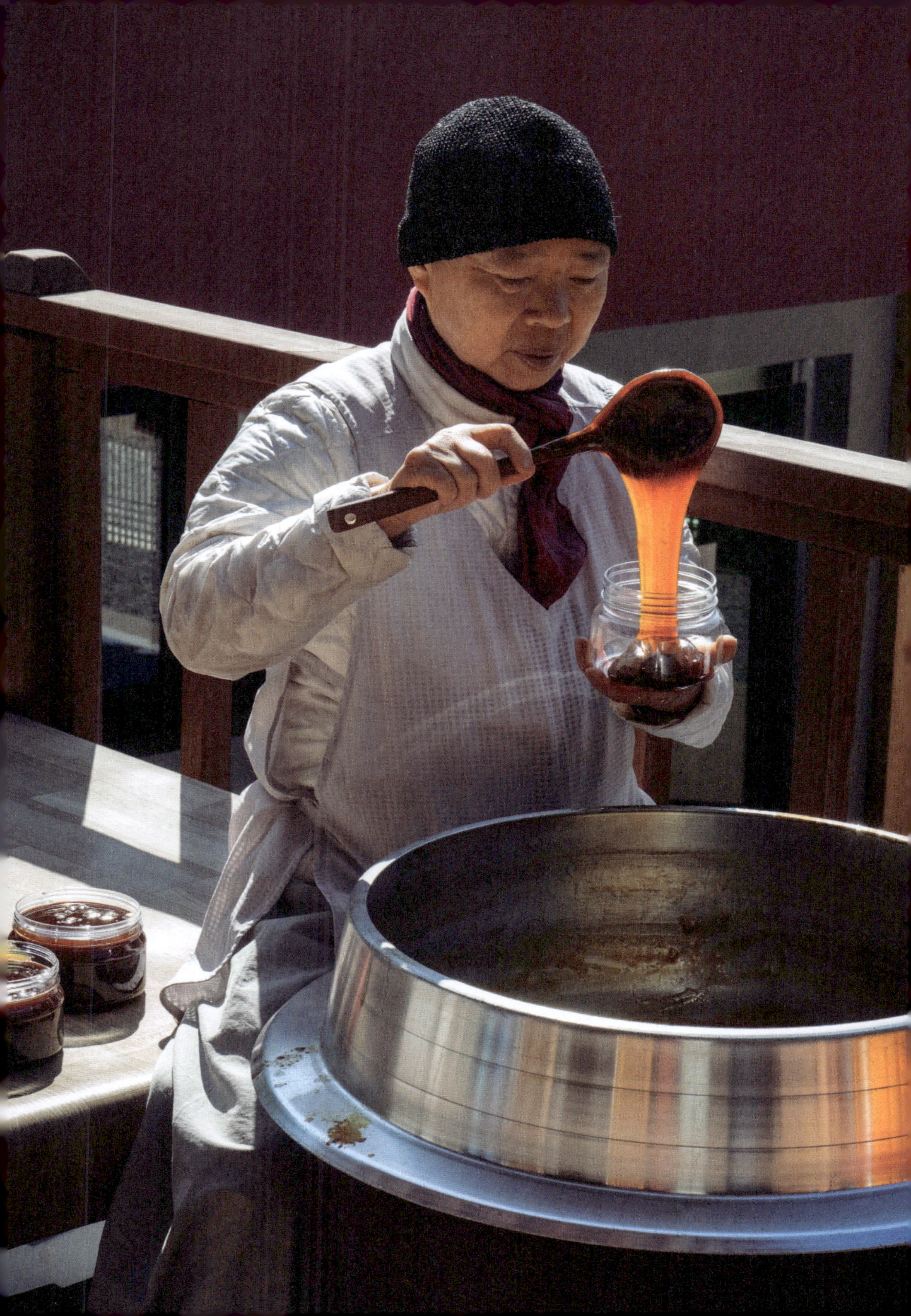

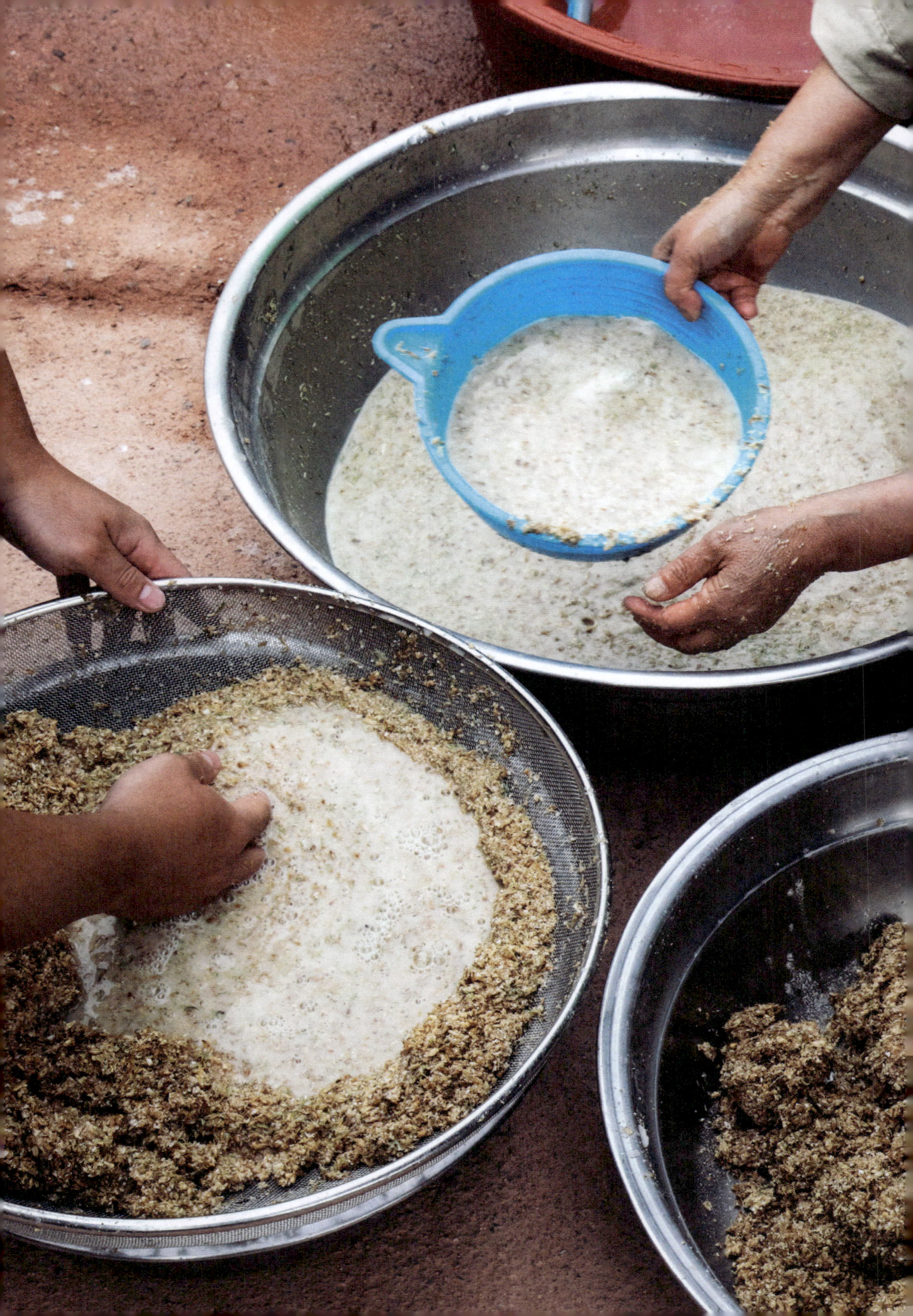

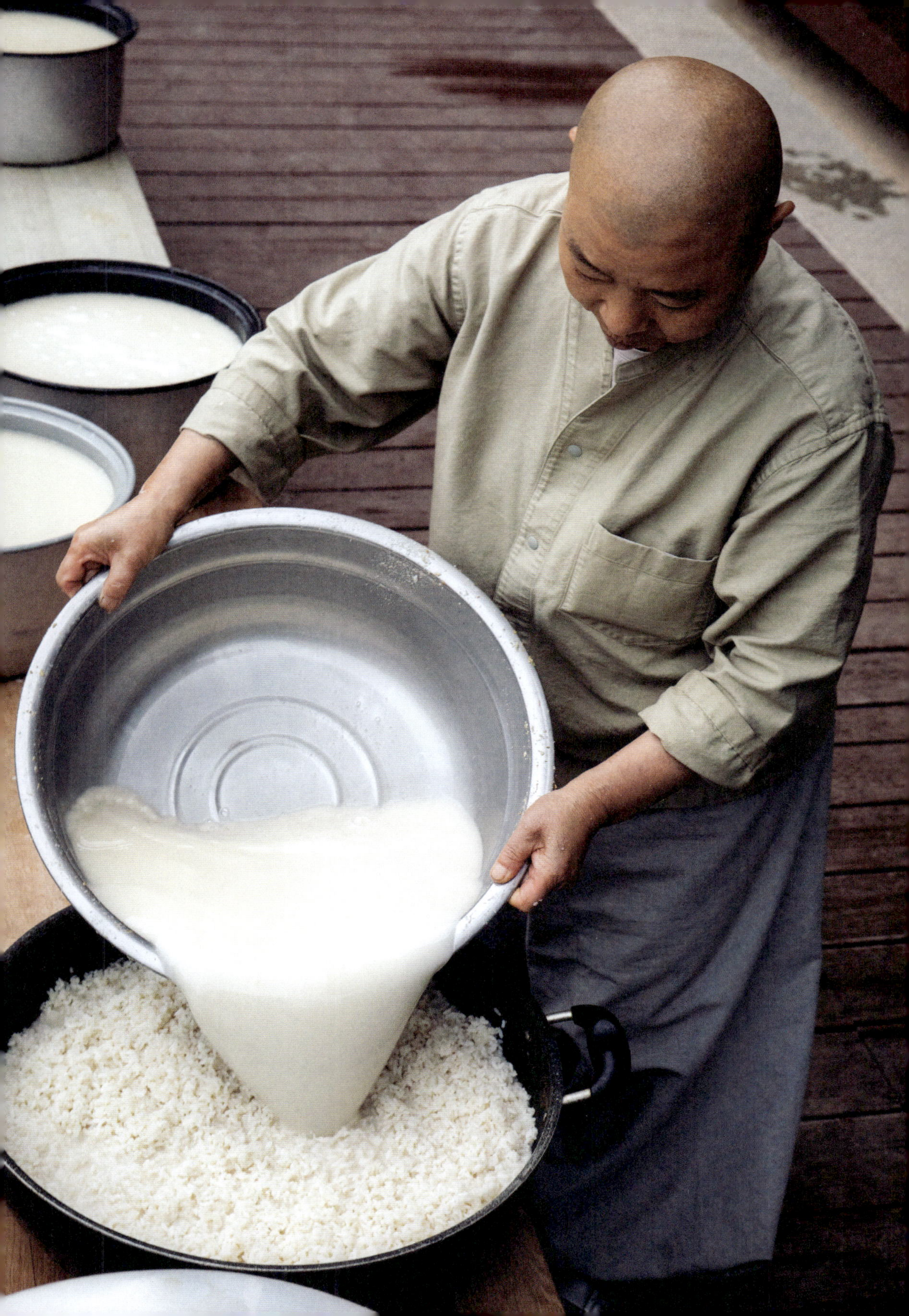

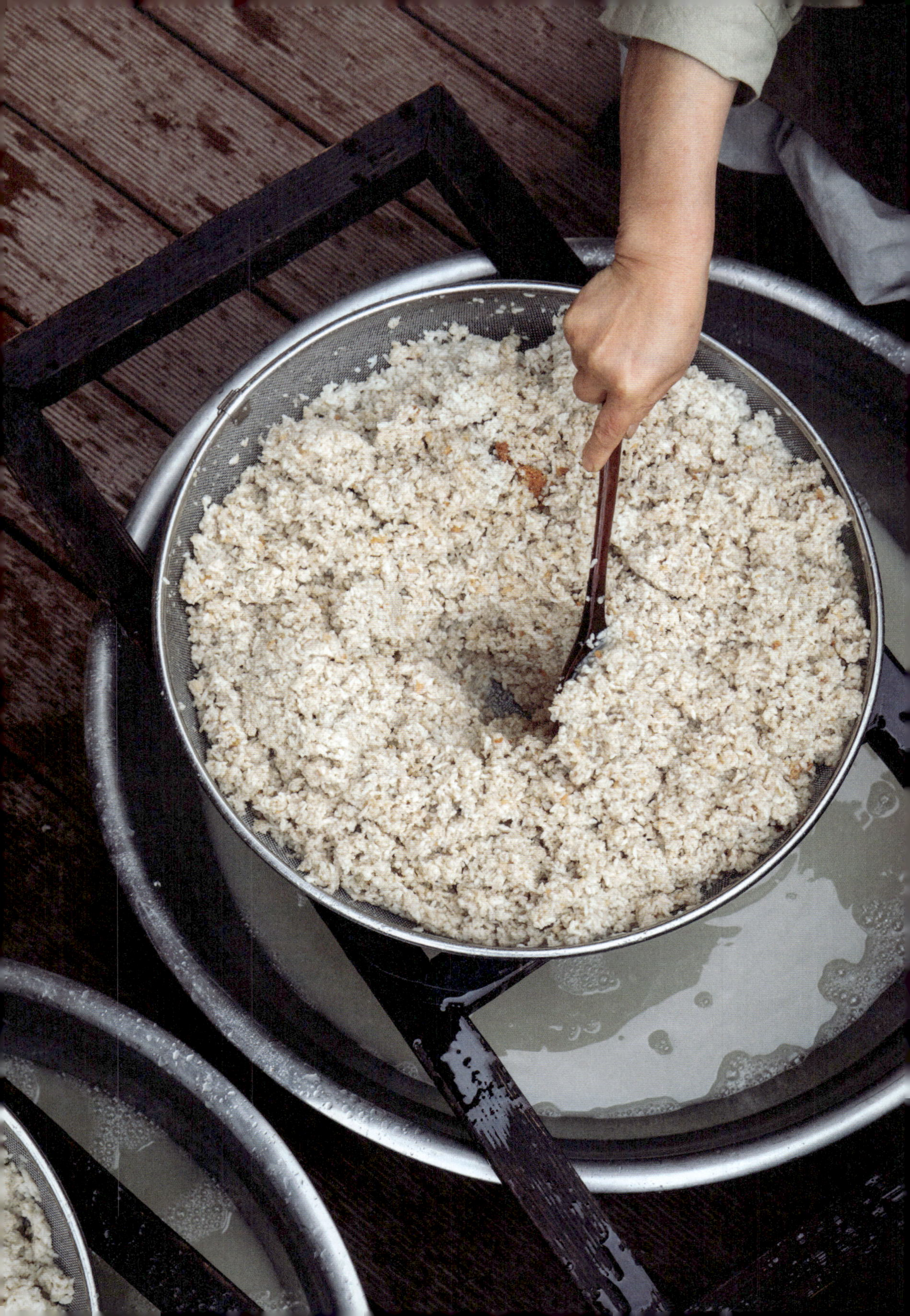

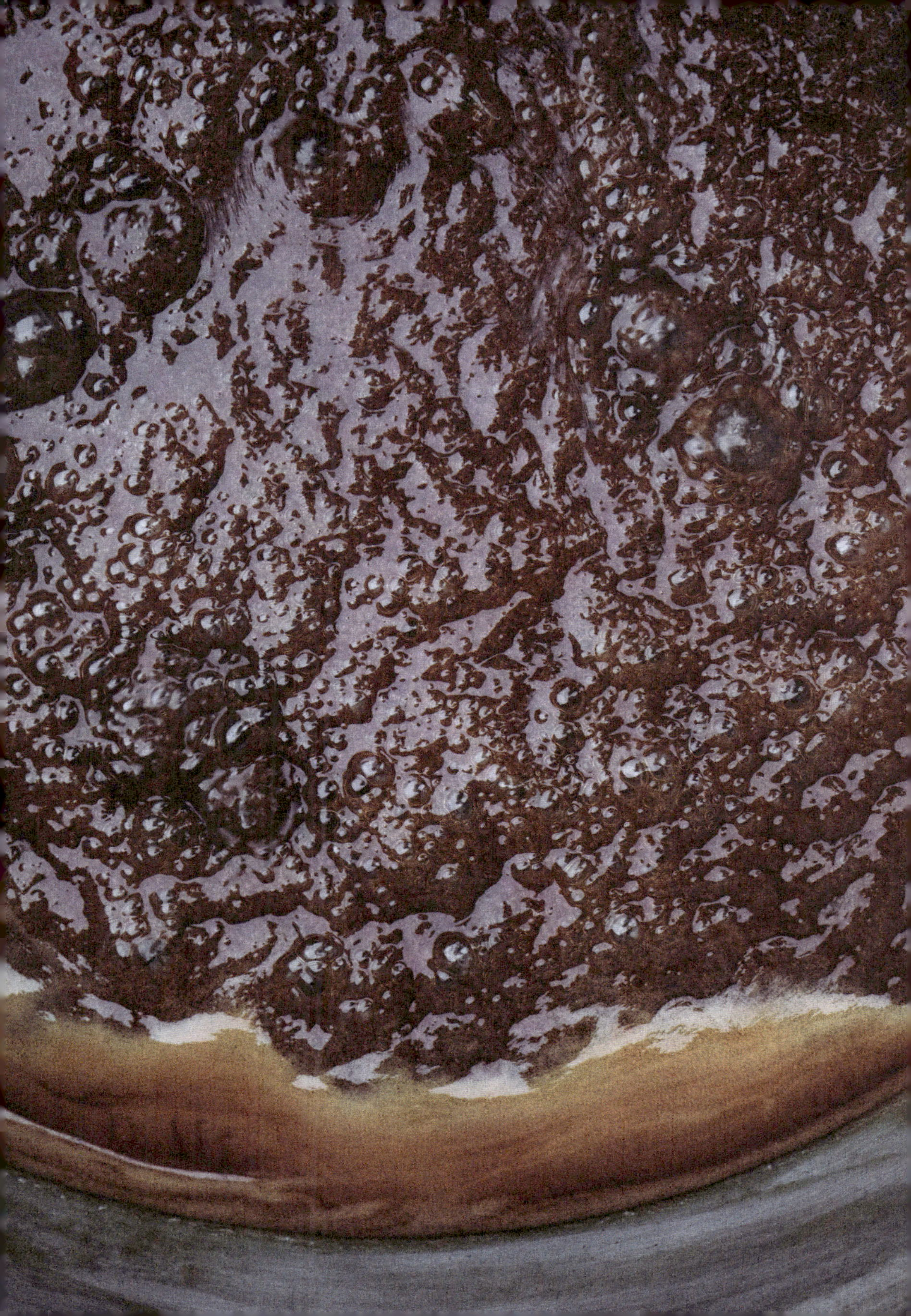

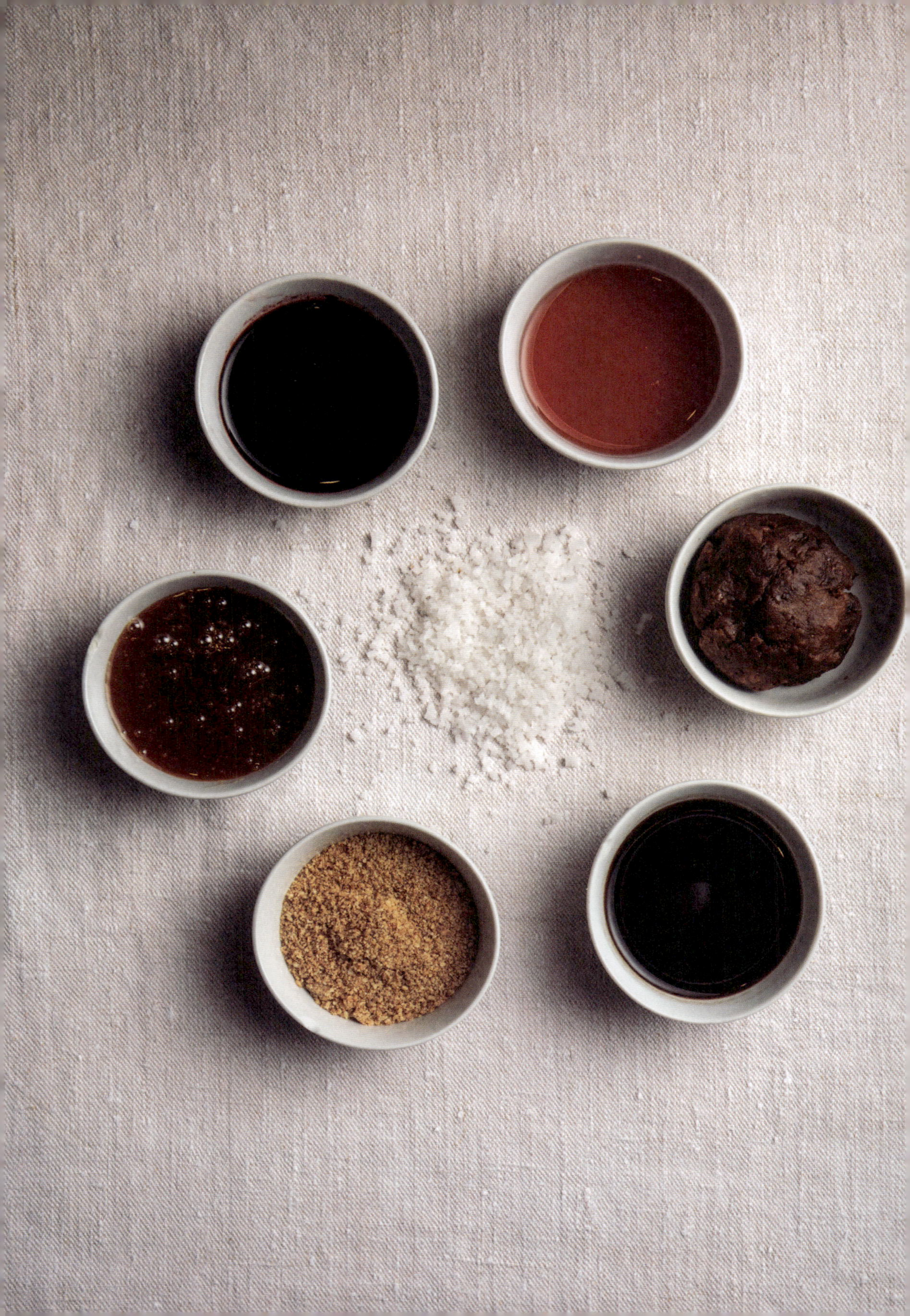

FLAVORINGS

Many people ask Jeongkwan Snim about the secrets behind her food—they want to know if she uses unfamiliar seasonings to create her incomparable flavors. But if you know a bit more about her cooking, two things stand out. One is that she doesn't use many flavorings, but she does make most of them herself. As is the case with temple cooking in general, her cooking is simple in terms of preparation methods, and she uses few ingredients. The other thing is that for Snim, the limits to what constitutes "flavoring" aren't clearly defined. Fruits and vegetables can serve as flavorings, or even products made from grains. How the ingredients are used also makes a difference: fruits and vegetables can be used in different ways depending on whether they're freshly preserved, fully dried, or just-harvested.

Snim mostly uses salt, soy sauce, doenjang, and gochujang as seasonings. She uses coarse sea salt, and because the salt still contains some water, she stores it in sacks for about five years to dry it out completely. Afterwards, the salt feels different; it's grainy and crunchy and tastes slightly sweet.

She makes her own soy sauce, doenjang, and gochujang. She says these seasonings are unique because they're flavored with yew due to her temple being located in the middle of a large, ancient yew forest. Because she prepares her flavorings fresh each year, she has different vintages of them that have developed different colors and various flavor nuances.

She uses a large number of different kinds of cheong that she makes out of fruits and grains and uses them as flavorings, too. Vinegar also forms an important seasoning, and every autumn, Snim makes vinegar from persimmons, grapes, and apples. These vinegars mature via a long process.

Sesame, an ancient crop whose seeds are usually roasted and ground and used as a spice (a highly aromatic oil is also extracted from the seeds) is indispensable. The oil isn't used for frying, only as a flavoring. Just as important is gochu, which has a great variety of flavors and sizes and ranges from tasting very mild to tasting very spicy. It can be prepared as a vegetable or used as a flavoring, often as either a coarse or fine powder. Snim's spice cupboard also contains mustard, *jepi* powder, *hamcho*, coriander, dried flowers, various powdered roots, and cinnamon. The magic of Snim's culinary skills may well lie in the fact that her flavorings are unique. Anyone who makes her recipes should be aware of this!

ABOUT THE RECIPES

Jeongkwan Snim rarely uses a scale or measuring cup. She often says that what you actually need in order to cook is a genuine interest in and in-depth knowledge of ingredients and homemade flavorings. This moves the cooking process along automatically, because then you know which ingredients go well together and what harmonizes best with what. It must be this familiarity with ingredients that gives her hands such confident instincts!

According to Snim, recipes can weigh us down with their overly detailed instructions, take away our curiosity, and inhibit our creativity. That's why our perception of recipes should never be too dogmatic—instead, we should nurture an open exchange with the ideas behind recipes. Not only does everyone have their own preferences, but the ingredients are also all distinct and differ significantly in flavor depending on when in the season we acquire them.

Nevertheless, Snim says that recipes can serve an important purpose when they demonstrate how to handle and prepare an ingredient to show off its individual flavors to their best advantage. Recipes can also give us information about which flavorings taste best with which ingredients. Recipes should also be as simple as possible— they should provide a foundation that gives everyone the opportunity to prepare food according to their own preferences. Having a solid foundation means that cooks will be able to come up with creative solutions whenever they lack particular ingredients. There's always a workable substitute! Still, it's best to always have some crucial basic flavorings on hand.

Snim maintains and honors culinary traditions, but she never stops there—she continues to experiment. The more often we try to develop a proper sense for ingredients in our hands, the better we will get at it, she says.

The recipes in this book have been compiled in this spirit as suggestions and instructions from Snim. Her knowledge and experience have made their way into these pages in a condensed form. Also note that in Korea, a meal is rarely only one dish—instead, there will be several dishes on the table alongside the rice. The more dishes that are available, the smaller the quantity of each dish gets.

The road from recipe to dish can be short or long, depending on how curious a cook is about making new culinary discoveries along the way.

"In the cycle of the seasons, there is actually no beginning and no end," says Jeongkwan Snim. In it, we see the wondrous course

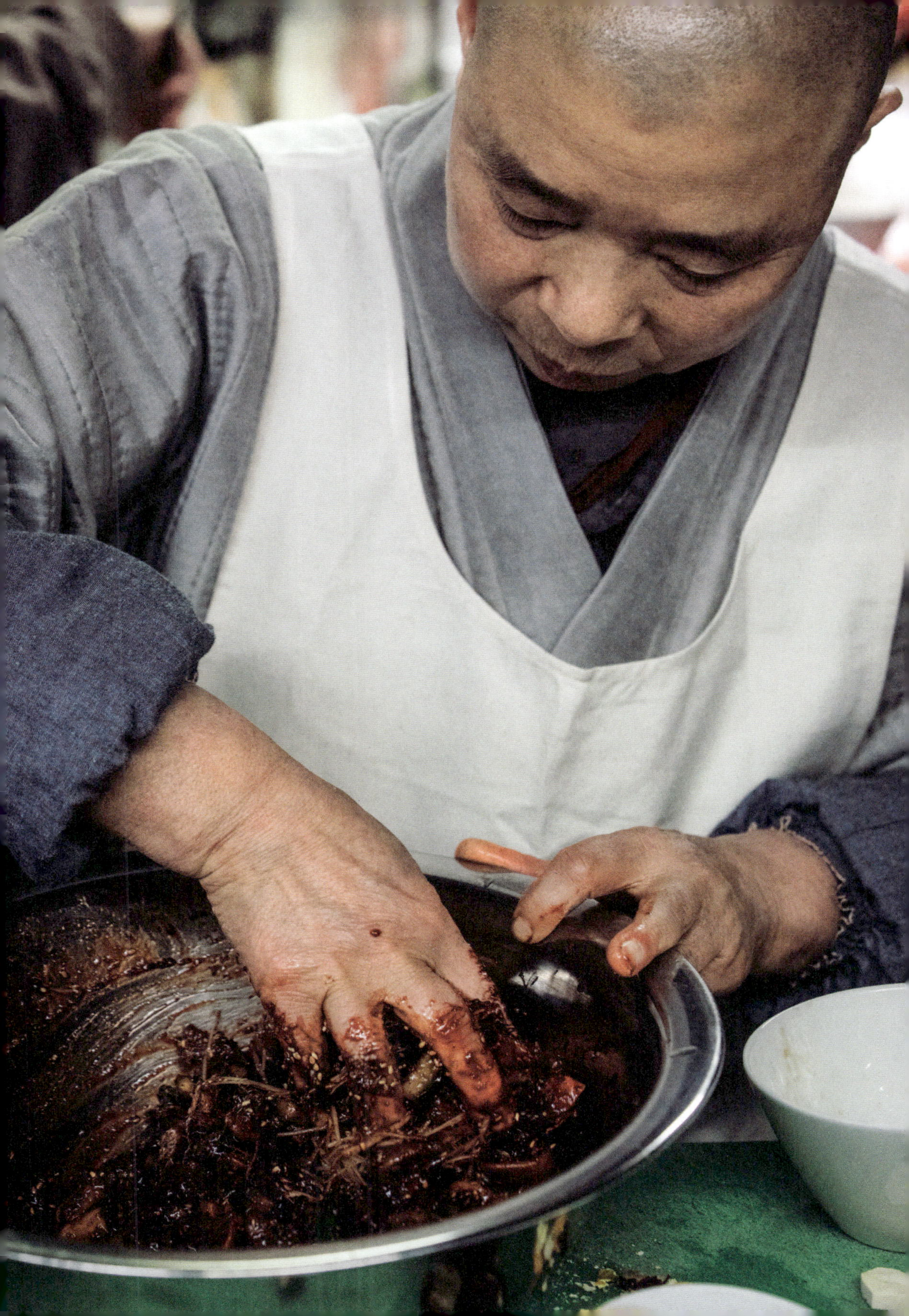

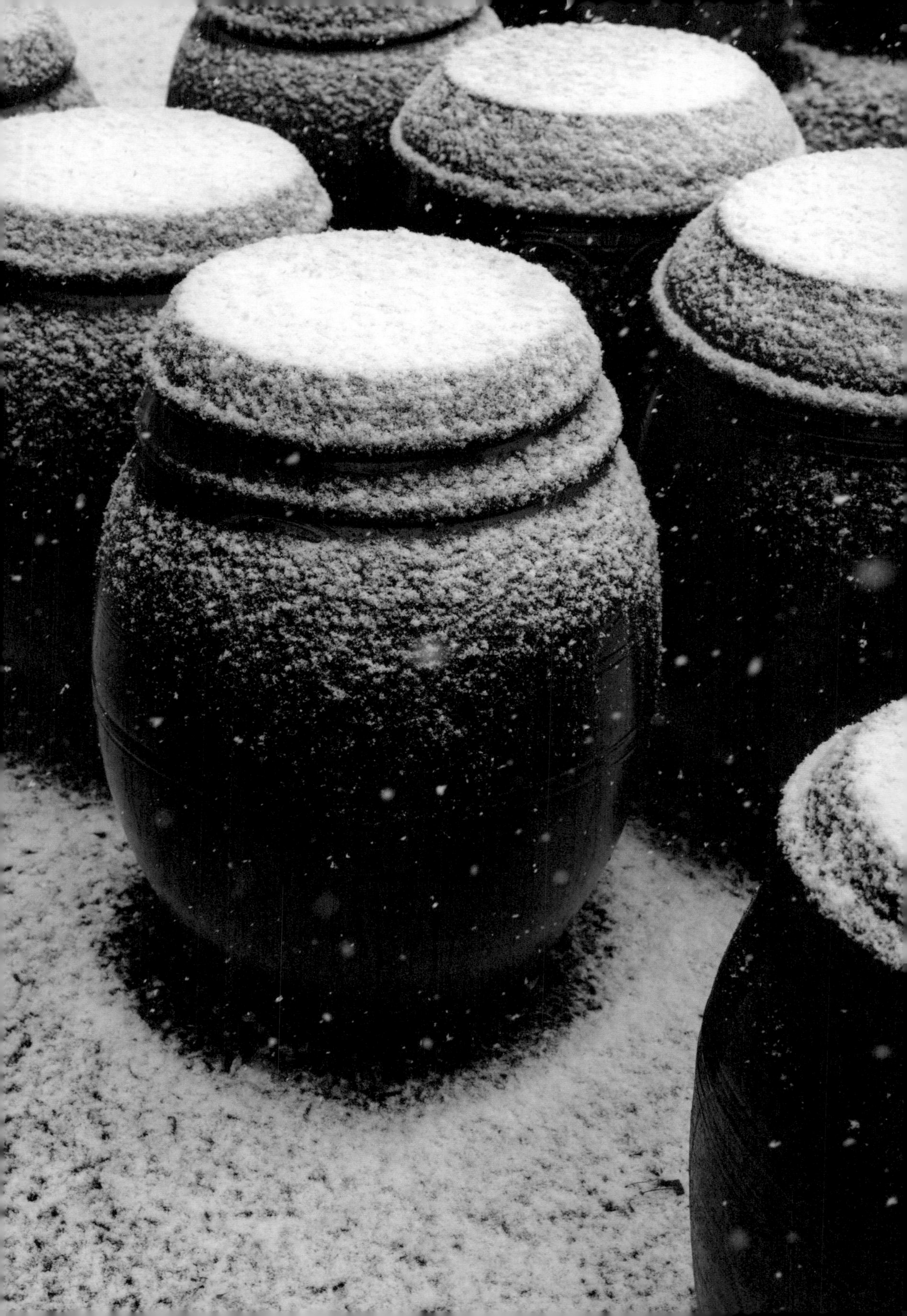

and vitality of nature. Our lives are embedded in it; nature provides us with food. It prescribes a rhythm for us, and it is sensible for us to follow it. The Buddha himself said that we should nourish ourselves naturally if we want to remain healthy.

The body requires different things as the seasons change. That means it's important to know what nature has available for us and how to use nature's bounty wisely. Each season lends our foods unique textures, colors, and beauty because each seasonal ingredient contains its own set of nutrients, aromas, and flavors.

WINTER

Snim says that winter is the time of waiting and endurance. Outside, it's cold, windy, and hostile to life. Nature withdraws into itself. Even so, seeds are already buried within the warm, protective soil, waiting to sprout again. New vital forces gather in the darkness. But we must rely on what we have stored! A few winterproof grains and vegetables exhibit a special vitality that allows them to defy the cold; these are the foods we observe and savor.

During winter, Snim likes to use winter vegetables like spinach, cabbage, and *naengi* alongside various dried items: namul, seaweed, mushrooms, beans, and fruits that she spent all of summer preparing. In spring or summer, when everything is available in abundance, she thinks ahead to winter and makes provisions accordingly. (For example, squash will keep well into the cold season.) Different holidays like the year-end party and New Year's occur during winter, and special dishes must be prepared for them, including in the temple. Communal meals dispel the cold and darkness!

Rice with Millet and Mushrooms — 202
Seaweed Soup — 204
New Year's Rice Cake Soup — 208
Squash Soup with Millet — 212
Dried Radish Slices with Doenjang — 214
Spinach with Soy Sauce and Sesame Seeds — 216
Dumplings with Mushrooms and Vegetables — 218
Tofu with Naengi Braised in Soy Sauce — 222
Pancakes with Napa Cabbage and Radish — 224
Deep-Fried Ginseng — 226

Modum beoseot gijang jobap

RICE WITH MILLET AND MUSHROOMS

2½ cups (500 g) short-grain rice (ssal)
½ cup (100 g) yellow millet (gijang)
4 white button mushrooms
4 fresh Korean shiitake mushrooms (pyogo beoseot)
2 king oyster mushrooms (saesongi beoseot)
½ pound (200 g) oyster mushrooms (neutari beoseot)
¼ pound (100 g) dried wood ear mushrooms (mogi beoseot)
1 tablespoon soy sauce (ganjang)
Salt for seasoning
1 tablespoon sesame oil (chamgireum)

Rinse the rice and the millet and soak them in water for 20 minutes.

Remove the stalks from the white button mushrooms and the shiitakes and slice the caps into ⅛ inch (3 mm) slices. Halve the king oyster mushrooms lengthwise and cut the pieces into slices of the same thickness. Tear the oyster mushrooms into bite-sized pieces. Soak the wood ear mushrooms in warm water for 20 minutes, then tear them into bite-sized pieces as well. Mix all the mushrooms together and season them with soy sauce and salt.

Add the rice and millet to a pot with an equal quantity of water. Layer the mushrooms over the top and drizzle them with sesame oil.

Bring the mushrooms to a boil. When the water bubbles, reduce the heat, cover the pot, and simmer until the mushrooms have absorbed the liquid.

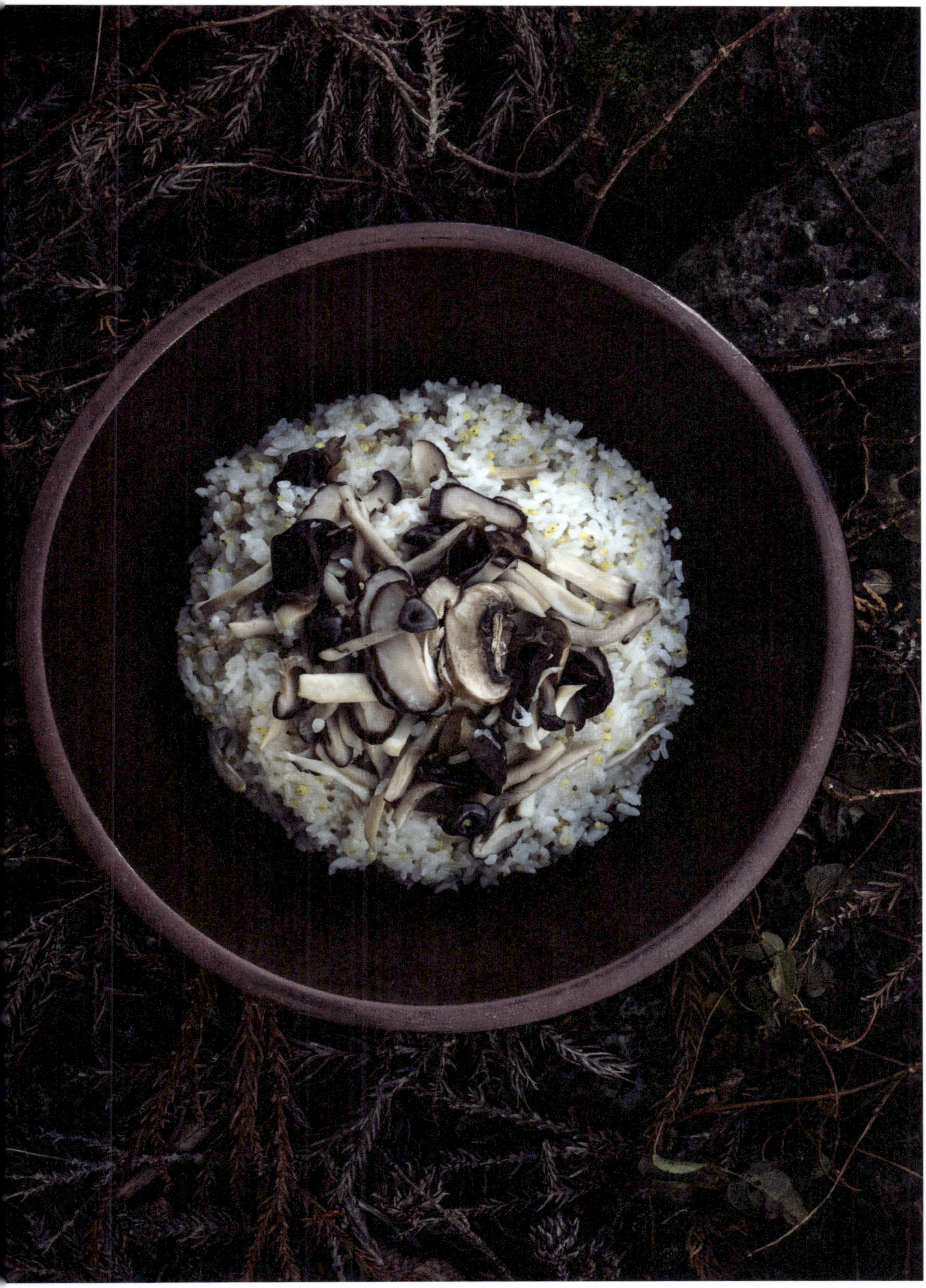

Fresh *miyeok* is simple to prepare, but when it's dried, it must be rinsed and soaked before cooking. Watch the quantity—soaking miyeok increases its volume significantly! Also, miyeok has a high mineral content. This soup is served for birthdays in Korea because mothers eat it for a while following childbirth.

Miyeokguk

SEAWEED SOUP

1 cup (15 g) wakame seaweed (miyeok), dried
2 medium potatoes (gamja)
2 dried Korean shiitake mushrooms (pyogo beoseot)
12½ cups (3 L) water, divided
2 tablespoons sesame oil (chamgireum)
2 tablespoons soy sauce (ganjang)
Salt for seasoning

Soak the dried seaweed for 20 minutes and then rinse it thoroughly.

Peel the potatoes and cut them into pieces with a knife. Remove the stalks from the mushrooms. Rinse them, then tear them into pieces.

Bring half of the water to a boil. Add the potatoes and mushrooms and bring them back to a boil.

Cut the seaweed into pieces 1¼ inch (3 cm) long and add it to the pot. If desired, you can sauté the seaweed, potatoes, and mushrooms in sesame oil before adding it.

The water should ultimately cover everything, but don't add the remaining water all at once! Instead, add it in two batches as you're boiling the soup. After the first addition, cover the pot with a lid and bring it back to a boil; after you pour in the rest of the water, leave the pot uncovered and let it boil for a bit longer. When it begins to smell of the ocean, season the soup to taste with soy sauce, sesame oil, and salt.

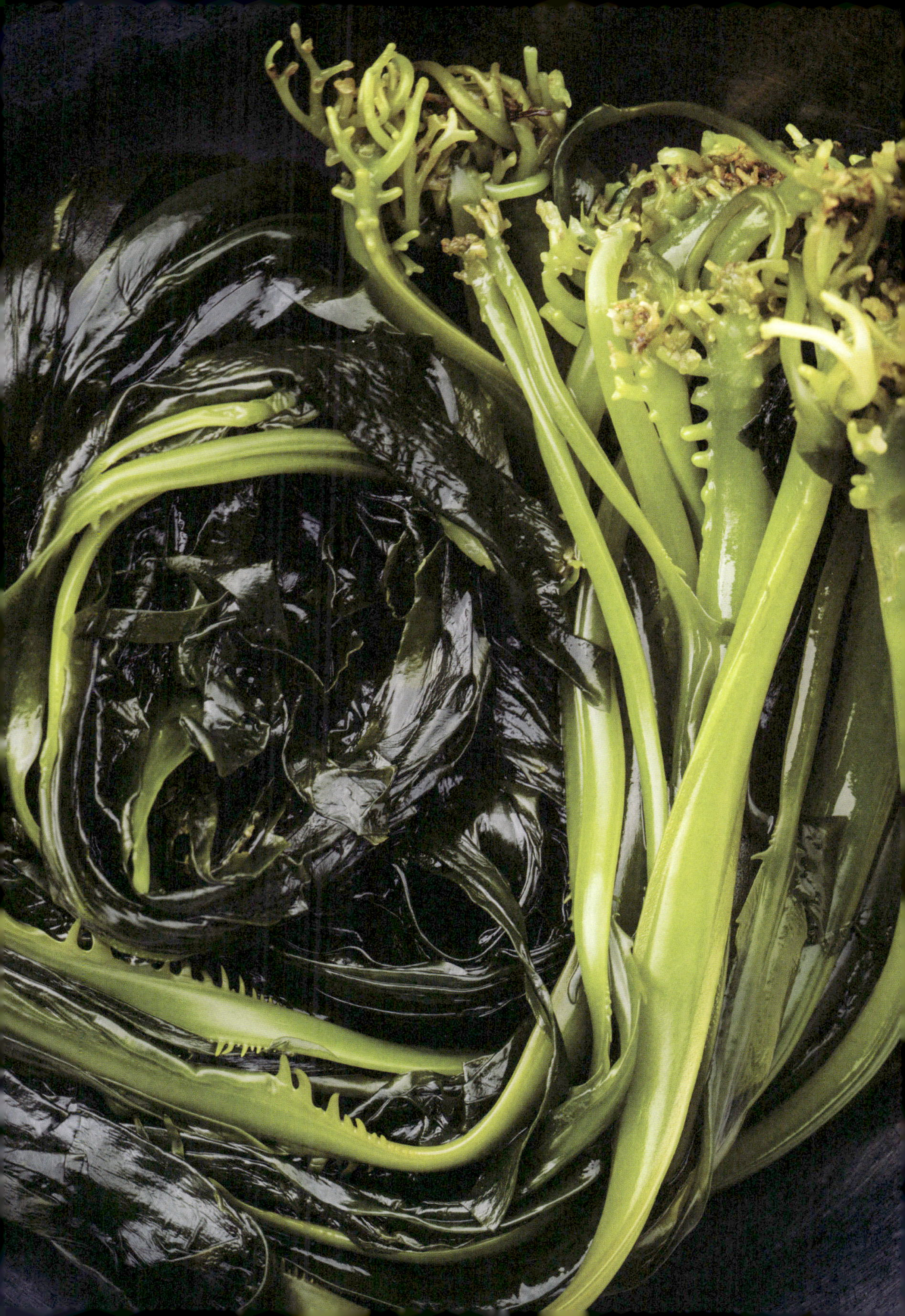

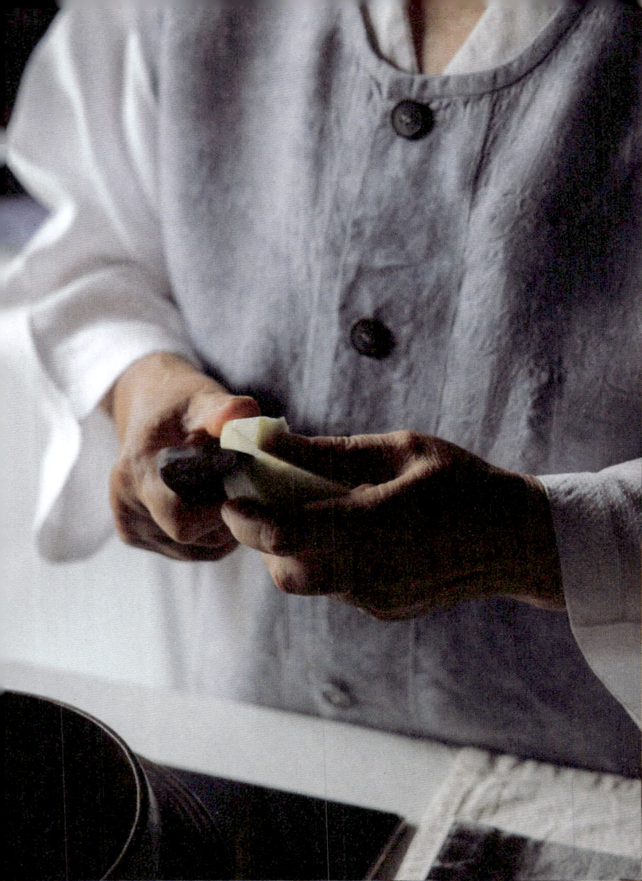
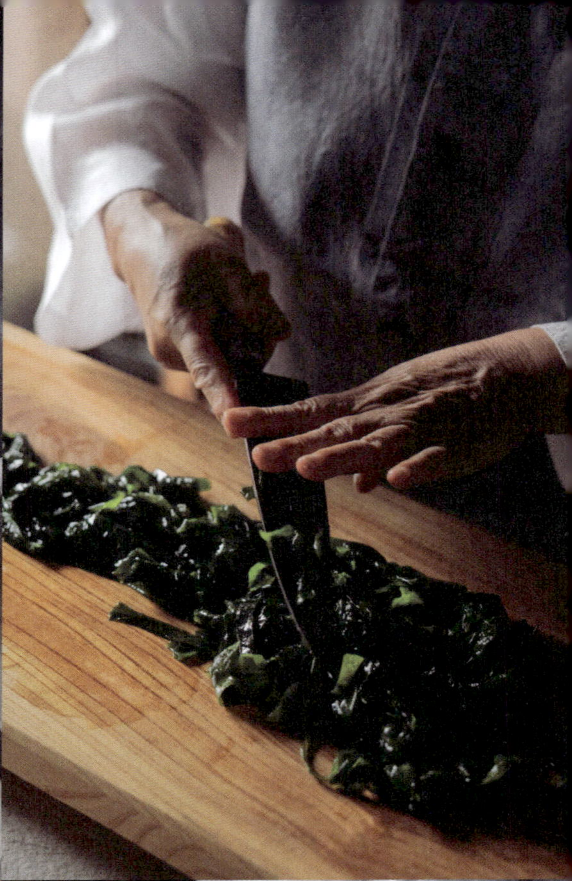
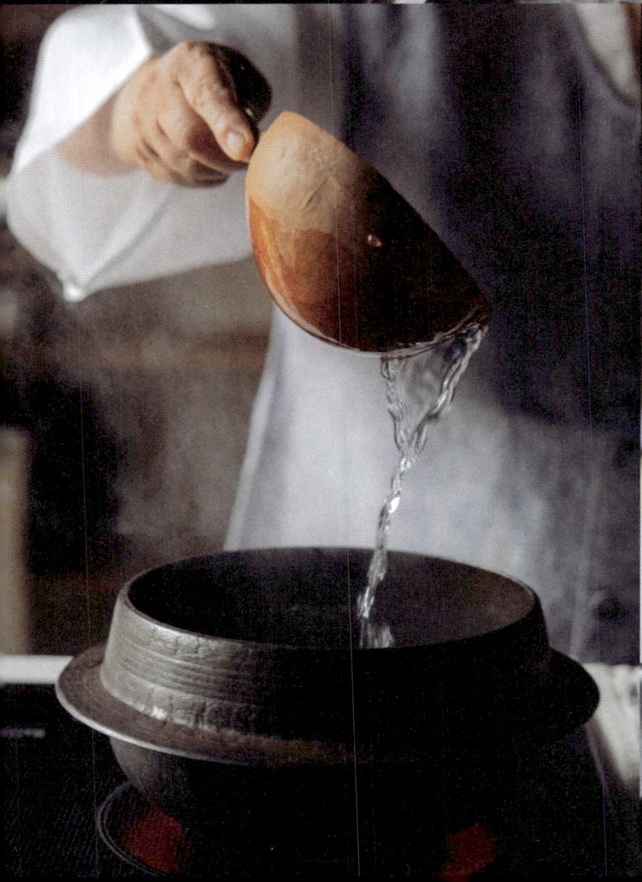
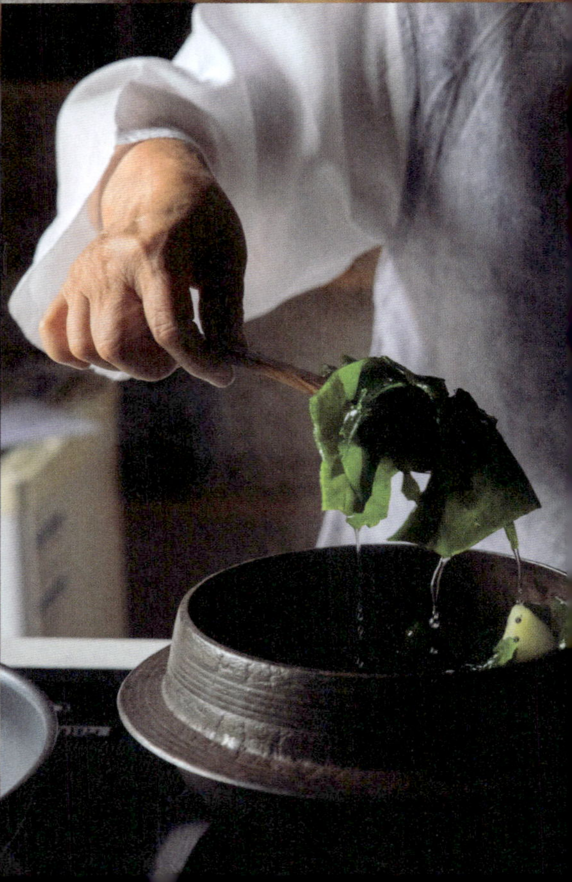

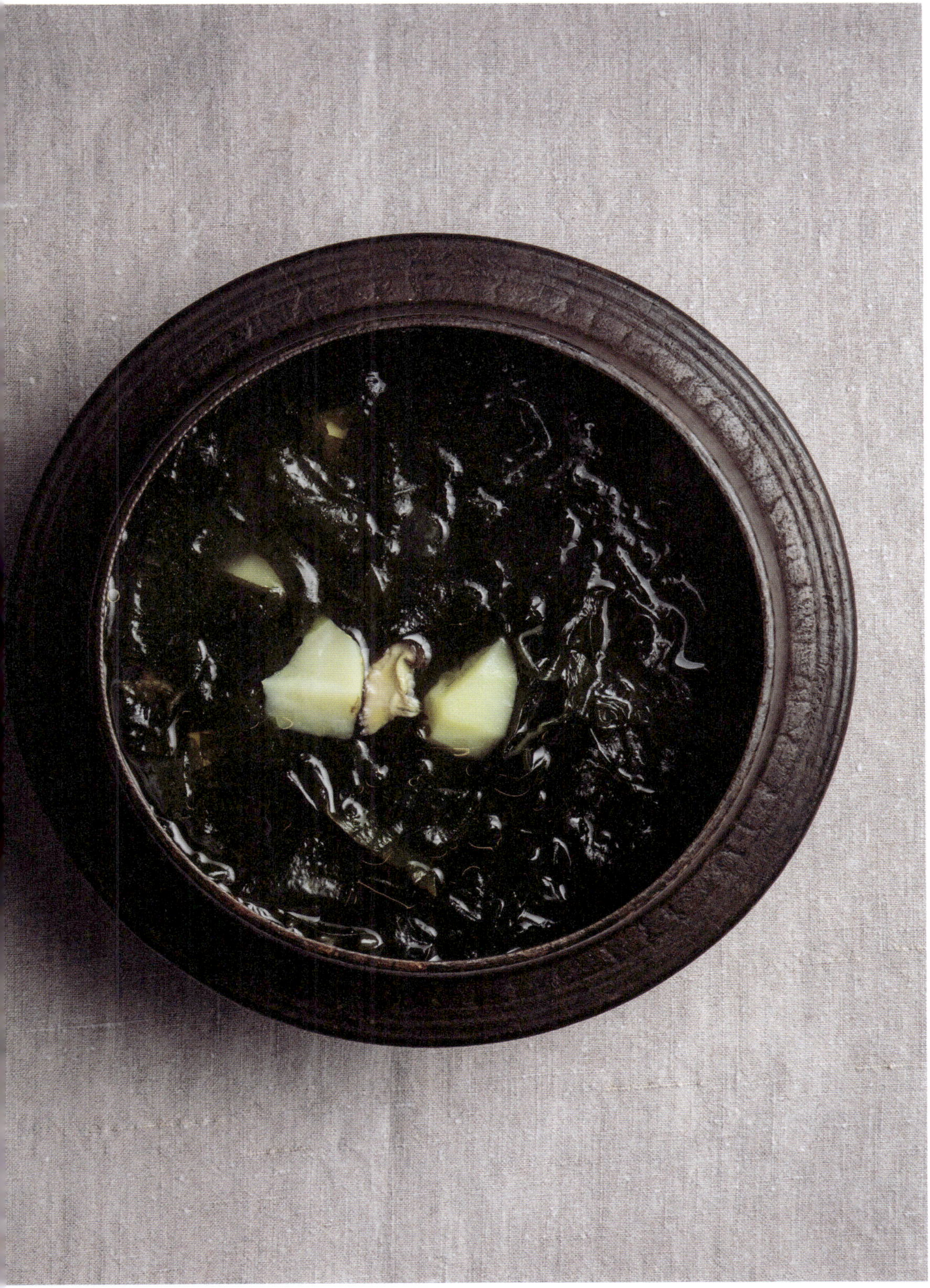

Jeongwol tteokguk

NEW YEAR'S RICE CAKE SOUP

7 ounces (200 g) firm tofu (dubu)
1 sheet of dried seaweed (gim)
8½ cups (2 L) water
3 tablespoons soy sauce (ganjang)
Salt for seasoning
Korean shiitake mushrooms (pyogo beoseot), fresh or dried
1⅓ cups (400 g) rice cakes (tteokguk tteok), sliced
1 cup (30 g) spinach (sigeumchi)
Soy sauce for seasoning
1 tablespoon sesame oil (chamgireum)

Soak the rice cakes in water for a few minutes.

Rinse the tofu with water and slightly pat it dry. Brown it slowly in a dry pan over medium heat until golden. Remove to a cutting board or plate.

Briefly toast the seaweed sheet in the same pan. Slice the browned tofu thinly on an angle.

In a pot, bring the water to a boil; add the soy sauce and salt.

Cut the mushrooms into strips (if using dried mushrooms, soak them before this step). Add the mushrooms and rice cakes to the pot. When the rice cakes float, they're cooked. Now add the tofu.

Rinse the spinach, separate the leaves, and add it to the pot. Bring the soup back to a boil. Season to taste with soy sauce and salt.

Crumble the seaweed by hand and sprinkle it over the soup, then drizzle the soup with sesame oil before serving it.

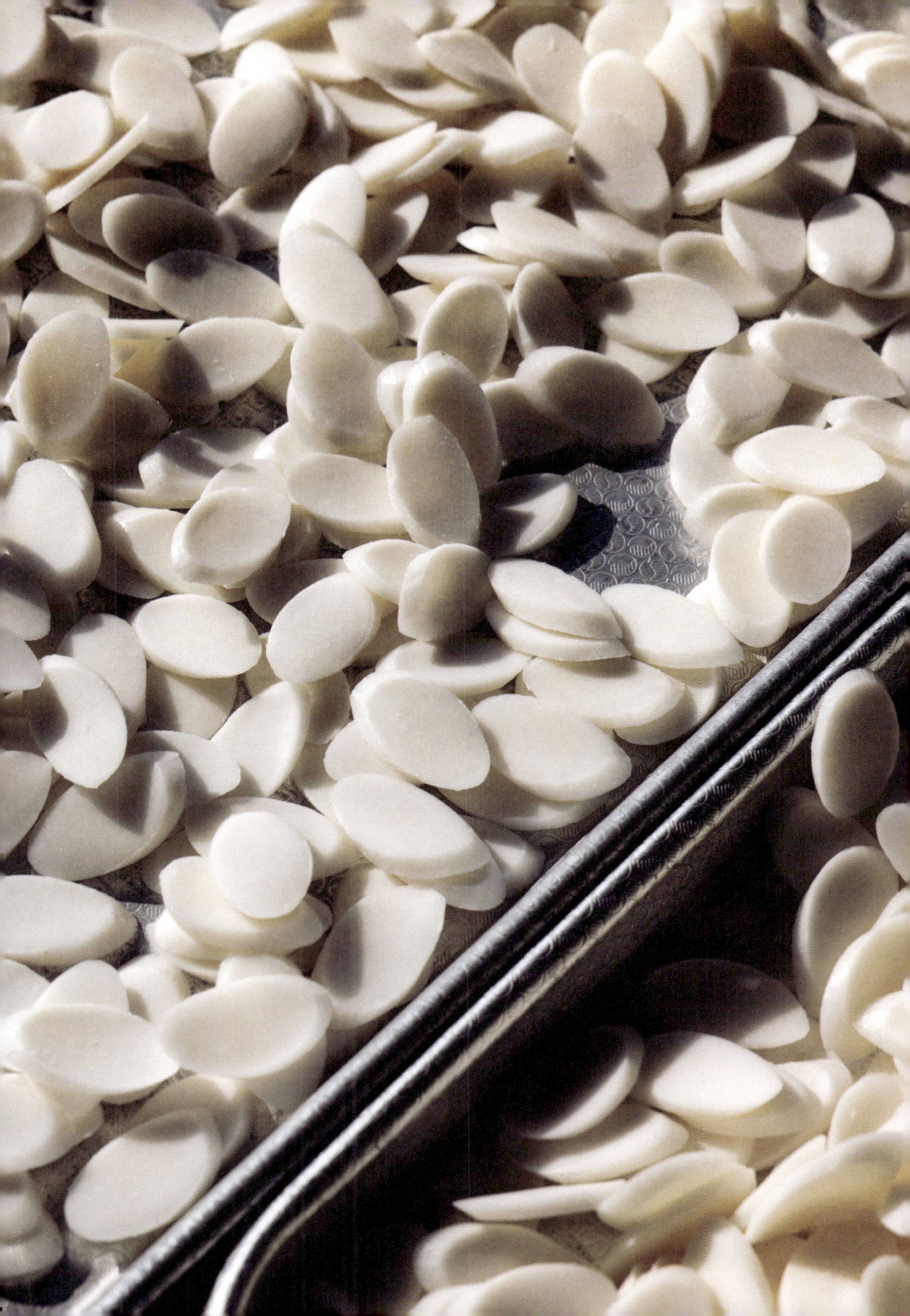

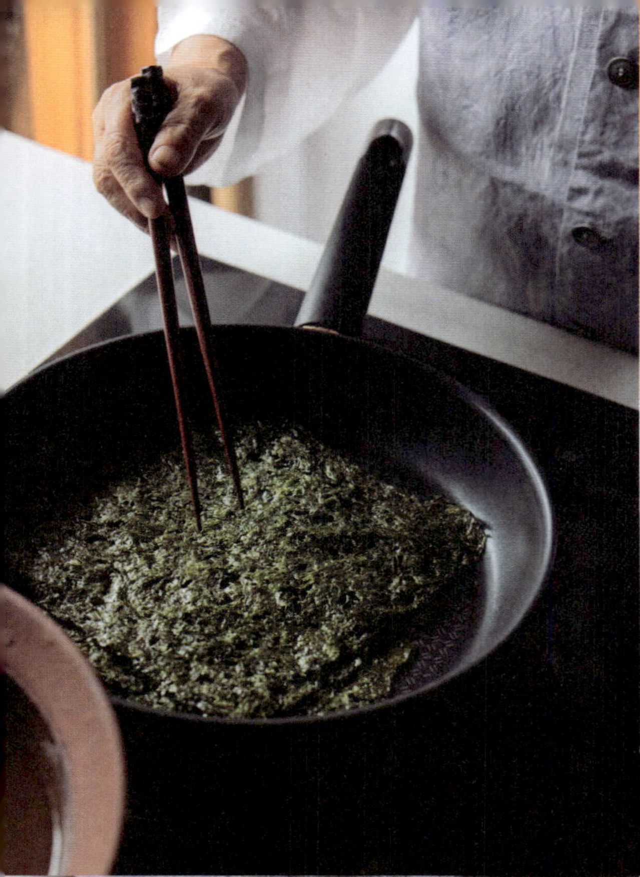
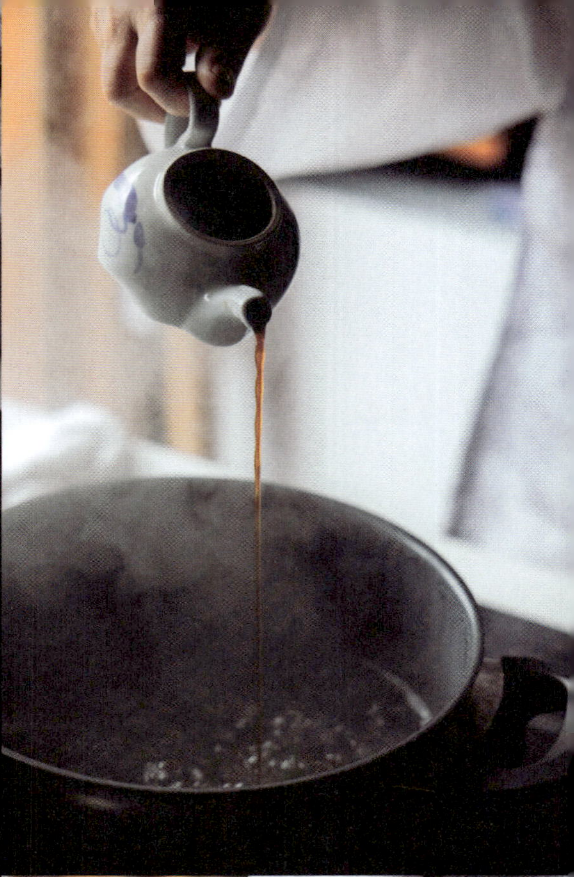
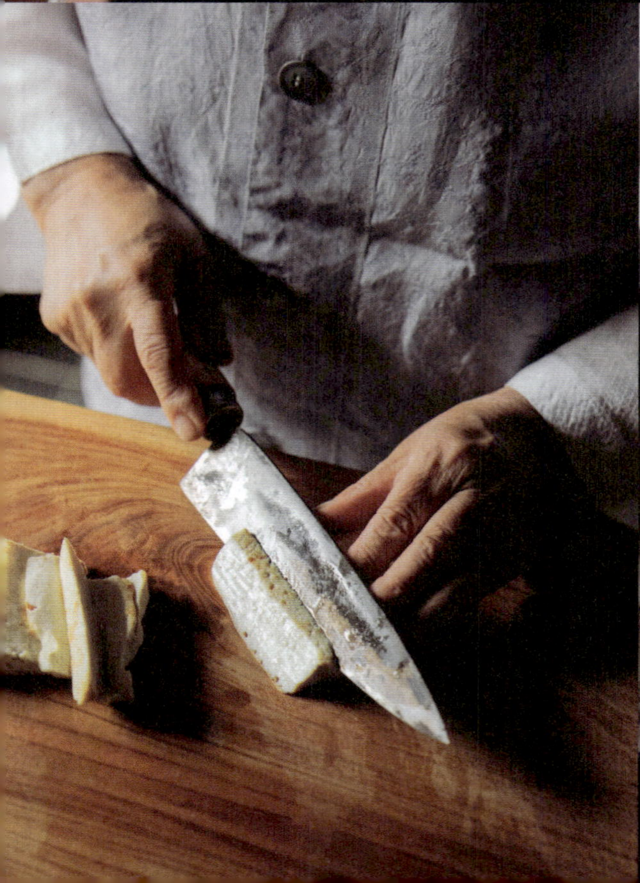
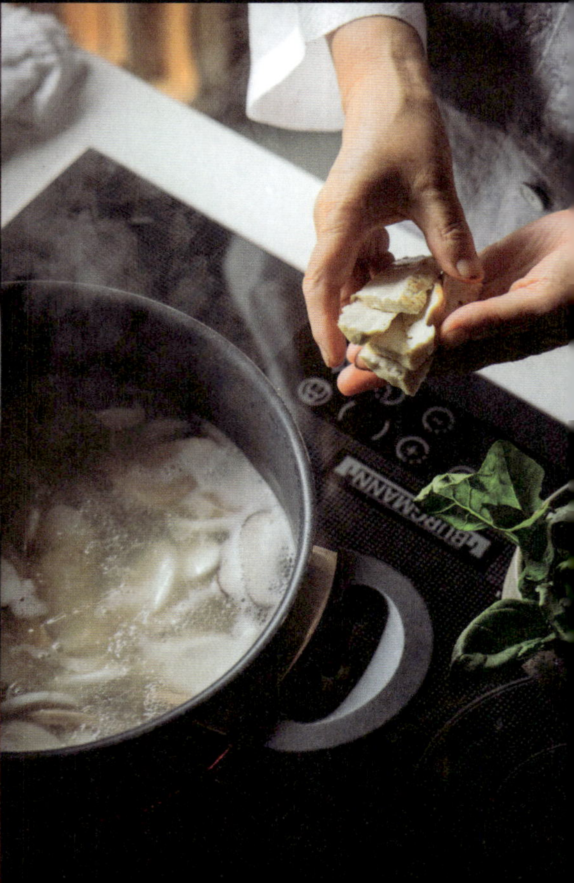

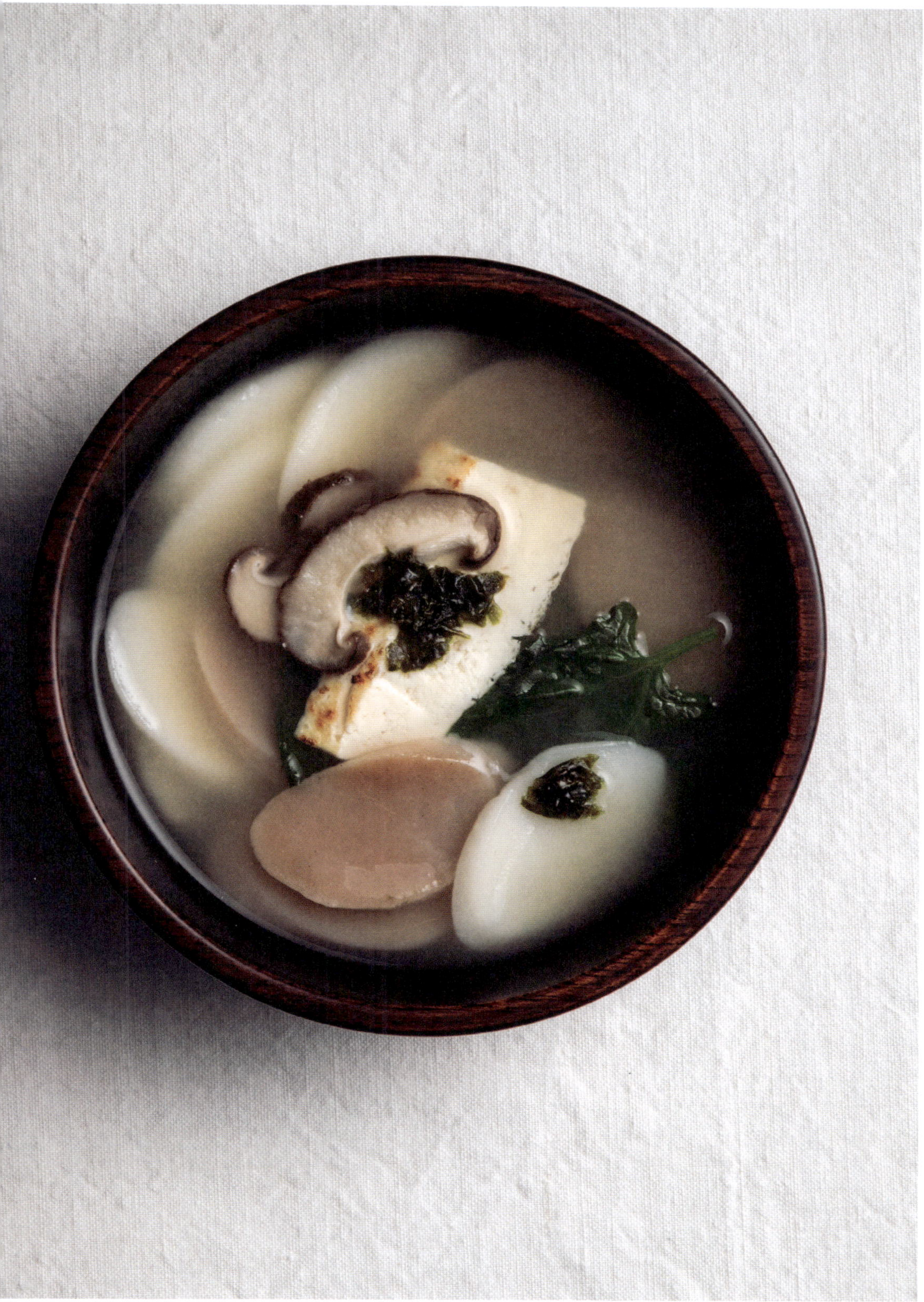

Neulgeun-hobak gijang-juk

SQUASH SOUP WITH MILLET

⅔ pound (300 g) calabaza or butternut squash (neulgeun-hobak)
4¼ cups (1 L) water
½ cup (100 g) yellow millet (gijang)
Salt for seasoning

Peel the squash and cut it into wedges. Scrape out the seeds and cut it into moderately thin slices.

Place the squash pieces in a pot and cover them with the water. Add the millet and simmer over medium heat, stirring frequently with a wooden spoon.

When the squash is tender and the millet is cooked, season the soup to taste with salt.

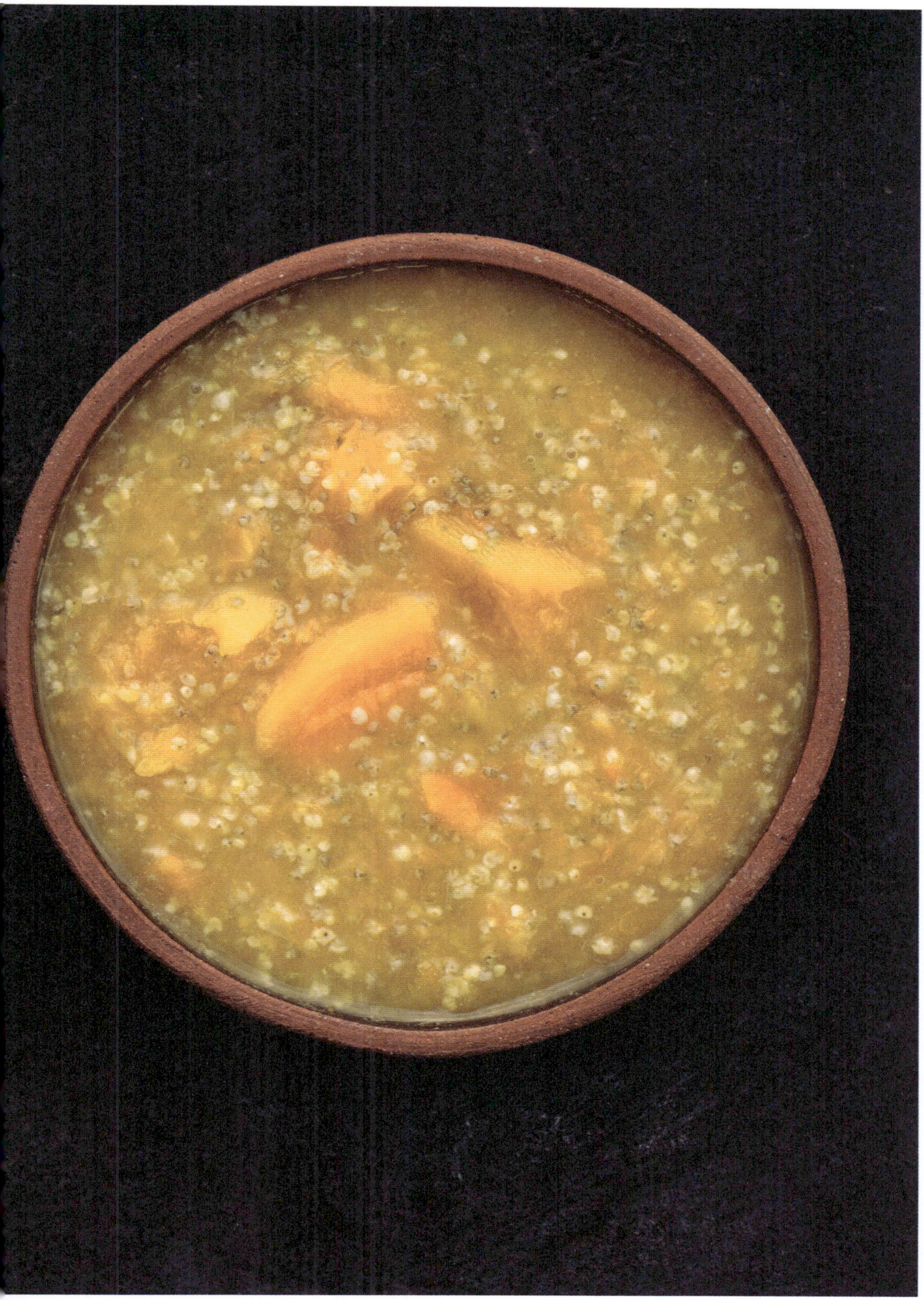

Mumallaengi doenjang muchim

DRIED RADISH SLICES WITH DOENJANG

3½ cups (400 g) white radish slices (mumallaengi), dried
5 teaspoons salt, divided
⅓ cup (70 ml) Maesil-Cheong (page 174), divided
⅓ cup (30 g) ginger (saenggang)
3 tablespoons sun-dried red chile peppers (hoenari-gochu), chopped
⅔ cup (150 g) glutinous rice paste (chapssalpul, page 412)
½ cup (150 g) fermented soybean paste (doenjang)
6 tablespoons (90 ml) Bokbunja-Cheong (page 180)
⅓ cup (100 g) Rice Syrup (Jocheong, page 190)
3 tablespoons sesame seeds (kkae), crushed
6 tablespoons (90 ml) soy sauce (ganjang)

Wash the radish slices and drain them, then mix 3 teaspoons salt with 4 teaspoons (20 ml) maesil-cheong. Pour the maesil-cheong over the slices, mix well, and let stand for 20 minutes. Then squeeze out the slices well.

Slice the ginger into fine strips and mince the chilies coarsely.

In a bowl, mix the glutinous rice paste, doenjang, bokbunja-cheong, remaining maesil-cheong and salt, jocheong, sesame seeds, and soy sauce to form a sauce.

Add the radish slices to a bowl along with the chilies and ginger and mix together. Pour the sauce over them and mix well.

Firmly press the radishes in a lidded container, cover, and let them mature at room temperature for 7 days. Afterwards, store them in the refrigerator. The radishes will keep in the refrigerator for 2 to 3 weeks.

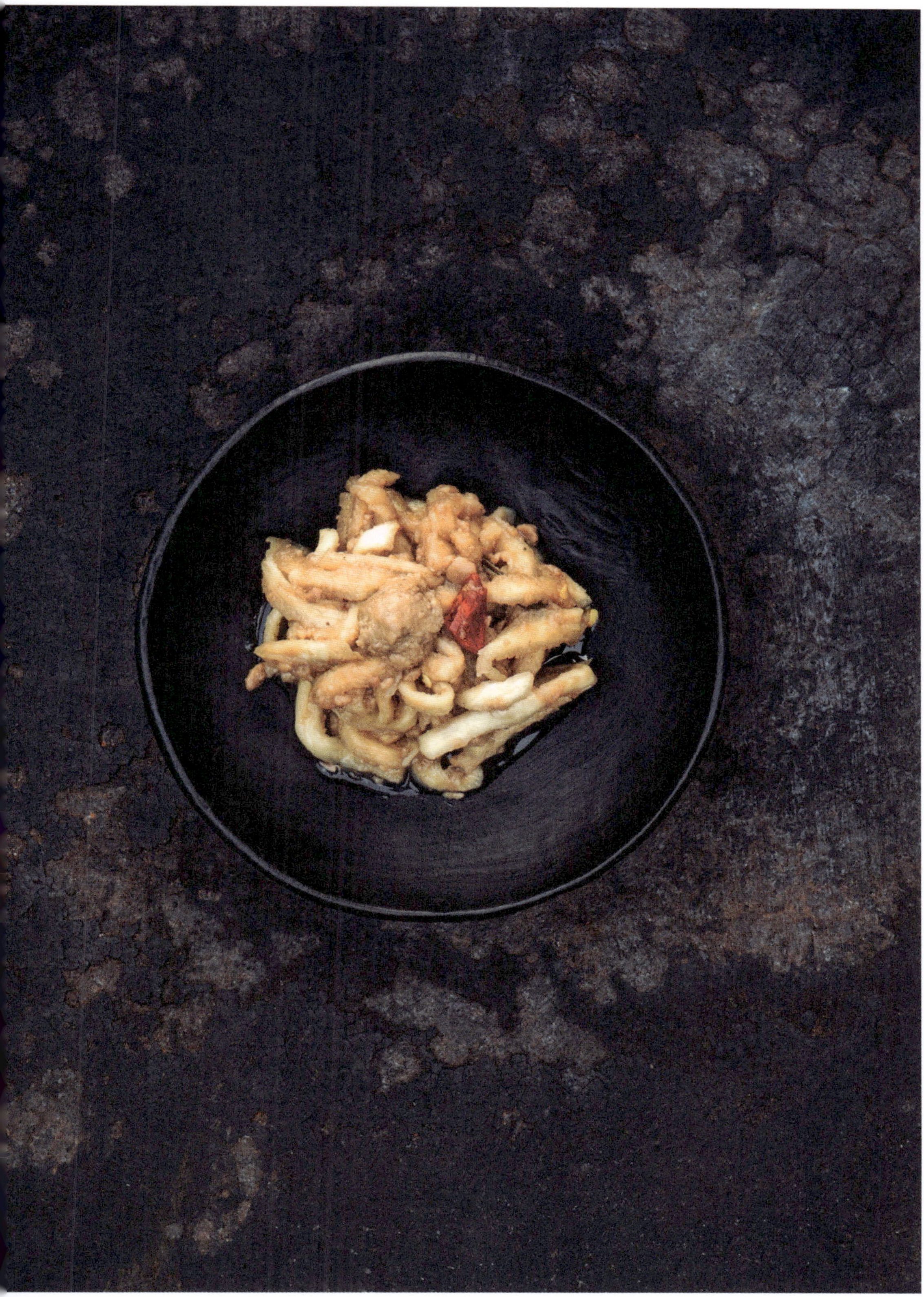

Sigeumchi muchim

SPINACH WITH SOY SAUCE AND SESAME SEEDS

7 cups (200 g) spinach (sigeumchi)
Salt for seasoning
1 tablespoon sesame oil (chamgireum)
1 tablespoon soy sauce (ganjang)
2 teaspoons toasted sesame seeds (kkae), (page 431), coarsely crushed

Remove the roots and the brown outer leaves from the spinach and rinse it well. Blanch it in boiling salted water, gently stirring it a few times.

Remove the spinach from the heat and immediately shock it in cold water to stop the cooking process. Drain it and squeeze it out well.

Add the spinach to a bowl and separate and loosen the leaves by hand. Season it with sesame oil, soy sauce, and sesame seeds. Shake it lightly and turn it gently with your hands.

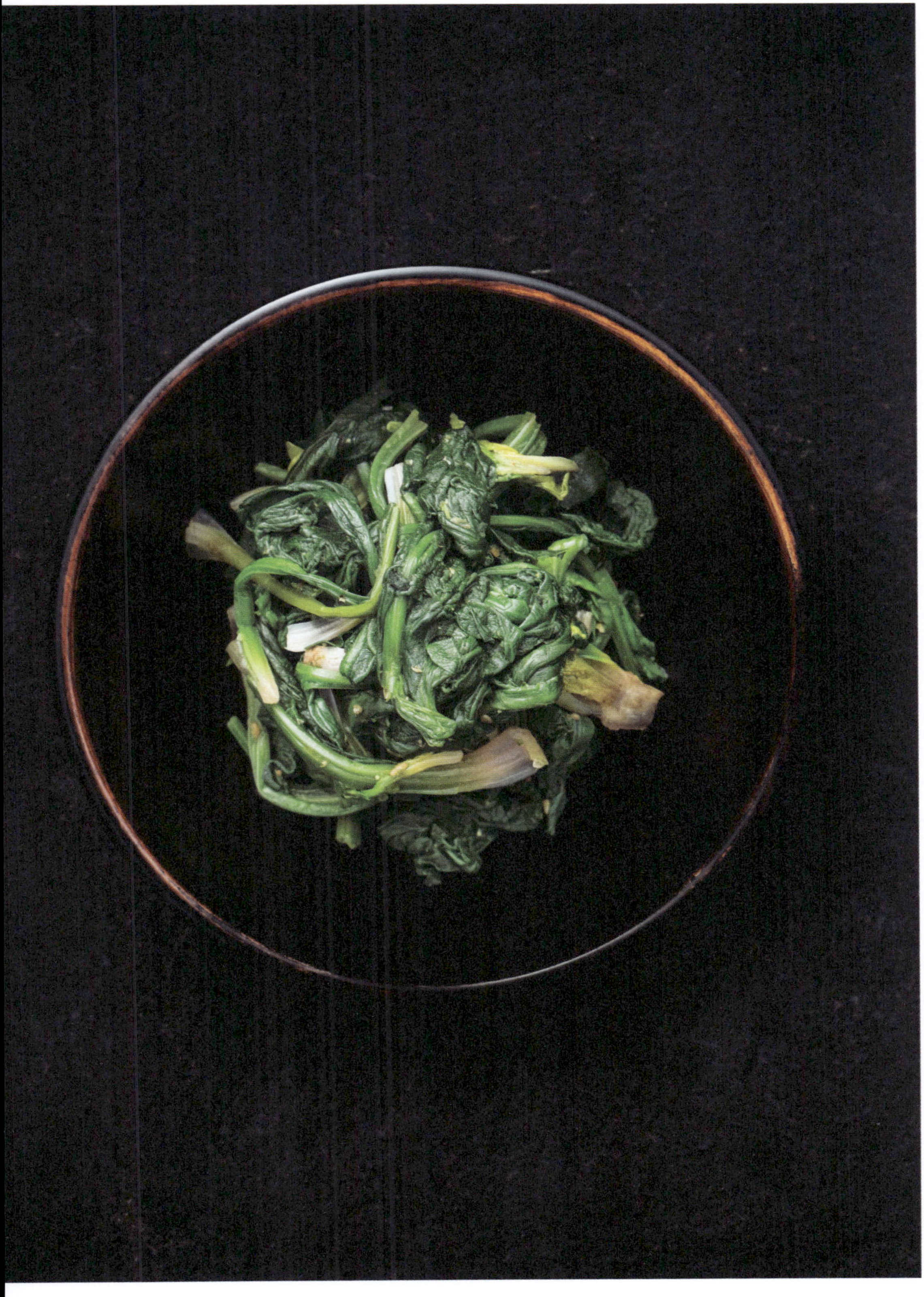

Mandu dumplings are eaten for holiday meals on *Chuseok*, the Buddha's birthday, New Year's Day, and the Moon Festival. Rice cake soup (page 208) and *nokdu* bean pancakes are also eaten on these days.

Neungi deulkkae sunmandu

DUMPLINGS WITH MUSHROOMS AND VEGETABLES

For the dough
2 ¼ cups (280 g) all-purpose flour
1 tablespoon salt
1 cup (250 ml) water
2 tablespoons perilla oil (deulgireum)

For the filling
½ cup (30 g) dried shingled hedgehog mushrooms (neungi beoseot)
2 tablespoons soy sauce (ganjang)
1 tablespoon perilla oil (deulgireum)
½ cup (50 g) zucchini (aehobak)
¾ cup (20 g) perilla leaves (deulkkaennip)
1 long red and 1 long green chile pepper (cheongyanggochu)
1 pound 1½ ounces (500 g) tofu (dubu)
Soy sauce for seasoning
2 tablespoons toasted sesame seeds (kkae, page 431), coarsely crushed
Salt for seasoning
2 tablespoons sesame oil (chamgireum)
Sichuan chili powder (jepi) for seasoning

Mix the flour and salt in a bowl. Gradually add the water and mix into a dough. Pour in the perilla oil and continue to knead.

Place the dough on a floured board and cut it into equal-sized portions. Roll out the individual dough pieces with a rolling pin and lay them out for filling.

Clean and rinse the mushrooms and soak them for 30 minutes. Squeeze them well and then chop them finely. Season them with soy sauce and perilla oil. Sauté them briefly, then set them aside.

Finely chop the zucchini, perilla leaves, and chilies. Rinse the tofu, pat it dry with a kitchen towel, pull it apart with your fingers, and form it into a soft mass.

Add the chopped vegetables to a bowl and mix well; add the tofu and mix again. The ratio of vegetables to tofu should be 1:2. Season with some soy sauce, sesame seeds, salt, sesame oil, and Sichuan pepper powder.

Working with one piece of dough at a time, place an appropriate amount of filling on it, wet its edges with some water, and fold it closed to form a dumpling. Place the dumplings in a steamer pot with some space between each dumpling so they won't stick together. Steam them for about 10 minutes.

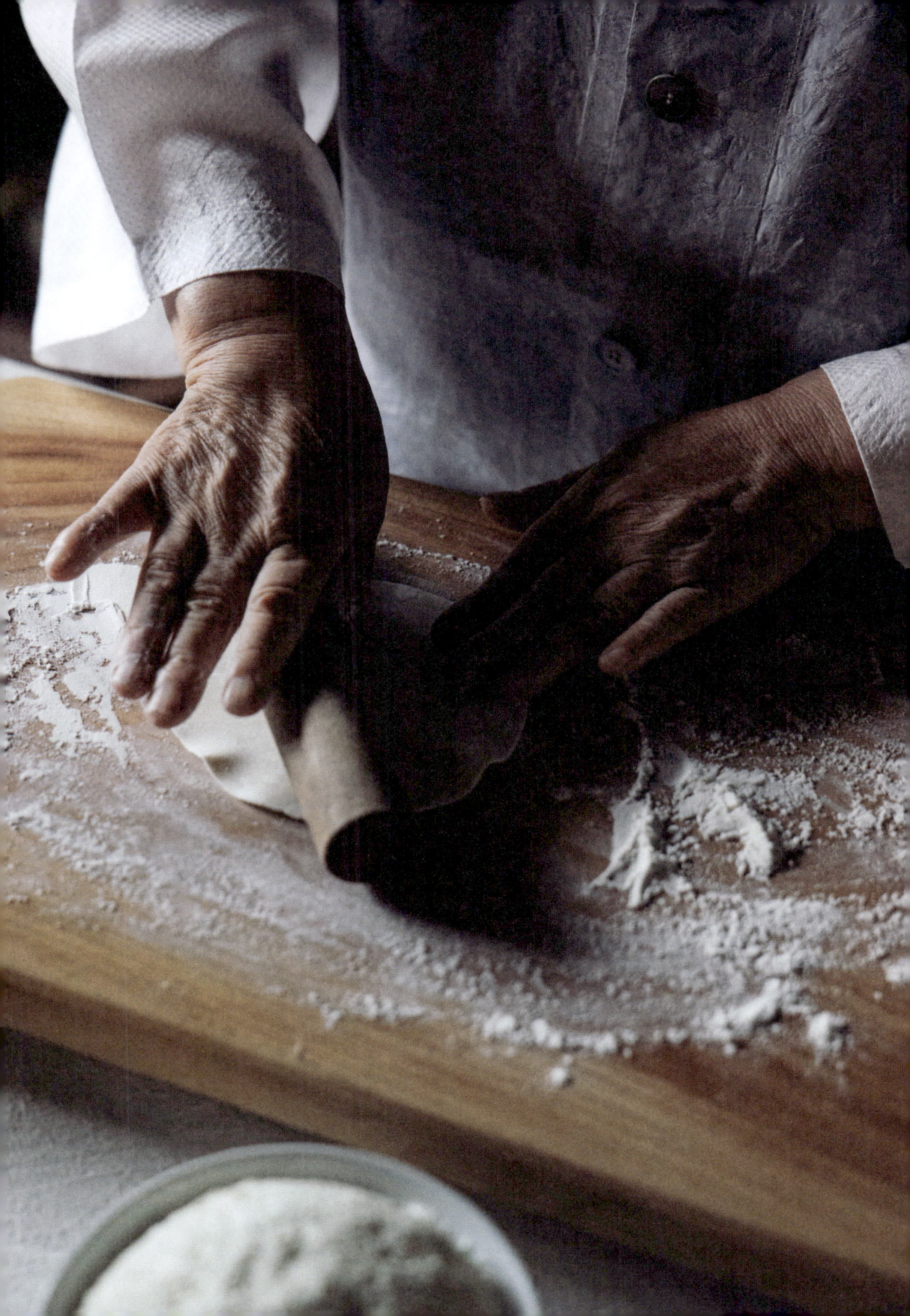

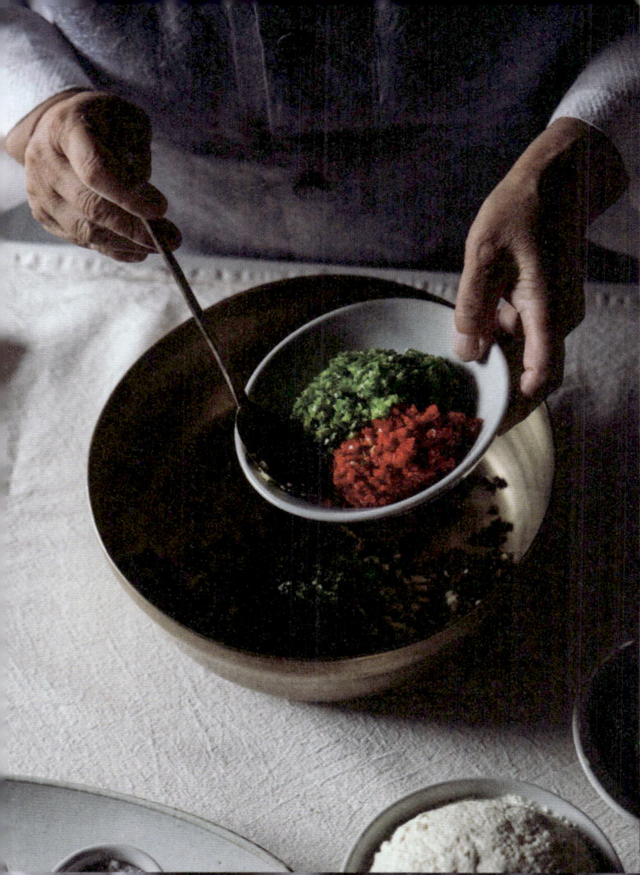
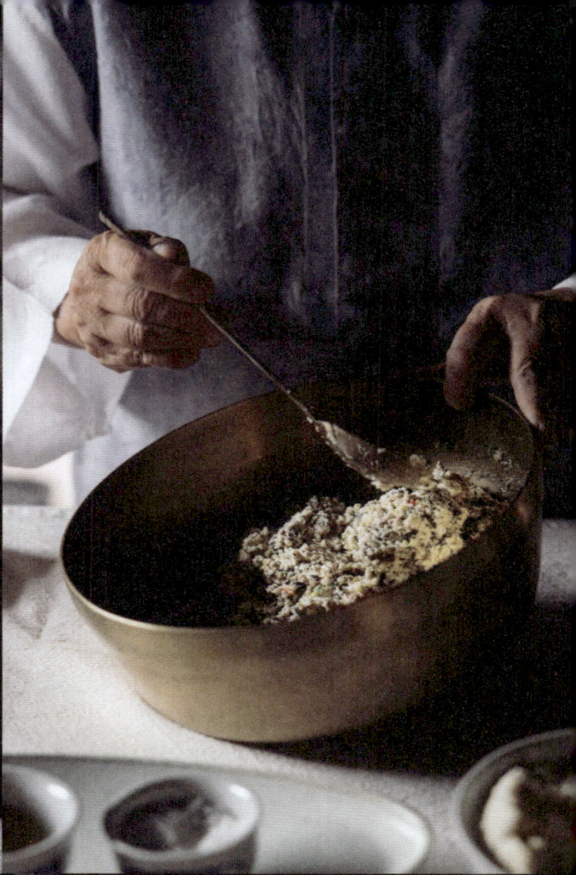
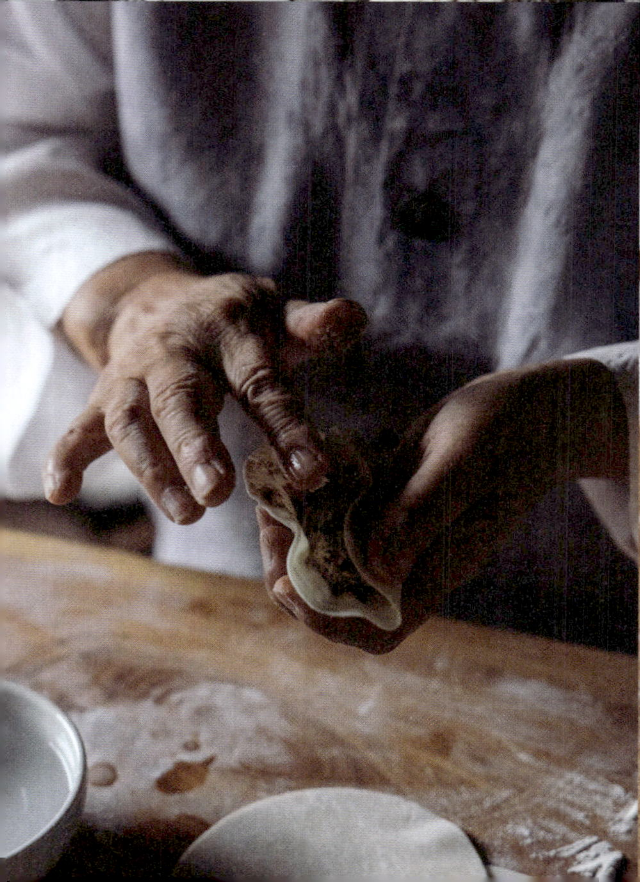
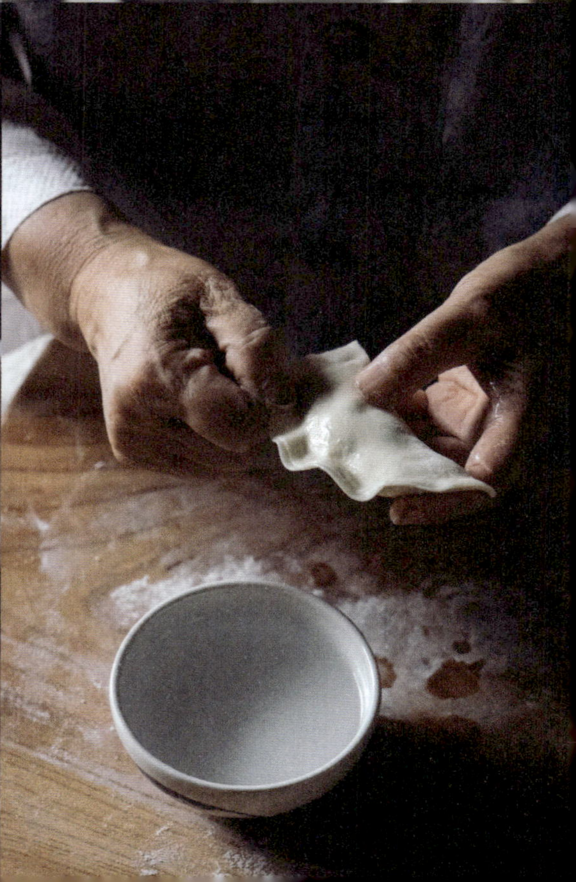

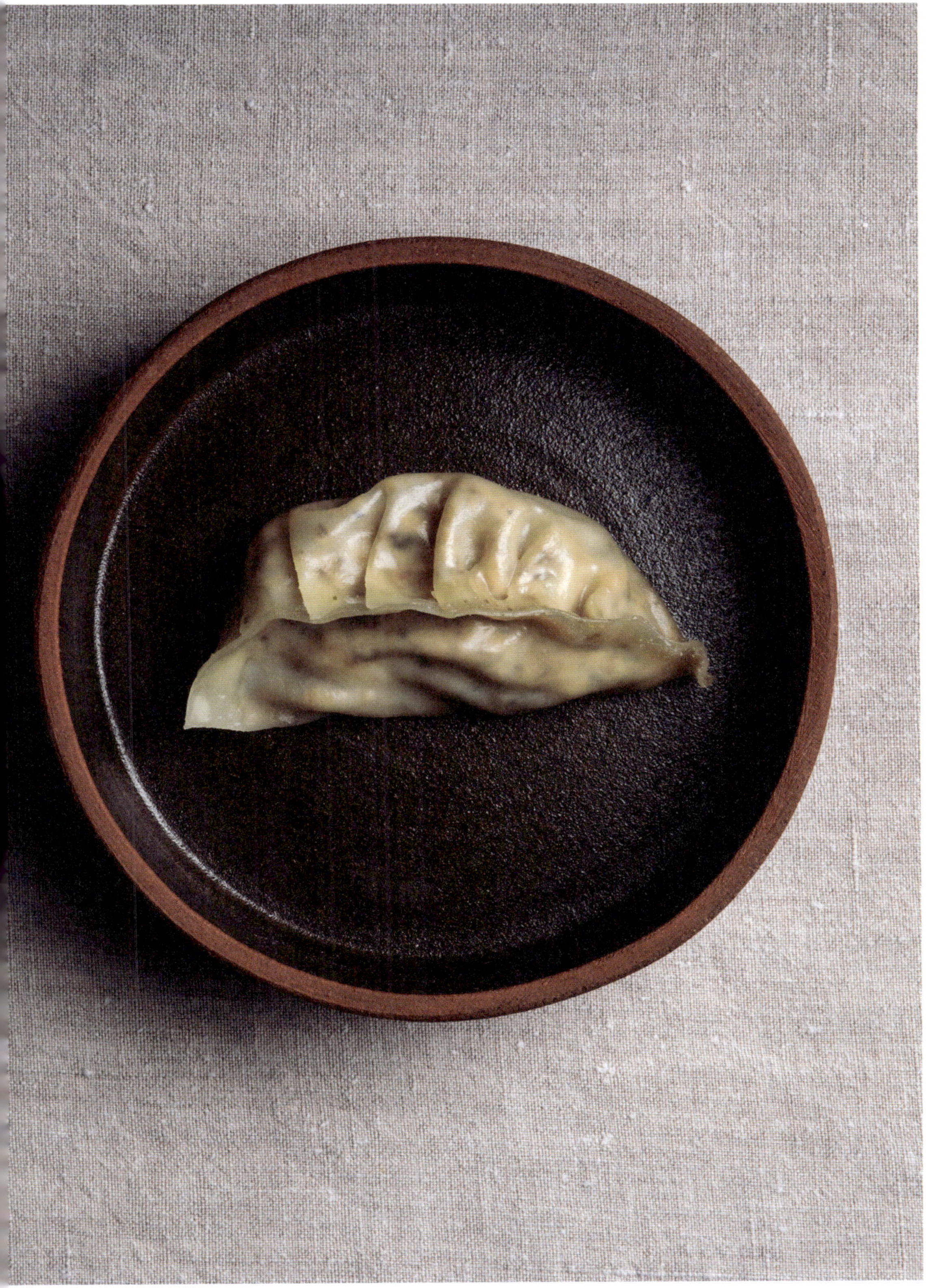

Guun dubu naengi ganjangjorim

TOFU WITH NAENGI BRAISED IN SOY SAUCE

For the tofu
1 pound 1½ ounces (500 g) firm tofu (dubu)
4 tablespoons perilla oil (deulgireum)
3 fresh Korean shiitake mushrooms (pyogo beoseot)
3 tablespoons (10 g) shepherd's purse (naengi)
Salt for seasoning

For the sauce
1 tablespoon soy sauce (ganjang)
1 tablespoon Bokbunja-Cheong (page 180)
1 tablespoon Omija-Cheong (page 186)
2 tablespoons Rice Syrup (Jocheong, page 190)
1 tablespoon sesame seeds (kkae), crushed
2 tablespoons (10 g) dried mandarin peel

Rinse the tofu with water, pat it dry, and slice it into pieces roughly ½ inch thick by 1½ inches long (1 cm by 4 cm), then salt it. Heat 2 tablespoons of the perilla oil in the pan and fry the tofu slices on both sides until golden. Remove the tofu and set aside. In the same pan, fry the mushrooms in the remaining perilla oil.

Add the sauce ingredients to a small pot and bring the sauce to a boil, then let it cool.

Finely chop the shepherd's purse. Halve the mushrooms, slice them thinly, and season them with salt.

Lay the fried tofu slices next to one another in a pan, layer the shepherd's purse and mushrooms over them, and pour the sauce over everything. Cover the dish and heat it briefly.

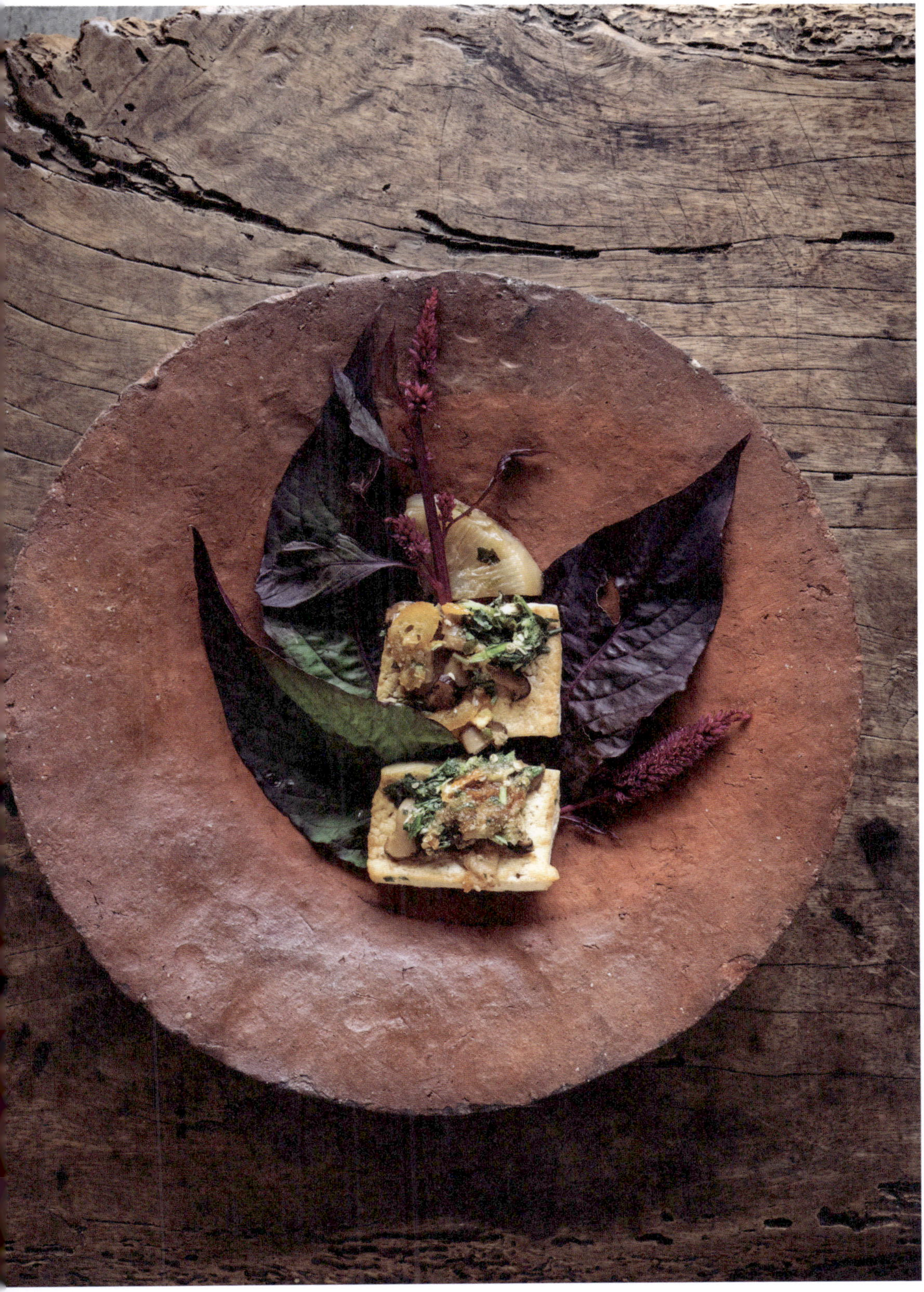

Baechu-mu-jeon

PANCAKES WITH NAPA CABBAGE AND RADISH

1 small white radish (mu)
1 small napa cabbage (baechu)
1 long red chile pepper (cheongyanggochu)
1 ¼ cups (150 g) all-purpose flour
6 tablespoons plus 2 teaspoons (50 g) buckwheat flour (maemil garu)
3 tablespoons perilla oil (deulgireum), divided
2 tablespoons soy sauce (ganjang), divided
Salt for seasoning
2 tablespoons soybean oil

Slice the radish into medium-thick slices and steam them briefly. Remove the leaves from the napa cabbage, press the stiff lower part of the leaves flat with a knife handle, and steam them as well until they're tender. Finely chop the chilies and set them aside.

Add the flour, buckwheat flour, 1 tablespoon perilla oil, 1 tablespoon soy sauce, and some salt to a bowl, then gradually add water to make a thick batter when you mix it.

Pour the soybean oil and the remaining 2 tablespoons perilla oil into a skillet over medium heat. Dip the radish slices into the flour batter and fry them in the oil.

Coat the napa cabbage leaves with a thin layer of batter and fry them until golden. Too much batter will overwhelm the flavor of the vegetables! (Variation: Mix some turmeric into the batter.)

Stir together the remaining soy sauce and the finely chopped chilies to make a sauce and drizzle some of it over the pancakes.

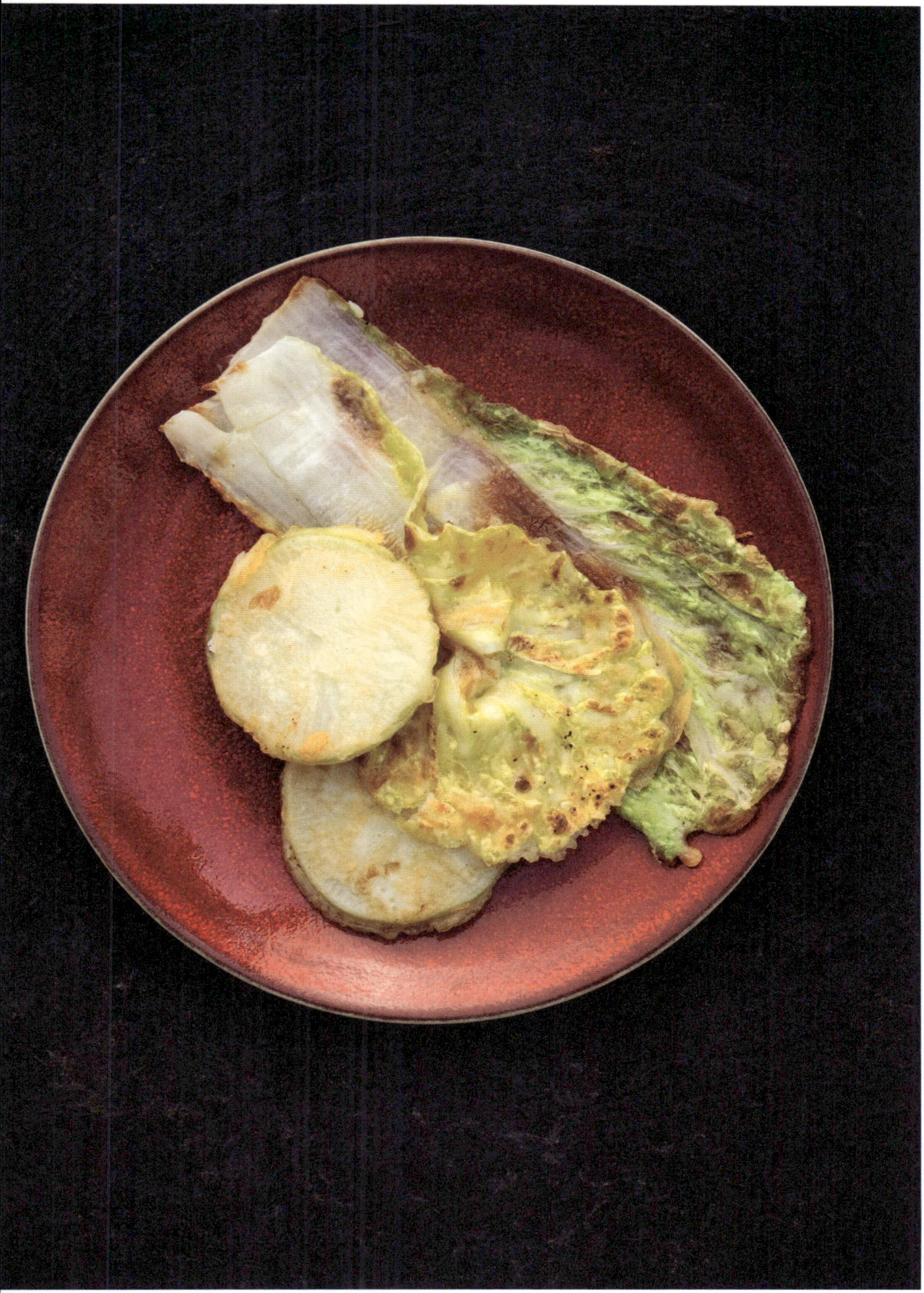

Susam twigim

DEEP-FRIED GINSENG

4 fresh ginseng roots (susam)
1 tablespoon soy sauce (ganjang)
2 tablespoons perilla oil (deulgireum)
Salt for seasoning
⅓ cup (50 g) rice flour (ssalgaru)
¾ cup plus 4 teaspoons (100 g) all-purpose flour, or Korean frying flour, divided
¾ cup (200 ml) water
Soybean oil for deep-frying

Rinse the ginseng roots well. Cut them in half and remove some of the lower ends if they're overly fibrous. Steam the roots for 5 minutes, then season them with soy sauce, perilla oil, and salt.

In a bowl, mix the rice flour and half of the flour with the water to make a smooth batter.

Heat the soybean oil to 350°F (180°C). First dredge the seasoned ginseng roots in the remaining flour, then dip them into the batter. Briefly deep-fry them in batches.

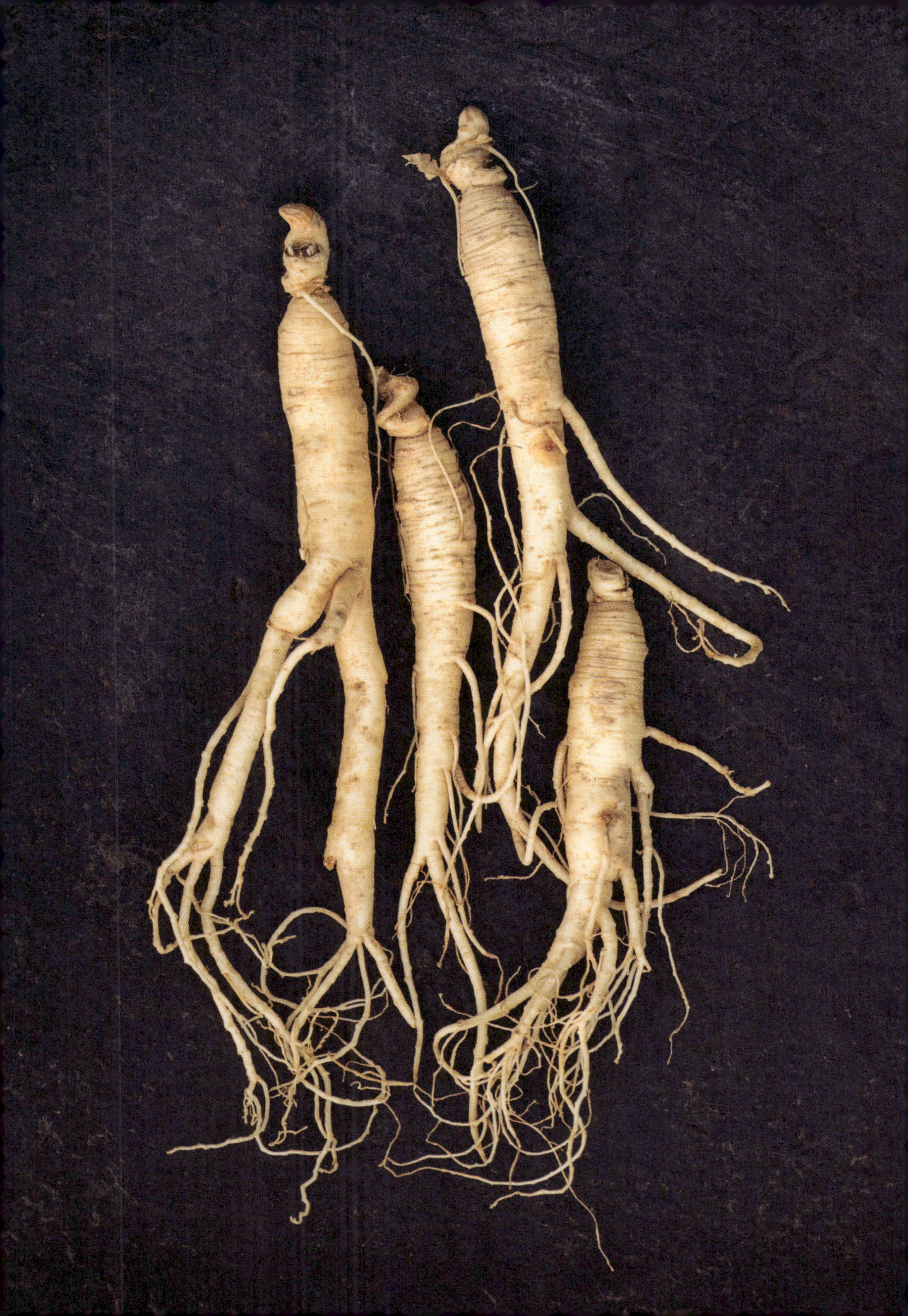

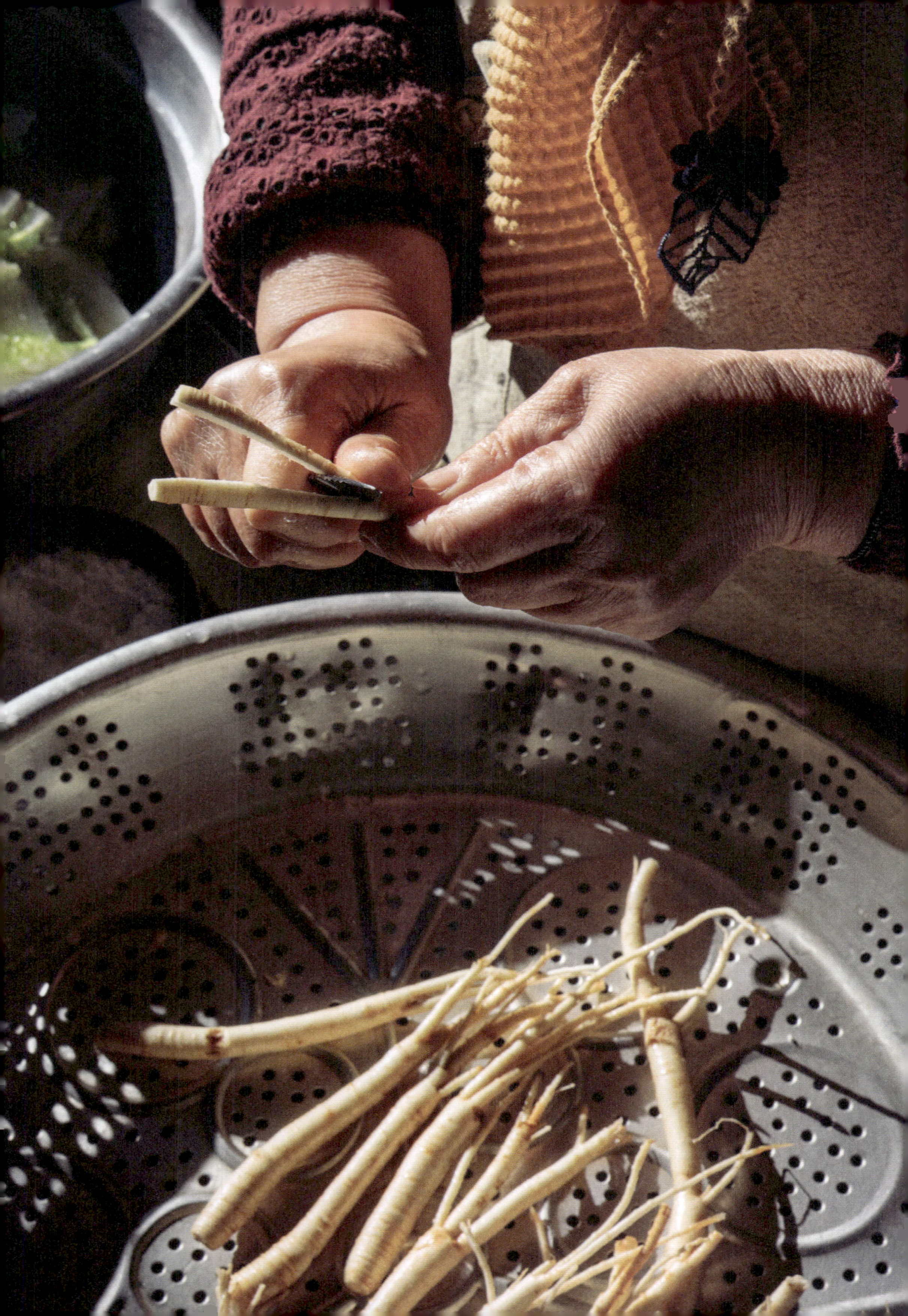

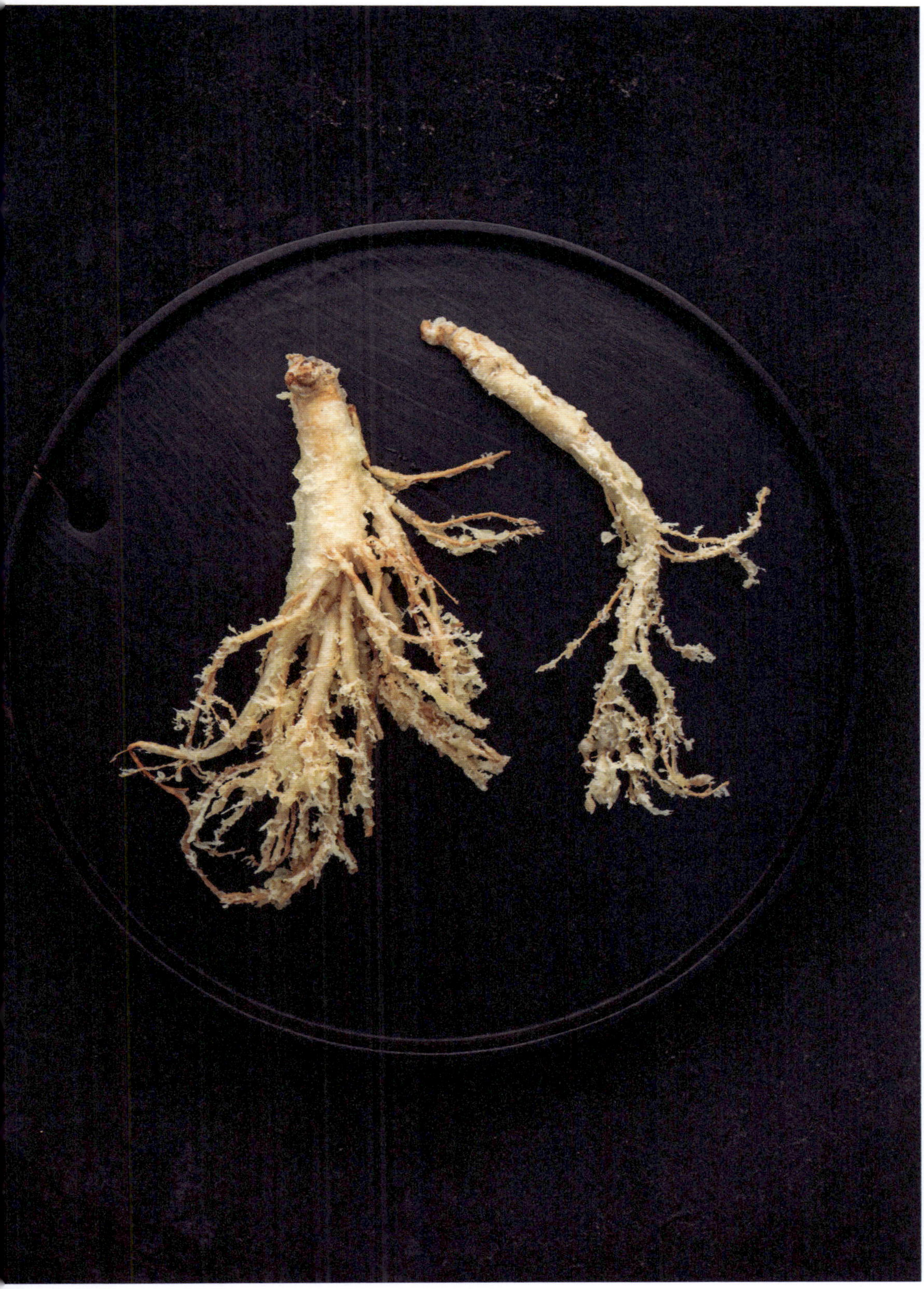

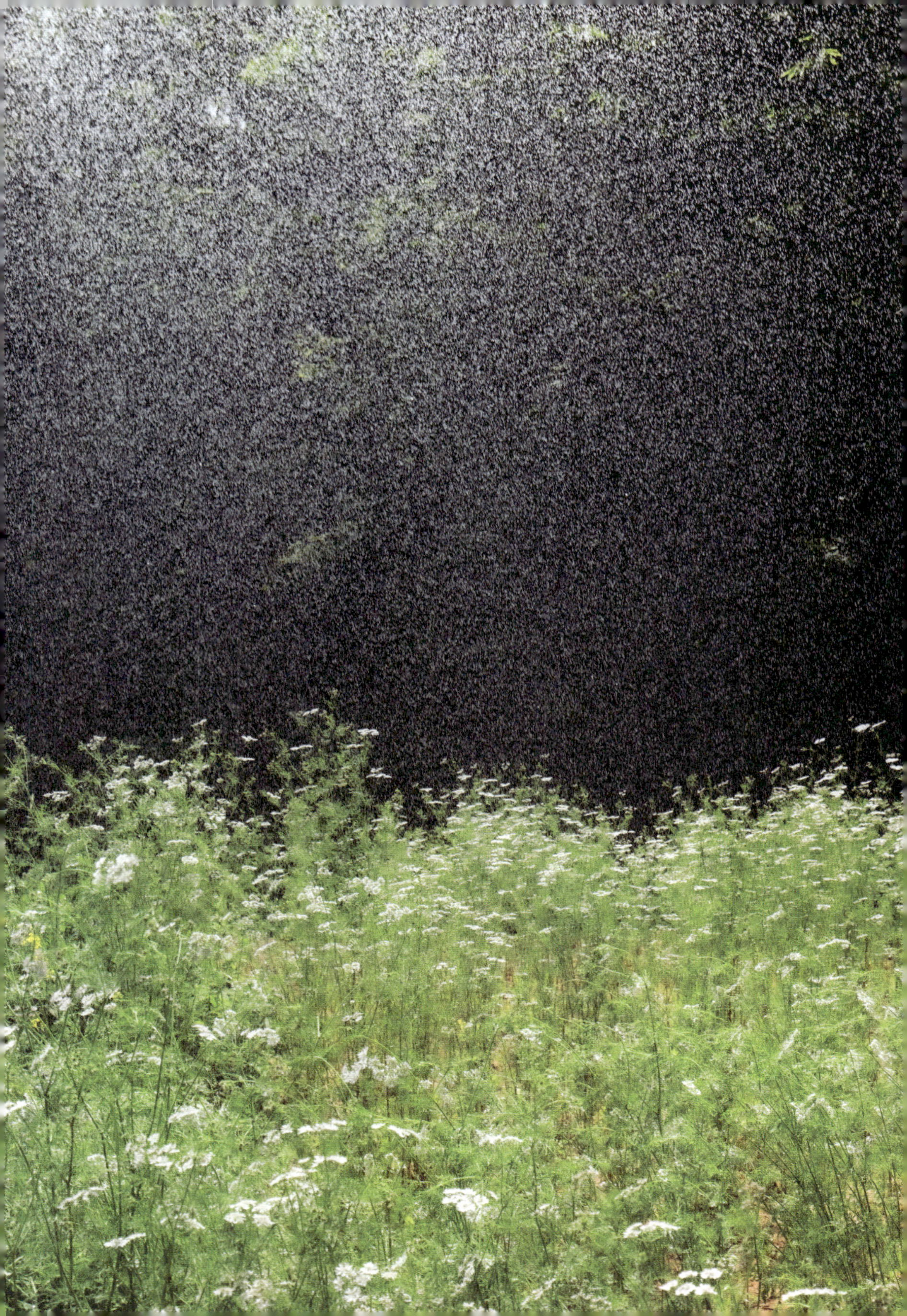

SPRING

The energy that has gathered during winter pushes outward as life opens up and stretches itself in the brightness and warmth of spring. It is tentative at first, but soon everything awakens, becomes green, and blooms. You can hear the shoots growing in the bamboo forest; *minari* announces its presence alongside the stream with its fragrance. Jeongkwan Snim goes out, sows seeds, forages, dries, and begins preserving. She must pick tea leaves and look for mushrooms early—she says it's important to supplement the new, light foods from spring with the old ones from last year. The old, dried roots, the namul, and the fruits from last autumn are richer in nutrients than the fresh leaves and shoots are at the beginning of spring. (Bibimbap is a fine example of using more mature ingredients to great effect.) Temple cooking maintains the tradition of combining fresh vegetables and namul with grains from last year (for example, in vegetable pancakes), and tofu can also be prepared with fresh vegetables.

Temple Bibimbap — 232
Soup with Soybean Sprouts — 238
Black Sesame Porridge — 240
Bamboo Shoot with Perilla — 242
Chinamul — 246
Mung Bean Sprouts with Minari — 248
Watery Mustard Green Kimchi — 250
Tofu Steamed in Zucchini with Fresh Green Tea Leaves — 252
Pyogo Mushrooms Braised in Rice Syrup — 256
Pancakes with Minari And Gochujang — 260
Bugak, or "Flower of Temple Food" — 262

Sachal bibimbap

TEMPLE BIBIMBAP

Serves 5–6

For the rice
1 ½ cups (300 g) short-grain rice (ssal)
½ cup (100 g) glutinous rice (chapssal)
1 tablespoon sesame oil (chamgireum)
Salt for seasoning

For the vegetables
¾ cup (40 g) Korean aster scaber (chinamul), dried
1 cup (40 g) Korean aster scaber (chinamul), fresh
1 tablespoon perilla oil (deulgireum)
1 tablespoon soybean oil
1 tablespoon soy sauce (ganjang)
1 tablespoon sesame oil (chamgireum)
2 tablespoons toasted sesame seeds (kkae, page 431), coarsely crushed

For the fernbrake
⅔ cup (20 g) dried fernbrake (gosari)
1 tablespoon perilla oil (deulgireum)
1 tablespoon soy sauce (ganjang)
2 tablespoons water
1 tablespoon sesame oil (chamgireum)
1 ½ tablespoons toasted sesame seeds (kkae, page 431), coarsely crushed

Rinse the short-grain rice and the glutinous rice several times in water until the water runs clear. Let the grains sit in water for 30 minutes, then drain them through a sieve. Add the rice to a pot and pour in 1 ¼ cups (320 ml) fresh water, add the sesame oil and salt, and bring to a boil.

Soak the vegetables separately in water for about 2 hours. Rinse them off and boil each of them individually in fresh water until they're tender. Afterwards, drain them, rinse them with cold water, and squeeze them out firmly. Add the perilla oil and the soybean oil to a pan and sauté the vegetables in separate batches. Add some water, cover the pan, and simmer the vegetables for 10 minutes. Season them with the soy sauce, sesame oil, and sesame seeds and mix lightly.

If using dried fernbrake, first soak it overnight. Boil it in fresh water for about 20 minutes until it's tender, then remove it from the stove and let it stand for 30 minutes. Drain the fernbrake, squeeze it out, and clip away any hard bits. Cut it into pieces 1 ½ inches (4 cm) long. In a pan, heat the perilla oil and fry the fernbrake for a while over medium heat. Add the soy sauce and water, cover the pan, and let the fernbrake simmer for a bit longer. Afterwards, add the sesame oil and sesame seeds and mix carefully.

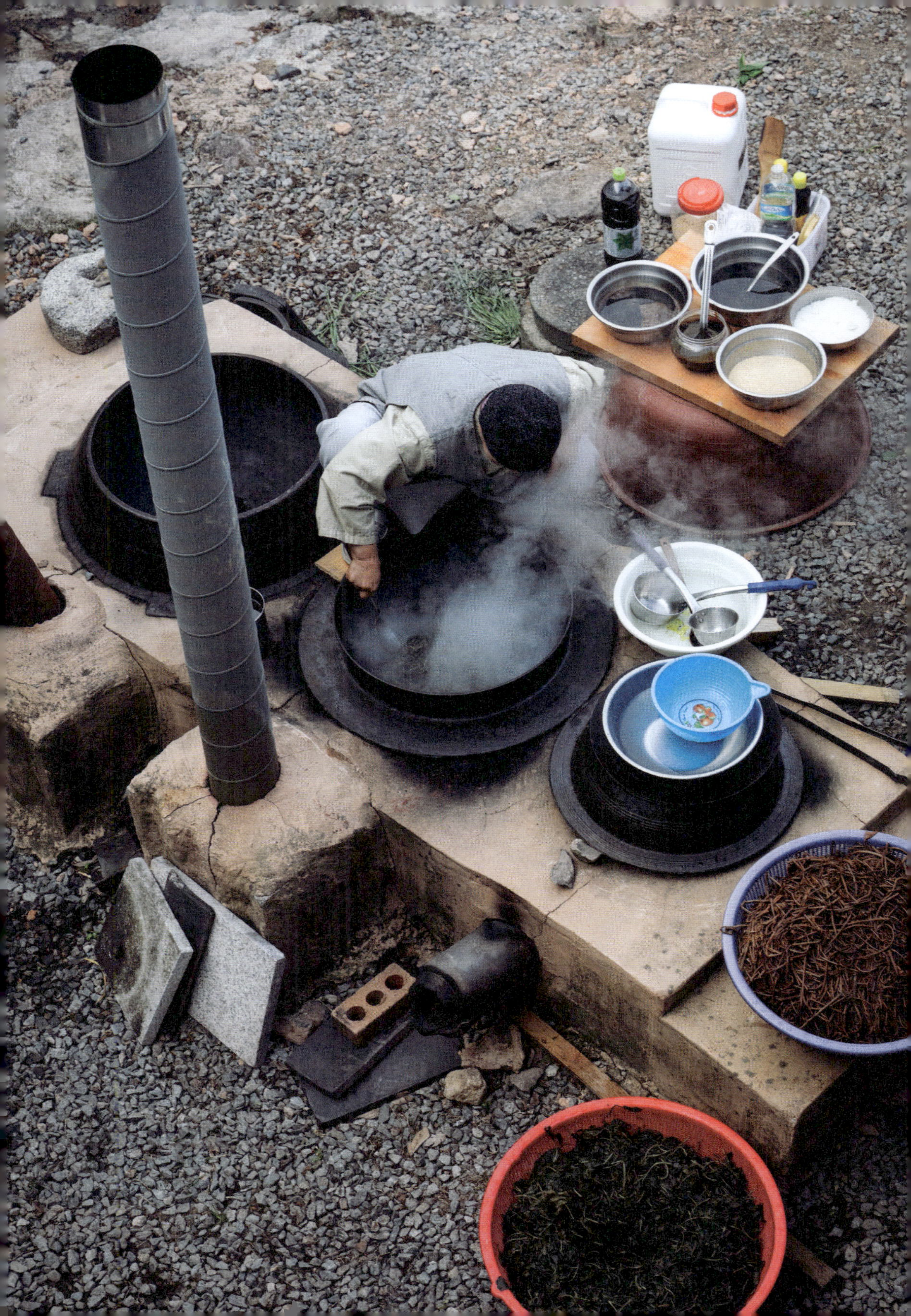

For the mushrooms
2 ⅓ cups (200 g) oyster mushrooms (neutari beoseot)
Salt for seasoning
1 tablespoon perilla oil (deulgireum)
1 tablespoon soybean oil
Soy sauce (ganjang) for seasoning

Clean the mushrooms and blanch them briefly in boiling salted water. Then shock them in cold water and squeeze them out gently. Tear them into bite-sized pieces. In a pan, heat the perilla oil and the soybean oil, then briefly fry the mushrooms in the oil. Season them to taste with soy sauce.

For the radish
1 medium white radish (mu)
Soy sauce (ganjang) for seasoning
3 tablespoons Omija-Cheong (page 186)
1 teaspoon fine chili powder (goun-gochugaru)

Rinse the radish well, slice it thinly, and then julienne the slices. Carefully mix it in with the soy sauce, omija-cheong, and chili powder.

For the spinach
10 cups (300 g) spinach (sigeumchi)
Salt for seasoning
1 tablespoon soy sauce (ganjang)
1 tablespoon sesame oil (chamgireum)
1 ½ tablespoons toasted sesame seeds (kkae, page 431), coarsely crushed

Rinse the spinach, then cut off the roots and any browned leaves. Blanch it briefly in boiling water and then place it in cold water. Once cooled, remove it from the water and carefully squeeze it out. Season with the salt, soy sauce, sesame oil, and crushed sesame seeds. Blend carefully.

For the tofu
3 ½ ounces (100 g) tofu (dubu)
Salt for seasoning
1 tablespoon perilla oil (deulgireum)

Cut the tofu into ¾-inch (2 cm) cubes, season them with salt, and sauté the cubes in perilla oil until golden.

For the seaweed
⅔ cup (10 g) wakame seaweed (miyeok), dried
Soybean oil for deep-frying

Cut the seaweed into small pieces with some kitchen shears, then deep-fry it briefly in soybean oil heated to 350°F (180°C). Crush the deep-fried seaweed with a mortar and pestle.

In each serving bowl, arrange some rice and all of the namul in an appealing way, set the tofu pieces in the center, and sprinkle everything with the fried seaweed.

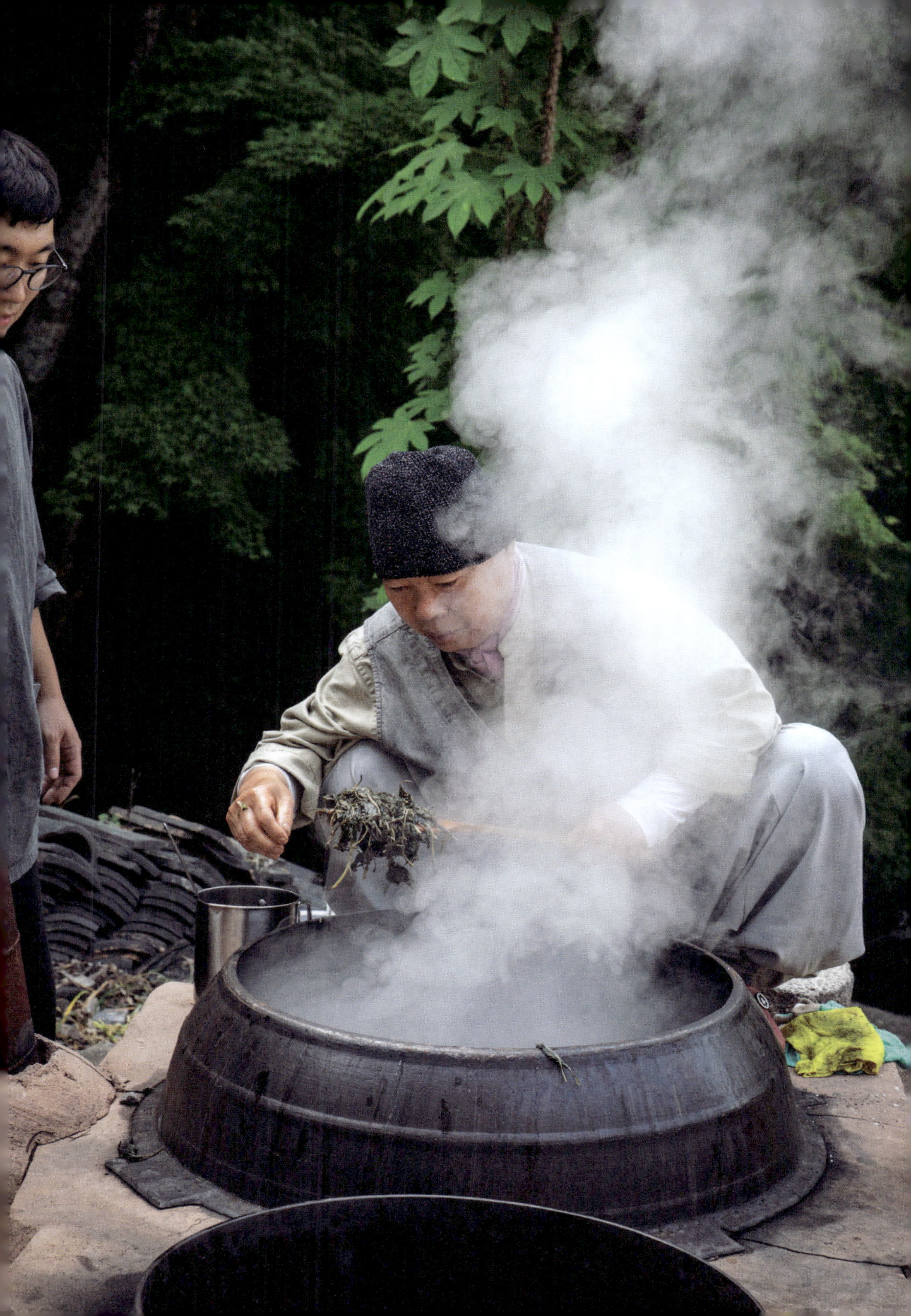

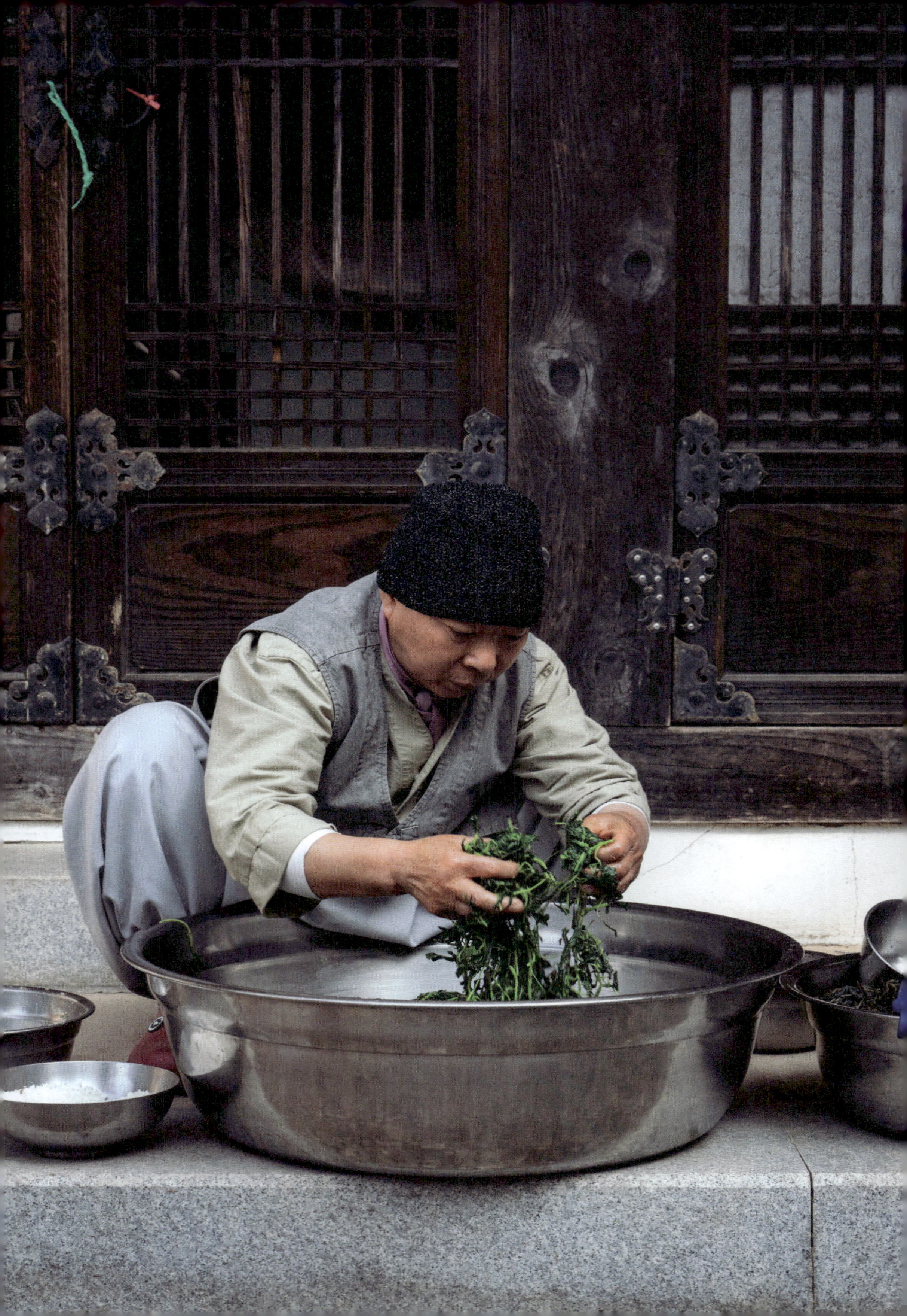

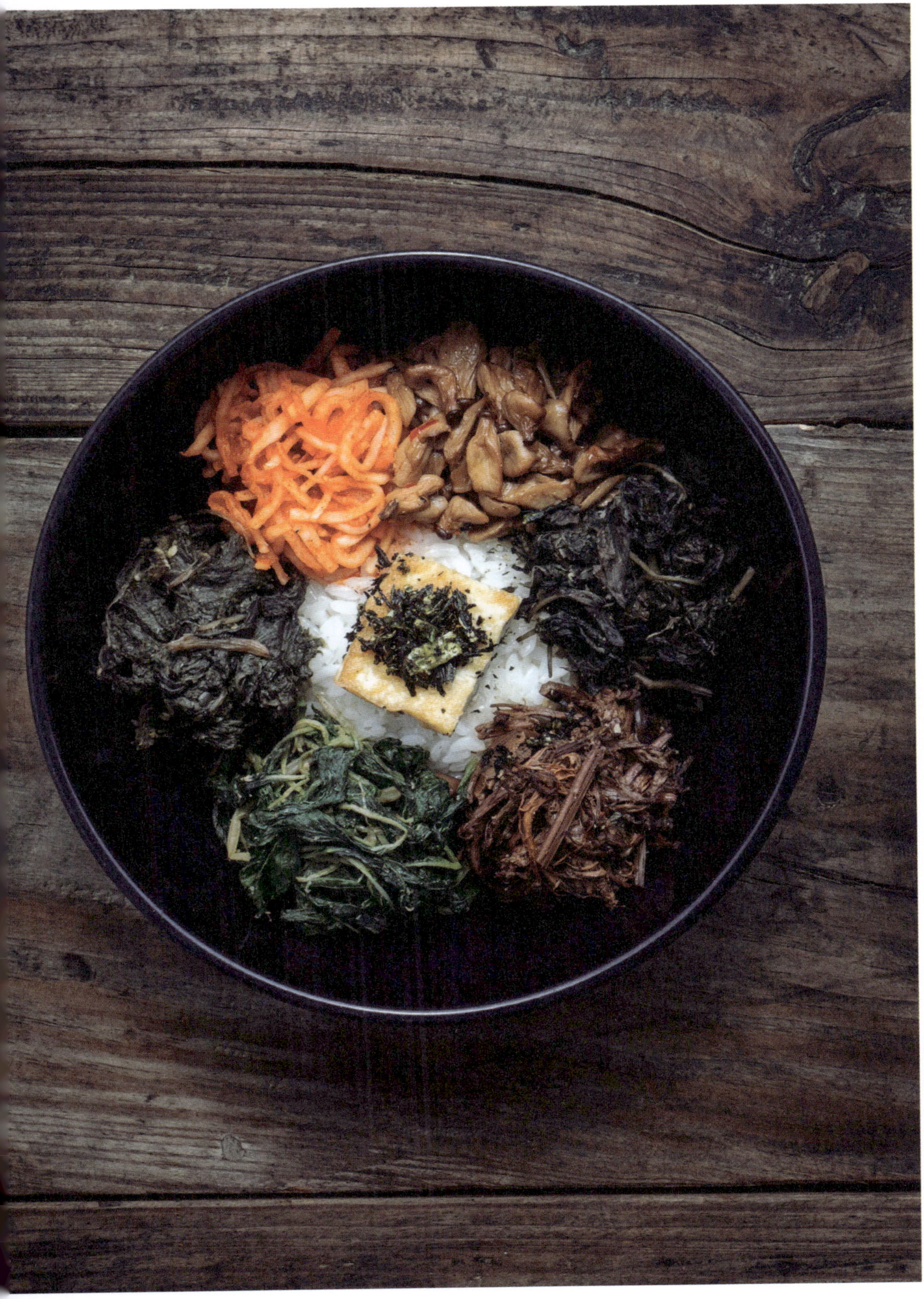

Kongnamul-guk

SOUP WITH SOYBEAN SPROUTS

3 cups (300 g) soybean sprouts (kongnamul)
1 cup (50 g) water celery (minari)
1 long red chile pepper (cheongyanggochu)
4¼ cups (1 L) water
Salt for seasoning
Sesame seeds (kkae), crushed

Rinse the soybean sprouts and remove any brown parts. Cut the minari and chile pepper into small pieces.

In a pot, bring the water to a boil, add the sprouts, cover, and boil for 3 minutes. Reduce the heat and simmer for an additional 5 minutes. Season to taste with salt.

Ladle the sprouts into bowls, add the minari and chili, and sprinkle with some sesame seeds.

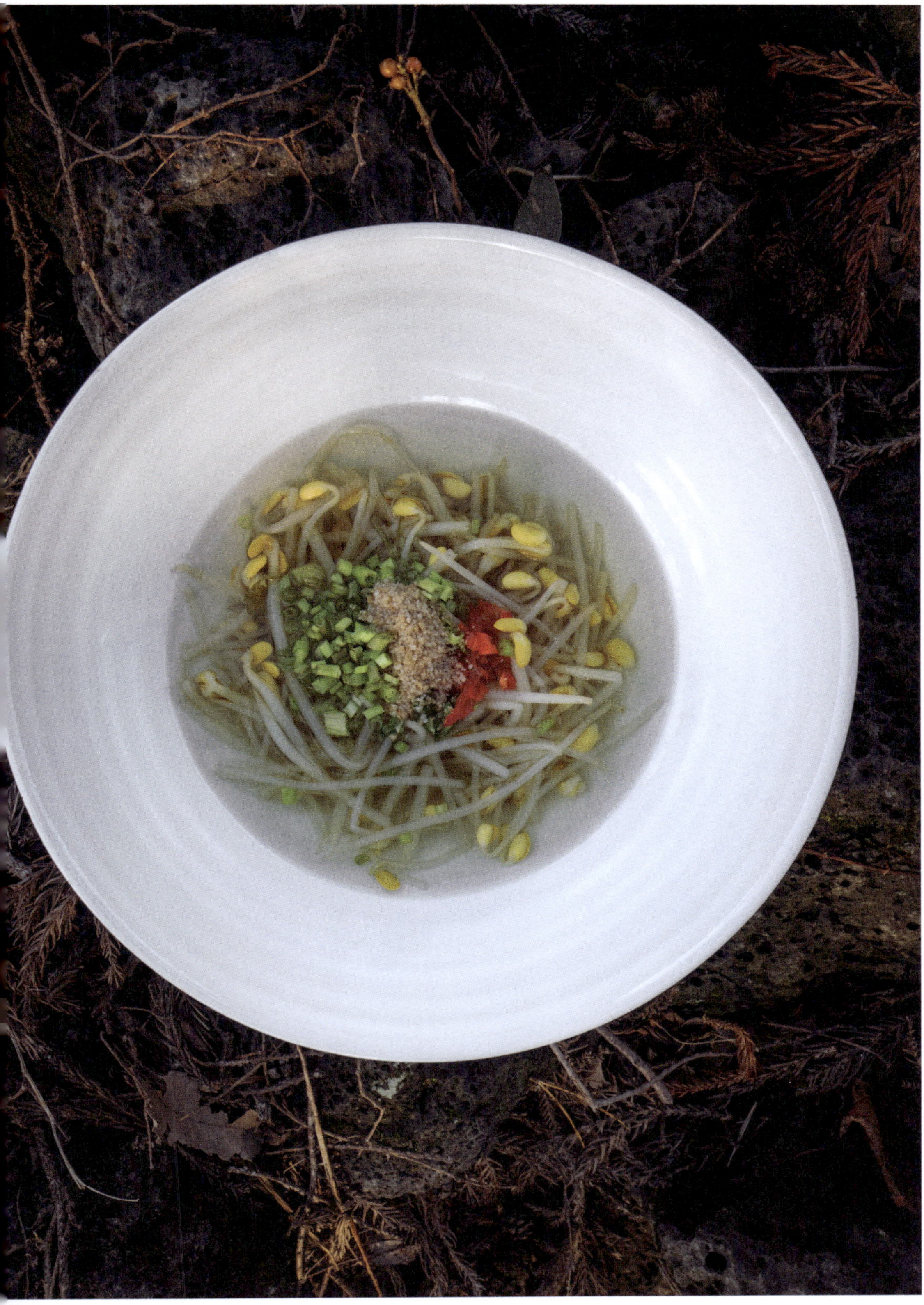

Juk is typically made from squash or sesame and is basically a thick, creamy soup. (Other versions are made from rice, millet, beans, or barley.) The consistency of this dish is similar to porridge, and like porridge, juk is believed to be easily digested. The simplest versions of juk are made from rice, salt, and soy sauce and are eaten in Korea during times of illness. Although juk can be made many ways, juk made from rice and accompanied by vegetables, mushrooms, mussels, fish, or meat is especially popular.

Heugimja-juk

BLACK SESAME PORRIDGE

6 tablespoons toasted black sesame seeds (heugimja, page 431)
6 tablespoons short-grain rice (ssal)
3 cups (720 ml) water, divided (plus more as needed)
Salt for seasoning

Toast the sesame seeds in a dry pan. Grind them and the rice together, then blend with 1½ cups (360 ml) of the water and let the mixture stand for 10 minutes.

Bring the rest of the water to a boil. Slowly add the sesame/rice mixture to the boiling water, stirring continuously. When the porridge begins to boil, reduce the heat to medium. If necessary, add more water until the desired consistency is reached.

Simmer 5 more minutes, then turn off the stove and let the dish stand a bit longer. Finally, season the juk to taste with salt.

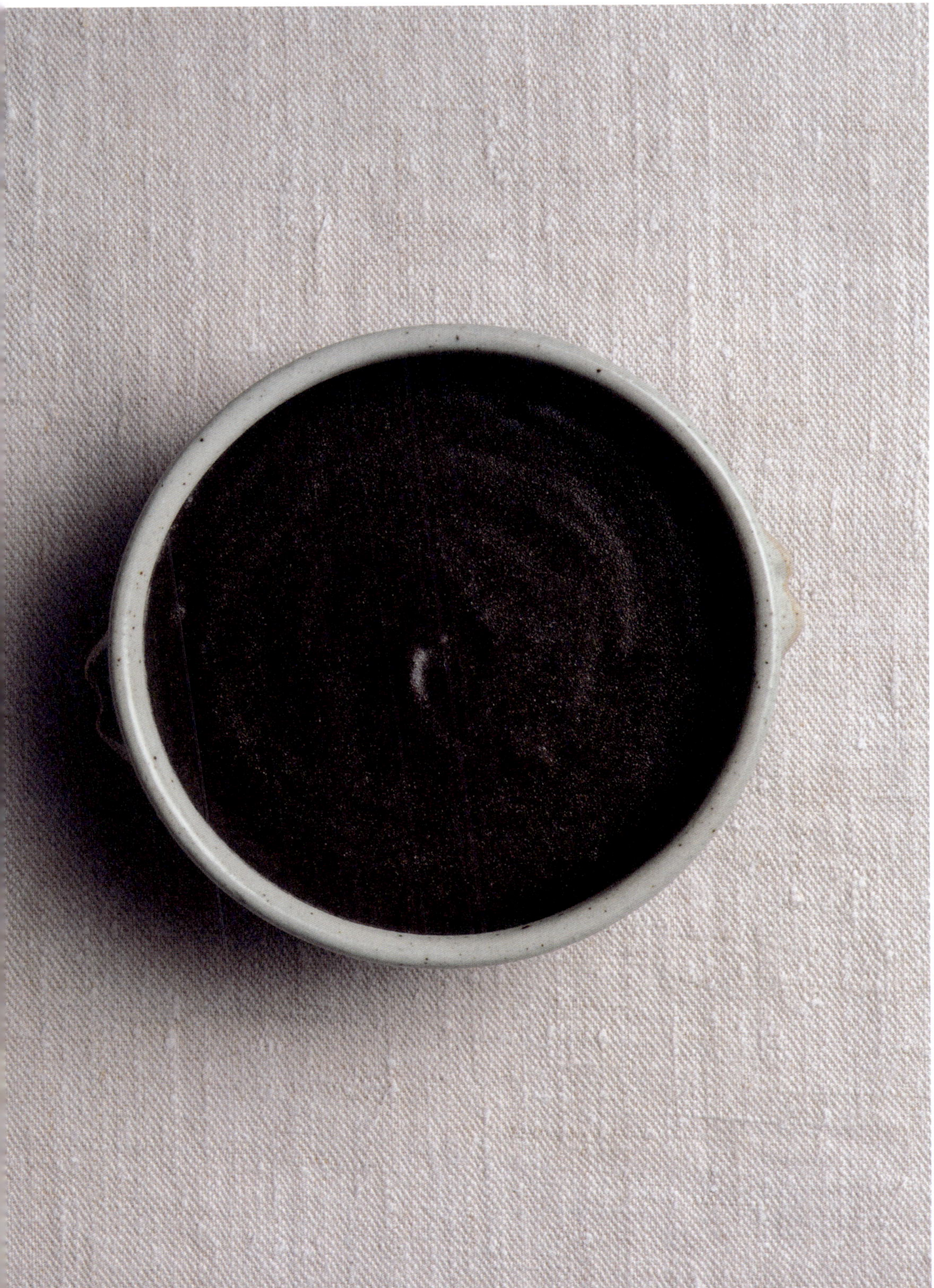

Juksun-deulkkae-namul

BAMBOO SHOOT WITH PERILLA

1 bamboo shoot (juksun), or pre-cooked bamboo shoot
Fermented soybean paste (doenjang) for seasoning
2 tablespoons perilla oil (deulgireum)
1 tablespoon perilla powder (deulkkae-garu), toasted
Salt for seasoning
Soy sauce (ganjang) for seasoning

Peel off the outer layer of the bamboo shoot, then halve the shoot lengthwise and rinse it. Use only the white inner part! Add both halves to a pot of boiling water. Either cook them with milky water previously used to rinse rice, or dissolve some doenjang into the water to season it.

Continue cooking until the shoot is tender. Let it cool, then tear it into pieces with your hands and firmly squeeze the water out of it.

Add the perilla oil to a pan along with the bamboo shoot pieces. Sauté the bamboo over medium heat. (Bamboo shoot does not have strong flavor of its own.)

Add enough fresh water to the pan to cover the bamboo pieces and simmer them slowly over medium heat. Once the water has evaporated, add the perilla powder and season to taste with salt and soy sauce.

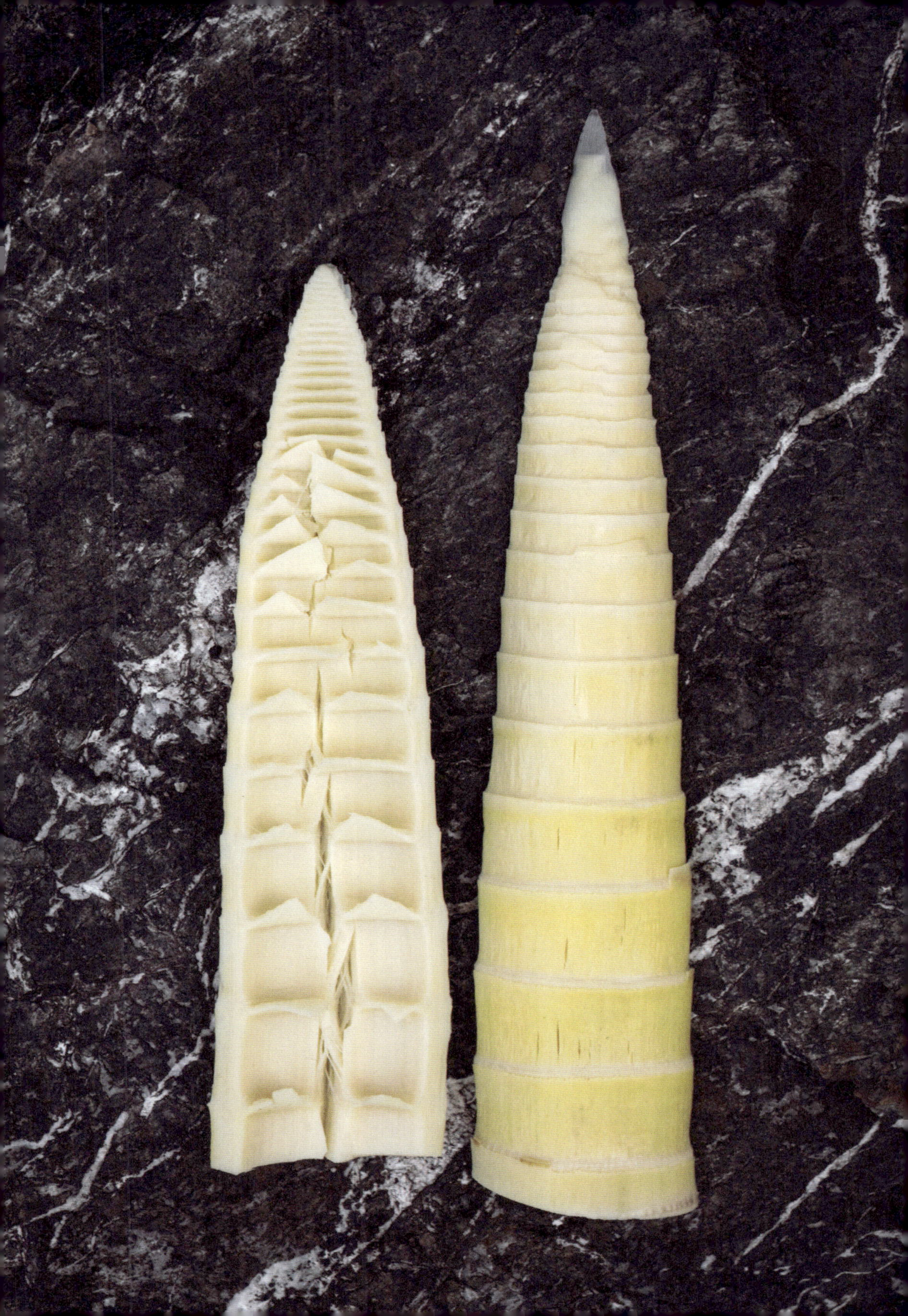

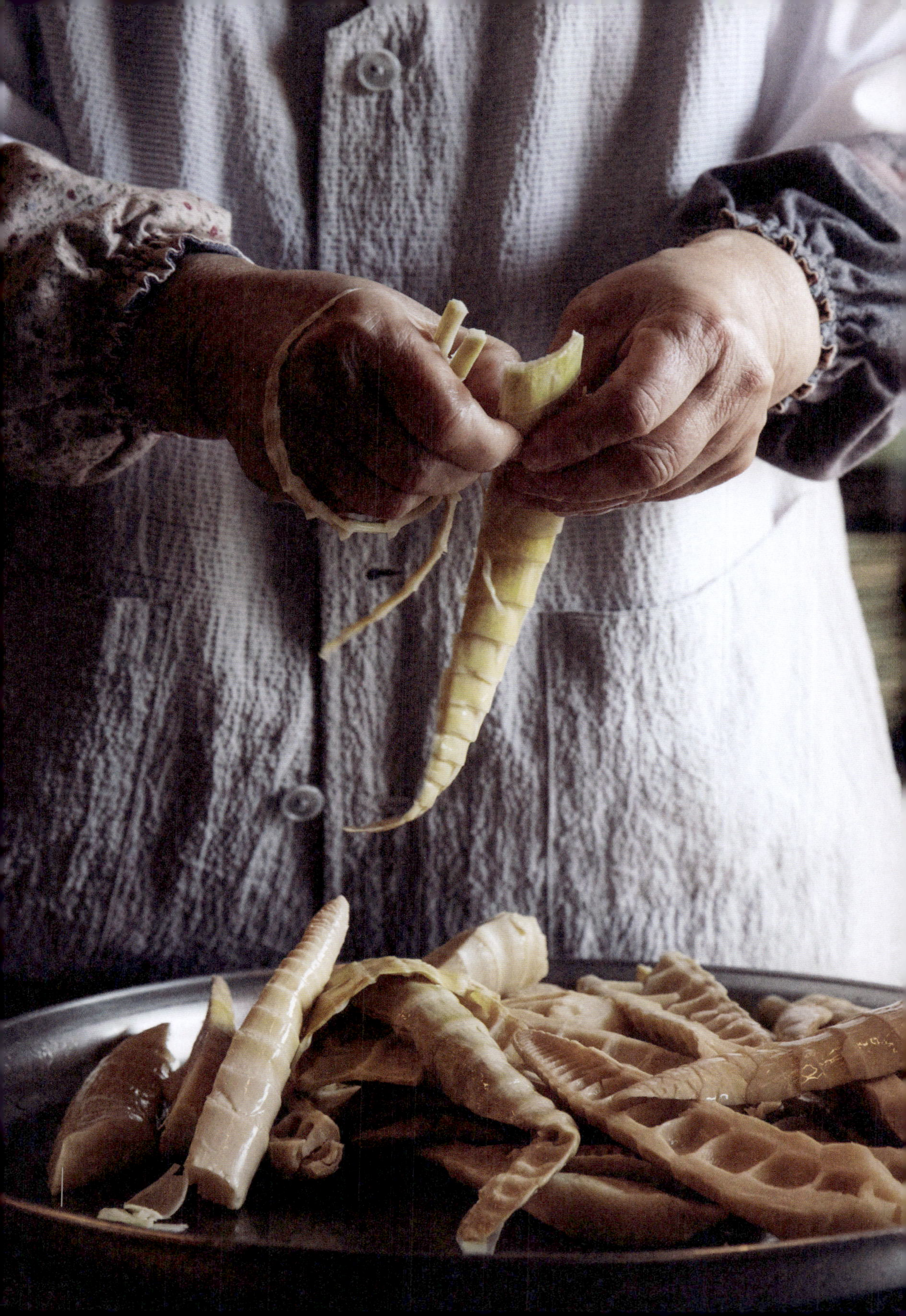

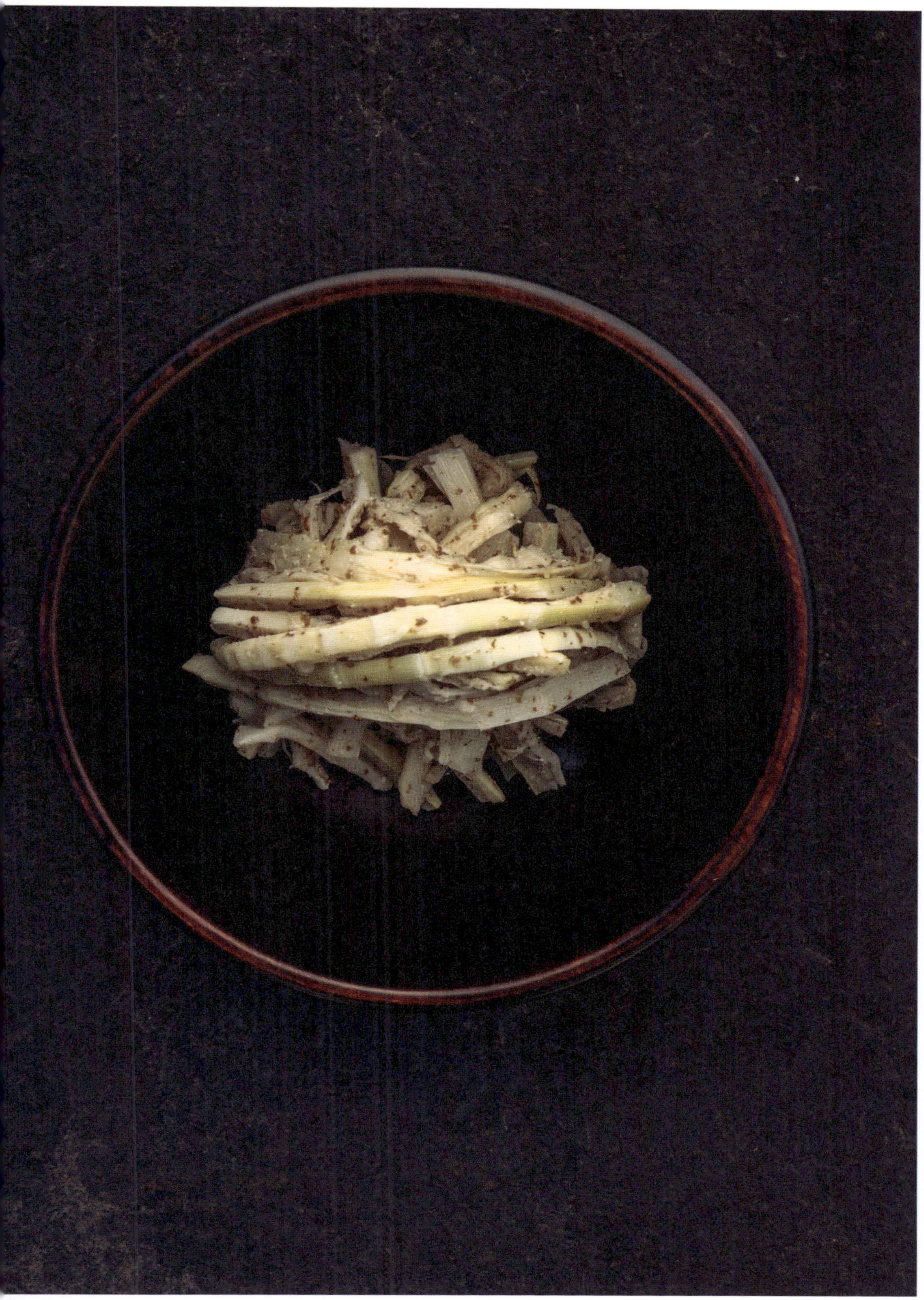

CHINAMUL

5 ½ cups (300 g) Korean aster scaber (chinamul)
¼ of a red bell pepper and ¼ of a yellow bell pepper (pimang)
1 tablespoon soy sauce (ganjang)
1 tablespoon toasted sesame seeds (kkae, page 431), coarsely crushed
1 tablespoon sesame oil (chamgireum)

Remove the hard bits from the *chinamul*, wash it, and then add it to boiling water for 5 minutes, cooking it until the stems are tender. (If using dried chinamul, first soak it for a few hours, then wash it and boil it.)

Remove the chinamul and place it briefly in cold water, then squeeze it out gently.

Finely dice the red and yellow bell peppers. Add the chinamul to a bowl, then pull it apart and loosen the leaves with your fingers. Add the diced bell peppers, soy sauce, sesame seeds, and sesame oil and mix carefully.

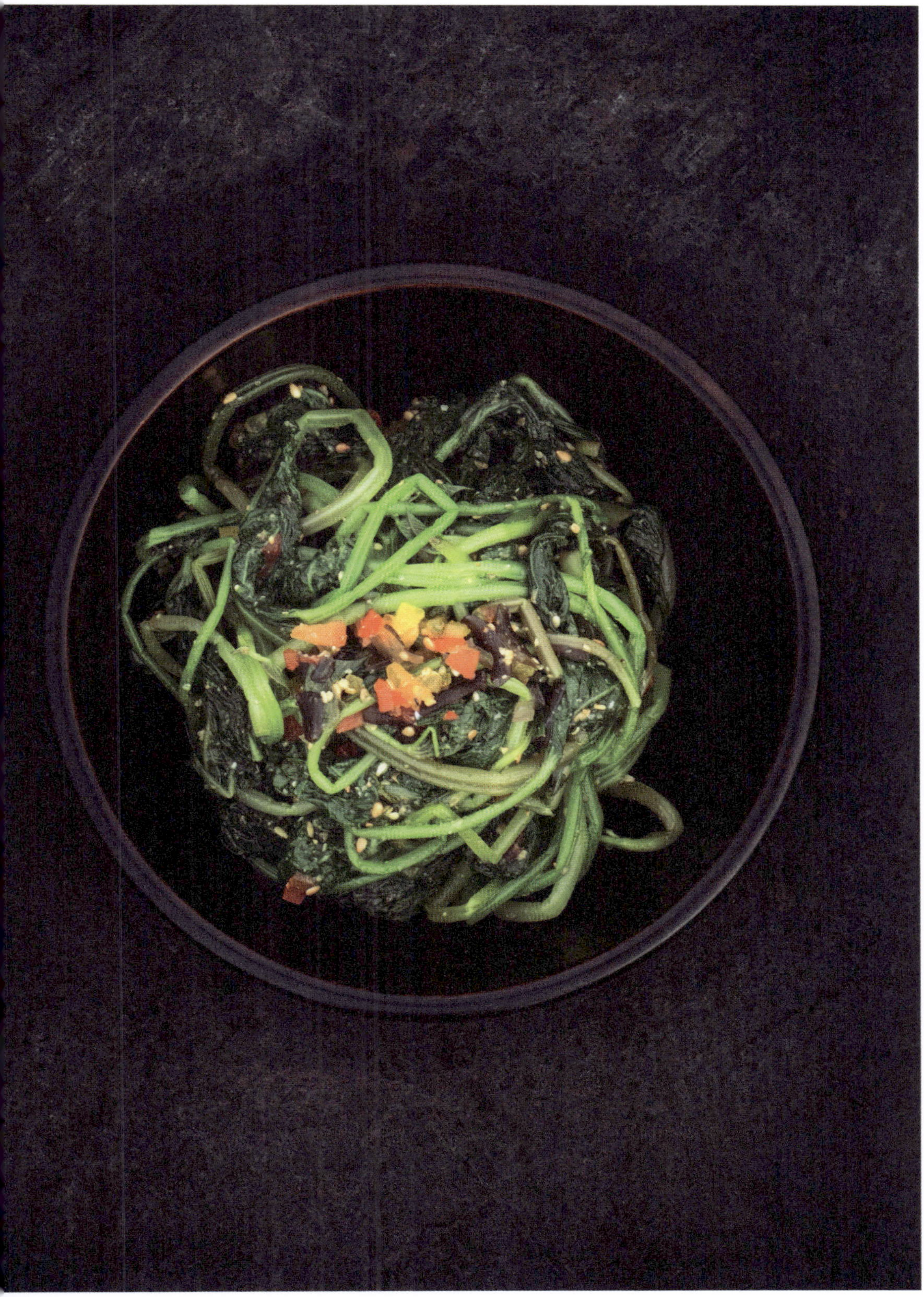

Sukju-minari-namul

MUNG BEAN SPROUTS WITH MINARI

3 ½ cups (200 g) water celery (minari)
5 cups (500 g) mung bean sprouts
1 tablespoon soy sauce (ganjang)
1 tablespoon toasted sesame seeds
  (kkae, page 431), coarsely crushed
Salt for seasoning
1 tablespoon sesame oil (chamgireum)

Rinse the minari stems and blanch them briefly in boiling water. Set aside the leaves to use for a different dish.

Rinse the sprouts and add them to a pot of boiling water. Blanch them briefly, then cool them off in cold water. Squeeze out the water from them.

Cut the minari into pieces. In a bowl, mix together the soy sauce, sesame seeds, salt, and sesame oil, then add the sauce to the vegetables and mix lightly.

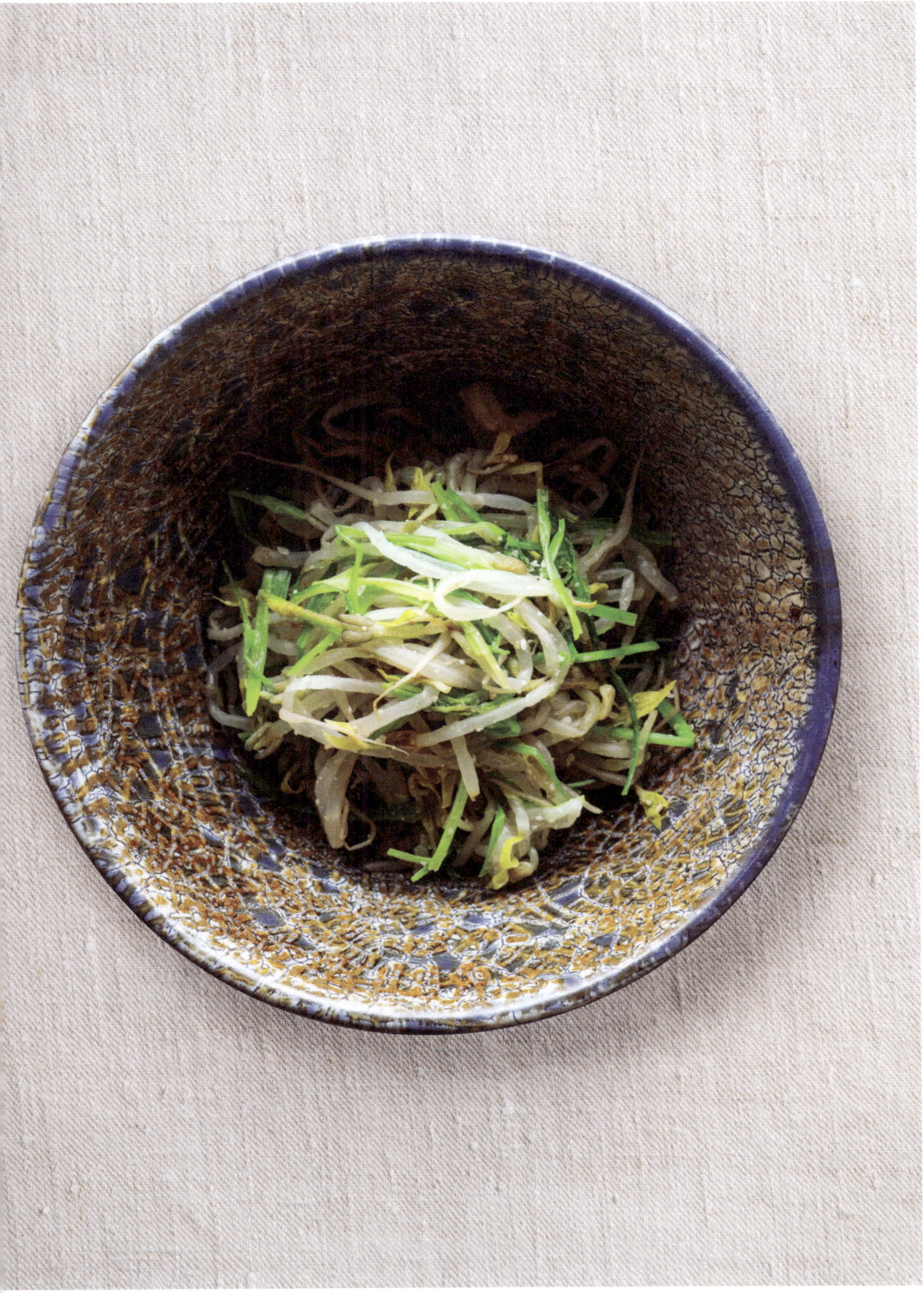

Gat-kimchi

WATERY MUSTARD GREEN KIMCHI

2 ¼ pounds (1 kg) mustard greens
8 ½ cups (2 L) water, divided
⅔ cup (200 g) salt, divided
1 dried long red chile pepper (cheongyang-gochu)
5 tablespoons glutinous rice flour
5 tablespoons Omija-Cheong (page 186)

Rinse the mustard greens and let them sit in a brine of 4 ¼ cups (1 L) water with ½ cup (150 g) salt for 10 minutes. Remove the greens, rinse and drain them, and squeeze them out carefully. Mince the chile pepper and set it aside.

Stir the glutinous rice flour into the remaining 4 ¼ cups (1 L) water and bring to a boil, constantly stirring. Let cool. Add the remaining salt and the omija-cheong, mix thoroughly, and season to taste.

Carefully mix the mustard greens into the flour mixture and place the kimchi in a container. Pour any remaining sauce over it and sprinkle on the minced chile pepper.

Let the kimchi mature for 2 days.

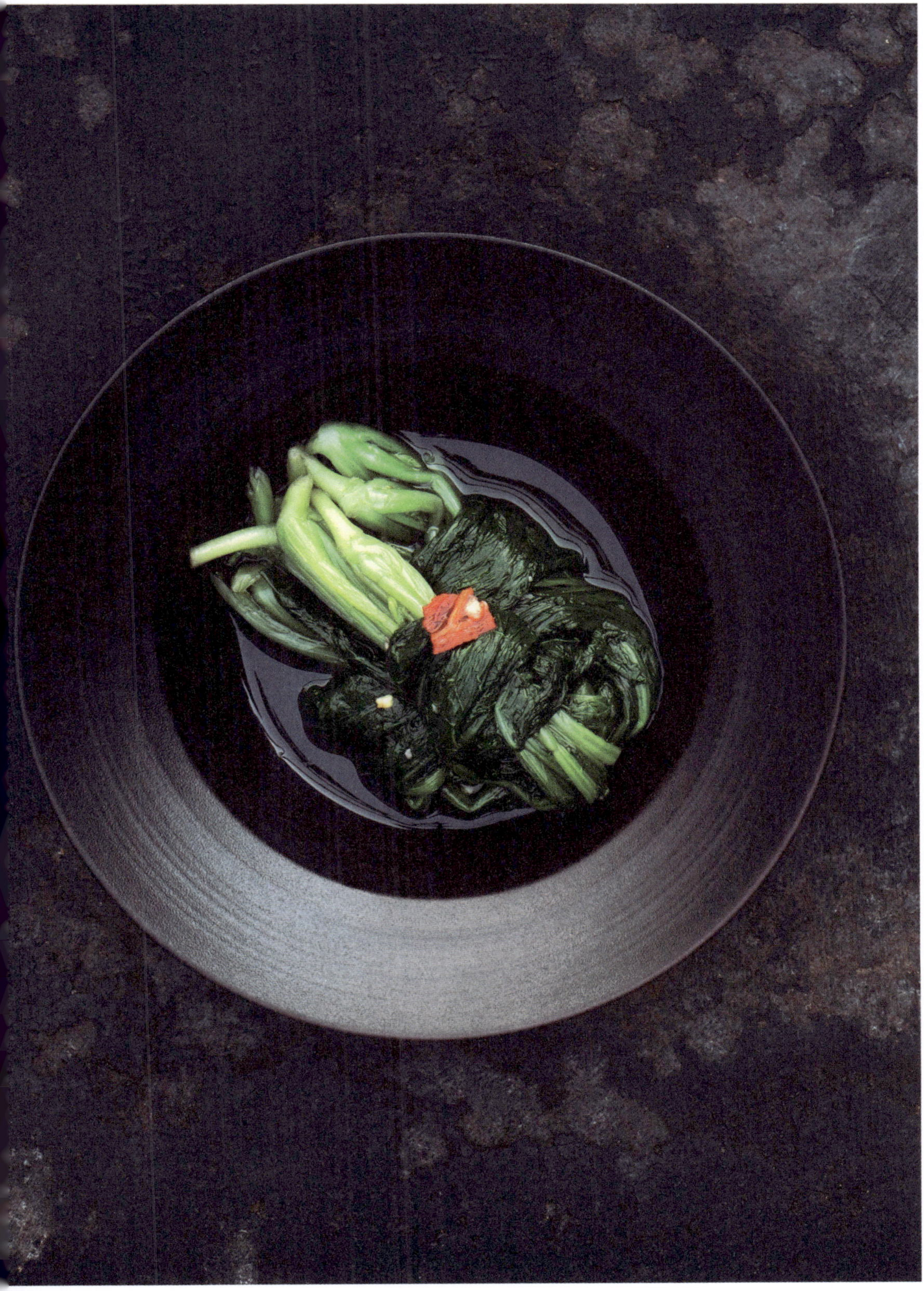

Nokcha oi-dubujjim

TOFU STEAMED IN ZUCCHINI WITH FRESH GREEN TEA LEAVES

A handful of fresh green tea leaves
1 zucchini (aehobak)
Salt for seasoning
1 cucumber (oi)
5 ⅓ ounces (150 g) tofu (dubu)
1 tablespoon toasted sesame seeds (kkae), page 431)
1 tablespoon sesame oil (chamgireum)
2 tablespoons soy sauce (ganjang)

Rinse the tea leaves. Cut the zucchini into ¾-inch (2 cm) slices, scoop out ⅔ of the seeds with a spoon, and season the zucchini with salt. Cut the cucumber into slices ¼ inch (5 mm) thick, season with salt, and let them sit.

Rinse the tofu with cold water and then pat it thoroughly dry with paper towels. Knead it into pieces with your hands, then season it with salt, sesame seeds, and sesame oil.

Form the tofu into small balls and place them in the troughs of the zucchini slices. Lay the tea leaves in a steamer basket, set the filled zucchini slices on them, and steam for 6 minutes.

Squeeze out the salted cucumber slices, then arrange them around the tofu-filled zucchini along with the tea leaves. Season with the soy sauce.

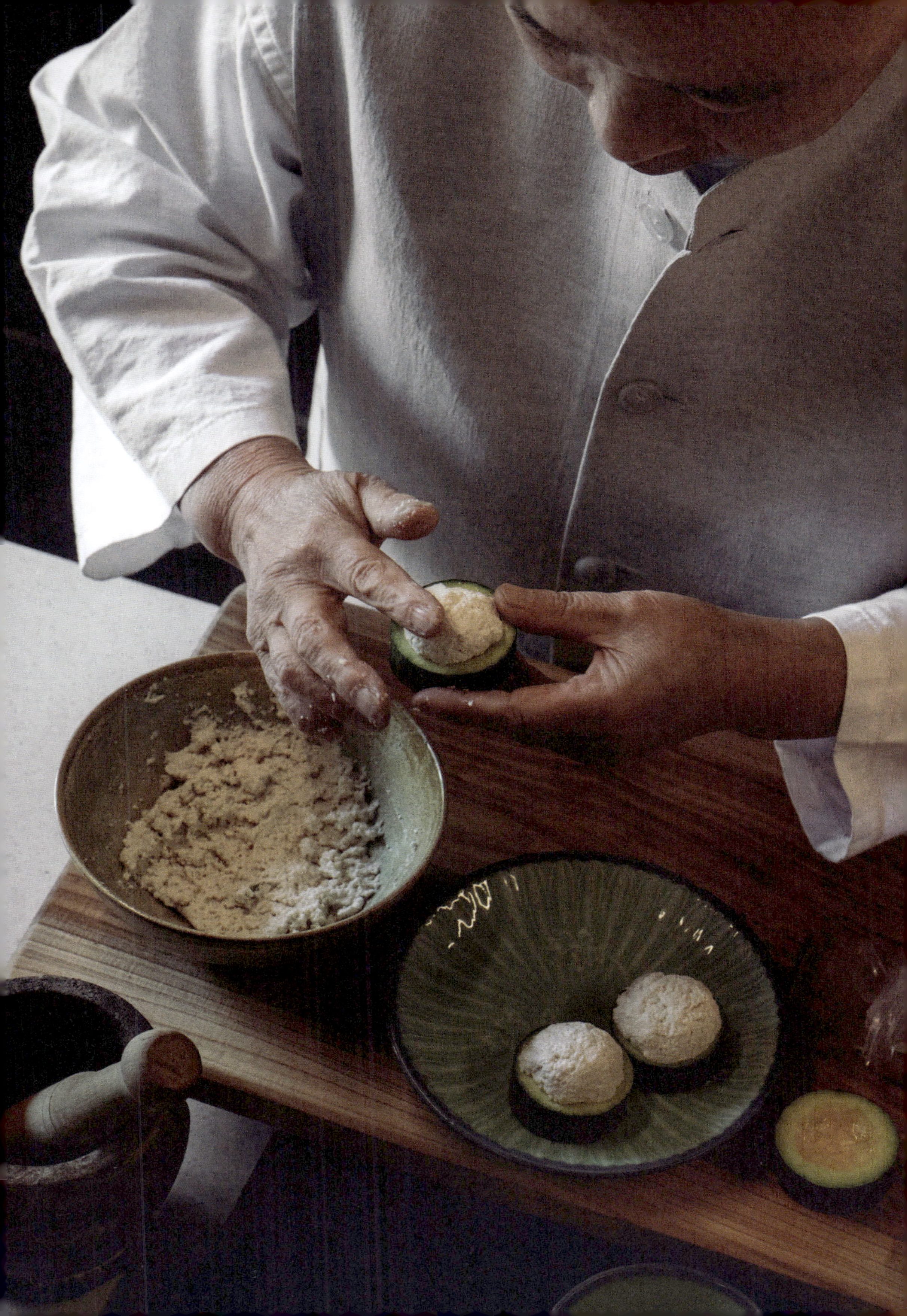

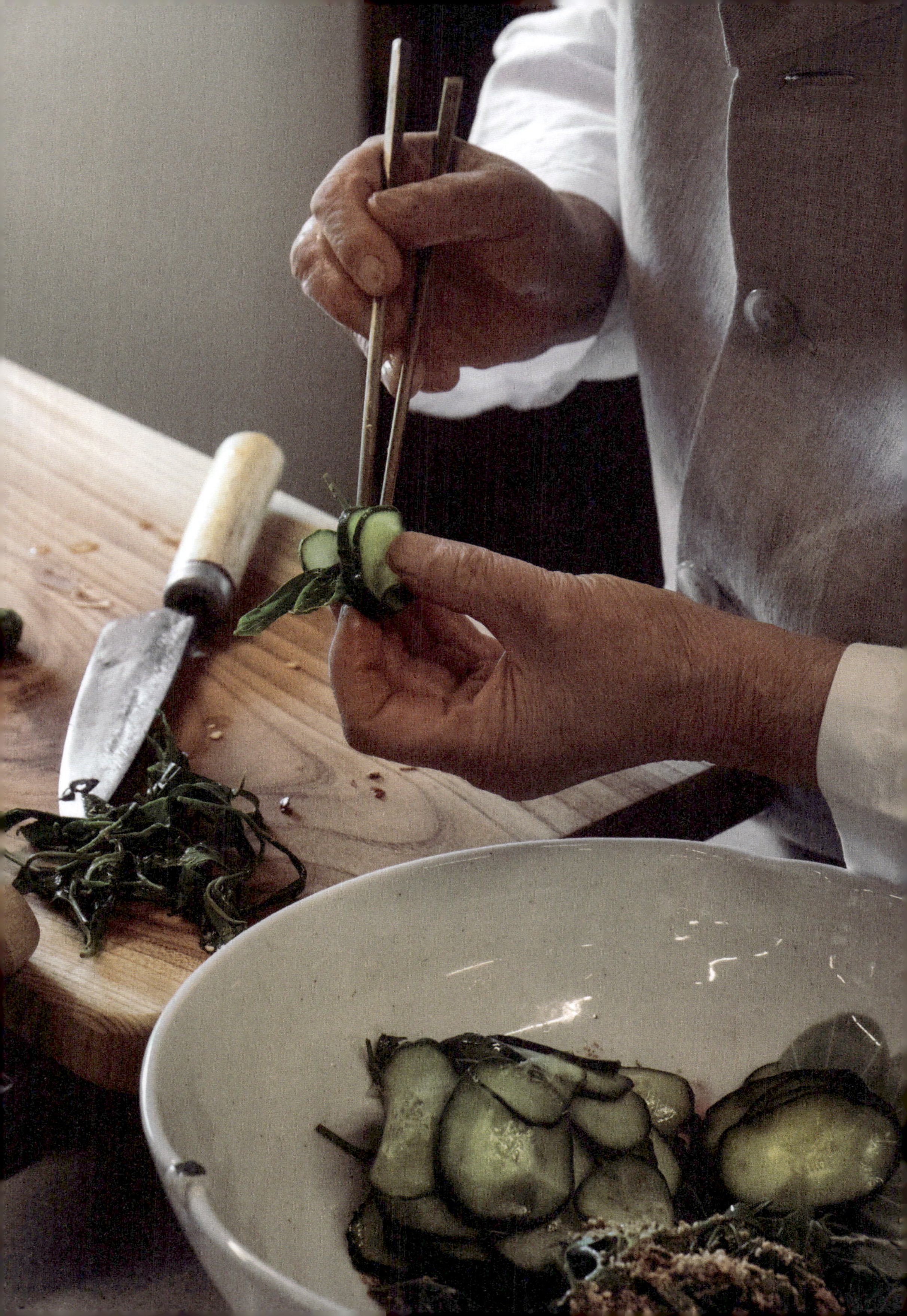

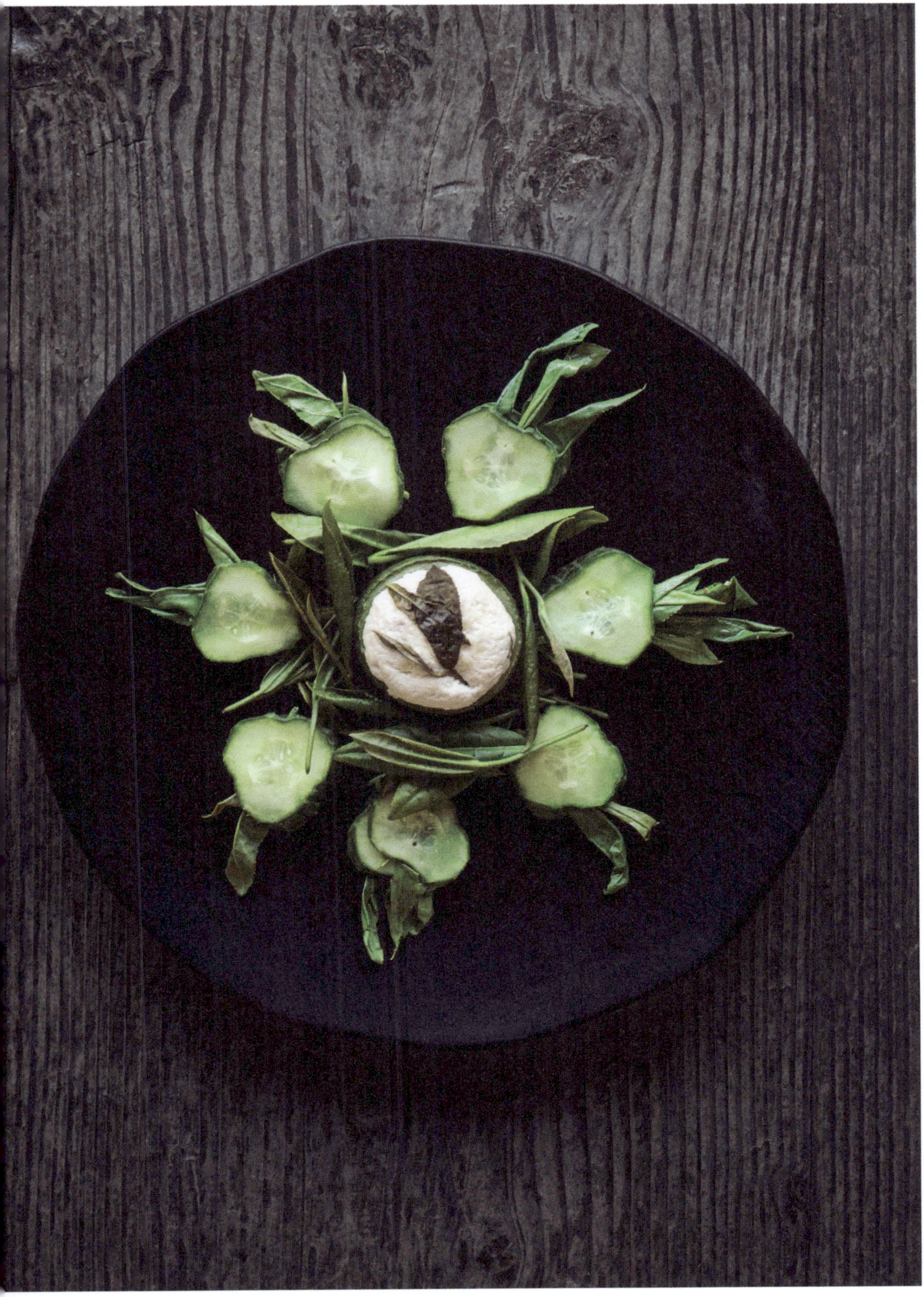

This dish has a special meaning for Jeongkwan Snim—it symbolizes her cooking skills and has become one of her signature dishes (page 56). She says that she's able to make it with her eyes closed and that she gets the best result when she does.

Pyogo beoseot jocheong-jorim

PYOGO MUSHROOMS BRAISED IN RICE SYRUP

20 Korean shiitake mushrooms (pyogo beoseot), fresh or dried
Salt for seasoning
2 cups (500 ml) water
2 tablespoons soy sauce (jipganjang, 5 to 7 years old)
1 tablespoon perilla oil (deulgireum)
2 tablespoons rice syrup (jocheong, page 190)

If using dried mushrooms, rinse them and soak them in water for 5 hours. Rinse them again and carefully cut out the stems. For fresh mushrooms, just rinse them before removing the stems.

Add a pinch of salt to a pot of water, then add the soy sauce and the perilla oil and bring to a boil. Add the mushrooms. The water should just cover the mushrooms.

Braise the mushrooms, periodically basting them with the liquid, until the sauce has thoroughly soaked into the mushrooms. Once the water has evaporated until about a third of it remains, add the jocheong.

Continue braising the mushrooms over low heat for a bit longer, stirring constantly, until they glisten. Remove from the stove and serve.

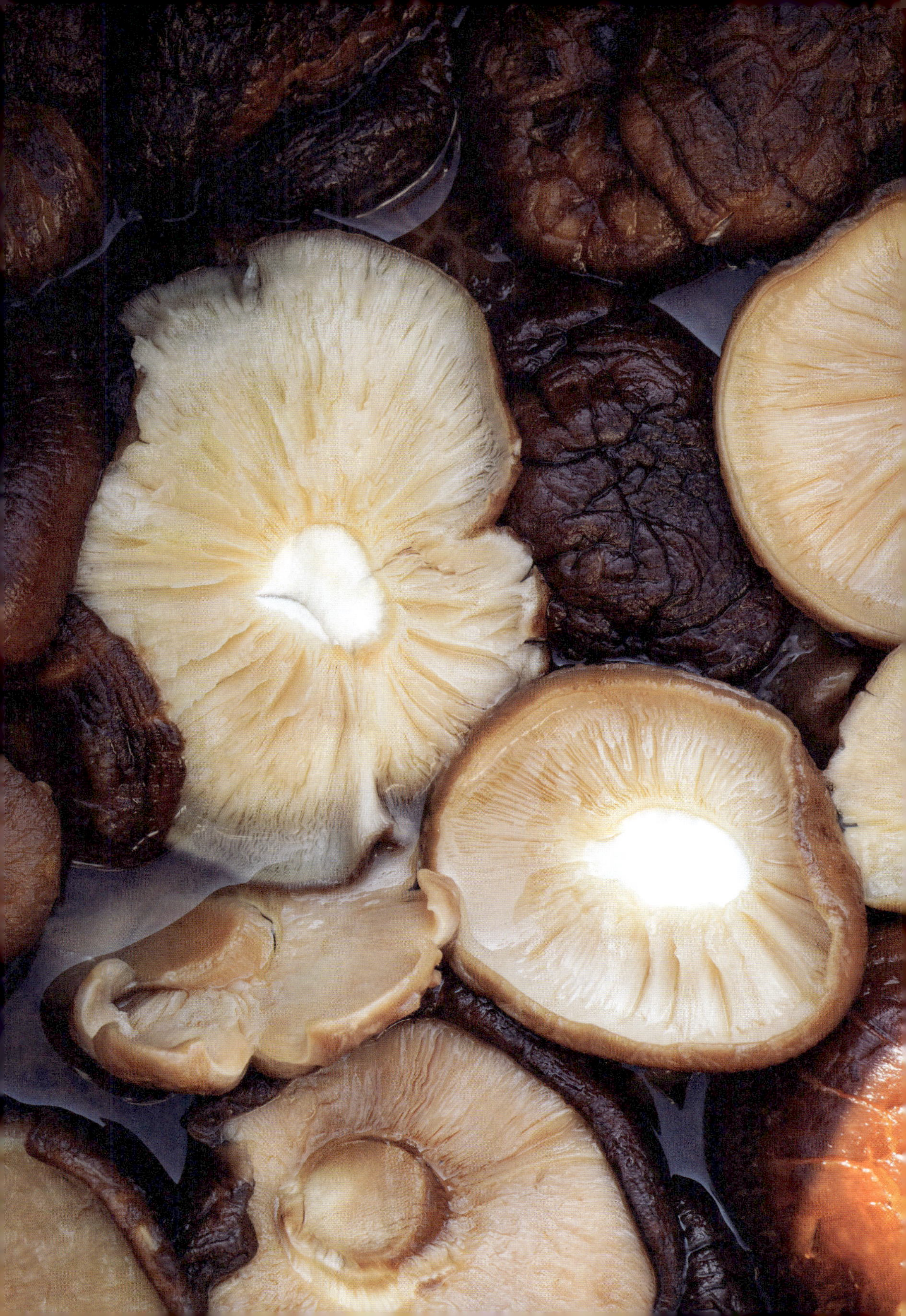

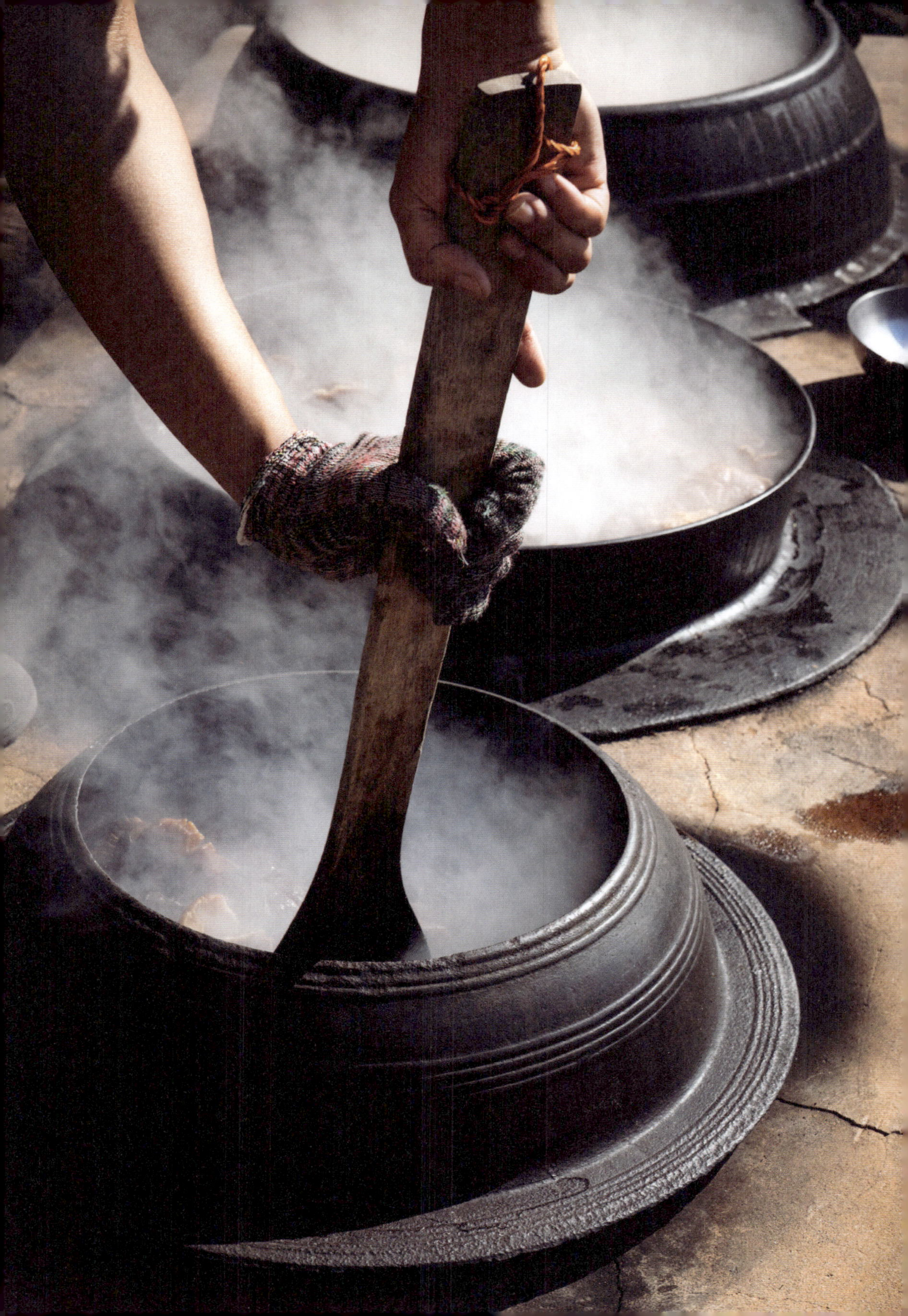

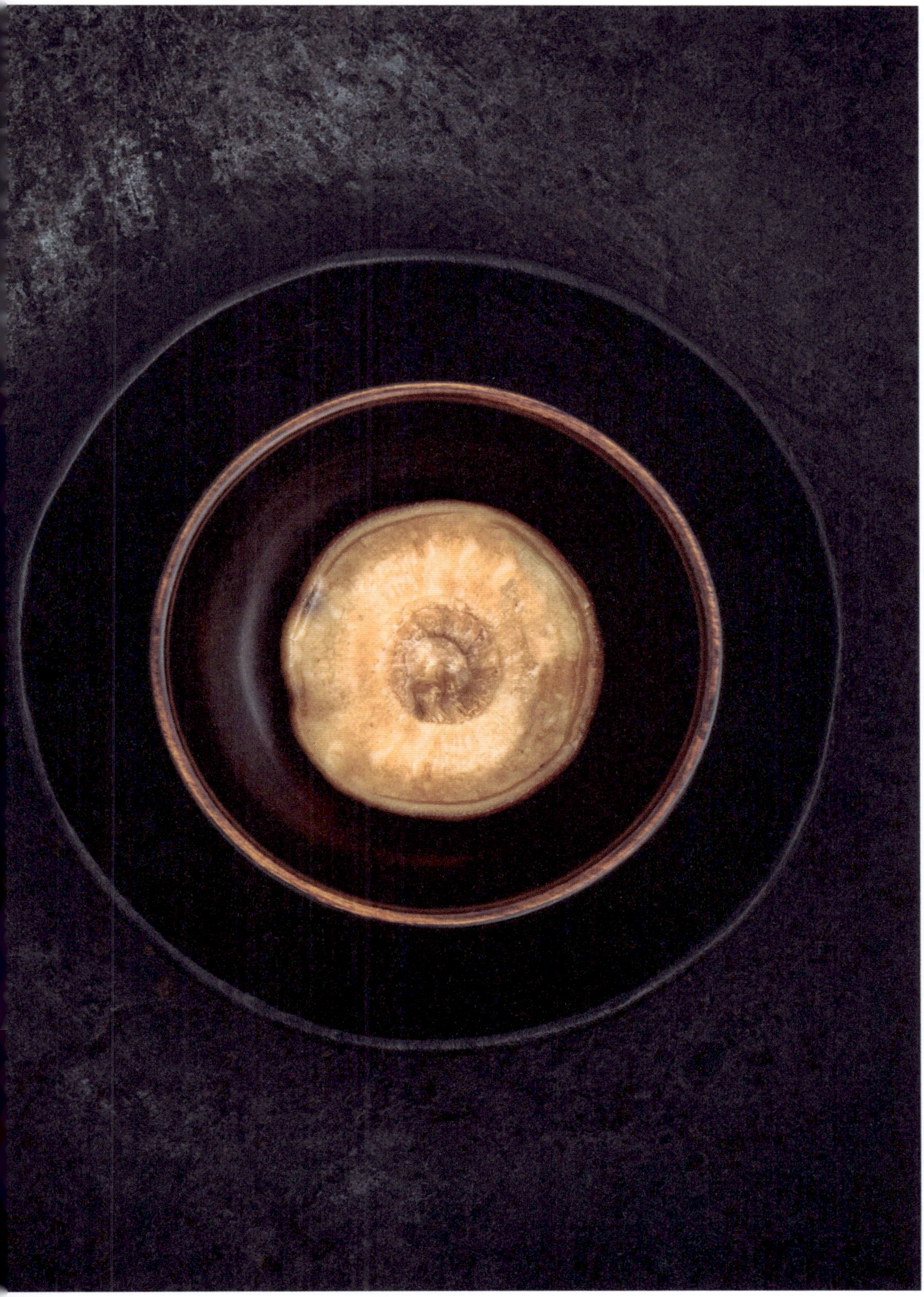

Minari-gochujang-jeon

PANCAKES WITH MINARI AND GOCHUJANG

5 cups (300 g) water celery (minari)
1 sun-dried red chile pepper (hoenari-gochu)
½ pound (200 g) potatoes (gamja)
¾ cup plus 1 tablespoon (100 g) buckwheat flour (maemil garu)
½ cup (60 g) pancake flour mix
Salt for seasoning
3 ½ teaspoons (20 g) Korean chili paste (gochujang)
2 tablespoons soybean oil

Rinse and halve the minari and cut the chili pepper into small pieces.

Grate the potatoes finely, mix them with the flour and pancake flour mix, and season them with salt. Mix with just enough water to form a batter. Pour half of the batter into a separate bowl and mix that half with the gochujang.

Heat the soybean oil in a pan. Coat half of the minari with the half of the batter that doesn't have gochujang and lay the minari in the pan. Sprinkle it with the minced chile pepper and fry it thoroughly. Coat the other half of the minari with the red gochujang batter and fry it as well.

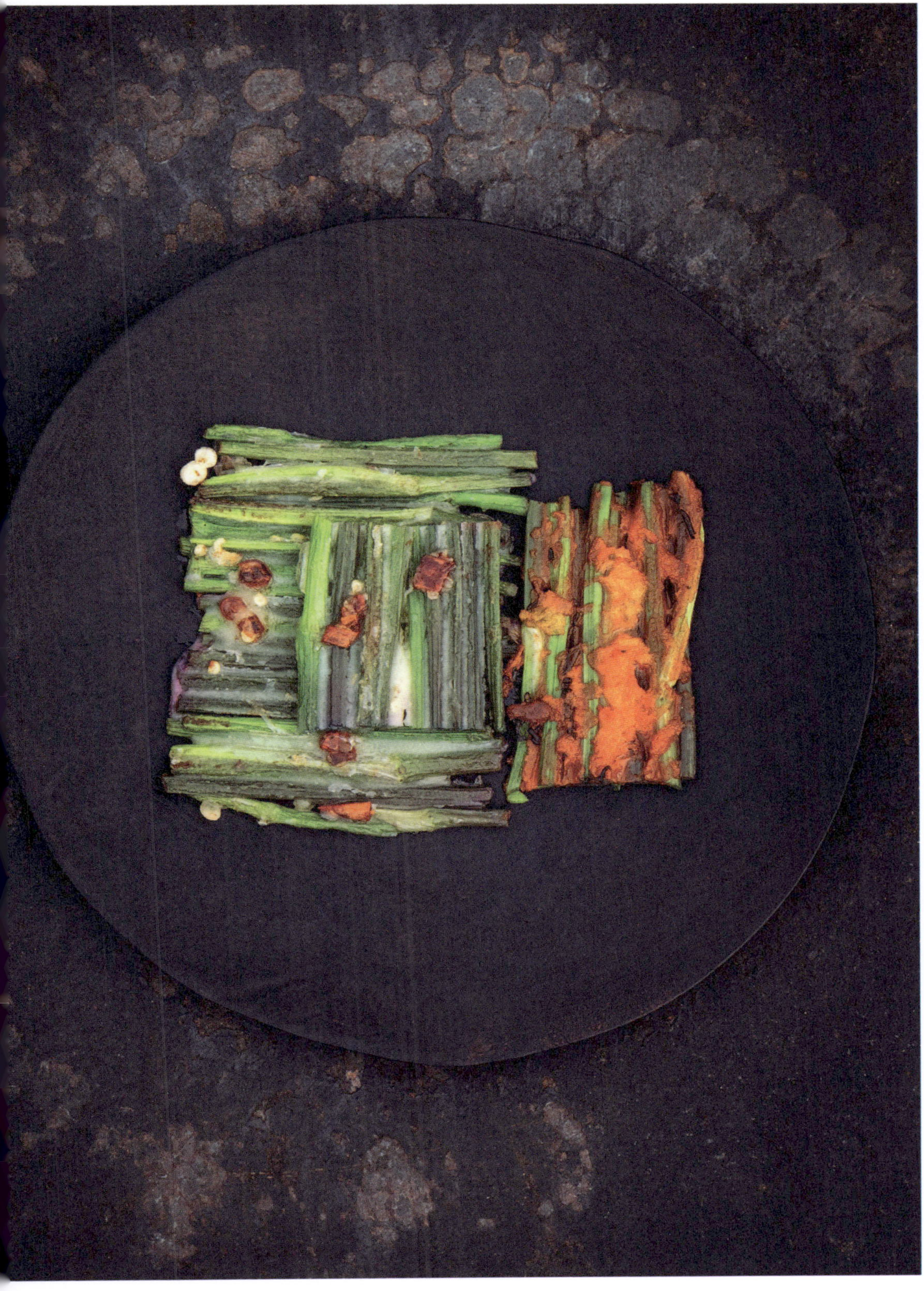

Jeongkwan Snim's *bugak* is distinguished by its natural ingredients and the yew-scented soy sauce and fermented glutinous rice paste she makes it with. Her bugak is quite popular and considered to be a delicacy. It's a bit easier and faster to make this with the glutinous rice paste on page 412.

Bugak

"FLOWER OF TEMPLE FOOD"

It's important that the oil temperature remain at a constant 425°F (220°C) throughout making this recipe. But only deep-fry the ingredients briefly! Otherwise, their color will become dark and they'll taste bitter.

For the glutinous rice paste (chapssalpul)
Glutinous rice (chapssal)
Salt for seasoning
Soy sauce (ganjang) for seasoning

Let the unwashed glutinous rice soak in a bowl with 3 times the quantity of water for 8 to 10 days. After a few days, bubbles will begin to form; that's a sign that fermentation has begun. After the 8 to 10 days, rinse the rice in cold water, drain it well, grind it, and boil it until a paste-like mass forms. Season it to taste with salt and soy sauce.

This is the way Jeongkwan Snim prepares her famous bugak with fermented glutinous rice paste, but if you want to make it easier to prepare this dish, you can make the paste with glutinous rice flour.

For the seaweed bugak
Dried seaweed (gim)
Glutinous rice paste (chapssalpul)
Sesame seeds (kkae)
Soybean oil for deep-frying

Using your hands, coat a seaweed sheet thinly with glutinous rice paste. Lay a second sheet on top and coat the second sheet with another thin layer of the paste. Scatter some sesame seeds onto the middle of each sheet of seaweed and let it dry for one day in the sun. (Or you can omit the sesame seeds.)

Cut the seaweed into suitably sized squares and deep-fry them very briefly in the oil. Drain them in a sieve and lay them out on paper towels.

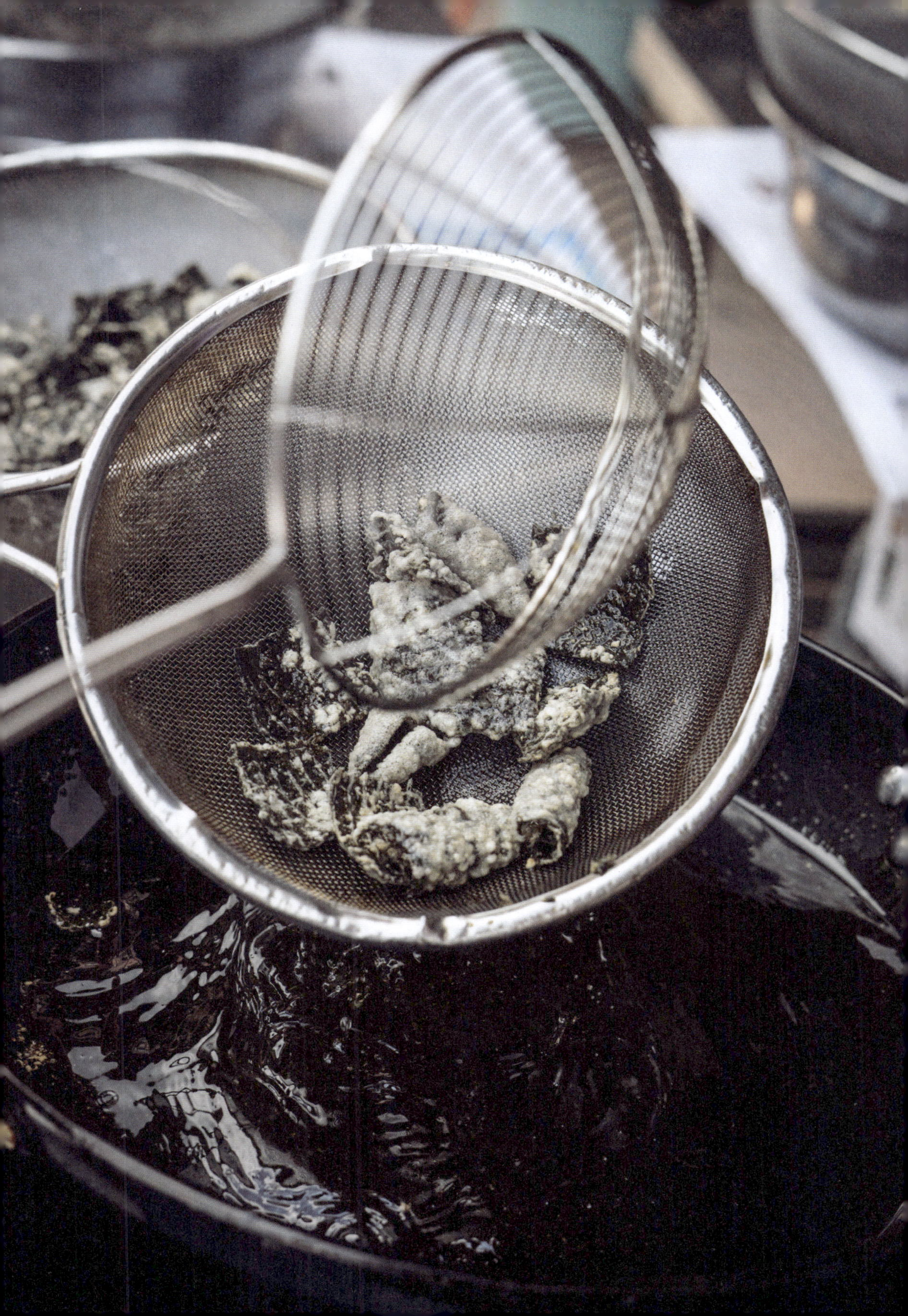

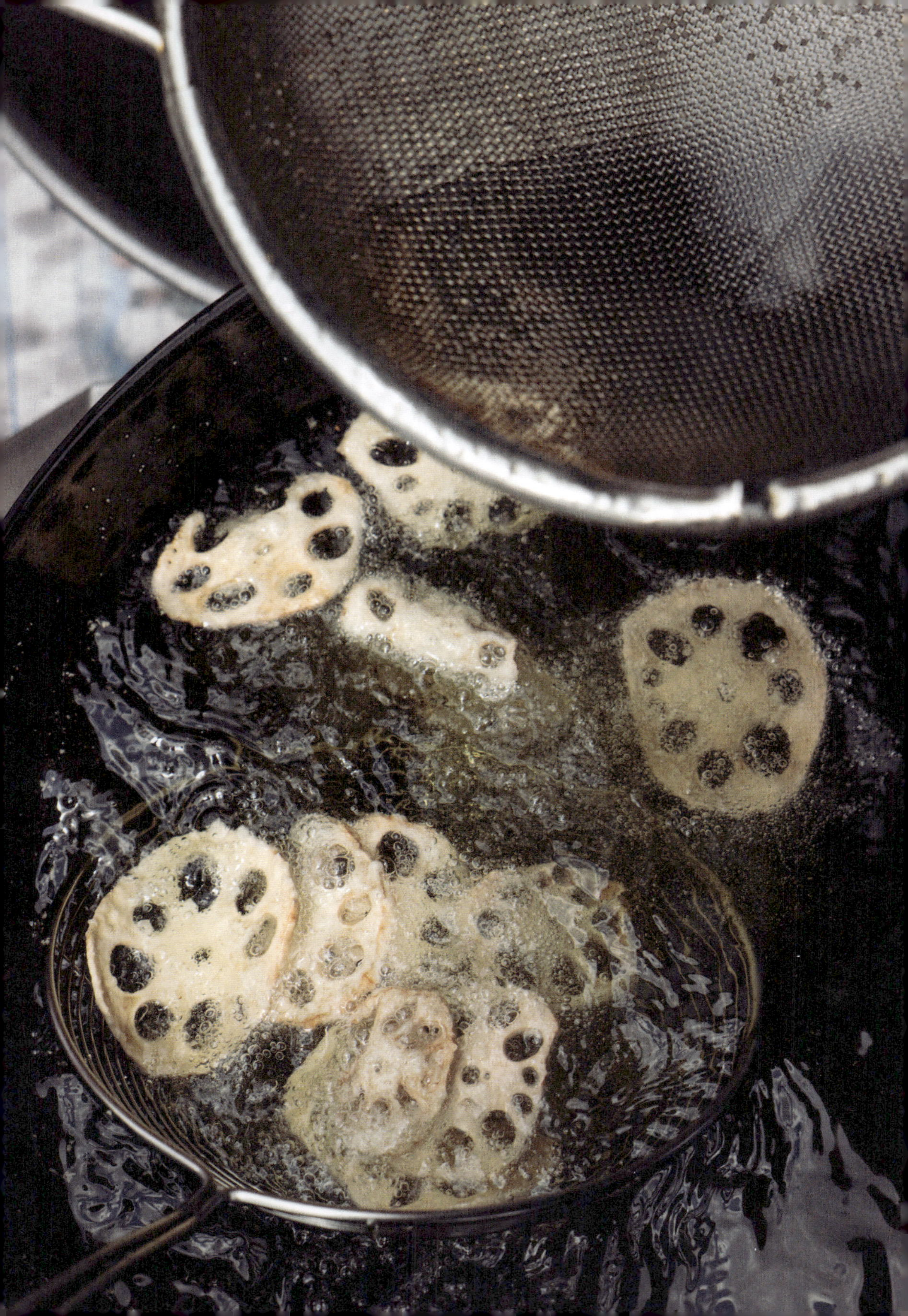

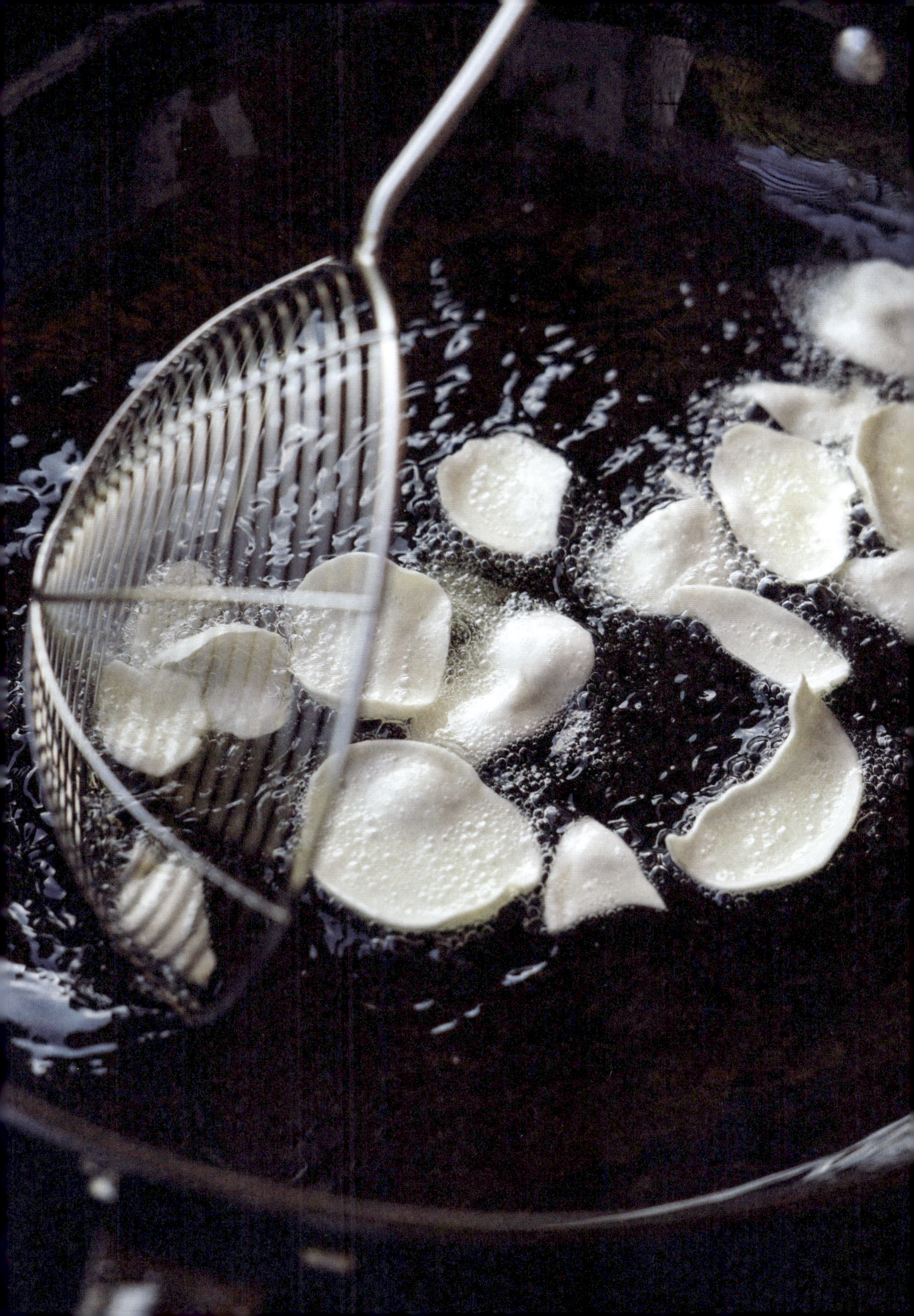

For the lotus root bugak
Lotus root (yeongeun)
Glutinous rice paste (chapssalpul)
Soybean oil for deep-frying

For the gajuknamul bugak
Fresh young leaves of Chinese toon
 (gajuknamul)
Glutinous rice paste (chapssalpul)
Sesame seeds (kkae)
Soybean oil for deep-frying

For the potato bugak
Starchy potatoes (gamja)
Salt for seasoning
Soybean oil for deep-frying

Peel the lotus root, rinse it, and slice it thinly. Boil it briefly in salted water for 1 to 2 minutes. (If desired, you can color the lotus root by including a slice of red beet in the boiling water.) Drain the slices and pat them dry with paper towels. Coat them thinly with the glutinous rice paste, then let them dry for one day in the sun. Deep-fry the sliced root briefly in batches. Drain them in a sieve and then lay them out on paper towels.

Rinse the fresh gajuknamul, then blanch it in boiling water. Shock it in cold water and squeeze it out thoroughly. Coat it with the glutinous rice paste, sprinkle it with sesame seeds, and let it dry in the sun for one day. Deep-fry it briefly in the oil. Drain it in a sieve and lay it out on paper towels.

Peel the potatoes, slice them very thinly, and let them sit in cold water for 5 hours to draw out the starch. Briefly blanch the potato slices in boiling salted water. Remove them and lay them out on a metal tray with holes in a single layer (or place them on a cooling rack). Let them dry for one day in the sun. Briefly deep-fry the slices; the color should remain pale. Drain them in a sieve and lay them out on paper towels.

Pack the bugak in an airtight container to keep it fresh and crispy.

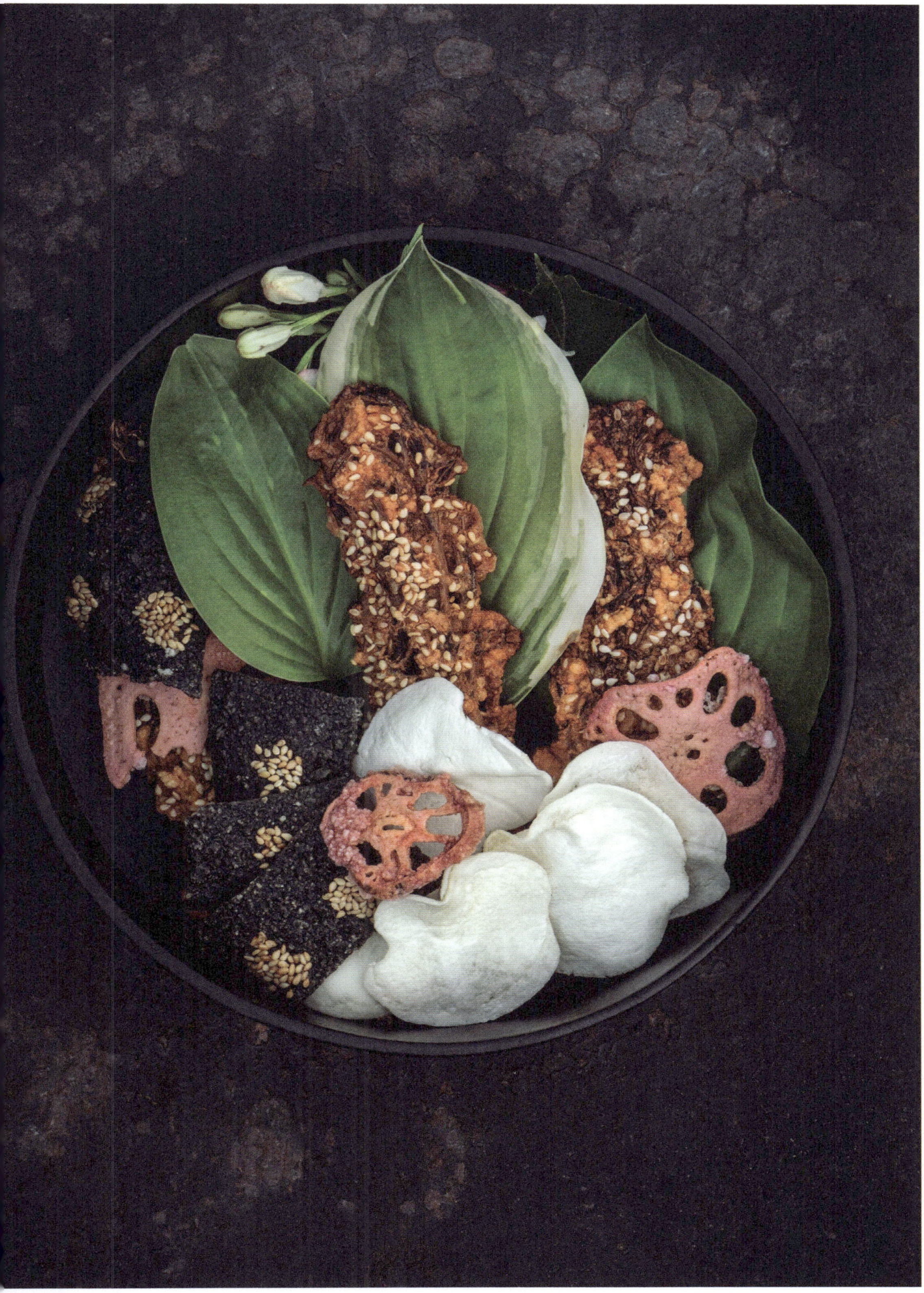

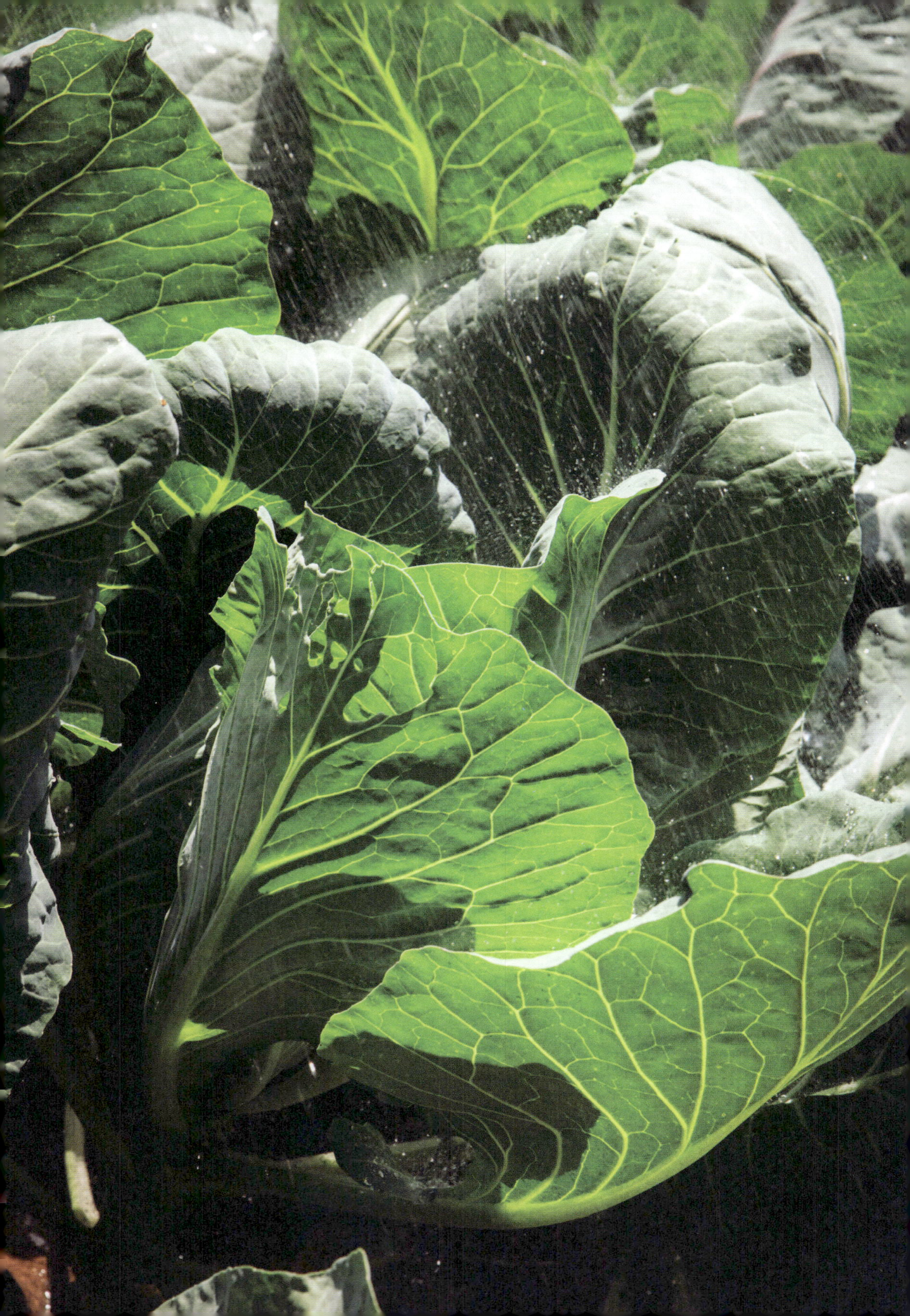

SUMMER

The summer heat ripens everything. The produce drinks in the warmth, transforming it into energy and storing it. Ears of corn form, their kernels emerge, and they gather fruitiness and sweetness.

However, the heat also seeps into the human body and causes it stress. Fortunately, there are cooling foods like cucumbers, napa cabbage, eggplant, zucchini, buckwheat, and tofu. Cooling the body from the inside out with proper nutrition helps us weather the summer better. If you then combine cooling foods with fermented ingredients like jangajji or doenjang, your meals will promote digestion and give your body relief from the heat.

Rice in Lotus Leaves — 270
Soup with Tofu and Napa Cabbage — 274
Tomato Jangajji — 276
Sansho Jangajji — 280
Fried Tofu with Pickled Sansho — 280
Cucumber Namul — 284
Soybean Sprouts with Turmeric — 286
Lotus Root with Yuja-Cheong — 288
Cold Vegetable and Mushroom Plate with Mustard Sauce — 292
Steamed Salted Eggplant — 294
Zucchini Breaded with Buckwheat — 296

Yeonnipbap

RICE IN LOTUS LEAVES

2 ¾ cups (500 g) glutinous rice (chapssal)
A handful of fresh kidney beans (gangnangkong) and shelled peas
5 whole lotus leaves (yeonnip)
Salt for seasoning

Cover the glutinous rice with cold water and let it stand for one hour.

Cook the kidney beans in boiling water for 10 minutes.

Remove the stems from the lotus leaves, lay the leaves out flat, and cut them into thirds.

Rinse and sieve the glutinous rice, then mix it with the beans and peas. Place a linen cloth in a steamer basket. Spread out the rice in the basket, fold the edges of the cloth on top of the rice, and let it steam over a small amount of water for 20 minutes.

Put the rice in a bowl, add some salt, and mix it carefully. Spread out a lotus leaf, shape a portion of the rice with your hands, and lay it on the leaf. Wrap it up snugly in the leaf.

Steam the leaves in a pot with a small amount of water (or in a steamer pot) for an additional 15 to 20 minutes, until the rice in the middle begins to take on the color of the leaf. Let it stand for a few minutes, then serve the entire closed leaf while it's still warm.

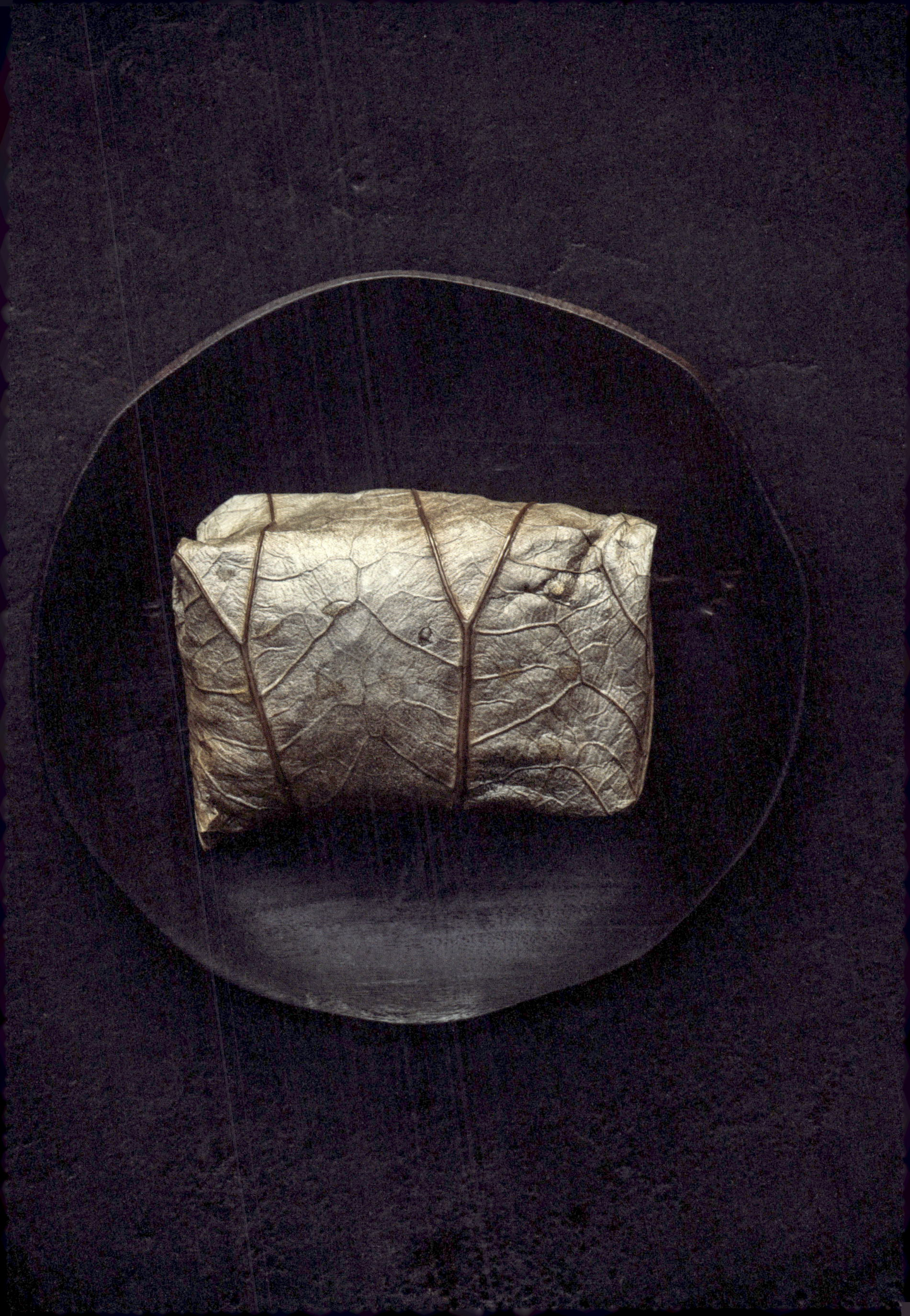

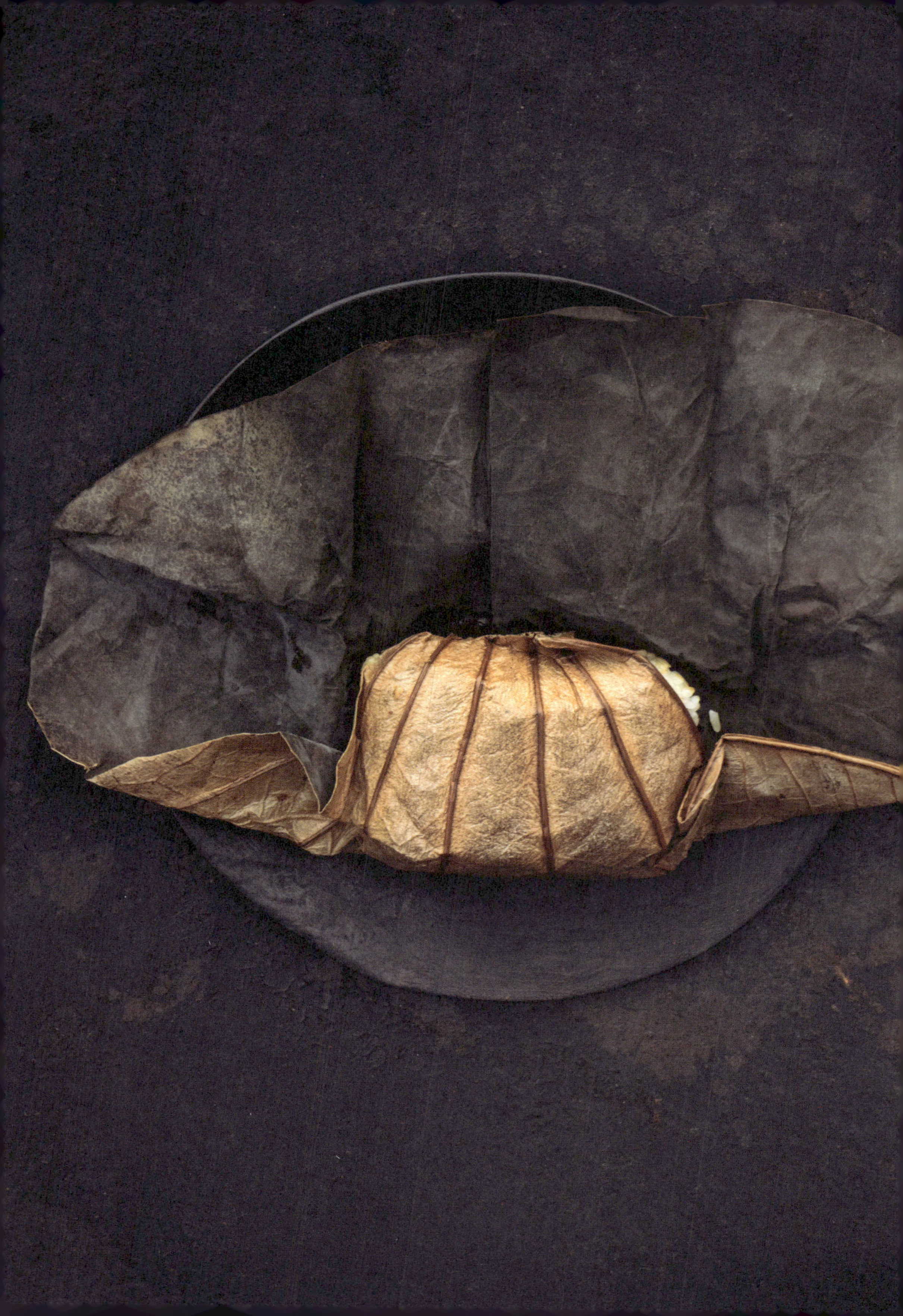

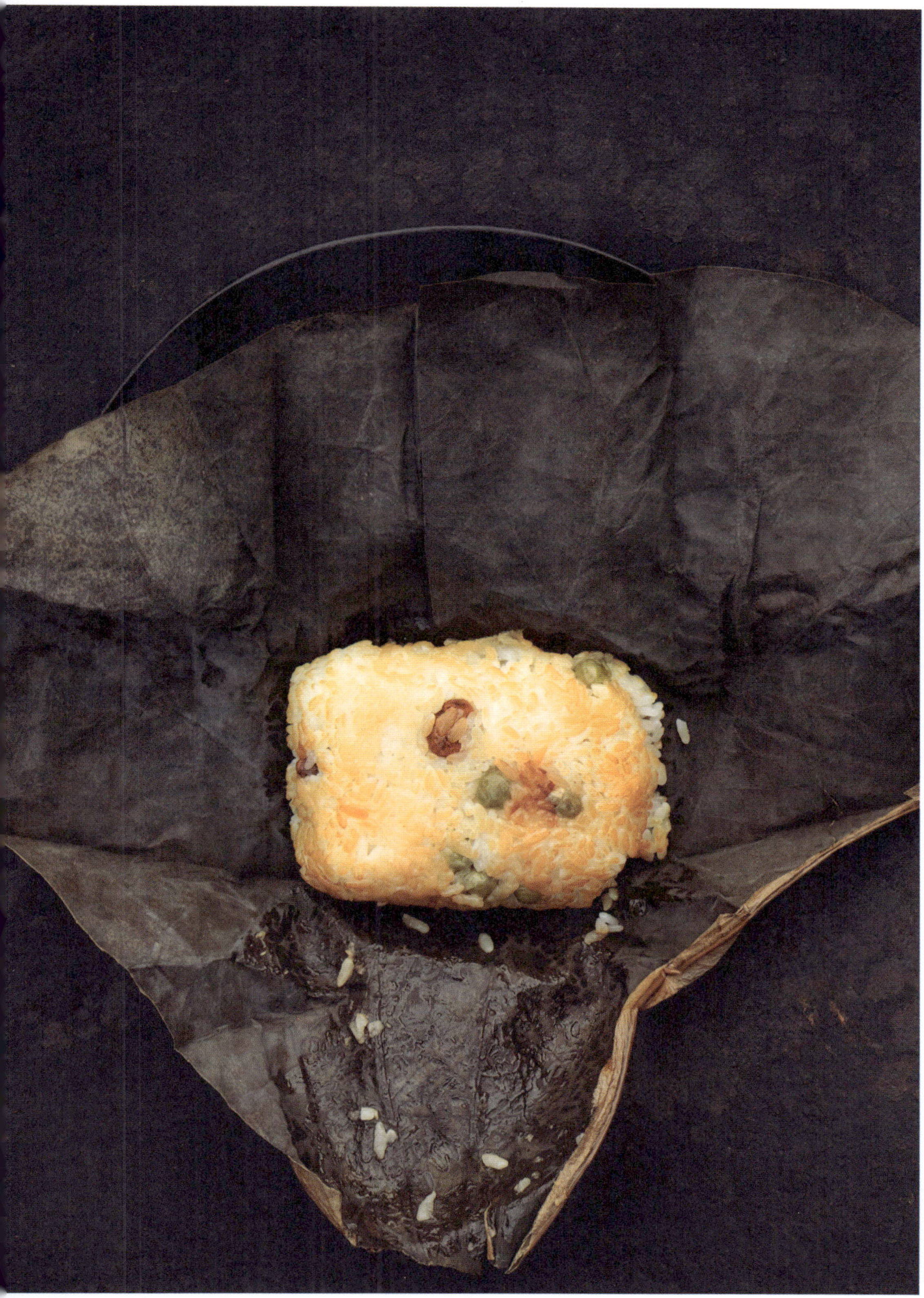

Malgeun baechuguk

SOUP WITH TOFU AND NAPA CABBAGE

6½ cups (1.5 L) water
10 ½ ounces (300 g) napa cabbage leaves (baechu)
7 ounces (200 g) tofu (dubu)
5 tablespoons soybean powder (konggaru)
Salt for seasoning

Bring the water to a boil.

Remove the stalks from the napa cabbage leaves, rinse the leaves, tear them into pieces, and add them to the boiling water. Cut the tofu in half. Cut one half into bite-size pieces and grate the other half. Add all of the tofu to the pot.

When the napa cabbage pieces are tender, slowly sprinkle the soybean powder into the soup and season to taste with salt. As soon as the soup begins to foam and little clumps form, it's ready to serve.

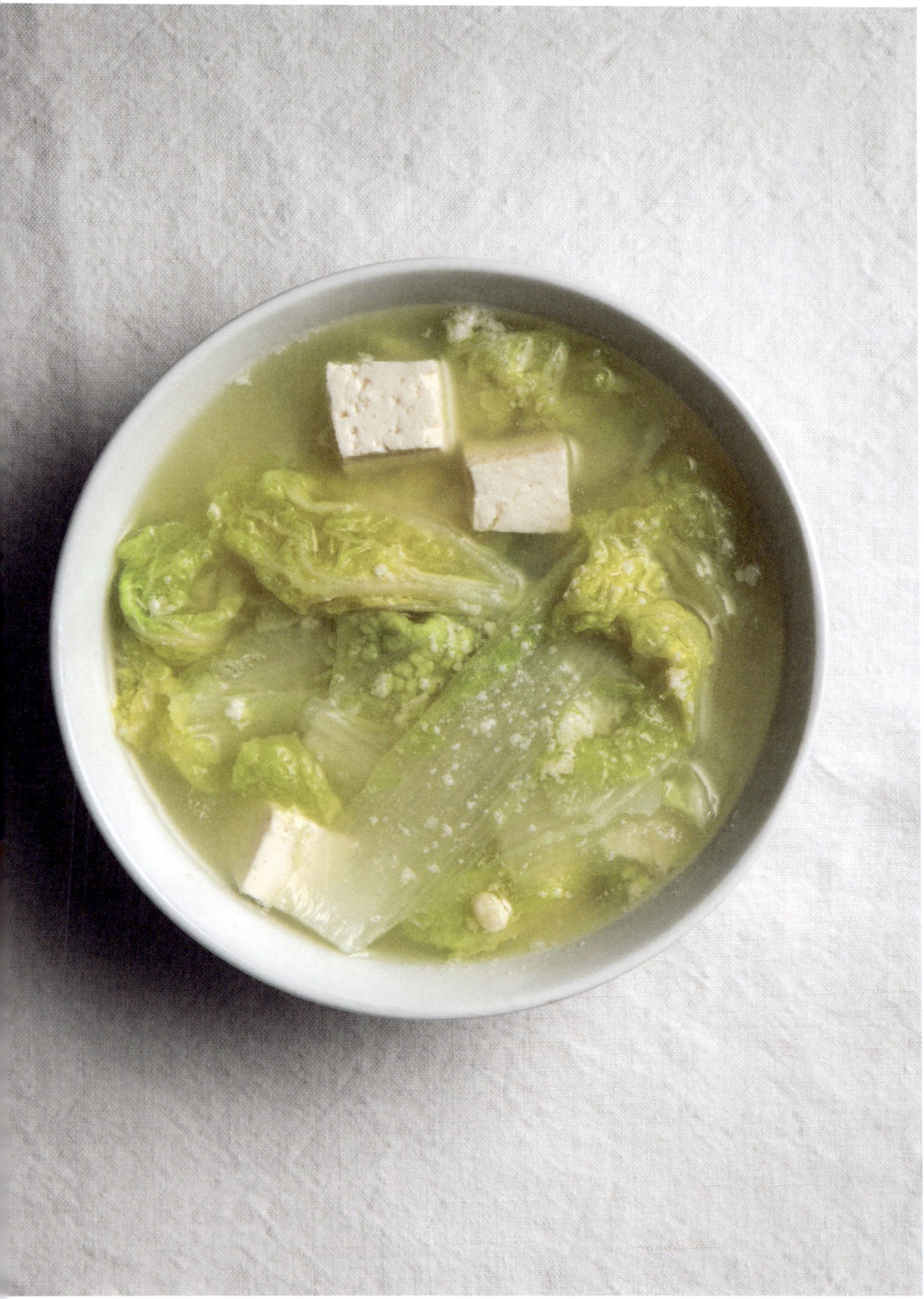

Tomato sogeum jangajji

TOMATO JANGAJJI

2 ¼ pounds (1 kg) green tomatoes (paran-tomato)
⅔ cup (200 g) salt, divided
2 cups (400 g) sugar, divided
2 ¼ pounds (1 kg) cherry tomatoes (bangul-tomato)

Rinse and halve the green tomatoes, then slice them into ¼-inch (5 mm) pieces. Mix them with ⅓ cup (100 g) of the salt and 1 cup (200 g) of the sugar and let stand for 3 hours.

Place the green tomatoes in a sieve and gently squeeze out some of the liquid. Dry them for 5 hours in a dehydrator (or oven) at 130°F (55°C).

Pour boiling water over the cherry tomatoes and let stand briefly, then tip them into cold water. Let them cool briefly and then peel.

Mix the remaining ⅓ cup (100 g) salt and 1 cup (200 g) sugar with the peeled cherry tomatoes and let stand for 3 hours.

Remove them with a slotted wooden spoon, drain them, and dry them in a dehydrator (or oven) at 140°F (60°C) for 5 hours. Turn them over and dry them in the sun for another 5 hours.

Store the dried green and cherry tomatoes in separate containers. They'll keep in airtight containers for a few months. The tomatoes can be eaten as *banchan*.

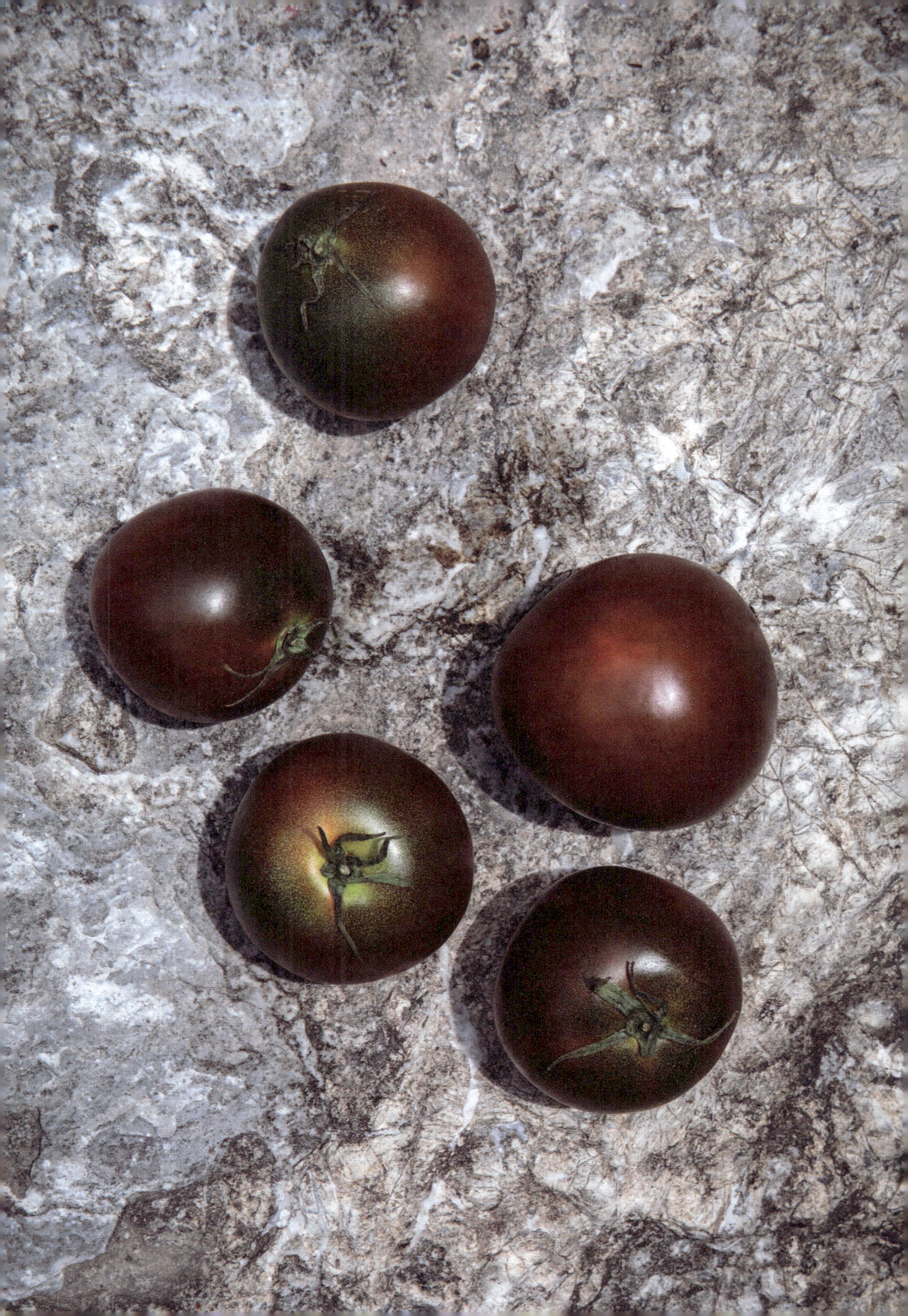

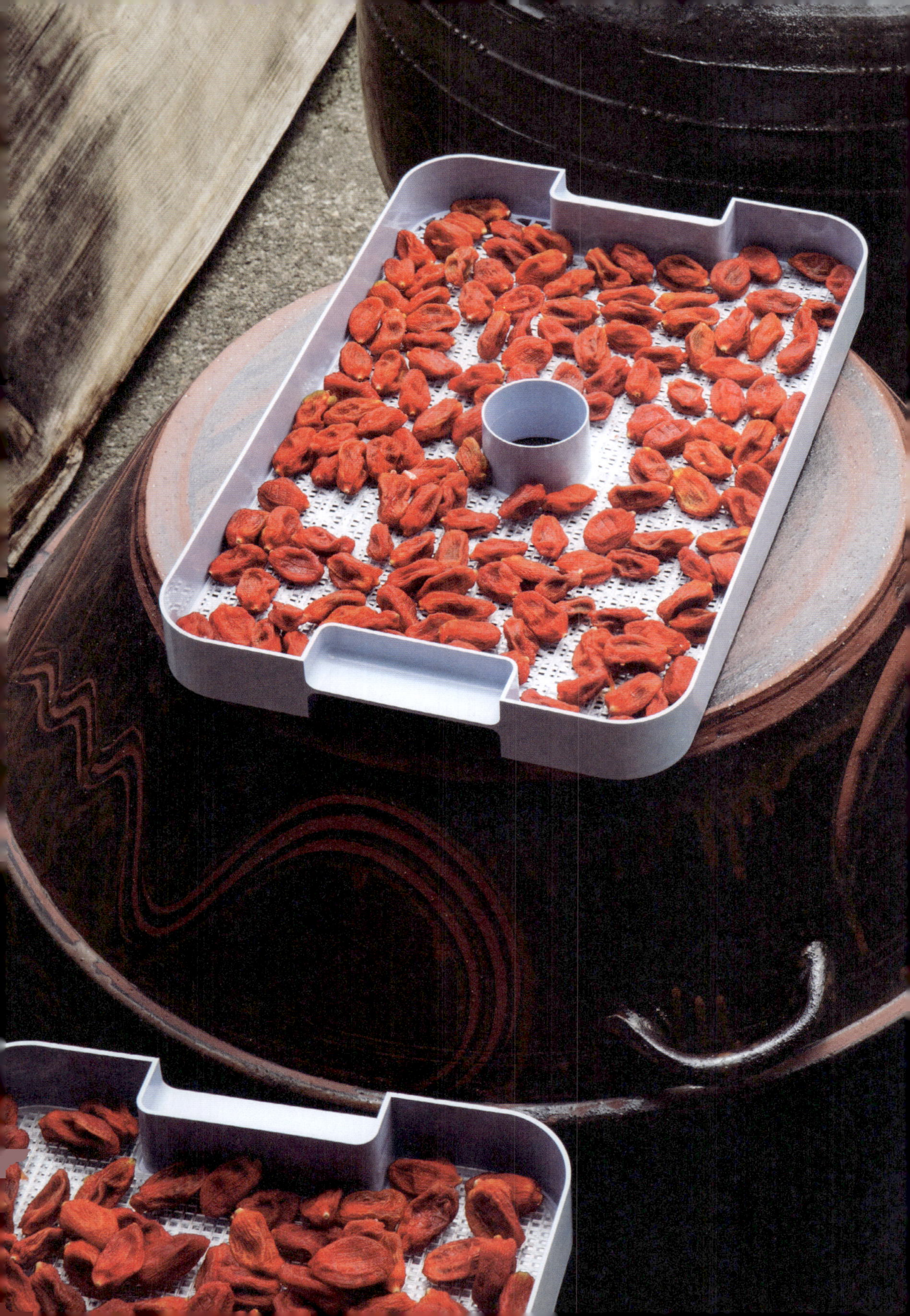

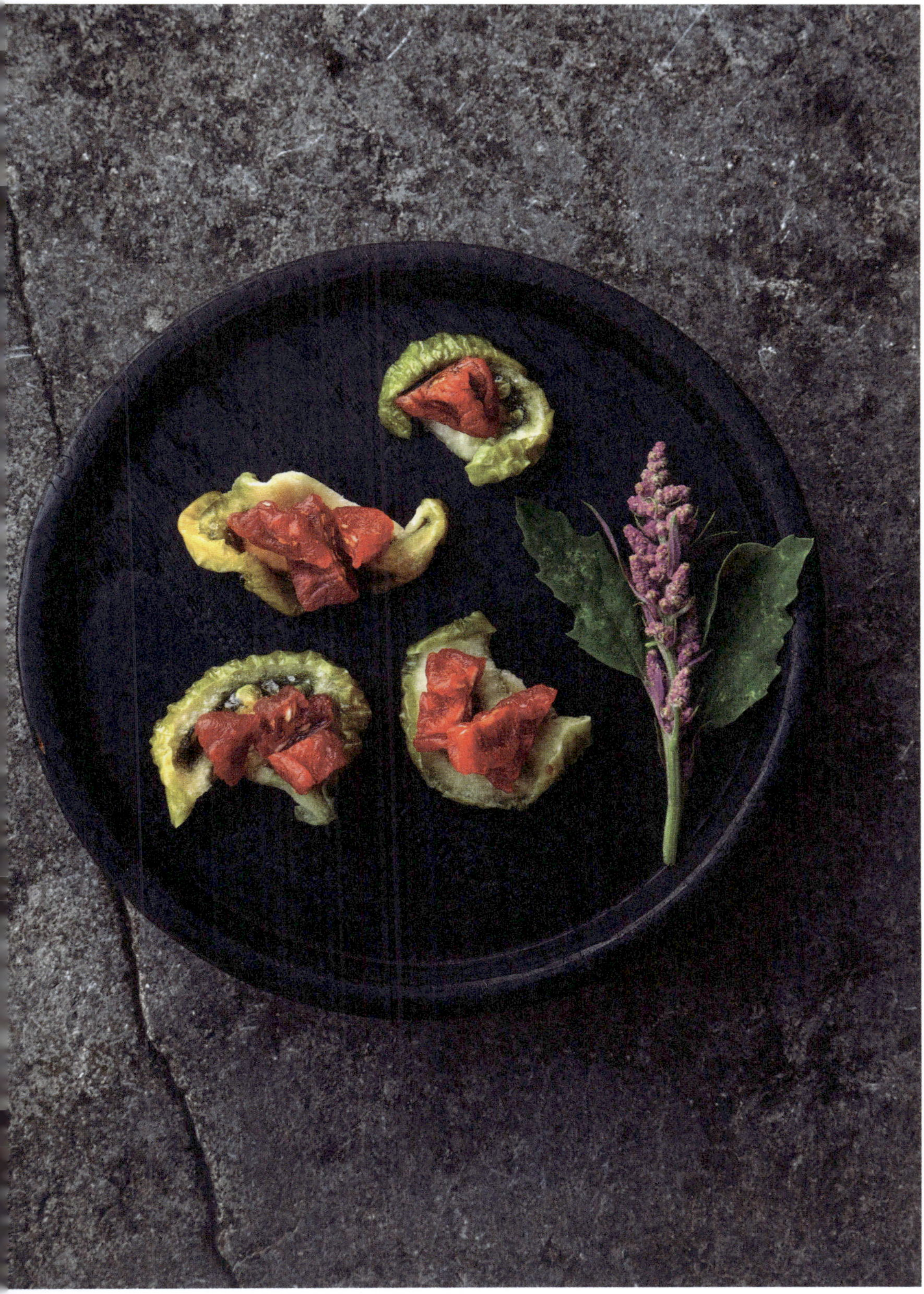

Sansho is also called "wild pepper." It consists of little berries that grow wild in southern Korea. They start off green but later become black, and they have an intense aroma. Sansho oil is popular, too, and Sansho Jangajji is a favorite dish among the snims.

Sansho Jangajji

SANSHO JANGAJJI

Wild pepper (sansho)
1 part soy sauce (ganjang)
2 parts water
Salt for seasoning

Pick the sansho in late summer when it's still somewhat green. Cut the berries into small pieces and rinse them.

Add them to boiling salted water and cook for one minute, then remove them and shock them in cold water. Let them sit in a bowl of water for five hours to remove their bitter flavor.

Drain the berries in a colander. Mix 1 part soy sauce with 2 parts water, bring to a boil, and salt it. Let cool.

Fill a container with the sansho and pour in enough liquid to cover the peppers, then use a clean stone (or other appropriate weight) to weigh the sansho down and keep everything submerged. Let the mixture stand in a cool shady place for one year. Combines very well with tofu.

Sansho guun-dubu

FRIED TOFU WITH PICKLED SANSHO

10 ½ ounces (300 g) tofu (dubu)
1 teaspoon salt
3 tablespoons perilla oil (deulgireum)
Pickled wild pepper (sansho) for serving
Rice for serving

Cut the tofu into 1 ¼-inch (3 cm) cubes and season it with salt.

Heat the perilla oil in a pan and fry the tofu cubes until they're golden brown on all sides. Let cool.

Place the tofu cubes on a plate and serve with sansho and rice.

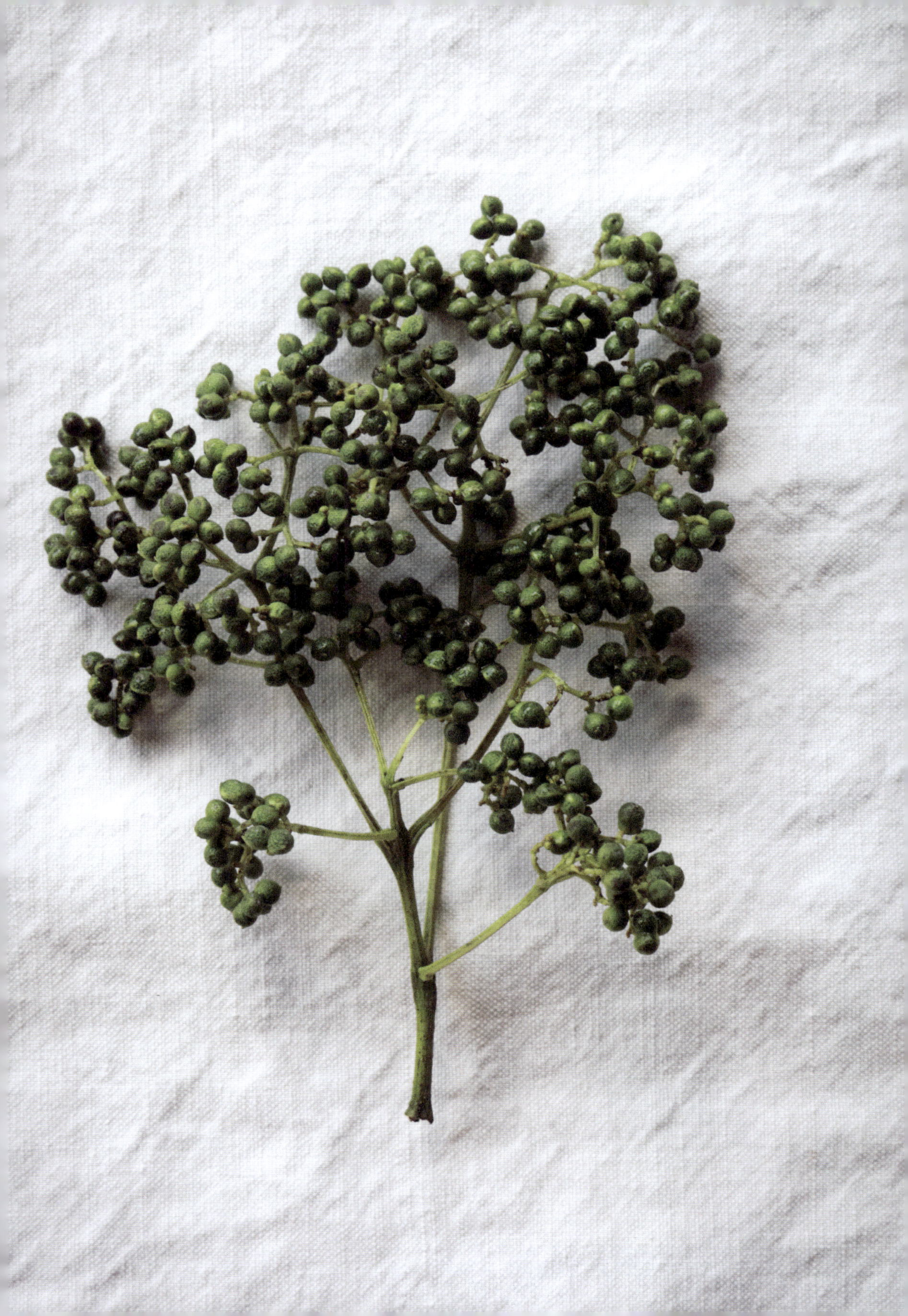

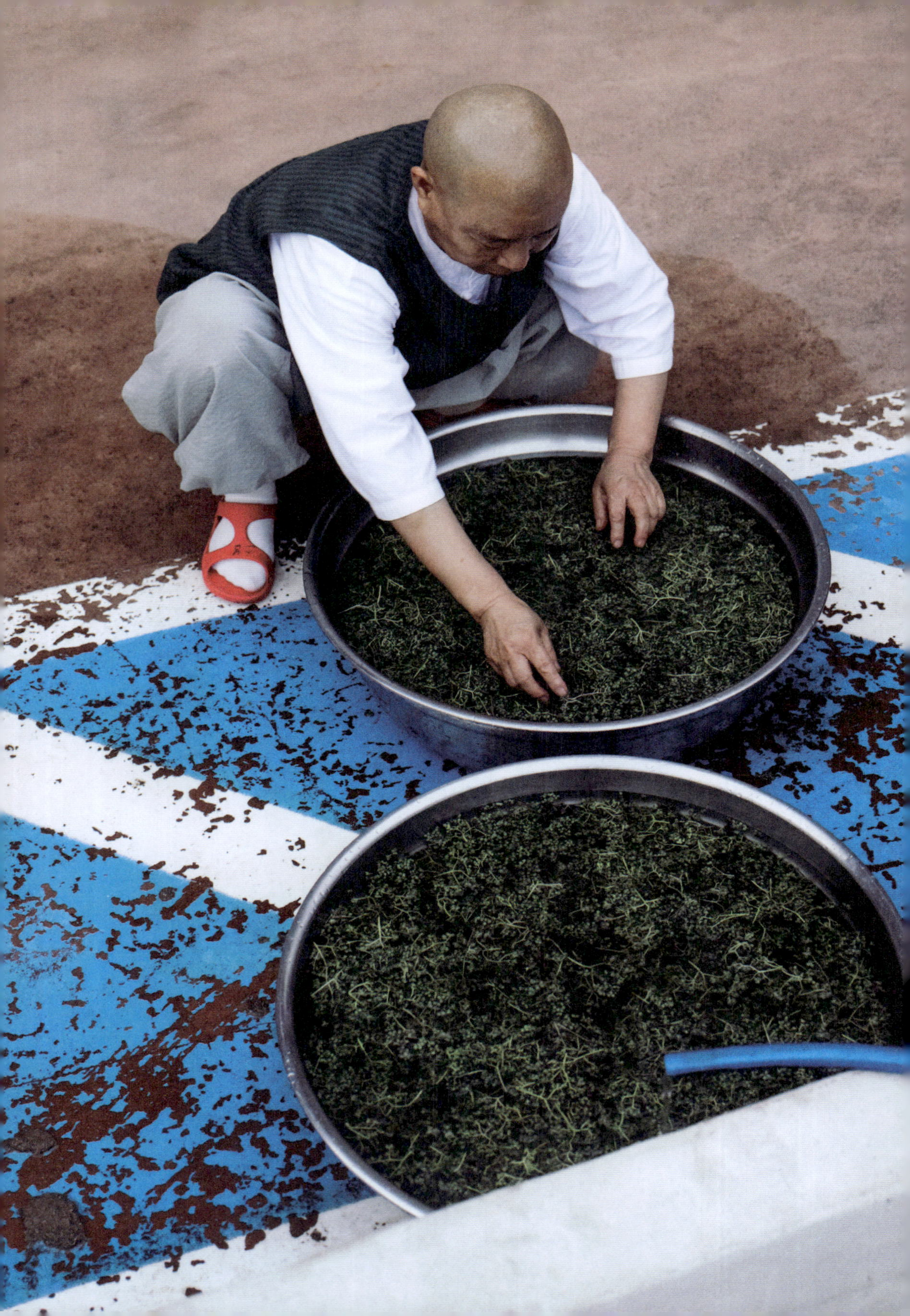

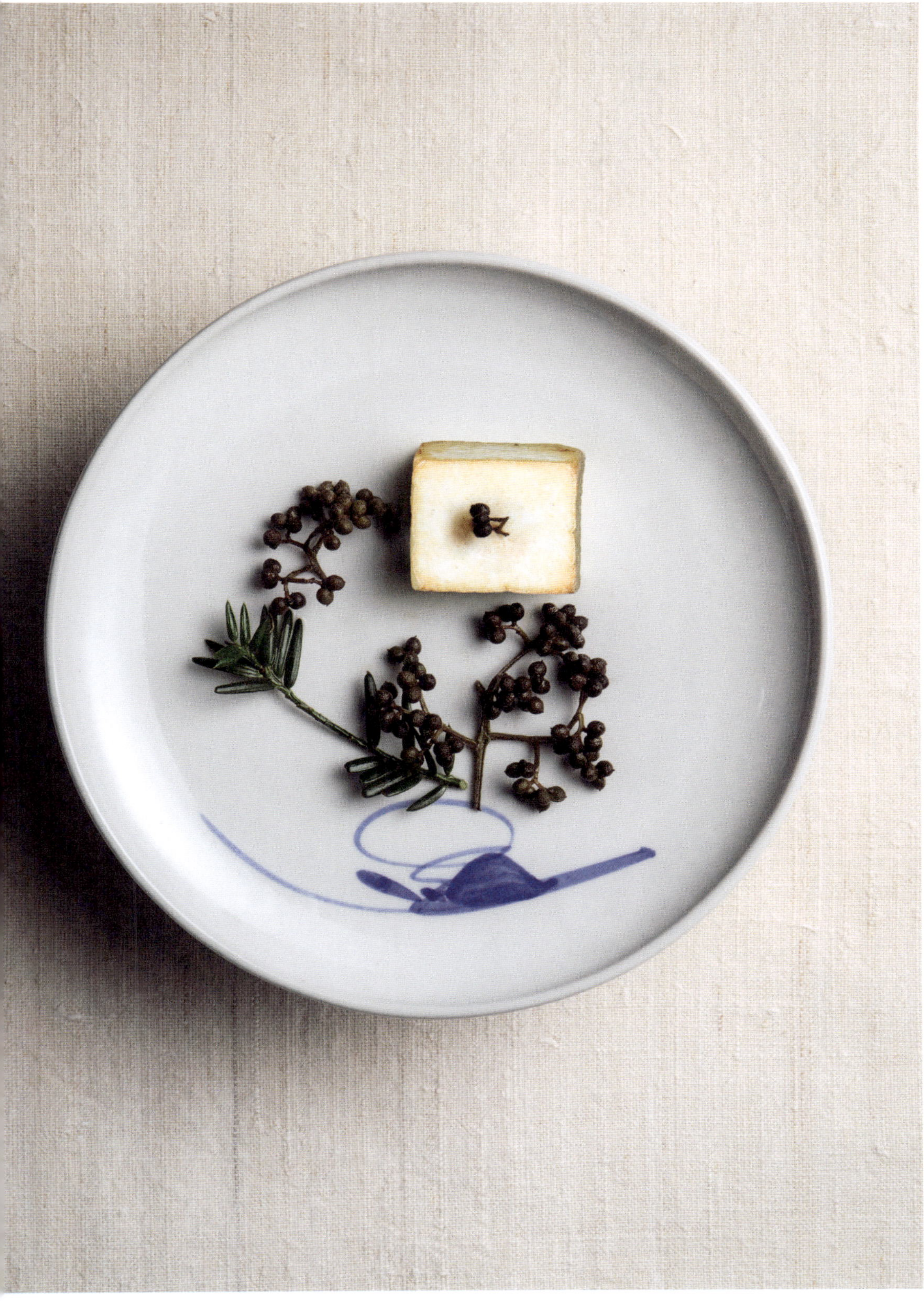

Oinamul

CUCUMBER NAMUL

2 cucumbers (oi)
Salt for seasoning
Soybean oil or perilla oil, for cooking
Sesame seeds (kkae), crushed

Rinse the cucumbers and slice them into ¼-inch (5 mm) slices.

Add the cucumber slices to a bowl, sprinkle with some salt, and add a splash of water. Mix well and let stand for 5 minutes.

Squeeze out the cucumber thoroughly and fry it carefully in a pan with some oil.

If necessary, season to taste with more salt, then sprinkle some sesame seeds over the cucumber to serve.

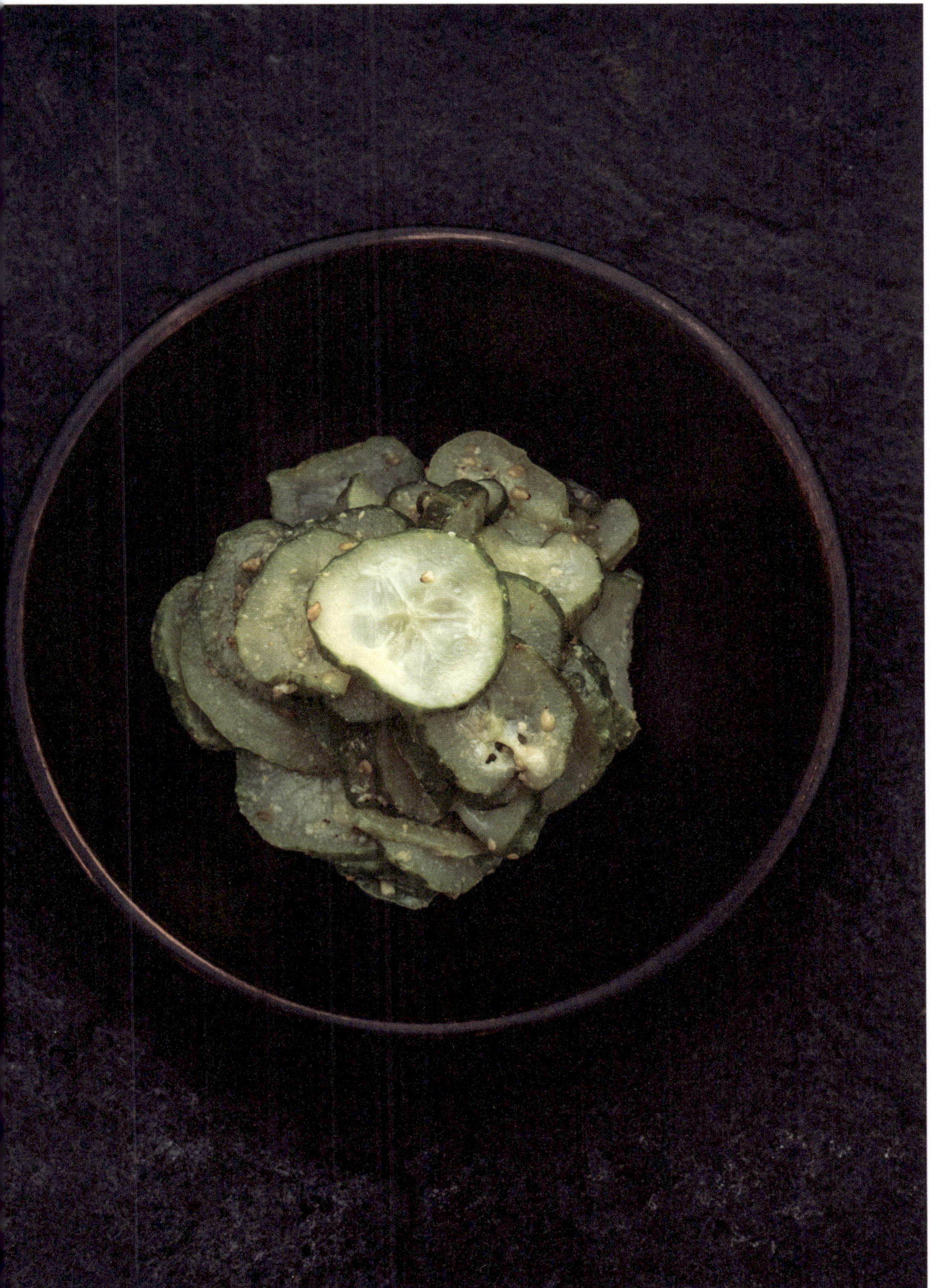

Kongnamul karebokkeum

SOYBEAN SPROUTS WITH TURMERIC

5 cups (500 g) soybean sprouts (kongnamul)
2 tablespoons perilla oil (deulgireum)
2 tablespoons turmeric (ganghwang)
Salt for seasoning
Edible flowers, such as blue chamomile (haneul gukhwa)

Clean the soybean sprouts, rinse them well, and drain them.

Warm the perilla oil over high heat and add the sprouts. Sauté them until their characteristic scent has dissipated. Add the turmeric and season with salt, and toss everything well in the pan.

Sprinkle with the flower petals to serve.

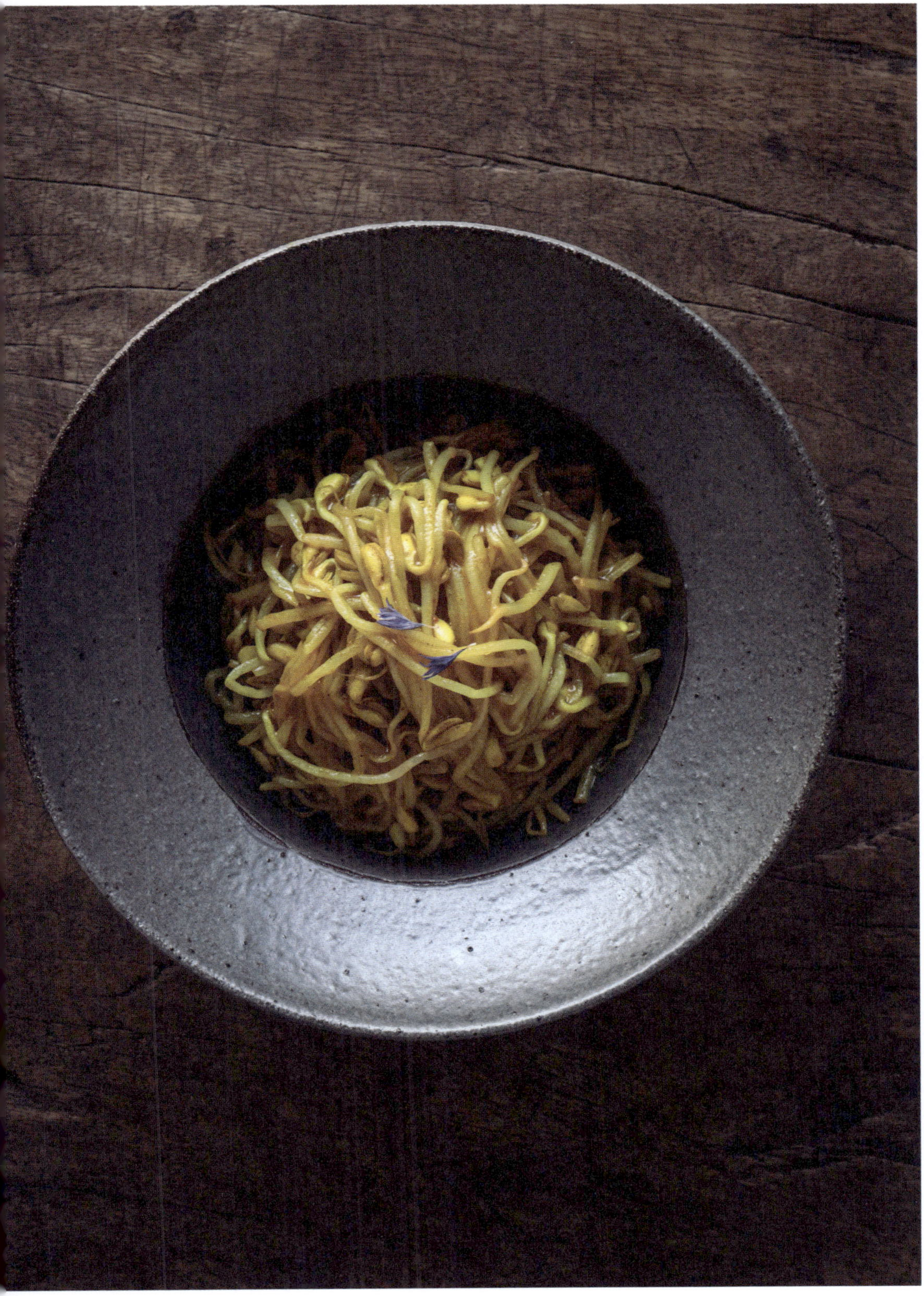

Yeongeun yuja-cheong muchim

LOTUS ROOT WITH YUJA-CHEONG

1 lotus root (yeongeun)
3 tablespoons persimmon vinegar (gamcho), divided
1 tablespoon Maesil-Cheong (page 174)
Salt for seasoning
2½ tablespoons (50 g) yuja-cheong (page 416)
1 tablespoon Rice Syrup (Jocheong, page 190)
1 long green chile pepper (cheongyang-gochu), dried (pages 403–404)

Peel and rinse the lotus root, then slice it into ¼-inch (5 mm) pieces. Bring a pot of water to boil and add 1 tablespoon of the persimmon vinegar. Cook the lotus root for a few minutes.

Mix 2 tablespoons of water, 1 tablespoon of persimmon vinegar, the maesil-cheong, and some salt and marinate the lotus root in the mixture for five minutes. Remove the slices.

In a bowl, mix the yuja-cheong, the remaining 1 tablespoon of persimmon vinegar and the jocheong to make a sauce.

Add the lotus root to the sauce. Tear the dried green chile pepper into pieces with your hands and carefully mix it with the lotus root

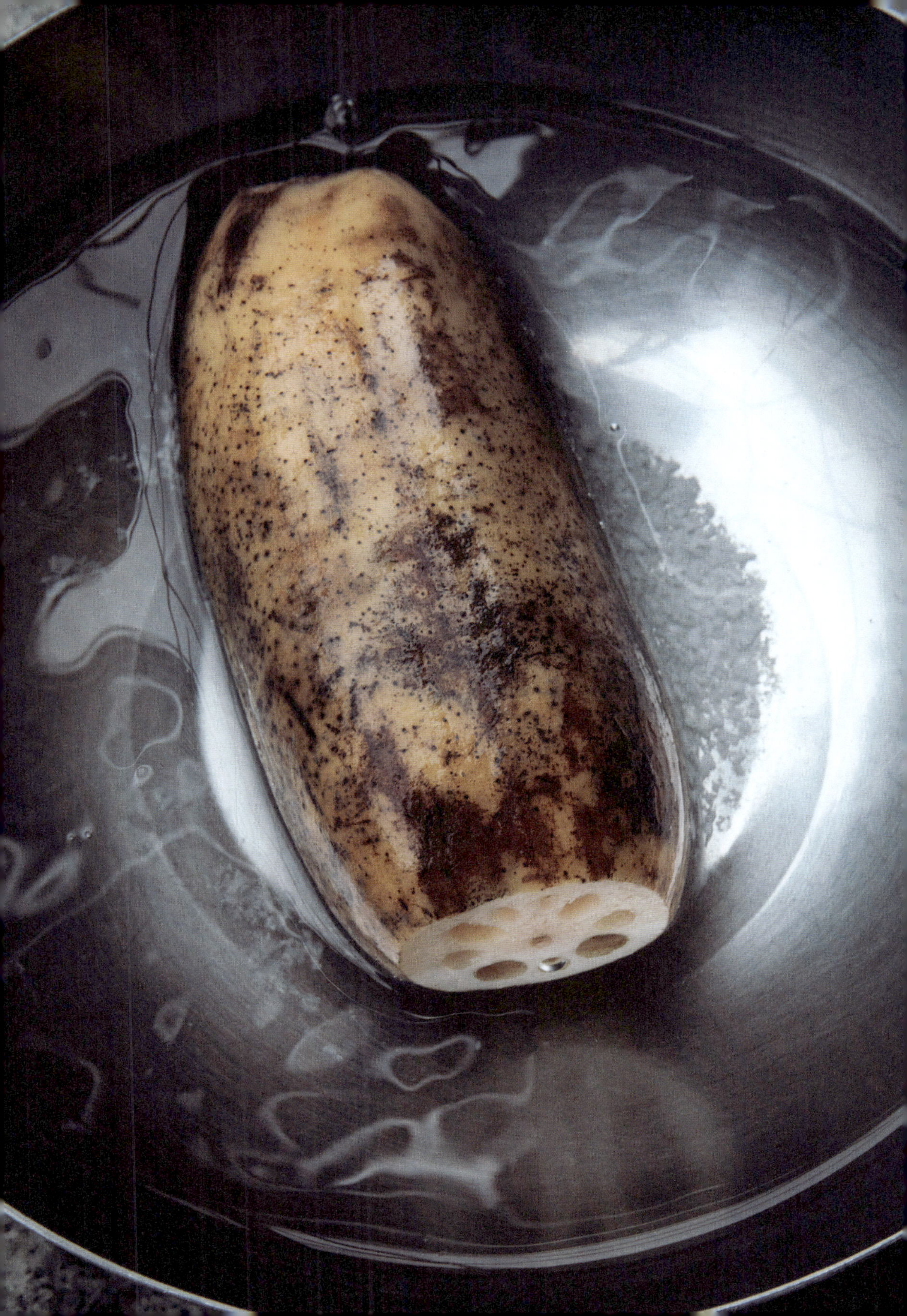

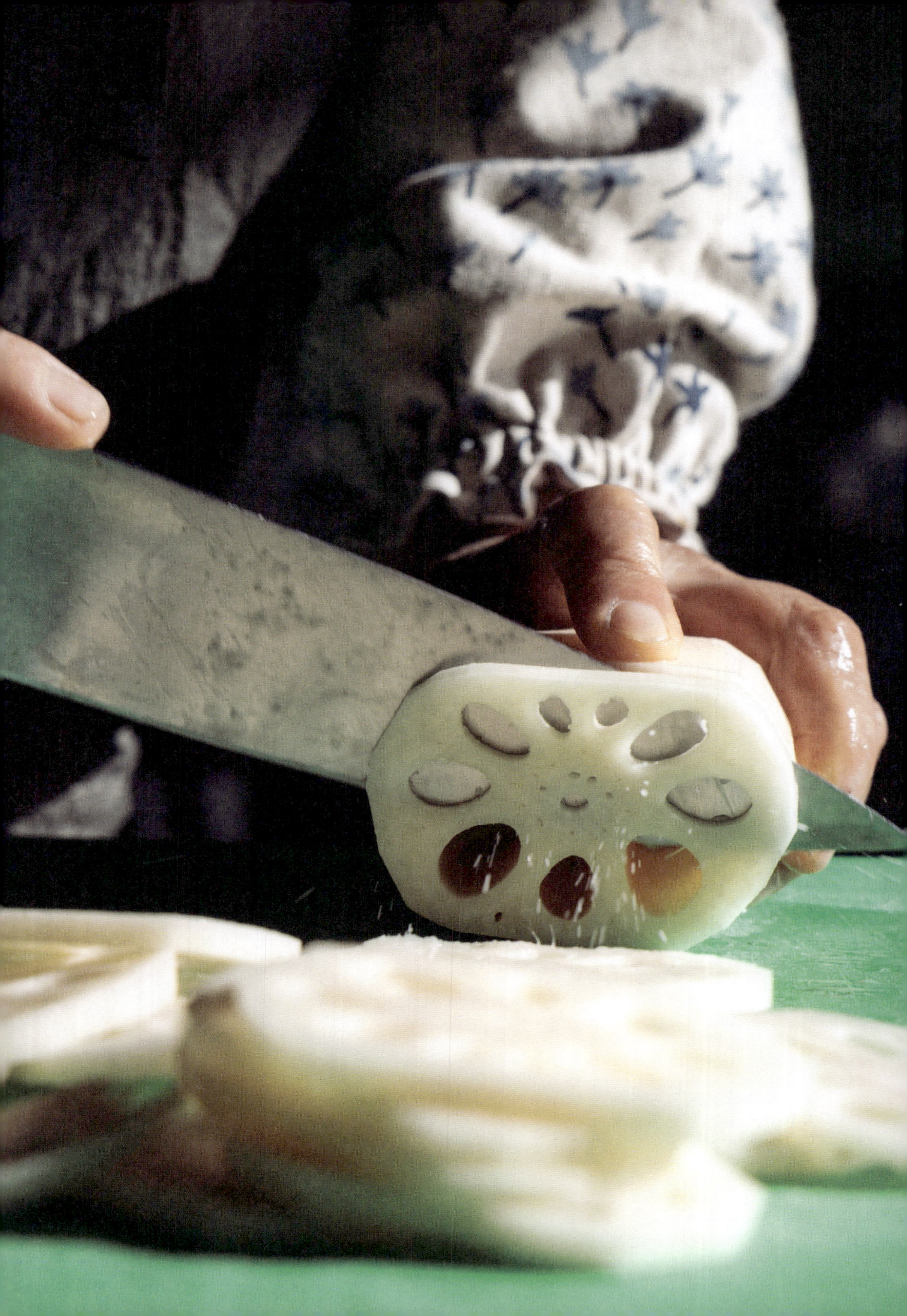

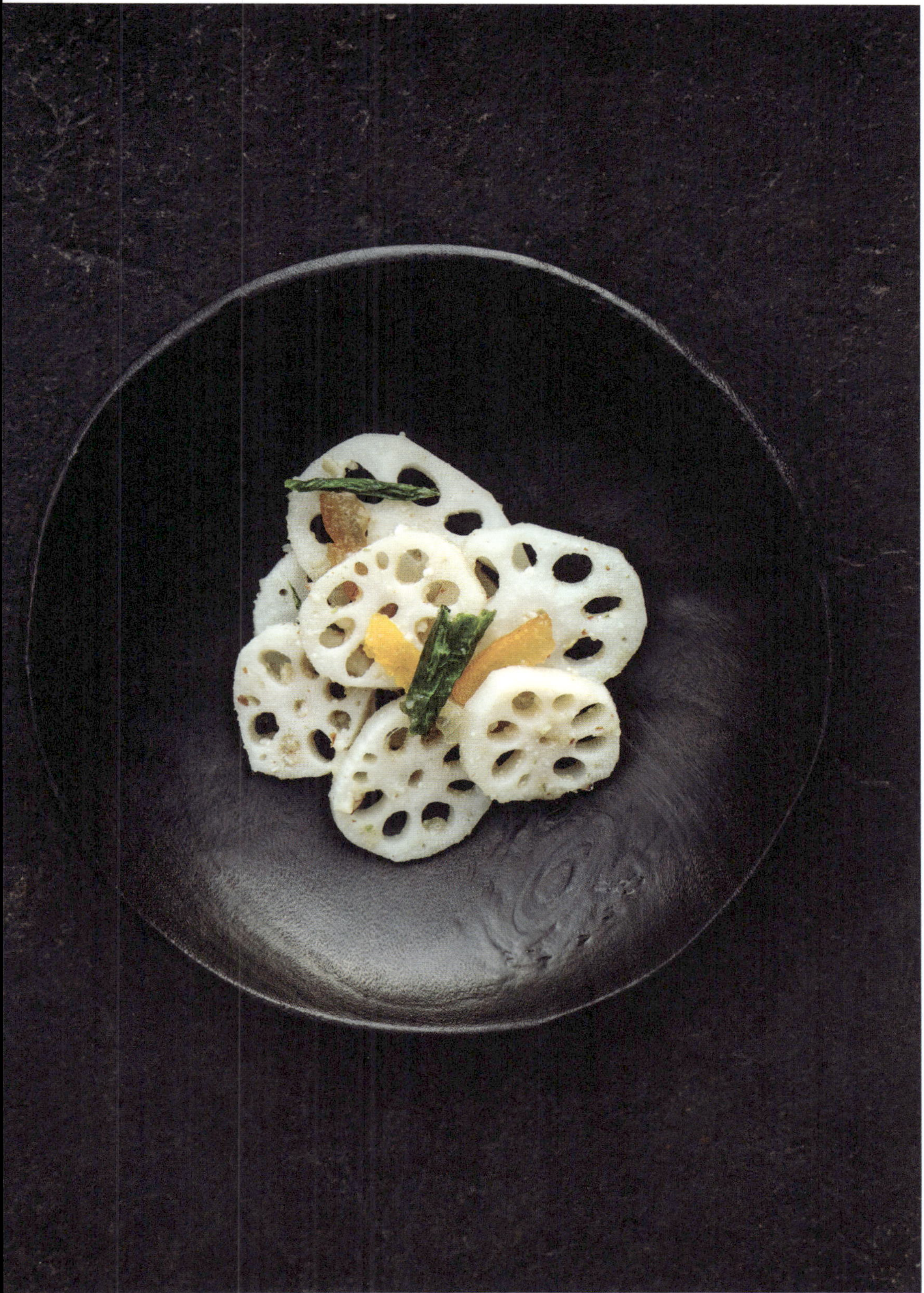

Modum jachae beoseot gyeoja naengchae

COLD VEGETABLE AND MUSHROOM PLATE WITH MUSTARD SAUCE

For the vegetables
1 carrot (danggeun)
½ cucumber (oi)
1½ cups (150 g) mung bean sprouts
1 cooked bamboo shoot (juksun)
4 wood ear mushrooms (mogi beoseot)
1 red bell pepper (pimang)
1 yellow bell pepper
7 ounces (200 g) mung bean jelly (nokdumuk)
⅓ pickled yellow radish (danmuji)
1 tablespoon perilla oil
2 tablespoons sesame oil (chamgireum) for seasoning
Salt for seasoning
Soy sauce for seasoning

For the mustard sauce
2 tablespoons mustard
2 tablespoons persimmon vinegar (gamcho)
1 tablespoon Maesil-Cheong (page 174)
1 tablespoon Omija-Cheong (page 186)
1 tablespoon Asian pear juice (bae)
1 tablespoon ginger juice
1 teaspoon black sesame seeds (heugimja)

Julienne the carrot and the cucumber into strips 2 inches (5 cm) long. Blanch the mung bean sprouts briefly in boiling water and then shock them in cold water. Do the same with the carrots. Squeeze out both vegetables.

Cut the bamboo shoot into pieces 2 inches (5 cm) long and tear the fibers away from it with your hands. Cut the mushrooms into small pieces and cut the bell peppers into thin strips. Cut the bean jelly and radish into thin strips.

In a pan, heat the perilla oil and briefly sauté the mushrooms in it. Remove them from the pan and let them cool.

Season the cucumber, bamboo shoot, bell pepper, sprouts, and mushrooms separately with sesame oil, salt, and soy sauce. Season the carrots only with salt.

To make the sauce, mix all of the ingredients together. Arrange the vegetables on a large plate and place a cup of the sauce in the middle.

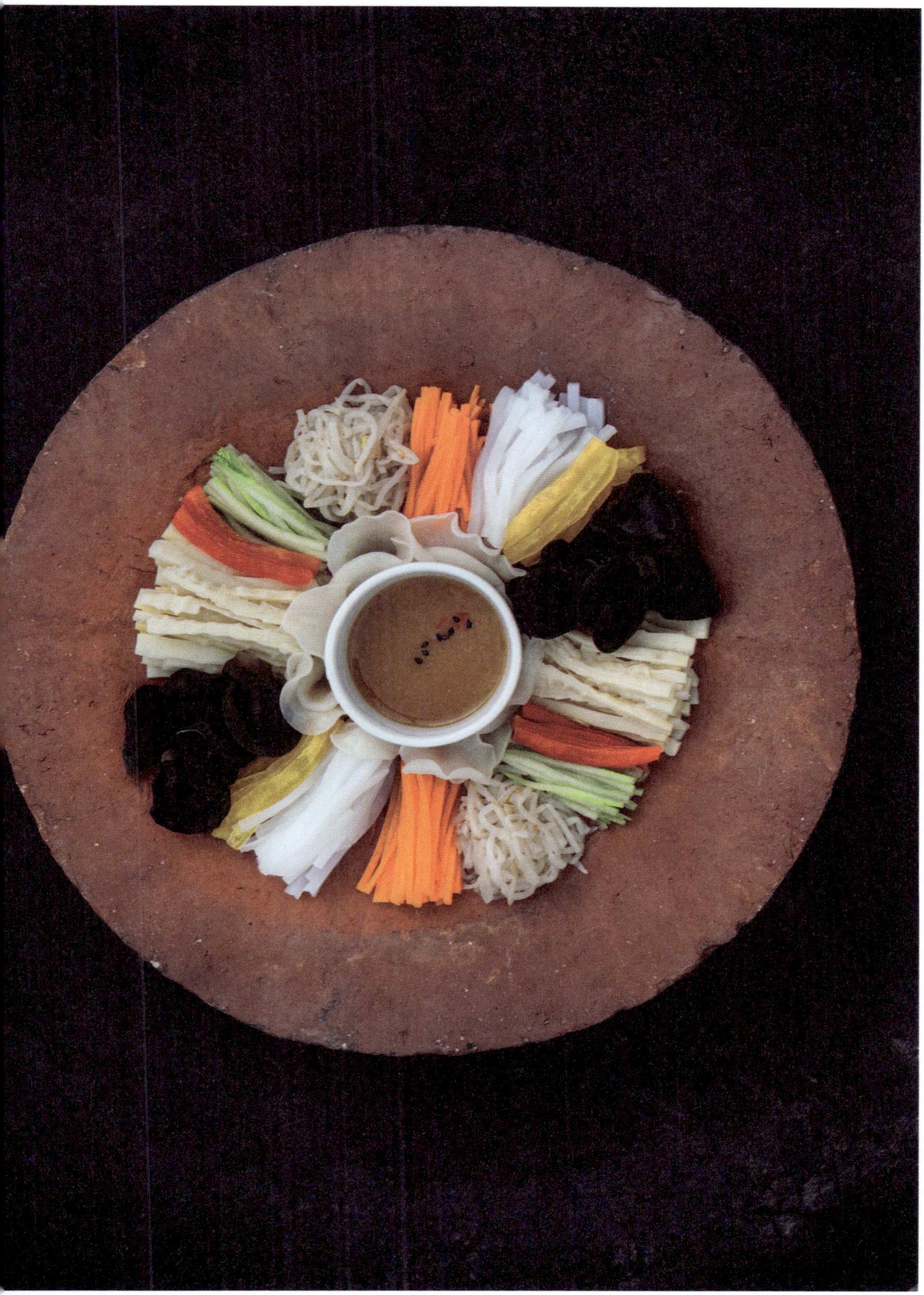

Gaji sogeumjjim

STEAMED SALTED EGGPLANT

2 slender, dark purple eggplants (gaji)
Salt for seasoning
1 tablespoon sesame oil (chamgireum)

Working with one eggplant at a time, make three slices most of the way through it lengthwise, but do not cut through the stem end. Soak them in salt water for 5 minutes.

Remove the eggplants from the salt water, path them dry, and then steam them briefly.

In a large pan, heat the sesame oil, carefully fan out the eggplants, and lay them in the oil. Briefly sauté them on both sides. Season to taste with salt.

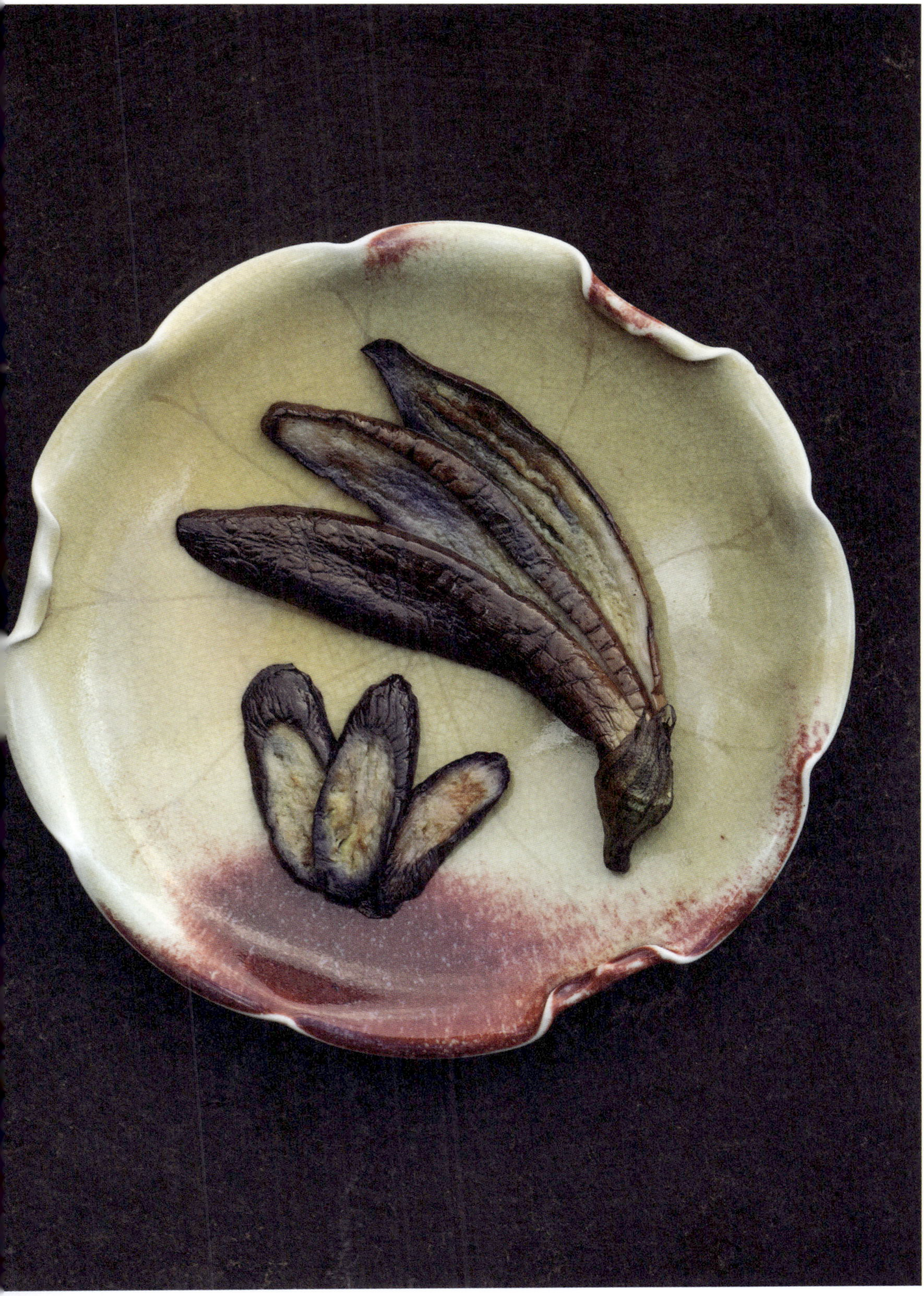

Aehobak maemil garu jeon

ZUCCHINI BREADED WITH BUCKWHEAT

2 medium zucchini (aehobak)
Salt for seasoning
¾ cup plus 1 tablespoon (100 g) buckwheat flour (maemil garu)
2 tablespoons perilla oil (deulgireum)
Edible flowers, such as blue chamomile (haneul gukhwa)
Soy sauce, for serving

Rinse the zucchini and slice them into pieces ½ inch (1 cm) thick. Lightly salt them and let them stand for several minutes.

In a bowl, mix the buckwheat flour with enough water to make a thick batter.

Heat the perilla oil in a pan. Dredge the zucchini slices in the batter and fry them briefly. Place three flowers on top of the zucchini, turn the slices over, and sauté the other side. Do not let the slices brown!

Serve with soy sauce, for dipping.

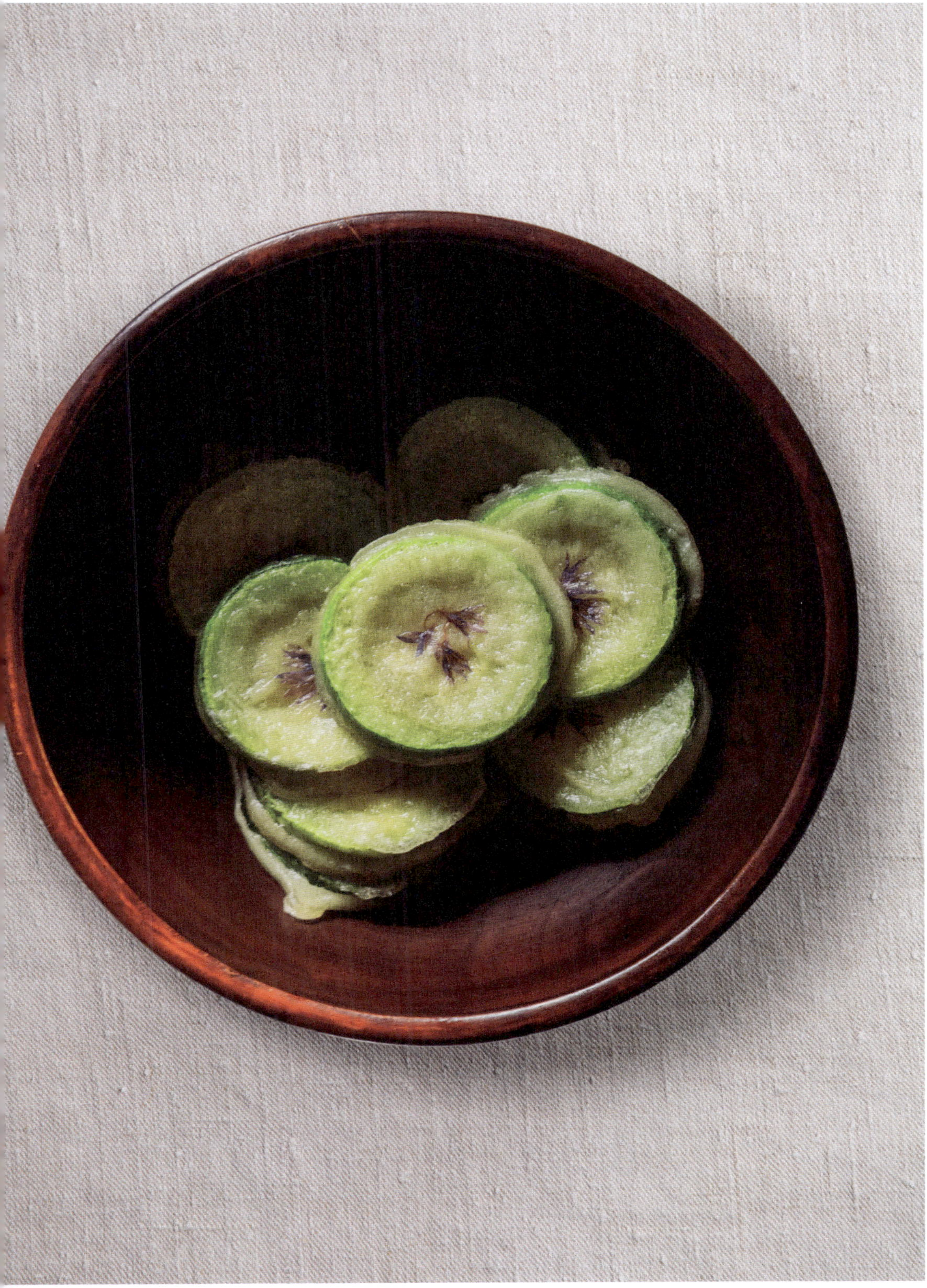

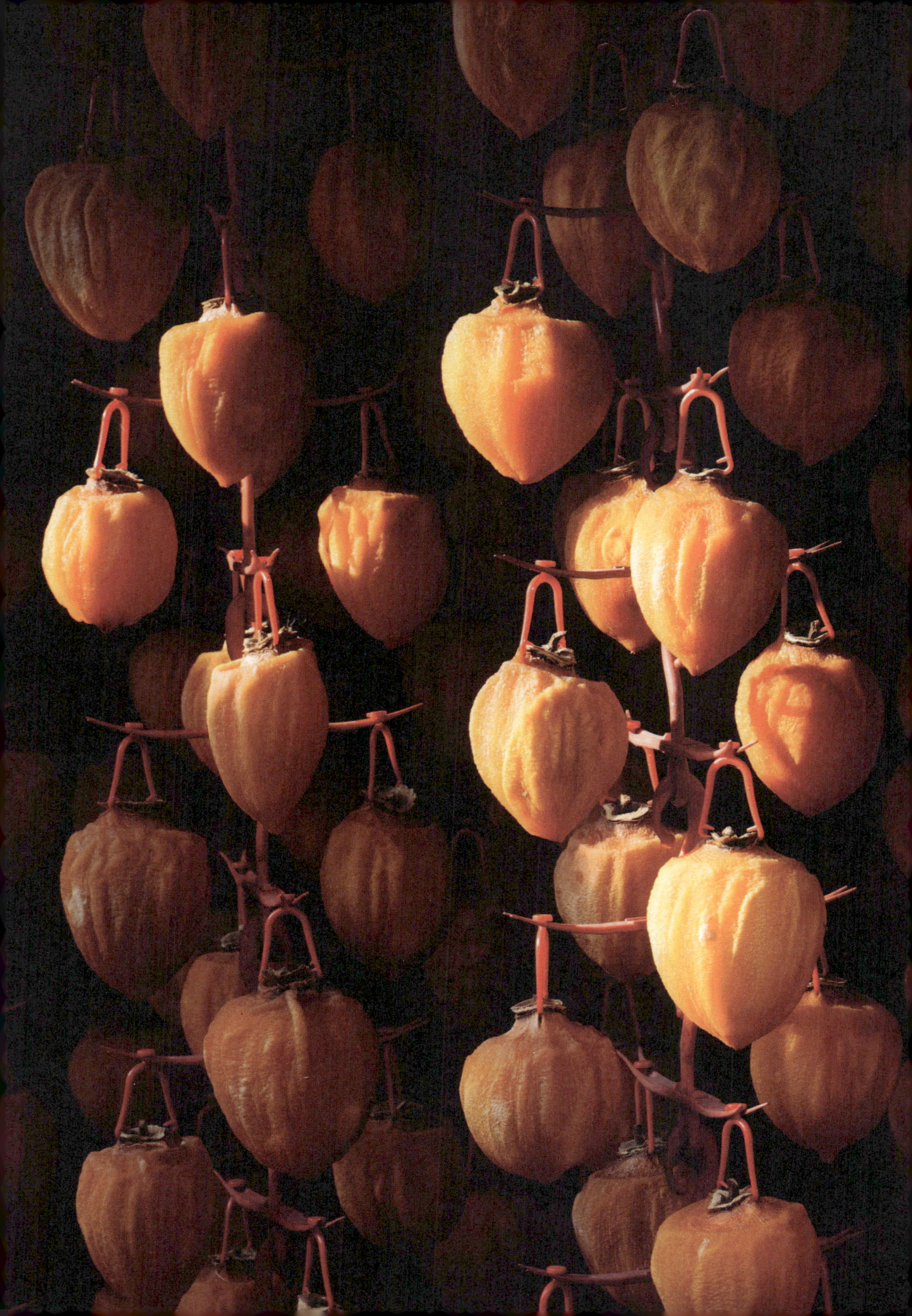

AUTUMN

Autumn is the time to harvest and lay away provisions because winter is looming. This is also the season when the colors and beauty of our food are plainly visible. It's when Jeongkwan Snim prepares her stores of kimchi and various jangajji, meju, and cheong for the cold winter months.

The different kinds of squash are now ripe and can be used for various dishes. Snim says that the main task in autumn should be gathering and eating roots, because they've stored up a lot of nutrients so that they can survive the long winter. We benefit from the work of the plants!

Many kinds of roots are eaten in Korea, whether dried or fresh, and lots of persimmon trees grow in the forest surrounding Snim's temple. The orange-yellow fruits lighten in the autumn sun and indicate that the season is coming to an end. Snim harvests them and makes vinegar from them, or she slices them and lets them dry in the sun so that she can prepare them later. The seasons have worked together to ripen the persimmons—the sweet fruits have a lovely color.

Steamed Sweet Squash with Tofu — 300
Stew with Neungi Mushrooms and Scorched Rice — 302
Doenjang Stew with Zucchini — 304
Tofu-Jang — 306
Fried Young Calabash — 312
Chinese Yam with Black Sesame Seeds — 316
Salad with Dried Persimmon Slices — 318
Salad with Ma and Persimmon — 318
King Oyster Mushrooms Braised in Rice Syrup — 320
Fried Eggplant with Sauce — 322
Fried Ueong with Gochujang Sauce — 326

Danhobak dubujjim

STEAMED SWEET SQUASH WITH TOFU

1 small kabocha squash (danhobak)
3½ ounces (100 g) tofu (dubu)
2 teaspoons sesame oil (chamgireum)
Salt for seasoning
2 red beans (gangnangkong)
1 pinch black sesame seeds (heugimja)

Rinse the squash, make a 1¼-inch (3 cm) radius cut around the base of the stem, and scoop out the seeds with a spoon.

Rinse the tofu, pat it dry thoroughly, and crush it with your hands into a pulpy mush. Season it with sesame oil and salt.

Use a spoon to fill the squash with the tofu mixture, press it in firmly, and place the beans on top. Steam until the squash is tender. Sprinkle the sesame seeds over the top before serving.

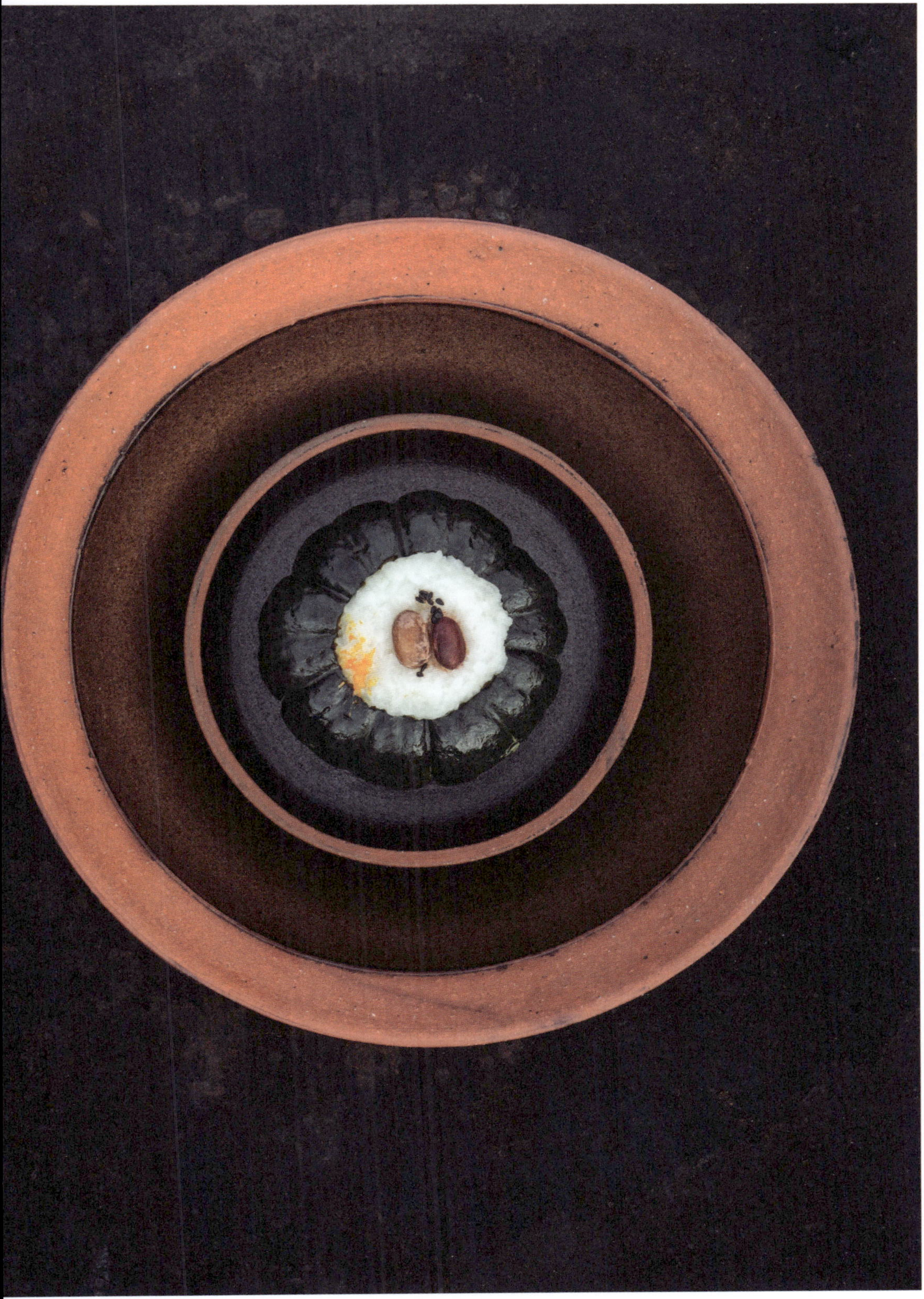

Neungi beoseot nurungji tangguk

STEW WITH NEUNGI MUSHROOMS AND SCORCHED RICE

For the mushrooms

½ cup (80 g) dried shingled hedgehog mushrooms (neungi beoseot)
1 red beet (bit)
2 medium carrots (danggeun)
1 small white radish (mu)
½ round green zucchini (aehobak)
1 small green cabbage (yangbaechu)
Salt for seasoning

For the soup

2 tablespoons soy sauce (ganjang)
Salt for seasoning
2 tablespoons kudzu powder (chik)
½ cup (100 g) scorched rice (nurungji, page 428)
Soybean oil for deep-frying

Rinse the shingled hedgehog mushrooms thoroughly and soak them in water for 3 hours, then cut them into 1¼-inch (3 cm) pieces. Keep the soaking water!

Peel and rinse the red beet, carrots, and radish, then cut them into ½-inch (1.5 cm) cubes. Rinse the zucchini and cut it into pieces. Remove the leaves from the green cabbage and cut them into pieces.

Working with one vegetable at a time (saving the mushrooms for last), briefly blanch each one in boiling water and season it with salt.

Add 4¼ cups (1 L) fresh water to the mushroom soaking water and pour it into a pot. Add the soy sauce, season with salt, and bring to a boil.

In a small bowl, stir the kudzu powder with enough water to make a slurry. Slowly stir the kudzu slurry into the broth, stirring until the soup has thickened slightly.

Deep-fry the scorched rice in the soybean oil at 375°F (190°C). Add the vegetables, mushrooms, and scorched rice pieces to a bowl and pour the hot soup over them.

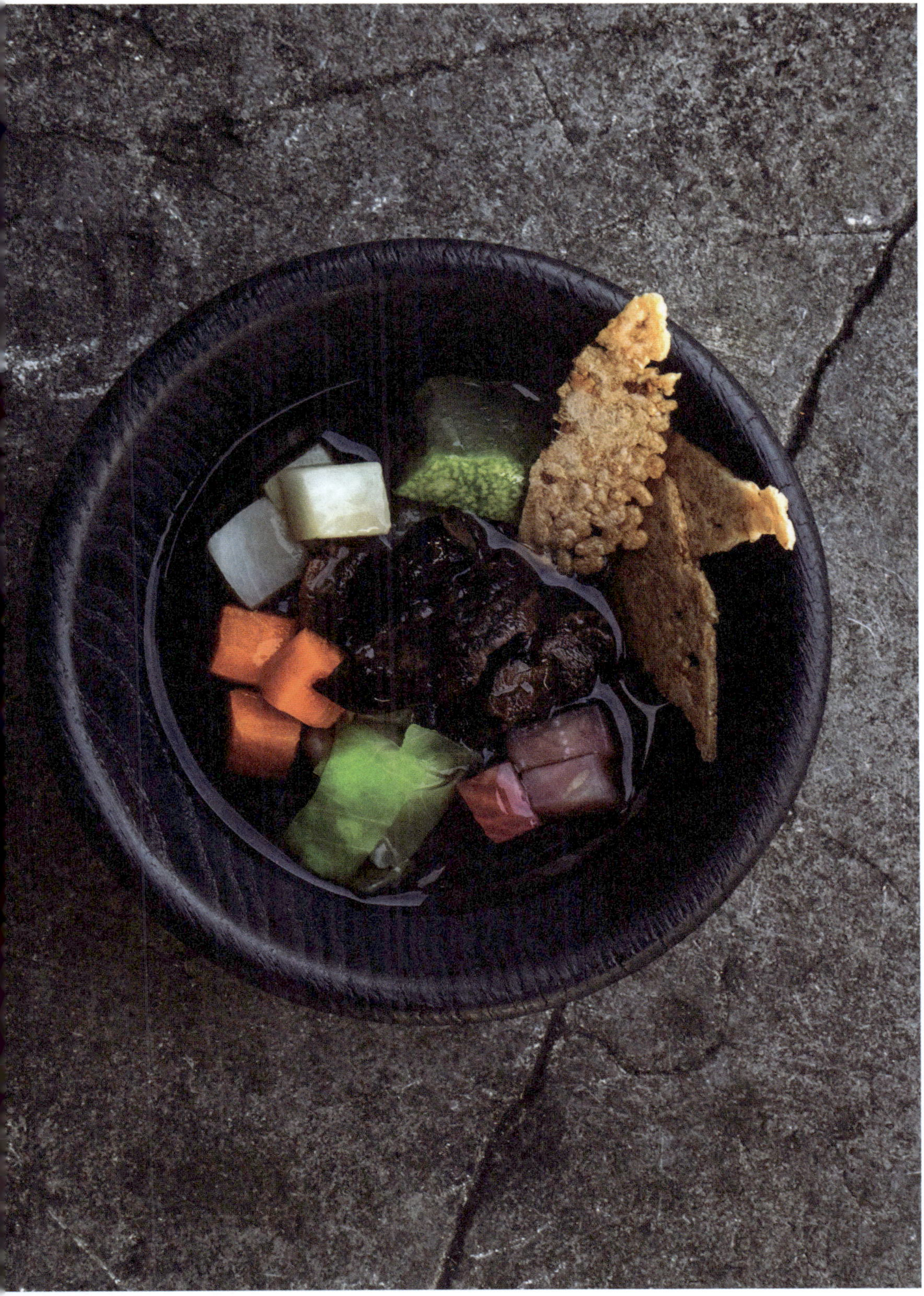

Aehobak doenjang-jjigae

DOENJANG STEW WITH ZUCCHINI

1 round green zucchini (aehobak)
3 long young chile peppers (cheongyang-gochu)
3 myoga ginger buds and shoots (yangha)
4¼ cups (1 L) water
4 tablespoons fermented soybean paste (doenjang)

Rinse the zucchini and roughly chop it. Chop the chile peppers and ginger.

In a small pot (preferably a Korean stoneware pot), bring the water to a boil. Add the zucchini, chili, and ginger and bring to a boil.

When the zucchini is tender, add the doenjang in batches, stirring continuously to dissolve it. Briefly bring the soup back to a boil, then ladle it into bowls and serve.

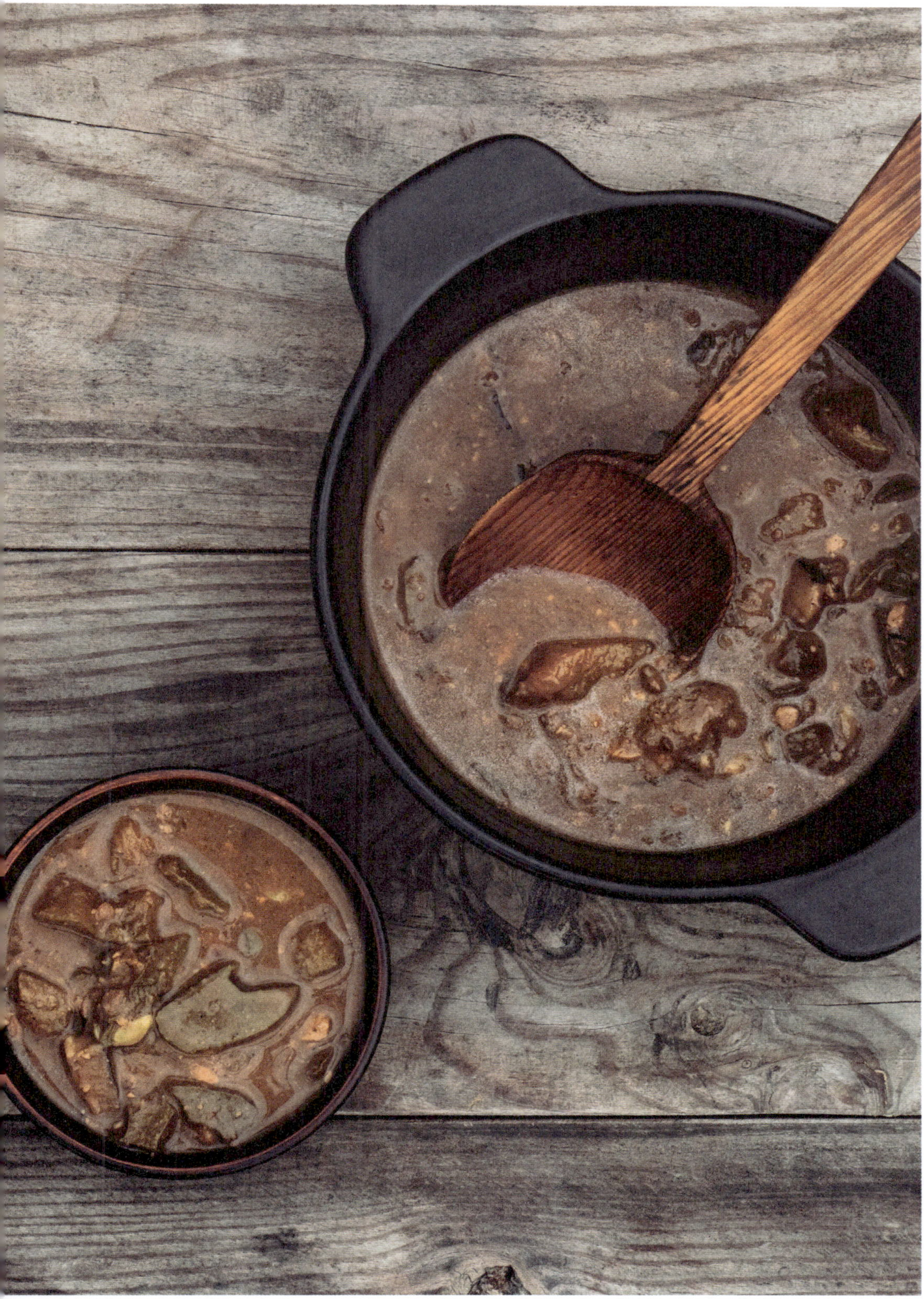

Dubu-jang

TOFU-JANG

1 pound (450 g) tofu (dubu)
1 tablespoons (20 g) salt
2 tablespoons soy sauce (jipganjang, 5 to 7 years old)
⅓ cup (100 g) fermented soybean paste (doenjang, 5 years old)

Fill a heatproof, round, bulbous ceramic container with water and boil the water to sterilize the container. Dry it well.

Rinse the tofu under running water, then wrap it in a cloth and squeeze out the water thoroughly. In a bowl, break the tofu apart with your hands and knead it into a pulpy mush. Add the salt and soy sauce and mix well. The tofu should be salty like cheese.

Fill the sterilized container with the tofu mixture, pressing down the tofu firmly so that no air is trapped inside of it. Smear the doenjang on top of the tofu, then seal the container with a lid.

Let the tofu ferment for 15 days at room temperature, then put it in the refrigerator. Serve it with rice or vegetables. After removing any tofu, seal it again with more doenjang. Maintained this way, it will keep in the refrigerator for up to 3 years.

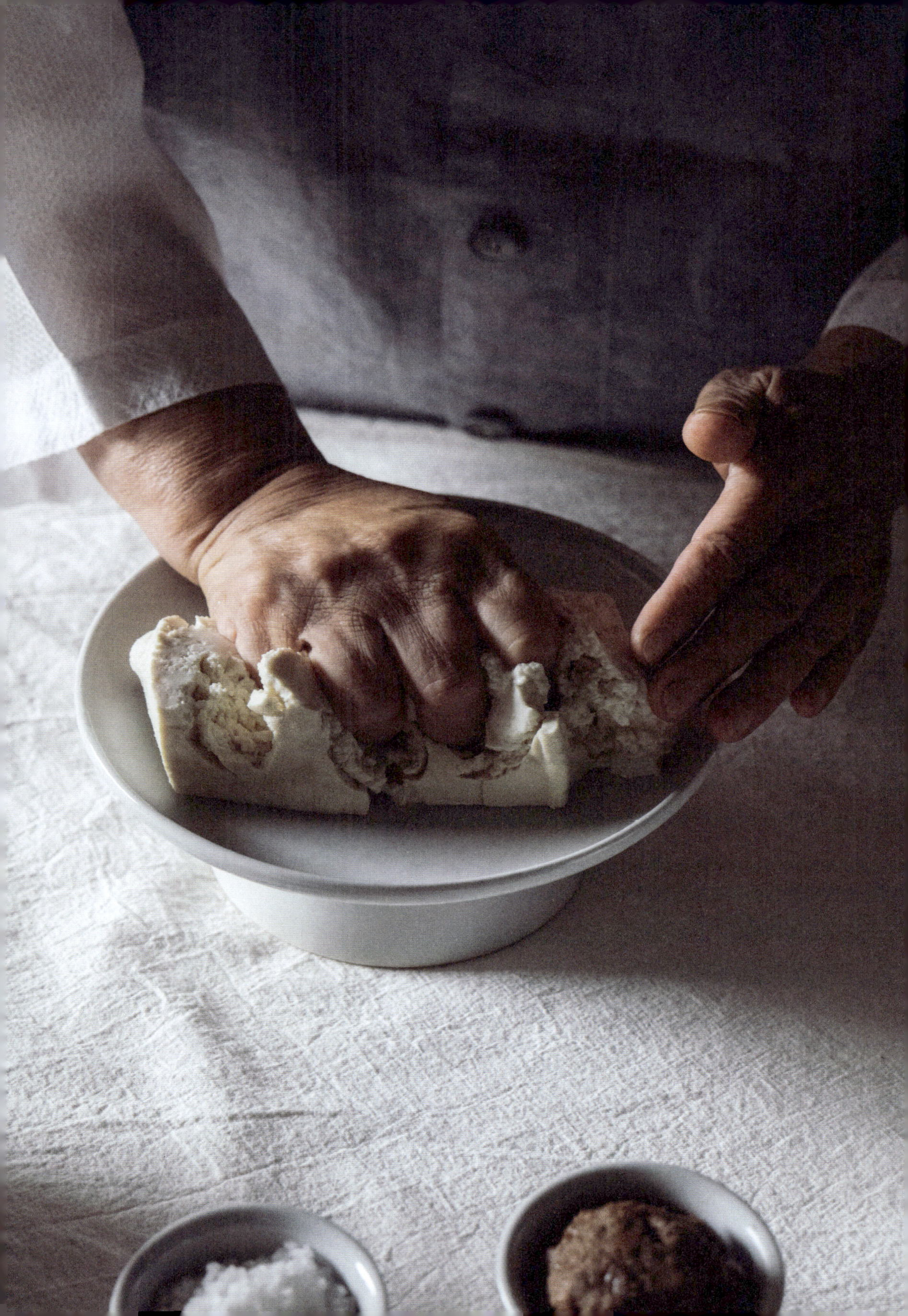

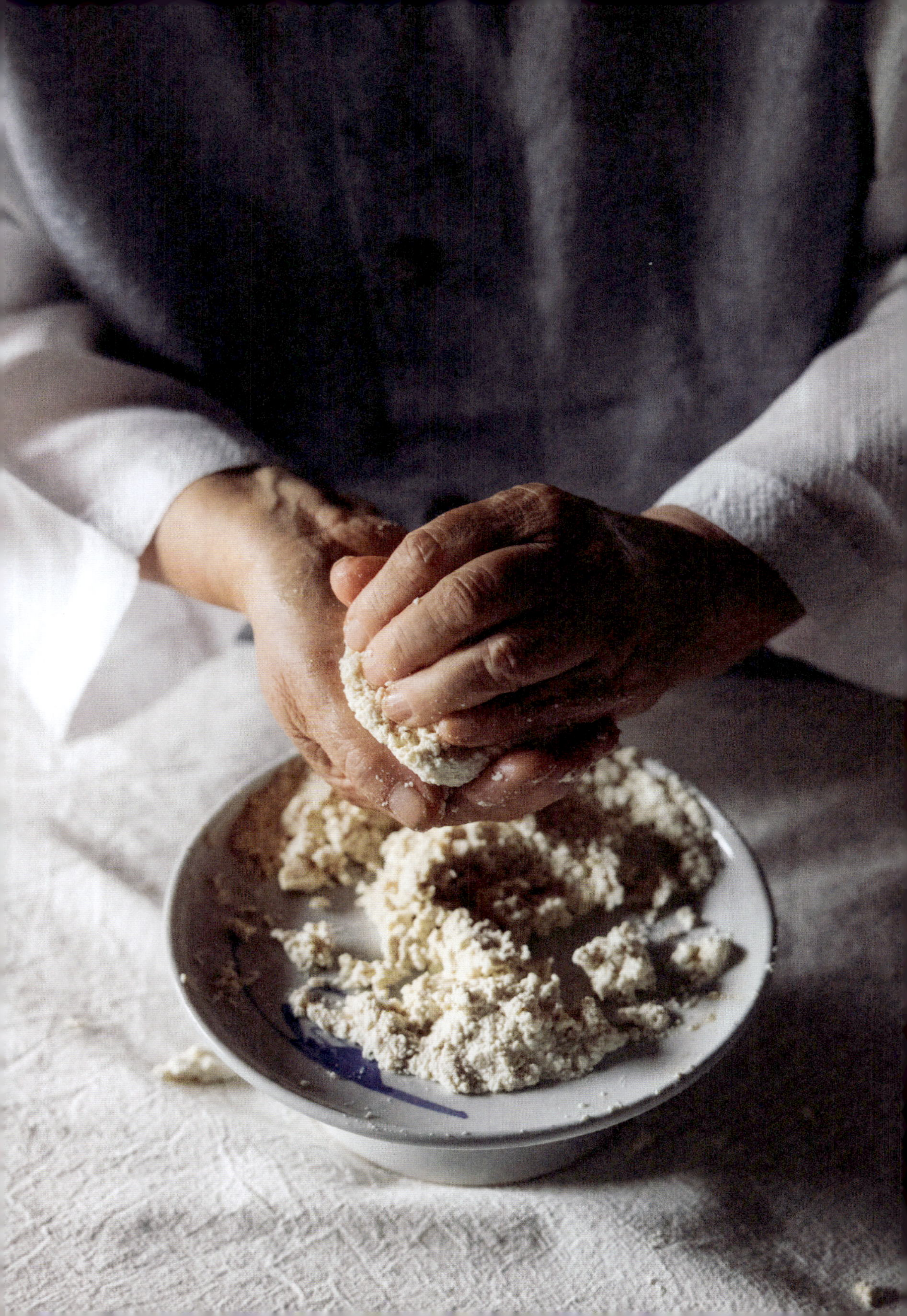

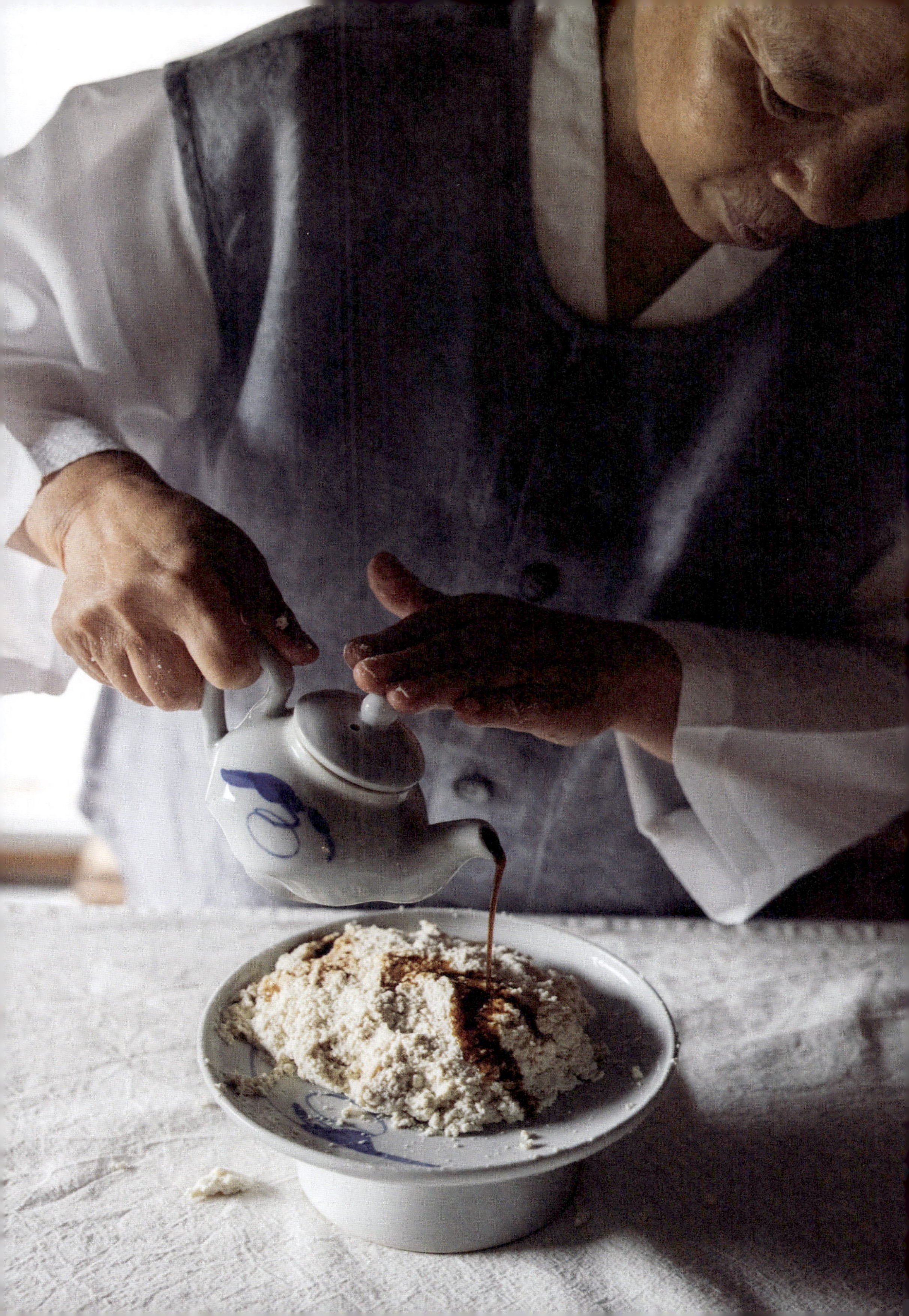

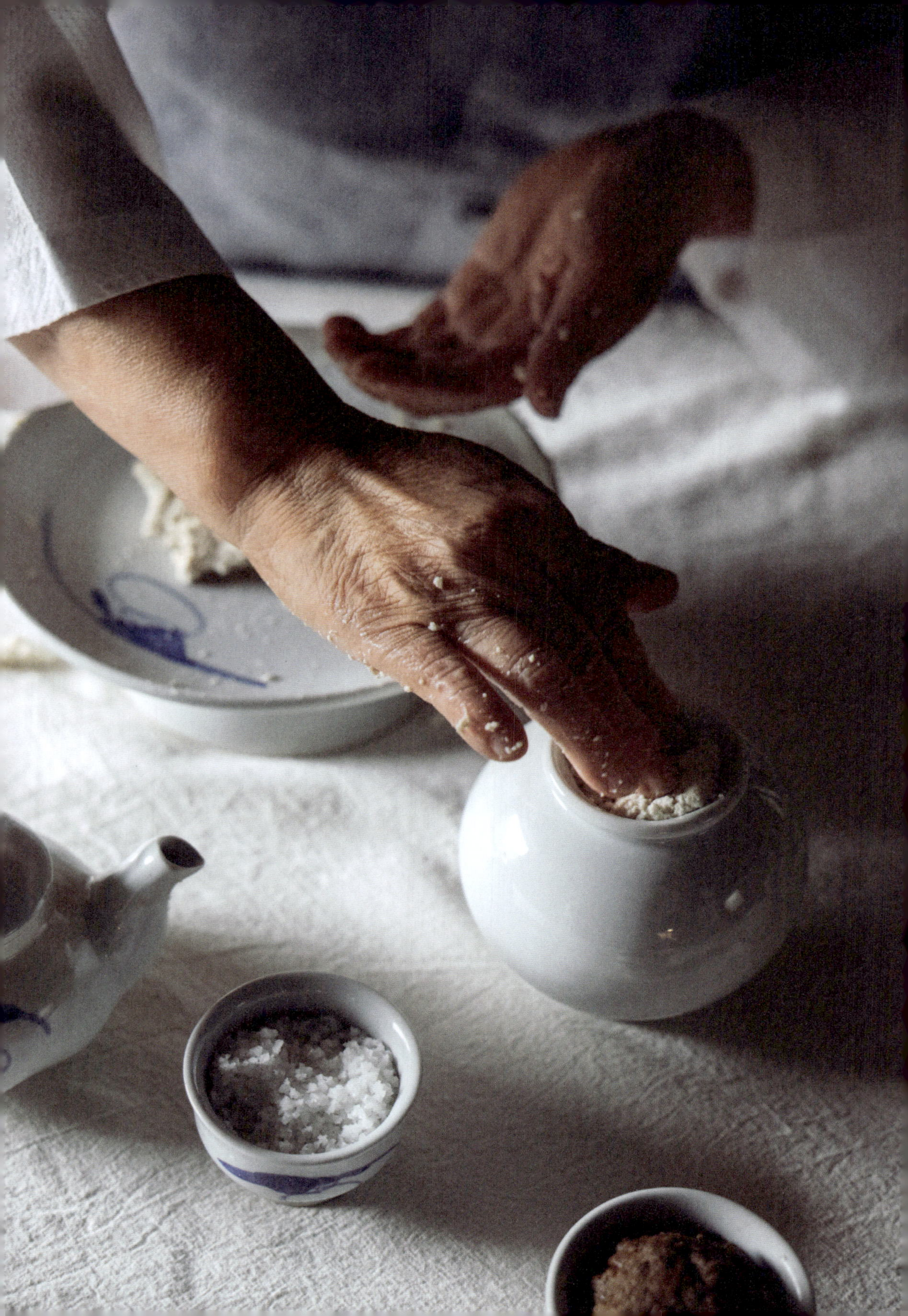

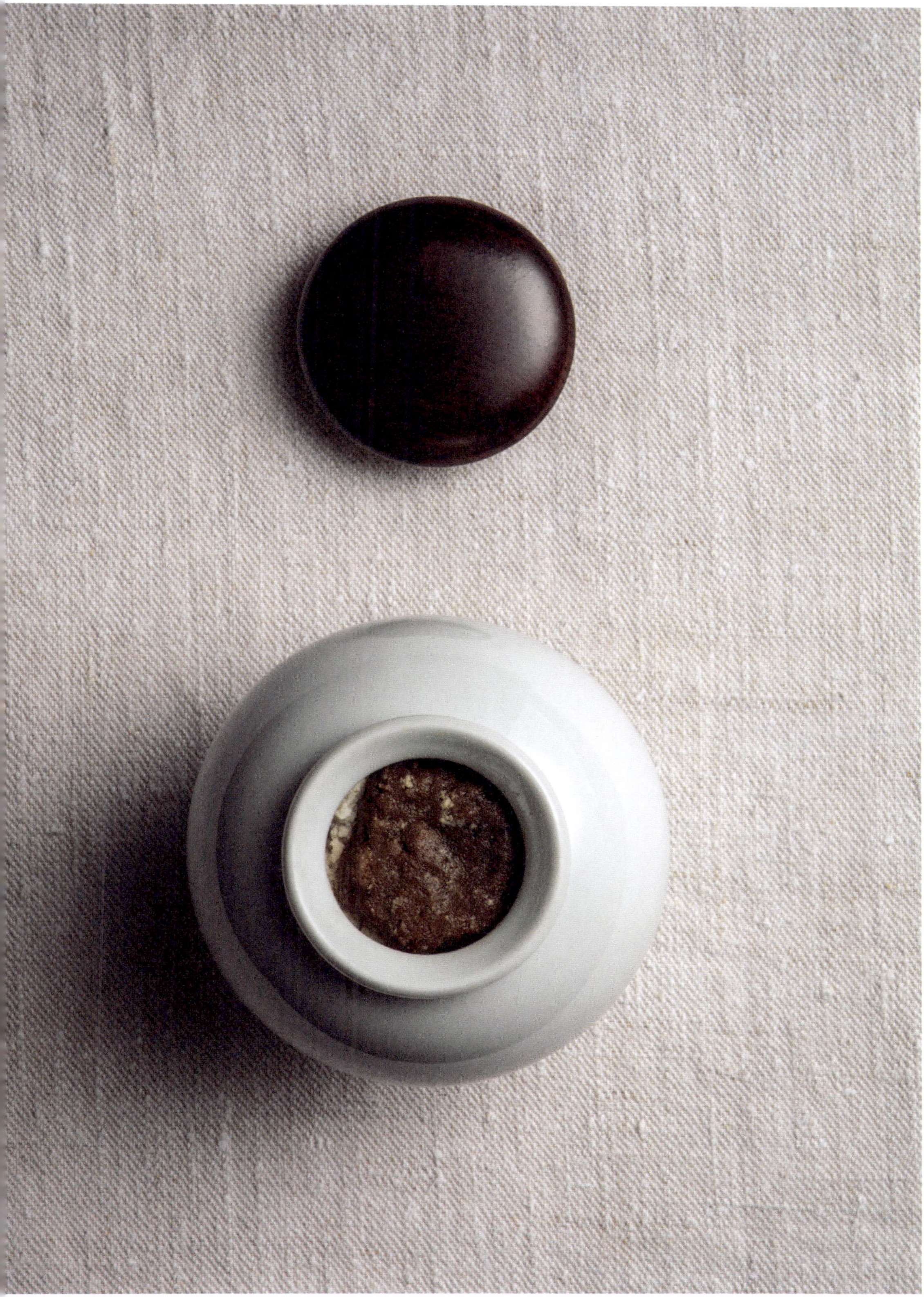

Yeonhan bak muchim

FRIED YOUNG CALABASH

1 young green calabash (bak)
1 to 2 tablespoons soybean oil or olive oil
Salt for seasoning
Dried red chili threads (sil-gochu)
1 teaspoon black sesame seeds (heugimja)

Halve the squash lengthwise and peel away the skin as thinly as possible to preserve the green color. Scrape out the inside with a spoon (skip this step if the inside is still very soft). Slice the squash halves into pieces ⅛ inch (3 mm) thick.

Add the oil to a pan over medium heat. Add the squash slices and fry them until they've absorbed the oil. Season them with salt, add a little water, and cover with a lid. Bring to a boil. Remove the lid and continue to cook until the squash glistens and turns translucent.

Serve the squash on plates with the chili threads and black sesame seeds sprinkled over the top.

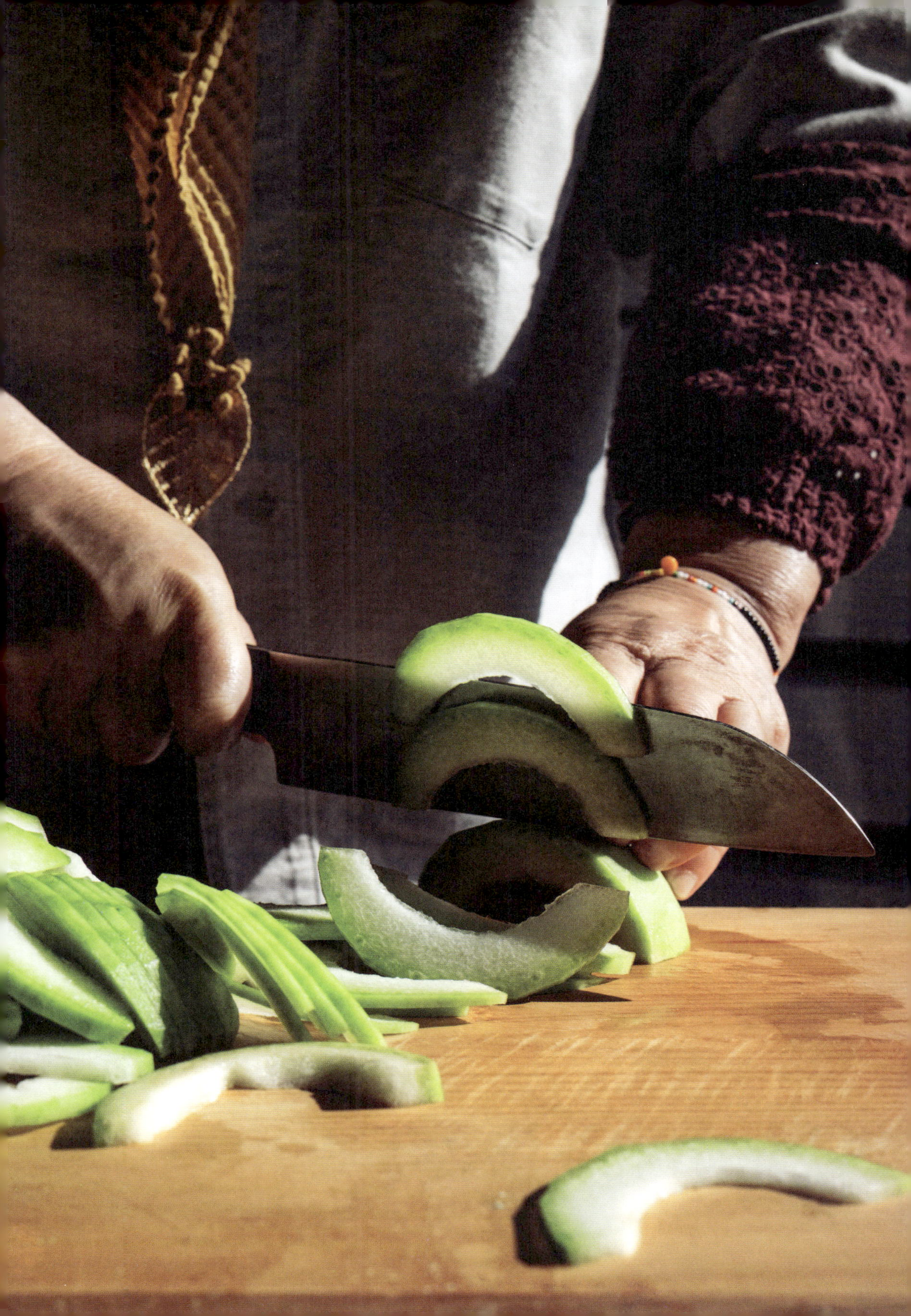

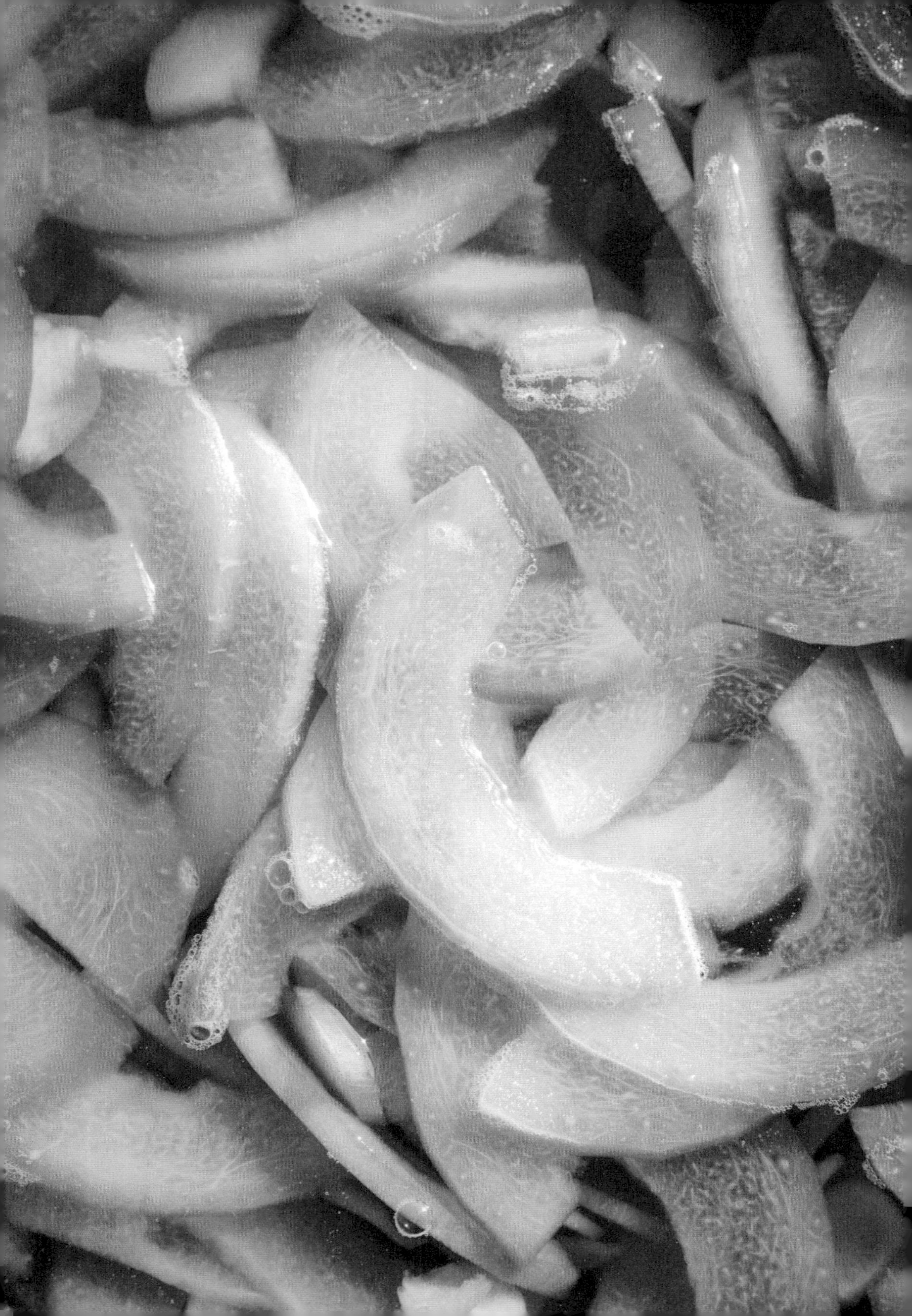

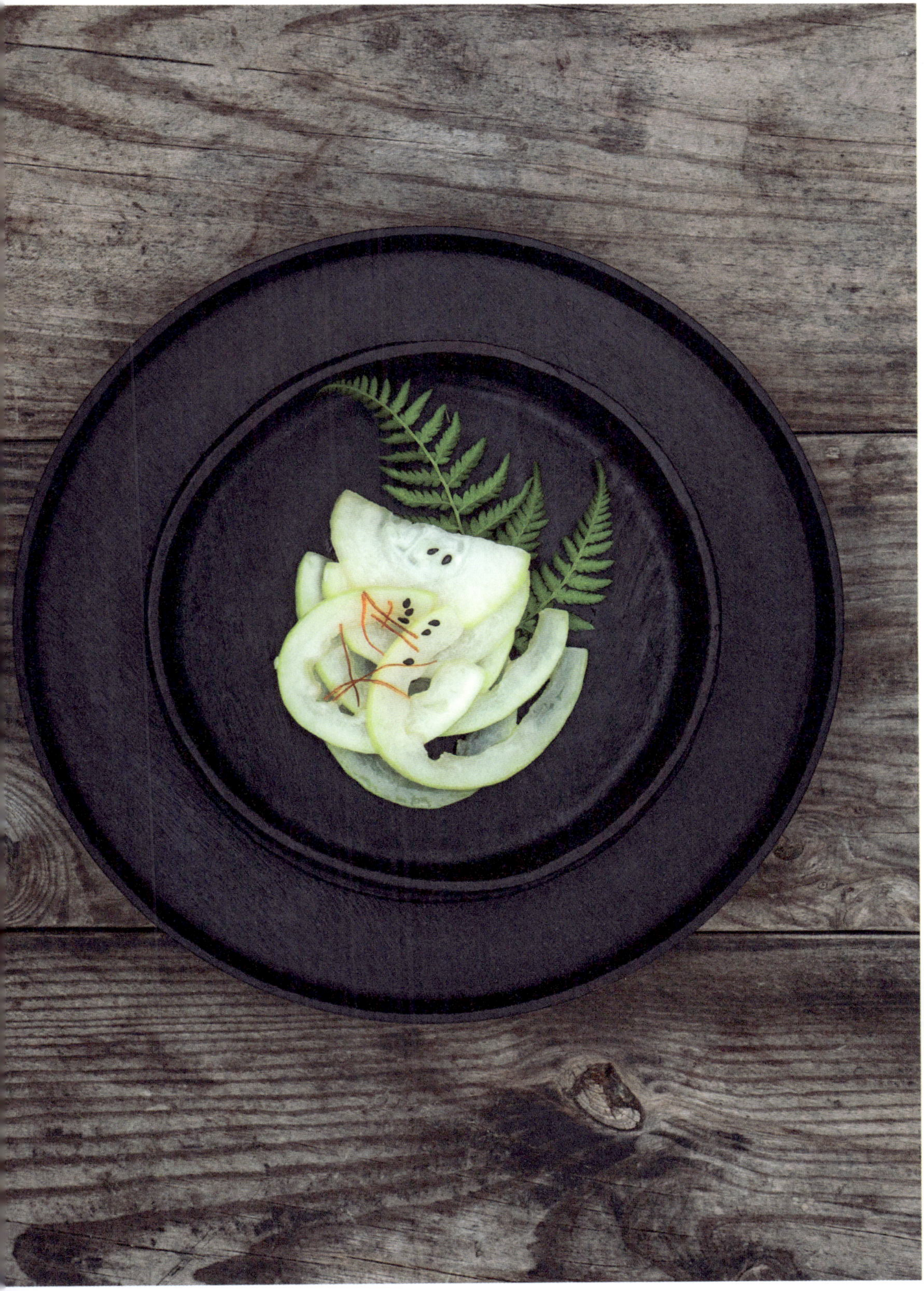

Ma heugimja gui

CHINESE YAM WITH BLACK SESAME SEEDS

1 Chinese yam (ma), about 10½ ounces (300 g)
1 tablespoon persimmon vinegar (gamcho)
1 tablespoon Omija-Cheong (page 186)
1 tablespoon salt
2 tablespoons toasted black sesame seeds (heugimja, page 431), crushed

Peel and rinse the yam, then cut it into slices ⅛ inch (4 mm) thick. Boil the yam in water for three minutes or until it turns white. Rinse the slices in cold water, then brush with the Omija-Cheong and salt them. Dip the edges in the sesame seeds.

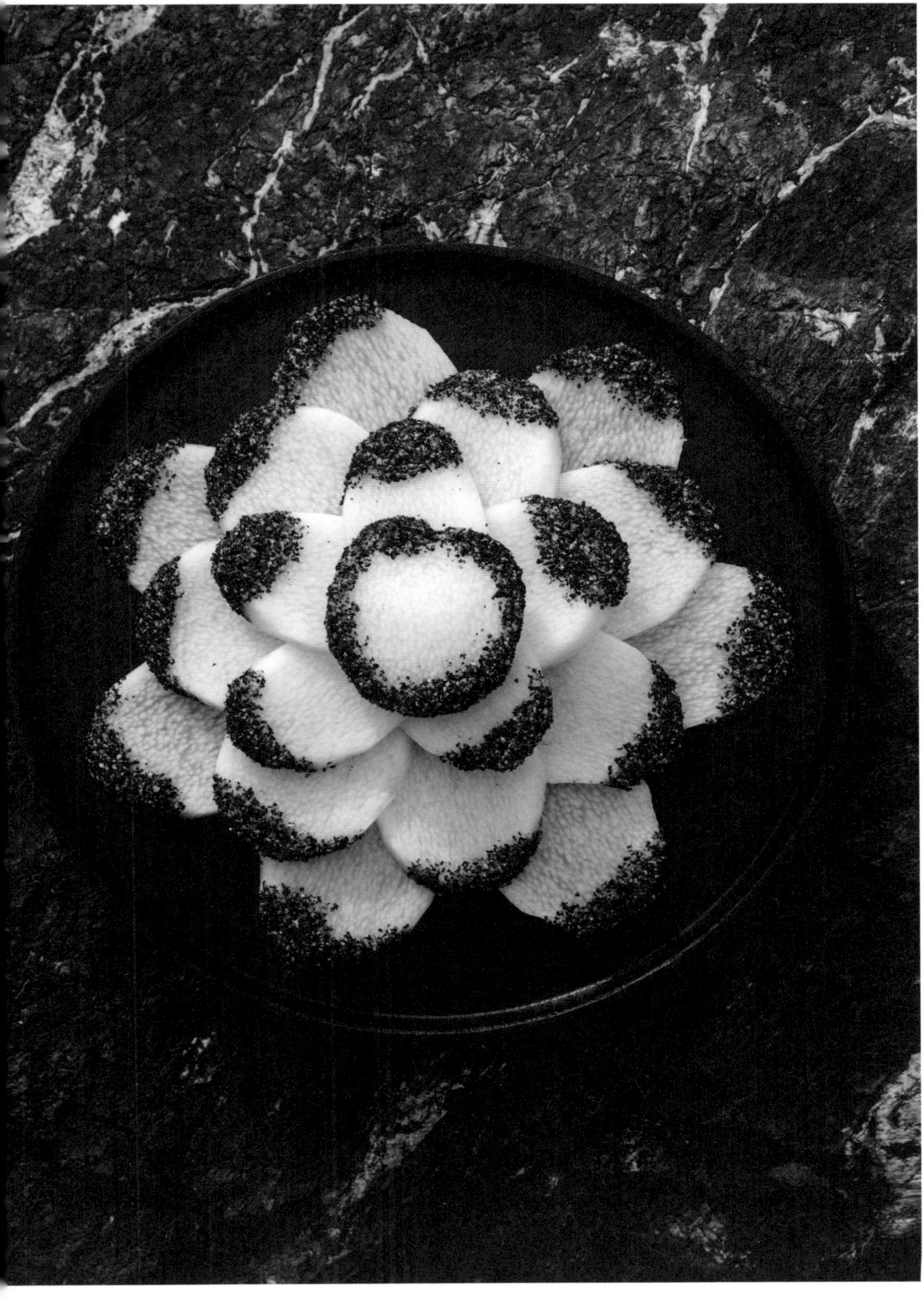

Persimmon is a popular fall fruit in Korea that's often eaten fresh, but it's also a treat when dried. The whole fruit is peeled, fastened to a string, and left hanging in the sun to dry. It's particularly delicious when the outside of the persimmon is dried but the inside is still somewhat tender and sweet! Persimmons are also often sliced and dried, preferably in the sun.

Gammalaengi muchim

SALAD WITH DRIED PERSIMMON SLICES

For the persimmons
2 cups (300 g) dried persimmon slices

For the sauce
2 tablespoons Rice Syrup (Jocheong, page 190)
1 tablespoon soy sauce
2 tablespoons Bokbunja-Cheong (page 180)
2 tablespoons Omija-Cheong (page 186)
½ tablespoon salt
1 tablespoon fine chili powder (goun-gochugaru)
1 tablespoon Korean chili paste (gochujang)

With your hands, pull the persimmon slices into halves or thirds depending on their size.

Mix all the ingredients for the sauce together in a bowl, then add the persimmon slices to the sauce and carefully mix with your hands.

Ma malingam saeleud

SALAD WITH MA AND PERSIMMON

For the salad
A mix of wild salad greens
⅓ Chinese yam (ma), about 1¾ ounces (50 g)
1 dried persimmon, about 1¾ ounces (50 g)

For the sauce
1 tablespoon persimmon vinegar (gamcho)
1 tablespoon Omija-Cheong (page 186)
1 tablespoon Maesil-Cheong (page 174)
1 tablespoon soy sauce (jipganjang, 5 years old)

Rinse the salad greens and drain them well. Rinse and peel the yam, then slice it thinly. The cut yam will secrete a sticky fluid, so the slices should be rinsed once in cold water and drained. (This fluid is good for the stomach.)

Cut the dried persimmon into fine strips, then add the yam and persimmon to the salad greens.

Mix all the ingredients for the sauce together and drizzle it over the salad.

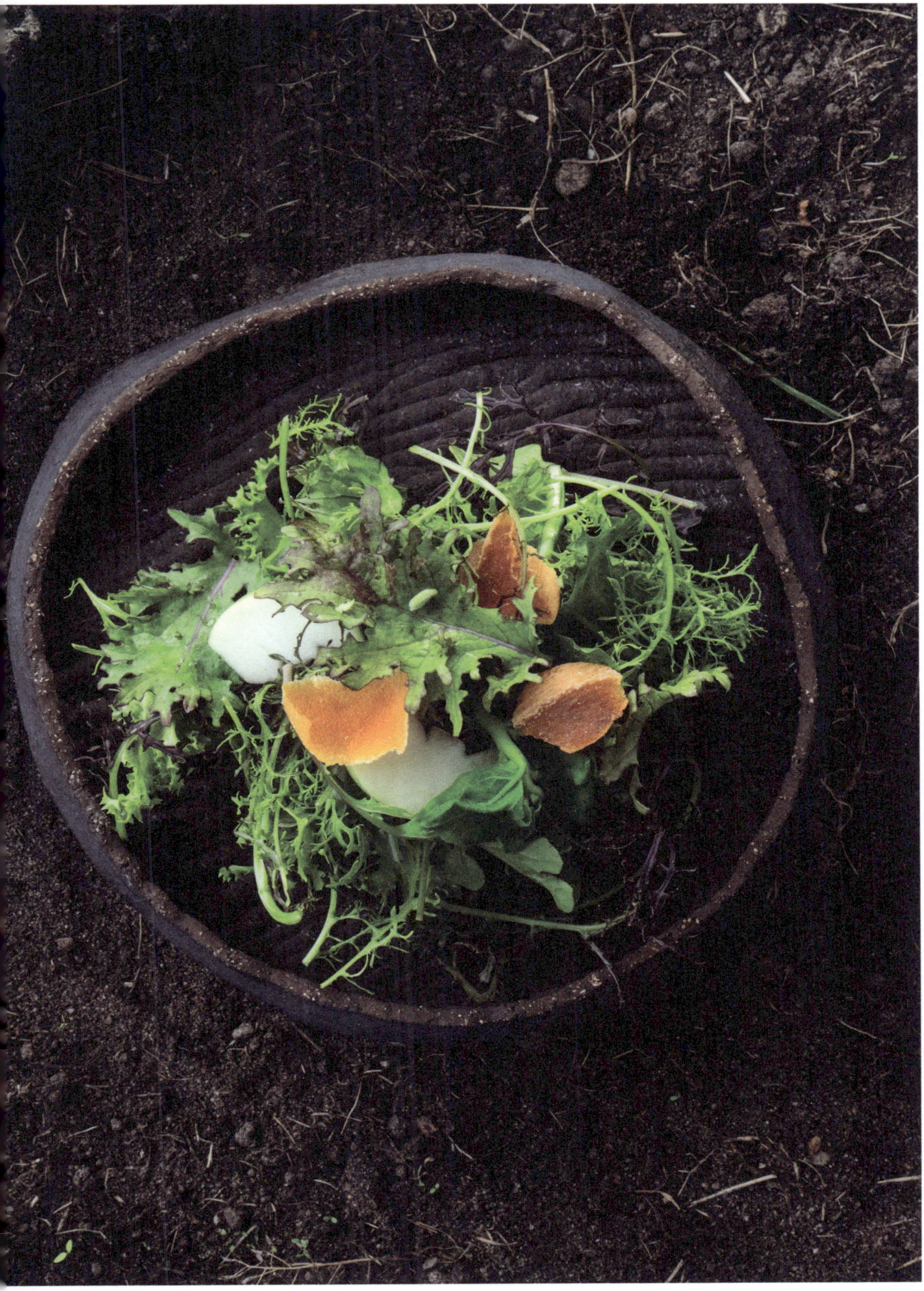

Saesongi beoseot jocheong jorim

KING OYSTER MUSHROOMS BRAISED IN RICE SYRUP

7 king oyster mushrooms (saesongi beoseot)
Salt for seasoning
2 tablespoons soy sauce (ganjang)
2 tablespoons perilla oil (deulgireum)
1 long red chile pepper (cheongyanggochu), dried
2 tablespoons rice syrup (jocheong, page 190)

Clean the mushrooms and cut them into halves or thirds depending on their size, then season them with salt and steam them briefly.

Fill a pot with enough water to cover the mushrooms and bring it to a boil. Add the soy sauce, perilla oil, and mushrooms. Once the mixture comes back to a boil, continue to braise the mushrooms over medium heat, stirring them occasionally.

When the liquid is reduced by half, reduce the heat and keep simmering. Every so often, ladle the liquid over the mushrooms with a spoon.

Once the water has boiled down and the mushrooms are tender, break the chile pepper into pieces and add it to the pot. Stir in the jocheong.

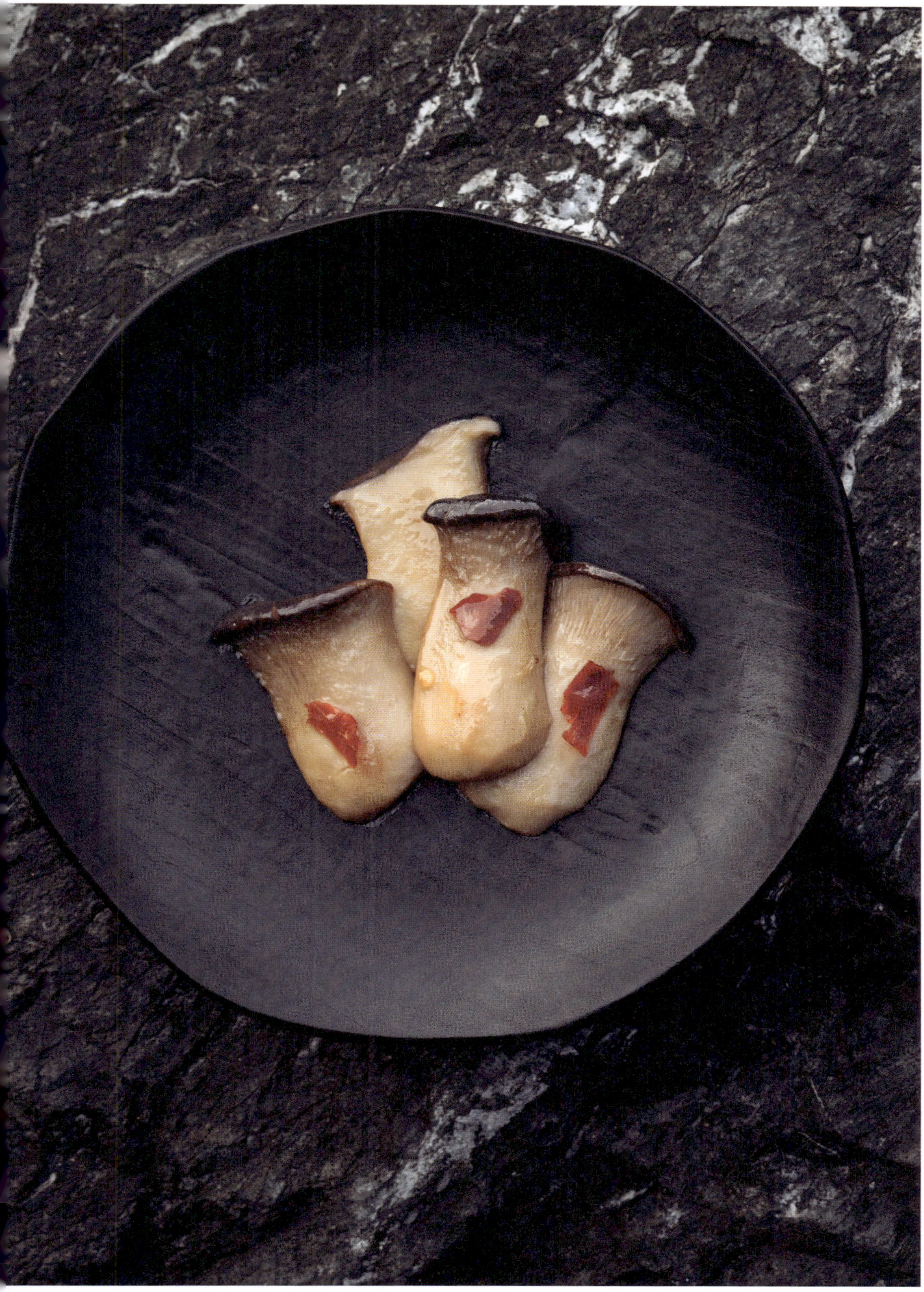

Gaji Yangnyeomjjim

FRIED EGGPLANT WITH SAUCE

For the eggplants
3 dark purple eggplants (gaji)
Salt for seasoning
1 tablespoon perilla oil (deulgireum)

For the sauce
1 long red and 1 long green chile pepper (cheongyanggochu)
2 tablespoons soy sauce (ganjang)
1 tablespoon Omija-Cheong (page 186)
1 tablespoon Bokbunja-Cheong (page 180)
½ tablespoon Rice Syrup (Jocheong, page 190)
2 teaspoons sesame seeds (kkae), crushed

Rinse the eggplants, halve them (or cut them into thirds, depending on their length), and then slice them lengthwise into moderately thin slices.

Salt the eggplant slices and let them stand for about 5 minutes.

Heat the perilla oil in a pan and sauté the eggplant slices on both sides.

Chop both of the chile peppers and mix them with the rest of the sauce ingredients, then pour the sauce over the eggplant. Let it sit briefly to absorb the sauce before serving it.

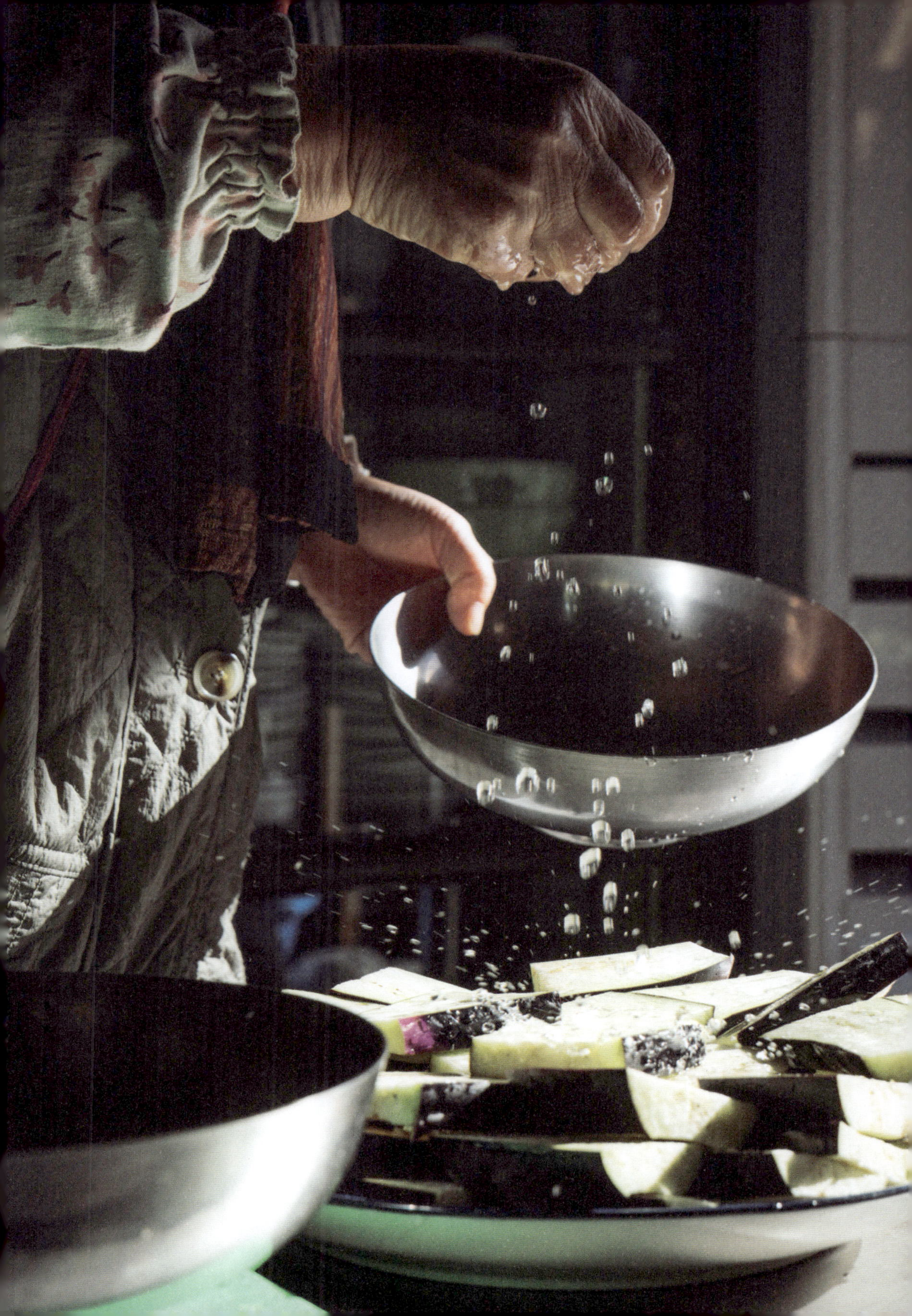

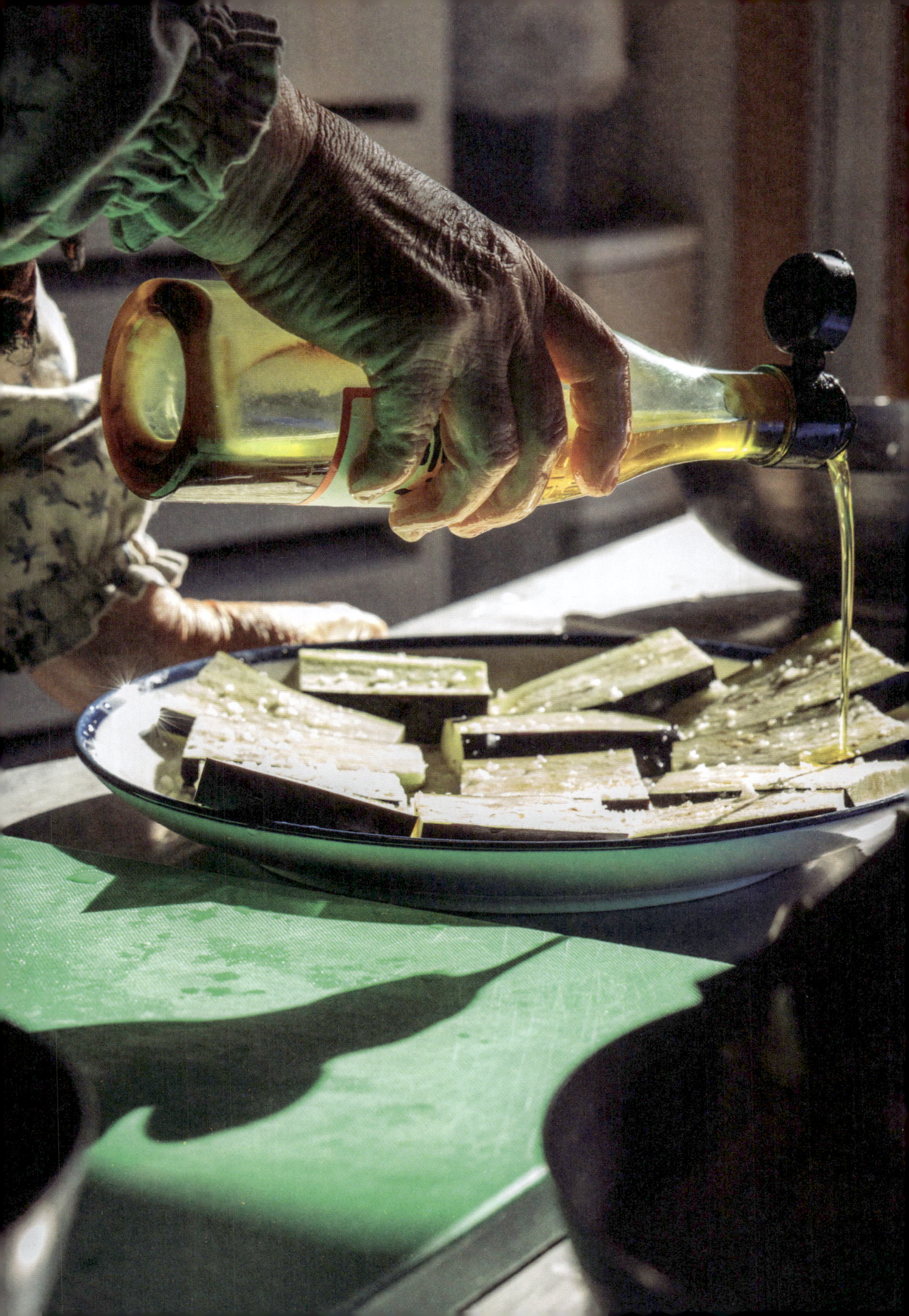

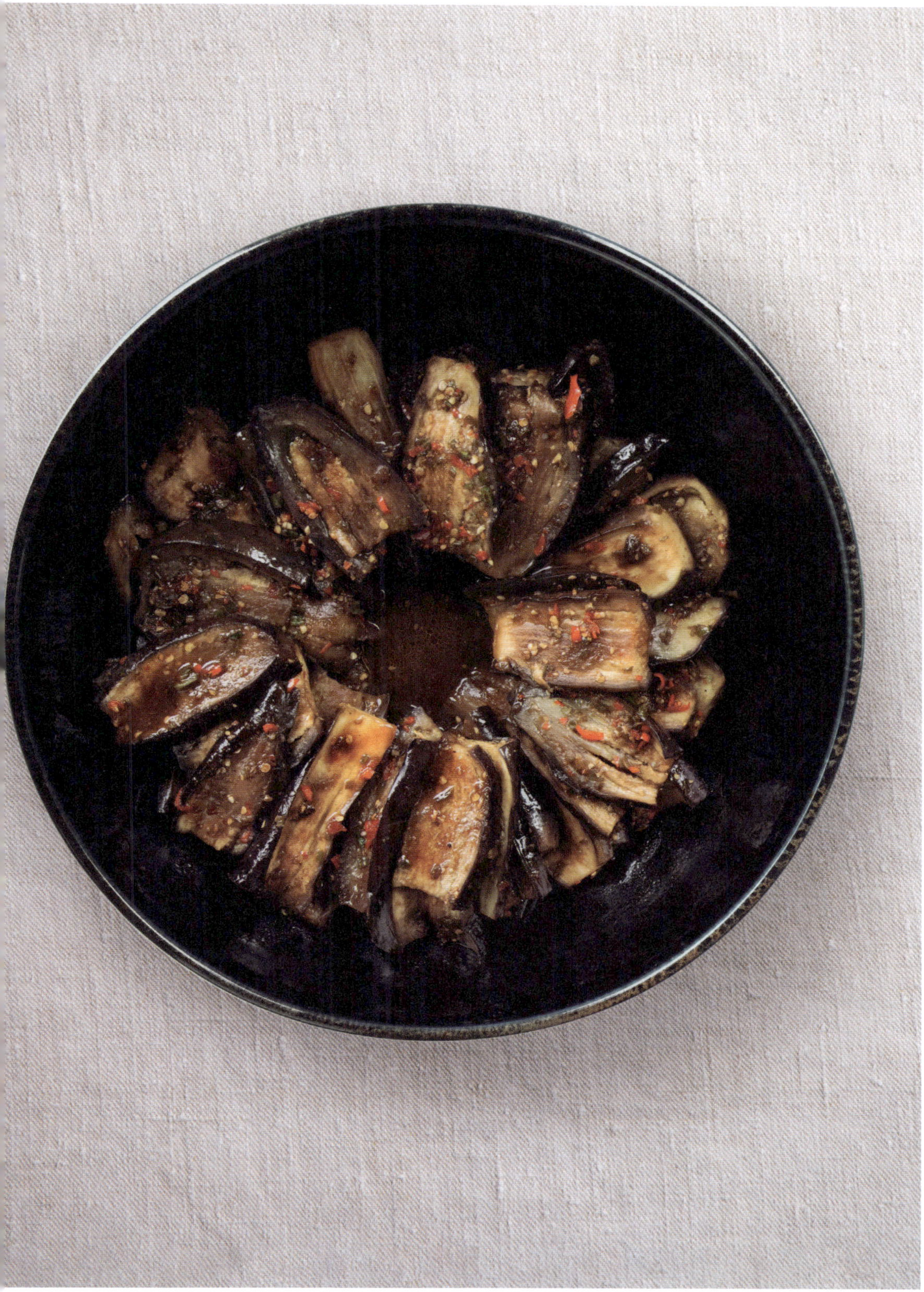

Ueong gochujang yangnyeom gui

FRIED UEONG WITH GOCHUJANG SAUCE

For the burdock
5 large burdock roots (ueong)
3 tablespoons perilla oil (deulgireum)

For the sauce
2 tablespoons soy sauce (ganjang)
1 tablespoon fine chili powder (goun-gochugaru)
2 tablespoons Korean chili paste (gochujang)
1 tablespoon Omija-Cheong (page 186)
2 tablespoons rice syrup (jocheong, page 190)
1 tablespoon sesame seeds (kkae)
1 tablespoon sesame oil (chamgireum)
Crushed black sesame seeds (heugimja) for seasoning
Radish sprouts (musun) for serving

Rinse the roots, scrape them with the spine of a knife, and steam them until they're half-cooked. Let them cool, halve them lengthwise, and carefully beat them with a wooden mallet to tenderize them. Heat the oil in the pan, sauté the roots until golden, and set them aside.

Add the soy sauce, chili powder, gochujang, Omija-Cheong, and jocheong to a pot. Add enough water to make a thick sauce, stirring constantly. Bring it to a boil. Remove the pot from the heat and stir in the sesame seeds and sesame oil. The sauce should taste sweet and spicy.

Cut the roots into 2-inch (5 cm) pieces and cover them evenly with the sauce.

Sprinkle with the crushed black sesame seeds and serve with radish sprouts if desired.

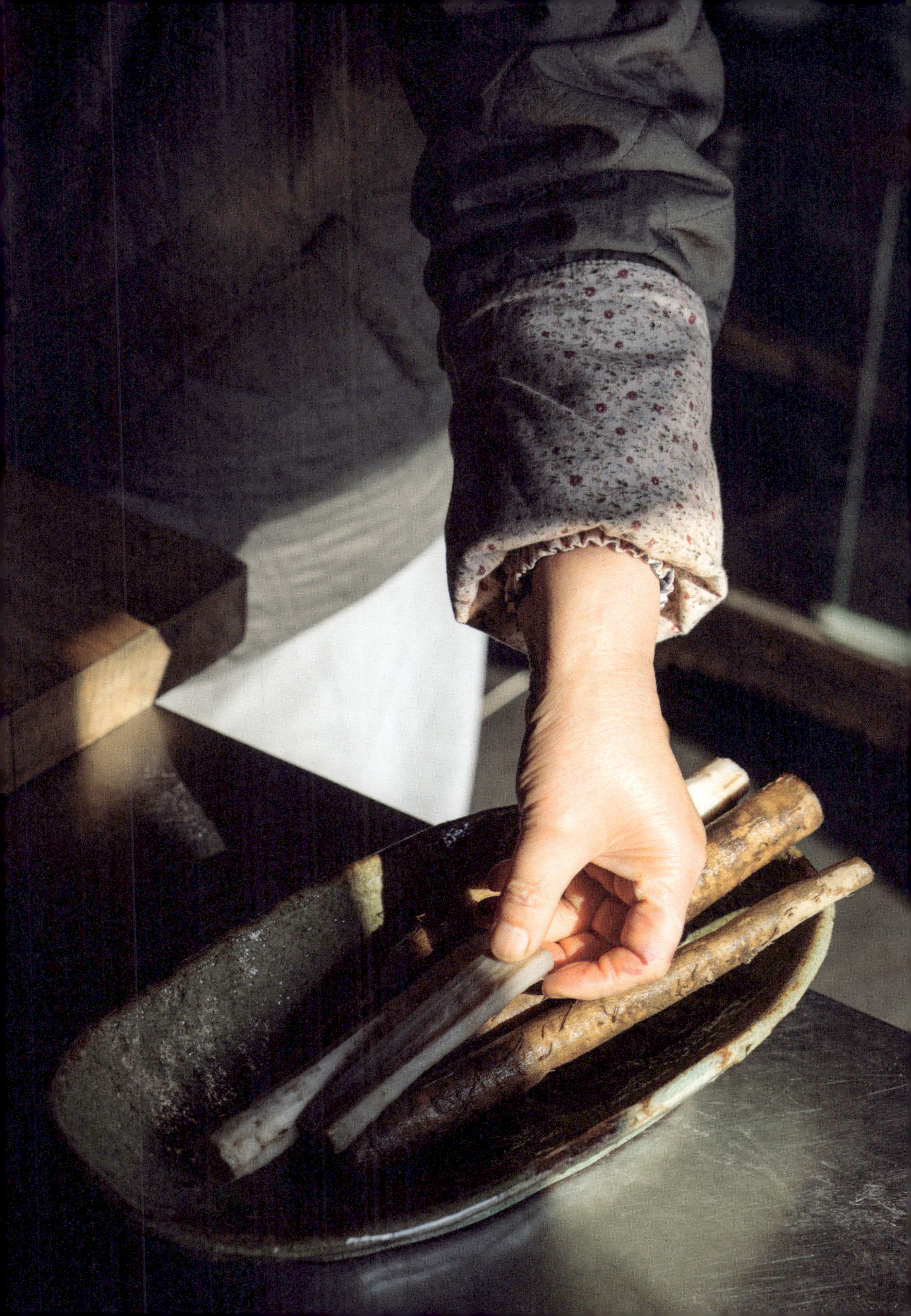

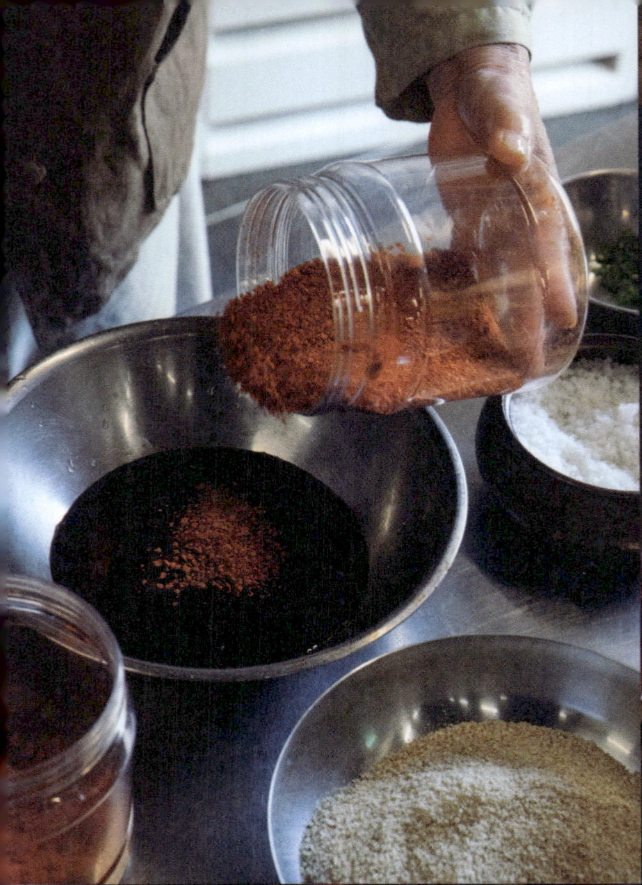
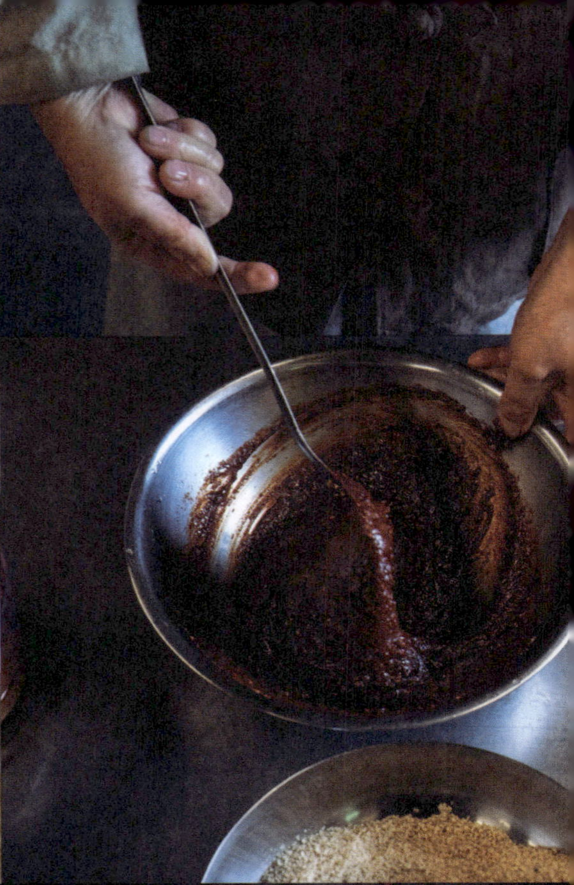
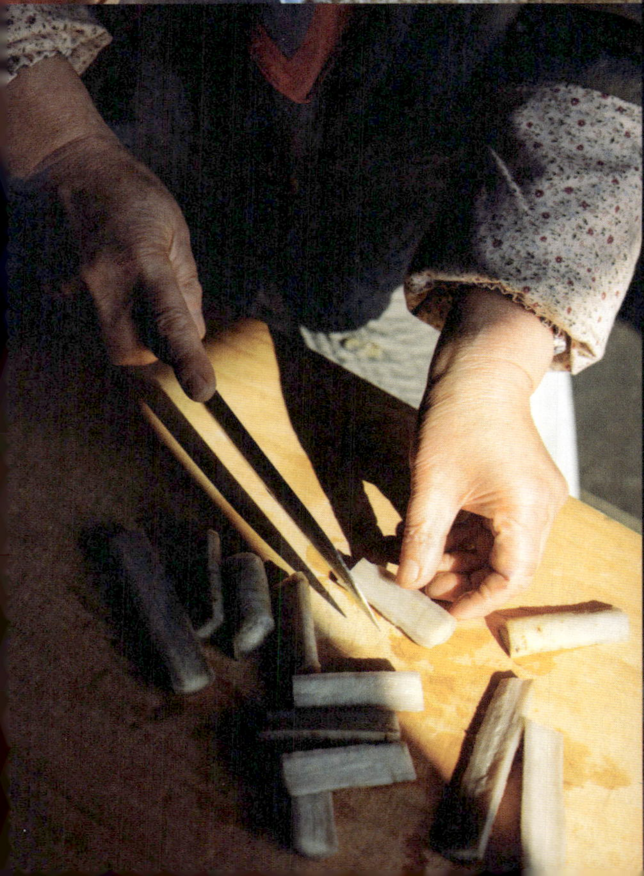
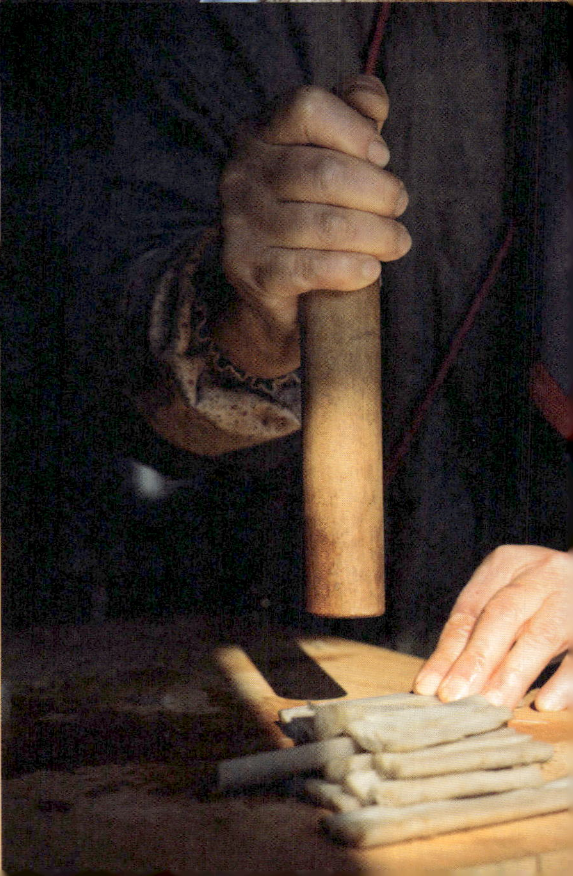

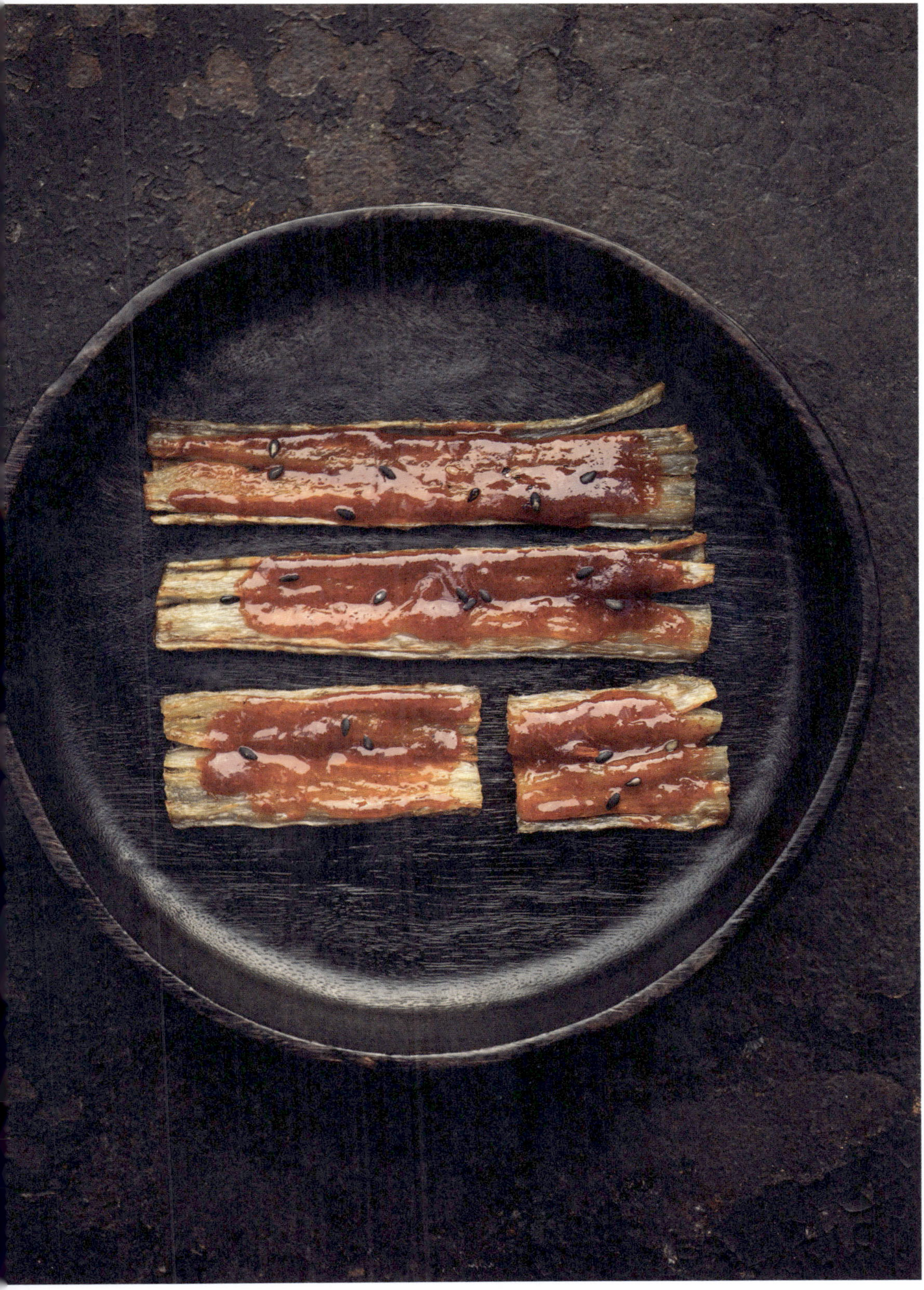

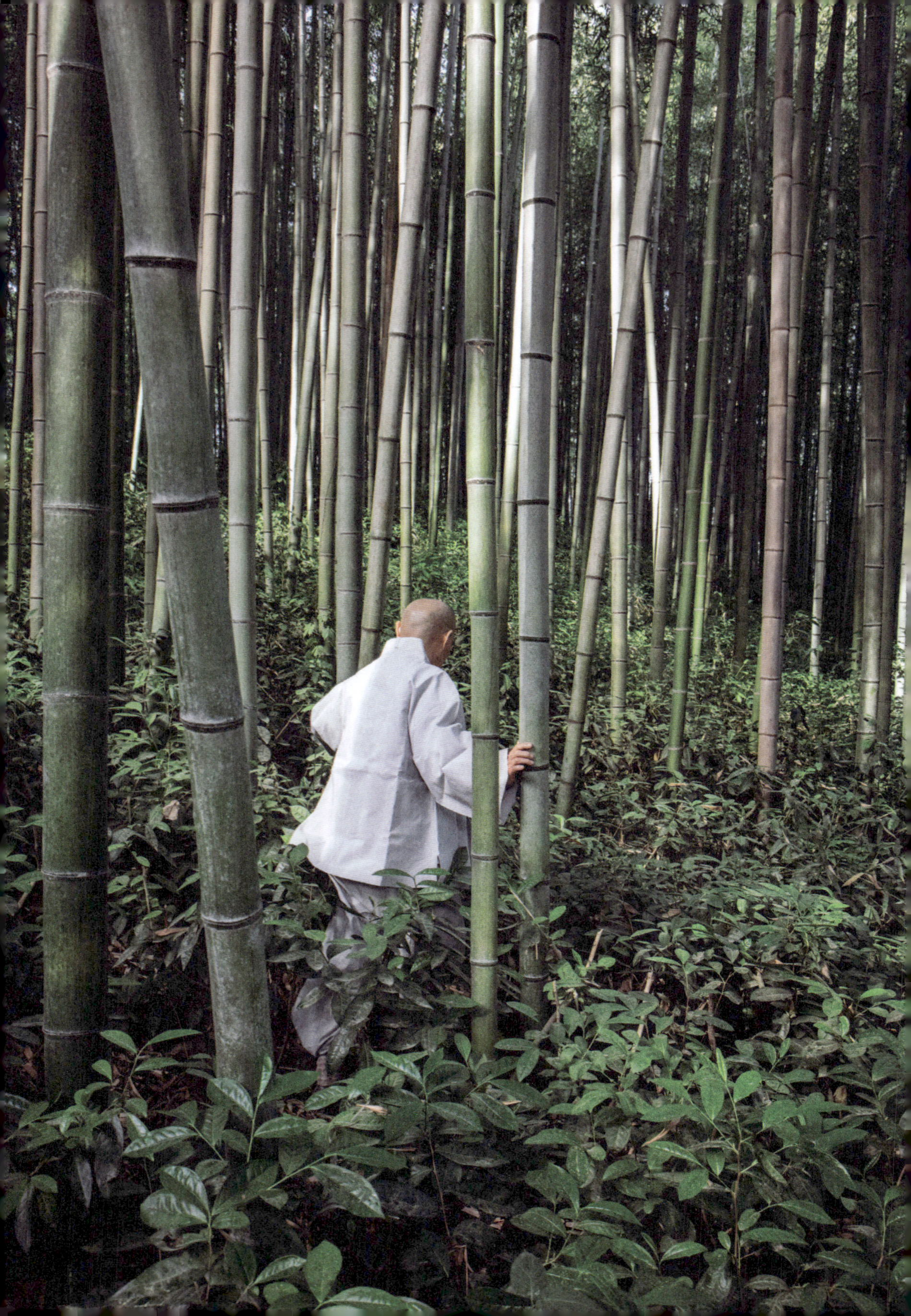

TEA AND BUDDHISM

Tea came to Korea with Buddhism, and together they became part of the local way of life—a plant and a religion developed an unusually close relationship and created a new culture. Jeongkwan Snim has her own tea room at her temple. It's small and modest, yet lovely. When the sliding doors stand open, they give a view of the mountains and into the valley. In this space, Snim receives guests and converses with the people who come to her for advice.

When she's chatting with her colleagues, there's invariably tea on the table. Snim always has different varieties of tea from Korea and abroad, and she also produces some tea herself, though not much. She knows all of the tea plantations in South Korea and visits them regularly.

In Korea, mostly wild plants grow in the areas around temples, jutting up between pine trees, maples, and bamboo. They bear witness to tea's first journey to Korea. It was snims who cultivated tea plants from China, tended them, and processed their leaves. Jeongkwan Snim talks often about where the teas came from, how they're produced, how they taste, and the effect they have on us. She also talks about the differences between oxidation and fermentation.

When you listen to her and try different kinds of teas—when you have their aromas in your nose and their flavors on your tongue—you feel yourself sink into the distant past. You can sense the warmth from the tea as it spreads slowly through your body, and you can feel the increasing clarity and alertness in your spirit.

A long, low table with the slightly crooked natural shape of a tree trunk occupies the central space of the tea room. A teapot, a canister of tea, a bamboo teaspoon, and small ceramic tea cups stand on the table. Everyone sits on the floor, with Snim sitting alone on one side and the others sitting next to each other on the opposite side. The first infusion is passed around, and then it's followed by additional infusions that have different colors and varying intensities of flavor.

East Asia's tea culture is one of the high points of Buddhism. The tradition of meditation is closely connected to tea; with its soothing effect and calming rituals, tea represents its own source of spirituality. In southern China, the home of tea, people discovered the mysterious aromas and healing effects of the green leaves early on—there, tea has long been used medicinally. It was Buddhism that first refined tea, carried it everywhere, and turned it into a cultural asset. Rituals developed

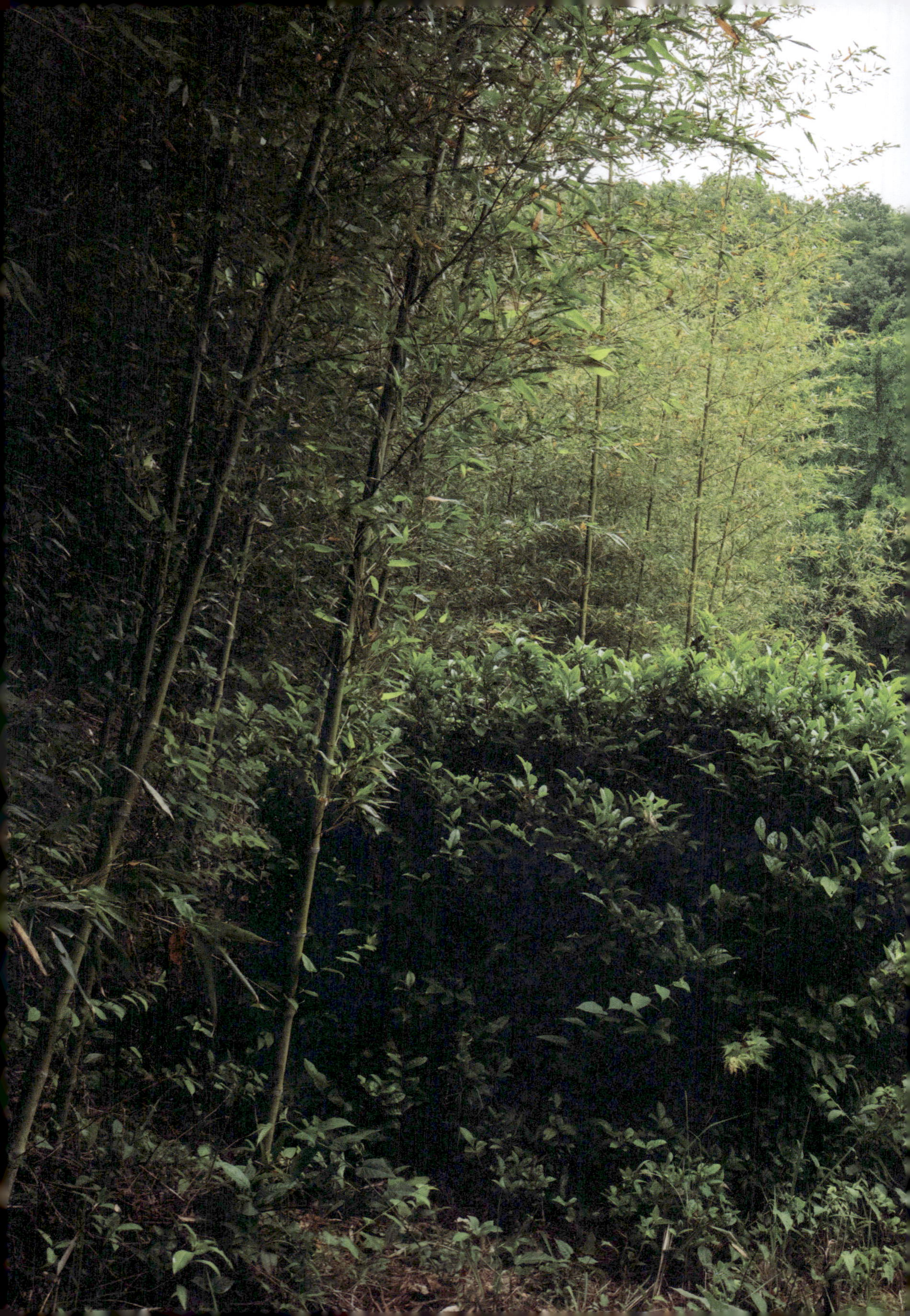

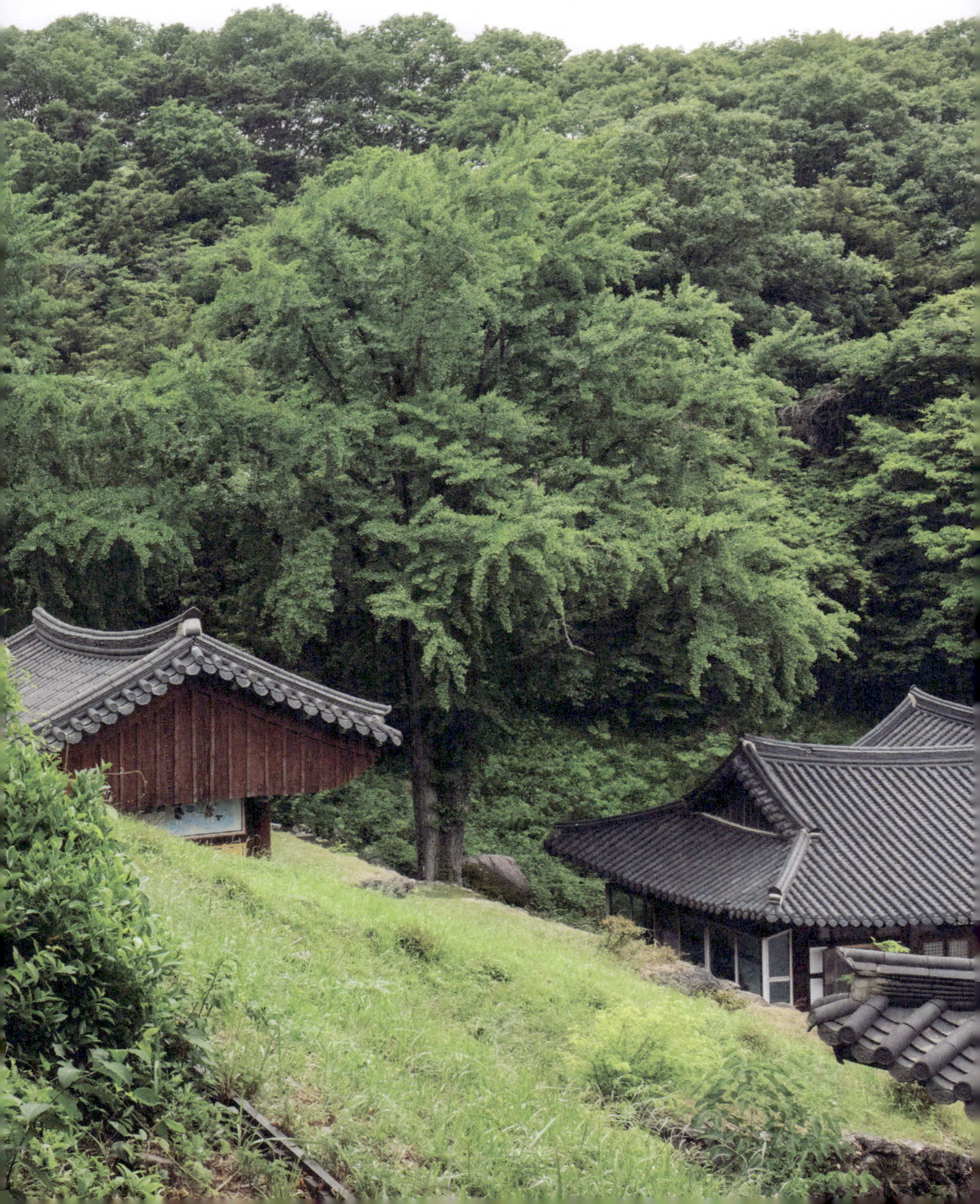

around it and a unique aesthetic emerged. Legends formed around the best teas. Celebrated by famous Buddhist masters and extolled by poets, tea acquired its own mystique.

Tea has been a faithful companion to Buddhism on the long road from China to the rest of the world; together, they have crossed many borders. By following Buddhism, the tea plant changed the landscape and way of life wherever it went. Drinking tea brought about new forms of socialization, and it created new meeting places and generated its own architecture. Together they thrived—a plant and a religion—and together they enriched one another. The tea plant became one of the most important crops in East Asia.

Tea drinking left temple grounds, spread out rapidly, and became part of everyday society. Not only did tea growing become a thriving industry, but a tradition of craftsmanship also grew up around the production of tea utensils—people needed tea cups, tea pots, and bamboo spoons, and tea quickly became a coveted good and a profitable commodity. With the onset of global trade, tea even started wars. However, far from the turmoil of the world, it remained an important component of temple life and a tonic for the Buddhist soul.

The three preparation methods for tea that are known today (boiling, frothing, and steeping) all originated in ancient China. They were cultivated and refined in the Tang, Song, and Ming dynasties. The methods have to do with various ways of processing the tea leaves, various preferences, and various trends: pressed cakes of tea are boiled, powdered and ground tea is frothed, and leaves are steeped.

Tea was being consumed in China long before the Common Era. During the Tang Dynasty (617–907), tea was boiled. The tea leaves were steamed, ground with a mortar and pestle, formed into flat cakes, dried, and stored. Some of these cakes were boiled with various ingredients, such as ginger, rice, salt, orange peel, and spices.

A significant shift in tea culture occurred in the middle of the eighth century with the emergence of poet and tea master Lu Yu (733–804), who lived at a time when Buddhism and Taoism were experiencing a symbiotic convergence and internal fusion. In the year 760, he published the first book about tea, *Chajing*, still considered to be a preeminent classic among tea literature. This volume (which concerned the drinking of tea) properly brought tea to the attention of the public. Not only did Lu Yu describe how to judge the quality of tea leaves and how important the water is, he also elevated tea drinking to an aesthetic experience. According to him, crockery should complement tea in color, refinement, and beauty. He highlighted the significance of the tea service and wound up influencing the developments of ceramics and porcelain. However, the real transformation that occurred at this time was the liberation of tea from other ingredients. Lu Yu initially kept the salt, only to abandon it soon after. The fine flavors of the tea could finally be savored without adulteration.

The Song Dynasty (960–1279) brought with it the fashion of frothing powdered tea with a bamboo whisk. The tart and bitter flavor, though toned down slightly by the foam, remains intense on the tongue because the leaves are being ingested whole. During this period of Chinese history, tea had become firmly established as a tradition to be maintained with great dedication. In the temples, drinking tea was a celebration, and strict rituals were observed in accordance with this celebration.

Tea culture was abruptly abandoned, however, when the Mongols conquered China and established the Yuan Dynasty (1279–1368). Originating from the north as a nomadic people, the Mongols had little appreciation for tea and its refined rituals. Much of the culture of the Song Dynasty was therefore lost, and so were many of the traditions around tea. The Song-era trend of frothing tea reached Japan in the twelfth century, where it's still beloved today. There, it's known as matcha.

During the Ming Dynasty (1368–1644) that followed the Mongolian reign, tea culture began to be revived. That was when the method of pouring hot water over tea leaves and letting them steep came into fashion. This preparation became generally accepted and established itself as the standard. At the beginning of the seventeenth century, tea left East Asia via trade routes and reached Europe. It had finally become a global commodity.

Tea (called *cha*) also accompanied Buddhism into Korea. The first tidings of Buddhism came to the country at the end of the fourth century and found their way into public awareness. Tea initially came to Korea as a finished product, but the plant also arrived in Korea as early as the sixth century due to brisk trade and a regular exchange of envoys between regions.

By the seventh century, tea drinking was widespread in Korea. Tea cultivation initially began in the areas around temples and—for climatic reasons—in the south of the country, particularly in the mountainous area around Jirisan. Ssanggyesa Temple, which is located in the Hadong tea cultivation area, is still an important site of Korean tea culture. This is where the oldest tea plants in Korea grow: it's been documented that in the year 828, tea plants brought by a Chinese

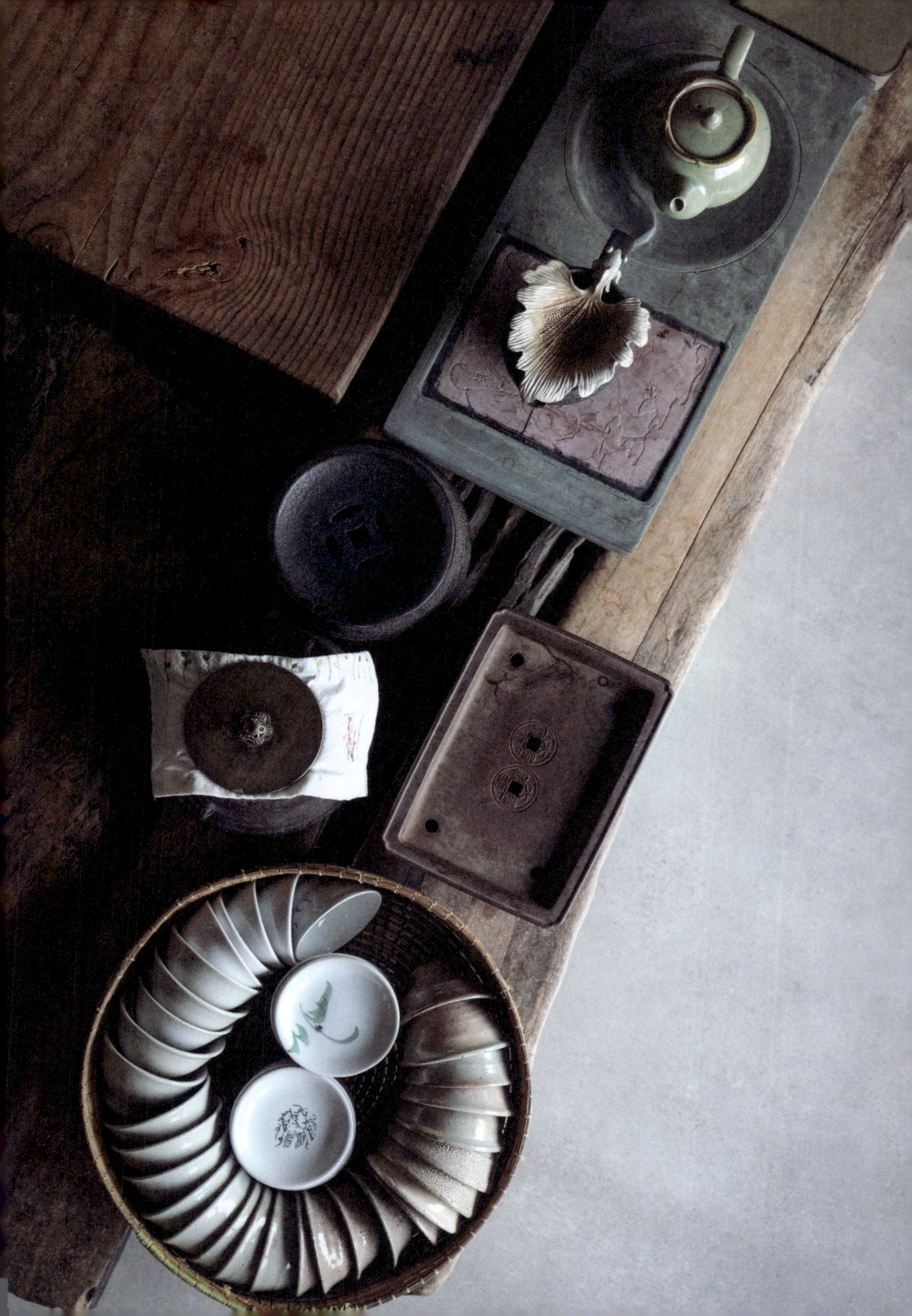

diplomat were planted on the slopes below the temple. Snims cared for the plants and produced tea from their leaves. Because it was a luxury good, tea consumption was initially limited to temple inhabitants, the royal court, and upper levels of the aristocracy.

As Buddhism flourished, tea spread throughout Korea and gained significance. When Seon Buddhism came to the country in the eighth century and became mainstream, *seon*, or meditation, was called the "way of tea." Tea was offered to the Buddha each day as a sign of veneration, and snims gathered to drink tea they had mostly grown themselves. There are numerous reports of how they competed with one another over whose tea was the best!

Tea varieties whose plants grew in bamboo forests or in rocky ground were highly prized, and teas made from the first shoots were and still are considered to be especially premium because they carry the concentrated energy that has collected in the plant all winter long.

Tea has always been drunk from a bowl. Tea was served at royal celebrations, weddings, and envoy receptions. More and more people discovered the joy of tea drinking, which stimulated and influenced the development of ceramic and porcelain. Many snims and poets have written poems and letters in which they proclaim their love of tea and describe its aromas and flavors. For centuries, tea was a popular gift among friends because it was a precious commodity; the gift-giver would often include a poem of their own composition along with the tea. Literati would meet amidst nature, drink tea, and write poetry. Tea and meditation and tea and poetry belonged together.

Between the eighth and fourteenth centuries, Buddhism experienced a period of expansion in Korea and shaped the entire culture. However, at the end of the fourteenth century, with the foundation of the last royal dynasty, the Joseon, tea suffered a mounting loss of importance because Confucianism was then elevated to being the state religion and Buddhism was increasingly suppressed. Snims retreated to remote mountains, lived in isolation, and devoted themselves to study and meditation.

At the end of the sixteenth century, a Japanese invasion ignited years of war that left the country completely devastated. Many temples went up in flames. Reports from the nineteenth century have led people to theorize that the cultivation of tea declined sharply. Not surprisingly, much knowledge was lost as a result. Some lamented this circumstance and tried to revitalize tea cultivation, but politically unsettled times followed.

In 1910, Korea became a Japanese colony, and Japan tried to create tea plantations in Korea to meet the increasing demand for tea. Plants were brought from Japan and planted in southern Korea—the famous tea-growing area of Boseong dates back to this initiative. Another important tea plantation lies on the island of Jeju, and the area around Hadong is also among the oldest green tea-producing regions. It still preserves this tradition today.

A plant and a religion converged through people and brought forth a unique cultural tradition. By touching our human senses, tea has created something spiritual.

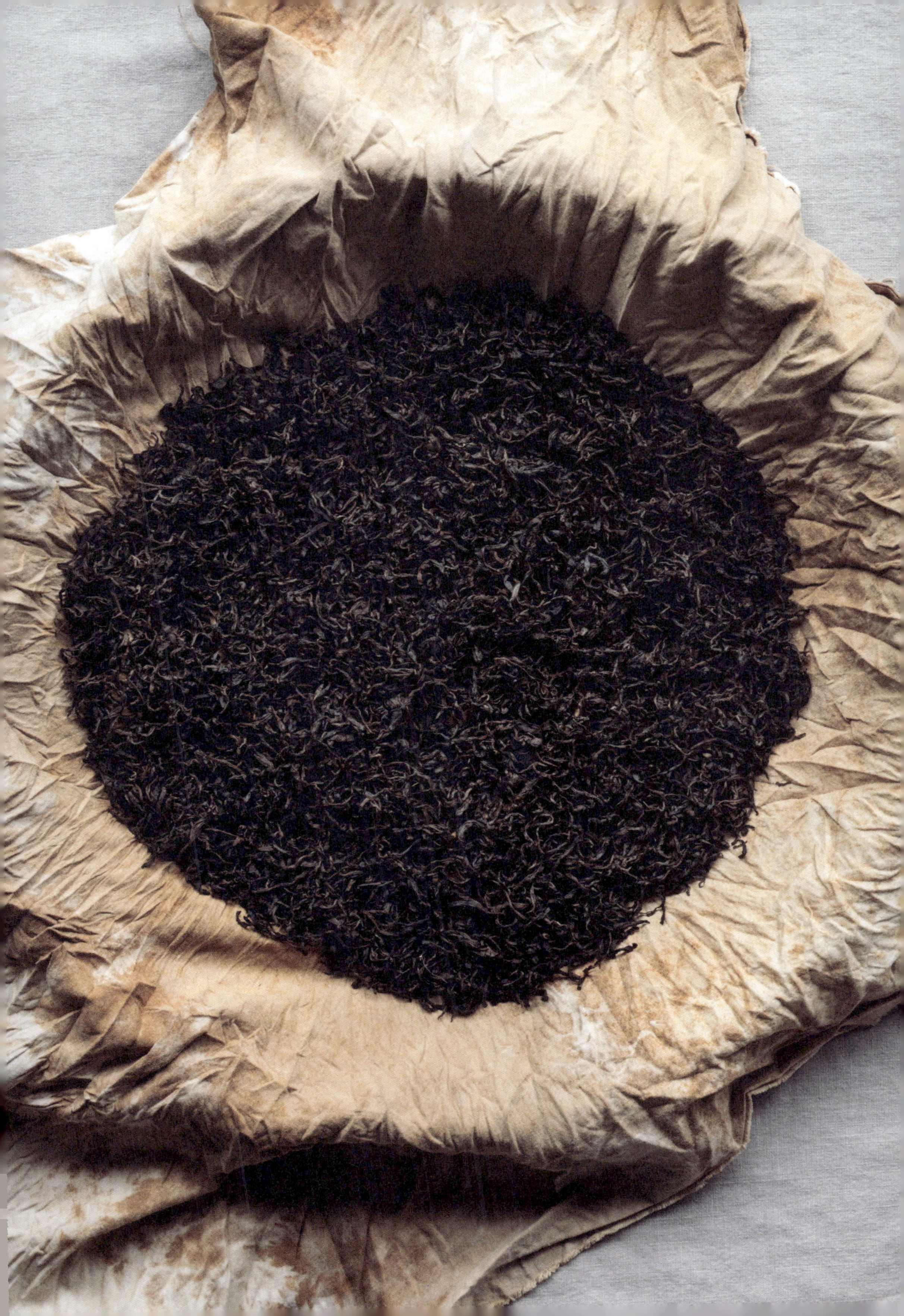

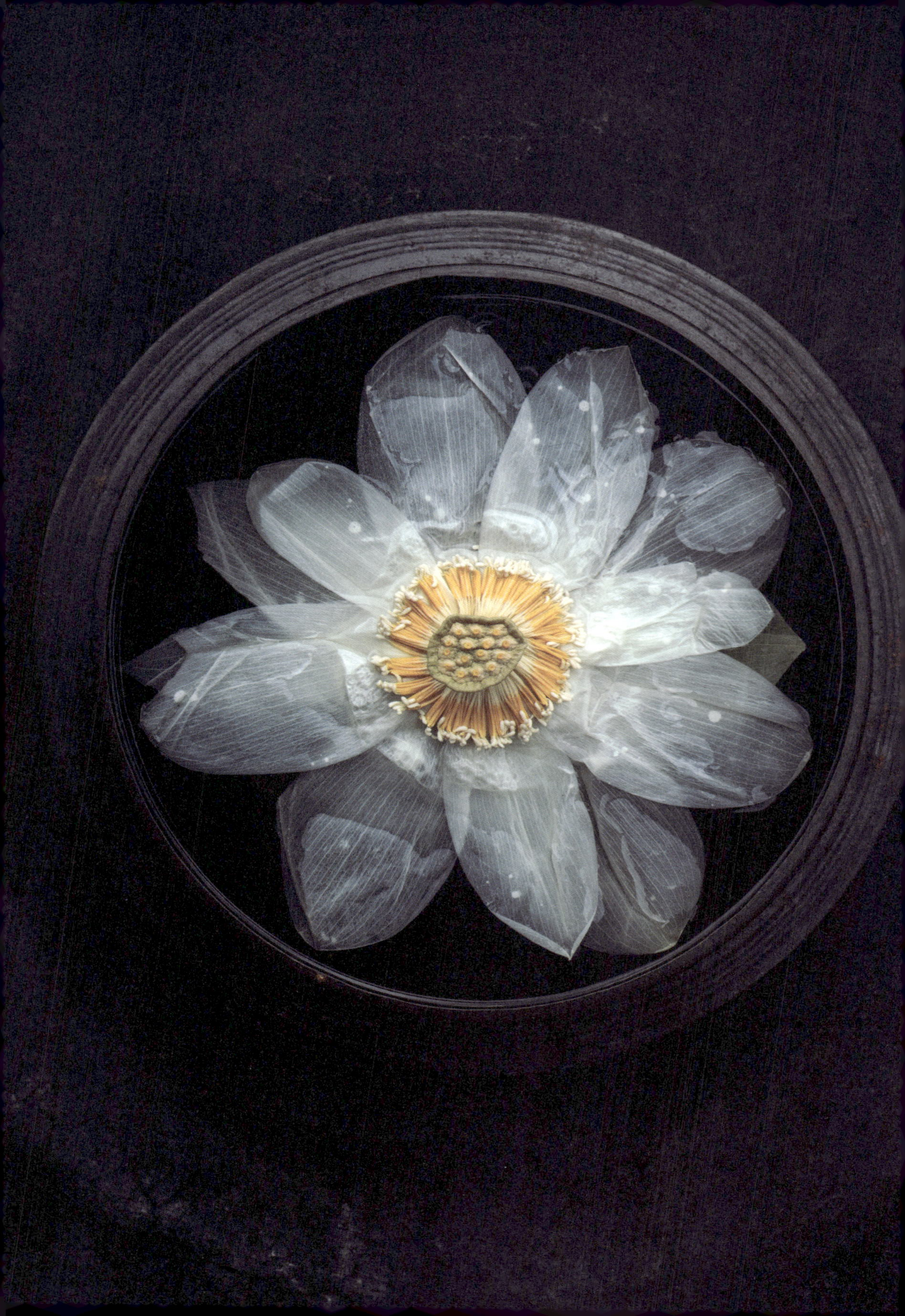

Has a blossom ever bloomed that has not swayed in the wind?

BUDDHISM IN KOREA

Buddhism began more than 2,500 years ago with a person who went searching and found a path. He had no idea at the time that a religion would grow out of his quest. But the Buddha's teachings have stood the test of time, because his search and his answers are still relevant today—we still experience the inner need that moved him back then.

The Buddha carved out a road that many people have since trodden. He was not a god but a teacher who continued to learn as he traveled his path. It was not his aim for people to believe in *him*—he wanted the understanding of his *teachings* to bring about change in their lives. He taught meditation, renunciation, and empathy for all living creatures, and he emphasized the necessity of studying and taking the right actions. Above all, he taught how to find a happiness that isn't fleeting but rather enduring and boundless.

The Buddha's teachings presume a certain view of humans and the world. He invites us to turn our insight toward ourselves first, toward what we think, feel, desire, and do. This alone will reveal how we should view our fellow humans and the world, because all things are interconnected. All change can only begin with oneself. This is especially true of the Buddhist path—when we ourselves change, then our environment will also change as a result.

The Buddhist mindset frees us and lets us see our interconnectedness with other humans and with nature. The Buddha gained deep insights into human nature and the psyche, and that knowledge is imperative for understanding humans and our behavior. The well-known Buddhist term *karma* simply means "to do, to act." Karma is important because we connect ourselves with other people and with the world through our actions. All actions bring consequences and leave traces, and these actions and consequences and traces determine the courses of our lives *and* the lives of others.

Where one person walks and others follow, a new path emerges from the wilderness. The Buddha opened a new way and proceeded along it. However, it's a profoundly individual path, and each of us must decide for ourselves whether we want to follow it. Buddhism has spread from its place of origin to many other countries while adopting to local conditions and changing its form during the passing of time.

If you want to understand Buddhism in concise terms, it's useful to engage with it on two levels: the historical and the doctrinal. Buddhism had already changed in form by the time it reached East Asia and therefore Korea, but once there, it continued to modify itself as it encountered natural and cultural influences. There, Buddhism took on a completely unique and distinctive shape.

HISTORY

Buddhism has its historic origins in Nepal, on the northern border of strongly Hindu India. Siddhartha Gautama (563–483 BCE) came from the Shakya clan and was the prince of a small kingdom. He founded the religious tradition of Buddhism, which centered not on God but on humans and their quest. Later, people called him *Buddha*, which means "the awakened one."

Siddhartha's life has been embroidered with many legends, making it difficult to tease out fact from fiction. He lived a sheltered life in the palace and enjoyed the upbringing of a prince. He was a polyglot with military training, and he learned how to lead people. As a young man, he realized that illness, age, and death are a part of life, and he embraced suffering and began to question its causes. To find an answer, he left his family, the palace, and his former life behind at the age of 29.

He searched for his answer in the teachings of the various traditional religions of his time. He studied the Brahman masters and went through the schools of asceticism. The ascetics viewed the body as an obstacle on the path to pure spirituality, and they sought freedom from fleshly shackles through asceticism. The Buddha ate hardly anything and lost weight. However, he soon saw that this wasn't the right path, because the longer he went hungry, the more his attention became fixed on his body—instead of being free from it, he felt imprisoned in it.

The Buddha recognized that hunger is a natural thing and that sound nourishment facilitates not only life but also study. He turned from the methods of the old schools and decided to find a new path. He began to eat again; he studied and meditated. At the age of 35, according to tradition, he was sitting underneath a bodha tree when he received the insights that survive as his teachings to this day, insights that went on to teach right ethical actions and grant inner peace, serenity, composure, and true happiness to whomever followed them.

After the day he spent underneath the bodha tree, the Buddha became a teacher for the next 45 years living his own life as he instructed others to do. His flock of disciples grew. His ideas about the equality of all humans and his deliberate rejection of the caste system (which still characterizes Indian society to this day) were revolutionary.

Buddhism followed the typical route of a new religion: it started small, and then it gradually acquired a fixed form and spread. A new tradition became established. Whenever this happens, institutionalization proves crucial because every religion requires organization—having an infrastructure helps preserve teachings, provides gathering space, formalizes rituals, sets rules, and provides for financing. Without this institutional support, no religion can last for long.

The Buddha's teachings had already taken on a recognizable form during his lifetime seeing as he taught for 45 years and died at the age of 80. His discourse was met with astonishment and interest due to the novelty of his thoughts, and it echoed far and wide. Many called themselves his students, teaching facilities were established, and a cloistered community grew. Later on, academies were founded that served as the intellectual centers of Buddhism. Disciples lived together, listened to the master, and discussed his teachings. Like his students, the Buddha lived on donated food that citizens placed in his bowl when he knocked on their doors, and he ate just one meal each day before noon. People followed him because he practiced what he taught. The prevailing tradition in India at the time was to pass on religious knowledge exclusively by word of mouth, so that's why for a long time, people internalized what the Buddha taught by rote learning and passed it on using that same method. The Buddha also traveled extensively to spread his teachings, and communities sprang up everywhere.

When the Buddha died, the situation shifted. His body was burned on sandalwood and the *sari* (or the ashes), bone fragments, and teeth were divided among eight kings. Each buried his share and erected a *stupa*, a tomb built in the Buddha's honor. That was when the veneration of relics in Buddhism began, primarily serving as a way to legitimize sites and buildings as being Buddhist. The stupas represent the earliest Buddhist monuments; later, they gave rise to pagodas. In all Buddhist countries, pagodas are erected as receptacles for saris and as such occupy a central place in rituals.

After the Buddha's death (known as entering *nirvana*, or "extinguishment"), the first gathering of students and disciples took place. According to tradition, instead of naming a successor, the Buddha had said that his teachings should be viewed as a torch that would light the way to the future. A controversy over the direction that Buddhism should take sprang up immediately, with two students, Ananda and Mahakashyapa, representing differing views. One topic was whether the ordination of women—which the Buddha had begun—should still be allowed. Ananda supported it.

The hole left by the Buddha's death soon became keenly felt. His disciples began to collect his teachings, although for a long time they continued to use the verbal method of passing along his teachings—they learned the sutras by rote and recited them from memory, ensuring that the sutras were passed along and preserved. This tradition is how some of the Buddha's quotes have survived word for word. The *Sutta Pitaka* collection supposedly traces back to Ananda and contains numerous ancient passages. The typical features of an oral tradition are recognizable in the texts today: they're short, simple, memorable, repetitive, verse-like sentences with great lyrical power. Because these teachings have been passed down by students and disciples of the Buddha, the sentences usually begin with "Thus have I heard . . ."

A century after the death of the Buddha, a second large gathering took place. Seven hundred participants came together to discuss various points of contention that had arisen, and it became apparent that they weren't going to find simple answers—by that time, no one still living had known the Buddha personally and therefore no one could invoke his authority. Conflicts arose among the various communities who had different living practices, and each of them claimed to be the legitimate successor to the Buddha.

An argument broke out about the banal activities of everyday life, an argument that ultimately led to a division in Buddhism. Outwardly, it was about the observation of monastic rules, but soon, deeper-seated rifts manifested themselves. In a nutshell, without the presence of an arbitrating entity, it was no longer possible to maintain the unity of the original Buddhism.

At this time, two large Buddhist communities had been established in northern India, one in the east and one in the west. The eastern community was the original one—that was where the Buddha was born, where he taught, and where he died. All of the stupas with saris were also located here. The western community had been founded later by the Buddha's students. It was conservative and traditional, while the eastern community wanted to handle the rules pragmatically and flexibly.

The dispute was about the interpretation of 10 issues within the monastic rules. For example, one question concerned mealtime. Tradition said that the one meal per day had to be eaten before the sun reached its midday peak, but how loosely that should be interpreted was a point of contention. Another question concerned how legitimate any collective resolutions were if someone arrived late to discuss the issue, because resolutions always had to be unanimous.

Two points of contention were especially central. One of those was whether a community was allowed to accept gold or silver coins instead of donated items. The Buddha had forbidden order members from taking coins into their hands, but building and maintaining temples and communities increasingly required money. The second point pertained to salt: was it permissible to carry it? At the time, many people carried salt around with them in a horn-shaped vessel because the Indian climate was hot and people sweated a great deal. But did salt count as food or medicine? Food could not be kept by order members, but medicine could.

In the eastern community, these things were handled pragmatically without violating the spirit of the rules. The western community, however, wanted to adhere strictly to tradition. And so unity was thus shattered not because of differences in the teachings, but because the 10 monastic rules were interpreted differently. This disunity made it obvious that the communities had developed differently and that no one wanted to surrender their independence.

The larger community in the west named itself *Theravada*, or "the way of the elders." The eastern group, which called itself *Mahayana* or "large vehicle," condescendingly referred to the western community as *Hinayana* or "smaller vehicle." Theravada Buddhism sought to legitimize itself by presenting itself as the protector of tradition. The split between Theravada Buddhism and Mahayana Buddhism took place slowly as the differences in beliefs gradually became more apparent. Throughout this schism, however, Buddhism continued to establish itself as a religion.

The great turning point for Buddhism came under King Ashoka (303–232 BCE), who was the first to unify India. Every religion obtains legitimacy and a boost in development when it earns political recognition and financial support, so it isn't surprising that Buddhism experienced its first period of expansion under Ashoka. He himself became a Buddhist after unifying the country using brutal methods to establish his dominance. To disseminate Buddhism, he had seven of the eight original stupas opened and the saris preserved inside of them distributed. From those, several thousand new stupas and temples were established all over India. Buddhism was embraced with an unexpected momentum; it spread south to Sri Lanka as well as northwest, where India's main trade route flowed.

Writing down the teachings also began in the first century BCE. It marked another turning point for the religion and contributed significantly to the spread of Buddhism outside India; along the way, it also incorporated lay people, allowing anyone to read the sutras. The oldest transcript is written in Pāli, a language native to Sri Lanka, but it was soon rendered into Sanskrit. Because holy teachings have traditionally only been passed on orally in India, for a long time, there was great reluctance to set them down in writing. After four centuries of Buddhism, however, the teaching texts had expanded so much that it was impossible to memorize everything.

The three sustaining pillars of Buddhism were finally in place. The first pillar is the teachings, called *sutras*. Metaphorically, the sutras are a string of pearls that symbolize the words of the Buddha. The second pillar is the rules that the order members must observe. The third pillar comprises the comments of the learned monks—the more time that passed since the lifetime of the Buddha, the more important it became to clarify and comment on the teachings that had been passed down. These three pillars are also called *tripitaka* or "three baskets," and they remain fundamental to Buddhism.

The first split in Buddhism resulted in additional branches of Buddhism. Theravada remained the dominant group until the first century CE, continuing to expand to Southeast Asia and Sri Lanka. It laid the foundation for the sutras and the theoretical disputes pertaining to them and offered little room for lay people. This school was also conservative and elitist—only monks and a select few could attain the goal of becoming *arhat* or "enlightened." Indian thought regarding the caste system continued despite the fact that it contradicted the Buddha's teachings. All of this resulted in disciples missing the rituals and the religious practice and them eventually turning away. Lay people too continued to turn to Mahayana Buddhism, because that branch of Buddhism taught that everyone could achieve enlightenment like the Buddha had if they made the effort. It was based on equality, and more and more, it was being sustained by lay people.

Mahayana Buddhism became mainstream in the second century. But meanwhile, Buddhism had constantly been under pressure from the start from powerful Hinduism—to Hindus, Buddhism was a reform religion. This amalgamation resulted in new forms of Buddhism. One of these was the so-called "secret Buddhism," also known as Tantrism. In this form, sutras are called *tantras*. It's considered to be a branch of Mahayana Buddhism, but Tantrism has increasingly developed into an independent movement. Its rituals include secret sexual practices and the belief that supernatural abilities can be acquired through meditation. The mandala—which symbolizes the Buddha and his world and is also said to be magical—is a central element of Tantrism.

Tantric Buddhism experienced a period of expansion in India in the seventh century and made its way to Tibet and Mongolia. However, as the newly established religion of Islam expanded further east and crossed into northern India, Buddhism fell under stiff pressure. In contrast to Hinduism, whose disciples were farmers, the Buddhists in India were mostly from the merchant class. As Muslims gained control of trade routes and only wanted to trade with Muslims, Indian Buddhists lost their core way of making a living. When Vikramashila, the last of the four Buddhist academies, was destroyed by Muslim conquerors in 1203, Buddhism disappeared completely from its home country of India. Many Buddhists fled to Tibet, strengthening the Tantric Buddhism movement there; what still remained of Buddhism in India was totally absorbed by Hinduism. However, Buddhism lived on outside of India: Theravada Buddhism in Southeast Asia, Tantric Buddhism (also known as Vajrayana) in Tibet, and Mahayana Buddhism (which includes Seon Buddhism) in East Asia. Today, Buddhism is present in various forms throughout the world.

The Mahayana variant of Buddhism came to China in the first century and spread from there to Korea and Japan. Mahayana Buddhism was successful because it recognized discontent early on and expressed the need for reform. It sought to break up the accumulation of obsolete ideas and practices and to renew Buddhism. The doctrinal system of Theravada that had dominated to that point was found to be bloated, overwrought, and too difficult to understand. The intention was to free the Buddha's teachings from what had been added to them later on and return Buddhism to its original simplicity. This school formed slowly over centuries, but it was apparent by the first century BCE. Its development accelerated once its adherents began to write down the teaching texts, and sutras unique to Mahayana Buddhism emerged. Old texts that had been transmitted orally were collected, reordered, interpreted, compiled, and expanded.

The emergence of Buddhist sculpture in Central Asia also helped draw new disciples to the religion. The first Buddha statues were created during the first century in the ancient region of Gandhara, under the influence of Greek culture. They soon became very popular and fundamentally changed temple architecture and Buddhist worship.

Although Mahayana Buddhism first acquired its own form in East Asia, where it experienced a period of expansion, its arrival proved to be anything but simple. Indian culture is fundamentally distinct from that of China in a number of respects, including its geography, climate, culture, and religious conditions. The arrival of Mahayana Buddhism in China was a lengthy process, one that was hindered or facilitated by various political and economic factors. During the first two centuries of its arrival, individual Buddhist monks came to China from India and Central Asia to spread the new religion. They spoke Chinese poorly or not at all, so their success varied. But many did go on to learn Chinese and attempted to translate the sutras they had brought with them into Chinese—after all, they couldn't proselytize without a text to work from.

The colossal task of translating the many sutras began in the third century and continued into the eighth century, when a canon was created. This achievement represented a unique transfer of culture that changed languages and cultures throughout East Asia, due largely to the fact that translating sutras became a very complicated endeavor in light of the cultural differences between India and China. Whenever a new religion or worldview comes to a country, the language will lack words to render the new ideas, and that was certainly the case in China. Terms like "enlightenment" and "nirvana"—and in fact the entire vocabulary of Buddhism—did not exist in the Chinese language. To permit the translation of the sutras, new terms had to be created, meanings of existing ones had to be expanded, and Sanskrit words simply had to be borrowed. Thus the language changed, and so did the way of thinking. (Interestingly, many words were borrowed from the vocabulary of Taoism because the content of its beliefs had a lot in common with Buddhism.)

The translation work was done in different phases; the translations were only gradually standardized, systematized, and harmonized. The way of thinking in China was taken more and more into account during the process in order to make the teachings easier to understand. Meanwhile, many Chinese monks traveled to India, studied there, and brought sutras back with them. They were then able to study the source materials themselves—help was no longer needed from India. Buddhism had already begun to show signs of deterioration in India in any case, but by then, Mahayana Buddhism had become part of the local way of life in East Asia and many Sanskrit words had been absorbed into East Asian languages. A new history of Buddhism began, one that carried unmistakable traces of East Asia. Those traces are especially apparent in Seon Buddhism, which started in China and soon developed into a powerful movement throughout East Asia.

As Buddhism spread from India to China, it had to leave behind everything Indian about it apart from the sutras. Its architecture also had to be abandoned. A unique form of temple architecture emerged in East Asia that was better suited to the climate, the local way of life, and the aesthetic ideas of the region. The Indian monastic rules also couldn't be transferred—the rules about clothing couldn't be observed, nor the commandment to go barefoot or collect food. Temples were mostly located in the mountains, and each temple community had to provide for its residents. A unique tradition of vegan temple cooking developed.

The Indian way of meditation also didn't find its way to China. That's why Seon Buddhism soon developed there, where the meditation is central. India has an ancient and diverse meditation tradition as well, but its hot climate required a different meditation technique than what was used in China's colder climate. In particular, breathing had to be different in colder areas than in hotter ones. (Breathing is a very important component of meditation because it also regulates body temperature, and meditation requires looking inward and immersing oneself in infinity.) While Indian thought is characterized by dualism, the dominant thought in East Asia focuses on unity, and this distinction is also reflected in the method of meditation.

Mahayana Buddhism saw its first explosion during the Tang Dynasty (617-907), which happened during China's Golden Age. Trade flourished and so did poetry. Some emperors became Buddhists and supported the new religion. Many famous Buddhist masters were active during this era; architecturally groundbreaking pagodas and temples were erected. Buddhism made its way into the people's thinking and attitudes toward living, becoming part of the local way of life. People's standard of living increased, tea culture emerged, and people were searching for personal happiness. This cultivation of life was particularly fostered in southern China, the home of Taoism, so it seems utterly natural that Seon Buddhism emerged there in the seventh century. It thrived until the Mongols conquered China in the thirteenth century and came to favor Tantric Buddhism. But because Seon Buddhism offered individuals the opportunity to find their own happiness with the help of meditation, that's likely why it has survived into the present day and has also found broad popularity in the West.

Starting in the fifteenth century, Buddhism saw its influence in East Asia begin to wane. That decrease was related to the revival of Confucianism, whose founder, Confucius, was a contemporary of the Buddha. Confucianism isn't a religion—it's more a combination of political philosophy, social theory, and ethics. That said, Confucianism does have a slight connection to religion because it includes the veneration of ancestors. Studying Confucian classics became a way to recruit elites and was how Confucianism maintained a constant political relevance. In contrast, without the protecting hand of politics, the influence of Buddhism waned. The fact that Confucianism borrowed a lot from Buddhism proved to be disadvantageous for Buddhism.

Buddhism came to Korea at the end of the fourth century. From there, it made its way to Japan. It spread slowly—it required about 200 years to really make its way to people and find a place in their culture. However, Buddhism was able to establish itself for two

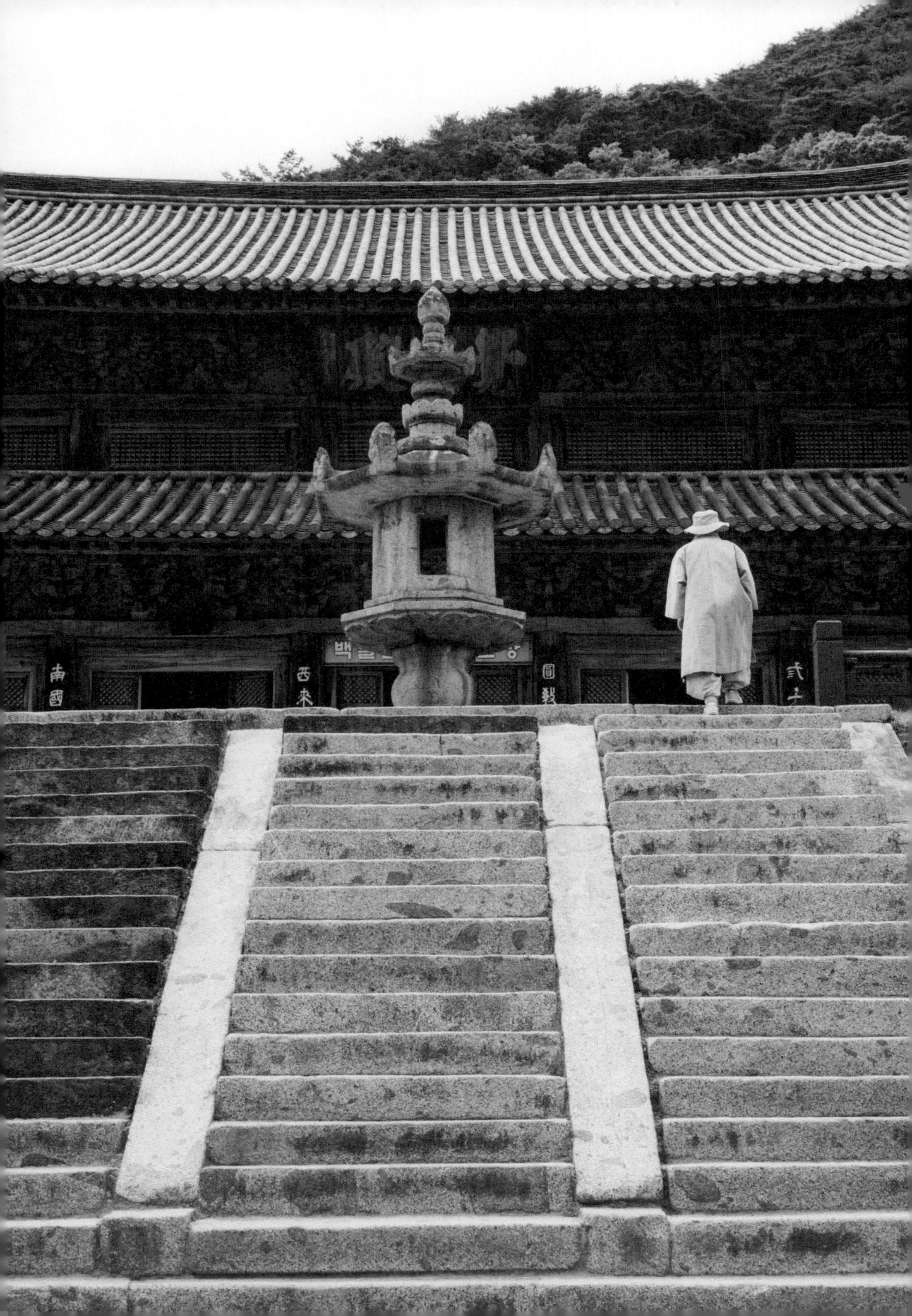
南國
西來
圓教

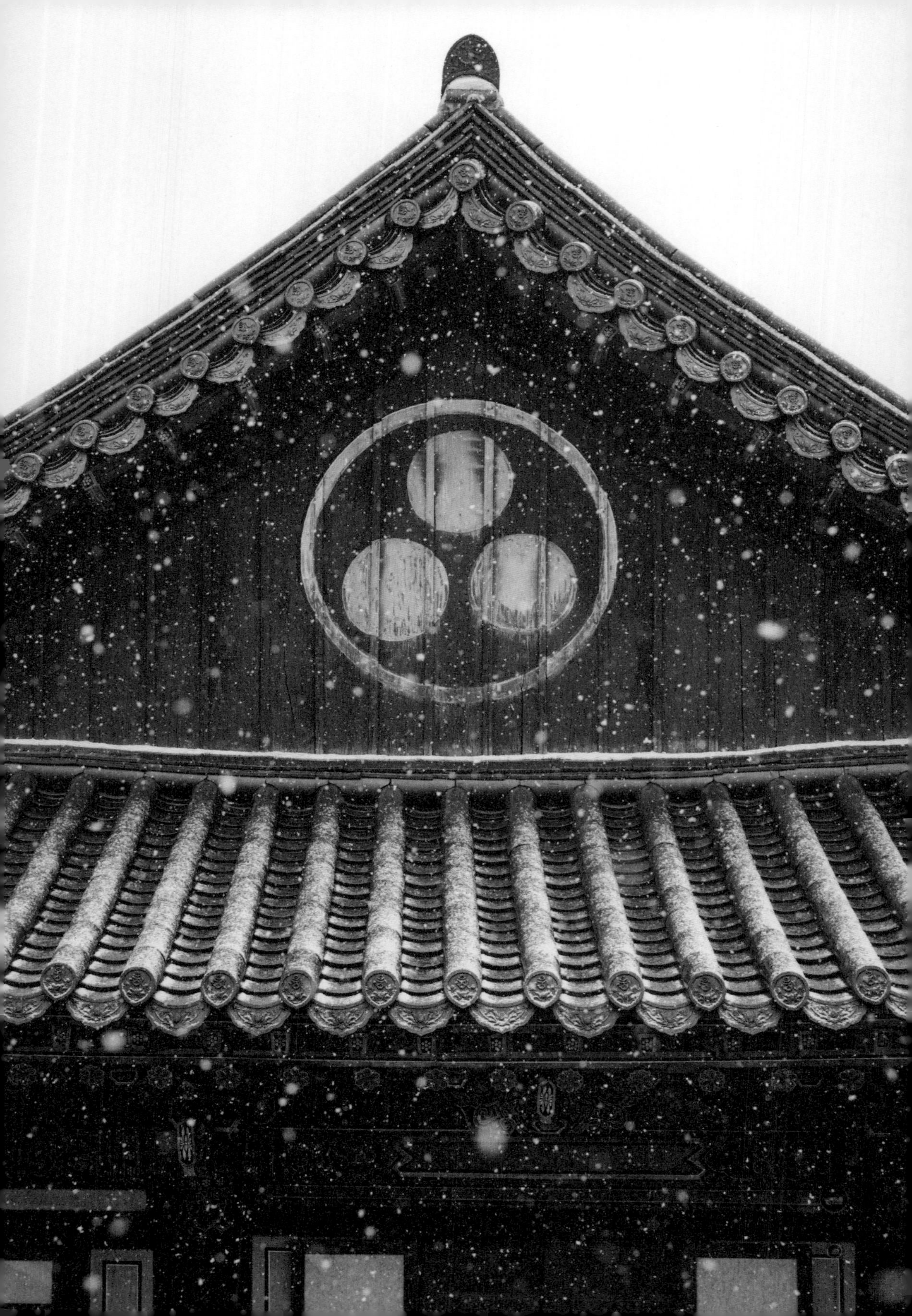

reasons: it was already in its assimilated form when it came from China, and Chinese script was used in Korea and Japan at that time. That meant that the sutras that had been translated into Chinese could be read in those two countries. Another advantage for Buddhism was that Korean elites were interested in it. Before then, no religion in Korea had had a written canon that was focused on spirituality and appealed to individuals—at that point, only shamanism and the veneration of ancestors (the latter influenced by Confucianism) were known. Kings converted to Buddhism and began to eat a vegetarian diet.

The most famous of the Buddhist masters in Korea was Wonhyo Daesa (617-686). He gave Buddhism a solid basis in Korea by bringing different movements together, and he significantly Koreanized them and then brought Buddhist teachings to the common people. A famous story exists about Wonhyo Daesa. On his journey to China—he was aiming to improve his study of Buddhism—one night, he fell asleep in a cave. Thirst woke him. He found a container of water nearby that smelled fresh, so he drank it and went back to sleep.

In the morning, he saw that what he had thought was a cave was actually a decaying gravesite and that the container he had drunk the water from was a skull. Suddenly, he felt uneasy and the place seemed eerie to him. That was when he realized that a person's internal attitude toward a thing is what determines how they perceive that thing. He went back home because he thought he then understood the Buddha's teachings.

In the seventh and eighth centuries, many Korean snims went to China. Eleven of them even traveled to India to study the Buddhist source texts. When Seon Buddhism reached Korea in the eighth century, it adapted to the cultural conditions of the country and quickly expanded and went mainstream, becoming the state religion until the end of the fourteenth century. Although Buddhism was repressed during the subsequent Joseon Dynasty (1390 to 1910) because Confucianism then became the state religion, Buddhism was able to maintain its influence thanks to its long tradition and the fondness people had developed for it. During its period of expansion, pagodas, temples, paintings, and books emerged all over the country. The *palmandaejanggyeong* or the *Tripitaka Koreana* is from the thirteenth century. It represents an incomparable testament to Korean Buddhism—it consists of more than 80,000 wooden tablets with sutras carved into them.

The Korean way of thinking, the Korean view of the world, and Korean aesthetics were heavily influenced by Buddhism. It wielded a formative influence over Korean culture and left many traces that are still visible today: it can be recognized in the language and the way of thinking and in architecture, philosophy, painting, literature, and food. Today, Seon Buddhism is one of the biggest orders of Buddhism. Jeongkwan Snim belongs to this order.

THE BUDDHA

Buddha began his quest with simple questions concerning human life. Those questions are timeless: why is the world the way it is, full of conflict, unhappiness, and suffering? Is it possible to find happiness of a sort that isn't fleeting but rather serene and enduring? Is it possible to live without suffering? How should we act to avoid increasing our own unhappiness and that of others?

After a long search, the Buddha found answers and began to tell others those answers. His teachings are known as the Four Noble Truths: there is unhappiness, dissatisfaction, and suffering in the world; there are causes for this and we are able to recognize these causes; overcoming suffering is possible; and there is a path that leads us there.

However simple his teachings may seem at first glance, we should not overlook the fact that these teachings have emerged from an ancient religious tradition. The renewal of Buddhism came from Hinduism, which during the Buddha's time occupied a central position. This historical context is important if we want to understand the cultural underpinnings of the Buddha's teachings and why they've taken on the particular shape we still recognize today. Since every religious teaching stands within a river of time, we cannot disregard the historical backdrop of Buddhism even though his teachings have fundamentally changed over time as Buddhism came under the influence of other cultures.

THE WORLDVIEW

The Buddha's teachings came about because he could not accept the most important basic assumptions of Hinduism. Like all religions, it had a very distinct worldview, and that worldview had a defining influence on the thinking and behavior of people in India at the time, especially with respect to the caste system, which governed India's social hierarchy. At the top were the Brahmans, who comprised the priestly caste. They were immigrants who referred to themselves as Aryans, and they represented the elite class of the country. Their worldview in particular was what the Buddha was challenging.

There are two fundamental metaphysical assumptions central to Hinduism: Brahman and Atman. *Brahman* means the one absolute and eternal ultimate reality; it's often described as the world's soul. Everything that exists can be traced back to it. *Atman*, on the other hand, means the part of an individual that is equally eternal and immortal. Brahman and Atman are thought to be similar in nature, allowing the individual to partake in absolute reality. It's assumed that something immortal resides in each person, a sort of eternal soul connected with the whole, with Brahman.

The Hindu teaching of reincarnation rests on this premise: each individual will be reborn because they have an Atman. However, the caste system remains untouched because the circle of rebirth plays out within the caste order and never transgresses the limits of it. In Hinduism, because religion is closely linked with the social order, it's virtually impossible for individuals to escape from the system—there's no way out of the closed chain of death and rebirth. This means that moral behavior doesn't have much impact on individual outcomes.

The Buddha disputed the existence of Brahman and Atman and rejected the caste system. His attitude toward the doctrine of reincarnation remained ambivalent, however—he didn't totally rule it out, although he did show people a way to free themselves from it entirely. His famous answer to it was nirvana, which means "extinguishment." Whether we manage to free ourselves or not depends entirely on our own behavior, he taught. This places the individual and their conduct at the center of religious life.

Karma comes from action, and it's important because it entails consequences: it connects the individual with the world and it can be ethically evaluated. This was a stark change and represented something new at that time, because rejecting Brahman and Atman meant that nothing was unchangeable and eternal. The Buddha thus negated the concept of the immortal soul and the existence of a self. According to him, language often implies the existence of an ego even though it cannot intrinsically exist. This view would later become central to Seon Buddhism; it led to the famous doctrines of emptiness and the no-self.

In his dispute with Hinduism, the Buddha developed his own worldview and introduced one principle as its basis. The principle superseded Brahman and Atman and grounded the Buddha's thinking and conduct. With it, he explained the world in which we live, how it functions, and how we're intertwined with it.

In Korean, the Buddha's principle is called *yeongi*, which can be translated as "dependent or conditional origin." It's meant to explain the impermanence of the world in terms of its relativity. The Buddha saw that things and phenomena are constantly being created and ceasing to be—everything changes and nothing stays the same. The world is seen as a kind of universal net and everyone takes part in it. When one thing moves, it displaces everything else. The famous butterfly effect is based on this and symbolizes how the world forms a single unit.

Thus, the world as the Buddha thought of it is not something static: it is a relationship. Nothing exists in isolation. Everything is connected to everything else, and everything is woven together. Embracing this way of thinking means that nothing can be eternal, because an eternal thing would be inherently enduring and unattached. Relatedness means openness and change.

The central tenets of Buddhism are: "If this exists, that exists. If this did not exist, that also would not exist. If this is created, that is also created. If this ceases to exist, that also ceases to exist." This means that everything owes its existence to external factors and does *not* carry the basis for its own existence within itself. Even the self depends on conditions that exist outside of the self—rather than being an autonomous entity, the self is dependent.

Under the right conditions, something is created, disintegrates, and disappears. Humans, for example, need parents, air, water, nourishment, language, etc. The Buddha says that what exists has no substance due to its instability and dependence on everything else. All on its own (which it cannot be), it is therefore inherently empty.

Through this worldview, Buddhism poses a stark contrast to monotheism, which considers God to be eternal and unconditional. God creates the world out of nothing, a world that is then segmented and full of dualism. Because Christianity founded a different tradition of thought and produced a distinct interpretation of the world, the languages spoken by people where Christianity became dominant developed in ways that are quite distinct from the languages spoken by people where Buddhism emerged. Not surprisingly, it's very difficult to translate the content of Buddhist teachings into European languages, and that in turn makes it harder for Westerners to understand Buddhist thought.

THE TEACHINGS

The Buddha sought inner peace and happiness. He began his search with a question about suffering: why does suffering exist, and how can it be overcome? Those who suffer cannot flourish. Of course, some suffering is inevitable—because we are physical beings, we are subject to illness, age, and death. However, violence, hate, greed, jealousy, and envy also make life difficult. The Buddha was sensitive to suffering and keenly felt people's unhappiness, and he wanted to reduce that unhappiness. In this respect, his quest followed the founders of other religions—we want religion to explain

Buddhism in Korea — 351

why our suffering continues and how we can free ourselves from it.

Christianity tries to explain how suffering came into the world with the construct of original sin. It's ultimately our hubris that condemns us to damnation, Christianity says. Jesus exemplifies suffering and how it can be overcome. Only faith in God makes salvation possible because God is the all-powerful creator of the world. Salvation is an act of divine grace, and people only experience salvation in the afterlife.

The Buddha's preoccupation with suffering, on the other hand, is entirely pragmatic. He focuses on life, not death. In Buddhism, the answer is not related to external salvation—the answer originates within the self. The Buddhist path is entirely concerned with individual behavior because we have the power to create suffering or happiness through our conduct. For example, eating the wrong food leads to illness, envy stokes conflict, and violence results in corporeal suffering. The Buddha's realization that everyone can alter their behavior for the better at any time is a core facet of Buddhism.

According to the Buddha, through our thoughts and actions, each of us shapes our lives and thus our environment and thus ultimately the world. This essential tenet makes Buddhism a radical and unique religion. The environment is another thing that we've shaped through our thoughts and actions. In everything we do, karma (or action) determines our fate, because for better or for worse, karma brings about consequences for ourselves and others, and these consequences branch out into other consequences. An abused child will often abuse their own child later on, for example, thereby bringing fresh unhappiness to the whole environment.

According to the Buddha, action incites a desire that we carry within ourselves, a desire that's difficult to subdue. It can take the form of hunger, thirst, or sexuality; it can be directed at material things like possessions or riches; it can center on immaterial goods like recognition, power, fame, and love. The latter might seem odd—after all, we think of love as a positive thing. But it also creates a lot of suffering. Losing love hurts! If love is disappointed or rebuffed, it can turn into aggression and hate and can manifest itself with great destructive power.

Desire is a powerful force within us. It can become obsessive and dominate our lives because it demands satisfaction. Desire is dangerous because it has no limit—it never stops needing. It leads us to constantly compare ourselves with others, but because what satisfies us can only come from the outside, desire makes us dependent—we can never really be free. Instead, we grow restless and unhappy and find that satisfaction and inner peace are difficult to achieve.

We must be aware of the nature of desire in order to be free of it. We must recognize that satisfying it grants only temporary happiness! We cultivate desire because we want to cling to the ego. But Buddha denies that there is an ego. And therefore the center is empty. This emptiness can never be filled with possessions, money, or fame. On the other hand, love, recognition, and friendship may appear without us seeking them if we love selflessly, achieve something, or remain sincere and trustworthy—that's when satisfaction, peace, and happiness will simply emerge.

Anyone who wants to be respected must start by respecting others. Anyone who seeks true peace must know that it consists of being aware of our desires and emotional shackles and not allowing ourselves to be ruled by them. We should pause and reflect before we act—what will the consequences of an act be for ourselves and for others? We can love, but we must love so selflessly that hate never grows from it.

The Buddha taught us to let go. That doesn't mean imposing a duty of renunciation and asceticism upon ourselves, though—the Buddha saw the difference between possessing things sheerly for the sake of possessing them and possessing them because we actually need them. Things can stifle and overwhelm us if we have too many of them, because when that happens, we forget to appreciate them. In a similar vein, there's also a difference between doing something for the simple joy of doing it and doing it for recognition. If we act without calculation, we're free, we enjoy more, and we have inner peace. We look at the world differently: without bias and with greater attention and serenity.

The Buddha was aware that letting go of desire is difficult. Practicing renunciation is stressful and requires a lot more strength than indulging in desire and demand. This dichotomy is especially apparent when we eat and drink! Likewise, it's also easier to hate than it is to meditate on our hate, to contemplate its source, and to let it go. But letting go instead of clinging brings freedom and means that we're not imposing our hate on others—instead, we're letting them be.

It's clear that today's world doesn't differ significantly from the time of the Buddha—if it were easier to let go, the world would be more peaceful! This is why the Buddha urged us to stay on the path and not stray from it. We also must remember that the Buddhist path is an individual one that depends entirely on the follower's own discretion. The Buddha showed us the way by sharing his own experiences and establishing concrete rules that we can follow.

THE PATH

The Buddha specifically describes what to do in order to follow him. This prescription is generally known as the Eightfold Path.

First, we need to acquire the right perspective on the world and on life. The Buddha believed that we must understand the principle of yeongi in order to grasp his teachings. Yeongi allows us to comprehend the connection between the world and the no-self.

Second, we must learn how to think correctly and wisely. Study was important to the Buddha because without knowledge, we cannot think correctly or act properly. The connection between thought and action is crucial: good thoughts lead to good actions, but reprehensible thoughts harm us and others because action begins with thought. Reflecting on our own thoughts is important! We must try to be aware of our negative thoughts and nip them in the bud. If we're full of hate inside, then we're imprisoned by it, we act according to it, and we cannot find any inner peace. Our perspective becomes consumed by hate and we cannot see the goodness and tenderness in the world.

The third aspect of the Eightfold Path to consider is right speaking. How we think determines how we speak, and how we speak betrays how we think. How we speak can either bring comfort to others or injure them and cause them pain—after all, speech is often used to express the deepest contempt. In contrast, speaking politely not only expresses respect to the other person, it also demonstrates self-respect and calms the speaker. Right speaking can have a positive impact on our own thinking as well as on the environment.

The fourth aspect is right action. Action always occurs within a greater context, thereby creating connections. We must always be aware of the consequences of our own behavior for ourselves and others; we must not harm others; we must not cause suffering. We should do the right thing even when no one is looking, and we should help others but say nothing about it. If we encounter suffering, we should try to reduce it, and we should show empathy and solidarity whenever possible.

Fifth, we should practice what we've realized and learned as right in our everyday lives. For the Buddha, it was important that people actually lived out what they understood to be right—abstract, theoretical knowledge isn't enough. What is understood is only truly understood when it is integrated into action. The Buddha was well aware of the great chasm between abstract knowledge and practice, between knowing that it's good to help others and *actually* helping them.

Sixth, we must stay on the path. The Buddha knew how strenuous it would be to follow his path and to align our own lives with it. Still, we must strive relentlessly and spend our lives working on ourselves despite being constantly tempted by desire and its comforts.

The seventh aspect of the Eightfold Path is that everything we do must be done with purpose—we must visualize our own actions.

Finally, the eighth aspect is that we must concentrate fully on everything we do or think and give it our full attention. We must meditate, because meditation enables us to look inside ourselves so that we can separate the unimportant from the important and free ourselves from distractions.

When we gain an understanding of the Buddha's Four Noble Truths and proceed along the Eightfold Path, we become companions of the Buddha.

SEON BUDDHISM

Seon Buddhism is a school of thought within Mahayana Buddhism that arose in sixth-century China and spread outward into Korea and Japan. In each of those countries, a unique traditional lineage developed that still exists today.

What's called *Seon* in Korea is named *Chan* in China and *Zen* in Japan. Seon Buddhism represents an East Asian variety of Buddhism; with its emphasis on meditation and the simplicity of its teachings, Seon Buddhism is considered to be a revival of the original Buddhism. Over time, the theoretical structure of Buddhism had grown more and more complicated and incomprehensible, which gave rise to calls for reform and a return to tradition. People said that the Buddha had spoken simply to people. His teachings should be free from restrictive baggage, they said.

Thus, the path to enlightenment was redefined rather than coming from the accumulation of knowledge, it's an intuitive experience that entails becoming aware of what's already inside of us. Meditation became the central focus; a refined meditation practice developed and was integrated into the everyday life of the temple inhabitants. This meditation is meant to enable true insight into oneself, mindful action, and inner equilibrium. (This is one of the reasons why most Seon Buddhist temples in East Asia are located deep in the mountains.) The study of the sutras became less significant, while experience, intuition, and practice became more important for living in the present. This formed the foundation of Seon Buddhism's particular affinity for art, because creativity thrives when the practice of living in the now is cultivated. Many Seon Buddhist masters were and are themselves poets and painters.

Seon Buddhism rapidly became mainstream. Bodhidharma, the Indian monk who came to China, is considered to be founder of Seon Buddhism even though there's little evidence of his historical works. There are many legends about him, however, likely because we don't know much about him as a person. In terms of the cultural history of Seon Buddhism, Taoist philosophy also played an important role in its formation. Taoist vocabulary was frequently used to translate the sutras from Sanskrit into Chinese, indicating a similarity of thought, and Seon Buddhism emerged in southern China, the home of Taoism. There, Buddhist teachings were transformed, and their content was adapted to local customs. Seon Buddhism thus arose from a convergence of linguistics and philosophy. That's also the case for the Taoist version of Buddhism.

Taoist philosophy is an interesting intellectual tradition that has significantly characterized East Asian thinking. It forms a kind of alternative model to Western thought and demonstrates that East Asian people have a fundamentally different view of the world. It's no coincidence that Tao is the central concept of East Asian thought and is also significant within the vocabulary of Seon Buddhism! In Europe, starting with the Greeks and later reinforced by Christianity, the entire focus is on the permanent and eternal. People were and are constantly searching for it. Ideas are eternal, God is eternal, truth is eternal, and so are being and substance. What's eternal is static and averse to change. In Europe, people sought an unmovable mover. Dualism is an inevitable result of these thought traditions: body and soul, substance and accident, being and manifestation. Substance is thought of as ever-enduring and impervious to change. In this intellectual tradition, changes can only affect the surface and not the core since substance must remain untouched by change.

In East Asia, however, the focus is always on change and transition. Nature is not a creation of God, but rather something that exists on its own. People ask with fascination: how is transformation possible? How do transitions come about? Transformation means those processes that are inherent to the world and simply continue without the help of humans, like growth, maturation, age, decay, life, the seasons, weather, digestion, etc. Transformation represents a continual metamorphosis of reality.

The Taoists saw the world from this perspective of innate, intrinsic transformation. From this point of view, there's no room for God, being, or substance because everything is in flux: the world is one big process of transition with its own rhythm. In the eyes of Taoism, acting against transition is not only laborious but also foolish. Pursuing transition, on the other hand, makes everything easier and better. Pursuing transformation means following *tao*, or "the path."

Laozi, the founder of Taoism, said that the mystical natural foundation that eternally brings about this transition is "mysterious." He also said that Tao is just a word, a simple name for this universal process. The process is larger than what language can capture—words cannot comprehend the entirety of it. Laozi used conceptual pairs like *yin* and *yang* or "emptiness" and "fullness" to describe how this universal process of transition functions.

It's fascinating that Laozi viewed emptiness as being significant for understanding dynamics and relationships. Only emptiness enables transformation and movement and ensures the function of things, Laozi said. This concept is expressed through the famous question: what is a tea cup? Is it the porcelain, or is it the emptiness in the middle? The porcelain surrounds the emptiness—without that emptiness, the cup is not a cup. In the same way, a house is not a house without the emptiness of its rooms.

The tradition of brush painting in East Asia is an especially prominent display of this dynamic of emptiness and fullness. Making the transition between the two visible—and thus making the transformation visible—subtly forms the foundational aesthetic of East Asian landscape painting. The Taoists' great love of nature is well known—they loved spiritual freedom and surrendered themselves to their own intuition and spontaneous impulses. In ancient China, Taoism was known as "the art of being in the world."

Within this spiritual environment, Seon Buddhism developed. Mahayana Buddhism's idea that each person carries the nature of the Buddha within themself and is capable of enlightenment forms the very foundation of Seon Buddhism. This is why equality between everyone was emphasized and quickly found widespread acceptance. The Buddha himself recognized the equality of all people, but during his lifetime, the dominant Indian caste system made that recognition of equality difficult to implement. However, the cultural diversity and material wealth that prevailed during the Tang Dynasty facilitated the development of the everyone-is-equal concept. Individualism grew more intense, and so did the search for happiness. The goal lies in the self, Seon Buddhism taught.

From that basis, a distinct Seon Buddhist meditation practice established itself. Indian-style meditation couldn't become part of the local way of life due to climatic and cultural differences, and Seon Buddhism resonated widely with people because it filled the gap. Life was celebrated and cultivated. Tea culture arrived and experienced its first great explosion. Tea—which is a spiritual drink—and meditation go together to this day.

The question of the true nature of enlightenment was again on people's lips. The teaching of *gong*, or emptiness, that's connected with the general Buddhist principle of yeongi remains central here: this thing exists because that thing exists and vice versa. Everything that exists is interdependent, and because of that inherent interdependence, anything considered in strict isolation is empty—on its own, it contains nothing. And nothing is eternal because everything changes with time.

These insights enabled a change in perspective that could be compared with the Copernican Revolution. The world remained as it always had been, but people's perspective of it changed. The famous heart sutra, a central text in Seon Buddhism, teaches about gong, emptiness, and *mu-ah*, the "no-self." If meditation leads to this realization, we can free ourselves from egoistic motivations, emotional shackles, and desires. We can succeed in letting go and staying in the present. We can relate to the external world differently, with greater serenity, openness, and freedom. All of this happens because we're no longer clinging to the self, we're less centered on ourselves, and we don't oppress others. More spontaneous actions become possible. Inner peace can develop because we face others with empathy. We don't find happiness because we know a lot about it or because want to find it—it's simply there when we choose the right action.

The great Seon Buddhist masters knew how difficult the Buddhist path would be—after all, the knowledge you gain through long meditation is not easy to pass on. Thus, silence is an important meditative practice, because words obscure much and conceal reality. Silence helps strengthen concentration and reveals the limits of what can be expressed in words.

The emergence of short tenets called *hwadu* (*koans* in Japanese), meaning "words at the borders of language," is related to this limitation. Although the hwadus came expressly from the Seon Buddhist masters, at first, they seem nonsensical and even contradictory. That's because they represent a kind of linguistic pitfall to show that one is searching in the wrong place and a radical change of perspective is needed. Hwadus expose the superficiality of supposed knowledge. Seon Buddhism teaches that enlightenment is not something that someone can directly will to happen—instead, enlightenment comes completely on its own when someone has the right understanding, restrains themselves, and acts with empathy.

Another characteristic that distinguishes Seon Buddhism is how very important work is for the members of the order. Alongside study and meditation, work is an important part of temple life. Every action we undertake with our full attention is considered to be a meditative activity, life itself becomes meditation. Work teaches modesty, humility, gratitude, and solidarity.

Although the Buddha and his disciples had lived off the donations of the people to whom they offered spiritual guidance, for members of the Seon Buddhist order, even though donations were accepted with gratitude, it was important to integrate work into temple life and to be self-sufficient as a community. The members farmed, grew tea, and gathered fruits, wild vegetables, and roots. This is the origin of the temple food tradition that Jeongkwan Snim carries on

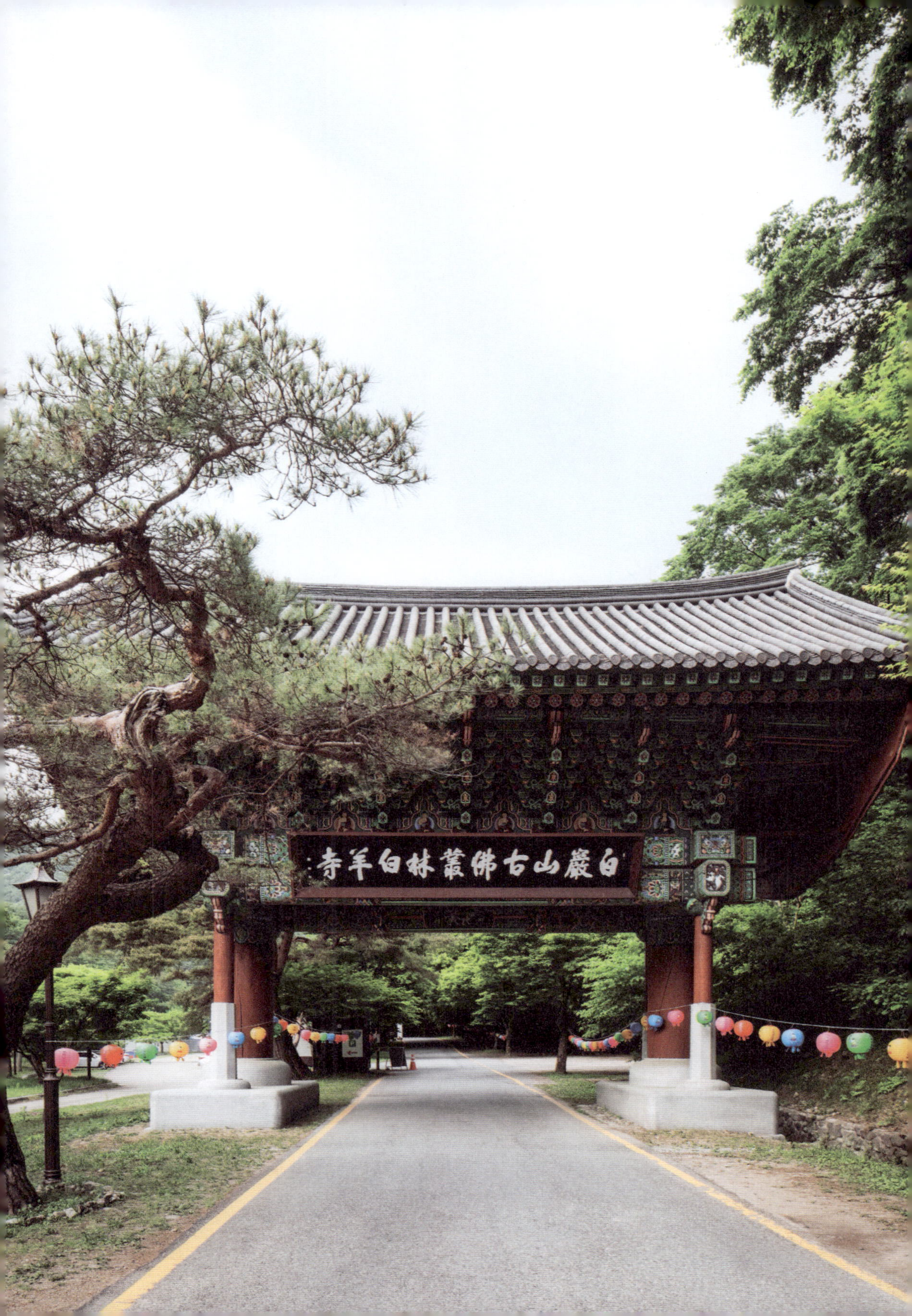
白巖山古佛叢林白羊寺

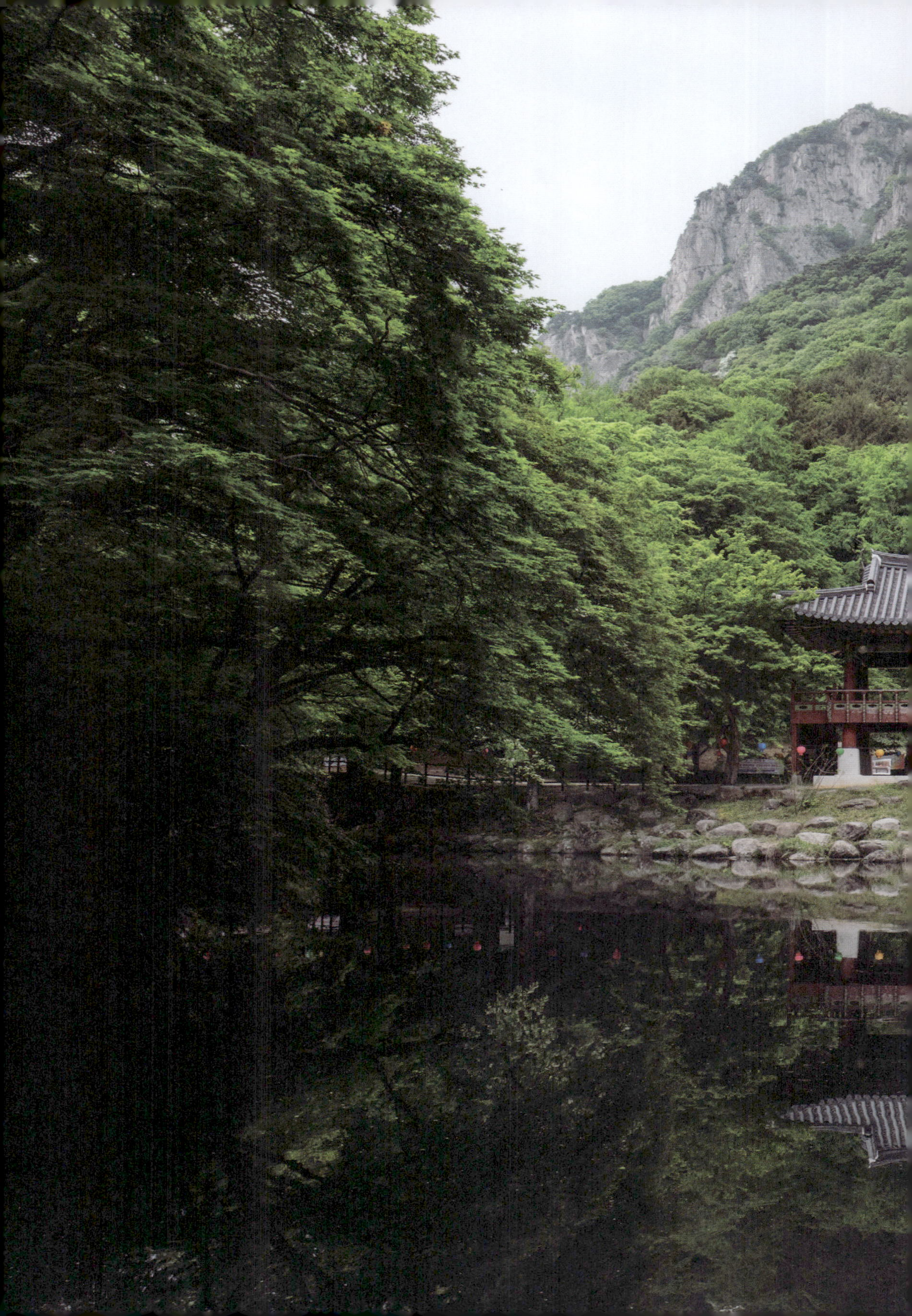

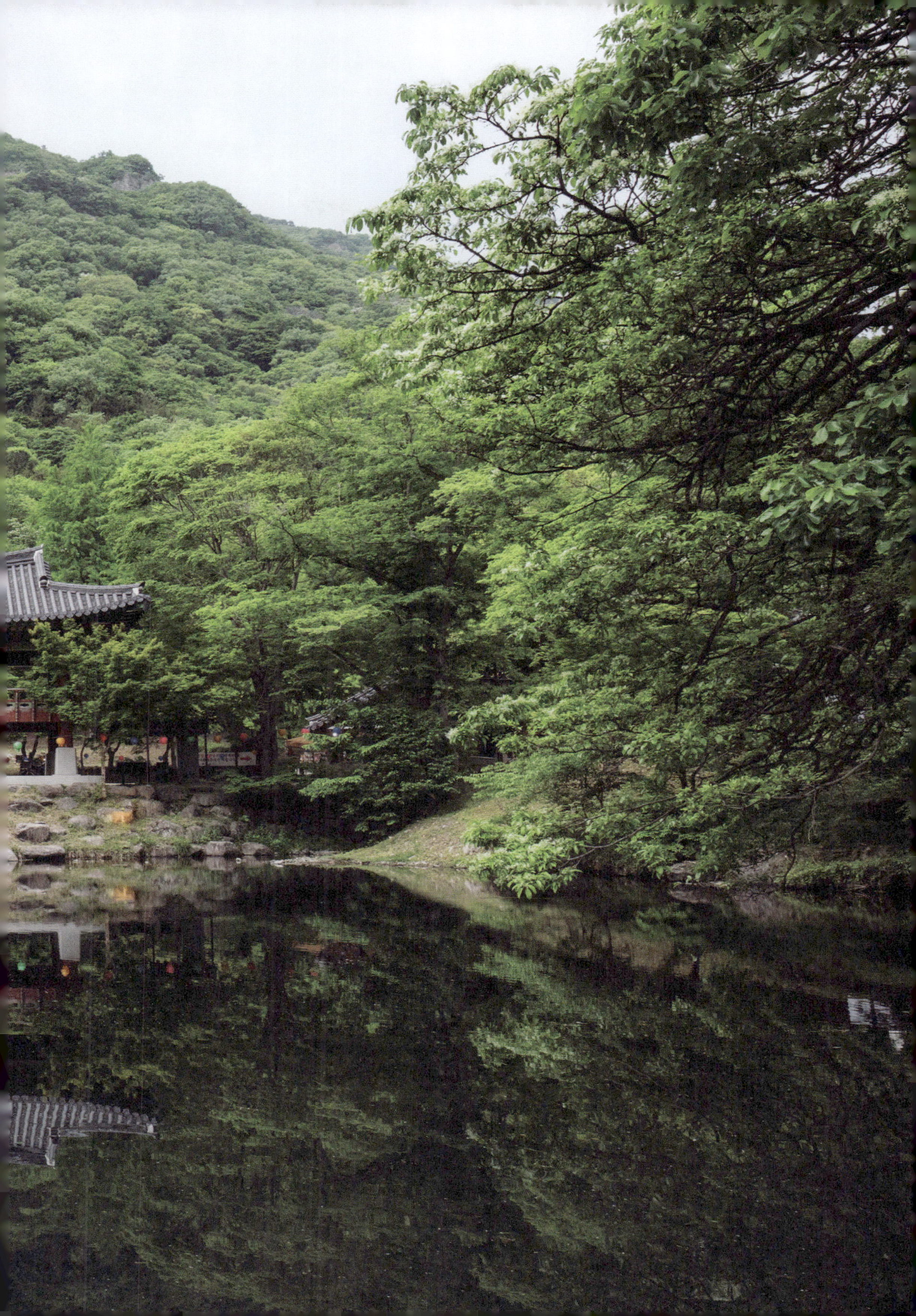

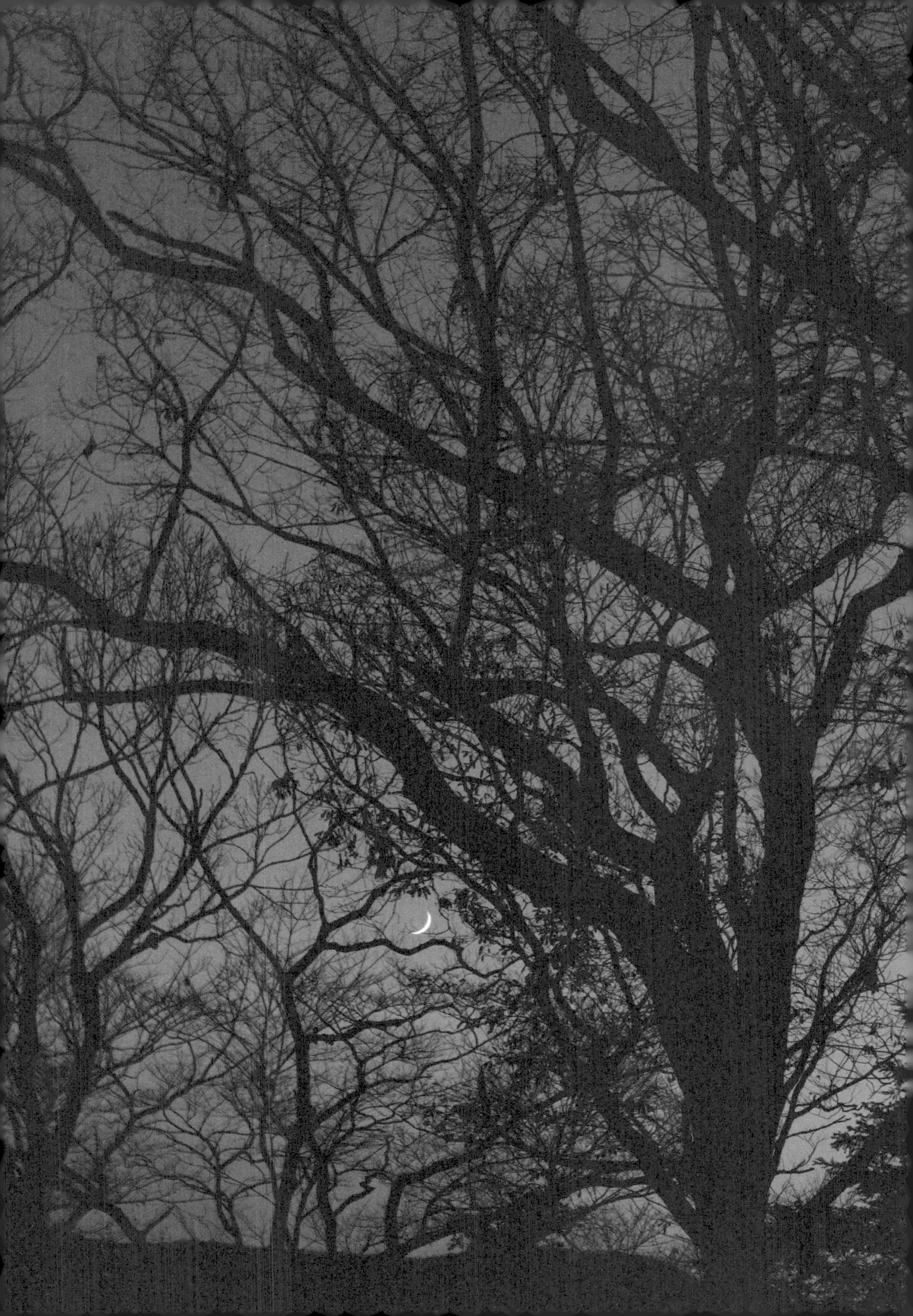

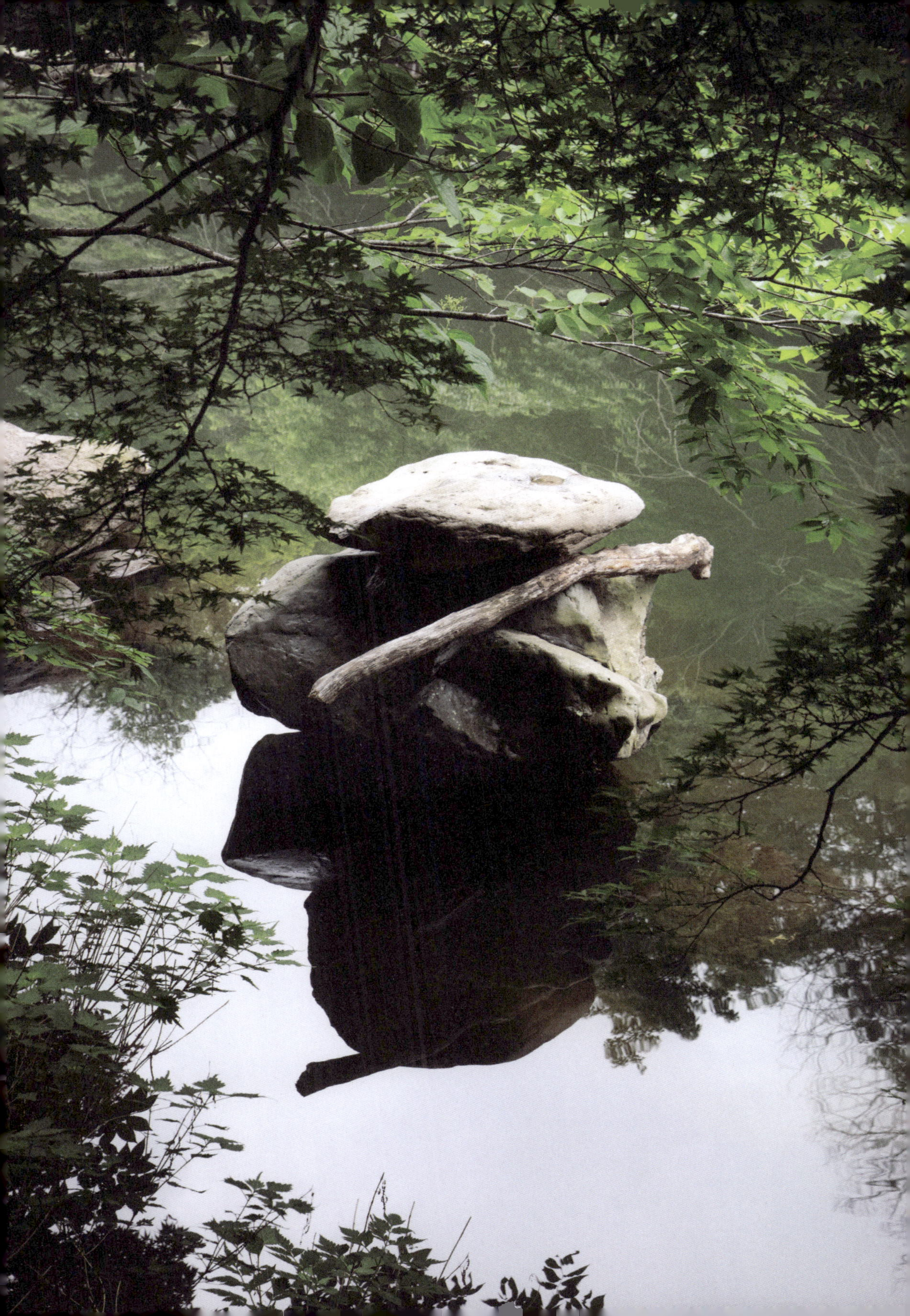

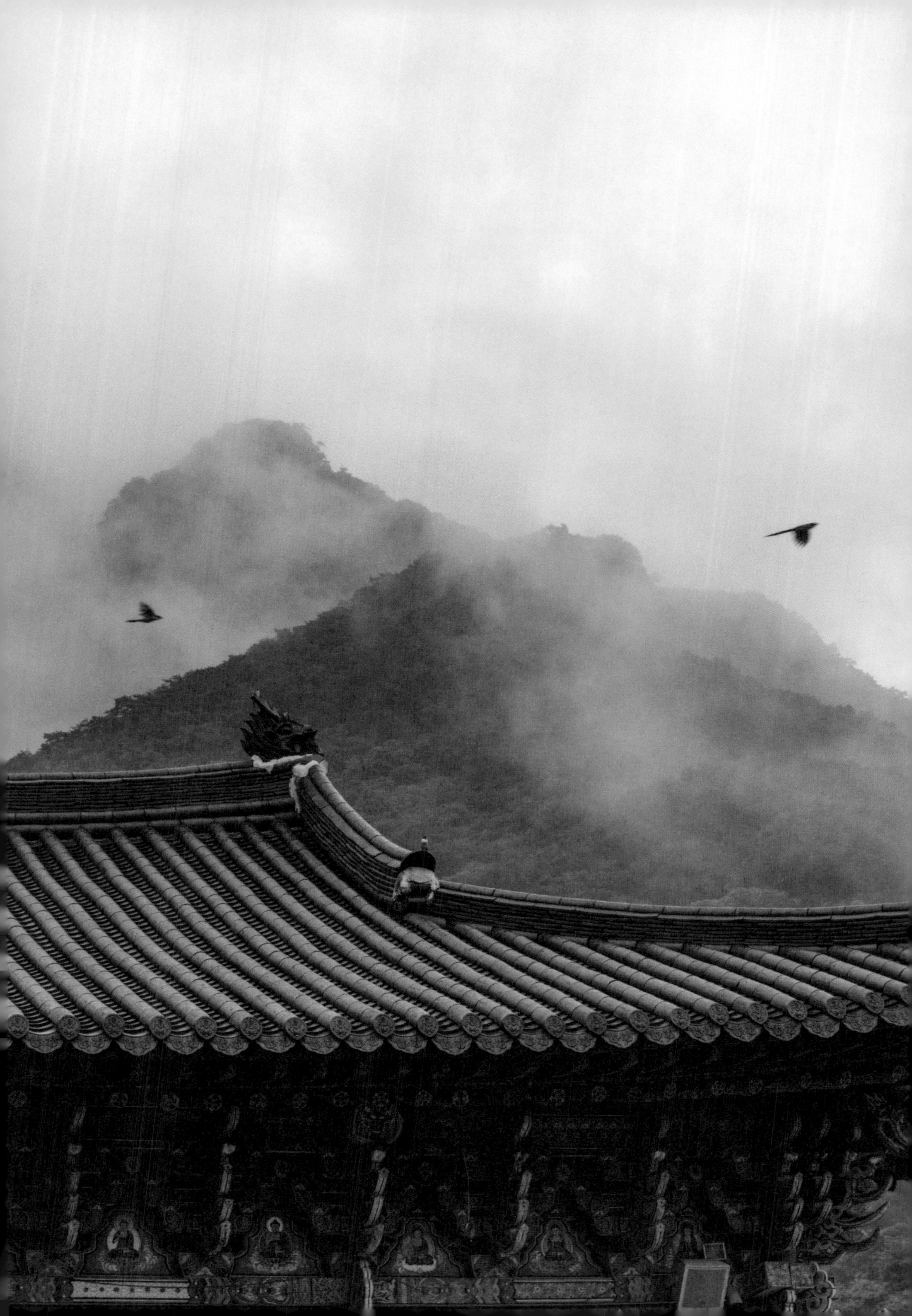

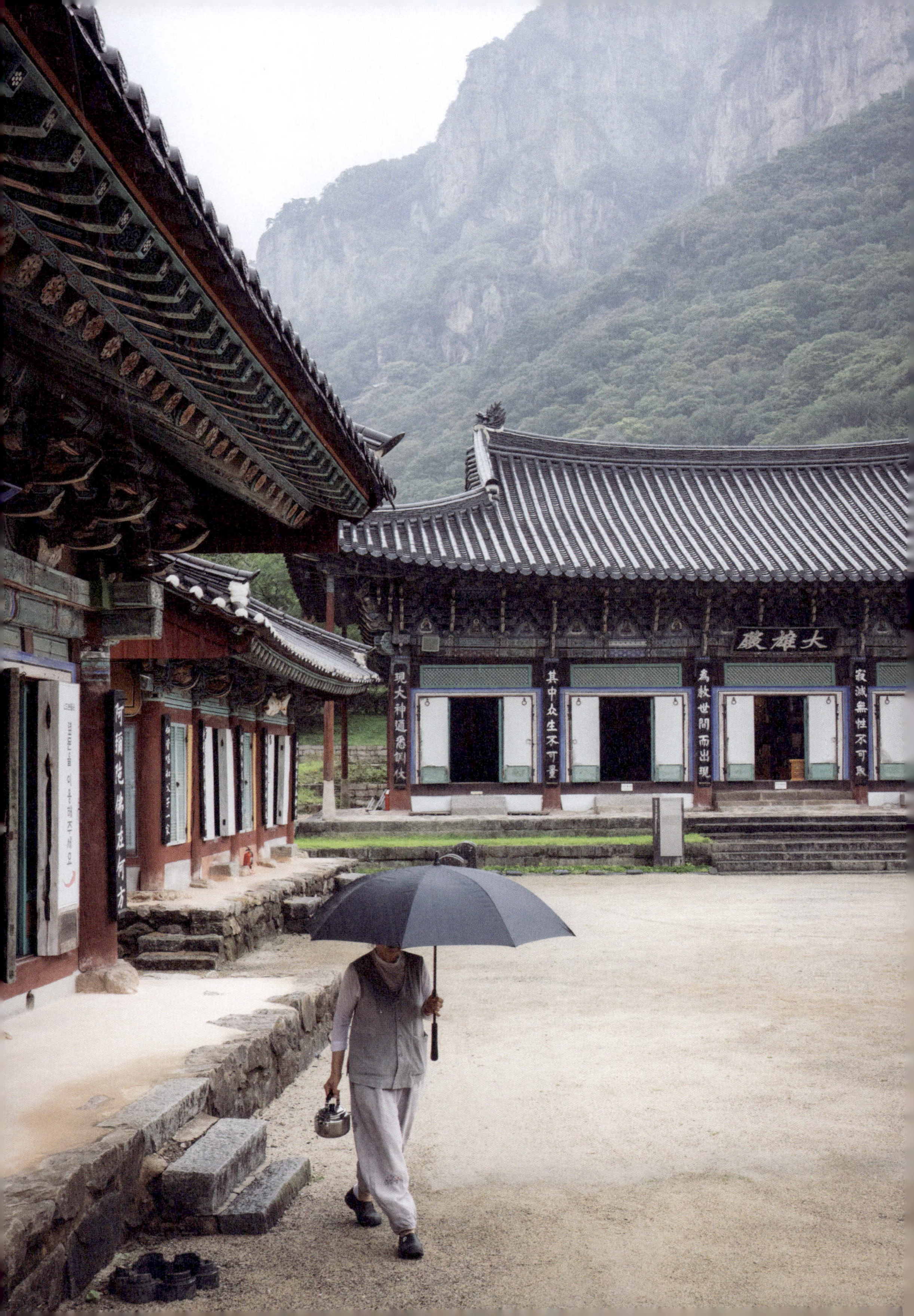
大雄殿
其中衆生不可量
爲救世間而出現
寂滅無性不可取

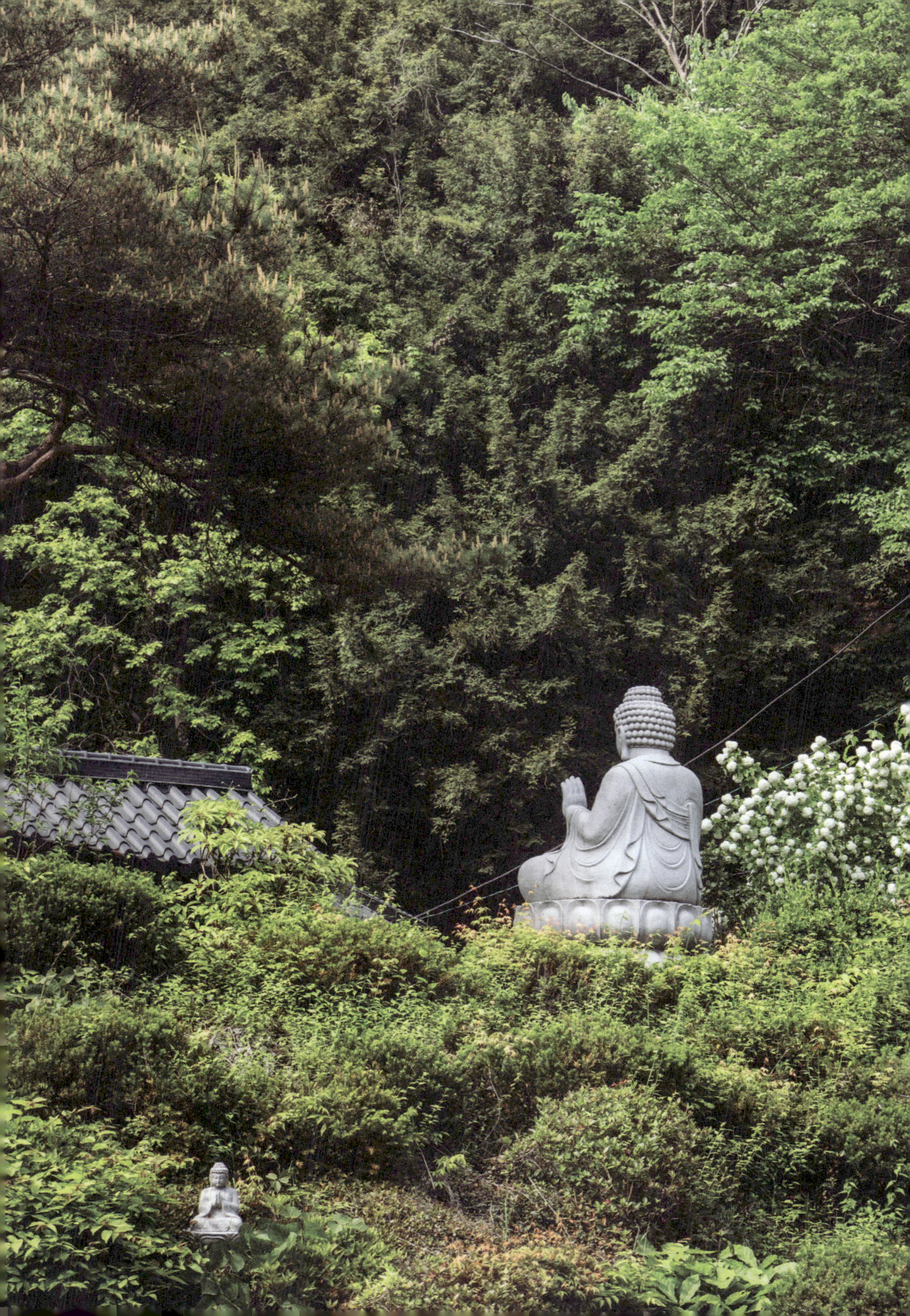

ARCHITECTURE OF THE TEMPLE COMPLEX

Korean Buddhist architecture demonstrates that it's a religion of paths. The search for understanding and right living is a journey that initially takes us inside ourselves, but it's also a journey through time and life. We are on our way to becoming a Buddhist when we want to follow the Buddha's teachings.

Korean temple architecture attempts to depict these ideas of paths and inner transformation through its buildings. A "temple" in Korea does not denote just one building—a temple is usually a spacious complex that includes various halls, pavilions, residential wings, pagodas, courtyards, gardens, ponds, streams, and forests. Temples can vary greatly in size; a large temple complex can include more than 60 different individual buildings. Most temples are in the mountains, but some of them are located on rugged coasts by the sea. The paths that wind through the complexes open up to spectacular views of the sea or into wide valleys and mountains. Nature's beauty is amplified by pavilions and temples that create space for spirituality. Fittingly, walking through landscapes has always had a special meaning in Buddhism—some rituals consist of circling around a pagoda or walking together from one temple to another.

A temple district in Korea is called "sachal" or "jeol." Due to the traditional style of building, each district has a unique atmosphere. The sachal is an unusual space: it's open, yet it's structured according to a particular pattern; it's harmoniously nestled into the surrounding natural landscape; and it possesses its own inimitable aesthetic.

Getting to a temple has always required traveling a certain stretch of road, and it still does today. Searching, lingering, being, and arriving are significant elements of Buddhism both in theory and in practice. If you're attentive as you walk the path, you'll notice that these elements manifest themselves in the architecture and configuration of the temple grounds—since each location has its own characteristics, each path that leads to a temple has a unique character that reveals a different face depending on the season. But although each temple has its own design, the basic ideas of Buddhism are visible at all temples. When you walk through the landscape, you can sense your own body; it can also become a spiritual experience if you properly compose yourself.

Visiting the temple begins before the visitor is even aware of it. If you come from the city, at first, you'll marvel at the natural landscape around you. The path will meander along a stream, heading deeper into the mountains; old trees will line the path. Your expectations will be ever-present, and you'll hope that at the end, you'll find something that brings calm or joy. You'll be searching for it at every turn.

Suddenly, as if from nowhere, a simple gate will appear, standing isolated in the landscape. The four wooden columns will be red, and the tile-clad roof will have load-bearing beams painted with patterns in five different colors. Gates organize spaces and signify transition; in Buddhism, spatial transitions should also be spiritual and internal. Another sphere is about to be entered. Buddhist architecture uses a lot of gates precisely because gates symbolize paths and transitions—they allow inner transformation and maturity in the spiritual realm to be felt in the physical world.

The gate indicates that the goal isn't far off. It's called an *iljumun*, and it marks the outer border of the temple area. Other gates will follow, until you reach the inner area of the temple complex. The distances between gates vary. The name of the gate comes from its form: it has two columns in a row, one after the other. Every kind of architecture emanates a particular atmosphere and is built in accordance with that spirit.

At the very first isolated gate, you can already sense the spirit of Buddhism. The gate has two features: it does not have any doors that can be closed, meaning it's always open, and it isn't enclosed by a wall or surrounded by a fence, meaning that anyone can walk through the gate or around it. Many will pass by the gate without a thought, simply marveling at its beauty. Few consider that a gate calls awareness to the existence of a path and to the importance of making individual choices in life.

On one hand, the iljumun represents the freedom to choose our own life path; on the other, it marks a transition into another space. In Buddhism, everything rests on the decision of the individual and their inner attitude, because seeing as there is no savior in Buddhism as there is in Christianity, everyone must find their own happiness. Therefore, the iljumun has a special meaning for those who pass through it mindfully.

Other gates will follow, and the more of them you pass, the closer you are to the inner temple area. The number of gates varies depending on the size of the temple. But even after you pass through the first iljumun, there's usually still a long stretch to travel before you'll see the next gate. A cultivated landscape will spread out before the visitor, making it obvious that humans and nature have worked together to create a unique cultural landscape.

The next gate looks like a small building; visitors pass through its center. It houses two figures on the left and two on the right, each standing watch and facing their own cardinal direction: the guardians of the east and the south stand to the left, and the guardians of the west and the north to the right. They gaze into their respective directions and are meant to ward off evil spirits. They also look upon the people who pass through the gate to ensure that the visitors observe the Buddha's teachings. These guardian kings originate from Hinduism, but they have since mingled with old Korean folk beliefs.

The third and last gate is called *bulimun*, "gate of non-duality," or *haetalmun*, "gate of enlightenment." Passing through it is meant to bring the awareness that everything is one and that separation contradicts nature. Buddhism has a unified worldview—it teaches that everything in existence forms a oneness. Nothing is created or exists alone; everything is interconnected and part of a complex network of relationships. This idea is one of the basic pillars of Buddhist thought. Once we realize this, we have arrived at the destination.

The third gate leads to the central square, and at the upper end of the square stands the Great Hall. Temple grounds are usually slightly hilly, making the path rise. Mountains in Korea can sometimes be quite rugged and steep, and visitors occasionally have to climb many steps to reach the central square. As they do so, visitors sense their body, their breath, and the strain of climbing—the entirety of the experience. The gradual ascent also carries the symbolic meaning of climbing into the Buddha's world and drawing closer to purification.

As the visitor slowly climbs the steps, the pagoda and the large square gradually come into view. Moment by moment, the view expands, just as the understanding and the insights gleaned by the visitors expand. This marks their arrival in the central square of the temple complex. It's the largest and most important part of the entire complex; several buildings stand there. To the left is the small pavilion that houses four instruments. Directly across the way at the other end is the elevated Great Hall. Before it are pagodas, which form an important part of the temple architecture and are ritually significant. A single pagoda can stand in the

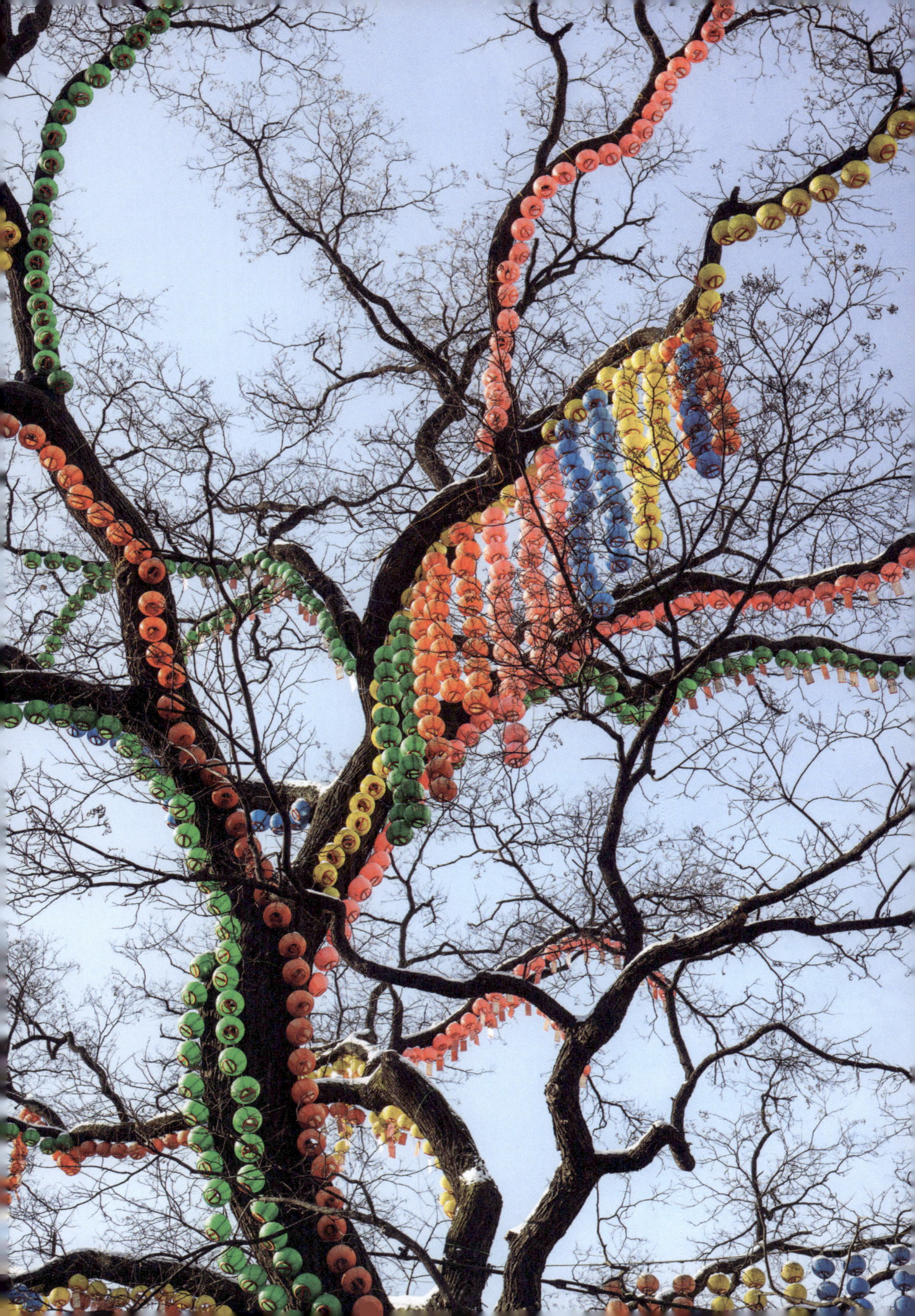

大雄殿

center of the square, or two pagodas may be positioned symmetrically. The sizes and structures of the pagodas vary greatly, although pagodas are mostly multiple stories and are made of stone.

Historically, pagodas are among the oldest elements of Buddhist temple architecture—their origin goes back to the Buddha's tomb. After the Buddha's death, his ashes were said to have been divided up and buried at various sites, and tombs were erected over each site in his memory. In India, these were called stupas; they later gave rise to pagodas. Stupas long served as the only physical symbol of the Buddha and the only pilgrimage destinations for his disciples. As the number of disciples grew and the rituals carried out in the Buddha's honor became more sophisticated and important, the need to have other physical signs to symbolize the presence of the Buddha also grew. An empty throne, footprints, a wheel chiseled in stone, and a lotus initially served this purpose.

Meanwhile, Buddhism was gradually spreading to all of Asia and the importance of ritual worship was increasing. Buddhist sculpture emerged in the first century CE, gained increasing acceptance, achieved a position of importance, and ultimately outshone the other symbols of Buddhism. As it spread to East Asia, the form of Buddhism changed, too. The construction of temples was adapted to local building customs, leading pagodas to develop a specific shape in Korea, and sculptural art also changed, with typical Korean Buddha statues emerging that expressed particular ideals of beauty. The greatest challenge for the artists was creating a specific smile on the Buddha's face, because their task was nothing less than to depict a visibly enlightened person. As the Buddha is free from suffering, his smile is meant to express cheeriness and meditative serenity but also a warm empathy toward all living things. Some statues of the Buddha are famous solely for the hint of an otherworldly smile on his lips.

As the oldest element of the temple architecture, pagodas had a special meaning. Various items of great historical value were contained within their foundations: saris in gold cases (glass spheres containing the ashes of famous snims), paper scrolls inscribed with the sutras, or documents concerning the building of the temple. But even though they contained such significant items, the importance of the pagodas began to decrease and continues to decrease. While pagodas towered over the entire complex of early temples and were the center of rituals because they symbolized the presence of the Buddha and his teachings, over time, the pagodas got smaller while the halls got bigger, more magnificent, and more important. This happened because performing complex rituals, practicing meditation, and carrying out temple life made the construction of new spaces necessary, necessitating different temple complexes with different proportions. Despite this, in modern-day Korea, many very old pagodas still stand and still form an essential component of temple architecture. During some rituals, participants circumvent the pagodas a specific number of times.

Directly behind the pagodas, the Great Hall—the largest building in the entire complex—rises up on elevated ground. This hall occupies a central position in the life of the temple: this is where the main ritual, the yebul, takes place, and where hundreds of snims regularly gather to study together and meditate. The Great Hall also houses statues of the Buddha and images that are important to the yebul. In all temples, this hall is constructed with the greatest care to make it the most beautiful and ornate building in the entire complex. The way the roof is constructed and adorned with ornamentation showcases the skill of Korean master builders and inspires great wonder in all who admire it.

Temple complexes also have numerous other learning and meditation halls of varying sizes, and there are hermitages where snims can retreat in solitude. Various courtyards, ponds, and small lakes weave themselves between individual buildings. Some temples are quite small, though, with only a few buildings.

In the lower section of the complex, the snims' residences are relegated to the side and are comprised of small, separate cells or rooms. In Korea, every temple is also a cloister, so it's always occupied by multiple snims. The rooms are compact and simple because snims don't have many personal possessions. A kitchen and a dining area are nearby, but they're in a separate building. There, three meals are taken at certain set times. Visitors are permitted to join the meal at no charge, although many give the temple a voluntary donation in return.

Every temple complex has a dual function: on the one hand, it has a religious side (expressed through symbolism and aesthetics), and on the other hand, it has a pragmatic side. That's because the temple must take the needs of the people who live there into account. Physical well-being must be well tended to, yes, but a temple must also be a place of study and meditation.

For a long time, it wasn't possible for visitors to spend the night at a temple, but today most temples offer a so-called Temple Stay program: visitors can stay overnight, participate in the yebul, meditate, and talk with the snims over tea.

Korean Buddhist architecture has several typical characteristics. One is the unique location: most temple complexes are situated deep in the mountains, where there's plenty of peace and quiet. This makes them appropriate for withdrawal and meditation. Openness is also important: the temple landscape isn't shut away behind walls or fences, and people are free to come and go as they please. If someone wants to stay, as long as they observe the rules, they are free to make that decision and determine that they're ready to stay; they cannot be forced to stay or leave. Although the Buddhist path is an individual one, the temple community is happy to help anyone find and walk it. The architecture reflects this spirit of openness.

The temple is traditionally made of wood; the roofs are curved and covered with tiles. The buildings are always modest, one-story structures. Over time, Korean temple architecture has adapted to climatic conditions and how the snims live. Traditionally, Korean buildings had no windows—instead, they had perforated wooden doors that were adorned with lovely carved designs and covered with traditional paper called *hanji*. Hanji is semi-transparent and lets the sunlight in while simultaneously dimming its brightness.

The front of the hall is usually comprised mostly of tall doors. In summer, they're all opened, removing the barrier between inside and outside. This displacement of borders is an interesting characteristic of traditional Korean architecture and can be found in other temple buildings as well. With these doors open, the view of the outside and of nature is unhindered. Only the back of the structure is securely walled in—that's where the statues of the Buddha stand on their pedestals.

Doors are on each of the two sides of the hall. Visitors are only permitted to use them when the snims are coming through the front doors. Before they enter, visitors must remove their shoes. They then sit on cushions on the wooden floor.

Historically, Korean culture has mostly not featured chairs—only a few public authorities possessed any. People always sat and slept on the floor, and tables for both eating and writing were small and low to the ground. This meant that rooms could be small because they served multiple purposes at the same time. Even though a lot has changed in modern Korea, the culture of sitting on the floor has remained in the temples (Although sitting cushions are needed for meditation.) In the past, not only did all of the snims sleep on the floor, so did all of the visitors.

More recently, tables and chairs have found their way into the dining facilities of temples. But the tradition of sitting on the floor is still observed when drinking tea—everyone sits around a snim at a low table. The traditional ways of tea are also still observed customs that are closely connected to meditation.

ROBES

Life as a snim starts with leaving the family and entering the temple with the intention of leading a new life focused on religion. This is how a person announces their wish to become a member of the order and of a new community—it signifies a break with their previous life, a caesura that creates the opportunity for a new one. The new beginning is made quite obvious: the aspiring snim's hair is shorn off, they discard their old name, they adopt a new daily routine, and they nourish and dress themselves differently.

These external changes are meant to be guided by internal changes. The latter begin to sink in deeply as they touch every aspect of the person's life: their way of speaking, walking, eating, sitting, thinking, and their conduct in general. The longer someone is in the

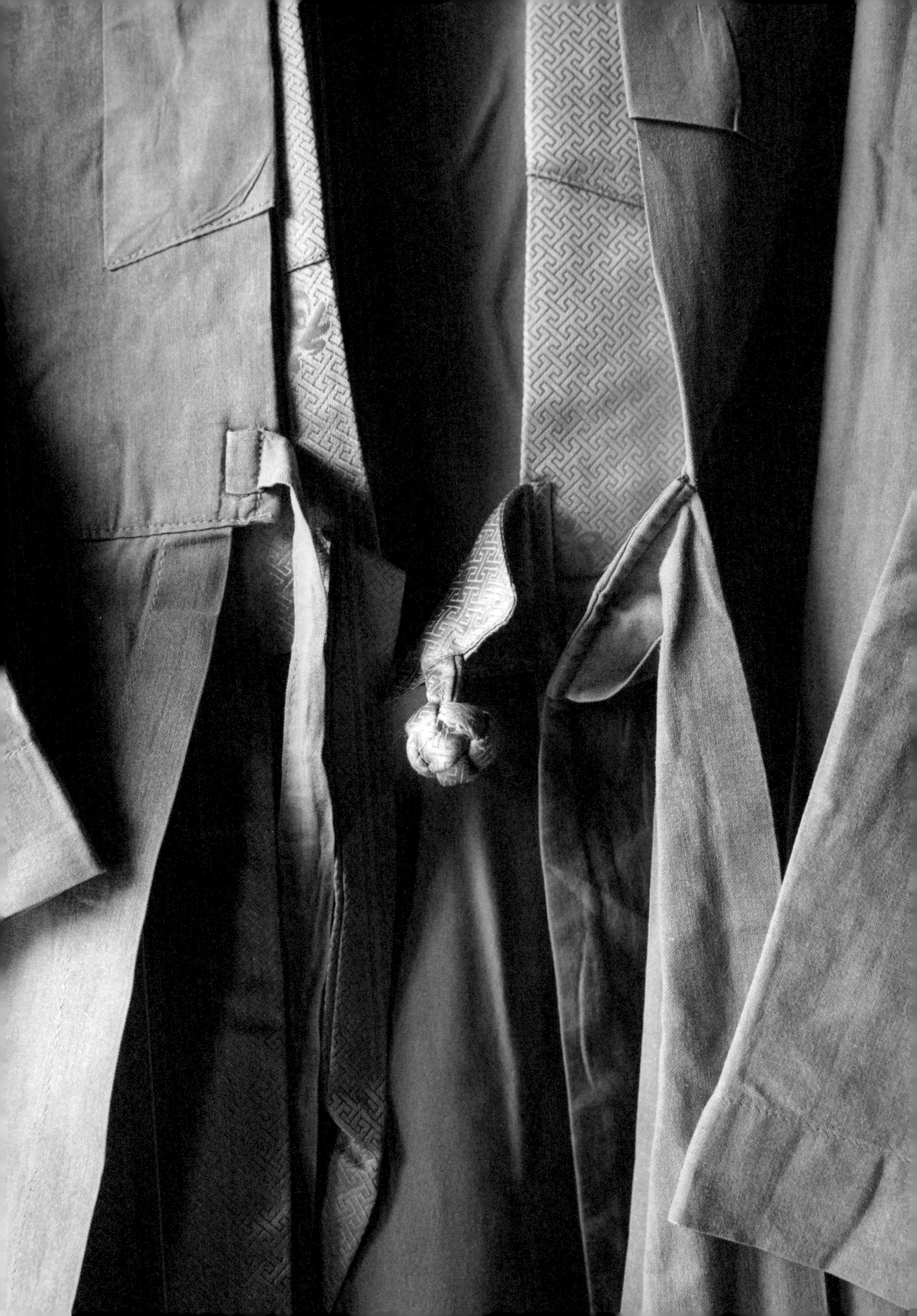

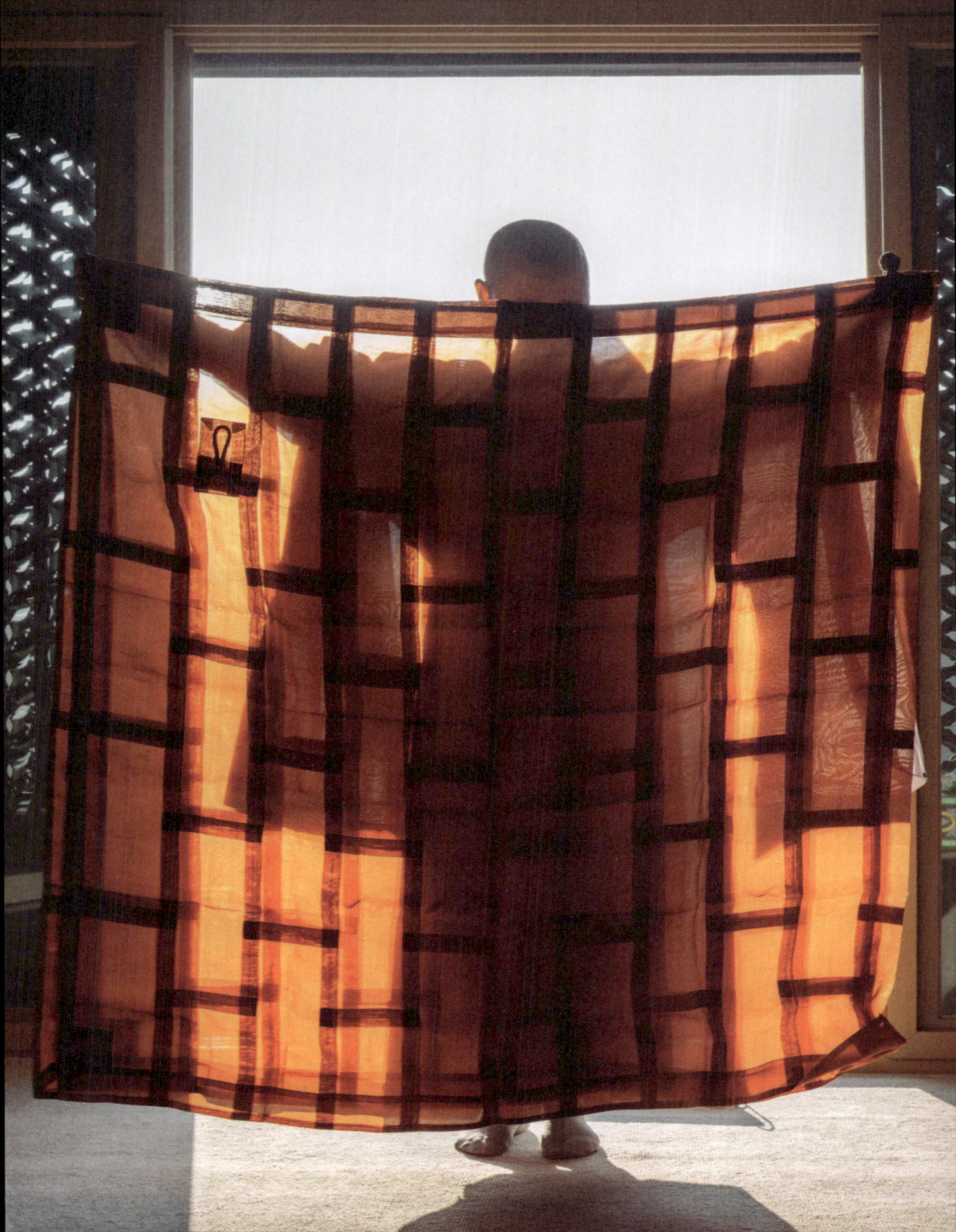

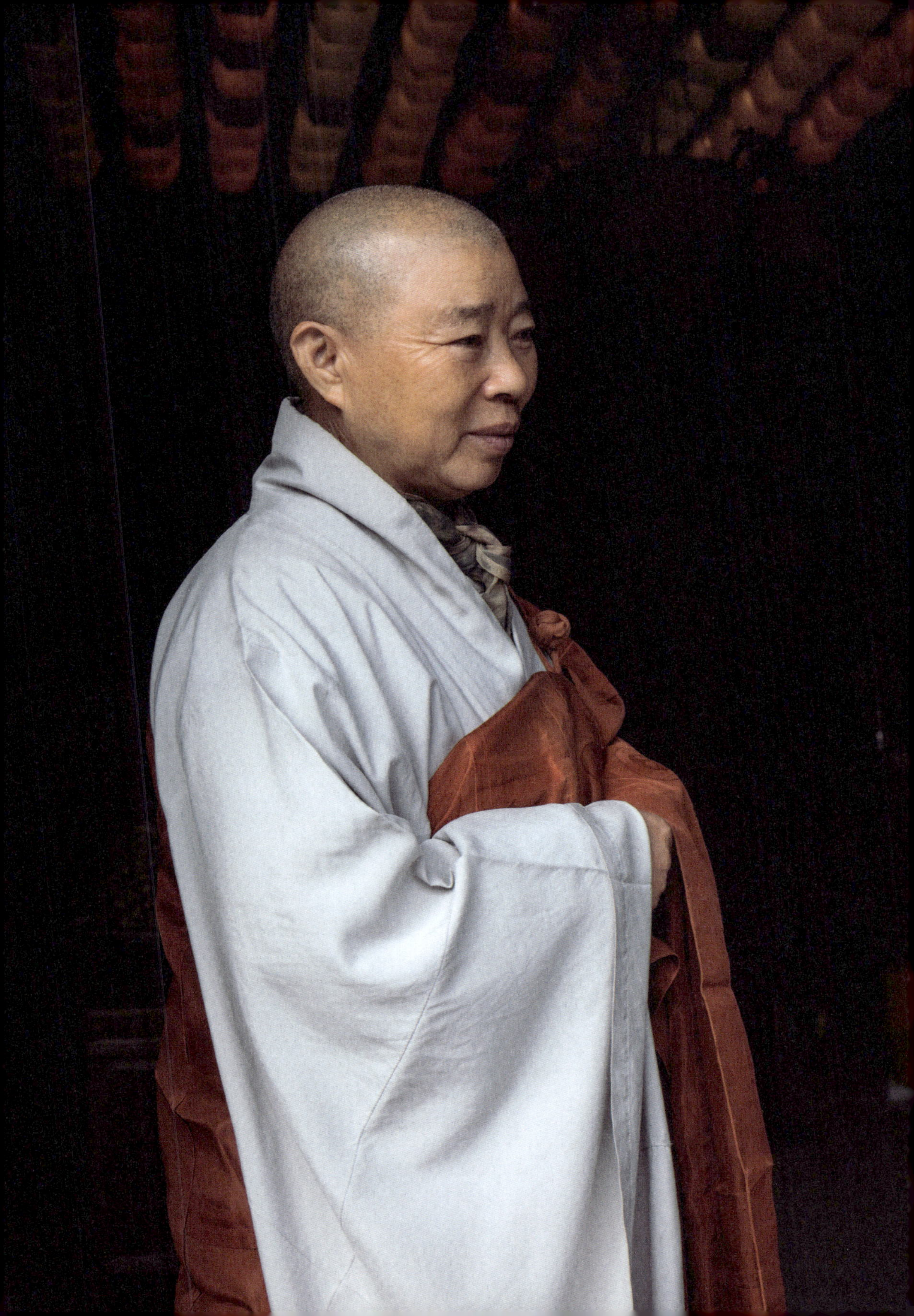

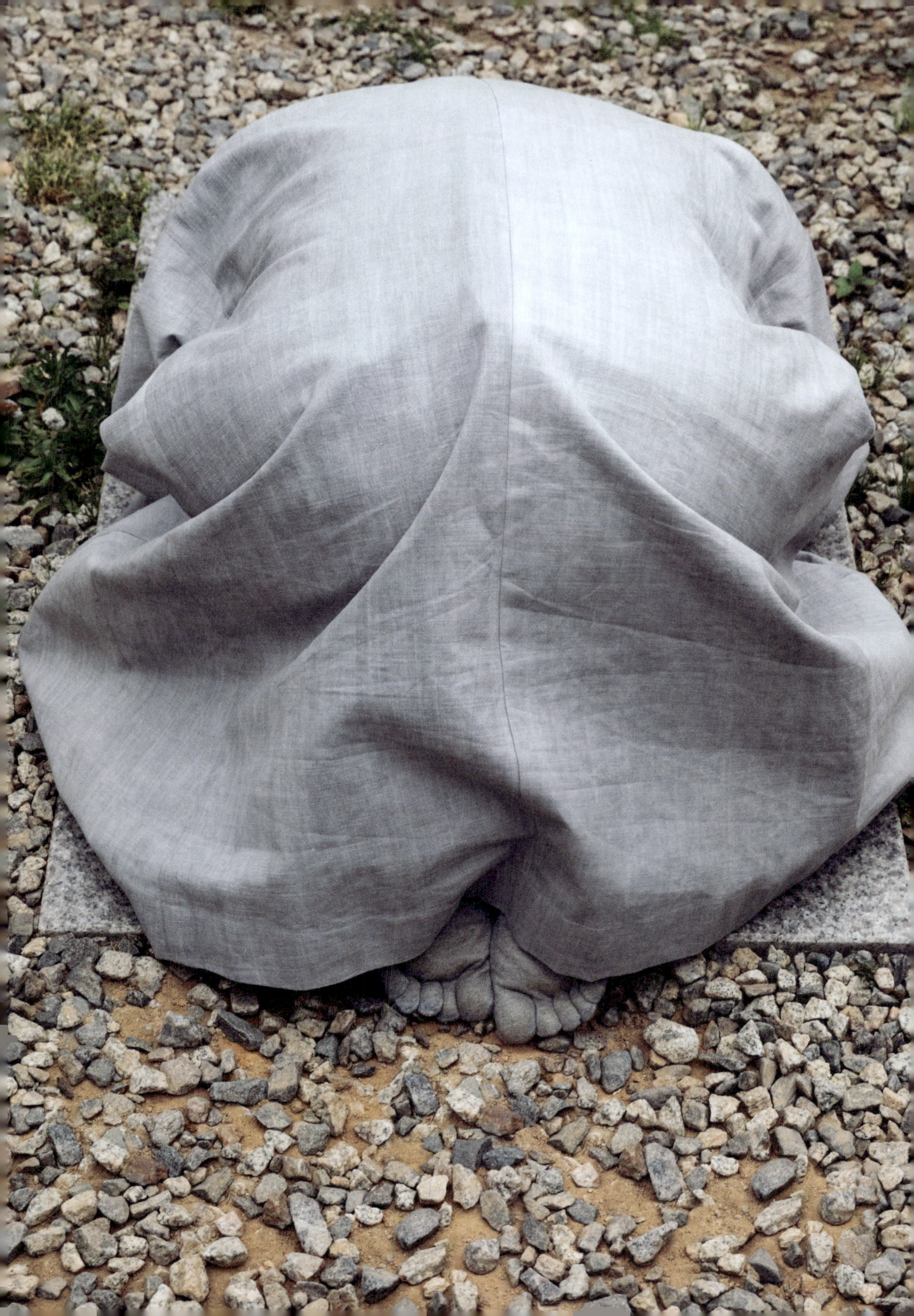

temple, the more their life is shaped by the temple and its daily rituals.

The robes, called *seungbok*, are mandatory for all snims and must be worn at all times. The main purposes of the uniform clothing are to externally symbolize membership in a group and to give the order members an internal sense of belonging. The homogeneous clothing enables the snims to truly recognize one another, practice solidarity with one another, and strengthen cohesion among themselves. Visible membership also influences the behavior of people toward the snims and vice versa because it gives the snims a sense of their own group affiliation. Mutual expectations come into play during each encounter, influencing behavior on both sides. In Korea, it's customary for snims to be addressed with a particular courtesy and greeted in a special way regardless of their age.

Although snims' robes are generally uniform, there are certain differences in form and color that visibly denote the various ranks. These correlate to the three levels one must pass through to become ordained, that is, to become a *bigu* or *biguni*. The rank of each snim is recognizable from their particular robes.

When a woman or man announces their wish to follow the Buddhist path and become a snim, certain conversations take place. To test how serious their decision is, applicants must kneel before the Buddha 3,000 times over several days and then have their hair shorn off. Then they begin their time as a *haengja*. This word means "someone who does a thing or who has set out on a path." This period typically lasts six months, but it can last somewhat longer. Their time as a haengja represents a kind of probationary period and is a necessary time of transition—it takes time to be able to tell whether someone has the personal maturity and personality traits they need to join the order and not just take the easy way.

The probationary period can be strenuous and full of privation. Haengjas have no names; they are called haengja because although they've left their old world behind, they have not yet properly entered their new world. They have to assimilate into the demanding everyday life of the temple, practice obedience, work hard (i.e., cooking and cleaning), study sutras, and learn rituals. They may not leave the temple without permission. Many aspiring snims quit in the middle of the probationary period. As haengja, women wear a simple two-piece orange-colored garment consisting of pants and a top and men wear dark brown robes. Their socks and shoes are gray, and their clothing—including their shoes—is provided entirely by the temple. Jewelry is not allowed, nor makeup or perfume.

If an applicant successfully completes their time as a haengja, they and the other applicants take a test that's administered at a fixed time. If they pass, they begin their novitiate, which takes four years. The men are called *sami* and the women are called *samini*. Women only receive their final confirmation after two years, when it's certain that they aren't pregnant. Their years as novitiates are a period of intense study and learning. Then, when their acceptance ceremony is celebrated, they each receive a Buddhist name that everyone must use to address them from then on. They're also given several items: the components of their robes, a four-piece set of wooden bowls called baru, cutlery, a wooden spoon, and chopsticks. The robes consist of multiple parts; in Seon Buddhism, they're typically light gray, and the collars and cuffs have narrow brown stripes that denote their status as a novitiate.

Once the novitiate has successfully completed that stage, they become a member of the order and are known as a bigu or biguni. Eventually, a celebratory ceremony will take place. They'll receive a new set of vestments that is also light gray and that they'll wear for the rest of their lives. The ceremonial robes have four pieces: pants, a top, a *jangsam*, and a *gasa*. The jangsam is a long, jacket-like outer garment that ties in front with two long ties; its sleeves are square and wide-cut and fall softly. The gasa is a reddish brown or brown cloth sewn together from a certain number of individual pieces and worn tossed over the left shoulder in a precise way. It's worn during daily rituals or on celebratory occasions.

The gasa is the only splash of color the members of the order wear—it's meant to be a reminder of the Buddha's original garments. However, since Korea has a different climate, the gasa isn't worn alone as it's commonly worn in warmer regions, but rather over other pieces of clothing. The history of the gasa goes back to what the Buddha's disciples wore—they collected rags, colored the pieces with earth, sewed them together into a large square cloth, and then wrapped themselves with it. Today, gasas are made from a unique fabric and are produced according to a particular pattern that displays the length of membership in the order—they're sewed together from a set number of 7, 9, 15, 19, 21, or 25 pieces, and the more pieces a gasa has, the higher rank its owner has. This tradition is a reminder of the origins of Buddhism. Along with the gasa, there are also meditation robes and study robes consisting of pants, a top, and the jangsam. For everyday life or for work, only simple pants and a top are needed.

Temple life requires that the robes vary depending on their function, but it's just as important to adjust them to the changing seasons. Summer vestments are made from light fabric like cotton or linen to mitigate the effects of the humid heat, but winter robes must keep the wearer warm, so they're usually made using traditional steppe techniques and are padded with cotton. Caps and hats must also be adapted to suit the weather.

In general, the robes should not fit snugly—they're loosely cut and comfortable. However, the cut must follow certain rules. For example, both men and women wear pants that are wide at the top and come together snugly at the ankles. Since the snims traditionally not only sit and sleep on the floor but also usually sit on cushions for rituals and meditation, their robes must be loose to avoid constricting the body or interfering with their circulation. If the robes were tight, moving during rituals and meditation would be difficult, and over time, that would have a negative impact on their health. The loose cut also has another purpose: the robes completely cover the contours of the body. Whatever could stimulate and awaken desire remains hidden. What meets the eye is only an unpainted face and unremarkable clothing.

The color of Korean Seon Buddhism is light gray. To be precise, nearly white. Gray is the color of ashes, nothingness, and emptiness. It's also the color of tusche, an indistinct and dull-colored ink.

On one hand, gray isn't a color, but on the other hand, it can be anything. It's created when something burns, completely losing its shape and disintegrating into ashes. Gray symbolizes withdrawal to nothing, but at the same time, it also symbolizes an origin. It's an unremarkable color that does not awaken desire, and it's neither luxurious nor completely pure. Gray is inherently modest and serene; it subdues emotion and brings calm. This is the color of the robes worn by Korean snims.

SOUNDS AND RITUALS

Korean Buddhism has its own rituals and a unique, instantly recognizable soundscape. What's made visible through its rituals is made audible through its music. By touching the senses, religion becomes a living experience—in a peculiar interplay, the sounds and the silence create a special experiential space for spirituality. Because we can only be aware of silence through sound, this varied soundscape enables us to appreciate Buddhism and helps bring the Buddha's teachings into the world.

The rhythmic sounds come from various instruments, ceremonial devices, and human voices and form an important component of the ritual. The tones and noises create a special atmosphere and cause us to experience the space differently. As the music floats between sensuality and spirituality, the sounds in the temple also connect the world of the senses with the world of the soul and spirituality; each ritual takes on a unique yet unmistakable form. The sounds also help guide the rhythm of everyday life in the temple: they mark transitions and divide the day in order to embed ancient rituals into the flow of time.

Life in the temple begins when the darkness turns into light, at three o'clock in the morning. It's

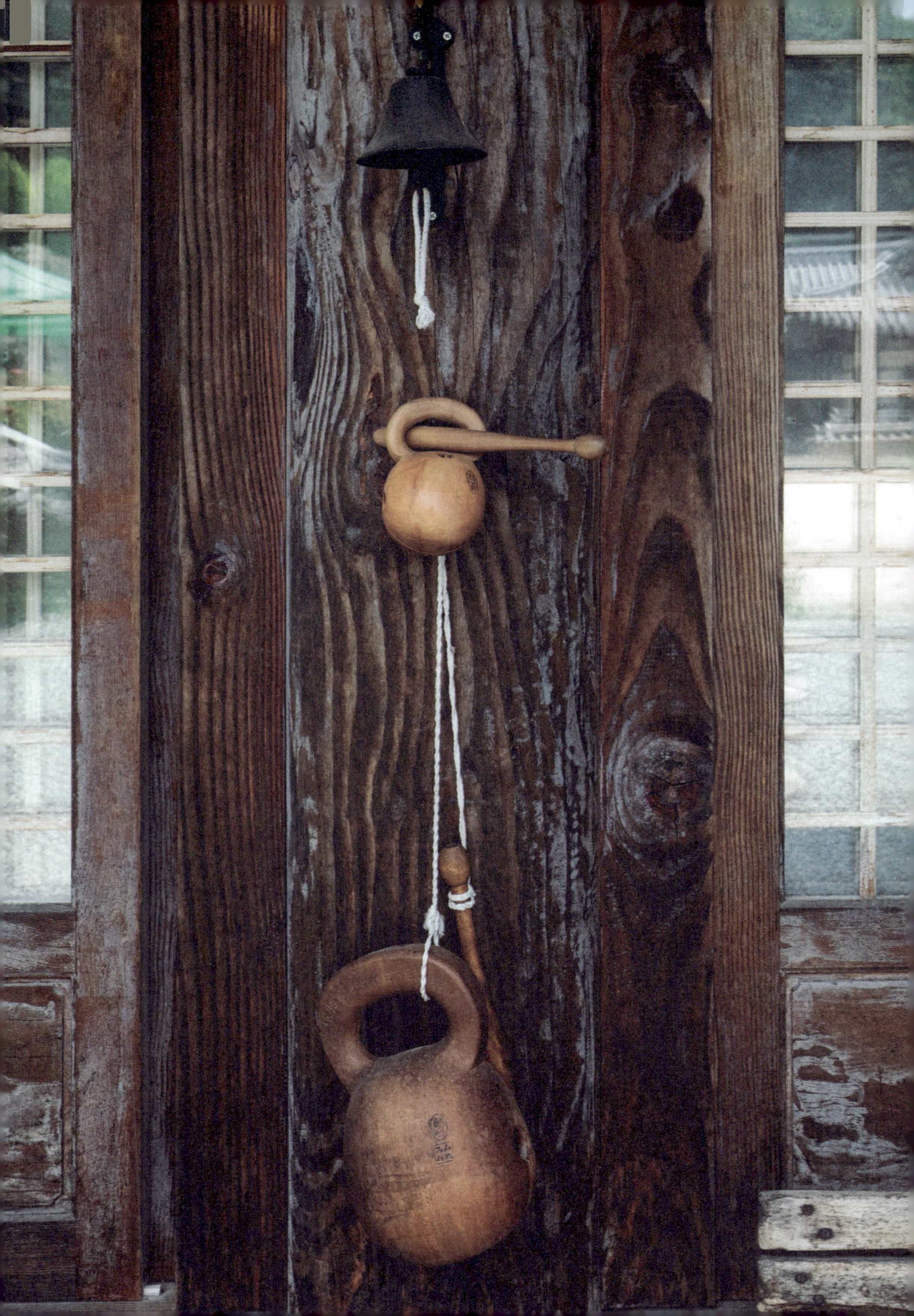

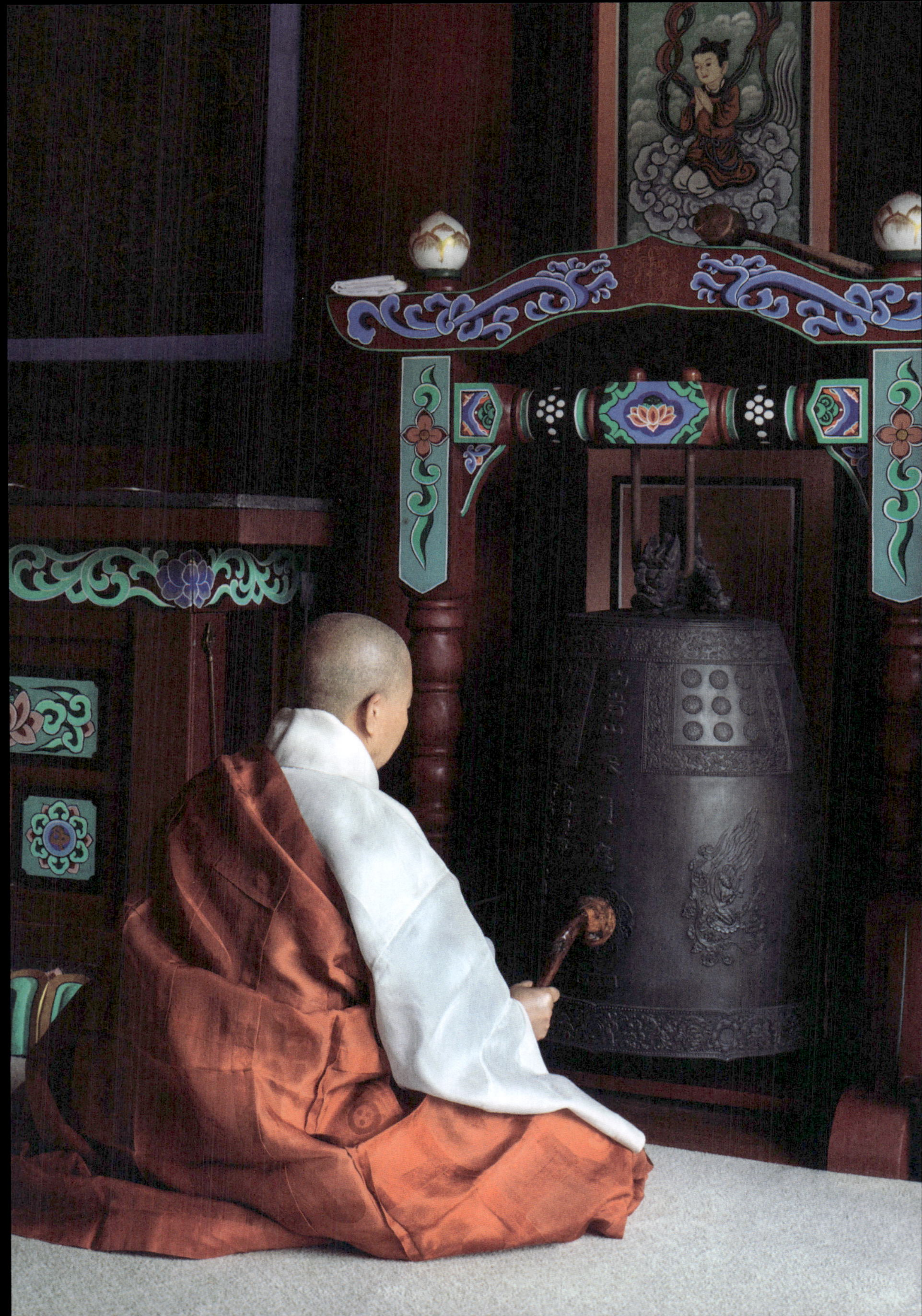

the time of transition; while the first light of day is growing in the distance, night withdraws. That's when the rhythmic sounds of the moktak resonate through the darkness and silence and suddenly fill the whole temple grounds, first softly and then with increasing volume. The sounds are meant to awaken not only the slumbering temple residents but also nature. The bright, clear tones and specific rhythms are a tonal representation of Korean Buddhism—everywhere the moktak can be heard, the Buddha is present.

This important ritual tool is made of wood and is struck with a short wooden mallet, and it has a distinctive form: it's shaped like a fish. It's said that this shape was selected because a fish is always alert and sleeps with its eyes open. This reference to vigilance is meant to remind meditators to remain attentive. The moktak also has a slightly rounded belly and is hollow inside. It's usually carved from the wood of a fig or ginkgo tree and is lacquered a warm, reddish-brown color. The size of a moktak varies depending on its function.

The moktak has a number of uses: it serves as a wake-up call, it can announce the start and end of a ritual, it calls temple residents to meals, and it proclaims the beginning of lessons. The moktak is struck with different rhythms, tempos, and volumes for different occasions. It's indispensable during the recitation of sutras because it supports the voices and sets the rhythm for the recitations. The physical act of steadily striking the moktak helps meditators maintain their concentration and drift slowly into a trance-like state; it exercises a peculiar pull that brings the body and spirit together. Memorizing and reciting various Buddhist texts is an important meditative activity, and all snims do it often, until deep into the night. Hearing the sound of the moktak and the melodic voices of the snims in the still of the night is an almost mystical experience.

One snim has the task of walking around the temple grounds while striking the moktak and reciting specific texts at three o'clock in the morning. It's the first ritual of the day, called *doryangseok*. The bright, clear sound rings throughout the temple grounds and wakes all those who are sleeping. It's said that the sound dispels the darkness and opens the ear.

The last tone of the moktak has hardly subsided when the bell from the Great Hall introduces the next ritual, the *jongsong*. A snim sits alone in the Great Hall with a bronze bell in front of themself. They use a small hammer to strike the bell slowly in a certain sequence while reciting a text loudly and rhythmically. With these actions and words, they express their wish for humans to overcome suffering and acquire wisdom, and they thank the Buddha for his teachings.

While the residents rouse themselves from their slumber, wash themselves, and get dressed, some of the snims go to a pavilion that stands on the left side in front of the Great Hall. There, an open pavilion with a lovely tiled roof sits atop high columns. It houses four instruments on its first floor; these are called the "four Buddhist items." The instruments are played in a particular order.

It starts with a giant drum called a *beopgo*. *Beop* means "the teachings of the Buddha" and *go* means "the drum." It's meant to carry the teachings of the Buddha out into the world. The drum hangs from the rafters and is covered with the hide of a cow on one side and the hide of a bull on the other: feminine and masculine, yin and yang, the two are thought to create harmony. But the hides must come from animals that died a natural death!

The rhythmic drumbeats are meant to awaken all living things on Earth so that they can receive the Buddha's message. Hearing the complex rhythms of the drum in the darkness and sensing its vibrations in your body is an unforgettable experience. During the winter nights, it's often cold; in summer months, it often rains during the monsoon season. No matter the season, if the sky is clear, a sea of stars ripples out overhead and the dark silhouettes of the mountains stand tall and firm.

At this time, the whole world vibrates and is filled with vitality as the drum is played with two long wooden mallets, its sounds creating a magical rhythm. Playing the drum is an exquisite art that demands strength and great mastery—it takes long practice to achieve a high level of expertise, musicality, and flowing movements. Because playing the drum is very strenuous, at least two snims must trade off to maintain the rhythms. Sometimes there are even three or four; a true master is often found among them. Both playing and listening become acts of meditation. The first player begins, and then several minutes later, that player gradually shifts to the rightmost edge of the enormous drum head while the second drummer begins to play on the left side. Then the first will leave the entire drum to the second. Play flows from one drummer to the next, until the final rhythm slowly concludes with specific beats along the edge of the drum. Each player has their own rhythmic pattern.

The next instrument to be played is the *mogeo*, or "wooden fish." It's literally a big, long fish carved from wood, painted, and hung from the rafters. The hollow space of its belly is beaten with two alternating wooden mallets in a staccato beat from the rear to the front. Its tone is powerful, dark, and earthy, meant to wake up all living things in the water so that they can receive the Buddha's message.

Next comes the *unpan*, the "cloud gong," a bronze instrument that consists of a plate in the shape of a cloud. It's embellished and hung from two columns, and it's struck with a wooden mallet. The tone is typically high, soaring, and metallic; it's meant to wake up all living things in the air so that they can receive the Buddha's message.

The ritual is completed by playing the large bronze bell. This is called the *beomjong*, or "universal bell." It's struck on the outside with a long tree trunk that's fastened to the rafters. Early in the morning, it's struck 33 times for all who cling to the world, and in the evening it's struck 28 times for the signs of the zodiac. Exactly how the bell is struck is precisely determined.

Many old bells reside in Korea whose sounds are famous—they're said to be pure and graceful. There are many legends about how some bells were created, which isn't surprising given that in ancient times, it wasn't easy to produce such large objects whose tones had the desired volume and timbre and that were viewed by people as being carriers of the Buddha's message. Striking the bell releases great, deep vibrations that travel far into the surrounding valleys, contrasting with the brighter, wafting tones of the drums. The tone of the large bell is deep and dark, allowing us to sense how the waves of its sounds spread out slowly through space; they remain close to the earth, permeate everything, and create a mysterious echo. The waves seem to disintegrate, gather strength again, and carry on into the distance. Due to the enormous reach of its tone, in earlier centuries, the bell served as a guide for those who had lost their way in the mountains—following the tone would always help them find the path to the temple, where they would be protected.

Beomjong encompasses earth, water, air, and sky; everything is unified into a great whole. The sounds of the four instruments are the words of the Buddha and a clarion call to the world. Buddhism wants to be there for all of us—it does not want to exclude anyone. Again, this mindset is expressed in the openness of the temple complex, a space that always remains open to the natural environment surrounding it.

One hour passes from the first strike of the moktak to the last tone of the bell. During that time, all of the snims will have dressed in their ceremonial vestments and gathered in the Great Hall. Once the last peal of the large bell fades away, the small bell in the hall chimes its response and the yebul begins, the main ritual of the early morning.

The Great Hall represents the heart of the temple and houses the most important statues of the Buddha. The snims sit before those on cushions in a certain order, listening to the last tone of the large bell outside and the answer from the small bell inside, preparing themselves internally. Once the yebul begins, they all stand. The snim who's leading the ritual has a small metal bell in their hand called *yoryong* that they use each time they need to announce a new phase of the ritual. A second snim strikes the moktak throughout the yebul.

The recitation of certain sutras is the most important part of the ritual. First comes the sound of individual voices, and then all of them come together in a harmonizing chorus. This creates a melodious recitation that's accompanied by the moktak. (On special occasions, another drum is also played that has a wholly different effect.) During the ritual, the participants kneel on the floor seven times and then rise. At the end, all of them turn right to a Buddhist painting called a *bulhwa* that hangs on the side wall and they recite the famous heart sutra in unison. (This is one of the most well-known Buddhist texts in Korea.) Reciting the heart sutra always comes at the end of the yebul, whether it's held in the morning or the evening. Reciting this particular sutra sounds especially melodious and beautiful, and its deep philosophical content represents the central teaching of Seon Buddhism: emptiness. The yebul ends when all of the participants turn forward to the Buddha statues again and bow three times. The entire ritual takes 30 minutes.

The recitation of sutras is a significant component of Buddhist traditions. For many years, Buddhist discourses were only transmitted orally, and so the snims have maintained a practice of loudly and rhythmically reading aloud, memorizing, and reciting from memory for themselves and for others. Recitation is central both for the various daily rituals and for the study of Buddhist texts; the words of the sutras possess their own musicality and beauty that cause them to linger longer with listeners. Reciting sutras beautifully in the traditional way is a high art that requires special skill—snims must dedicate themselves to much study and practice in order to bring the sutras to life and lend them spirituality through finely modulated recitations.

Once the yebul has ended, most of the snims withdraw and meditate while some novices and snims go to the kitchen to prepare breakfast. Some of the visitors perform the ritualized bowing in the hall, called *bae*, bowing 108 times with a long string of wooden beads in their hands: they kneel down on a cushion, touch their foreheads to the floor, and stand again. Each repetition flows into the next. Every visitor does this three times when they come into the hall to demonstrate respect for the Buddha.

The Buddhist religion is a sensual, bodily religion, and the number 108 represents possible mistakes that we can make in life. When performing this ritual, we should reflect on our own acts as well as the consequences of our acts for ourselves and others. We should also sense our bodies during this reflection—the depression we may be feeling inside can be lightened in this way.

When the moktak announces breakfast at 6 a.m., everyone gathers in the dining room. After breakfast, many of the snims go to the community meditation hall, where the sound of a ritual device called a *jukbi* is inextricably linked with the ensuing meditation session. The jukbi is made from a thick stem of bamboo about 16 inches long; two-thirds of it is cut through lengthwise. It's gripped in the right hand and struck on the palm of the left hand. The left hand immediately closes around the jukbi so that the sound doesn't spread out into the space but instead sinks into itself. A short, muffled, yet pleasant tone is created that ends abruptly. It indicates the start and end of a long meditation session.

Sometimes the master—who paces between the rows of those who are sitting—will softly tap the shoulder of a snim if they sense that the snim is restless or losing their concentration. Whenever the tap of the jukbi sounds in the silence of the meditation room, the tone develops an especially magical effect because the transition from silence to sound happens so suddenly . . . and then the stillness once again completely absorbs the sound, as if it had never been there to begin with.

Dinner is usually eaten at 6 p.m. After that, the evening yebul is celebrated. In Korea, there's no twilight—darkness comes swiftly and suddenly. The four instruments in the pavilion are played once again in the same sequence while all of the snims gather in the Great Hall. The drum beat vibrates through the air again as the light transforms into darkness. Then the mogeo and the unpan follow. Finally, the heavy tone of the large bell resonates once more through the valleys, announcing the coming night. Just as all of the living beings of the earth, water, and air are awoken in the early morning to receive the teachings of the Buddha, they are laid to rest in the early hours of darkness, when they can sink into sleep so that everything can begin anew once again. From the Great Hall, the beating of the yoryong and the moktak is heard, as well as the voices of the snims; finally, the order members recite the heart sutra together.

In these transition times, one can experience a magical moment in the temple. Darkness comes over the mountains and spreads quickly to the valleys. The visitors and tourists leave the temple complex and the motley, raucous world disappears with them into the valleys. Their voices are almost inaudible; only their laughter is occasionally heard. The footsteps of people hurrying fade away gradually . . . and then, suddenly, it's night. The voices of the night birds are heard and the stars emerge.

While every temple in Korea has a large bell, not all of them have a pavilion with the four instruments—many temples are small, consisting of only a few buildings and with a few snims in residence. But a large bell is a necessary requisite for every temple, as are the small bell and the small ritual devices like the yoryong, and every snim has their own moktak. However, anyone who wants to get acquainted with the entire musical side of Korean Buddhism must seek out a large temple complex. This is also where the great masters reside who conjure up unforgettable rhythms on the giant drum.

But of course, when cataloging everything that belongs to the soundscape in a Buddhist temple, the sounds and noises of nature also feature prominently. Since temples are mostly in the mountains, they're surrounded by nature, so there's one sound that's familiar to all visitors: the wind generates it by making the many small bells that hang from the curved roof gables and pavilions ring. The little bells have clappers with fish figures fastened to them, and these sway to and fro in the wind, prompting the bells to give a soft, pleasant tinkling. That's why they're called *punggyung*, or "the sound of the wind."

The punggyung remind us that the wind is there, and so is nature; time passes, and everything changes. The soft sound of the little bell is an audible token of Korean Buddhism.

DEATH IN BUDDHISM

Death has a very distinct character in Buddhism because it's part of the cycle of rebirth. However, we must free ourselves from the cycle, and the Buddha told us how to do this. Life is connected to suffering. If a person remains in the cycle, death represents a transition, but if they've broken away from the cycle and are free, death means extinguishment and equates to nirvana.

We are born with a body; soon, consciousness develops. With the help of the senses, consciousness develops a relationship with the external world. Emotions form and knowledge is acquired. Living requires doing and acting, which cause various consequences and leave traces. When someone dies, their actions determine whether and into which form they will be reborn. The more unsatisfied wishes, desires, or resentments someone is carrying inside at the moment of death, the more likely they are to be reborn. However, what's reborn is not the individual as they were, but rather a negative energy acting within the person that takes on a new form because the person has adhered to life and has refused to let go. The unmet desires and unamended consequences of actions create an energy that acts as the engine of rebirth. Rebirth is not desirable, because as Buddhism teaches, life is full of suffering. We should strive to free ourselves from this cycle.

This view of death has inspired the creation of a particular death ritual in Korea that's still maintained to this day. If someone wants a Buddhist burial, their body is cremated, and then starting on the day of death, a ceremony takes place every seven days, the core of which is the recitation of particular sutras, especially the diamond sutra. This ceremony is repeated seven times on every seven days. On the 49th day, a great parting ritual is held. The sonorous recitation (accompanied by the moktak) is for the deceased so that they'll heed the teachings of the Buddha, look back on life, repent of their bad deeds, and strengthen their good intentions.

The first 49 days after death are the transition period that determines whether and in what form the

>>> Page 389

大雄殿

제 나름 중생들로

진리의 이모습은

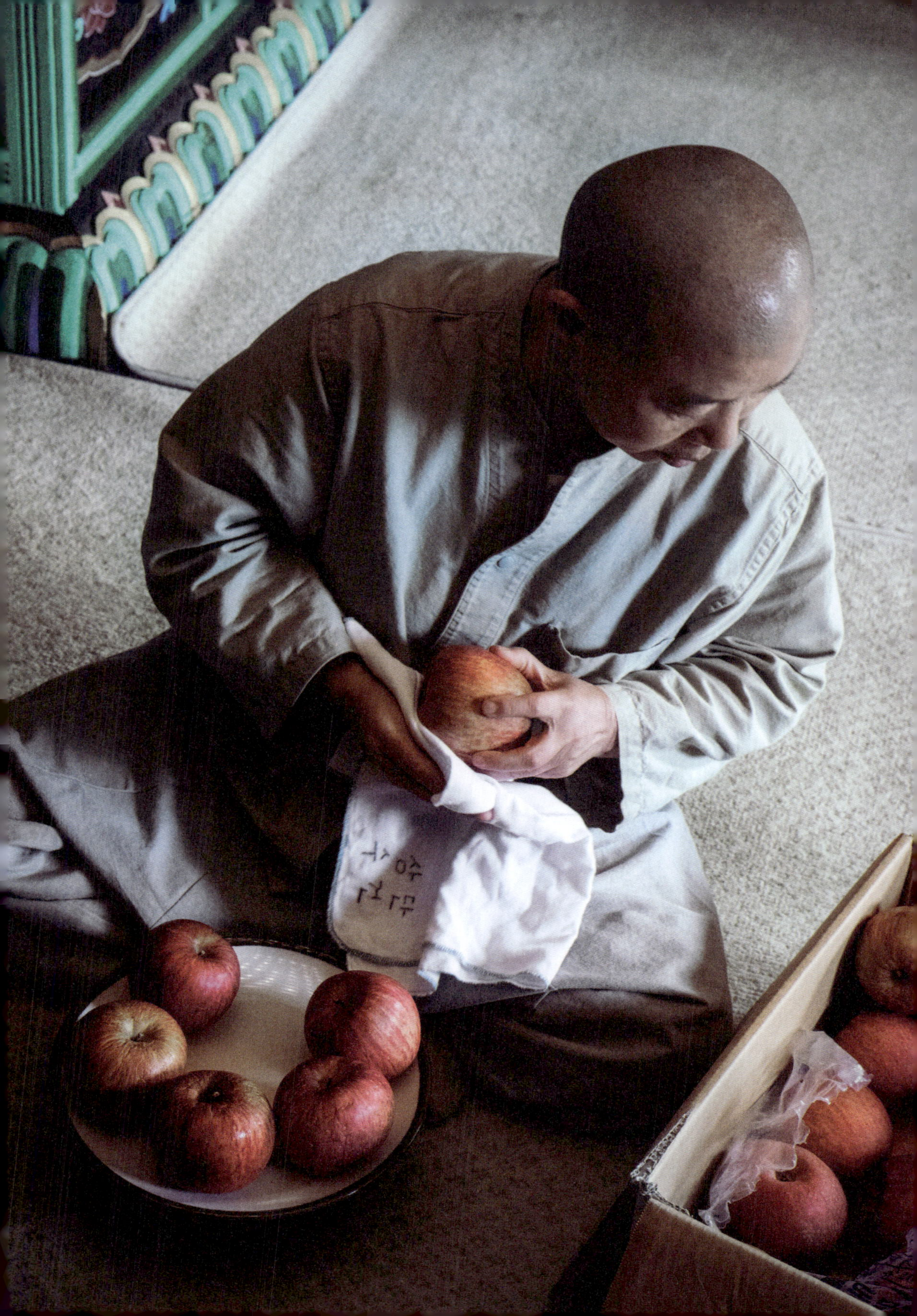

佛 殿 函

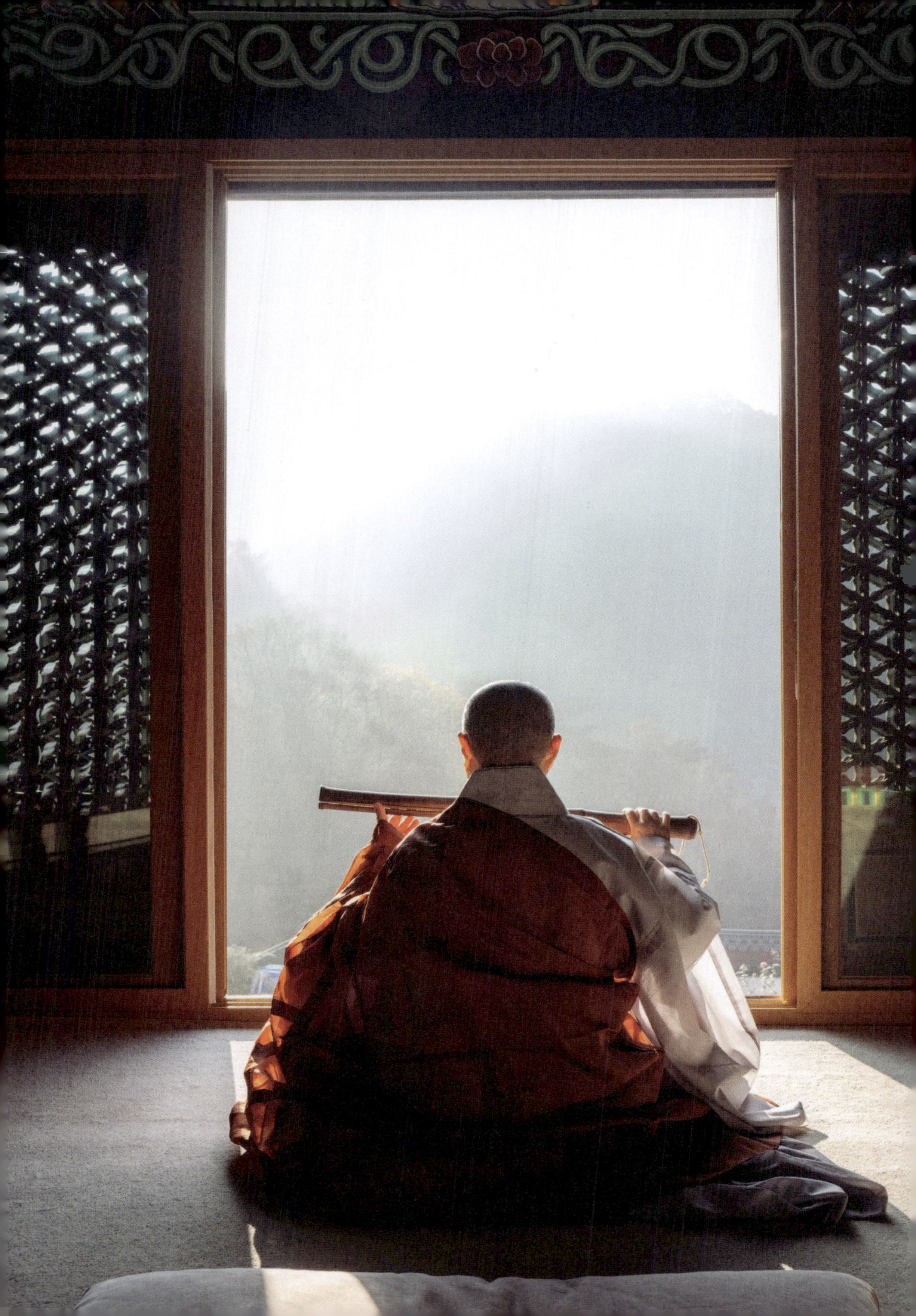

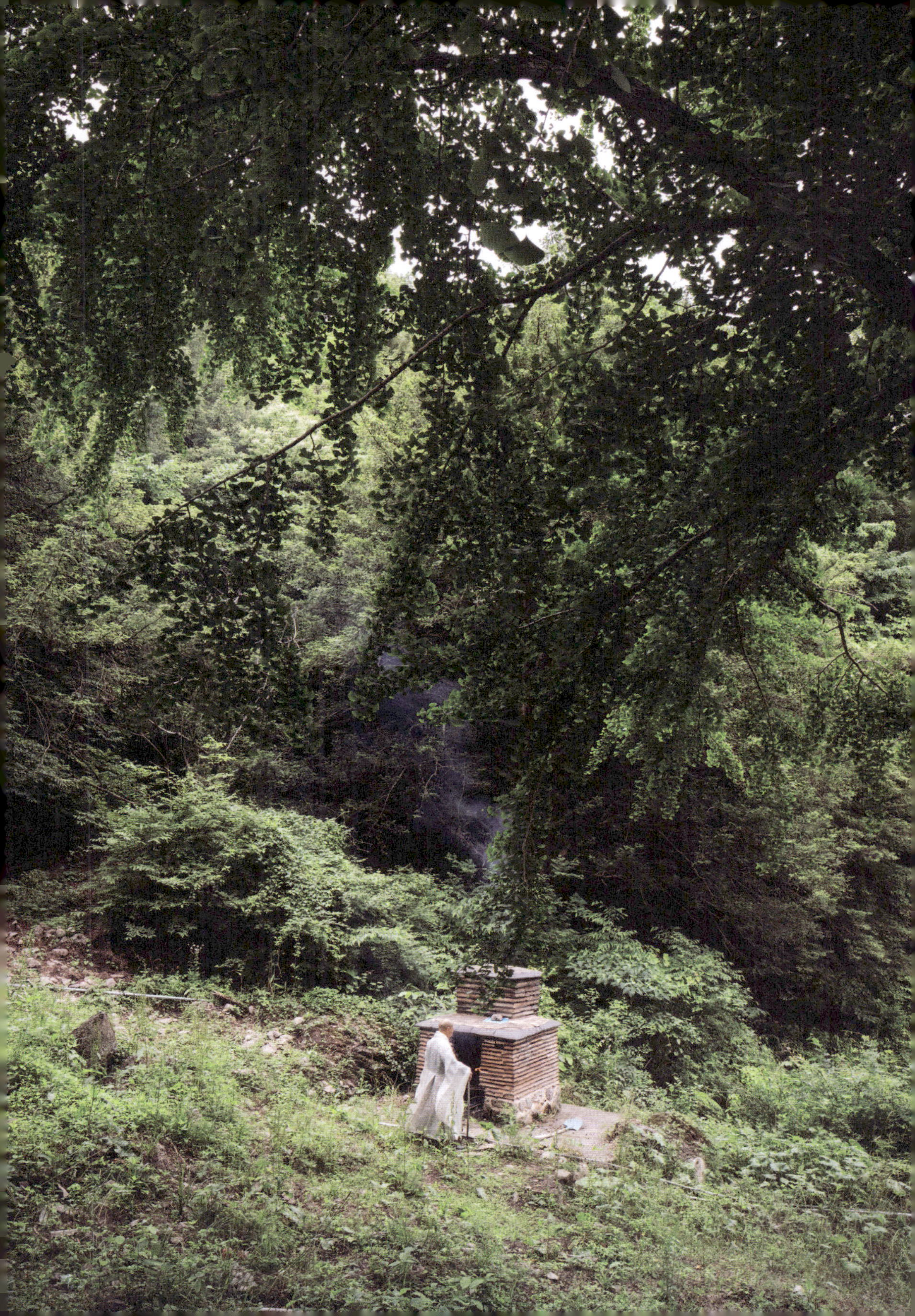

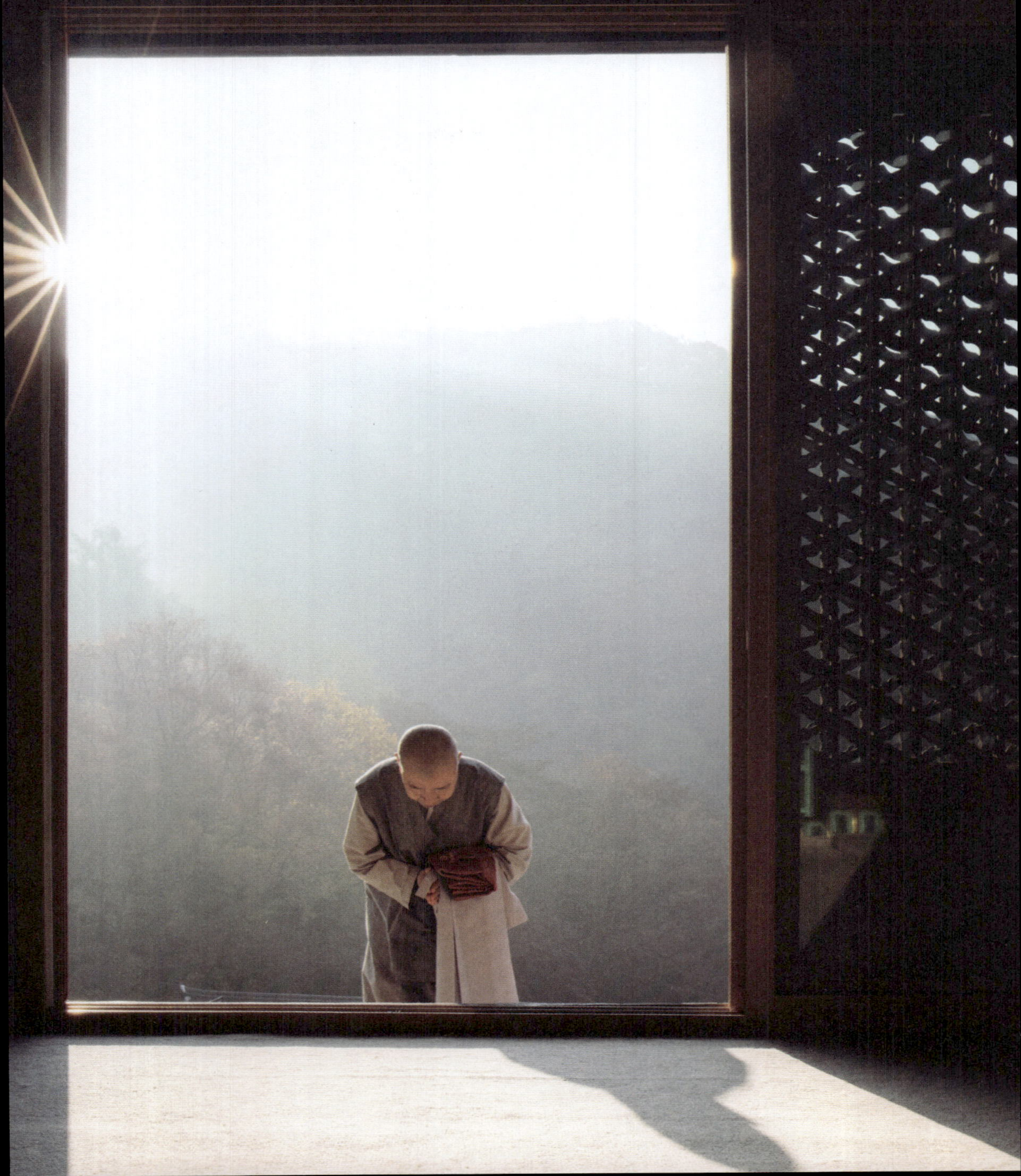

person will be reborn. If the deceased hears the sutras and absorbs them, they have a chance of improving their fate. The deceased alone is able to change things, in death just as in life. Family members can join in, too, and wish the deceased success. (Over the years, some folk beliefs have emerged with respect to this belief—for example, the western paradise of Amitābha Buddha, who is so compassionate that he won't rest until all have been freed from the cycle of rebirth.)

Although the recitation of the sutras is the main event of the death ceremony, an altar featuring particular foods is also set up. This aspect of the ritual comes from the Confucian tradition of ancestral worship: a core element of Confucianism was to offer rice, meat, fish, fruit, and wine to the ancestors, and ancestor veneration is celebrated at home. This veneration makes it clear that family is important and that we receive our own lives from the ancestors. It expresses gratitude for the gifts of life and care. By honoring the ancestors, we take our own place in the ongoing cycle of birth and death, creation and destruction, and at the same time, we honor the mystery of life.

In Korea, Buddhist and Confucian traditions have mixed and created symbiotic relationships. Notably, the food offered on the altar differs from Confucian tradition: there are rice, vegetables, and fruit and no animal products or wine. The altar is in the temple, not the home, and the food is simple. It must not be colorful nor have too strong a smell, so sesame oil isn't used.

Once the parting ritual is over on the 49th day, the death ceremony is complete. The clothing and personal belongings of the deceased are burned at a separate ceremonial site on the temple grounds. The dead person should no longer cling to life—they should renounce it. The family should say goodbye and return to living. That said, a small electric candle may be lit in the temple and the name of the deceased may be attached to it. The family can return there to remember their loved one whenever they wish. Grief takes time.

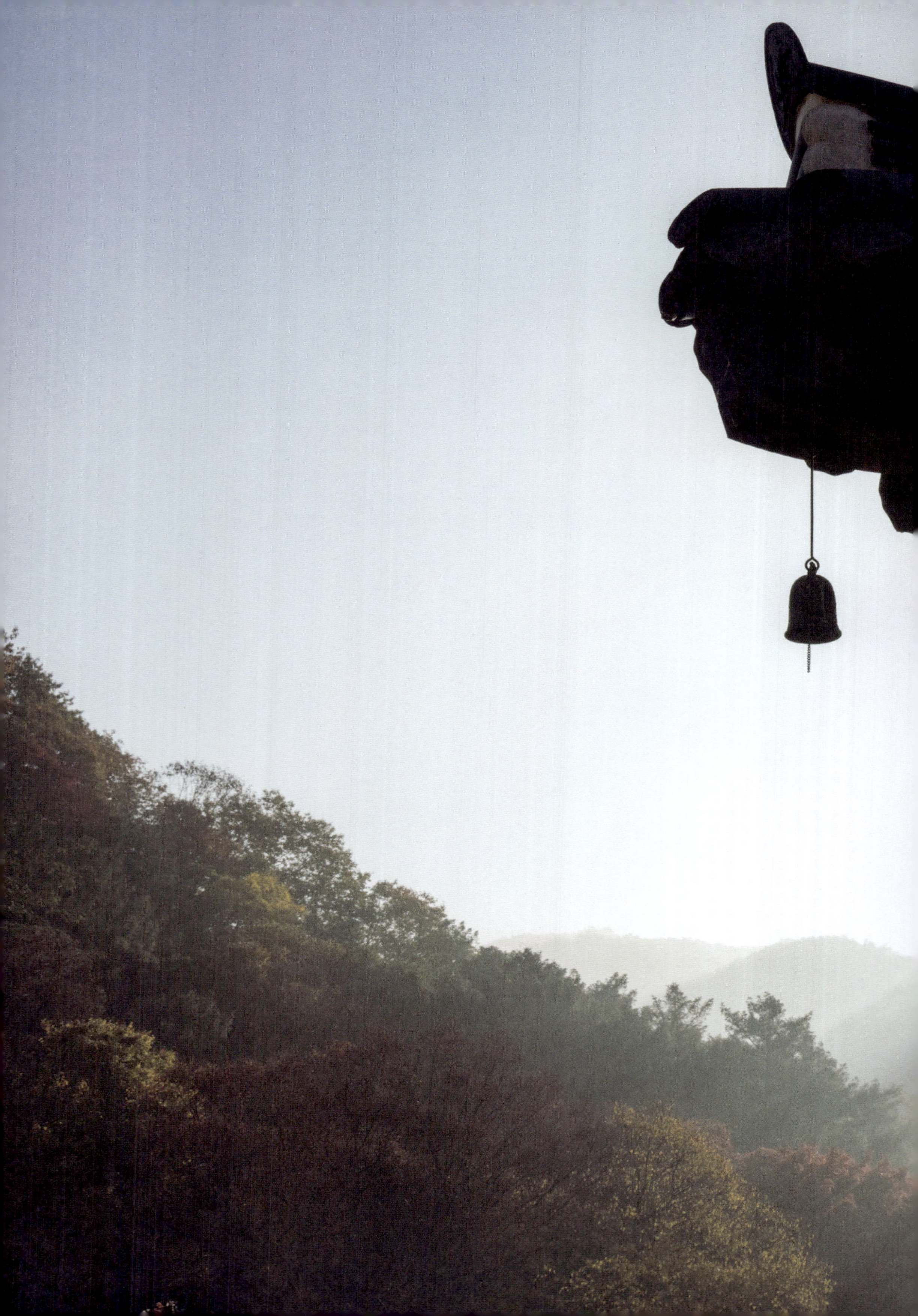

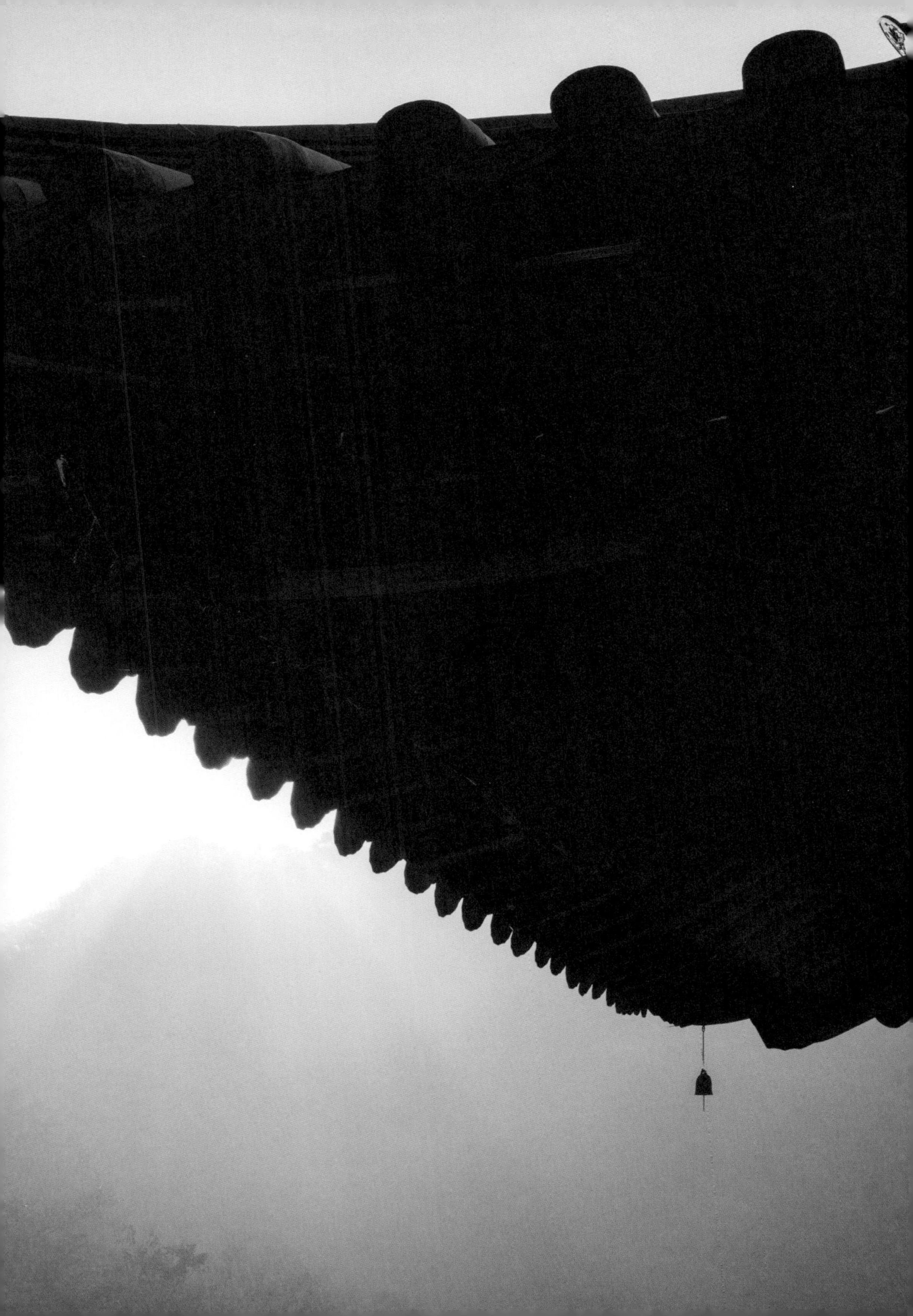

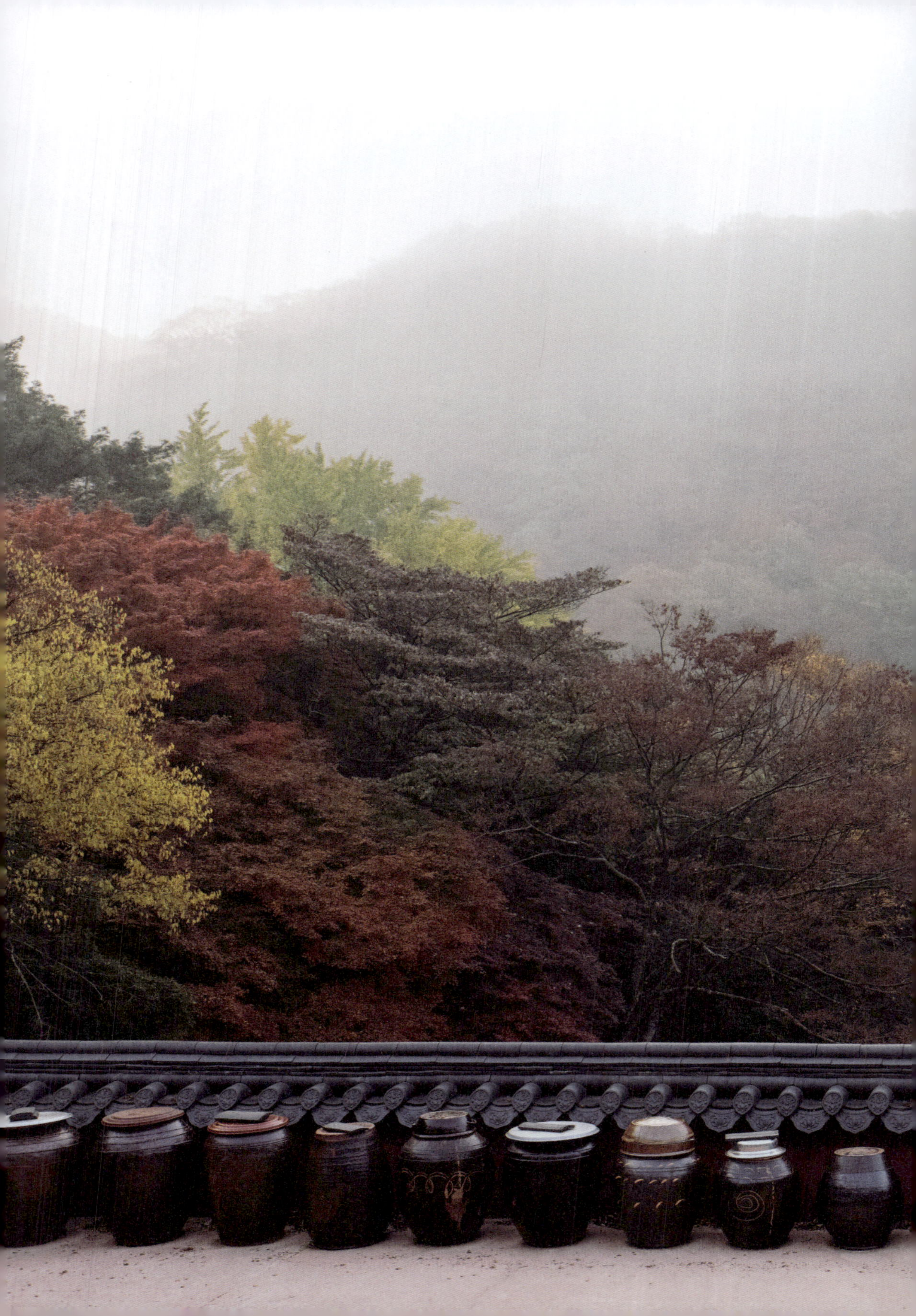

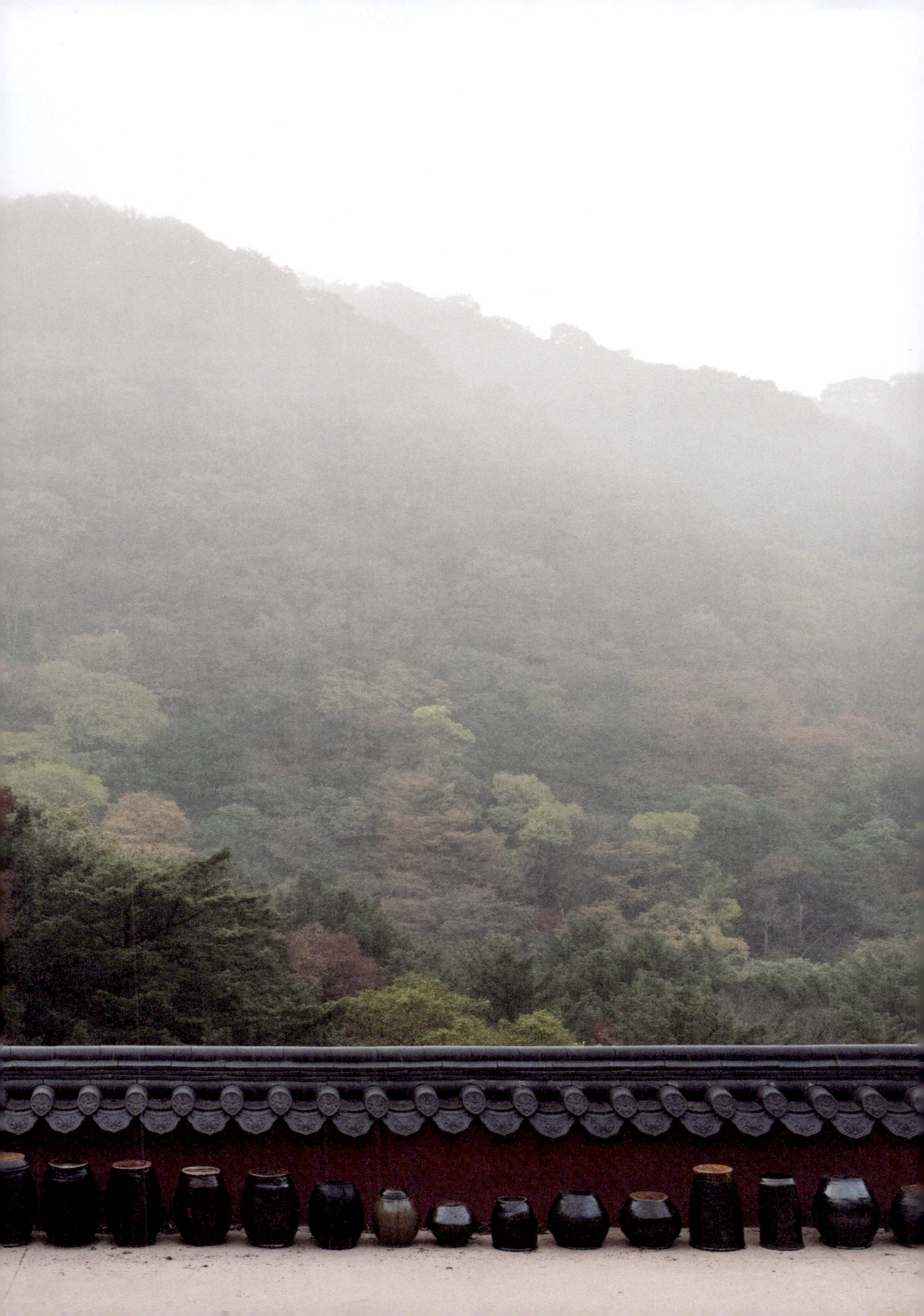

미나리, 야채의모든것   중앙청

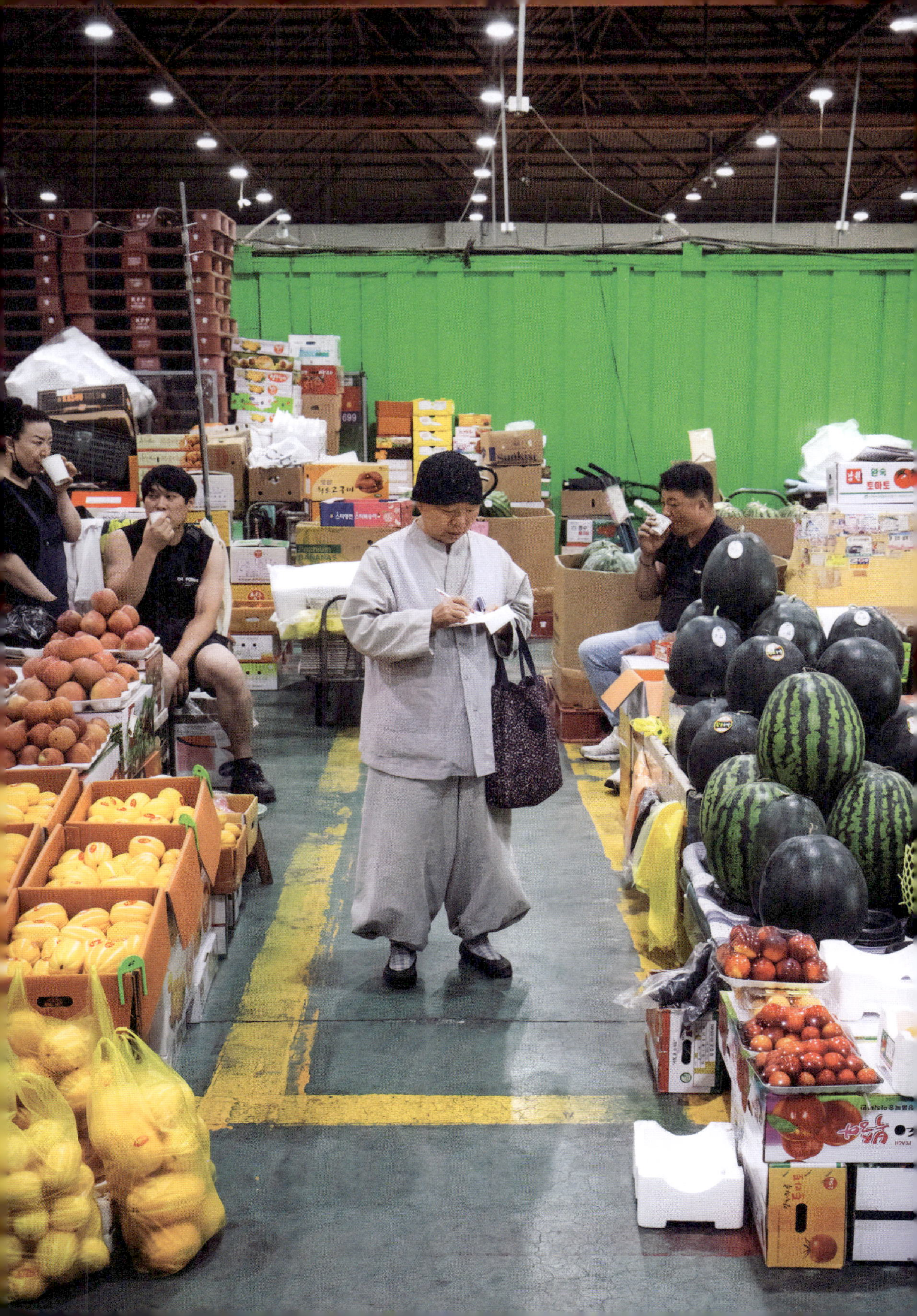
Sunkist
완숙 토마토

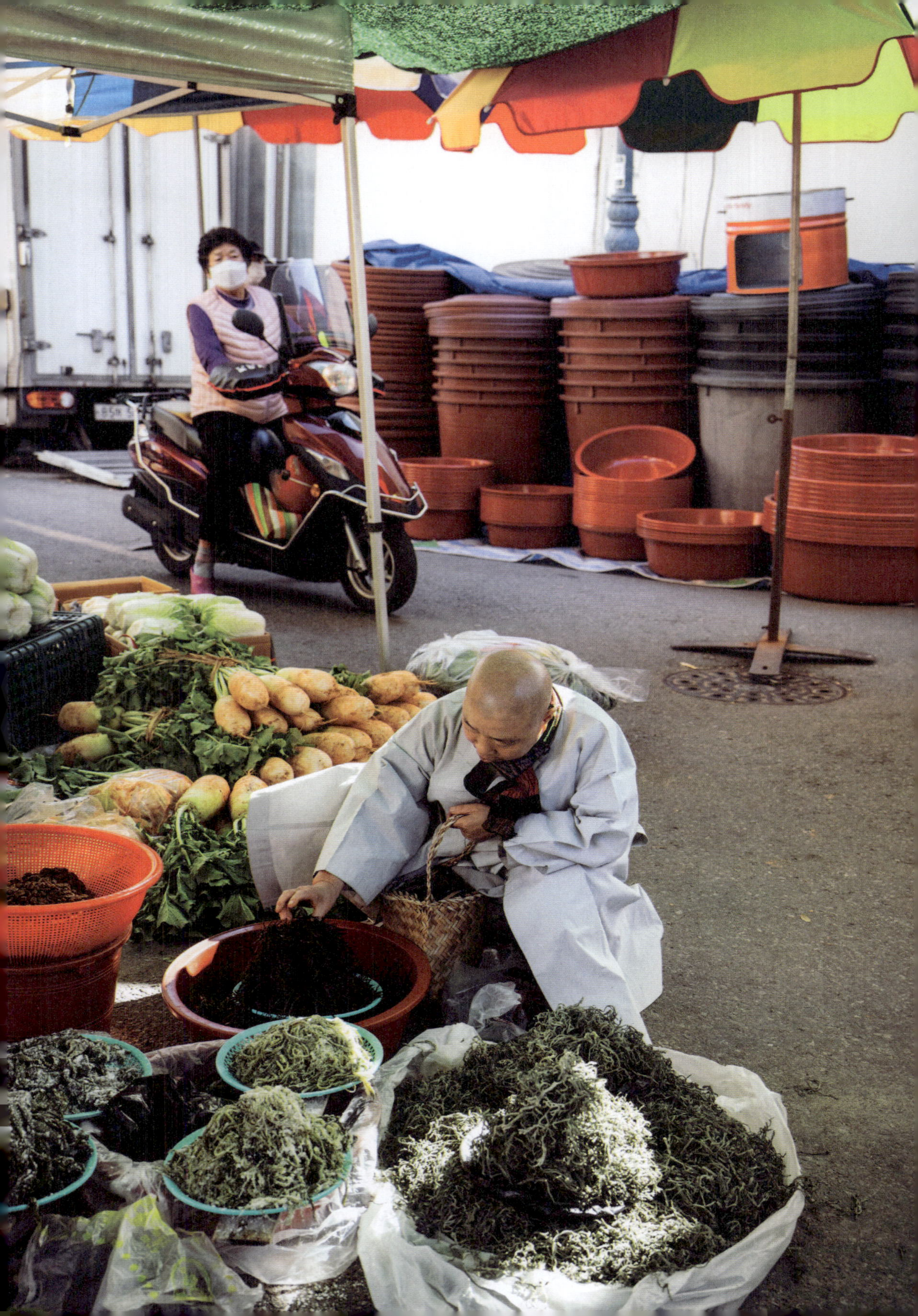

3-15-18

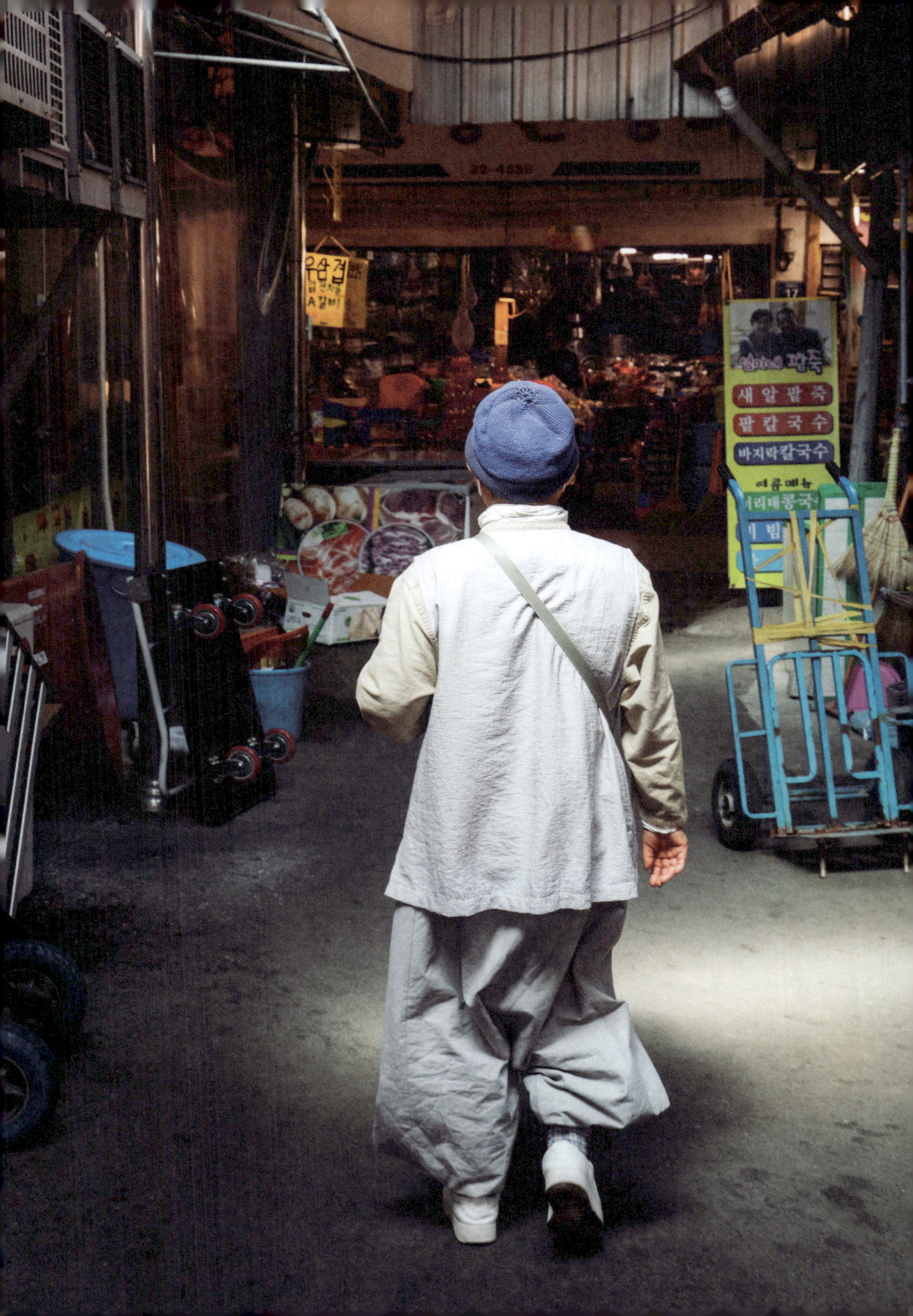
새알팥죽
팥칼국수
바지락칼국수

GLOSSARY OF INGREDIENTS

Geography, climate, and culture determine what the people of a country eat. Korea is a very mountainous peninsula with a continental climate and four distinct seasons, and Buddhism has left deep cultural traces in the country's food traditions. Because this book concerns Jeongkwan Snim's vegan temple cooking, all of the ingredients that she uses and that are listed here are plant-based. As numerous as these may seem to be, they actually represent only a small number of all the ingredients used in Korea.

Some of these foods may already be well known in Western cooking, but not all of them are. This glossary is intended to act as a guide to an unfamiliar world of foods and flavorings—use this list to orient yourself. Cooking begins with becoming familiar with ingredients so that you can handle them properly!

Aehobak see Squash

Apple (sagwa): Apples are a popular fruit in Korea—they're often cut into artistic shapes and served as a dessert. In the past, many more varieties of apples existed, but that variety has unfortunately diminished because nowadays people prefer sweeter varieties (although some regional varieties still exist). Today's apples are primarily large, sweet, juicy, red apples. In Korea, apples are also dried, made into juice, or used in cooking.

Bae see Pear
Baechu see Napa cabbage
Bak see Squash

Bamboo shoot (juksun): In spring (particularly after the rain), bamboo shoots sprout up from the soil. They must be pulled up then because in a very short time, they'll grow too high to be useful—they can shoot into the air with unbelievable speed! That's because they have gathered enough energy from four or five years underneath the soil to sprout and break through the earth once again. People say you can hear bamboo growing. In Korea, the shoots have been eaten for about 800 years.

The shoot is cut through the middle to expose the inner white flesh, which holds a bitter liquid that must be rinsed out. The edible parts are boiled until tender and then cooled in cold water before they're incorporated into dishes. *Juksun* goes well with other ingredients because it has no distinct flavor of its own—it can be combined with meat or eaten in a stew or as a savory seasoned vegetable. Today, bamboo shoots are very easy to find canned.

Bangul-tomato see Tomato

Beans (kong, pat): Korean cooking uses a wide variety of beans. They're separated into two groups: *kong* and *pat*. Kong (also called *daedu* or "big head") is the yellow soybean indispensable to Korean cooking: soybeans form the basis for tofu, soy sauce, soybean paste (doenjang), oil, sprouts (kongnamul), soy milk, soybean powder, and syrup. Kong is also seasoned, braised, and eaten as a banchan. Its leaves can be made into kimchi or jangajji.

Kong contains high amounts of protein (40 percent), fat (20 percent), carbohydrates (35 percent), and vitamin B. Kong sprouts contain vitamin C even though the soybeans themselves don't contain any. Because of its high protein content, kong is called "beef of the field."

The black beans that are so popular in Korea also belong to the soybean family. In addition to these, there are various other kinds of beans, like kidney beans (*gangnangkong*), peas, borlotti beans, and mung beans (*nokdu*), all of which can yield sprouts, flour, or jelly. Bean pods aren't eaten in Korea—only the ripe beans themselves are eaten. They're cooked together with rice or used as a filling for various rice cakes. Lentils were unknown for a long time in Korea but have since been introduced from the West.

Pat or *sodu* (meaning "small head") is the small red bean also known as the *adzuki* bean. Pat has little protein or fat, but it has a higher carbohydrate content. It's boiled or steamed, mashed, and lightly sweetened and used as a filling for rice cakes, steamed wheat cakes, and pastries. It's also made into jelly and ice cream. *Patjuk*, a creamy soup made from pat, is eaten on New Year's Eve.

In Korea, because prisons often mix beans into rice instead of using expensive meat to feed the incarcerated population, the expression "to have kongbap," or "to eat bean-rice" means that someone is in prison. When a prisoner is released, family members or friends welcome them with a piece of tofu that they must eat—in fact, they should eat enough so that they never have to go to prison again.

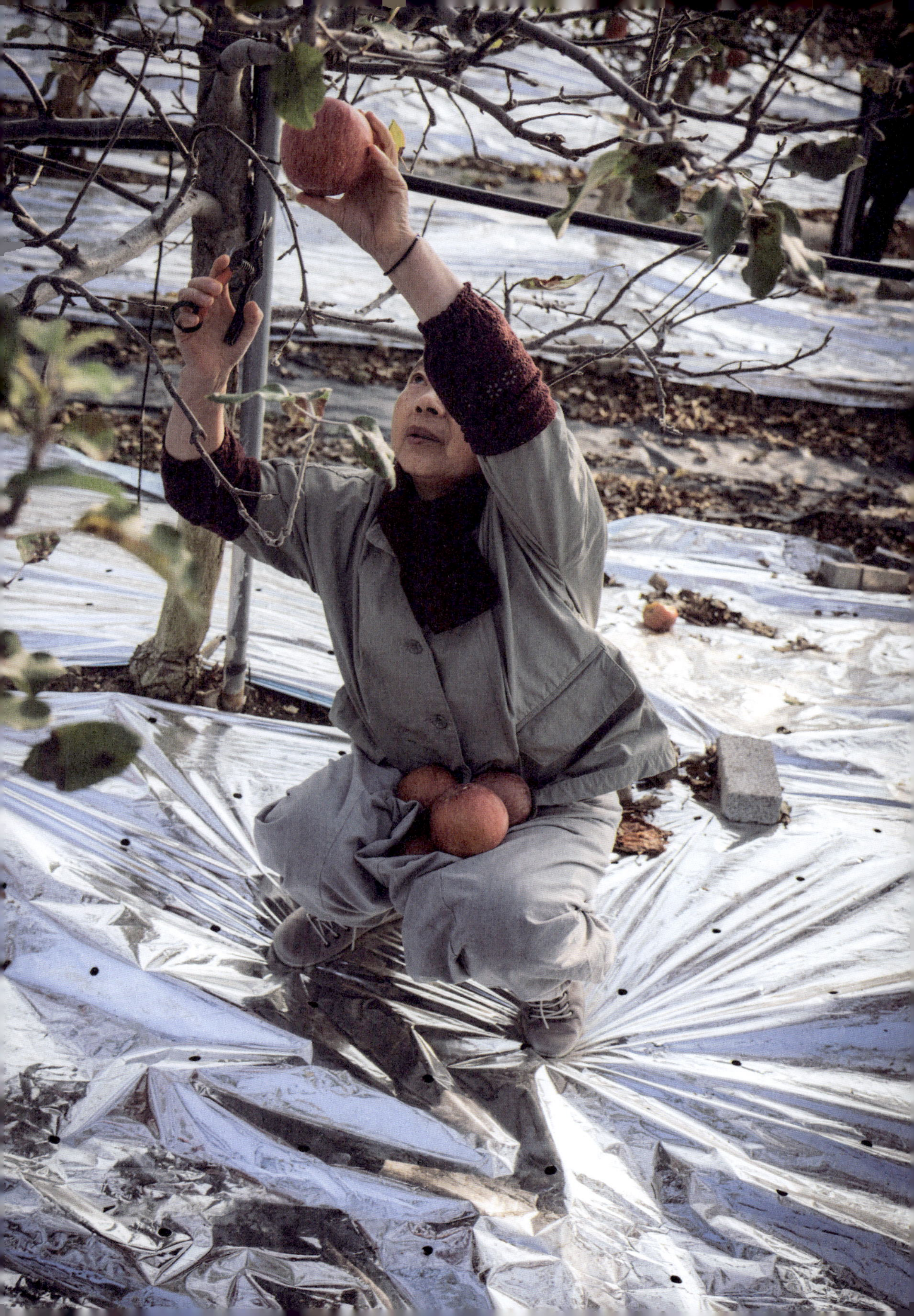

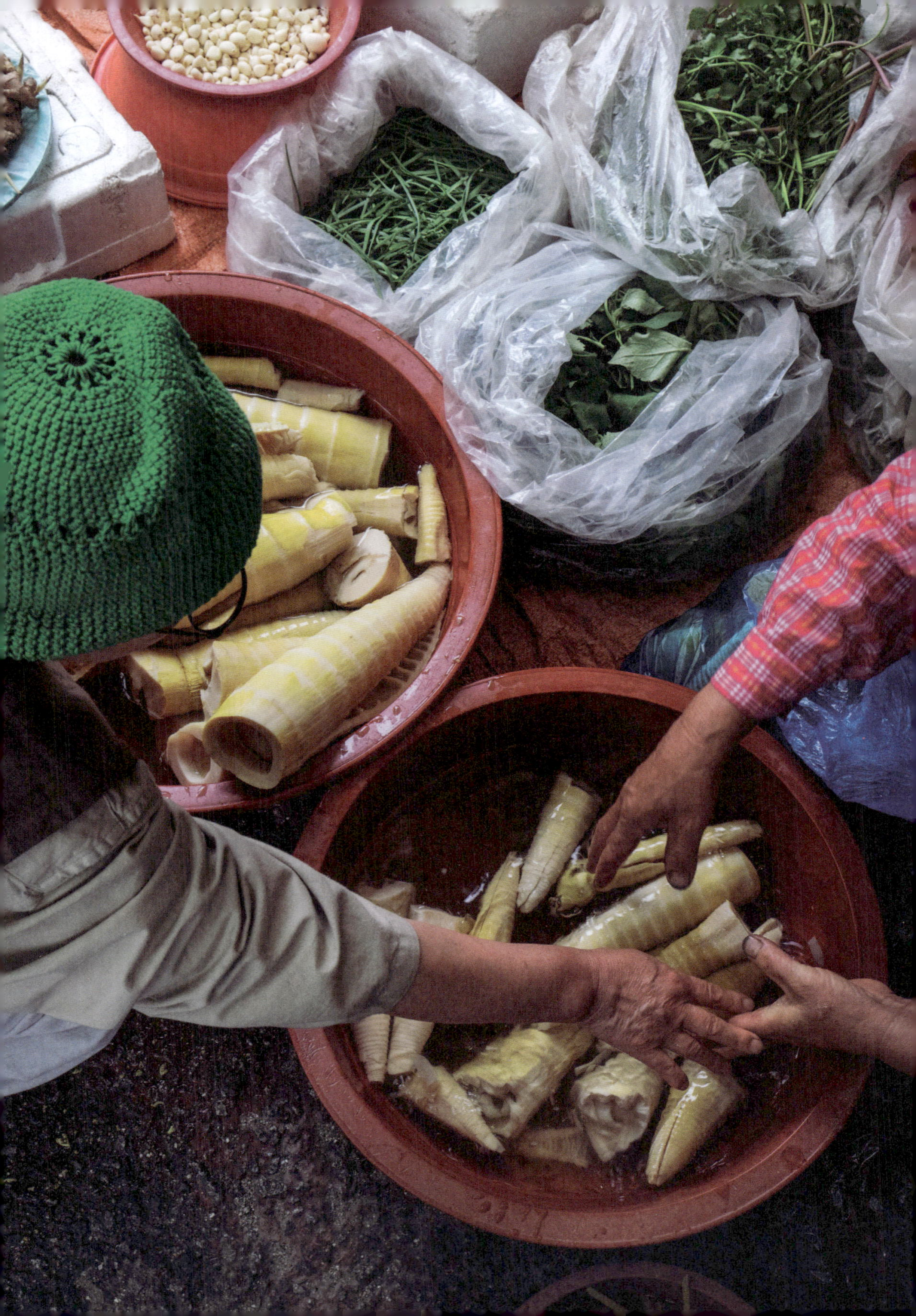

Beoseot see Mushrooms
Bit see Red beet
Bitter orange (taengja and **Taengja-Cheong)** see page 168
Blackberry (bokbunja and **Bokbunja-Cheong)** see page 180

Buckwheat (maemil): Buckwheat (which is a pseudocereal rather than a grain) is cultivated extensively and used in a variety of ways in Korea. It thrives easily all over the country, even in mountainous areas. In September, buckwheat plants bloom white and fields transform into lovely flowering meadows. (There's a famous Korean short story by Lee Hyo-Seok titled "When Buckwheat Flowers Bloom.") Noodles made from dark buckwheat flour (*maemil garu*) are very popular in summer dishes because they remove heat from the body. The noodles can be eaten either cold or in a warm broth. In Korea, buckwheat flour is also mixed with wheat flour and made into vegetable pancakes, and a pleasant, mild-flavored tea is made from toasted buckwheat. Buckwheat can also be fermented into liquor. Also note that despite its name, buckwheat is gluten-free.

Calabash (bak) see Squash
Calabaza squash (neulgeun-hobak) see Squash

Carrot (danggeun): Carrots can be used in a wide variety of ways. Julienned, briefly sautéed carrots are a bibimbap filling (page 232), or they can be diced and used in fried rice. They're also a must for juk (porridge), soups, and omelets. Due to their vibrant color, carrots are often added to other dishes.

Castor leaves (pimaja): In Korea, the leaves of the castor bean plant are picked in spring and eaten as a vegetable. Oil is derived from castor seeds.

Chajo see Millet
Chamgireum see Sesame seeds
Chapssalpul see Glutinous rice paste
Cheong (see page 167)
Cheongyanggochu see Chili

Chili (gochu): Gochu is considered to be an indispensable spice and is also popular as a vegetable. The word *gochu* covers a broad palette of different varieties: green, yellow, and red; large and small; spicy and mild. Each kind has its own name. Korean cuisine has many savory dishes that call for the spicier kinds. The powdered form (gochugaru) is needed to make the paste (gochujang) and kimchi. In short, different kinds of chili powder are used for different dishes.

Dried gochu can be ground fine (*goun-gochugaru*), medium, or coarse. Making gochujang requires a fine powder; making kimchi requires a medium powder. Sun-dried gochu (hoenari-gochu) are usually coarsely chopped or used whole. Less spicy varieties are eaten raw, steamed, pan-fried, grilled, or stuffed. The leaves are blanched and eaten as a vegetable. Bell peppers (*pimang*) are recent arrivals from the West and don't count as gochu.

Cheongyanggochu is a popular variety of chili from South Korea that's spicy yet also somewhat sweet and flavorful. (The spiciness protects the plant from predators.) Gochu is a popular addition to stews, meat dishes, and vegetables; it has antibacterial properties and helps preserve foods. Dried gochu is also kept and used in a variety of ways. One popular ingredient is *sil-gochu*, or "gochu threads," which are dried red gochu cut into extremely thin strips. *Kkwarigochu* is a small, somewhat wrinkly variety with a mild flavor. It's eaten steamed or sautéed.

Chili paste (gochujang): To make gochujang, boil 1 cup (200 g) of glutinous rice until al dente, then let it cool a bit. Add ⅔ cup (100 g) of barley malt powder, mix well, cover, and let the mixture ferment in a warm place for 2 hours. One after the other, add 2 ⅓ cups (300 g) fine chili powder, ⅓ cup (70 ml) jocheong, and 5 teaspoons (30 g) salt and mix well. Season to taste with salt. Transfer the paste into an earthenware container and leave it in a cool place for about 3 months to mature. Then it will be ready!

Chinese toon (gajuknamul): The young shoots of Chinese toon are called chamjuknamu in Korean. *Namu* means "tree" and *chamjuk* means "the true vegetable that snims eat." The leaves have a very distinct aroma and can be harvested from April to June. They stimulate the appetite and are considered a delicacy. They also contain a lot of vitamins and nutrients and serve as a healing plant. They're eaten as jangajji (page 161), as a vegetable, as bugak (page 262), and as jeon (pancakes). Gajuknamul combines well with soy sauce.

Chinese yam (ma): Ma is the root of the alpine plant known as Chinese yam. The root looks like a sweet potato, but it's white and slick when

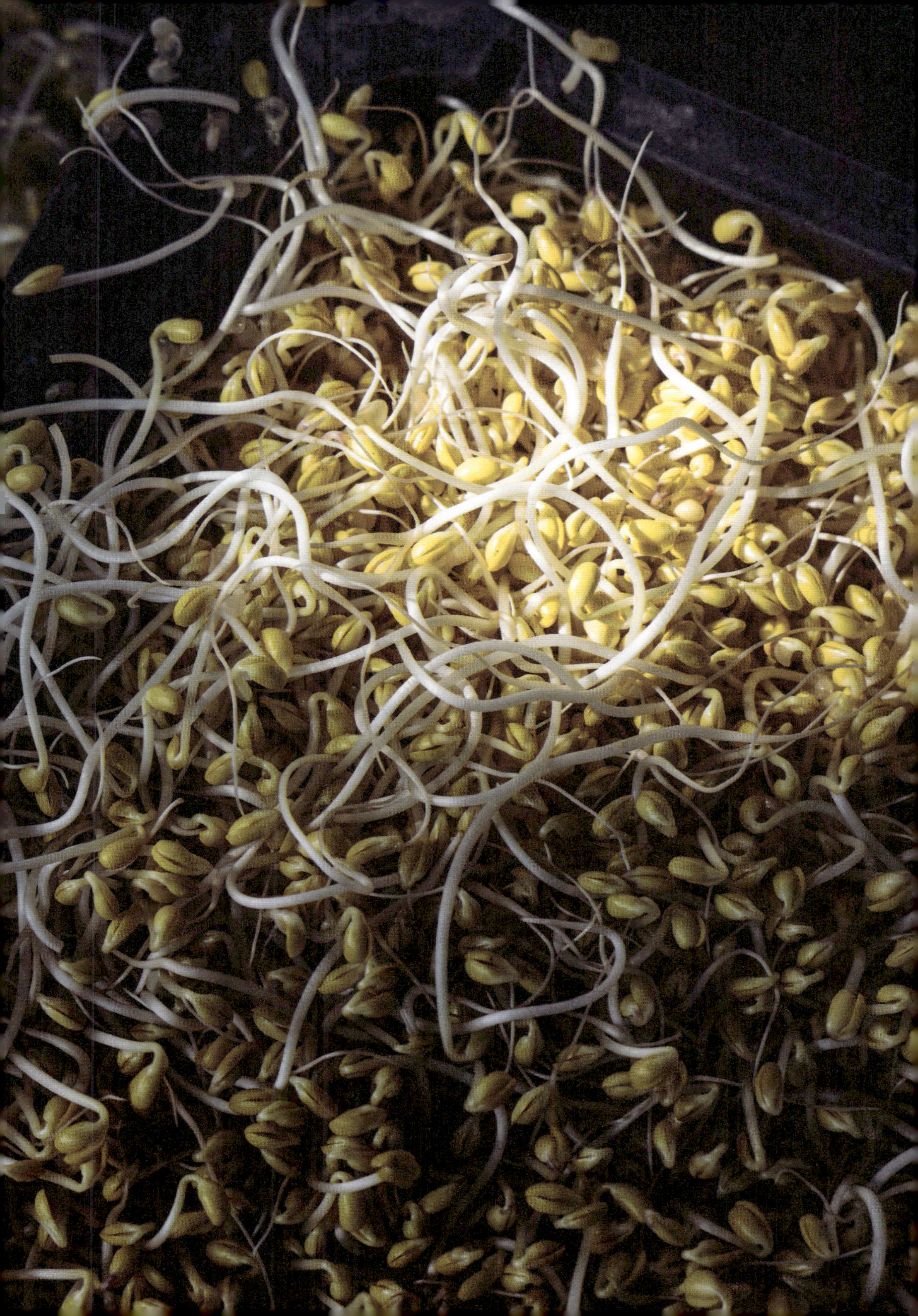

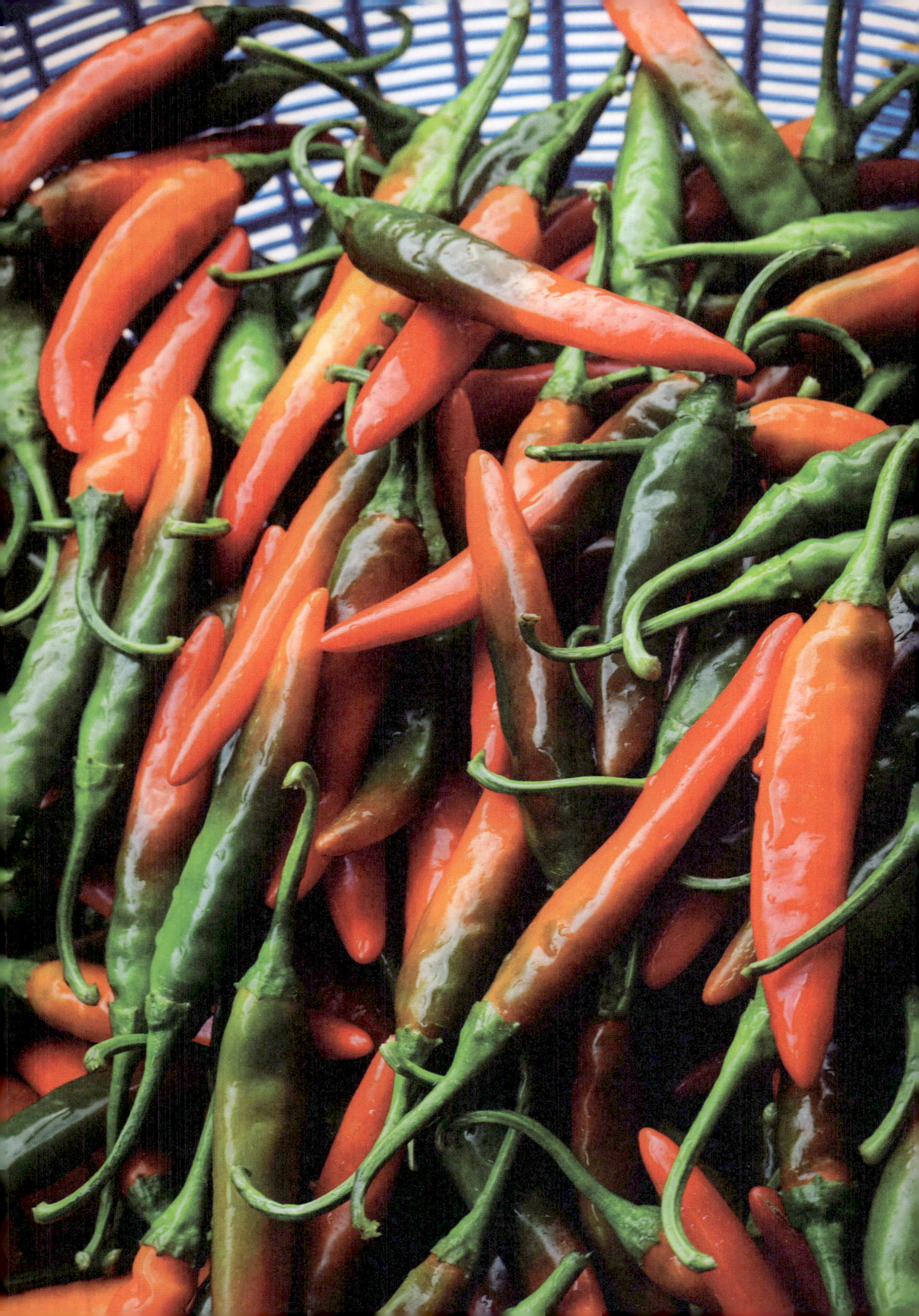

peeled. It can be eaten raw, steamed, or deep-fried, or it can be added to stew.

Chinamul see Korean aster scaber

Cucumber (oi): Korean cucumbers are easy to distinguish from the varieties available in the West: oi is light green, slim, and has a rather firmer flesh. It can be made into kimchi or a savory, spiced salad. Cucumber is a must for gimbap, and it can also be made into jangajji (page 161). Cucumbers can also simply be cut into spears and dipped in a sauce made from doenjang and sesame oil. The cucumber has a cooling effect in the body and is therefore a summer vegetable.

Daechu: Korean dates are red when ripe, and they taste sweet yet somewhat tart—an unusual and unique flavor. They can be eaten fresh, but they're usually eaten dried. Since time immemorial, daechu have been used medicinally for insomnia and rheumatism. They're rich in vitamins and help with colds because they warm the body from within. Tea made from daechu is one of the best-known traditional teas and is drunk during the winter months and when people have colds.

Daechus are added to many dishes to lend their sweet, characteristic flavor note. *Samgyetang* is a popular summer food prepared by slow-cooking an entire young hen in broth with ginseng and daechus. Beef ribs are braised with daechus for a dish known as *galbijjim*. Daechus are used as a filling for rice cakes, and rice can be steamed with daechus, chestnuts, raisins, and pine nuts. Daechus can also be used to make cookies and even liquor. They're indispensable in the preservation of meju in salt water as well as in the production of soy sauce and doenjang.

Danggeun see Carrot
Danhobak see Squash
Danmuji see Radish
Deulkkae see Perilla
Doenjang see page 138
Dubu and **sundubu** see page 99

Eggplant (gaji): Eggplant is one of the oldest kinds of vegetables in Korea—it was already known there in the sixth century. Korean cooks prefer the slender, dark purple or white oblong varieties as their inner flesh is white and tender and has few seeds. Eggplant was traditionally steamed, torn into pieces by hand, and served with a sauce. Today, it's also sautéed, grilled, or deep-fried. It combines very well with garlic and with beef. It can be cooked with rice, or it can be sliced and dried. Eggplant also makes very good kimchi.

Eunhaeng see Ginkgo

Fernbrake (gosari): Fernbrake is one of the most popular foods in Korea. There's a wide variety of fernbrake plants (360 varieties!), but only the young shoots of a particular type *(pteridium aquilinum var. latiusculum)* are eaten. Raw gosari is toxic—the young shoots must be cooked before they can be eaten. Gosari is also available dried. It must be soaked in water before being used in recipes. Gosari is eaten on holidays and is an important ingredient in bibimbap (page 232). It can be eaten as namul (page 105) or added to stew with meat. It contains vitamins B and C, calcium, and iron.

Five-flavor berry (omija and **Omija-Cheong)** see page 186
Gaji see Eggplant
Gam see Persimmon
Ganghwang see Turmeric
Ganjang see page 137

Gardenia (chija): *Chija* is the fruit of a tree that belongs to the gardenia family and is native to East Asia. The blossoms are white and the ripe fruit is orange. The flowers have a similar fragrance to jasmine. The fruits have been used as a remedy in traditional medicine since ancient times because among other things, they reduce fevers. And because chija fruits create a fiery or reddish-yellow color, they've also been used as a food coloring and to dye paper and textiles. Radish pickled in chija water (called *danmuji*) is known for its intense yellow color and is a popular food.

Gat see Mustard greens
Gijang see Millet
Gim see Seaweed

Ginger (saenggang): For more than 1,000 years, this tuberous root has often been used in Korean cooking and also medicinally. Ginger warms

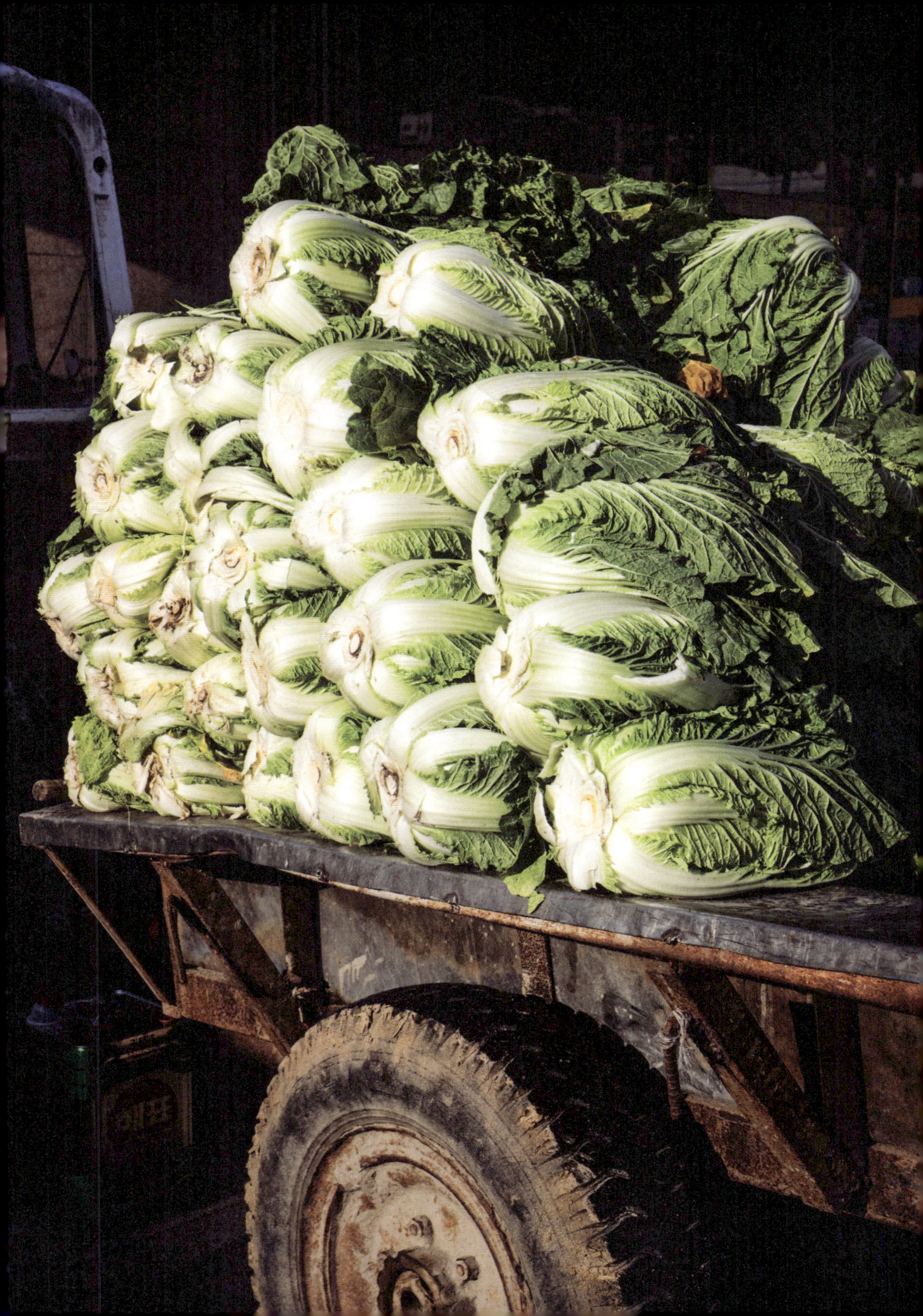

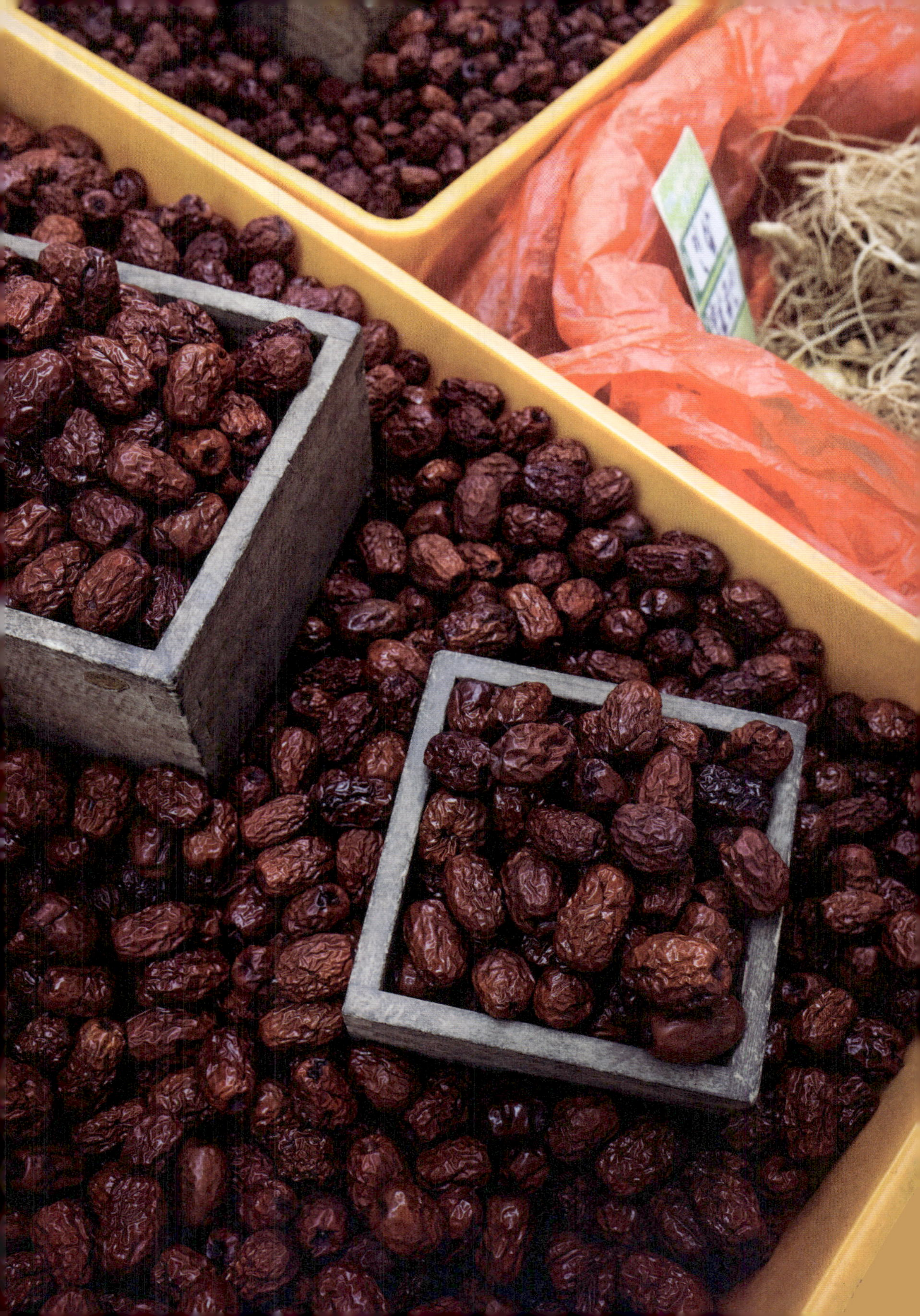

the body from the inside, so it's good if someone has a cold. For someone with cold feet or hands, ginger can help, too. The spicy root lends a special character to dishes—ginger and ginger juice are important flavorings for kimchi. Along with garlic, onion, and leek, ginger helps temper and neutralize the smell of meat, and tea and liquor are also made from ginger. In East Asia, myoga ginger (*yangha*) is a local variant prepared as a vegetable. Sugared ginger slices called *pyengang* are a popular snack in winter.

To make pyengang, peel 14 ounces (400 g) ginger and slice it diagonally into ⅛-inch (3 mm) pieces. Let the ginger slices sit in water for 2 hours, changing the water periodically. Pour out the water and boil the ginger for 15 minutes in a pot of fresh water, then pour off the water again. In a pan, cook the ginger with 1 cup plus 3 tablespoons (235 g) sugar over medium heat until a foam forms. Reduce the heat and stir continually to prevent the ginger from burning. When the syrup has boiled down and crystallized, turn off the stove and continue to stir. Spread the ginger slices on a rack, shake off the remaining sugar, and let the slices dry for about an hour. The rest of the sugar can be used in another dish. Store the ginger slices in a lidded glass container.

Ginkgo (eunhaeng): In Korea, the nuts of the ginkgo tree (called *eunhaeng*) are eaten. Ginkgoes are one of the oldest trees on Earth, and today, the trees are planted in cities because they're so robust and their leaves turn a beautiful gold in autumn. Their nuts have a soft outer shell and a hard nut inside. Unfortunately, they smell very unpleasant when they ripen and fall from the trees, and the soft outer shell is toxic and can cause an allergic reaction. Because of this, ginkgo nuts shouldn't be picked up with bare hands. However, once the nuts are rinsed and then dried and cracked open, they taste wonderful when sautéed or grilled. They're often mixed into rice, rice cakes, and meat dishes.

The nuts are used medicinally because they lower blood pressure and help open airways when someone is ill. But they must not be eaten raw! And you cannot eat too many at once: adults shouldn't eat more than ten nuts and children shouldn't eat more than five.

Ginseng (insam): This root is one of the most famous healing plants in Korea, and it's also an important and lucrative export. *Insam* means "human-shaped root"—when ginseng is several years old, the root actually does resemble a human form. Insam has been cultivated since 1392, but it was used in traditional medicine long before that. Previously, the plant only grew wild and was difficult to find, making the root very precious and costly. Even today, there are professional *sansam*, or "mountain ginseng" hunters.

Wild roots can cost tens of thousands of dollars—the older they are, the more expensive they are. The plant is sensitive to direct light, so cultivating it requires a lot of care. Although the root is most potent when it's six years old, it can be harvested and used as a cooking ingredient before then. Insam tastes very bitter, has a strong fragrance, and contains agents like ginsenoside that strengthen the immune system and support resistance to illness. Research has indicated that the root may have a positive impact on health and can protect the body from illness.

Fresh roots (*susam*) are breaded and deep-fried. They can also be added to *samgyetang*. Syrup is made from the juice of insam mixed with honey, and the roots are steamed and dried several times to make *hongsam* (red ginseng) or *heugsam* (black ginseng). Thinly sliced ginseng preserved in honey is a popular treat, and it's also made into candy.

Glasswort (hamcho): In English, this plant is known as glasswort or sea asparagus. The Korean name comes from its salty flavor. Hamcho grows in seawater or along the coast and is green in spring and summer but dark red in autumn. The saltier the ground is where it grows, the more the plant thrives and the more it's able to absorb minerals from the soil. This characteristic makes hamcho a particularly healthy food. The tender parts of the plant can be eaten as a vegetable or made into a salad. In Korea, it's also ground into a powder to be taken medicinally. Hamcho has been an important ingredient in East Asian traditional medicine since ancient times; it's considered to be effective against respiratory disease, high blood pressure, and diabetes and especially constipation and bowel blockage. Jeongkwan Snim likes to use hamcho as a vegetable, and she also makes cheong from it.

Glutinous rice paste (chapssalpul): Glutinous rice is a variety of rice with a matte white color and a unique characteristic: it's very starchy due to its high amylopectin content, so it becomes very sticky when cooked. In Korea, paste made out of powdered glutinous rice is called *chapssalpul*, which is properly translated as "glutinous rice paste." In the past, it was used as a paper adhesive in Korea.

Glutinous rice paste has two primary functions in the preparation of kimchi. One is that it helps the various sauce ingredients mix

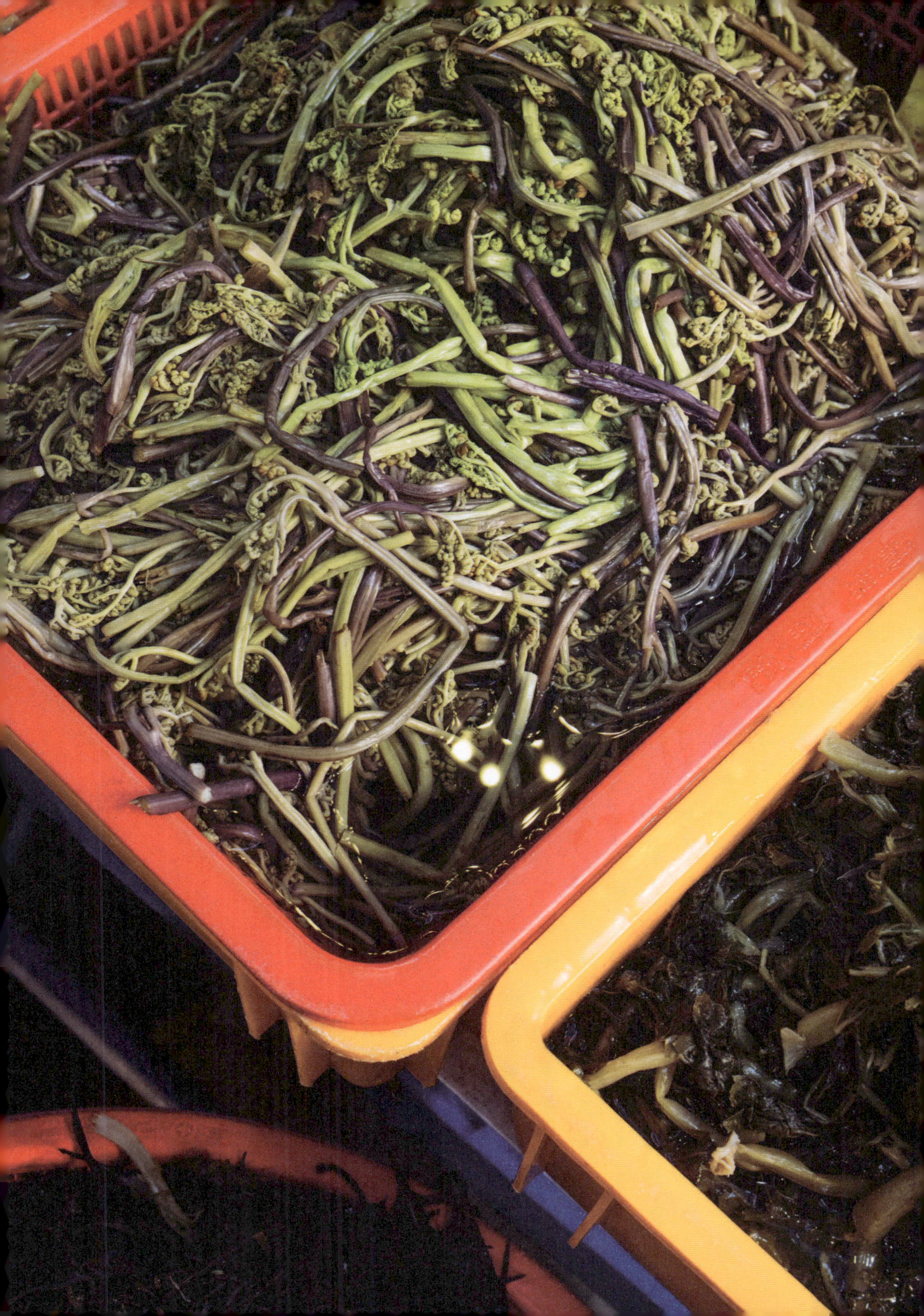

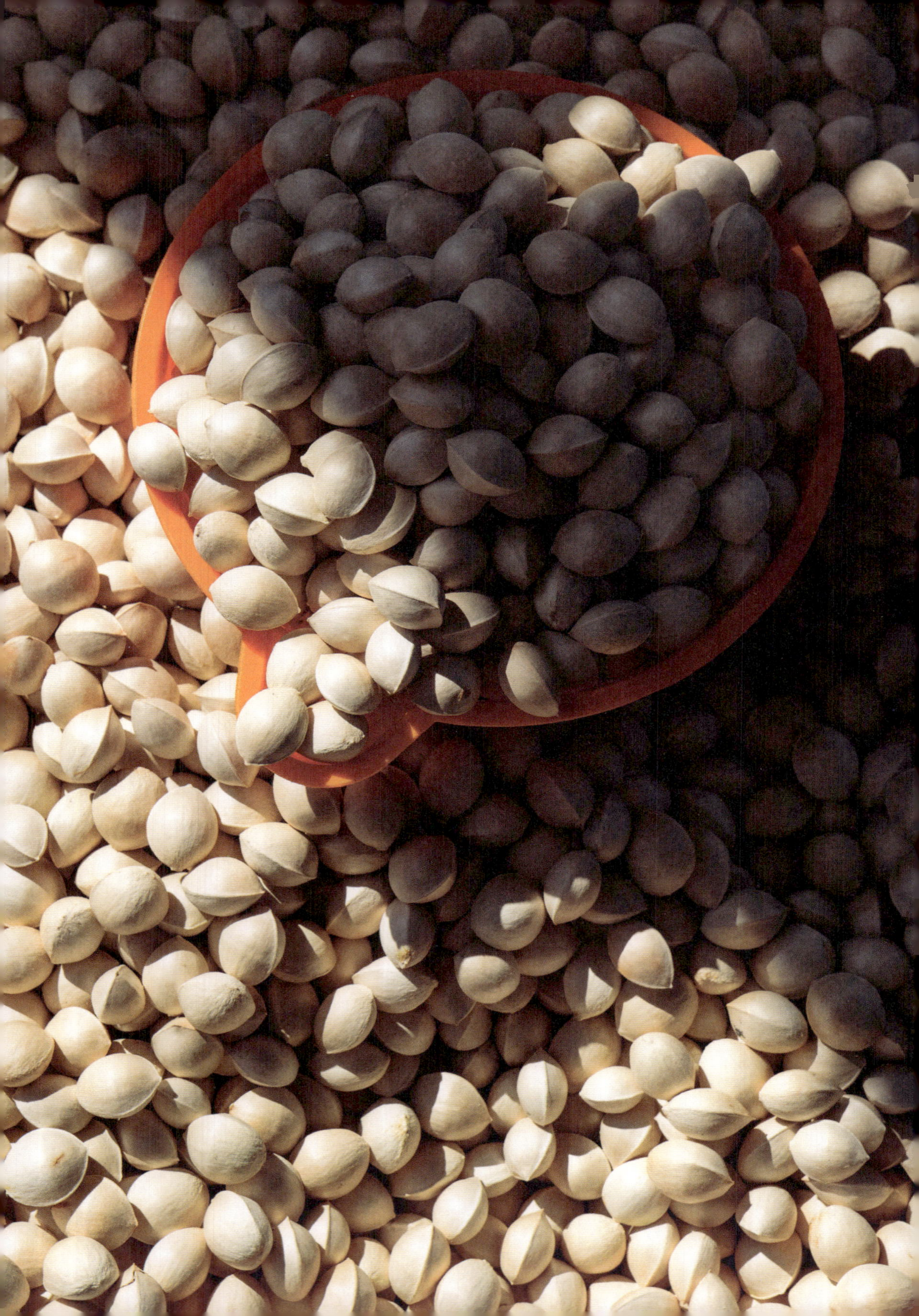

uniformly and make the sauce creamier. This is especially important when it comes to the chili powder (gochugaru), which must not clump. That's why the chili powder is usually mixed with the paste before the other ingredients are added. The other function is to promote fermentation. (Other grains do this as well.)

To prepare glutinous rice paste, slowly bring 1 tablespoon glutinous rice flour and ½ cup (125 ml) water to a boil over medium heat, stirring constantly, until a uniform paste forms. It will taste mild and lightly sweet. Once cooled, it will form the basis for the kimchi sauce yangnyeomjang.

Gosari see Fernbrake
Goun-gochugaru, gochu, gochugaru, and **gochujang** see Chili

Grains: Grain varieties like rice, barley, wheat, millet, and corn have traditionally been grown in Korea, but the country grew very little rye and oats—those were introduced later. Historically, not much wheat has been grown; without a bread-baking tradition, there wasn't much use for wheat. Wheat flour was primarily used to produce noodles and yeast doughs that were filled with beans and steamed.

Greater burdock (ueong): *Ueong* is a round, crunchy root. It can be eaten steamed, braised, deep-fried, or simply seasoned. It's very good in gimbap, in *jjigae* (page 304), and in a stew called *jeongwol*.

Green cabbage (yangbaechu): This variety of cabbage isn't native to Korea, where it's called *yangbaechu*. Things that come from the West usually bear the prefix "yang," which means "came from across the ocean." (What's called baechu in Korea is called napa cabbage in the West.) Today, green and red cabbages have a variety of uses in Korean cooking, from being used to make kimchi to being eaten raw, steamed, sautéed, pickled as jangajji (page 161), or cooked as ssam (page 432).

Hamcho see Glasswort
Heugimja see Sesame seeds
Hobak see Squash
Hoenari-gochu see Chili
Insam see Ginseng
Jangajji see page 161
Jocheong see page 190

Glossary of Ingredients — 415

Juksun see Bamboo shoot
Kabocha squash (danhobak) see Squash
King oyster mushroom (saesongi beoseot) see Mushrooms
Kkae see Sesame seeds
Kong and **kongnamul** see Beans

Korean aster scaber (chinamul): Korean aster scaber is a type of wild spring namul that's now cultivated because there's such a great demand for it. It's considered to be very healthy because it contains high levels of calcium, iron, and vitamin A. Because chinamul is particularly tasty and aromatic, the leaves and stems are eaten fresh as a salad green, or they're fried, pickled, or blanched and then served with a sauce. *Chinamulbap*—chinamul cooked with rice—is popular in spring. Chinamul is also used as a remedy for pain and when someone has an iron deficiency or bowel inflammation.

Lemon (yuja): *Yuja* is the Korean lemon that's used to make cheong (page 167). The lemon is washed, sliced, and preserved with sugar. This preserve can then be enjoyed primarily as tea in the winter months by stirring a spoonful of it into hot water. If the preserved yuja is left to sit for longer than three years, it will ferment and become cheong. In Western markets, this kind of lemon is sometimes labeled with the Japanese name, yuzu.

Lotus root (yeongeun): Lotus grows in ponds and blooms in the summer. Nearly every part of the plant is used: the root, the seeds, the leaves, and the flowers. The root is harvested in late October and early November. Its white inner flesh is shot through with many holes—the quality of a given root is judged by how uniform its holes are. To get rid of its slightly bitter taste, the root should be peeled and then immediately placed in salted water (or water mixed with vinegar). Although it's quite crisp and sweet when fresh, the root should not be eaten raw. It can be eaten braised, deep-fried, or steamed, or it can be prepared as soup, salad, or kimchi. It can also be cooked with rice. Because lotus root is starchy, its starch is also used to make juk. Its leaves can be wrapped around prepared rice and steamed.

Lotus root is a traditional medicinal remedy and is effective against cough and nausea. It also helps wounds heal faster and promotes circulation.

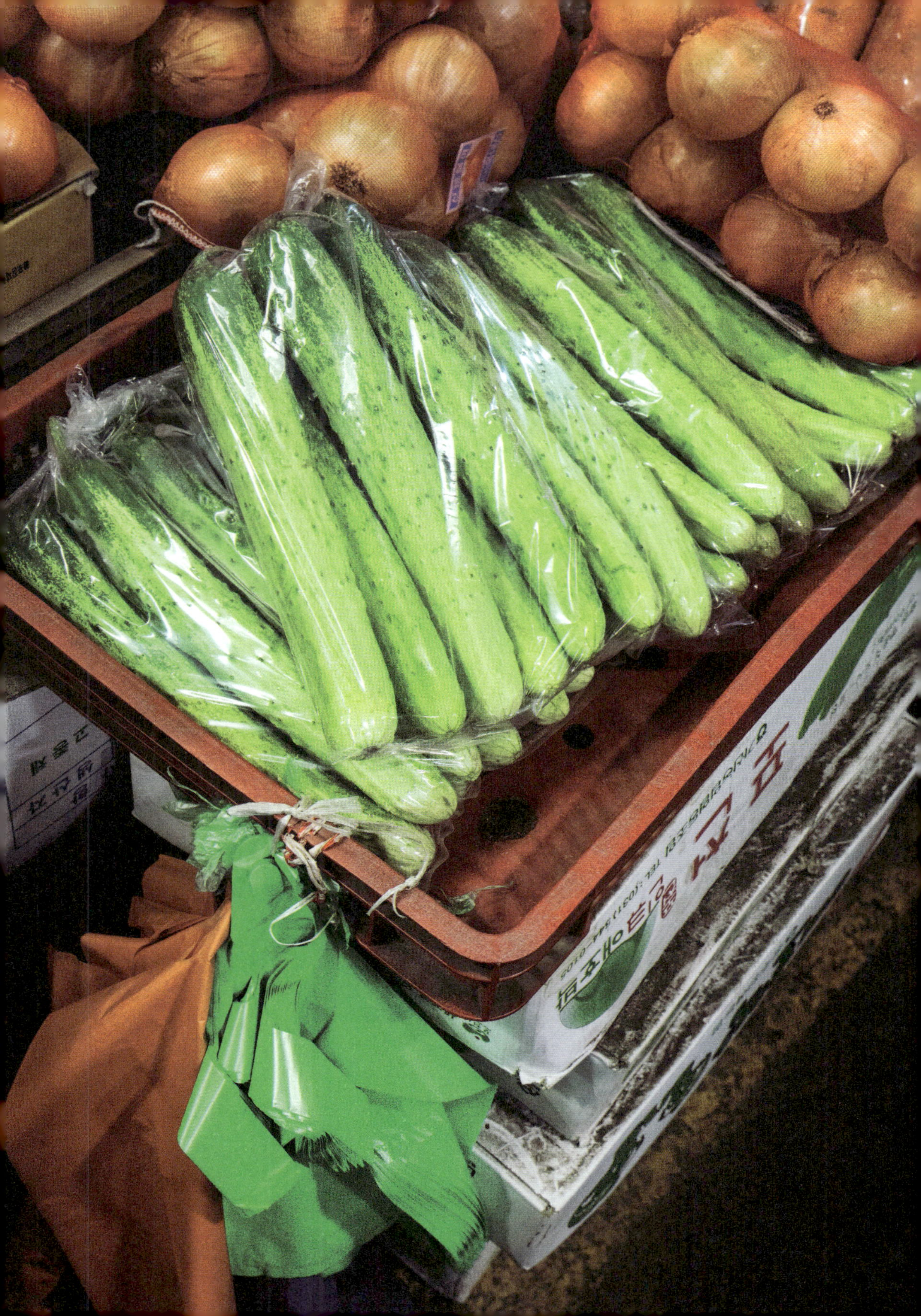

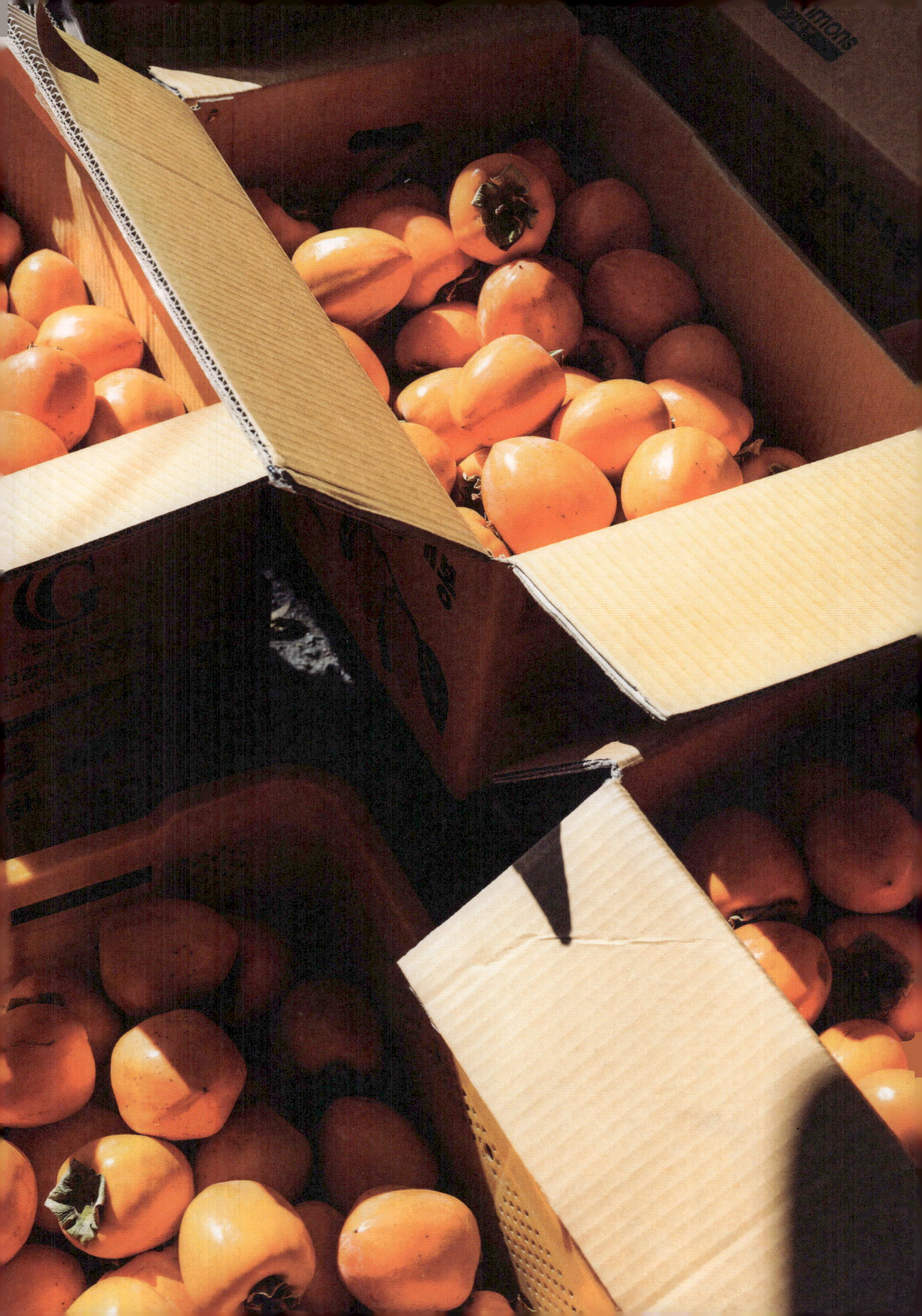

Because the lotus represents the Buddha, it symbolizes Buddhism. Its roots, leaves, and flowers are often used in temple cooking, especially the roots. Tea is made from its flowers; they have a lovely aroma that also symbolizes Buddhism.

Ma see Chinese yam
Maemil and **maemil garu** see Buckwheat
Maesil and **Maesil-Cheong** see page 174
Meju see page 137

Millet (gijang, chajo): Millet is a type of grain that's been grown in Korea for a long time. Some types of millet feature yellow grains; some feature green grains that are aromatic and contain more starch. Millet is cooked with rice or can be made into cakes, syrup, or liquor. Like buckwheat, millet is gluten-free.

Minari see Water celery
Mogi beoseot see Mushrooms
Mu and **musun** see Radish
Mung beans (nokdu) see Beans

Mushrooms (beoseot): Korea is home to many types of mushrooms—about 1,100. Of those, about 30 are eaten. Mushrooms appear on Korean tables a lot more frequently than they do in the West. Some popular varieties include chanterelles (in Korean, "nightingale mushroom"), *neutari beoseot* (oyster mushroom), *yeonggi beoseot* (said to prevent aging), *paengi beoseot* (enoki mushroom), *mogi beoseot* (wood ear), *neungi beoseot* (shingled hedgehog mushroom), morel, shimeji, *saesongi beoseot* (king oyster mushroom), clustered coral, *pyogo beoseot* (shiitake), and white button mushrooms.

Songi beoseot (pine mushrooms) are popular and are foraged in pine forests in autumn. They're considered to be a delicacy because they possess a distinctive pine flavor. No one has managed to cultivate them, though, so they're only available in the wild. This makes them especially valuable. These mushrooms are eaten sautéed on their own or with meat or tofu. They can also be braised.

White button mushrooms recently came to Korea from the West and are called *yangsongi beoseot. Yang* indicates goods that have come from the West. Mushrooms that are called king oyster in English-speaking countries are called saesongi beoseot in Korea; the syllable *sae* means "new."

Glossary of Ingredients — 419

Pyogo beoseot grows on the dead trunks of oak and chestnut trees and can only be harvested in spring. It's considered to be the king of mushrooms. During the winter months, these mushrooms gather their energy before emerging in spring. It takes two or three years for them to send up their fruiting bodies, so they're an expensive mushroom variety. They contain a lot of protein and are very tasty. (Jeongkwan Snim's dish of braised pyogo-beoseot is famous!) Pyogo beoseot are used often in temple cooking and are said to be useful against high blood pressure and colds.

Different kinds of mushrooms are prepared in different ways: they can be sautéed, braised, steamed, or grilled, or they can be included in soups, jjigae (page 304), and stews. Many varieties are also dried. Virtually all mushrooms have curative effects and are used in traditional medicine.

Mustard greens (gat): *Gat* is a leafy green whose seeds are made into mustard. Gat can also be made into kimchi, and its leaves can be eaten in salads or as a vegetable. They have a distinct, slightly spicy flavor.

Myoga ginger (yangha) see Ginger

Napa cabbage (baechu): Baechu is the most important variety of cabbage in Korea because it's used to make kimchi. When it came to Korea via China at the end of the nineteenth century, the cabbage was small and slender, but the modern-day baechu that's cultivated in Korea is a large, heavy variety with mild, sweet, slightly nutty-tasting leaves. The yellow inner leaves in particular are crispy and very sweet.

In late autumn, when everyone's making kimchi, heaps of baechu are in stores. As kimchi makes it obvious, baechu pairs very well with gochu. Baechu can also be made into soup when combined with doenjang (*baechuguk*), or it can be made into pancakes (*baechujeon*). It can also simply be sautéed and eaten. The dark green outer leaves are also collected, cooked, and dried (they're called *ugeoji*) and are used in soups and stews.

Koreans cannot do without kimchi! This makes the price of baechu a hot political topic—if the price increases too much, people talk about *geumchu*, or "gold baechu," and that can land the government in hot water. The Korean 10,000 *won* bill—which serves as a benchmark for price fluctuations—is greenish and known colloquially as a "baechu leaf."

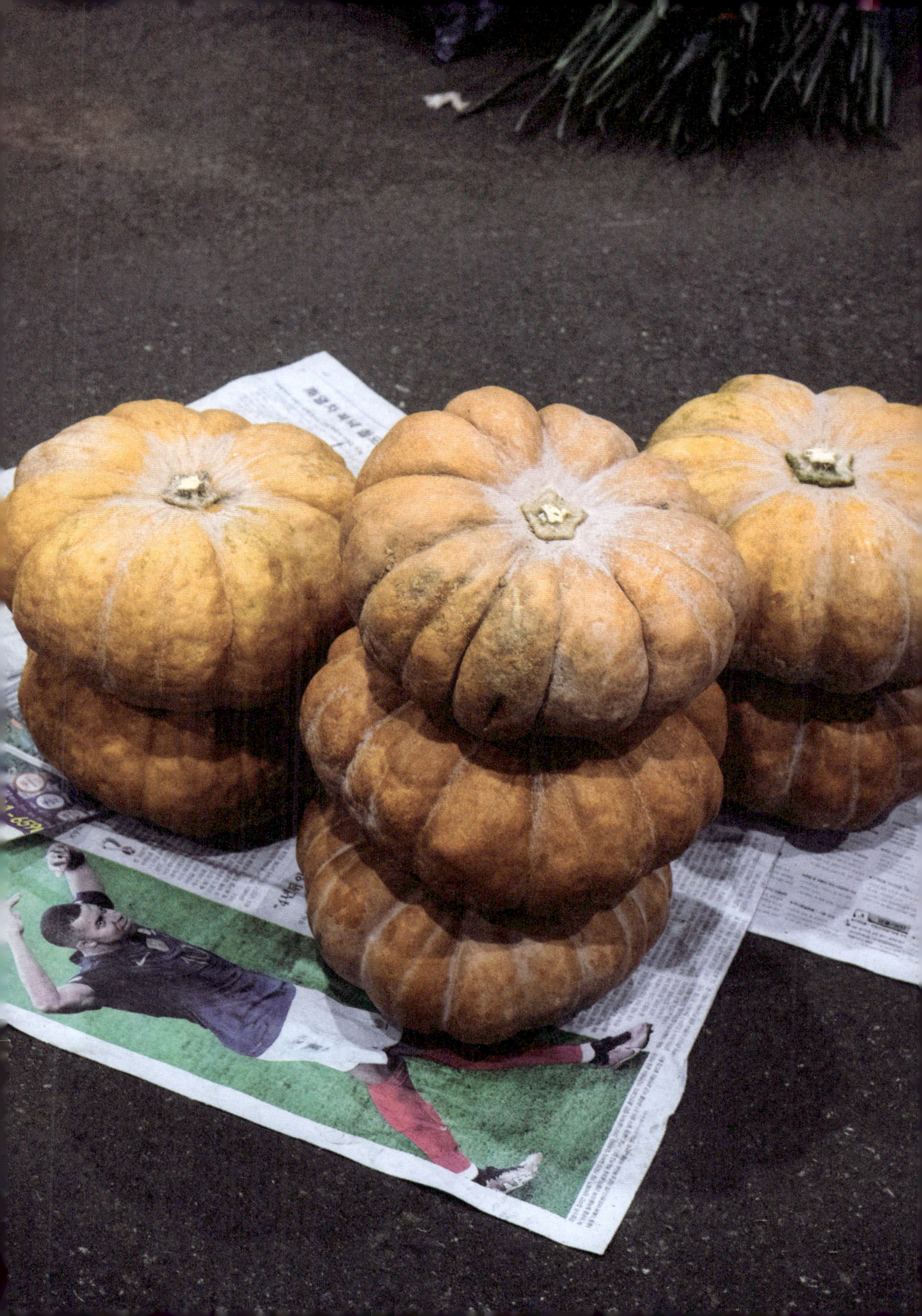

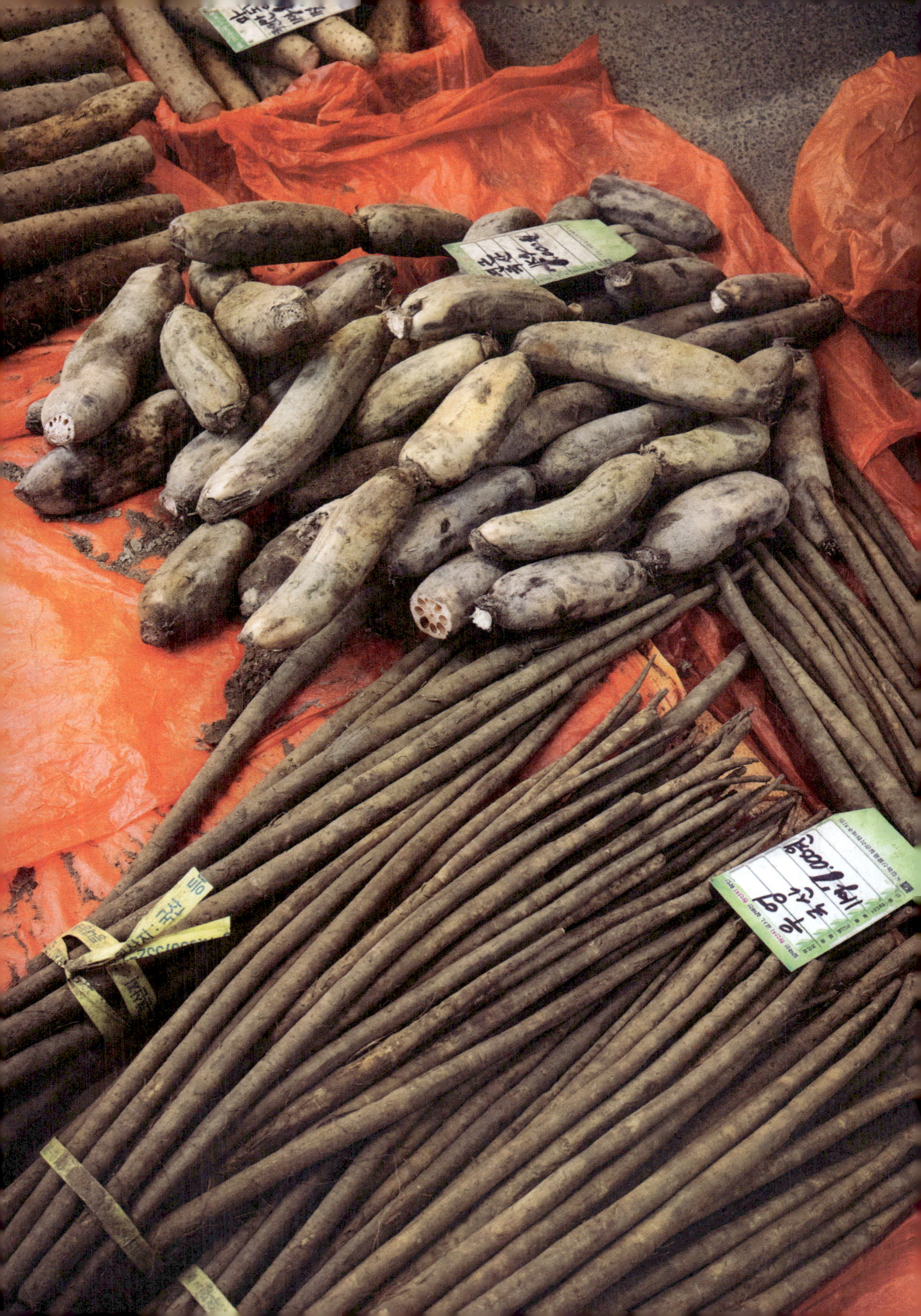

Neulgeun-hobak see Squash
Neungi beoseot and **neutari beoseot** see Mushrooms
Nurungji see Scorched rice
Oi see Cucumber
Omija and **Omija-Cheong** see page 186
Oyster mushrooms (neutari beoseot) see Mushrooms
Paran-tomato see Tomato
Pat see Beans

Pear (bae): The Korean pear (often called Asian pear in the West) is a local variant of the kind that's native to East Asia. It's large, bulbously round, tan with faint white spots, juicy, and sweet. Other varieties have almost disappeared because Koreans greatly prize this pear due to its sweet, fruity flavor. Bae is eaten as a fruit or used as an ingredient in cooking. It's an essential ingredient for kimchi sauce and in beef marinades.

Perilla (deulkkae): In Korea, perilla is called *deulkkae* or "meadow sesame" (meadow seeds) even though the two plants aren't related. (The leaves are sometimes erroneously called sesame leaves.) Perilla seeds are round and can be reddish-brown or gray-black. The flavor of sesame seeds and perilla have a certain similarity, but sesame's flavor is somewhat finer and subtler. The leaves of the perilla plant are eaten fresh as a salad or as ssam, but they're also treated as a vegetable and sautéed, deep-fried, or preserved as jangajji (page 161). Perilla seeds can be crushed into an aromatic oil that has a variety of uses. When they're toasted or crushed, the seeds can be used to season stews, noodles, soups, and vegetables. Note that they must be toasted with great care because they burn easily!

Perilla seeds, toasted: Toasting perilla seeds is comparable to toasting sesame seeds (page 431). Perilla seeds are somewhat softer, though, and during toasting, they should be stirred often and closely watched as they can easily burn and become bitter.

Persimmon (gam): Persimmon is a typical fall fruit in Korea. Different varieties have different shapes and flavors, but when persimmons are ripe, they turn orange. While the unripe fruits often have an unpleasantly bitter flavor, that can be removed by placing them in salted water. The two main varieties sold in the United States are fuyu and hachiya. Fuyu

Glossary of Ingredients — 423

persimmons are round and look like tomatoes; hachiya persimmons are pointed at the bottom. Fuyu persimmons have much lower levels of tannin than hachiya persimmons and consequently can be less bitter. They can be eaten raw, or peeled and dried, either whole or in slices. The dried fruit can also be used in salads or served as a dessert. Persimmons are also fantastic for making vinegar and sauces for kimchi.

Plum (maesil and **Maesil-Cheong)** see page 174

Potato (gamja): The potato is native to the Andes mountains in South America; it came to Korea via China at the beginning of the nineteenth century. (Corn and sweet potatoes came to the country somewhat earlier than that.) Today, potatoes are prepared and eaten as a vegetable in a variety of ways: steamed, boiled, and braised; sliced thinly, sautéed, and seasoned. Potatoes can be finely grated and made into pancakes, or they can be added to stews with other vegetables. Some steamed cakes are made from potato flour and filled with beans. Most recently, French fries have made their way to Korea.

Pyogo beoseot see Mushrooms

Radish (mu): Korean cooking uses radishes much more frequently than Western cooking does. Not surprisingly, there's a correspondingly greater variety of radishes in Korean cuisine. Not only is the root used, but also the leaves, which are called *mucheong* or "radish greens." A Korean type of white radish that's somewhat rounder and juicier and with a sweeter flavor is popular. It's used to make radish kimchi, kkakdugi, or *dongchimi*, a mild radish water kimchi. Kimchi made this way is considered to be the original kimchi because napa cabbage only came to Korea in the nineteenth century. Mu is also grated or finely chopped and then added to Baechu Kimchi (page 126). Because radish neutralizes both fish and meat odors, it's a popular addition to dishes with those ingredients. Mu tastes good in soup, stews, and jjigae (page 304). Radish is also cut into slices, dried, and eaten during the winter.

The stems and leaves of the white radish (called *siraegi*) are dried whole in the sun and boiled in soups and stews in the winter. Siraegi combines well with doenjang. Danmuji, or white radish pickled in a vinegar-sugar-water mixture and dyed yellow with gardenia (chija) is popular. Radish sprouts (*musun*) are used as an ingredient or garnish.

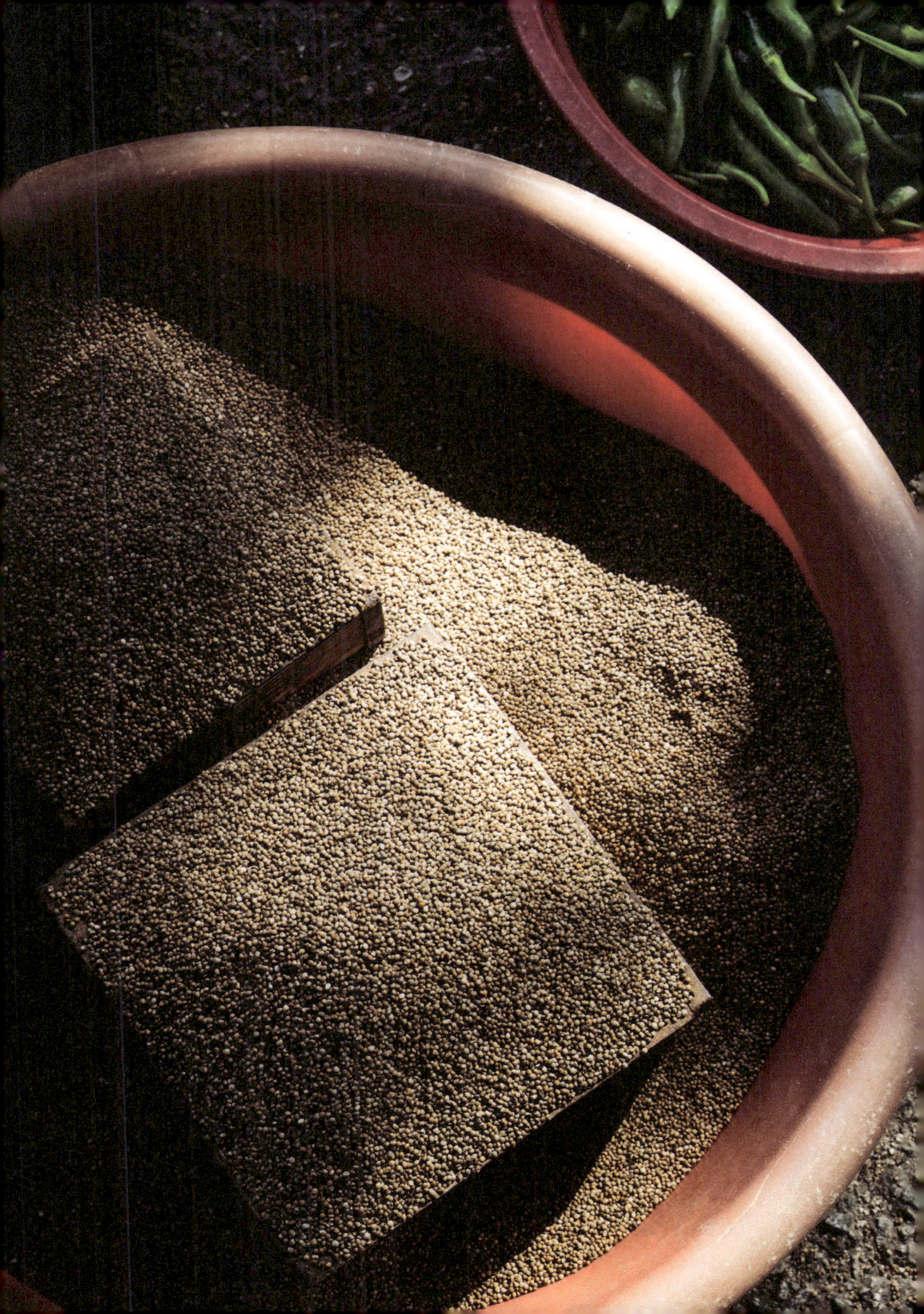

표고 (제주산)
10,000

10kg

Some radish varieties are smaller. The whole radish and the leaves of one smaller variety are made into a popular kind of kimchi called *chonggak* kimchi, which means "bachelor kimchi." Another variety, *yeolmu*, has a very small root but long leaves. The entire plant is used to make yeolmu kimchi. It's mild, not spicy, and it's served with noodle dishes, steamed sweet potatoes, or rice cakes. The saying "Do not drink the kimchi liquid when no one is thinking of giving you rice cakes" is based on yeolmu kimchi. That means one should not rush to be happy about something that's not yet definite. This kind of kimchi is a bit watery and goes well with dishes that are dry or that contain a lot of carbohydrates.

Red beet (bit): Although this root vegetable is relatively new to Korea, it has become quite popular. It can be pickled or eaten in salad or as a vegetable.

Rice see page 83

Rice cakes (tteok): The word translated as "rice cakes" doesn't actually represent a baked good, but rather a steamed, rice flour-based food. Many varieties exist: rice cakes with filling made from red beans (pat), nuts, honey, chestnuts, and sesame seeds, and rice cakes mixed with squash, mugwort, dried fruits, and beans. The simplest variety, called *garaetteok*, is made of a dough consisting of rice flour and water that's shaped into a cylinder and then steamed. After that, the garaetteok is sliced diagonally, dried, or deep-frozen. These slices are called *tteokguk tteok* and are used for the dish tteokguk.

Rice Syrup (Jocheong) see page 190
Saenggang see Ginger
Saesongi beoseot see Mushrooms
Sagwa see Apple

Salt (sogeum): In Korea, salt is primarily derived from seawater and salt fields. Today, there are also newer methods for pumping out clean deep-sea water and extracting the mineral-rich salt via a special process that involves evaporating the water with hot air. Jeongkwan Snim buys a large quantity of sea salt at once and stores it for many years to dry it. The remaining water in the salt evaporates completely, and the salt feels crunchier and tastes more pure.

Since salt is necessary for life, it has taken on a variety of cultural meanings. In Korea, great purifying power is attributed to salt, so to this day, when someone walks away from an argument, it's customary to loudly call out that "a ton of salt should be scattered!" to express annoyance.

Sansho see page 280

Scorched rice (nurungji): *Nurungji* refers to the thin layer of rice that remains in the pot after the rice has been cooked and removed. This layer especially used to form when rice was cooked in a cast iron pot. The lightly browned layer of leftover rice could be loosened and eaten in small pieces like crackers. Today, however, rice is cooked in rice cookers, where nurungji won't form. Some time ago, a nostalgic trend emerged to make nurungji artificially. It can be eaten like a cracker, boiling water can be poured over it to make a beverage, or it can be added to stews.

Seaweed (miyeok, gim): *Miyeok*, also known as *wakame* in Japan, is one of the better known types of edible algae. When it's fresh, it's light or dark green, but when it's dried, it looks almost black. It grows on the ocean floor in shallow, rapidly flowing water with a lot of sunlight and botanically falls into a division called *thallophytes*.

The leaves reach a length of between 20 and 31 inches (50 and 80 cm). In Korea, the best miyeok comes from the southern coast, where it still grows natively and where it has been harvested the same way for 600 years: with long poles. Miyeok tastes like the ocean and has a somewhat slick mouthfeel. This algae has been eaten in Korea for a very long time—it was mentioned in a written chronicle as early as 1123. (After the birth of a prince, the mother received miyeok as a gift to help her heal faster.) Miyeok is rich in minerals, including iron, calcium, and iodine. To this day, women in Korea eat a soup called *miyeokguk* after childbirth, and everyone eats it on their birthday to commemorate this tradition.

Miyeok may be prepared in a variety of ways, including made into soup along with beef, tofu, or mushrooms. (Leek shouldn't be added since it doesn't pair well with miyeok.) Miyeok is also popular when made into *miyeokjuk*, a kind of porridge made with rice, and it can also be combined with minced beef and perilla seeds. Miyeok is popular as a vegetable: briefly blanch it in boiling water, rinse it in cold

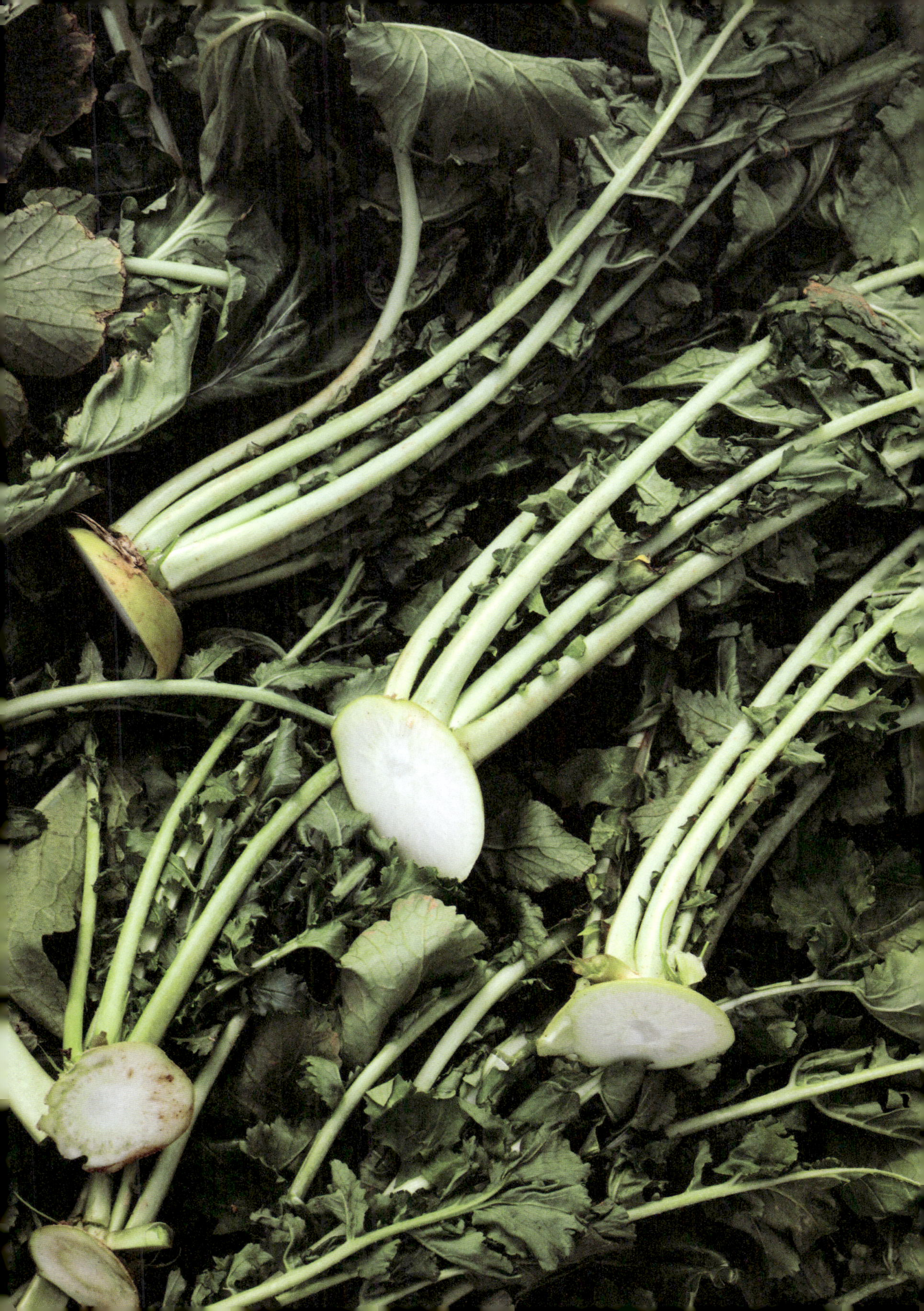

국산천일염

「소금산업진흥법」제37조에 따른 품질표시

염의 종류	식용 천일염
중 량	20 kg
생산년월	2017년 월
성분표시	NaCl 70% 이상
중금속 적합여부	적합
포장재질	폴리프로필렌

※ 보관 및 취급방법 ※

- 직사광선을 피하고 습기가 적은 곳에 보관하십시오.
- 본 제품은 장기간 보관하여도 품질에 이상이 없어 유통기한을 별도로 표기하지 않았습니다.
- 유통과정 중 간수가 빠지면 자연감량 될 수 있습니다.
- 순수자연에 의해서 생산된 (햇빛, 바람) 천일염이므로 이물질이 들어갈 수 있습니다.
- 본 제품은 소비자피해보상규정에 의거 교환 또는 보상받을 수 있습니다.
- 부정·불량식품 신고는 국번없이 1399번

생산지	전남 신안군
생산자	

water, squeeze out the liquid, and season it with soy sauce or vinegar mixed with gochujang. If you use dried miyeok, be careful with the quantity, because once it's soaked in water, it will expand a *lot*! Don't use too much of it.

Gim is a light red marine algae that grows on stones; today, it's cultivated on Korea's southern coast. (In the West, gim is known by its Japanese name of *nori*.) The young plants are formed into paper-thin squares and placed on straw or wooden mats to dry. Mineral-rich algae have been eaten in Korea since the sixth century. Today, gim is used along with rice and other ingredients to make gimbap, a traditional picnic food.

To prepare gim, the thin sheets are brushed with oil, sprinkled with a little salt, and quickly toasted or baked. The result is crispy sheets. That said, if gim is left uncovered for very long, it gets limp and soft. But when it's cut into small pieces, coated with glutinous rice paste, dried, and deep-fried, then gim becomes *gim bugak*, a tasty snack that's much less prone to softening. Noodles and tofu can be served garnished with crushed gim sprinkled on top. Korean gim has become very popular and is now exported all over the world.

Sesame seeds (kkae): There are two versions of sesame seeds: light beige and black (*heugimja*). Sesame has been used as a flavoring in Korea since ancient times; it's primarily paired with soy sauce and doenjang. Jeongkwan Snim likes both sesame seeds and sesame oil (*chamgireum*) and uses them often. Sesame seeds only show their real potential when they're toasted! That's when you can smell a distinct, unique aroma called *kkoso hada*. It's the epitome of deliciousness, although it's also used to convey a sense of schadenfreude. Because toasted sesame seeds taste so much better than untoasted seeds, in Korea, sesame oil is always extracted from toasted seeds.

Sesame seeds, toasted: Add a small quantity of seeds to a stainless steel pot and toast them over medium heat while stirring constantly. The seeds will gradually turn brown and begin to jump around. Don't let them get too brown! They'll become bitter. Remove them from the stove and let them cool a bit, then use a mortar and pestle to grind them. It's said that the seeds taste best and are easiest for the body to absorb when they're crushed but not completely crushed into powder. It's best to prepare sesame seeds fresh whenever you need them, but if you've toasted more seeds than you need at the moment, you can mix a little

Glossary of Ingredients — 431

salt with the leftover seeds and store them in a small glass container for later use. The toasted and cooled seeds can also be fully ground in a mill.

Shiitake mushroom (pyogo beoseot) see Mushrooms
Shingled hedgehog mushrooms (neungi beoseot) see Mushrooms
Sigeumchi see Spinach
Sil-gochu see Chili
Soybeans (kong), soybean sprouts (kongnamul), soybean powder, and **soybean oil** see Beans
Soybean paste (doenjang) see page 138
Soy sauce (ganjang) see page 137

Spinach (sigeumchi): Spinach is a popular vegetable. It's usually prepared by blanching it in boiling water, placing it briefly in cold water, and then squeezing it out. After that, it's seasoned with soy sauce, salt, toasted sesame seeds, and sesame oil. Spinach also pairs well with doenjang in soups.

Squash (hobak): Many different varieties of squash exist in Korea, although Koreans don't distinguish between zucchini and squash—zucchini is also considered hobak. Not only are the fruits of hobak varieties eaten, but also their flowers, seeds, and leaves.

Aehobak—or young, tender hobak—is the most commonly used variety. It's small and long and similar to zucchini, but it's light green and more tender. Aehobak also includes the small, round squash used for jjigae (page 304), jeon, and guk (soup). The large, yellow-brown wrinkled calabaza squash (*neulgeun-hobak*) is also popular. It tastes sweet and is therefore used in juk (page 212) or steamed. It's also mixed into rice cakes or baked into cakes, and it can also be made into kimchi. Syrup and tea are made from it.

Green kabocha squash (*danhobak*) is good when steamed, and the calabash (*bak*) is eaten as a vegetable when it's still young and tender. Squash can be dried for later use. Its leaves are eaten steamed as ssam. It can reduce edema, which is useful for women after childbirth.

Ssam: The word *ssam* actually means "to wrap"—in Korea, many green leaves are eaten wrapped around something, and those are collectively called ssam. Any salad green can be used for ssam, plus steamed squash leaves, napa cabbage, and green cabbage are also used. Grilled meat, mushrooms, vegetables, and rice can be eaten wrapped up, either alone

상긋
만 원

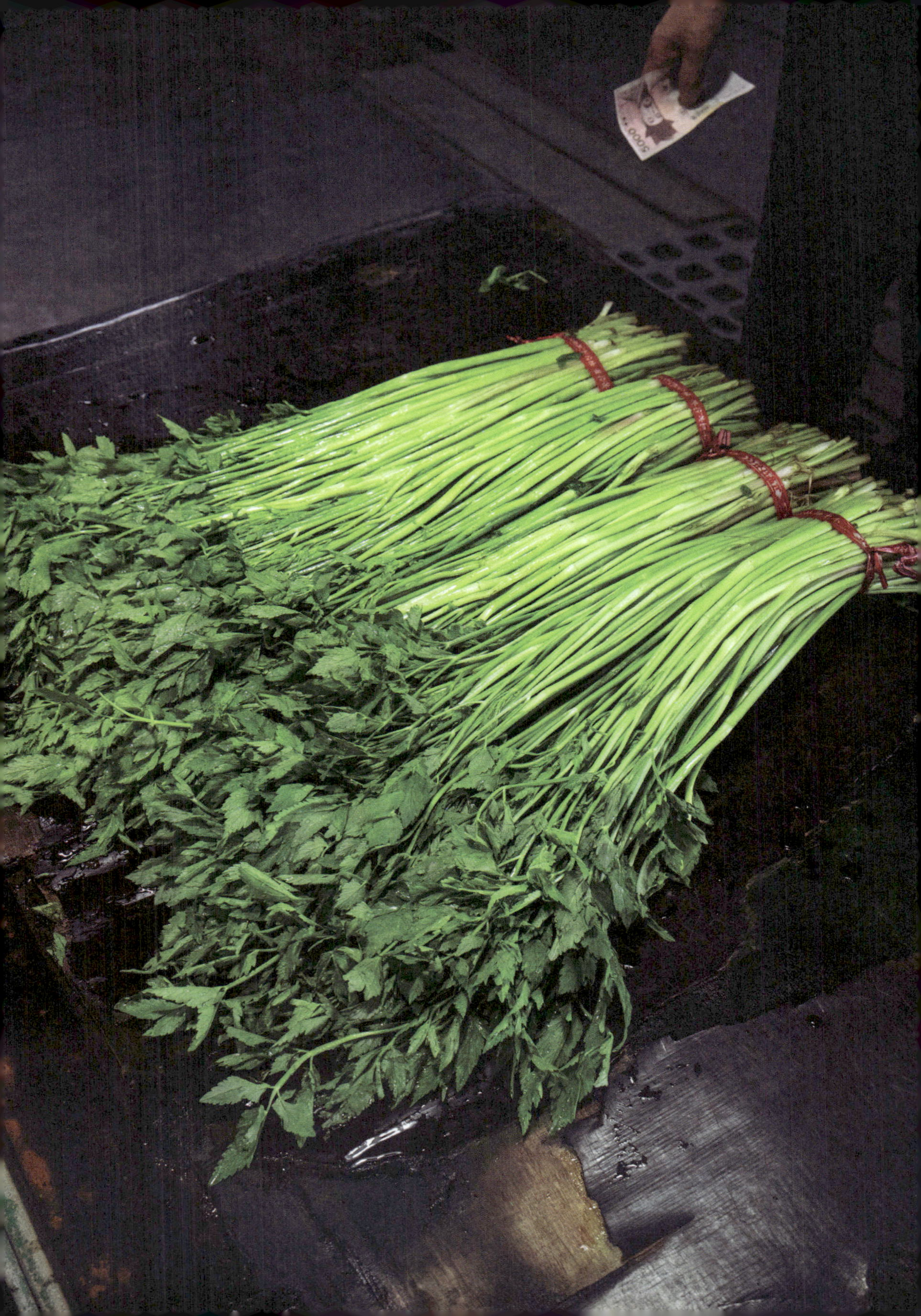

or combined. Sauces made from doenjang or gochujang (page 404) mixed with sesame oil are served with these dishes. Ssam is very popular in the summer.

Taengja and **Taengja-Cheong** see page 168

Tea leaves (cha-ip): South Korea is home to tea plantations that produce primarily green tea. However, wild tea plants still grow in the areas around Buddhist temples because tea culture and Buddhism are historically very closely connected—tea leaves are used not only to make tea, but also for cooking. For example, they can be cooked with rice or eaten as a salad green. Find more information about tea starting on page 331.

Tofu (dubu), fresh tofu (sundubu) see page 99

Tomato (tomato): Tomatoes are also called *tomato* in Korean, indicating that tomatoes aren't native to the country. That said, Korean tomatoes do differ somewhat from those found in the West: they're greenish-light pink and also larger. There's also a green variety called *paran-tomato*. Ever since it came to Korea, many more varieties of tomatoes have been grown and eaten, including cherry tomatoes (*bangul-tomato*). Because tomatoes generally aren't cooked or made into sauces in Korea but are eaten raw like fruit, they contain more water and are juicier. They've long been eaten sprinkled with sugar, and today they're eaten in salads, as jangajji (page 161), or dried. Although seeing as pasta is becoming more popular in Korea, people now do in fact make fresh sauce from red tomatoes.

Tteokguk tteok see Rice cakes

Turmeric (ganghwang): The turmeric plant is related to ginger and grows in subtropical areas. In Korea, it's grown in the south. The roots have not only an intense color but also a strong, unique scent. They're used as both a flavoring and a coloring agent. Turmeric tastes slightly bitter, so don't use too much! Traditional medicines of East Asia recognize turmeric as a healing plant; it's been proven to reduce inflammation and protect the liver.

Ueong see Greater burdock

Wakame see Seaweed

Water celery (minari): Minari is a plant that grows in shaded spots near water. The plant possesses everlasting vital energy! Its stalks are 8 to 20 inches (20 to 50 cm) tall, with brachiated leaves on the ends, and are hollow inside. The plants bloom in the summer and have a very peculiar aroma that makes them good for a variety of uses. As a vegetable, they're blanched and seasoned, but they're also a popular ingredient in fish stew because they neutralize the odor of fish. They go well with vinegar-gochujang sauce and also with pork. They're best used as an ingredient in jeon (pancakes).

Wild pepper (sansho) see page 280
Wood ear mushroom (mogi beoseot) see Mushrooms
Yangha see Ginger
Yeongeun see Lotus root
Zucchini (aehobak) see Squash

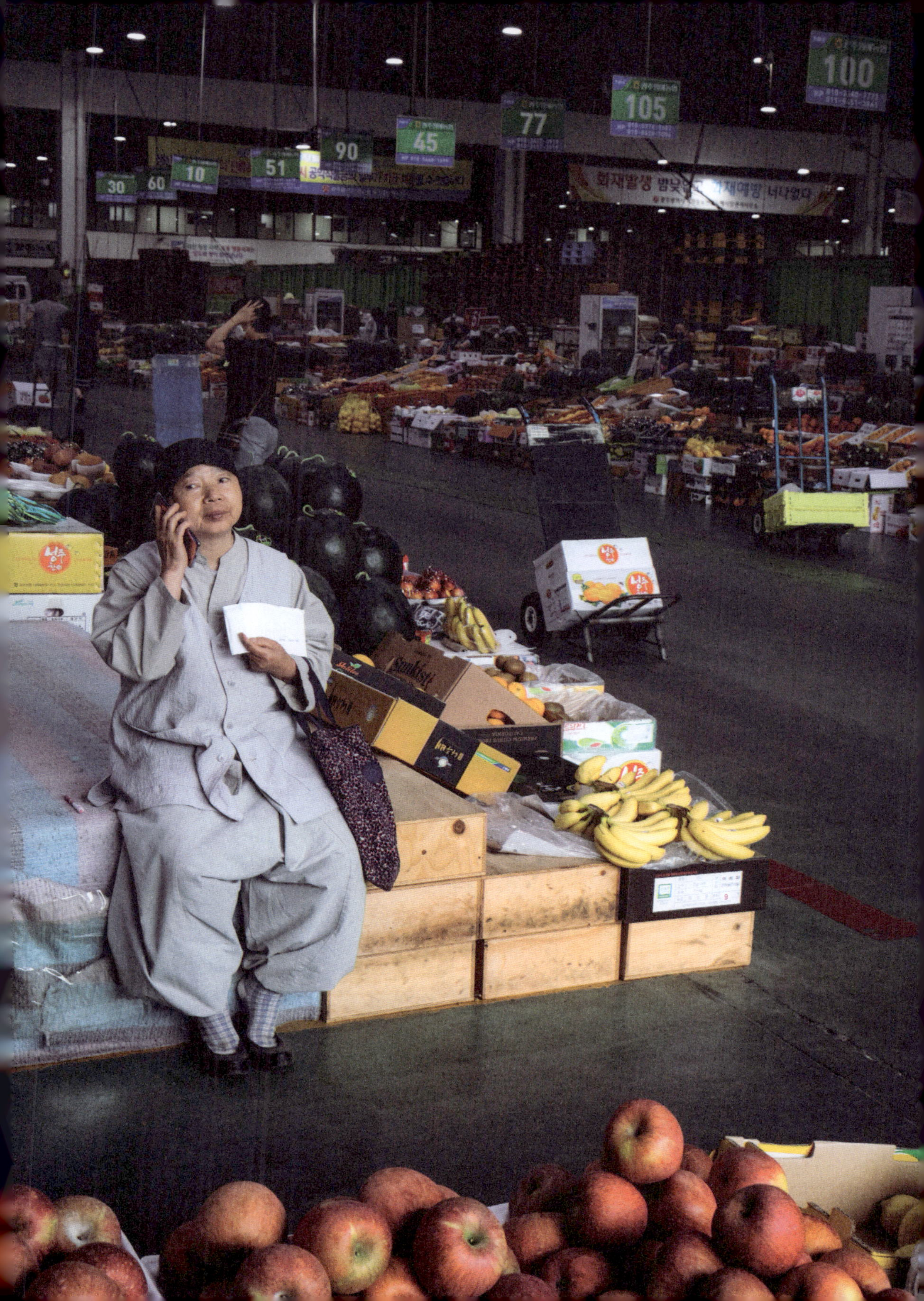
100
105
77
45
90
51
10
60
30

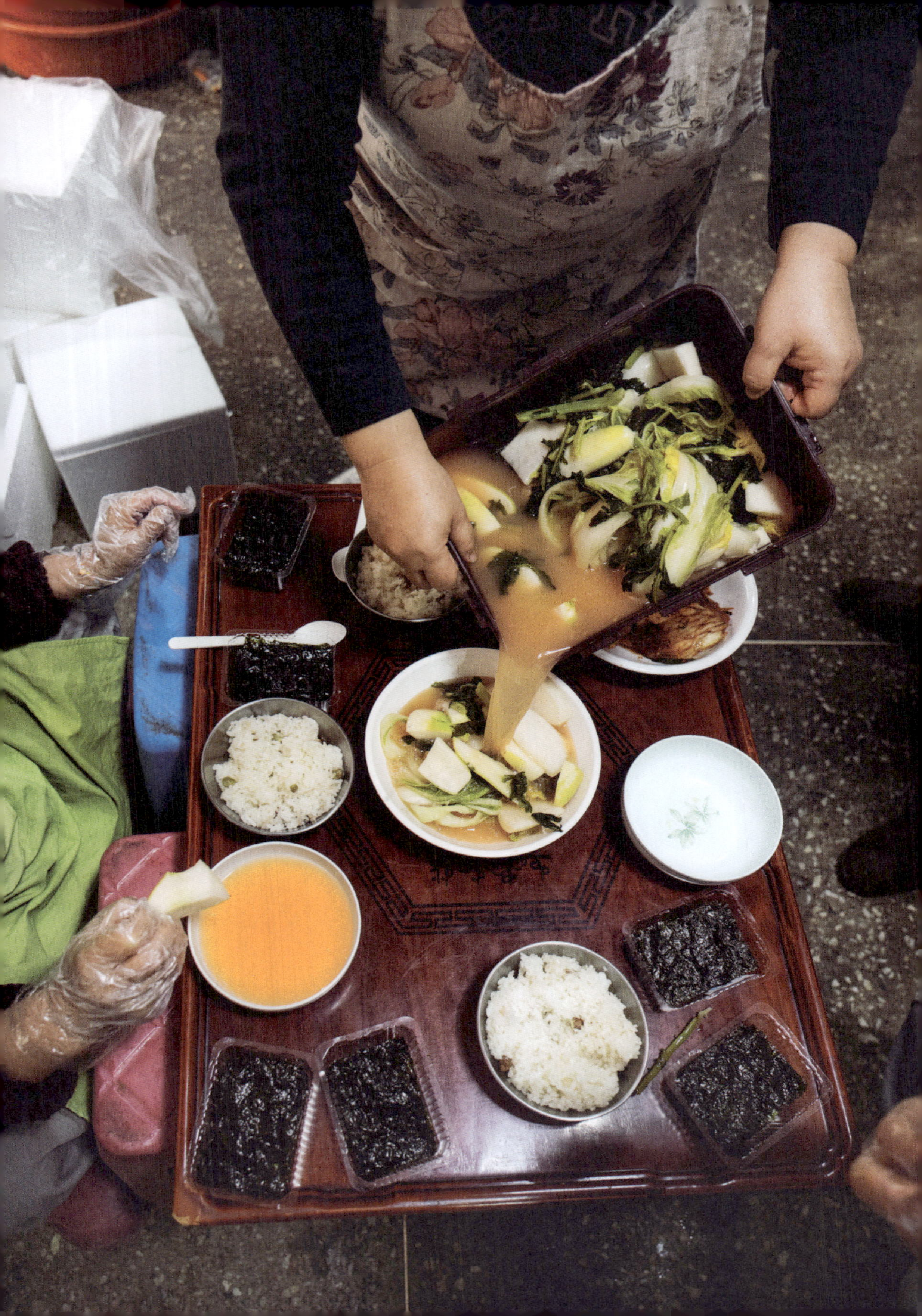

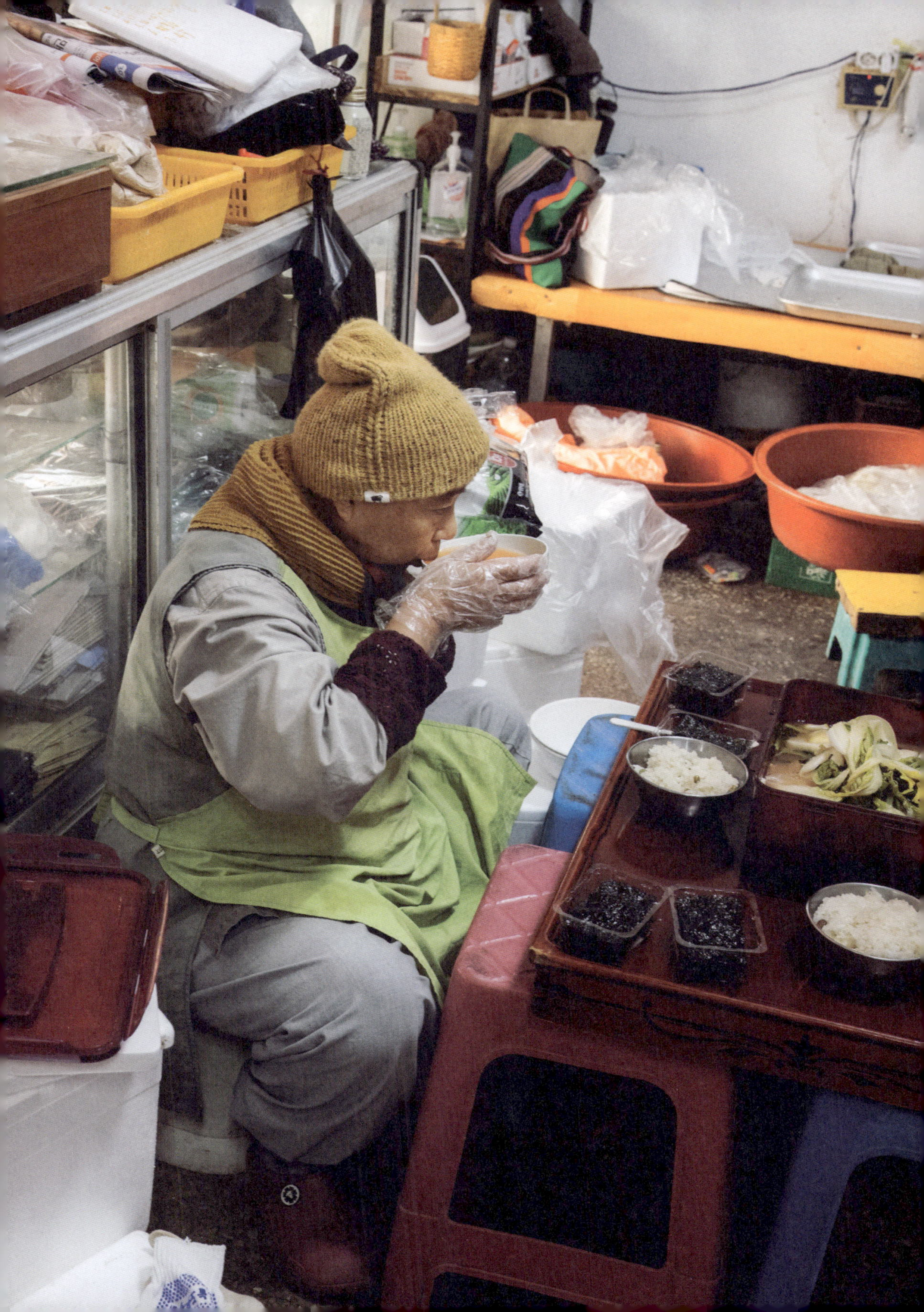

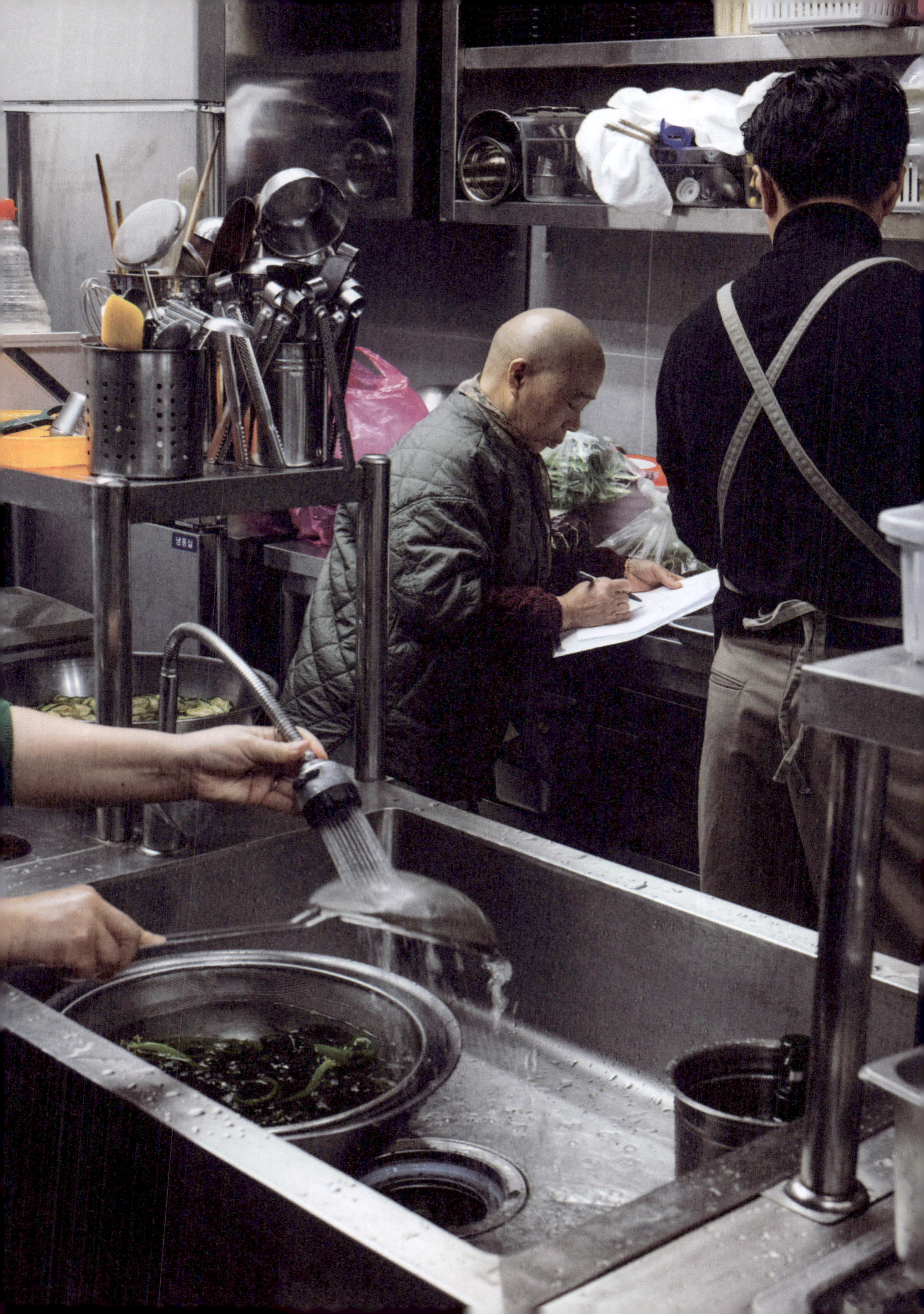

INDEX

A
Aehobak see Squash
Apple (sagwa) 399
B
Bae (pear) 423
Baechu see Napa cabbage
Bak see Squash
Bamboo shoot (juksun) 399
Bamboo Shoot with Perilla 242
Bangul-tomato see Tomato
Beans (kong, pat) 400
  Mung Bean Sprouts with Minari 248
  Rice in Lotus Leaves 270
  Soybean Sprouts with Turmeric 286
  Soup with Soybean Sprouts 238
Beoseot see Mushrooms
Bit (red beet) 427
Bitter orange (taengja),
  Taengaja-Cheong 168
Blackberry (bokbunja),
  Bokbunja-Cheong 180
Braised dishes
  Braised Three-Year-Old Kimchi 132
  King Oyster Mushrooms Braised
    in Rice Syrup 320
  Pyogo Mushrooms Braised
    in Rice Syrup 256
  Tofu with Naengi Braised in Soy Sauce 222
Buckwheat (maemil) 403
  Pancakes with Napa Cabbage
    and Radish 224
  Pancakes with Minari And Gochujang 260
  Zucchini Breaded with Buckwheat 296
Bugak 262
  Seaweed bugak 262
  Gajuknamul bugak 266
  Potato bugak 266
  Lotus root bugak 266

C
Calabash (bak) see Squash
Calabaza squash (neulgeun-hobak)
  see Squash
Carrot (danggeun) 403
Castor leaves (pimaja) 403
  Temple Bibimbap 232
Chajo see Millet
Chamgireum see Sesame seeds
Chapssalpul see Glutinous rice paste
Cheong 167
  Bokbunja-Cheong 180
  Jocheong (Rice Syrup) 190
  Maesil-Cheong 174
  Omija-Cheong 186
  Taengja-Cheong 168
Cheongyanggochu see Chili (gochu)
  Fried Ueong with Gochujang Sauce 326
  Gochujang 404
  Pancakes with Minari And Gochujang 260
Chili (gochu) 403
Chinese toon (gajuknamul) 404
Chinese yam (ma) 404
  Chinese Yam with Black Sesame Seeds 316
  Salad with Ma and Persimmon 318
Chinamul 246, 416
Cucumber (oi) 415
  Tofu Steamed in Zucchini with
    Fresh Green Tea Leaves 252
Cucumber Namul 284
D
Daechu (Korean date) 407
Danggeun (carrot) 403
Danhobak see Squash
Danmuji see Radish
Deep-fried dishes
  Seaweed bugak 262
  Deep-Fried Ginseng 226

Index — 441

Gajuknamul bugak 266
Potato bugak 266
Lotus root bugak 266
Deulkkae see Perilla
Doenjang 138
Doenjang Stew with Zucchini 304
Dried Radish Slices with Doenjang 214
Tofu-Jang 306
Dubu see Tofu
E
Eggplant (gaji) 407
Fried Eggplant with Sauce 322
Steamed Salted Eggplant 294
Eunhaeng (ginkgo) 411
F
Fernbrake (gosari) 408
Chinamul 246
Temple Bibimbap 232
Five-flavor berry (omija),
Omija-Cheong 186
G
Gaji see Eggplant
Gajuknamul bugak 266
Gam see Persimmon
Ganghwang see Turmeric
Ganjang see Soy sauce
Gardenia (chija) 408
Gat see Mustard greens
Gijang see Millet
Gim see Seaweed
Ginger (saenggang) 408
Sugared ginger slices 411
Ginkgo (eunhaeng) 411
Ginseng (insam) 411
Deep-Fried Ginseng 226
Glasswort (hamcho) 412
Glutinous rice paste (chapssalpul) 412
Glutinous rice paste 262
Glutinous rice paste,
easy method 415
Gosari see Fernbrake

Goun-gochugaru, gochu, gochugaru, and
gochujang see Chili
Grains 415
Greater burdock (ueong) 415
Fried Ueong with Gochujang Sauce 326
Green cabbage (yangbaechu) 415
H
Hamcho (glasswort) 412
Heugimja see Sesame seeds
Hobak see Squash
Hoenari-gochu see Chili
I
Insam see Ginseng
J
Jangajji 161
Sansho Jangajji 280
Tomato Jangajji 276
Jocheong see Rice Syrup
Juksun see Bamboo shoot
K
Kabocha squash (danhobak) see
Squash
Kimchi 113
Baechu Kimchi 126
Braised Three-Year-Old Kimchi 132
Quick Kimchi with Oak Leaf Lettuce 130
Summer Water Kimchi 120
Watery Mustard Green Kimchi 250
Yangnyeomjang 120, 126, 130
King oyster mushroom (saesongi beoseot)
see Mushrooms
King Oyster Mushrooms Braised
in Rice Syrup 320
Pyogo Mushrooms Braised
in Rice Syrup 256
Kkae see Sesame seeds
Kong and **kongnamul** see Beans
Korean aster scaber (chinamul) 416
Chinamul 246
Temple Bibimbap 232
Korean pear (bae) 423

L
Lemon (yuja) 416
Lotus leaf (yeonnip)
  Rice in Lotus Leaves 270
Lotus root (yeongeun) 416
  Lotus Root with Yuja-Cheong 288
  Lotus root bugak 266
M
Ma see Chinese yam
Maemil and **maemil garu** see Buckwheat
Maesil (plum) 174
Meju 137
Millet (gijang, chajo) 419
  Squash Soup with Millet 212
  Rice with Millet and Mushrooms 202
Minari see Water celery
Mogi beoseot see Mushrooms
Mu see Radish
Mung beans (nokdu) 400
  Mung Bean Sprouts with Minari 248
Mushrooms (beoseot) 419
  Stew with Neungi Mushrooms
    and Scorched Rice 302
  Cold Vegetable and Mushroom Plate
    with Mustard Sauce 292
  King Oyster Mushrooms Braised
    in Rice Syrup 320
  Pyogo Mushrooms Braised
    in Rice Syrup 256
  Rice with Millet and Mushrooms 202
  Dumplings with Mushrooms
    and Vegetables 218
  Temple Bibimbap 232
Mustard greens (gat) 420
  Watery Mustard Green Kimchi 250
Musun see Radish
Myoga ginger (yangha) see Ginger
N
Naengi see Shepherd's purse
Namul 105
  Bamboo Shoot with Perilla 242

  Chinamul 246
  Cucumber Namul 284
  Mung Bean Sprouts with Minari 248
  Soybean Sprouts with Turmeric 286
  Spinach with Soy Sauce
    and Sesame Seeds 216
  Soup with Soybean Sprouts 238
Napa cabbage (baechu) 420
  Baechu Kimchi 126
  Noodles with Vegetables In Broth 92
  Pancakes with Napa Cabbage
    and Radish 224
  Soup with Tofu and Napa Cabbage 274
Neulgeun-hobak see Squash
Neungi beoseot and **neutari beoseot** see
  Mushrooms
Noodles with Vegetables In Broth 92
Nurungji see Scorched rice
O
Oi see Cucumber
Omija (five-flavor berry) 186
Oyster mushrooms (neutari beoseot) see
  Mushrooms
P
Pancakes
  …with napa cabbage and radish 224
  …with minari and gochujang 260
Paran-tomato see Tomato
Pat see Beans
Perilla (deulkkae) 423
  Toasted perilla seeds 423
  Bamboo Shoot with Perilla 242
Persimmon (gam) 423
  Salad with Dried Persimmon Slices 318
  Salad with Ma and Persimmon 318
Plum (maesil),
  Maesil-Cheong 174
Porridge
  Black Sesame Porridge 240
Potato (gamja) 424
  Potato bugak 266

Pyengang see Ginger
Pyogo beoseot see Mushrooms
R
Radish (mu) 424
   Dried Radish Slices with Doenjang 214
   Pancakes with Napa Cabbage
     and Radish 224
Red beet (bit) 427
Rice 83
   Cooking rice 84
   Rice in Lotus Leaves 270
   Rice with Millet and Mushrooms 202
Rice cake (tteok) 427
   New Year's Rice Cake Soup 208
Rice Syrup (Jocheong) 190
   Temple Bibimbap 232
S
Saenggang see Ginger
Saesongi beoseot see Mushrooms
Salad
   Salad with Dried Persimmon Slices 318
   Quick Kimchi with Oak Leaf Lettuce 130
Salt (sogeum) 427
   Sansho see Wild pepper
   Sansho Jangajji 280
   Fried Tofu with Pickled Sansho 280
Sauce
   …for fried eggplant 322
   …for Salad with Dried Persimmon
     Slices 318
   …for Salad with Ma and Persimmon 318
   …for tofu with naengi 222
   Gochujang sauce 326
   Mustard sauce 292
   Yangnyeomjang for kimchi 120, 126, 130
Sautéed dishes
   Fried Eggplant with Sauce 322
   Fried Tofu with Pickled Sansho 280
   Fried Ueong with Gochujang Sauce 326
   Fried Young Calabash 312
   Cucumber Namul 284

Scorched rice (nurungji) 428
   Stew with Neungi Mushrooms and
     Scorched Rice 302
Seaweed (wakame, gim) 428
   Seaweed bugak 262
   Seaweed Soup 204
   Temple Bibimbap 232
Sesame seeds (kkae) 431
   Toasted sesame seeds 431
   Black Sesame Porridge 240
   Spinach with Soy Sauce
     and Sesame Seeds 216
Shepherd's purse (naengi)
   Tofu with Naengi Braised in Soy Sauce 222
Shiitake mushroom (pyogo beoseot) see
   Mushrooms
Shingled hedgehog mushroom (neungi
   beoseot) see Mushrooms
Sigeumchi see Spinach
Sil-gochu see Chili
Soup
   Seaweed Soup 204
   Squash Soup with Millet 212
   Noodles with Vegetables In Broth 92
   New Year's Rice Cake Soup 208
   Soup with Soybean Sprouts 238
   Soup with Tofu and Napa Cabbage 274
Soybeans (kong), **soybean sprouts, soybean
   powder, soybean oil** 400
   Soybean Sprouts with Turmeric 286
   Soup with Soybean Sprouts 238
Soybean paste (doenjang) 138
   Doenjang Stew with Zucchini 304
   Dried Radish Slices with Doenjang 214
Soy sauce (ganjang) 137
   Spinach with Soy Sauce
     and Sesame Seeds 216
   Tofu with Naengi Braised in Soy Sauce 222
Spinach (sigeumchi) 432
   Spinach with Soy Sauce
     and Sesame Seeds 216

Temple Bibimbap 232
Squash (hobak) 432
    Doenjang Stew with Zucchini 304
    Fried Young Calabash 312
    Steamed Sweet Squash with Tofu 300
    Tofu Steamed in Zucchini with
        Fresh Green Tea Leaves 252
    Squash Soup with Millet 212
    Zucchini Breaded with Buckwheat 296
Ssam 432
Steamed dishes
    Steamed Salted Eggplant 294
    Steamed Sweet Squash with Tofu 300
    Tofu Steamed in Zucchini with
        Fresh Green Tea Leaves 252
    Dumplings with Mushrooms
        and Vegetables 218
    Cold Vegetable and Mushroom Plate
        with Mustard Sauce 292
Stew
    Stew with Neungi Mushrooms
        and Scorched Rice 302
    Doenjang Stew with Zucchini 304
Sundubu see Tofu
T
Taengja (bitter orange) 168
Tea leaves (cha-ip) 435
    Tofu Steamed in Zucchini with
        Fresh Green Tea Leaves 252
    Tea and Buddhism 331
Temple Bibimbap 232
Tofu (dubu), **fresh tofu** (sundubu) 99
    Tofu with Naengi Braised in Soy Sauce 222

Homemade Tofu 100
Tofu-Jang 306
Fried Tofu with Pickled Sansho 280
Steamed Sweet Squash with Tofu 300
Tofu Steamed in Zucchini with
    Fresh Green Tea Leaves 252
Soup with Tofu and Napa Cabbage 274
Temple Bibimbap 232
Tomato (tomato) 435
    Tomato Jangajji 276
Tteokguk tteok see Rice cakes
Turmeric (ganghwang) 435
    Soybean Sprouts with Turmeric 286
U
Ueong see Greater burdock
W
Wakame see Seaweed
Water celery (minari) 435
    Pancakes with Minari And Gochujang 260
Watery Mustard Green Kimchi 250
Wild pepper (sansho) 280
Wood ear mushroom (mogi beoseot) see
    Mushrooms
Y
Yangha see Ginger
Yeongeun see Lotus root
Z
Zucchini (aehobak) see also Squash
    Doenjang Stew with Zucchini 304
    Tofu Steamed in Zucchini with
        Fresh Green Tea Leaves 252
    Noodles with Vegetables In Broth 92
    Zucchini Breaded with Buckwheat 296

Hoo Nam Seelmann: Born in South Korea, she studied philosophy, German philology, and art history in Germany and did her doctorate on Hegel's Philosophy of History. Since 1997, she has been writing about Korea and East Asia for the Neue Zürcher Zeitung. Ms. Seelmann lives in Riehen, Switzerland, where she works as a publicist and author.

Véronique Hoegger: Born in Lausanne, she studied photography in Vevey and Zurich. She has worked as a freelance photographer since 2001 and lives with her family in Zurich.

The authors would like to thank: The employees and all of the volunteer helpers who were at Cheonjinam Temple during our time there. A big thank-you to Echtzeit Press, to Wendelin Hess for his trust, patience, and spirit of adventure. Many thanks go out to Gianin Walter, Jesse Wyss, and Alex Herzog for their fantastic work. Special thanks to Kurt Seelmann, Susanne Märki, Chris Niemeyer, and Athina Hoegger.

The press and the authors would like to thank: Jeongkwan Snim for the trust she placed in us and for her generosity.

Hardie Grant

NORTH AMERICA

Hardie Grant North America
2912 Telegraph Ave.
Berkeley, CA 94705
hardiegrant.com

Copyright © Hoo Nam Seelmann
Photographs copyright © Véronique Hoegger

All rights reserved. No part of this book may be reproduced in any form without written permission from the publisher.

Jeongkwan Snim: Ihre koreanische Tempelküche written by Hoo Nam Seelmann with photos by Véronique Hoegger
First edition in German published by Echtzeit Verlag, 2024 / ISBN: 9783906807355
© Echtzeit Verlag GmbH, Basel

This edition published in 2025 by Hardie Grant North America,
an imprint of Hardie Grant Publishing Pty Ltd.

Library of Congress Cataloging-in-Publication Data is available upon request.

ISBN: 9781964786186
ISBN: 9781964786193 (eBook)

Printed in China
Design: Müller+Hess+Walter+Wyss, Basel
Translation: Kelly Burt-Candelaria
Typesetting: Hadley Hendrix

First Edition

MIX
Paper | Supporting responsible forestry
FSC
www.fsc.org FSC® C020056